Armenian Golgotha

Grigoris Balakian, Vienna, 1913

Armenian GOLGOTHA

Grigoris Balakian

Translated by Peter Balakian with Aris Sevag

ALFRED A. KNOPF NEW YORK 2009

THIS IS A BORZOI BOOK
PUBLISHED BY ALFRED A KNOPF

www.aaknopf.com

Originally published in Armenian in two volumes as *Armenian Golgotha: Episodes from the Armenian Martyrology from Berlin to Zor, 1914–1920* (Vienna: Mekhitarist Press, 1922) and *Armenian Golgotha, Volume 2: Episodes from the Armenian Martyrology from Berlin to Der Zor* (Paris: Imprimerie Araxes, 1959.)

Library of Congress Cataloging-in-Publication Data
Palak'ean, Grigoris, d. 1934.
[Hay goghgot'an. English]
Armenian Golgotha / by Grikoris Balakian ; translated by Peter Balakian.
p. cm.
Includes bibliographical references and index.
ISBN 978-0-307-26288-2 (alk. paper)
1. Armenian massacres, 1915–1923—Personal narratives.
2. Armenians—Turkey—History—20th century. 3. Palak'ean, Grigoris, d. 1934. I. Balakian, Peter, 1951– II. Title.
DS 195.5.P3413 2009
956.6'20154—dc22 2008039957

Manufactured in the United States of America
First Edition

Contents

Constantinople
Izmit
Bursa
Angora
Yozgat
T U R K
Aegean Sea
Afyonkarahisar
Smyrna
Caesarea
CILICIAN ARMENIA
Adana
Musa Dagh
Armenia, 500 B.C. – Present
Cilician Armenia, 1080–1375 A.D.
Armenian Provinces of the Ottoman Turkish Empire
Republic of Armenia, 1991– (formerly Soviet Armenia, 1920–1991)
0 MILES 200
0 KILOMETERS 200
Beirut
Mediterranean Sea
Jerusalem
EGYPT
Cairo

Constantinople
Izmit
Bursa
Angora
Yozgat
T U R K
Aegean Sea
Afyonkarahisar
Smyrna
Caesarea
CILICIAN ARMENIA
Adana
Musa Dagh
Armenia, 500 B.C. – Present
Cilician Armenia, 1080–1375 A.D.
Armenian Provinces of the Ottoman Turkish Empire
Republic of Armenia, 1991– (formerly Soviet Armenia, 1920–1991)
0 MILES 200
0 KILOMETERS 200
Beirut
Mediterranean Sea
Jerusalem
EGYPT
Cairo

Black Sea
Batum
Tiflis
RUSSIA
Ani
Kars
Lake Sevan
NAGORNO KARABAGH (ARTSAKH)
Trebizond
Etchmiadzin
Yerevan
RUSSIAN ARMENIA
Tokat
SIVAS
Sivas
Erzerum
ERZERUM
Mt. Ararat
E
Y
Harput
BITLIS
Lake Van
Van
Tabriz
Bitlis
HARPUT
VAN
Diyarbekir
Lake Urmia
Zeytoun
DIYARBEKIR
Ourfa
Aintab
Aleppo
ALEPPO
PERSIA
Der Zor
SYRIA
Tigris River
Euphrates River
Baghdad
Syrian Desert
Damascus
N

Introduction

The literature of witness has had a significant impact on our understanding of the twentieth century. What we know about our age of catastrophe we know in crucial part from memoirs such as Primo Levi's *Survival in Auschwitz*, Elie Wiesel's *Night*, Michihiko Hachiya's *Hiroshima Diary*, Nadezhda Mandelstam's *Hope Against Hope*, and many others, stories that have taken us inside episodes of mass violence and killing, genocide and torture. They have allowed us acquaintance with individual victims and perpetrators, offering insights into the nature of torture, cruelty, suffering, survival, and death. By the end of the twentieth century some scholars had referred to our time as an age of testimony.

Grigoris Balakian's memoir *Armenian Golgotha*, for decades an important text of Armenian literature, belongs to this group of significant books that deal with crimes against humanity in the modern age. Balakian, a priest and later a bishop in the Armenian Apostolic Church, was an esteemed clergyman and intellectual. On the night of April 24, 1915, along with about 250 other Armenian cultural leaders (writers, clergy, teachers, journalists), he was arrested in Constantinople, the cultural center of Ottoman Armenians, and deported by bus and then train to a prison in Chankiri, about two hundred miles east, in north central Turkey. Bewildered and terrified, he could not have imagined that he was at the beginning of an odyssey that would last nearly four years, the duration of World War I. He was one of only a handful of the original group to survive the ordeal; against all odds, he would manage to escape Turkish officials, police soldiers, and killing squads.

From Chankiri, he was driven south on a forced march amid continual horrors and extremity. At various intervals he lived amid bedraggled groups of survivors; he listened to escapees, often children, tell stories of massacres and atrocities; he spent time with Islamized Armenians who poured out their anguish and inner conflicts over their predicaments. He also listened carefully to Turkish perpetrators and collaborators who, knowing that he was marked for death, opened up to him with candor that was tinged at times with gloating and at other times with guilt. His long interview with Captain Shukri, on the road from Yozgat to Boghazliyan, is particularly poignant. He spoke as well with righteous Turks, like the *mutasarrif* Asaf of Chankiri, who, revolted by the plan to exterminate the Armenians, warned Balakian of what was about to happen.

Along his many roads of exile, Balakian witnessed slaughter, fields of corpses, and starving women and children. He gathered invaluable first-hand testimony from numerous survivors as well as eyewitness accounts from German, Swiss, and Austrian engineers and administrators who were constructing the Berlin-to-Baghdad railway through the Amanos and Taurus mountains. Through an unusual encounter with *mutasarrif* Asaf in the summer of 1915, he read an official telegram from Talaat inquiring about the efficiency of massacres in the region—a moment he would recall when he testified at the trial of Soghomon Tehlirian, who assassinated Talaat Pasha in Berlin in 1921.

For about two months Balakian was one of a group of threadbare survivors forced to walk hundreds of miles south along a central deportation route. Traveling from Chankiri through Choroum, Yozgat, Kayseri, Hajin, and Sis, all the way to Islahiye (not far from today's northern Syrian border), he became the unofficial leader of these deportees, who were being taken by Turkish police soldiers to die in the desert region of Der Zor, in northeastern Syria—a place that was to become the epicenter of death in the Armenian Genocide. Through wild, harsh, and remote terrain, he helped keep them alive, caring for their physical and spiritual needs. For the next year and a half he was a fugitive.

In order to understand the circumstances of Balakian's survival, it is important to understand the political and cultural role the Armenian Apostolic Church (the mother church, as Balakian commonly refers to it) played in Armenian life in the Ottoman Empire. The Church was the basis of much of Armenian political power in Turkey, and the Church and particularly the patriarchate in Istanbul conducted its own diplomatic relations with officials in foreign countries. Balakian, who was an emissary for the patriarchate, had considerable experience as a church diplomat with both Ottoman and foreign officials. As a *vartabed* (a celibate priest), he occupied a position of leadership and prestige in Armenian life, and so it is not surprising that fellow Armenians went to great lengths to protect him and aid in his escapes, often risking their own lives.

Because he had been educated in Germany, first as an engineering student at Mittweida University in Saxony and later as a graduate student in

theology at the University of Berlin, his fluency in German enabled him to engage the German engineers and administrators along the railway; it would later prove vital to his disguise and ultimate escape. With wit and ingenuity, Balakian took on various identities: a German worker on the railway, a German Jew, a German engineer, a railway administrator, a German soldier, and a Greek vineyard worker.

As he managed to stay alive through an extraordinary chain of circumstances, Balakian became an observer of what one might call the inner life of the Armenian Genocide. Thus the perspective of witness here is more multifarious and broad than in most survivor memoirs. We see, in process, the "government planned, systematic, race extermination," as *The New York Times* referred to it in 1915, from conception to execution; from its impact on the victims—women, children, and men of all ages—to its impact on the perpetrators and bystanders.

Structure of Genocide

It will be clear to any reader that *Armenian Golgotha* is more than a personal story, for Balakian brings together a survivor account, eyewitness testimony, historical background and context, and political analysis. Throughout the narrative he discloses essential elements of the politics, sociology, and ideology of the Turkish extermination plan. His analyses of Turkish culture and of the structure of the CUP's* (Ittihad government) plan to exterminate the Armenian population are astute and soberly accurate for the most part, upheld by decades of scholarship since. In a crucial chapter, "Plan for the Extinction of the Armenians in Turkey," Balakian gives us an eleven-point outline of the Young Turks' "final solution." While decades of good scholarship have explored the causes, contexts, and morphology of the Armenian Genocide, his outline remains a general blueprint for an understanding of this event.

Balakian depicts the arrest and deportation of the 250 Armenian cultural leaders on April 24 with such vivid detail and texture that we see how well planned and orchestrated the whole scheme was. We also recognize the importance that the CUP placed on killing off the intellectuals, first in Constantinople and then throughout the country (thousands of cultural leaders were killed), so as to mute the potential outcry and to silence the voice of the culture.

As one of the 250 initially arrested, Balakian gives us a valuable piece of Armenian intellectual history via his report on the torture and murder of

**Ittihad ve Terakki*, the Committee of Union and Progress, the ruling government of the Ottoman Empire in 1915.

many of its most important figures, including Daniel Varoujan, the poet, and Krikor Zohrab, the novelist and Ottoman parliament member. On the deportation to Chankiri, Balakian reports how his carriage mate, the fellow priest and composer Komitas, began to break down. Balakian recounts praying for Komitas, at his request, as terror and anxiety were overwhelming him. Balakian also documents the Ottoman government's repeated use of the infamous blacklists, rolls of targeted cultural and community leaders that had been carefully prepared with the help of Armenian informants. Such lists exemplify how methodical the Turkish government's bureaucracy was in classifying the Armenian population in their extermination plan.

Grigoris Balakian reveals other fundamental structures of the extermination plan. He shows how important the nationwide network of Ittihad (CUP) clubs and bureaucracy were to the plan, and how the CUP's mobile killing squads (*chetes*) were created by releasing some thirty thousand prisoners throughout Turkey for the express purpose of massacring the Armenian population "on the pretext of protecting the rear of the Ottoman army." He describes their tactic of planting weapons in Armenian homes to trump up charges of disloyalty as a pretext for arrest. The parliamentary legislation that legitimated the deportations (Temporary Law of Deportation) and the confiscation of wealth (Temporary Law of Confiscation and Expropriation) resulted in organized, as well as ad hoc, acts of plunder and theft of Armenian goods in addition to the movable and immovable wealth of "the Armenian people and their cultural institutions." Throughout, Balakian describes a frenzied general cupidity in some segments of the Muslim population as Armenian homes were pillaged, women were robbed of their jewelry, and businesses were looted of every last object of value.

Balakian's understanding of the political context surrounding the Armenian Genocide is perceptive and essential to understanding Turkey's sense of vulnerability. He notes how German and European imperialist designs on Turkey created resentment among the Turks and betrayed the Armenians in the end. He is shrewd, as well, in explaining, before the term "total war" was coined, how the Turkish government exploited the chaos of the war and the pretext of wartime security in order to implement their final solution for the Armenians. The war, Balakian notes, was "their sole opportunity, one unprecedented."

There are chilling portrayals of how the actual killing was done. The perpetrators often used the tools of the farmer, butcher, and tanner—axes, hoes, meat cleavers, pitchforks, knives, and gouges—to kill and mutilate. The variety of tortures included eye-gouging, hair-plucking, beheading, genital mutilation, and disemboweling. There are scenes of mass terror as well as individual grief, and some of the gruesome details that Balakian gives us were related to him by the perpetrators themselves, speaking with bravado. These tactics and organized efforts were not ineffective: by the end of 1915 three-fourths of the Ottoman Armenians were extinct.

The unfolding depth of Balakian's narrative brings us closer to scenes of atrocity and massacre in ways that were unprecedented in modern history to this point. The account of the massacres in Ankara province by a girl who had been left for dead in a pile of corpses; the mounds of hastily buried bodies of tens of thousands of Armenians at Islahiye, which bring the deportees to despair and suicidal feelings; the piles of bodies dismembered and disgorged on the Marash-Baghche road that spurred a German nurse to jump off her horse and fall to the ground, embracing the decapitated body of a six-month-old infant; the killing zone of the Kanle-gechid gorge in the Amanos mountains, through which 450,000 Armenians were deported, a huge portion of whom were slaughtered and thrown into the valley and river below, while thousands more froze to death or died of dysentery, diarrhea, and famine, so that the fields were covered with mounds of unburied bodies; or the desert of Der Zor, where tens of thousands of half-naked, emaciated women and children were eating the rotting corpses of animals. These scenes and others comprise one of the most extraordinary accounts of mass killing in the modern era, and any student of genocide will find them invaluable as evidentiary witness.

As Balakian reveals, the CUP's commitment to race extermination was comprehensive. Through the testimony of perpetrators, victims, bystanders, and his own experience, he makes clear that deportation "was synonymous with murder" and that the "relocation" of Armenians was merely a charade—as the Constantinople postwar courts-martial trials would confirm from Turkish testimony. Catholic Armenians (most were Orthodox or Protestant), who had previously been exempt from persecution and massacre, were zealously massacred in Yozgat, where the majority of them lived. And, Talaat was determined to kill every last Armenian working on the Berlin-to-Baghdad railway, despite their importance to the Germans and thereby the Turkish war effort.

Sexual violence was also an integral part of the mass killing program, and Balakian relays firsthand accounts of the abductions and gang rapes of women, and abductions as a component of the deportation. The absorption of Armenians into Islamic Turkish life through forced conversion and abduction is a recurrent theme of the genocidal process. In a moving scene in the chapter "Gazbel to Hajin," Balakian finds himself sitting at a dinner table with a family of Islamized Armenians who beg him to bless their table, give them Holy Communion, and hear their confessions. Full of anguish, they all break down weeping. It is a vivid lesson in the cruelty and violence suffered by those who survive but are nevertheless robbed of their culture and identity. An estimated 5 to 10 percent of the Armenian population was assimilated into Muslim households.[1] In another scene, we observe the spectacle of hundreds of newly converted Armenian boys paraded in carriages through the streets of Ankara during circumcision ceremonies.

Balakian was the first survivor to give us this depth of understanding about what happened in the deserts of northern Syria and especially in Der Zor—a name synonymous with death that haunted all Armenian deportees. He portrays in detail an often unexplored dimension of the Genocide—the second wave of massacres aimed at surviving Armenians (between 160,000 and 200,000) in camps in the summer of 1916. Balakian's statistics suggest that more than 400,000 perished in Der Żor, making it a kind of Auschwitz of the Armenian Genocide.

Armenian Golgotha gives us further insight into how the CUP's pan-Turkic ideology—its advocacy of a homogeneous Turkey, free of Christian minorities, especially Greeks, Assyrians, and Armenians—was not only a racist and xenophobic platform but a motivating factor in the final solution for the Armenians. Balakian hears German soldiers referring to Armenians as "Christian Jews" and "bloodsucking usurers of the Turkish people." Such remarks demonstrate the ideological relationship Germans and Turks were forging in their shared view of Armenians, to whom the Germans extended and applied anti-Semitic notions. He observes that Turkish government officials often justified their violence against all Christians—Greeks, Assyrians, and Armenians alike—as "just retribution for the dominance of these groups in Turkey's economic life," characterizing Christians as "ferocious leeches."

In the intensity of Balakian's depiction of Turkish atrocities and his rage against both the country and the people, sometimes he essentializes Turks in a racialist way characteristic of the period and sometimes he veers away from essentializing them, underscoring instead the morally courageous behavior of righteous Turks. He shows us the "kind and thoughtful" governor Reshid Pasha of Kastemouni; Ali Suad, lieutenant-governor of the Der Zor district; Mehmed Jelal, governor-general of Aleppo Province; and *mutasarrif* Asaf of Chankiri, all of whom were forced from their posts because they resisted Talaat's orders to kill all the Armenians in their jurisdictions. Balakian notes the beneficence of the Turks of Konya (led by a monastic group of Mevlevis, or Sufis) who treated the Armenians well, and he depicts with care an elderly Turkish woman in Ankara who cursed her government for its treatment of the Armenians and a Turkish carriage driver who could no longer cope with deporting Armenians and watching them be killed.

Nevertheless, *Armenian Golgotha* is not a scholarly history but a memoir that documents this large, complex history in the immediate aftermath of the event. Although he refers to having read some of the classic texts of the period, such as James Bryce's *The Treatment of the Armenians in the Ottoman Empire* and *Ambassador Morgenthau's Story*, U.S. Ambassador Henry Morgenthau's memoir of his years in Turkey during the war, one is left to conjecture what other sources he might have had access to, including the published texts of the 1919–20 Constantinople courts-martial in the Ottoman *Parliamentary Gazette (Takvim-i-Vekayi)*, which include numerous Turkish confessions concerning the extermination plan.

Since the publication of *Armenian Golgotha* in 1922, the Armenian Genocide has given rise to a significant scholarly discourse, especially in the past thirty years. An extraordinary body of research has been produced by a wide range of scholars in countries that include Armenia, Australia, Bulgaria, Canada, France, Germany, Greece, Ireland, Lebanon, Russia, Syria, Turkey, the United Kingdom, and the United States, among others.

And from the time of the event, there are numerous eyewitness accounts from American and European missionaries and diplomats, Armenian survivors, and various European bystanders. The Armenian Genocide is abundantly documented by thousands of official state records of the United States, France, Great Britain, and Turkey's wartime allies Germany, Austria, and Hungary, and by Ottoman court-martial records.

Yet for all this, one might suggest that no single book has brought us closer to the experience of this event, as social and political process, than *Armenian Golgotha*. It is a seminal text, personal, and much of the scholarship of the succeeding decades corroborates and is corroborated by it.

Raphael Lemkin, the Polish Jewish legal scholar who pioneered the concept and conceived the term "genocide," did so in large part on the basis of what happened to the Armenians. Reading *Armenian Golgotha*, one gets a deeper insight into why Lemkin was so focused on the Turkish extermination of the Armenians, and why the Armenian event was, for him, a template for genocide in the modern era. Looking back at the twentieth century, we can see the Armenian Genocide as the paradigm from which the Holocaust and other genocides, for example, in the Ukraine, Cambodia, Rwanda, the Balkans, and Darfur, can be more deeply understood.

In *Armenian Golgotha*, we see what Elaine Scarry has called "the thick agony of the body"—the torture, the sexual mutilation, the rape and abduction of women, the murder of children and infants and we also see the destruction of cultural leaders, institutions, and artifacts. As Lemkin noted, genocide is an act that involves the "organized destruction of the art and cultural heritage in which the unique genius of a collectivity are [*sic*] revealed in fields of science, arts and literature."* In the breadth of Balakian's deportation experience, we encounter in vivid detail not only mass slaughter but the murder of cultural leaders and writers, the destruction of cultural institutions, and the massive ruins of an ancient and once vital civilization. While it is most likely that Lemkin never read *Armenian Golgotha* because of the obstacle of translation, he had accrued a depth of understanding of the events of 1915 such that his own knowledge of the Armenian Genocide is vividly borne out by and embodied in Balakian's memoir.

Tragically, the Turkish government today spends millions of dollars annually in an effort to falsify the facts and reality of the Armenian Genocide, and while it has lured a few scholars into colluding with its denial campaign, the mainstream scholarly world and many nation-states and political institutions have responded with moral redress at this state-sponsored propaganda.† The mainstream scholarly community has pointed out that the denial of the Armenian Genocide is a manifestation of an extreme Turkish nationalism, and part of Turkey's very poor human rights record today. Many readers will find that *Armenian Golgotha*, because of its intimacy with Turkish culture and the Anatolian landscape, will be another important text that tells the story of the eradication of the Armenians from inside Turkey and reveals Turkish denial as a continued assault on truth.

*Raphael Lemkin, *Acts Constituting a General (Transnational) Danger Considered as Offences Against the Law of Nations*, 1933, available at http://www.preventgenocide.org/lemkin/madrid1933-english.htm.

†In order to make clear the resolved record on the Armenian Genocide, The International Association of Genocide Scholars (the largest organization of genocide scholars) has issued several open letters that underscore that the historical record on the Armenian Genocide is overwhelming and unambiguous, noting Raphael Lemkin's first use of the term "genocide" to describe the Armenian case and the applicability of the 1948 United Nations Convention on the Prevention and Punishment of the Crime of Genocide (see www.genocidescholars.org/home.html). Elie Wiesel has called Turkish denial a "double killing" that strives to kill the memory of the event. Deborah Lipstadt has written: "Denial of genocide whether that of the Turks against the Armenians or the Nazis against the Jews is not an act of historical reinterpretation. . . . The deniers aim at convincing innocent third parties that there is another side of the story . . . when there is no 'their side' of a legitimate debate. . . . Denial of genocide strives to reshape history in order to demonize the victims and rehabilitate the perpetrators."

Bystander Witness

During his underground journey through the tunnels of the Berlin-to-Baghdad railway in the Amanos and Taurus mountains, Balakian encountered German, Austrian, and Swiss engineers and administrators who became rescuers and resisters. As he receives aid and protection from some of them, we see through their eyes both various Turkish atrocities and acts of bystander resistance. Their part in the second half of this story is extraordinary: Klaus (the superintendent civil engineer surveyor) and his wife, Hugnen (director of the railway in Constantinople), Morf (Austrian architect and engineer); and others such as Litzmayer, Winkler, Kegel, Koppel, Kuterlen, and Leutenegger disobeyed their government's policy, took risks to help Armenians, expressed moral outrage, physically fought off Turks in order to give bread to the dying, and went to creative lengths to hide and protect Balakian in his escape. Despite the German administrators' best efforts to save the remaining 11,500 Armenian railway workers sent to deportation and death by Talaat in 1916, in the end only a few hundred were saved.

Writing

In his late thirties when the Genocide began, Balakian, a dynamic personality by all accounts, was nevertheless seen by many as a potential future patriarch (head of the Armenian Apostolic Church in Turkey). Already the author of several books on Armenian culture and current affairs, he found it natural to intersperse his narrative with historical and political analysis.

Throughout the narrative readers will find that Balakian is reflective about his need to write about his experience. On the night of his arrest, while on a train carrying deportees out of Constantinople, he describes what would be the beginning of his writing process:

> It was dark outside and inside the train, and our hearts were just as dark, as the specter of death stood before us. No one on the train was in the mood to talk; we were all silent, absorbed with torment and worry.
>
> After midnight the chief of the train, a noble and selfless Armenian official, approached me and said softly: "Reverend Father, please write the names of your arrested friends on this piece of paper and give it to me." With a surreptitious motion of his hand, he slipped a pencil and a piece of paper into my hand and, leaving the lamp with me, went to distract the police officials supervising us. With a trembling heart, under the flickering rays

> of the dim light, I hastily wrote the names of all the friends that I could remember. Then I secretly gave this list to the official without saying a word.

What would become a defining moment for Balakian is reminiscent of a moment that the Russian poet Anna Akhmatova describes during the worst years of Stalin's terror. A woman waiting in line outside a prison in Leningrad asks her: "Can you describe this?" When Ahkmatova answered that she could, "a smile passed fleetingly over what had once been the woman's face."

During the summer of 1915, after a long period of illness, while Balakian was being held with his comrades in the town of Chankiri, he felt dismay at their squabbling over money just received from the patriarchate. He explains: "I withdrew to an orchard near the town and began to busy myself with literary work; it was the only way I could forget our worrisome condition." It is an arresting statement, and one that suggests how naturally writing came to him as a response, in the midst of disaster and chaos.

Near the end of that year, Balakian told his friend Diran Kelegian that he had "decided not to die at all costs." His will to survive was fortified both by his hope of seeing an independent Armenia after the war and by his drive to tell the story of this "unprecedented historical event." By 1917, during the first phase of his escape, Balakian was making mental notes in preparation for his book, and by September 1918 he was hiding out in his mother's and sister's houses in Constantinople to work on *Armenian Golgotha.*

Intensely self-aware about what it meant to write this story, in his preface* he confesses to feelings of inadequacy—of being "weak of both heart and pen"—and notes the limitations of language. Indeed, in the face of such "untellable suffering," one would need a "supernatural pen" to bear witness. On various occasions fellow deportees pleaded with him to stay alive and write their stories. Although the challenge was psychologically overwhelming because it required reliving everything—"going on the exile a second time" and bringing to "mind and eye again more than a thousand days, more than three years filled with death and blood"—he saw it as a sacred obligation.

Addressing the Armenian nation in the preface, he declared, "I put this into writing, because I have a holy inheritance from your saintly, perished children." The martyrs compelled him in so many ways and "requested that I should write about their exile and tortures." "The only thing I could

*See Appendix.

do," he lamented, "was be an eyewitness to the martyrdom of my race . . . a testifier to this great crime."

Given Balakian's often painful musings on death without burial, his book seems driven by a need to bury his unburied nation, reminding us of Hegel's assertion that burial is the first act of civilization, an act that genocidal killing negates. Unlike large, secure nations that have monuments and memorials to their dead, Armenia, he notes, at that time had none, and so he calls his book "a humble monument, a simple grave-cross of black history in honor of the one million two hundred thousand."

He was also aware that writing in what now can be called a modern age of mass atrocity (Raphael Lemkin would coin the term *genocide* in 1943, in large part on the basis of what happened to the Armenians in 1915) had changed the idea of self, individual, and human experience. "Though I have written," he notes,

> it was not to become a hero; only in the good old days could our heroes be counted on one hand or two. Today everyone—from the suckling Armenian baby in the cradle to the eighty-year-old grandmothers and grandfathers—has truly become a hero. Because they endured such unheard-of suffering and tortures and died such heroic deaths in the name of their nationality and religion, I am ashamed even to call my tribulations suffering.

The Armenian Genocide and the survivor experience that ensued altered our idea of modernity; and Balakian articulated this phenomenon long before a genocide-survivor discourse emerged in the 1970s. In many ways his assessments anticipate the post-Holocaust era: "There was a time when the Armenian nation had one collective history. But today, oh . . . every martyred or surviving Armenian has his or her own special story of black days, and this is only one of those hundreds of thousands of stories."

Balakian was fiercely patriotic and dreamed of a new Armenia that he hoped would emerge after the war, a vision that sustained him in the worst of times. But he does not refrain from critical scrutiny of his own culture. Although he extols Armenia's past and present achievements, there is no sentimentality in his evaluation of the failures of Armenian leadership during this crucial period. Nor does he spare his beloved Armenian Apostolic Church or its patriarch, Zaven Der Yeghiayan, in ascribing ineptitude and corruption.

With an acid pen he exposes the Armenian traitors who aided the Turkish government with their arrest and deportation plans, foolhardy romantics like Armen Garo, who advertised himself as a revolutionary in the British press, and miserly misanthropes like the wealthy Nalbandians of

Sis who wouldn't spare a penny to help the starving deportees passing near their properties. Nor is Balakian coy about expressing his disappointment in the lack of vision and the excess of emotionalism that defined Armenian politics of the time.

Readers, I think, will find Grigoris Balakian's persona large and passionate. His vitality, gusto, and intelligence are inseparable from his shrewd survival instincts, and his sense of irony helps him mediate his anguish and disbelief at what is happening to the Armenian people. While he sees himself always as a humble servant of God, he is a dynamic figure who understands when to take risks and when to lie low, when to speak and when to be invisible. He calls himself a "shepherd of a dismembered flock, an exiled clergyman in a caravan of exiles." He is devoted first and foremost to his flock, whether they be his intellectual comrades from Constantinople in prison at Chankiri or the emaciated group of about one hundred from Yozgat whom he cares for on a several-hundred-mile deportation march in the face of extraordinary violence and cruelty. For a period of time he refuses to consider the idea of escaping on his own because of his sense of responsibility to his fellow deportees.

There is a certain transparency about him that may owe something to his being a man of God, at times an open book to his Lord. He invites the reader into his prayers and nightmares, his tormented, death-saturated consciousness: corpses of children, the sexual mutilation and rape of women and girls, fields of dead, plains of mass grave mounds for miles, acres of unharvested wheat (the farmers all having been murdered), stray orphans and waifs with stories of massacre—all leave him in such anguish that he racks his mind for language. These images define the nightmarish landscape of his journey, and yet amid this horror he remains a clear-eyed observer.

We also experience the psychological dimensions of Balakian's conflicts; he is caught between knowing something awful is going to happen to the Armenians (as he does when he summons his brother-in-law to Constantinople from the eastern provinces in the fall of 1914) and his astonished disbelief about what is happening to him when he is arrested and imprisoned at Chankiri. Thus, we find Balakian in what Robert Jay Lifton has called a "common state of dissociation" that people facing extreme situations often manifest, as they hold within themselves contradictory feelings: intellectual understanding coexists with helplessness, confusion, and inability to accept the brutality of unfolding events.

Balakian evinces a keen awareness about how living in extremity has affected his mind and body. Upon his return to Constantinople in the fall of 1918, he describes (long before the term was coined) post-traumatic stress disorder: "I had become suspicious of everything, and I had developed a persecution complex . . . a telling sign of mental illness," and "despite the fact that my mind was clear, I could not free myself of my nightmares."

Notwithstanding his immersion in death, Balakian's engagement with nature provides an unexpected counterforce to the killing fields. His knowledge of and passion for landscape, geology, flora, and fauna inform his narrative. Embedded in the density of the Anatolian terrain, Balakian lived like an animal for close to four years, sleeping in mud, rain, and snow. In the forests of Injirli, he sustained himself with cedar sap, wild grasses, and the water he could suck from bark. This same knowledge of nature shows us how shrewdly the Turkish government used the severe and rocky terrain of Anatolia—with its cliffs, ravines, canyons, and gorges—to kill hundreds of thousands of Armenians and leave their corpses where they would be hidden from view. For example, the dramatic Kanle-gechid gorge in the Amanos mountains and the arid desolation of northern and eastern Syria were used to kill almost half a million.

Yet mingled with Balakian's dark report on land and topography is a pietistic feeling for the natural world. His psychological and emotional engagements with nature are infused with a kind of Hopkinsian or Wordsworthian sensibility. In nature he finds corollaries for human feeling and thought. He measures his psychic life in accord with and in contrast to the seasons, the weather, and the textures and vibrancies of flowers, trees, and animals. He describes rivers and streams with precision and sometimes waxes passionate over the natural beauty of Cilicia or the ruins of historic Armenian buildings in a haunted landscape. At one point, when in hiding, working in a vineyard owned by a Greek in Adana, he exclaims:

> I was living in such a peaceful state in Mother Nature's marvelous and tranquil environment that I would sometimes forget I was a deported and fugitive clergyman . . . the vineyard was giving me new vitality. On warm nights I would lie on the roof of our cottage and sleep peacefully—relaxing my nerves and maintaining my mental balance. So many individuals had lost their minds in similar circumstances! My life on the vineyard was a providential blessing, an oasis in these mortifying deserts of grief, tears, and blood.

It was here, in the bosom of nature, that Balakian decided he would write "the horrific story" and call it *Amenian Golgotha*.

Biography

He began to write *Armenian Golgotha* under the eaves of his mother's and sister's houses in Constantinople in the fall of 1918, even before the war had ended. But much of the writing seems to have been done in Manchester, England, where Balakian was the parish priest of the Armenian church from about 1921 to 1923, before he left for Marseilles to become bishop of southern France. The first volume was published in 1922 by the press of the Armenian Mekhitarist monastery in Vienna. The second volume fell into a void for lack of funding. It was found among his sister Rosa Antreassian's papers after her death in 1956 and was published in Paris in 1959 with the aid of the Armenian General Benevolent Union. (The precariousness of the voyage into the world of a book this important is hard to imagine.)

Grigoris Balakian was born in 1876* in Tokat, a small, multicultural city in the north-central highlands of Turkey, about seventy-five miles from the Black Sea. His father, Garabed, and his uncle Hovanness were merchants, both married to educated and dynamic women. Grigoris Balakian's mother, Varvara, from the well-known Huesisian family of Shabin Karahisar and Tokat, was unusually well educated for a woman of her time and place, and she often wrote for Armenian publications and encouraged him to pursue his clerical and intellectual career. After his graduation from Sanassarian Academy of Erzerum in 1894, which he attended on scholarship, Grigoris went to Mittweida University in Saxony, Germany, to study engineering. After a year there, feeling called by God, he returned to Turkey and entered the Armash Seminary to study for the priesthood; he was ordained in 1901.

By the following year Grigoris was a pastor in Kuzgunjuk and vicar of Bilejik. For a short time he was patriarchal vicar of Kastemouni, where he tried to organize a new diocese that, in the end, was not recognized by the Ottoman government; so he returned to Constantinople in 1906 as the personal secretary of Patriarch Maghakia Ormanian. Soon thereafter he was elected a member of the National Religious Assembly.† In 1908 he became a catholicossal envoy. On a historic mission in 1909, which he recalls in the early part of *Armenian Golgotha*, he accompanied Catholicos Matheos Izmirlian to St. Petersburg and Etchmiadzin, the Holy See of the Armenian Apostolic Church. He was involved on various fronts of Armenian cultural life. By 1912, as a member of the Izmiriantz Literary Committee, he became superintendent of the National Library and was

*The birthdate is disputed; accounts range from 1873 to 1879. In chapter 20 (vol. 2), he refers to himself as age forty in January 1917.

†Body of ecclesiastics overseeing the religious affairs of the Armenian nation.

responsible for its move to Pera. In that same year, he was sent to Erzerum by the board of trustees of the Sanassarian Academy to oversee the relocation of the school to Sivas. He was also elected the visiting pastor of the Armenians in Bulgaria, although his post was not approved by the Bulgarian government.

Intensely involved in both national and international Armenian issues, he negotiated with the German embassy in 1912–14 regarding Armenian reforms in Turkey. In 1913 he went to Berlin to study theology, only to return to Constantinople when World War I broke out in August 1914. The story of his life from that moment on is the subject of *Armenian Golgotha*. After the Armistice, he went to the Paris Peace Conference with Archbishop Yeghishe Tourian, Professor A. Der Hagopian, and Dr. Armenag Parseghian to join the Armenian delegations. He then apparently returned to Constantinople. He went to Cilicia (historic Armenia in southern Turkey) to evaluate the remnants of Armenian life there, but in 1920 his mission was aborted with the evacuation of Cilicia by the Kemalists.

By 1921 he was the pastor of the Armenians in Manchester and London. The catholicos charged him to organize a diocese of the Armenians in Europe, a daunting project that he was unable to complete, despite his energetic efforts. Greatly disappointed by the failure of the European Armenian diocese, he went to Marseilles around 1923, to become bishop of the Armenian Apostolic Church of southern France. There he pursued his lifelong passion for architecture. His training as a civil engineer led him to plan and organize the construction of two churches, one in Nice and one in Marseilles, as well as seven chapels and seven Armenian schools in Marseilles. In 1933, embittered by church politics, he resigned from this post. He lived in seclusion in Marseilles until he died in 1934 from a heart attack, which he suffered after lifting a foundation stone at the construction site of a new church. His death seemed inseparable from his love of building.

He appears to have been as intensely engaged with the Armenian scene as any intellectual of his generation, and given the numerous national and civic responsibilities he took on beyond his work as a clergyman, his productivity as a writer is impressive. Unfortunately, among the books he wrote, only *Armenian Golgotha* and *The Ruins of Ani* (1910) are in existence. His unpublished or lost manuscripts or books include "My Memoirs: Current Events, Conditions, Historical Moments, 1894–1914," "The Armenian Question in the Balkan War, and the Rebuilding of the Six Major Armenian Regions, 1912–1914," "The Armenian Hero, 1914–1918" (incomplete), "The Armenian Grand Chaos, 1918–1922," "Morsels of Armenian Politics," and "The Need for Reform of Holy

Etchmiadzin." He notes in *Armenian Golgotha* that during the massacres the Turks confiscated two other manuscripts, "The Armenian Family" and "Armenian Church Law." His works of memoir, current affairs, and nonfiction show his commitment to chronicling what he understood to be a momentous period in Armenian history, at a time when few historians seemed to be writing about it.

While accounts of Balakian describe him as "warm," "good-hearted," "fearless," "fiery," "kind," "sincere," "passionate," "dedicated," and "patriotic," it is clear that he was also outspoken and controversial. He believed his role as a public intellectual meant being a critic of the existing religious and political establishment, and his acuity often seemed to override a requisite acquiescence to authority. Direct, trenchant, and eloquent, Balakian manifested a reformist impulse toward what he regarded as the outmoded institutional mechanisms of his church and his nation.

Translation

Bringing *Armenian Golgotha* into English has involved a complex collaborative process of translation that began in 1999 when Anahid Yeremian, a particle physicist at Stanford University, generously offered to start translating the first chapters of *Armenian Golgotha* for me to translate further. The process was halted due to my work on other books and when it recommenced around 2004, I was working with Aris Sevag as the primary translator, though Yeremian continued to provide assistance. Sevag's expertise has been invaluable. Not only is he a seasoned professional translator, with several dozen books from Armenian into English to his credit, but his knowledge of Armenian history and literature enriches the process, and his commitment to this text was invaluable.

Because Grigoris Balakian had had no editor or professional publisher, my editor George Andreou at Alfred A. Knopf, Aris Sevag, and I assumed editorial roles, making various small cuts in the text. The Armenian literary style of the period, which lent itself to long, multiclause sentences, was sometimes so involuted it required trimming. At times when Balakian's emotions overwhelmed him, he repeated himself or drew the same conclusion in different terms; in reliving his anguish through writing, he could be redundant, for example, employing excessive modifiers *(merciless, wretched, bloody, horrific)*.

Some editorializing and sermonizing passages were deleted—moments of patriotic sentiment, clerical blessings of the dead, rage at Turkey, and the like—because, while they revealed the intensity of Balakian's emotions, they digressed from and interfered with the organic flow of the narrative. We left enough of these passages intact so that the reader will have an ample sense of these moments. Never did we interfere with fact or sentiment, voice or style. Balakian's vivid and detailed account of his experience is rendered faithfully, as are his ideas and analyses.

Balakian's early-twentieth-century Armenian demanded a precise and adaptive translation to twenty-first-century English. The compulsive process of sifting and culling, of finding nuanced meaning and idiomatic correctness in word, clause, and sentence, the fine-tuning of syntax, diction, and punctuation was continually challenging for me as collaborative translator and editor. With a book of two volumes and seventy-one chapters, this adventure has engaged me for nearly ten years. After my discovery of my great-uncle Grigoris Balakian (about which I wrote in a chapter, "Reading a Skeleton," in *Black Dog of Fate*), it has been a particularly poignant and rich experience for me to bring his book into print in English, eighty-seven years after its initial publication. I have done my best to view his story with an editor's objective eye and a poet's demand for precise language.

Peter Balakian
Hamilton, New York
April 2008

Black
Adrianople
(Edirne)
Rodosto
(Terfirda)
CONSTANTINOPLE
Adapazar
Sea of Marmara
Izmit
(Nicomedia)
Dardanelles
Bandirma
Bursa
Bilejik
Kastemouni
Chankiri
Ayash
ANGORA
(ANKARA)
Kizil River
Eskishehir
Kutaya
Aegean
Sea
Kirshehir
Lake
Tuz
Afyonkarahisar
Kara
Punar
Konya
Eregli
The 1915 Armenian Genocide
in the Turkish Empire
Principal routes of deportation
Railroad lines
Centers of massacre and deportation
Concentration camps
Principal points of transit
Principal destination points of deportation
Boundaries of the eastern provinces
0 MILES 200
0 KILOMETERS 200
Mediterranean Sea
CYPRUS

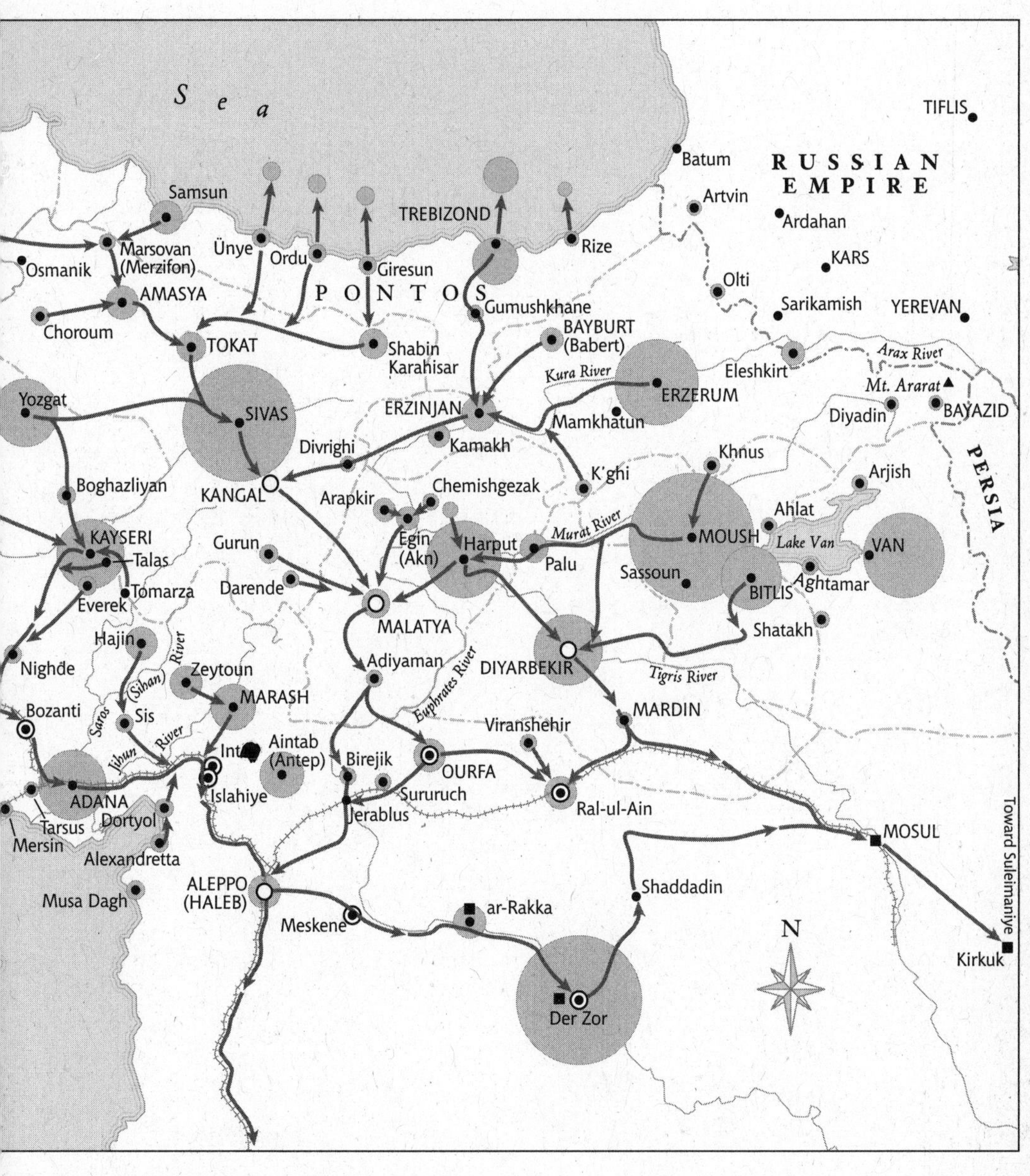
Sea
RUSSIAN EMPIRE
TIFLIS
Batum
Artvin
Ardahan
KARS
Olti
Sarikamish
YEREVAN
Samsun
Marsovan (Merzifon)
Osmanik
Ünye
Ordu
Giresun
TREBIZOND
Rize
PONTOS
AMASYA
Choroum
TOKAT
Shabin Karahisar
Gumushkhane
BAYBURT (Babert)
Kura River
ERZERUM
Eleshkirt
Arax River
Mt. Ararat
BAYAZID
Diyadin
Yozgat
SIVAS
ERZINJAN
Mamkhatun
Divrighi
Kamakh
K'ghi
Khnus
PERSIA
Arjish
KANGAL
Boghazliyan
Arapkir
Chemishgezak
Ahlat
KAYSERI
Talas
Tomarza
Everek
Gurun
Darende
Egin (Akn)
Harput
Palu
Murat River
MOUSH
Lake Van
VAN
Sassoun
BITLIS
Aghtamar
Shatakh
MALATYA
Hajin
Nighde
Saros (Sihan) River
Zeytoun
MARASH
Adiyaman
Euphrates River
DIYARBEKIR
Tigris River
MARDIN
Bozanti
Sis
Jihun River
Aintab (Antep)
Birejik
Viranshehir
OURFA
Islahiye
Sururuch
Jerablus
Ral-ul-Ain
ADANA
Tarsus
Mersin
Dortyol
Alexandretta
Musa Dagh
ALEPPO (HALEB)
Meskene
ar-Rakka
Shaddadin
MOSUL
Toward Suleimaniye
Kirkuk
N
Der Zor

Chronology

1876*

Balakian is born in Tokat. (Various sources give dates ranging from 1873 to 1879). His given name is Krikor (Gregory). During his childhood, the family moves to Constantinople.

1894

Balakian graduates from the Sanassarian Academy in Erzerum and leaves Turkey for Germany, where he studies engineering for a year at Mittweida University.

1894–1896

Sultan Abdul Hamid II wages an empire-wide campaign of massacres of the Armenian population, in reprisal for largely peaceful protests for reform; approximately 200,000 Armenians are killed. The sultan is called the "bloody sultan" in the Western press.

1896

Balakian returns to Constantinople and enters the Armash Seminary.

*Dates conform to the Gregorian or Western calendar.

1901

Balakian is ordained a *vartabed* and takes the classical form of his name, Grigoris. He begins as a minister but soon is called to administrative service by the patriarch of Constantinople.

1906–1913

Balakian serves in diplomatic positions in the Armenian Apostolic Partriarchate of Constantinople; he travels widely.

1908

JULY 24 The Young Turks (Committee of Union and Progress [*Ittihad ve Tarakki*], or CUP) force Sultan Abdul Hamid II to reinstate the constitution, which leads to the promise of reforms for Armenians and the other minorities of the empire.

1909

APRIL 13 A counterrevolution by the sultan's supporters and the military in Constantinople stirs anti-Christian feelings throughout the empire. In this context, massacres of Armenians take place in Adana and spread throughout Cilicia, resulting in the deaths of 15,000 to 25,000 Armenians and the destruction of the Armenian sections of towns and villages.

APRIL 23 The counterrevolution is quashed by the CUP's forces, and the sultan is deposed.

1912–13

In the Balkan Wars the Ottomans lose more than 80 percent of their European territory and suffer heavy casualties. A mass influx of Muslim refugees into Turkey creates increased political animosity toward Christians, and Turkish nationalism intensifies.

1913

JANUARY 26 The triumvirate of Ismail Enver, Mehmed Talaat, and Ahmed Jemal stages a coup, taking over the government in the name of an extreme nationalist ideology.

1913–14

Balakian studies theology at the University of Berlin.

1914

FEBRUARY 8 The Armenian Reform Agreement, whose passage is overseen by the European powers, allows European inspectors to oversee the condition of Ottoman Armenians, angering Turkey.

JULY 28 Austria-Hungary declares war against Serbia.

AUGUST 1–4 Germany declares war on Russia and France.
Turkey signs a secret military alliance with Germany.
Ottoman troops are effectively placed under German command.
World War I begins.

AUGUST In the cities of the western coast, vandalism and looting of Armenian and Greek shops takes place. Many Greeks are driven out of western Turkey.

MID-SEPTEMBER Balakian returns to Constantinople from Berlin.

NOVEMBER 5 Russia declares war on the Ottoman Empire.

NOVEMBER 9 In Constantinople the Sheikh-ul-Islam proclaims *jihad* against Christians to incite religious war against the Allies, but also igniting animosity toward the Armenians at home.

1915

JANUARY The Russian army routs the Turkish army in the Battle of Sarikamish. The presence of Armenian volunteers in the Russian army stirs more anti-Armenian passions. Armenians in the Ottoman army are disarmed and put into labor battalions, in which they will be massacred in the coming weeks and months by fellow soldiers.

FEBRUARY Interior Minister Talaat tells German ambassador Hans Freiherr von Wangenheim that he is going to resolve the Armenian Question by eliminating the Armenians.

FEBRUARY–MARCH Under the direction of the Interior Ministry, Dr. Behaeddin Shakir organizes *chetes* (mobile killing units) of the Special Organization (*Teshkilati Mahsusa*), mostly comprising thirty thousand criminals released from prison. This is a major component of the government's plan to annihilate the Armenians.

MARCH Ittihad (CUP) leaders convey through the Ittihad party network across the empire that Armenians must be deported.

APRIL Looting, rape, mass arrests, imprisonment, and executions of Armenians take place throughout the empire. In Zeytoun, Armenian mountaineers resist disarmament and tax extortion by Turkish troops; they are deported.

APRIL 15 Armenian resistance to massacre begins in Van province; they will hold off the Turkish troops for five weeks.

APRIL 24 In Constantinople, as British, Australian, New Zealand, and French troops prepare to land at Gallipoli, some 250 Armenian intellectuals and community leaders, including Grigoris Balakian, are arrested and sent under armed guard to a prison in Ayash and Chankiri, two hundred miles east. Similar arrests of Armenian intellectuals will continue in other cities throughout the year, and hundreds more will be arrested in Constantinople over the next few days. Fighting at Gallipoli fuels Turkish rage toward Armenians inside Turkey.

MAY 6 *The New York Times* reports: "The Young Turks have adopted the policy of [sultan] Abdul Hamid, namely the annihilation of the Armenians."

MAY 27 The Ittihad government passes the Temporary Law of Deportation, allowing the forcible deportation of all Armenians.

JUNE–AUGUST Armenians throughout Turkey are arrested in their homes, put on deportation marches, tortured, and massacred or abducted. Children are Islamized. Property is confiscated. Turkish refugees from the Ottomans' former European territories are resettled on Armenian lands.

JUNE 15 In Constantinople, twenty Hunchak Party leaders are publicly hanged.

JULY–AUGUST Many of the remaining leaders from Constantinople who were arrested on April 24 are killed.

JULY 16 U.S. Ambassador to Turkey Henry Morgenthau cables the secretary of state about "deportation of and excesses against peaceful Armenians," reporting that "a campaign of race extermination is in progress under a pretext of reprisal against rebellion."

AUGUST U.S. Consul Jesse B. Jackson reports to Ambassador Morgenthau that more than a million Armenians are believed to be lost.

SEPTEMBER The Ittihad government passes the Temporary Law of Confiscation and Expropriation, allowing it to confiscate all real estate and other property belonging to Armenians. In Musa Dagh, Armenians resist deportation and massacre. They hold off Turkish troops for several weeks until 4,058 persons are rescued by English and French warships and taken to Port Said, Egypt. This is one of four failed resistances—the others are at Van, Ourfa, and Shabin Karahisar.

1916

MID-FEBRUARY Balakian leaves Chankiri on a forced deportation march, along with the few surviving Constantinople intellectuals and the Armenian men of Chankiri, about fifty in all. Later they are joined by the remnants of the Armenian men of Yozgat, bringing their group to about one hundred.

APRIL Balakian escapes the deportation caravan in Islahiye and begins his life as a fugitive.

MAY 19 Britain and France sign the secret Sykes-Picot agreement, apportioning a good part of western Armenia to Russia.

JULY 15 The Russian army defeats the Turkish army in the Caucasus. Russian troops occupy most of western Armenia.

JULY–AUGUST Talaat orders a second wave of massacres of Armenians who are still alive in Der Zor. The total killed there exceeds 400,000.

AUGUST The Interior Ministry abolishes the Armenian Patriarchate of Constantinople.

1917

MARCH 15 In Russia, Tsar Nicholas II abdicates.

APRIL 6 The United States declares war on Germany and Austria-Hungary

APRIL 20 Turkey breaks diplomatic relations with the United States.

NOVEMBER The Interior Ministry orders all Armenians who are working on railroad lines to be deported.

NOVEMBER 7 In Russia, the Bolshevik Revolution ends the monarchy, soon beginning a civil war. Russian troops leave the Anatolian front, abandoning the Armenians.

1918

JANUARY In the United States, President Wilson presents his Fourteen Points, including assurances of security and "opportunity of autonomous development" for nationalities under Turkish rule.

MARCH 3 Germany, Russia, and Turkey sign the Treaty of Brest-Litovsk, in which Russia drops out of the war and, among other things, cedes three Armenian provinces to Turkey.

MARCH–APRIL Turkish forces reoccupy the historically Armenian provinces of Erzerum, Kars, and Van.

MAY 22 Turkish forces advance toward Yerevan and Etchmiadzin, the heart of historic Armenia in Russia. At Sardarabad, Armenian forces turn back the Turkish army and save what remains of Armenia.

MAY 28 Georgia and Azerbaijan, Armenia's partners in the short-lived Transcaucasian Federation, declare their independence from the federation. Armenia is left with no choice but to do the same. In Tiflis, the Democratic Republic of Armenia is declared.

SEPTEMBER 25 Disguised as a German soldier, Balakian returns to Constantinople, where he begins to write *Armenian Golgotha*.

OCTOBER The Allies capture Damascus, Beirut, and Aleppo. The surviving Armenians are rescued.

NOVEMBER 2 The ruling triumvirate—Talaat, Enver, and Jemal—flees the country.

NOVEMBER 11 Armistice.

1919

JANUARY 4 With Archbishop Yeghishe Tourian, Professor A. Der Hagopian, and Dr. Armenag Parseghian, Grigoris Balakian boards the British admiral's ship for the Paris Peace Conference.

FEBRUARY 1 Under British pressure, Ottoman courts-martial of perpetrators of the Armenian massacres commence in Constantinople. The Ittihad leaders will be sentenced to death in absentia in June; several convictions will result in imprisonment or execution. Although the trials will fall apart by 1920, they will yield hundreds of pages of confessions by perpetrators, which will be recorded in the Ottoman *Parliamentary Gazette* (*Takvim-i-Vekayi*).

MAY 15 Greece invades Turkey. The Allies have sanctioned the invasion in order for Greece to take back historically Greek territories along the western coast of Asia Minor.

JUNE President Wilson sends the King-Crane Commission, and later the Harbord Mission, to Turkey to assess the viability of a U.S. mandate for Armenia. The commissions will verify the extermination of the Armenians and place the death toll at more than one million.

JUNE 10 A military tribunal convicts Talaat, Enver, Jemal, and Dr. Nazim of war crimes and sentences them to death in absentia.

1920

APRIL 22 The United States recognizes the Democratic Republic of Armenia.

APRIL 23 In Ankara, Turkish nationalists form a separate government and elect Mustapha Kemal as their leader.

The Allies, negotiating the Treaty of Sèvres, ask President Wilson to draw the boundary lines of the Armenian Republic.

MAY 24 President Wilson goes before Congress seeking a mandate for Armenia. The Senate will reject it on June 1.

SEPTEMBER Kemalist forces launch a major offensive against the Republic of Armenia. They capture the Armenian lands formerly occupied by Russia.

NOVEMBER 22 President Wilson submits the boundary lines for a postwar land settlement for Armenia, including the provinces of Ererum, Trebizond, Van, and Bitlis and an outlet on the Black Sea. Turkey is to renounce claims to the ceded lands. The Wilson award reiterates the award to Armenia made in section 6 of the Treaty of Sèvres.

DECEMBER 2 The Democratic Republic of Armenia capitulates to the Turkish Republic and signs the Treaty of Alexandropol, which forces Armenia to relinquish the territory awarded in the Treaty of Sèvres.

DECEMBER 2–4 Soviet forces capture Yerevan, the Armenian capital. The Armenian Republic collapses after a little more than two and a half years in existence. Later, it will become the Soviet Socialist Republic of Armenia; it will reemerge as an independent republic in 1991, at the collapse of the Soviet Union.

1921

Balakian is serving as pastor of the Armenians in Manchester and London, England.

MARCH 16 Turkey and the Soviet Union sign the Treaty of Moscow, wherein they divide the significant parts of historically Armenian lands in the Caucasus between themselves.

MARCH 21 Soghomon Tehlirian, a young man who saw most of his family massacred in 1915, assassinates Talaat Pasha in Berlin.

JUNE In Berlin, Balakian testifies at the trial of Soghomon Tehlirian, who is acquitted in the assassination of Talaat.

1922

SEPTEMBER 14 Kemalists drive the Greek army out of Turkey. In the process, they burn Smyrna and massacre the Greeks and Armenians there.

1923

JULY 24 At Kemal's insistence, the European powers sign the Treaty of Lausanne, annulling the Treaty of Sèvres. The new treaty recognizes the Republic of Turkey as successor to the Ottoman state and establishes new borders for Turkey. The award to Armenia is scrapped; the word *Armenia* does not appear in the Lausanne treaty.

OCTOBER 29 The Kemalists proclaim the modern Turkish Republic.

1923–33

Balakian is bishop of the Armenian Apostolic Church of southern France. He resigns in 1933 and dies in 1934 in Marseilles.

Translator's Note

We have made a concerted effort to give the most commonly used form of place-names in order to ensure the greatest number of readers will be familiar with them. Therefore, the Armenian names of certain cities and towns have been replaced by their Turkish counterparts, which have existed in English-language literature for the past century and a half. Both forms are given in the Glossary under Place-Name Variants.

As for the spelling of Turkish place-names, again, we have given preference to the most widely used variants. Also, Turkish names are given in the style commonly used before the Turkish alphabet reform of 1928; thus, Erzinjan rather than Erzincan.

Generally speaking, Armenian personal names have been transliterated based on Western Armenian pronunciation, inasmuch as the overwhelming majority of individuals mentioned in this memoir were of Western Armenian origin. We have made exceptions in the case of a few, including the author himself, who were known to prefer the classical morphology; for example, Grigor instead of Krikor, Komitas instead of Gomidas.

Except for April 24, (the night of the arrest of the cultural leaders in Constantinople and the day on which the Armenian Genocide is commemorated worldwide, and the immediate days following) we have left the dates as Grigoris Balakian presented them in accord with the Julian calendar used in the Ottoman Empire. Exceptions are the chapters about Berlin and the events following the Armistice in 1918, in which he uses the Gregorian calendar. In the twentieth century, the difference between the Gregorian and Julian calendars is thirteen days.

Aris Sevag

VOLUME ONE

The Life of an Exile

JULY 1914–APRIL 1916

O God, the heathen have come into thy inheritance;
They have defiled thy holy temple; they have laid Jerusalem in ruins.
They have given the bodies of thy servants to the birds of the air for food,
the flesh of thy saints to the beasts of the earth.
They have poured out their blood like water round about Jerusalem,
and there was none to bury them.

PSALM 79:1–3

PART I

July–October 1914

1

In Berlin Before the War

Ever since the day of the assassination of Ferdinand, the heir to the Austro-Hungarian throne, by a Serbian youth in Sarajevo, the political atmosphere of Europe had been extremely gloomy. On July 25, 1914, Serbia gave an unsatisfactory reply to the harsh forty-eight-hour ultimatum issued by Austria-Hungary. Austria's declaration of war against Serbia was imminent.

Finally the horrible pan-European war—which had been expected for many years—was erupting, and it will remain a permanent blot on the illustrious European civilization.

On the main boulevards of Berlin, and particularly on the grand Unter den Linden, which runs from the Kaiser's palace to the Brandenburg Gate, the people displayed great enthusiasm for the war. The prevailing sentiment was that Russia would not simply sit back and watch an Austro-Hungarian-Serbian war. Large oil portraits of Kaiser Wilhelm and Emperor Franz Joseph were displayed side by side in the windows of the big stores. Everywhere the Austro-Hungarian flag was waving along with the German flag, and there was great hustle and bustle at night on the major boulevards of the city.

On Sunday, July 26, the crowd was large enough to cause congestion on Unter den Linden, Friedrichstrasse all the way to Leipzigerstrasse, and Potsdamerplatz. Hundreds of thousands of additional copies of the main daily newspapers were distributed free, for the purpose of preparing the minds of the German people for the great historical events about to happen.

All the daily newspapers of the capital, irrespective of political sympathies, defended the views of Germany's ally Austria-Hungary, firmly and openly advocating support for meeting the responsibilities of an ally, if needed. Only the German socialist (Social Democratic) party organ *Vor-*

wärts did not defend the Austro-Hungarian cause, coming out in absolute opposition to the war. All the capital's other daily papers used language that, if not quite threatening, was still hostile toward Russia, declaring that the origins of the Sarajevo crime were better sought in St. Petersburg than in Belgrade.

On Sunday night the main buildings of Berlin were lavishly illuminated, and the people, fired with military fervor, maintained a mood of carefree celebration all night long.

By July 27 the papers of Berlin large and small had adopted outright menacing rhetoric toward Russia. They announced that in the event of an Austro-Hungarian-Russian war, Germany would immediately carry out its sacred responsibility as ally. The people of the capital now considered war against Russia inevitable. The government organs, led by the *Norddeutsche Allgemeine Zeitung*, the largest official daily, were preparing the ground for blaming Russia in case of war.

At half past eight on the evening of July 28, the Social Democratic Party of Berlin had organized a huge meeting against the war; it took place simultaneously at twenty-seven different meeting halls in the capital. Half an hour before the designated starting time, I went to the large meeting hall, called Volkshaus, at the Charlottenburg community center, located close to my apartment, not wanting to miss this historic opportunity to study up close the psychology of the organized German working class. Truly the scene was impressive, as the huge meeting hall, along with its adjacent wings and garden, was filled with tens of thousands of working-class men and women. They had all come in festive clothing, but no one was drunk or noisy; a mysterious silence prevailed. It seemed to me that on the face of each worker I could read the nightmarish expression of impending danger.

Just as in the other twenty-six meeting halls, here as well the slogan was "Speak against the war." To summarize the thoughts of the speaker, a socialist member of the Reichstag:

> We don't want war because in the present century such a war is an insult to European civilization; the entire burden of it shall be borne by us workers, through our honest sweat and blood. We, being the large mass of working people, will not permit the capitalists and owners of arms factories to exploit us and, trampling over our carcasses, make additional millions for themselves. No, we don't need war, and why should we go to war? So that Austria-Hungary can succeed without fail in squashing a small independent Serbia?
>
> We don't want to become the tools of the adventurous policy

> pursued by Austria-Hungary for years in the Balkans. No matter how small and weak Serbia is, as an independent and self-respecting nation, is it really possible for it to accept conditions that Austria-Hungary itself has trouble enforcing in its own country? We don't want war to become the tool of Austria-Hungary, which, wishing to condemn and punish the Sarajevo incident, would, in exchange for the death of one person, commit the greatest of crimes, subjecting all of Europe to the unprecedented horrors and carnage of an all-encompassing war.

From all directions shouts went out, "Down with war! Long live world peace and the brotherhood of the working class! Yes, we are opposed to the war, and we stand in unity with those hundreds of thousands of laborers in St. Petersburg, who are demonstrating against it, like us. We have no hatred for the French people, who share our feelings and thoughts."

The speaker, the socialist member of Parliament, then began to enumerate serious accusations against the major arms factory owners, the capitalists, the prowar political parties, and the military.

A resolution against the war was immediately composed, to be sent to German prime minister Theobald von Bethmann-Hollweg and the International Socialist Bureau in Brussels. Police officers, who had been deliberately lingering outside, were greeted with whistles upon entering the hall. But the popular gathering ended and, in a perfectly orderly manner, we went down to the street, where the scene was even more impressive. A crowd of more than fifteen thousand working-class people, who had been intently listening to the speakers in the large meeting rooms of the various *Volkshäuser* and the four speakers in the large garden of the community center, had united and formed a procession. Moving at a solemn military pace and in an orderly fashion, the procession advanced from Bismarckstrasse, one of Berlin's largest boulevards, toward the Tiergarten. The destination, according to the secret watchword of the day, was the imperial castle, where the 150,000 to 200,000 organized socialist workers of Berlin who had participated in the day's meetings at twenty-seven different locations were scheduled to assemble.

However, agents faithful to despotic and militaristic Germany—such as policemen on horseback, foot, and bicycle, and military police—had gathered at the intersection of Bismarckstrasse and the large boulevards of Kurfürstendamm and Kantstrasse. Carrying iron chains tied together, these forces, with their bodies and horses, sought to disperse the crowd because it was protesting against war.

Despite the most circumspect crowd-control measures, between 60,000 and 70,000 working-class people reached the imperial palace from the side streets, singing the "Internationale." The Kaiser, for his part, having prior knowledge of it all, had departed at dawn by train for the old royal city of Potsdam, an hour away.

I was quite impressed, because I had been witness to the demonstrations and processions of the Muslim people in the wake of the Ottoman constitution, but really there was no comparison. What took place in Constantinople had been a demonstration by a mob, while the one in Berlin was respectable and methodically planned. The former, like a low comedy, caused the onlooker to laugh, while the latter earned the regard and sympathy of even Germanophobic foreign witnesses.

The working folk of Berlin had gathered calmly and coolly for a grand celebration of peace. They could not be blamed if their peaceful efforts were futile, owing to a bellicose and adventurous Kaiser intent on ruling over the ruins of neighboring countries. Future criminal and tragic events would serve to vindicate those who lived by the honest sweat of their brow and refused to follow the warmongering camarilla.

I found more good judgment and foresight in these people, who bore the heaviest burden of life's struggle and received the least, than in the German and Austro-Hungarian ministers and government officials. These lines are reprinted from my unsigned series of articles entitled "The Berlin Diary of an Armenian, on the Occasion of the European War":[1]

> The day is not far off when, in the wake of war, this working class will appear as the greatest actor in the great internal revolution and rebirth to take place within a *crushed* Germany, with a completely new structure and based on new foundations . . . Instead of merely sobering up after the disaster, they said and did everything to clear the dangerous black clouds of worldwide hatred of the German race from the German skies, and so they are not responsible if no one heeded them . . . The eminent German prime minister Bismarck had not been mistaken when he considered the German socialists the biggest enemy of German "Imperialism," who today already have 111 deputies in the Reichstag, *and who will certainly play decisive roles in tomorrow's Germany.*

Today, six years later, as I write these lines, my predictions are already a reality.

The next day, July 29, all the papers of Berlin reporting on those huge peace demonstrations pronounced them antinationalist! Only the *Vorwärts*, the main organ of the socialists, while giving all the details of the peaceful demonstrations, stridently criticized the excesses of the police.

Although the antisocialist and chauvinist elements, as well as the promilitary and imperialistic groups, wanted to organize counterdemonstrations, luckily, except for youths attending school, they could find no followers.

At this time feverish negotiations, mediated by the king of England, were going on via telegram among the three emperors. A noble proposal for an agreement, made by the English foreign secretary, was received with contempt in Berlin. The German military party and the pan-German federation, with the Kaiser at its head, secretly carried out all sorts of measures to abort every peacemaking effort and stir up savage prowar sentiment among the German people.

Berlin's daily newspapers were promulgating news of the Russian mobilization. It was even said that Russia had already taken up a threatening position on the borders of Germany and Austria-Hungary, and on July 31 popular opinion had it that war was inevitable.

The anger and resentment of the German people was directed against Russia, though by contrast there was no obvious ill will toward France. The German government was spreading false rumors via its secret service that Russian spies had come to Germany to murder the Kaiser and blow up bridges, that Germany and Austria-Hungary were overrun with Russian secret agents, and that the Sarajevo incident had taken place at Russia's behest to provide a pretext for attacking Austria-Hungary. By means of these and other such false reports, the masses were stirred to prepare the ground for the official declaration of war against Russia the very next day.

And so the fate of Western civilization hung on the words of the German Kaiser. He, in turn, caught up in such wild dreams of victory as only world conquerors dream, did not care to foresee the widespread misfortune of millions, whom he considered merely cannon fodder.

The European peoples stayed up on the last night of peace, July 31, 1914, unaware of the horrific mourning that was to prevail—from the imperial palaces to the most remote village huts—at the loss of the 30 million innocents who would soon be led to the slaughter.

2

In Berlin

August 1, 1914, was the last day of the semester at the University of Berlin. As a divinity student, according to tradition, in the morning I had gone to the university to listen to the famous professor Adolf von Harnack, the lecturer for the first hour, after which the annual vacation so dear to us students would begin.

But instead of beginning his lecture, Professor Harnack launched an exhortation about the war that inevitably would be declared in a day or two. He said he expected the German students to take their honorable place in this historic war, which jealous neighboring nations were forcing upon the Germans in the hope of destroying the German people along with German civilization. Abandoning his calm and scientific demeanor, this world-famous scientist suddenly sounded like a general leading his troops to the front. The lecture hall, with more than eight hundred listeners of both sexes, was thus transformed into a war rally, and the blood of the German youth was already boiling with vengeance. In their violent passion they had forgotten for a moment that there were numerous foreigners of all nationalities among us.

Professor Harnack tried to continue his lecture, but the students, now bursting with enthusiasm for the war, were no longer interested and began to leave. The University of Berlin, located on Unter den Linden, became clogged from dawn on with an ever-growing crowd that made a loud, raucous noise and impeded any normal flow of workday traffic. A few decades earlier Germany's world-famous philosopher Friedrich Nietz-sche had preached that pity and compassion were mental illnesses . . . and he proclaimed that the doctrine of brute force was the dominant factor in Germany's present and future glory.

The generations since Nietzsche were instilled with this spirit. Professor Harnack, a devotee of this destructive doctrine, wanted to push the German university students to the front, since the time had come not only to sing "Deutschland, Deutschland über alles!" but also to make it a reality.

When I left the university, I saw that the boulevard, more than a hundred meters in width, was so congested that—except for military officers of any rank, who were shown respect and greeted with shouts of praise ("*Hoch!*")—it was impossible to walk along it or cross it.

Large oil portraits of the two great German generals, Bismarck* and Helmut von Moltke, who had been victorious in 1870–71, were displayed in the windows of all the major stores. A sea of humanity overflowed the huge square of the imperial palace, Berlin's cathedral, and the museums. Aware of the significance of these historic days, and taking upon myself every hardship, I tried to get close to the large balcony facing the cathedral of the imperial palace, from which, it was said, the Kaiser would be making the official declaration that same day.

The people were shouting, "We want to see our beloved Kaiser!" Finally, after we'd waited for four and a half hours, the curtains of the large balcony were opened, and the Kaiser, like some new Napoleon, appeared, along with the empress, surrounded by palace guards. A cemetery-like silence descended over that united crowd of more than a hundred thousand. He was the citadel of the people's patriotism, and every German believed that the fate of the European peoples depended on their all-powerful Kaiser. I think that if, God forbid, he had in the end emerged victorious, his people would have made a saint out of him, if not a god, just as the ancient Romans had done.

In his clear bass voice the Kaiser spoke:

> I did what was possible to preserve the peace, but our jealous neighbors have crossed our borders, trampling upon the sacred soil of our fatherland.
>
> I forgive all the passionate struggles waged up to now [referring to the socialists]; irrespective of party or denomination, the German nation needs to stand as one to wage that inevitable critical fight, which our enemies thrust on us, with the sole intention of destroying us.
>
> Today, I pull out my sword, which I had put down for over 25 years, in the name of and for the love of peace, and I am not going to put it back in its sheath until I win.
>
> Well, go to church tomorrow, get down on your knees and pray to our God for speedy victories for our troops.

The huge capital vibrated with the thunderous hurrahs and *Hoch*s from hundreds of thousands of lips, and the sea of people, in waves, gradually dispersed, singing their two national songs, "Deutschland, Deutschland

*Best known as chancellor of Germany, 1871–90.—trans.

über alles" (Germany, Germany above all others) and "Die Wacht am Rhein" (The Watch on the Rhine).

It was the death sentence of civilized mankind that this modern-day Caligula had pronounced, without any understanding that he and his warmongering people would soon drown in a pool of innocent blood. And in his demagoguery he deceived the ignorant people into believing that their enemies had entered their land, whereas it was he who was about to make a sudden incursion onto Belgian soil.

The people passed the time on Sunday, August 2, in gaiety and laughter, drunk with the anticipation of victories. Then the following day they evaluated the weighty consequences of the situation more soberly and descended on the banks to withdraw their savings.

On the second day after the declaration of war, all foodstuffs became more expensive, then disappeared from view. Red conscription announcements were posted, and the general opinion was that five million soldiers, ready and waiting within seven days, would be able to rush into the neighboring enemy countries, sweeping aside and trampling underfoot all impediments.

On Sunday, August 2, the *Norddeutsche Allgemeine Zeitung* had published the declaration of war against Russia, reporting that the Kaiser had issued the order for general mobilization. All the large and small Berlin papers threw wood into the already raging furnace, each trying to surpass the others in publishing false news. In order to kindle patriotic enthusiasm, they wrote that the Ottoman government had ordered a general military conscription, that a major revolt had broken out in the Caucasus, and that the Muslims of India had started to stir. In reality, it would have been impossible to get such news in twenty-four hours.

Truly Sunday, August 2, was a historic day for every German when, in accordance with the Kaiser's request, solemn services were conducted in churches throughout the country, praying for military victory. At 9:30 A.M. the bells of the hundreds of churches in Berlin were almost deafening, inviting the people to *Gottesdienst*. I went half an hour early to the extraordinary Kaiser-Wilhelm-Gedächtniskirche near my apartment, the second-largest church after the Berlin cathedral. It had been built by Wilhelm II as a memorial to his famous grandfather Wilhelm I; with its Gothic exterior, golden mosaic interior, and a bell tower 150 meters high, the marvelous temple was admired by all foreign visitors.

The scene that day was indeed impressive. The long, wide boulevards leading to the huge square of the church—Tauentzienstrasse, Kantstrasse, and the Kurfürstendamm, the arteries of the major traffic in Charlottenburg that stretch all the way to the church square—were crammed with people, and all traffic had stopped.

Meanwhile inside the church, which I reached only with great effort, the majestic solemnity of a sanctuary prevailed. On the eastern side stood the life-size snow-white marble statue of Jesus under a white marble apse with pillars; to the untrained mind and eye, it left the impression of a pagan idol, fundamentally contrary to the spirit of the Old and New Testaments. In front of it, there were three large candleholders on each side, with all the candles lit. And on either side of the altar were winged silver crosses. The entire church was flooded with the light of hundreds of electric lamps, under whose rays sparkled the precious images of the Bible and the gold-plated mosaics and the stained-glass windows.

Since it was the second day of the mobilization, no young people [meaning men] could be seen in the church. The twenty-one-to-thirty-five-year-olds had already rushed to respond to the fatherland's call for military duty. In attendance were men and women past the age of forty, and young ladies. Many were quietly crying over being separated from their loved ones—whose return was uncertain at best.

The day's eloquent preacher, following orders, used martial words exhorting the people to the defense of the trampled fatherland! Then, at the preacher's request, the congregation obeyed the Kaiser's command to kneel down to pray to the God of peace for military victories for the German armies.

Similar solemn prayers were being said at the same time in the church square, and tens of thousands had also fallen to their knees on the asphalt of the large boulevards and on the tracks of the tramcars, to pray for victory. Then, singing familiar patriotic favorites, they dispersed, confident of quick and decisive successes.

Meanwhile in Petersburg similar solemn religious ceremonies were taking place before the tsar, as many thousands of Russians asked for the victory of the Russian troops.

On the next day, August 3, inasmuch as the railroads had been commandeered for troop transport, communication was cut off. The Berliners pursued any Russians in sight, often with sticks, raining blows on the heads of these poor people who were just innocent merchants, or getting the police to arrest them.

Out of curiosity I rushed to the Charlottenburg railway station to see for myself the scenes of the soldiers, having responded to the call of military service and now leaving Berlin to join their battalions, parting from their loved ones. Hundreds of soldiers, carrying their small bundles, had come to the railway station to take their final leave of their families.

Truly the scene was moving: affectionate hugs, unending kisses, a husband being separated from his wife, a father from his young sons, the groom from his new bride, a young fiancé from his fiancée. Only two parting words were heard from everyone's lips: *auf Wiedersehen*, "till we see [each other] again." No tears, no regrets, no sighs . . . the soldiers, saying their goodbyes with smiles, went joyfully to the borders as if to a party, so confident were they of their victory.

I was amazed at the patriotism of the Germans, but I felt sorry for these young men, many of whom would never return, because the leaders of the nation, for the sake of their own personal glory and profit, were sending them to the slaughter. Many young soldiers went to war asking their loved ones not to forget to send gift parcels care of the *Zentral-Postlagernd Paris*, or General Delivery in Paris. Those sending these youths to die had convinced them that, as if on some pleasure trip, they would be in Paris by September 2, the historic anniversary of the Battle of Sedan.*

When, however, on August 4 England suddenly declared war on Germany, the mood in the German capital quickly changed, and general concern supplanted the air of festivity. It was as if a bomb had been dropped on the once-jubilant German public. No one had expected England to intervene, and so they believed that in a few months they would flatten France and Russia. Now the German papers began to viciously attack England, blaming the Francophile English king, Edward, for paving the way for this horrible war against Germany by befriending France and, through the mediation of the latter, reaching an agreement with Russia. The papers also claimed that Edward's goal was to eliminate German trade, along with the German fleet, and in this way to secure uncontested control over the seas.

Now England was considered the source of all evil, whereas no demonstrations of disrespect were mounted against the representatives of Russia and France. So enraged were the German people against England that a large crowd attacked the British embassy on Wilhelmstrasse, smashing all the glass windows, while the ambassador and his wife were inside. Mocking the mercenary character of the Germans, embassy officials threw large bags of pfennigs at the crowds, provoking even more anger.

Responding to a directive they received from above, the German papers, wanting to brighten the dark effect of England's declaration, began to spread the false rumors that 300,000 Russian workers had rebelled against the tsar in Petersburg and that the tsar had been forced to flee his capital city to Moscow. In reality, the emperor of Russia had gone to Moscow to kindle the martial enthusiasm of the *muzhiks* by visiting the historic church of the tsars in the Kremlin to pray for the victory of the Russian forces. The German papers also wrote, likewise falsely, that rebel-

*Sedan (1870) was a decisive battle in the Franco-Prussian War during which Napoleon III was captured.

lions had broken out in Poland and Finland. During the course of the war the papers gradually perfected the art of rumor, until all these lies came crumbling down like a house raised on sand.

It was the fifth day of the war, and I was sitting in a café called Yost on Potsdamerplatz with a few compatriots, watching the procession of newly enlisted soldiers bound for the front, when a policeman came to invite me to the police guardhouse, because a few Jews had, on account of my beard, mistaken me for a Russian spy and sought my arrest. As I followed the German policeman through the crowd to the guardhouse, individuals pursued me; their number gradually increased and posed a threat, until they delivered a few blows to my neck with sticks. I hastened to show them my Ottoman passport and declared that I was from a country friendly to theirs. I then quickly became the object of kindly gestures from all sides, as many, including the policeman, sought forgiveness for the misunderstanding—which, unfortunately, was not the last I would experience.

The German papers gleefully announced that the large German battle cruiser *Goeben* and the light cruiser *Breslau* had bombarded the French Algerian shore. These same warships would later play a critical role when they fired upon the Russian men-of-war in the Black Sea, thus forcing Turkey to plummet into the burning abyss of war.

On Thursday, August 6, I was sitting in one of the familiar cafés in Charlottenburg with two professor friends from the University of Berlin, talking about the burning issues of the day. Two German strangers, upper class, came in and sat right next to us, and the younger of the two, who we found out later was a lawyer, expressed the following thought as an aside: "How great it would be if the Armenians in the Caucasus revolted now! . . . The Armenians are an enterprising, daring, and active people; if they revolt, and the twelve million Muslims in the Caucasus quickly follow their example, it will be big trouble for the Russians." If this German had been aware of the presence of an Armenian . . . I would have considered his a comment of polite affectation; however, as he knew nothing of this circumstance, I couldn't help but recall the fable about the lion and the mouse.[1]

On the seventh day of the mobilization, five million soldiers, in their various formations, were already positioned on the two war fronts and engaging in combat against the French and Russian armies. In Berlin every foreigner not of enemy nationality had to wear on his lapel a little flag of his country.

The Americans were treated with great respect, as the Germans were making every effort to attract the sympathy and neutrality of this great nation. At that time fifty thousand Americans lived in Berlin. In these days, by chance, I met my tailor, who had become a reserve officer and was headed to the front in two days; I asked him what he expected regarding the duration of the war. He answered with certainty, "If it were only Russia and France involved, it could be over in two months. However, since England has also come in, perhaps it will last a few months longer." When I asked him when the Germans could hope to enter Paris, he hastened to reply, "We are going to celebrate this year's Sedan anniversary in Paris on September second." Indeed, this was now the firm conviction of every German.

On the day after the declaration, more than forty thousand Russians of military age had been jailed as prisoners of war, and the German government now sent them to the fields, under strict surveillance, to gather the harvest. To fulfill their duty to the fatherland, more than sixty thousand German women and young unmarried ladies applied to serve in various divisions of the Red Cross, for which service they were prepared in specially organized classes.

The people began to manifest a fanaticism unbecoming a civilized nation, demanding that signs in French and English be removed from the stores and cafés in the city and replaced with German-language signs. Thus, during the first week the foreign-language signs were gradually removed. The sign on one of Berlin's most famous and wonderful cafés, the Piccadilly, which also happened to be one of the most glorious buildings in the capital, was changed to read "Fatherland Café."

On any given day everyone was waiting for news of victory, the Germans confessing regularly to foreign friends: "We have been preparing for this war for the past forty years." Such an arrogant confession was a condemnation of the German nation.

The police made an official announcement inviting the people to pursue and facilitate the arrest of Russian spies; this led to harsh persecution of innocent Russians. From then on you could frequently see in the streets of Berlin crowds persecuting or even thrashing Russians—contrary to the most basic tenets of twentieth-century civilization.

On Sunday, August 9, trains full of Slavic soldiers passed through Berlin on their way to the French border. The Austro-Hungarian government was transferring them from the Russian front to Germany's French front, fearing that these troops might turn traitor and join their fellow Slavs on the other side.

The illustrated German newspapers, in a calculated way, published articles about the German siege of Paris in 1871. They depicted dogs, cats, mice, horses, and so on hanging by their feet for sale in the desperate butcher shops. They hoped to spur the troops' patriotic zeal, hastening them to the gates of Paris.

On the ninth day of the declaration I had an argument with a German friend who made a frank pronouncement that seemed to express the conviction of every German: "When we enter Paris this time, we will not want to come out with just five billion, but rather we will demand thirty billion, so that France will not be able to afford to enlist, through loans, allies against us and prepare for new wars of revenge."

By now this mentality had become a national mantra, without even a consideration that the opposite might also come to pass . . . which it did—after the war Germany would be forced to pay huge fines and reparations.

It was just ten days since the start of the war, and already the poor were having trouble obtaining the most basic necessities. Every item of foodstuff had increased in price. The savings institutions and banks were barely able to pay 5 percent interest. Contrary to prohibitive government laws, the bread-bakers' union wanted to increase the price of bread, arguing that the old price was impossible, given the unusually high price of flour.

The movie theaters, racetracks, and other places of amusement were automatically closed because of the war. On Sundays the people of the capital did not rush to the railway stations or take walks in the nearby parks and gardens as before. Everywhere one could see extreme seriousness and thrift. Even the number of those going to restaurants in the afternoons diminished; in the name of frugality, everyone now prepared their own lunches and tried to spend as little money as possible. Customers were hardly to be seen in the shops, which were frequented only by buyers of urgently needed items or by travelers.

My apartment was exactly at the edge of Lietzensee in Charlottenburg, facing the Grünewald, the fantastic grove of cedars that was the favorite promenade of Berliners. Once artillery training began there, all day long I could hear horrific thunderous booms that shook the multistory houses of the marvelous suburb nearby, terrifying the mothers and other women with loved ones on the battlefields.

During these days I had the chance to meet with a high-level officer who lived in our building and was getting ready to go to the front. I asked him how long the war might last. He answered,

> *Hochwürdiger,** we cannot tell our women and people the concern we feel; however, you are a confessor and a trustworthy person; I don't want to pretend: whether we win or lose, Germany is going to be a poor country; our paradise of a country is going to be filled with our own corpses. Even though we had been prepared for this war for the past forty years, we had never anticipated that so many

*Reverend.—G.B.

> powerful enemies would be attacking us at once. With the participation of England and Japan in the war, the balance is upset . . . In particular, we never expected the English attack, and the serious class of the German people is very worried, since the English are a stubborn nation. But no one can express an opposing view at this time, since special secret police have been assigned to arrest those who speak against the war and to render them to the courts-martial as traitors . . . It is a shame, the marvelous civilization, which is the result of our forty years of peaceful work, is going to be ruined.

It was thus that I first met a German—a senior officer at that—who, refusing to get caught up in the prevailing enthusiasm, was viewing the realities coolly and calmly, assessing and analyzing them, and predicting horrible disaster.

The English and French papers condemned Germany's fruitless violation of Belgian neutrality; as if in response, all the German daily papers wrote, "*Not kennt kein Gebot und kein Verbot*" (Urgency knows neither law nor obstacles). This principle, which seemed to apply only to the German state, would be taken to extremes to justify violating every treaty and agreement in the name of "urgency." And in this way Germany would earn worldwide hatred.

The problem of the poor tenants of apartment buildings had become a pressing issue. The mayor's office and the newspapers recommended that landlords treat their poor tenants with compassion. With the working members of families gone off to war, the soldiers' wives could not live on the small sum of ten marks they received for each child monthly from the government. Ladies' auxiliary committees began to form and, through special campaigns, raised considerable sums to help the families of the soldiers, thus bringing relief to the mothers whose onerous concern was feeding their children.

I visited two soup kitchens operated by ladies' auxiliary committees and I was favorably impressed to see society ladies serving nutritious hot food free to all the innocent children, young and old of both sexes, during lunch and dinner hours. I also saw special restaurants where unfortunate unemployed laborers received two kinds of food with plenty of bread for ten pfennigs, which amounted to twenty paras at that time. The government also did everything possible to help the poor, hoping to keep the number of war-related malcontents low. It knew quite well that these individuals would otherwise swell the ranks of the socialists.

Already quite riled up against the Russians, the Germans became further incensed by reading in the newspapers that their marvelous embassy in Petersburg had been largely destroyed—burned and plundered by the Russian mob, which act had also resulted in the death of a longtime and elderly embassy employee. And so they began to persecute Russians in the street more viciously, tormenting them without mercy.

On the thirteenth day of the war, to conserve coal, the municipal government cut back on electricity in the capital and called on its residents to conserve water, natural gas, and electricity in order to reduce the use of pit coal in the giant plants that furnished these utilities.

The poor were already afflicted by unemployment, as many stores and offices had begun laying off employees, both male and female. The majority of these workers were young girls, who, now in extreme need, wandered the crowded streets of the capital prostituting themselves and creating a public scandal. In order to maintain public morality, the police began to employ the strictest of measures. In addition, ladies' societies were formed to zealously uphold the morality of these young unfortunate girls, by gathering and protecting them.

It must be noted that communal German family values were quite strong, and anyone who dared to violate them was subject to the most severe punishment, without regard to position, rank, or wealth. The capital of imperial Germany was the only one on the continent without houses of ill repute, and as was not the case in Paris, the police sought out any house even suspected of being such.

The result of this moral and religious way of life was that the German population—of barely 36 million in 1871—had reached the unbelievable size of 68 million, setting an example of rapid growth unprecedented among all nations. Meanwhile France, with a population of 46 million in 1871, experienced exactly the opposite trend, and its current population was only 37 to 38 million.

On the fifteenth day of the declaration of war, news of the initial German victory on the Belgian and French fronts reached the capital, making the city of more than three million people (a million of whom were stationed at the central army headquarters) drunk with excitement. Everywhere there was a festive mood, as on holidays, and thousands of flags waved.

There were popular processions everywhere, and strident voices sang patriotic songs to enliven the capital's peaceful, sad, and heretofore deserted streets. The German people were waiting from day to day for news of their army's entrance into Paris. The Kaiser—the incarnation of the self-confidence and self-sacrifice of the German people—had already departed for the French border.

Already, too, black plaques bearing the names of the German war dead had appeared on the doors and walls of official buildings. Large crowds gathered before them, searching for the names of their loved ones. The wives of the many officers who had been killed were now wearing black. Everywhere there were "room for rent" signs, every family having set aside a few rooms in their home to create a new source of income. Only the photographers prospered, because every person who went to war rushed to have his picture taken, as a final memento for his family.

The movement of the electric trams and railways resumed, with the distinctive regularity of normal days. By an ordinance of the ministry of education, the secondary schools and *Volksschüle* reopened, whereas the technical schools and institutions of higher education would remain closed pending further orders. In any case, the secondary schools (gymnasiums and *Realschüle*) and the public schools (*Volksschüle*) opened on August 1, while the institutes of higher specialized education and the universities didn't open before September 15.

The military authorities, bearing red signs, now started to invite thirty-five-to-forty-six-year-olds to join the army as well, and for this reason widespread alarm, if not panic, began to mount. The newspapers, in turn, were encouraging people to endure every great sacrifice, to save the fatherland from the pan-Slavic inundation! One by one the heads of the German federated states, including the kings of Württemberg and Bavaria and numerous dukes, went to the front to lead their respective armies.

The patriotic vigor was extraordinary among all classes of the populace, but especially admirable was the heroic sacrifice of the German mothers. Some had sent four and even six young sons to the front. The newspapers were full of stories of heroic and self-sacrificing German mothers who had given birth to many children. The true foundations of German power and greatness, they wrote, were "German multibirthing mothers," without whom neither the tens of thousands of giant cannons nor the rapid-firing Mausers of the Krupp firm of Essen—even the most perfect weapon—would have no value. Were it not for the German mothers, it would be impossible to field five million soldiers as a human bulwark against the enemy.

I heard from one member of the German-Armenian Society that during these days the president of that group, a well-known Armenophile, Dr. Johannes Lepsius, had written a petition to the German foreign minister, Gottlieb von Jagow, asking that the Armenians, no matter their citizenship, be safe from police pursuit, and apparently the minister had replied favorably. Thus an Armenian of Russian citizenship was able to reach Petersburg via Sweden. But this agreement could not be trusted for the long term; after Germany became allied with Turkey, Armenian youths of military age were turned over to the Turkish military administration.

It was apparent, even from the beginning, that Germany had not put much hope in the military capability of Austria-Hungary. Furthermore, it was highly suspicious of Italy, considering it an "unfaithful ally" that would defect to the side of the most powerful country at the first opportunity. The military censors, however, had forbidden any anti-Italian expression whatsoever, so that in the event Italy were no longer with Germany, at least it would not turn against them. From the first month on, Germans had such sympathy for Turkey that they considered it an associate of their cause, their natural ally in this war.

The military administration, having drafted those who were of legal military age, twenty-one to forty-six, now invited those between seventeen and twenty years of age to take up arms as volunteers, training them under the supervision of retired officers.

In order to break the mighty stride of the German armies that were rapidly advancing toward Paris, the Russian army forced them to defend their rear by rapidly invading East Prussia, sweeping aside everything in its path. The German people, who expected only news of victory, were terrified to learn the details of the Russian advance into Prussia. And the Germans living in these regions, paralyzed with fear by stories they had heard about the brutality of the Russian Cossacks, took flight with great urgency, leaving behind all their property and possessions.

Most of these people, whose condition was wretched, came to Berlin seeking refuge, and Berliners, upon hearing these shocking stories about the Russian Cossacks, also became panic-stricken.

A month had passed since the declaration of war, and the entire German population was impatient for the vanguard of the German army to enter Paris by September 2. Now, however, news of defeats on the French front began to reach Berlin, disheartening the people, who had been drunk with news of earlier victories. The military censors made every effort to magnify news of victories and proportionately minimize defeats.

We were reading in the German newspapers the first account of the Armenian volunteer movement's activities in the Caucasus. Turkey, in turn, was continuing the military draft with vigor, supposedly in order to withstand a probable attack from the Russians.

Other articles that had appeared before the war in British and French dailies were now reprinted in the German papers, of course with sarcastic commentary, to the effect that if Turkey made any move, it would pay the price of the broken glass of a pan-European war. And that the time had come for a radical solution to the Eastern Question, which had become gangrenous. Again and again the European powers, with their conflicting interests in Turkey, had conjured the specter of world war to pressure the Sublime Porte to come to a solution to the Eastern Question.[2] But now, with the events at Sarajevo, the war had exploded; thus unbidden, the opportunity presented itself to plunge the surgeon's lancet deep into the abscessed wound of Turkey.

3

Return to Constantinople from Berlin

Following the start of the world war, amid the frightful clamor of thousands of thundering cannons, the panic gradually became more intense and widespread. Irrespective of sex and age, not one individual was unaffected by this all-encompassing storm. All the twenty- to forty-six-year-old foreigners of different nationalities who were in Berlin received compulsory notices from their respective consulates to return to the homeland and prepare to meet their obligations. Germans abroad, in turn, hurried back to Germany and, putting on military uniforms, enthusiastically went with their respective regiments to the front. Thousands of German laborers who had been working on the Baghdad railway line were arriving in Berlin, headed for the front.

It was impossible not to be affected by this swell of patriotic fervor. No one thought about desertion. The moment had also come for us Armenians; at gatherings of compatriots, we too had started to think about duty. I was considering a return to Turkey, and scarcely had I expressed this intention to a few of my closest friends than everyone expressed the opinion that it would be dangerous for me to return to Constantinople. Many advised me to go to the Caucasus and join the Armenian volunteer groups, and then cross over into Turkish Armenia.

I, for my part, felt that such a bold step was risky. I considered the volunteer movement, which had been hastily conceived in the very first months of the war, an extremely dangerous development likely only to irritate the Ittihad government and lead to grave consequences for the more than two million Armenians living in the Turkish empire.

Some felt extremely encouraged by the Armenophile policy of the Russian government and thought that, thanks to the all-merciful tsar, it would be possible to save Turkish Armenia. I reminded them of the Russo-Turkish War of 1877–78, in which the Russian army, with the help of [Russian] Armenian commanders, captured Erzerum; then, due to a sudden shift in policy, the Russian troops withdrew, leaving the local Armenian population of some eight thousand exposed to the raging vindictiveness of the Turkish government and mob.

But Armenians, inflamed by their centuries-old hopes, did not want to hear suggestions that stemmed from logic. Caught up in their nationalist sentiment, they were loath to miss this unique opportunity to redress the wrongs committed by the Turks against the Armenian people.

On the other hand, no perceptive Armenian living in Germany could fail to notice the fervent Turcophilism of the German government and people, and it was impossible not to be concerned about future difficulties and misfortunes. Contrary to the reassurances of Dr. Lepsius of the German-Armenian Society, the Germans did not much like us Armenians, the enemies of the Turks. Meanwhile the German-Armenian Society, formed in Berlin at the suggestion and with the endorsement of the German foreign minister, von Jagow, and his assistant Arthur Zimmermann, was intended not so much to protect the interests of the Armenian people as to prevent the two million Armenians living in Turkey from becoming tools of the tsar's government, and to prevent the Russians from using the Armenians as a pretext for interfering in Turkey's internal affairs.

The latter concern had become firmly rooted in the minds of German politicians, so much so that during the Balkan War, as a member of the patriarchate's central committee for Armenian reforms, I had sometimes made official visits to the German ambassador von Wangenheim, who had emphatically advised me of his worries and expressed his wish that we Armenians distance ourselves from the Russians, jumping instead into the lap of the Germans.

Even as the German Foreign Ministry secretly used the German-Armenian Society to further its covert plan of winning over the Armenians and alienating them from the Russian government, a German-Turkish Society, through the overt initiative of the same government office, was being formed under the chairmanship of [Baron] Rüdiger von der Goltz Pasha, who had reorganized the Turkish army during the past twenty years [1883–96]. In February 1914, five months before the declaration of war, this von der Goltz Pasha, who was German by race but truly Turkified in heart and mind, defended the following position in his opening speech as chairman at the first official meeting of the German-Turkish Society. He delivered it in the presence of the Turkish ambassador and his entire staff, as well as well-known German political and business figures:

> The Russian government has in this past century used the subject Christian peoples living in the Turkish Empire as a pretext to interfere in the internal affairs of Turkey, and thus has been

> the cause of Turkey's dismemberment. Considering that all of Turkey's subject Christian nations have already been liberated, now the Russian government has taken up [the cause of] the Armenians as well and, taking advantage of the Balkan War, has put forth a reform plan, with the hidden purpose of subjecting Turkey to a new dismemberment. In order to save Turkey from a new calamity, it is necessary to once and for all remove the half a million Armenians living in the provinces of Van, Bitlis, and Erzerum, contiguous to the Russo-Turkish borders, and move them from those border areas southward, to the vicinity of Aleppo and Mesopotamia. In exchange, the Arabs from these regions should be moved to the Russo-Turkish border areas.

He was hereby pursuing two political agendas with one blow: separating the Arabs and the Armenians from their ancient historic homelands, and killing in them every hope and expectation of present or future national independence.

When a professor who had been present at the meeting confided this monstrous plan to me, I hurried to write about it to the patriarchate.

However, at that time no one gave any credence to the possibility of such a huge political plan, because in human history from prehistoric times, there had never been a forced displacement of an entire nationality.

But as we will unfortunately see, that which had seemed impossible to everyone at that time, and even became a subject of derision, became possible during the world war, as did a litany of other tragic and criminal events, as well as widespread human slaughter unprecedented in the annals of mankind.

Thus, as a clergyman who had served among the Armenians in Turkey for fifteen years, I preferred to return to Constantinople to be as useful as possible to those whom I indeed saw as being in immediate danger, standing on the edge of a frightening precipice.

The patriotic fervor around us contributed to my inner voice of responsibility, which overcame the other voice of fear. Thus, in mid-September 1914, I departed Berlin for Constantinople.

Just an hour after I left Berlin, two German women, a mother and daughter, sitting near me in the compartment of the train (incidentally, it was scarcely possible to encounter German men on the trains, since all had been conscripted except for young adolescents and the elderly), asked me my nationality, so that (no doubt in accordance with the secret order of the police) they could keep an eye on me.

Hearing that I was from Turkey, and thinking that all Turkish nationals must invariably be ethnic Turks, they accepted me as a representative of a friendly nation and spoke with me unguardedly about the events of the day.

Still fresh in my memory is the compassion of the young German woman, who, criticizing those responsible for this war, said, among other things:

> Too bad that we Germans have many famous generals and military men, but we don't have any politicians. We don't have any because all those holding political office are military people, whether prime minister, minister, ambassador or consul. Therefore we don't have seasoned diplomats with a serious understanding as they do in Britain, and under these conditions we will not be able to produce them either. If we had at least one diplomat, and if he were to tell us that we Germans are now hated all over the world, the responsible people of our nation would, of course, not have jumped into this war so rashly and lightly. None of us believed that Britain would suddenly join our enemies, and in doing so upset the balance of power so that whether we win or lose this war, Germany is lost in any case.

The mother, her national pride offended, was angry with her daughter for having been so open with a foreigner and tried to change the subject. Nevertheless, I was able to get a sense of the view and psychology of those Germans who were against the war. A few hours later we reached Breslau, where the mother and daughter got off, since it was their home. Having relocated to Berlin on business, they were now returning to their birthplace because of the war, hoping to endure it in as peaceful an environment as possible.

The Russians' victorious entry into East Prussia had stoked such fear and confusion that the top German military brass had given the order to entrench Breslau, the large city nearest to the Russian-German border. Thousands of workers were cutting down the surrounding forests and digging trenches to defend against an invasion from Moscow.

Our Berlin-Constantinople express train raced on, passing military trains—loaded with huge cannons, vehicles, iron ovens, kitchens, thousands of soldiers, and animals—rushing to the borders. They were headed mainly toward East Prussia, which at that time seemed to be the Germans' weakest and most vulnerable flank.

We reached the Austro-German border at midnight, where there was a military checkpoint. According to the new arrangement, we had to leave the German train and wait for an Austrian one, which, however, was late in arriving. After a five-hour delay, we departed for Budapest in a dirty and slow Austrian train. All the curtains of the train windows were closed so that foreign travelers could not see the secret military transports, and furthermore it was forbidden to look outside.

After an oppressive sixty-hour journey in a fetid atmosphere we reached Budapest, whereas before the war it had been possible to reach Constantinople in the same time. All of us travelers were asked to present ourselves with official papers to the central military commander of Budapest to confirm our identity. After rather lengthy formalities, it was easy for me, as a citizen of a friendly nation, Turkey, to get a military permit document and then buy a railway ticket and board the train.

The scenery was the same during the entire trip—long rows of railroad cars loaded with cannons, weapons, ammunition, supplies, soldiers, horses, and so on. The sight of these transports provoked fear in all of us, as we easily imagined the bursting fire and flames from the thundering muzzles of these hundreds of cannons spreading death everywhere.

Soon we entered the wide fertile plains of Hungary, which were as flat as the surface of a calm sea. In some places the harvest had been completed and the sheaves of grain stacked up in piles had become a mass of heaps. In other spots, the peasants had only now been able to harvest the crop with the help of Russian soldiers, who were prisoners of war. In all the stations at which we stopped in Austria-Hungary, hundreds of soldiers were leaving their loved ones with embraces of final farewell. While we had not seen tears or heard the sighs in Germany, we were witnesses of lamenting, wailing, and crying in Austria-Hungary.

In Germany soldiers had said goodbye to their loved ones with joy, with the indestructible hope of victory. In Austria-Hungary, however, the soldiers parted from their loved ones with crying and mourning, as if going to their inevitable deaths.

On the fifth day of our journey we reached Bucharest, the capital of Romania. Romania, having taken a neutral position, was not thought to be engaged in any war preparations, but we heard the horrific thunder of cannons—the maneuvers of the artillery men—in the capital itself.

Inasmuch as we had changed trains at the Romanian border, we departed Bucharest for Constantsa after a few hours via the Romanian railway. An extraordinary hustle and bustle of war preparations could be seen everywhere, as if Romania were indeed at war. On the opposite bank of the Danube, the Bulgarian side, we could see preparations too, and mysterious transports in covered railway cars.

Finally, crossing the large, marvelous iron bridge over the Danube, we arrived in Constantsa at night. Like other travelers, we were forced to wait five to six days before we could depart by steamship for Constantinople. And in Constantsa as well, the loud thunder of cannons; here too maneuvers were being conducted, but no one knew by whom or against whom. With great fear all nationalities, the whole populace, were taking preparatory steps to get as far away as possible and, if necessary, to escape by some means, either unscathed or with minimal damage.

I went to the central office of the Romanian steamship company on the quay, where there were a great many travelers and the crowd was so dense that the office allocated tickets only to those who had been referred by official places and persons. In order to get such preference, I was forced to petition the director of the company, and when he learned that I had come from Berlin, he became extremely interested and asked for news.

Thinking that the Romanians were Germanophiles—their king was descended from the imperial German Hohenzollern dynasty—I began to praise the German nation and their yet-to-be-deified emperor, and I told the director about the German victories, thus hoping to win his favor and secure a ticket to Constantinople. To my great disappointment, however, he interrupted me and said confidentially, "Monsignor, you think that the Romanians are going to go to war on the side of the Germans? No, not at all; we like the French, and if we make money, we don't go to Berlin to eat; rather, we go only to Paris."

Discontinuing my forced Germanophile defense, I tried to take a middle road, this time speaking about the fine qualities of the French and recalling the Battle of the Marne, praising General Joffre, who had saved the French capital by defeating the Germans there. I no longer had any doubt that the Romanians would be fighting on the side of the Entente, since every Romanian thought and felt like this director of the steamship company. Having achieved mutual friendly respect with the man, I acquired a first-class ticket on the steamship and went to the hotel. Finally, after a tortuous fifteen-day journey, I reached Constantinople. Though the sea had been calm, my soul was agitated.

I had just entered the customs house on the Galata Quay when the officials, who had had the opportunity to make my acquaintance (or, to use the Oriental word, *befriend* me) owing to my frequent travels, learned I was returning from Berlin. They immediately left off inspecting the goods of the multitude of travelers, gathered around me, and asked with great interest for news of German victories.

Since Turkey had not yet officially entered the war, the French and English papers that reached Constantinople, as well as the Greek and Armenian papers of the capital, had reduced the Turks to despair by exposing the false rumors of German victories.

Naturally, not wishing to express myself in an indiscreet manner, on the day that I entered Constantinople, I encouraged the Turkish officials with accounts of real and hypothetical German victories.

My Germanophile manner of speech was so pleasant to them, so close to their hearts, that the chief of the customs house inspectors praised my common sense, saying,

> *Effendi*, give your compatriots in Constantinople, whose views are completely opposite yours, a little advice so that they will renounce their love for Russia. They have gone to such extremes in their affinity and love for the Russians, French, and English that on the day that the Russians win, the Armenians smile . . . but when the Russians have been defeated, they are sad. This much sincerity will cause them much trouble later on.

Already, right on the quay, I became aware that a large breach had opened between the Turks and the Armenians. With agonizing fear, I saw that the Armenians of the capital, by giving in to their emotions and self-destructive sincerity—in only the second month of the war—had stirred the Armenophobic feelings of the Turkish people. And this, despite knowing what a horrible pitch the frenzy of the Turks could reach and what criminal consequences it could have. The bloody experience of the last thirty years had not made the Armenians any more prudent; nor had it made them less earnest or more self-contained.

PART II

The First Deportation

APRIL 1915–FEBRUARY 1916

4

The General Condition of the Armenians at the Beginning of 1915

The all-encompassing terror of the world war, like the devouring flames of a fire, spread gradually from the imperial palaces to the wretched village huts. Besides the five great powers involved (England, France, Russia, Germany, and Austria-Hungary), all the remaining nations large and small, having a profound grasp of this extraordinarily grave situation, had lost no time in declaring neutrality.

Even Italy, whose thirty-year treaty obliged it to participate in the war with its allies Germany and Austria-Hungary, was extremely wary about taking a decisive step, not wanting to subject itself to the uncertain outcome of an adventurous policy.

Yes, all of them were pursuing a reserved course and did not want to express sympathy or antipathy toward either side, attentively awaiting the development of military events, which were escalating on a daily basis. Each nation had quickly appointed its most experienced elder politician as head of state, and each nation, prudently and anxiously, had taken serious measures to resist the worldwide storm of blood gradually approaching its borders.

Each nation, to the best of its ability, was bent on concealing its true mind and heart, and all the governments went to impossible lengths to prevent their neighbors from guessing their secret political, administrative, and military undertakings.

And so during these frightful historical days, we Armenians alone failed to heed this overall prevailing concern, and we alone neglected to address the imperative to act with judgment and farsightedness; on the contrary, according to our custom of giving way to our feelings, we threw ourselves as a nation blindly into a precipitous adventure. Whereas the most powerful governments remained noncommital, not wanting to offend this or that side, and played their diplomatic or strategic cards close to the vest, we Armenians alone began, from the first day, to show our self-destructive sincerity and rashness.

In this way we provoked the Turks, who had for a long time been looking for an excuse to correct the big political mistake of their Ottoman predecessors in not [completely] massacring the Christians and, in one blow, annihilating the entire Armenian population in Turkey.

From the very first day, Armenians abroad, the unorganized groups of volunteers rushing to the Caucasus, and Armenians from the Caucasus hastened to declare active sympathy for the Triple Entente powers and particularly for tsarist Russia.

Meanwhile these countries, who we thought were our friends, were engaged in shameful bargaining to cultivate and prepare for the secret treaty of 1916.[1] By that treaty they would divide our ancestral lands among themselves by putting our national fate and our four-thousand-year-old homeland up for auction, even as they called us their brave little ally. We Armenians, imprudently and without forethought, put our already-drained blood in the service of these very same powers.

In solemn public ceremonies in Paris and in Sofia, Constantinople Armenian clergymen blessed the weapons from America intended for regiments of Armenian volunteers [in Russia], as secret informers for the Turkish embassies looked on. Moreover the Turkish ambassadors reported all such goings-on on a daily basis to the appropriate officials of the Sublime Porte in Constantinople.

The Armenian population of the capital, about 120,000, failed to take its very delicate situation into consideration and follow the reserved and circumspect course that its Greek and Jewish neighbors took. It had already begun to consider itself saved.

These Armenians expressed their inner feelings in such an open manner that Turkish newspapers, like *Karagoz*, wrote that if one wished to know the military successes or failures of the day, one had only to look in the face of the first Armenian one encountered. If he was happy, then Russia was the victor; if he was sad, then Germany was the victor—so the Turkish officials had told me at the customs house the day I arrived in Constantinople.

The Armenian dailies of Constantinople, propelled by the general current of this enthusiasm, extolled the victories of the Entente powers, both spurious and actual, with grandiose headlines and exaggerated accounts, while they ignored or minimized the initial successes of the Germans, never missing an opportunity to express anti-German sentiment. One need only peruse the editions published at the outbreak of the war, in July, August, and September 1914, to confirm this fact.

However, during this critical period the Armenian Turks had no set Armenian national policy—individuals and political organizations wrote, spoke, and acted as they wished, according to their own points of view. This was irresponsible because no one considered that innocent Armenians living within the borders of Turkey would pay the price. Meanwhile the Armenian population of Constantinople, believing that the hour of its redemption was finally at hand, was in a state of great excitement. Traditional solemn festivities were observed with a new fervor by people who were carried away by their illusions. Sensational theatrical performances based on the lives of national historic figures, large concerts organized under the direction of the Archimandrite Komitas, matinee recitals presented by the Essayan Alumni Association of Pera, literary gatherings, neighborhood evening parties and daytime parties on Sundays, nighttime dances, autumn soccer matches, public processions of Boy and Girl Scouts, frequent lectures organized in the name of the Red Cross, and other such gatherings, recitals, and competitions followed one another, in the excitement of unrealistic enthusiasm.

Like all tyrannies, the conniving Ittihad government [Committee of Union and Progress] did not obstruct the celebrants; on the contrary, it provided more accommodating conditions than were usually possible for the Armenian people within the limits of the law, thus ensuring they would not have time to think perceptively about the secret plans the Ittihad government was hatching in the dark.

So widespread were the excitement and demagogy that no one worried about tomorrow. Besides me, just a few national representatives were trying, in vain, to point out the imminent danger to the Armenians in Turkey. But we dissenters had been silenced with threats of exile handed down from the all-powerful Osman Bedri, the chief of police of Constantinople. Anyway, what was the use of terrifying people and driving them to desperation over circumstances that boded ill when everyone was so excited? After all, weren't the mighty English and French fleets already at the Dardanelles? Each day now they destroyed some solid bastion of Kilit El Bahr in the straits of Chanak Kale. And after all, wasn't Constantinople on the verge of falling in a couple of days?

Indeed, at this time the daily newspapers of Constantinople were reporting that the Turkish government, under the leadership of Sultan Reshad and his ministers, was making preparations to move to Eskishehir and then, if necessary, to the old Turkish capital of Konya. The papers of the government record offices were being gathered up and stored in trunks or iron chests, awaiting the order for final departure. Therefore, what cause was there to worry?

Popular enthusiasm reached such a pitch as to surpass that of the first

Armenian exultation back in 1894.[2] Now once again groups of Armenians were running every day to the shores of the Sea of Marmara to watch the majestic British fleet pass toward the Bosphorus, its mission to save the Armenians, of course. We had quickly forgotten the historic words of the British government officials who said that the English fleet could not climb Mount Ararat (5,560 meters). But they had no problem getting their men-of-war to climb Mount Everest. In the meantime, while the Armenians in Constantinople were frolicking and rejoicing, more than two million elsewhere were abandoned to a black fate.

The Turkish government was censoring the mails in the name of martial law and the state of siege, reaching the limit of stringency, since the day the Turks entered the war, while travel had become so restricted that all communication between Constantinople and the provinces had ceased. Thus all communications between the Patriarchate of Constantinople and the more than thirty large and small provincial archdioceses and dioceses were severed.

The Armenians of the capital were uninformed about the Armenians in the provinces and vice versa. For this reason the provincial population did not know what the overall national [Armenian] position was or in what manner they should proceed. Still the Armenians of the provinces, like the Armenians of Constantinople, believed that the historic hour had come for the realization of their age-old national dreams and hopes, and so they too were in a state of unprecedented euphoria. But in the provinces they were waiting, confident that the leaders in Constantinople were doing all that was needed to make it happen.

The largest, most heavily Armenian-populated archdioceses and dioceses, such as Sivas, Diyarbekir, Van, Erzinjan, Arapkir, Agn, Moush, Ankara, and other secondary dioceses, as well as the nine dioceses of Cilicia,* had been left without a shepherd for many years, because of the transfer or death of prelates, who were bishops and archimandrites [*vartabeds*]† or vicars.

Only after the start of the war between Russia and Turkey, on the first day of Bayram‡ in the autumn of 1914, did it dawn on people that there was an urgent need to send shepherds to the more than twenty provincial dioceses and archdioceses that were without spiritual leaders.

The Ittihad government, or the real government of the Ittihad committee that was hiding behind it, opened all the gates of the Turkish pris-

*Not literally a province of "historical Armenia," Cilicia—a region southeast of the Taurus mountains to the Mediterranean coast—was ruled by Armenian kings from 1199 to 1375 and has been known as Little Armenia and Armenia Minor.—trans.

†*Vartabed:* Celibate priest, ranking below a bishop.—trans.

‡General Turkish word for *festival* on any nationally celebrated holiday.—trans.

ons under a general pardon, thereby releasing thousands of professional criminals, who then formed bands of *chetes.** These bands began to infest all the roads in Asia Minor, making them impassable, and disrupting all traffic, especially of Christians.

During this time I received an invitation from the patriarchate to assume the position of *locum tenens* of the Diocese of Erzinjan and to travel immediately to my new post via Sivas. I tried in vain to convince those who were making these hasty, shortsighted, eleventh-hour arrangements that it was impossible for me to assume this position and travel to that province under the prevailing circumstances. It was not a matter of my not wanting to go, I stated, but of my not being able to go.

And so a certain faction of the clergy stirred up a storm against me. As I had turned down the assignment, they believed they had found the opportunity to satisfy their own interests and cleverly accused me of aiming to depose the patriarch. Meanwhile, with Police Chief Bedri† standing over all of our heads like a Damoclean sword, it was not the time to move; nor were there means to do so.

I consider it extraneous to delve into more detail than this; thus let it suffice to present here the copy of the two official letters exchanged between us.

ARMENIAN PATRIARCHATE CONSTANTINOPLE

Constantinople, October 22, 1914

Mixed Assembly
National Central Administration
Number 528

Your Grace Rt. Rev. Grigoris Balakian
Locum Tenens of Erzinjan
In Constantinople.

Considering the vacant state of the diocesan throne of an important province like Erzinjan in the present, delicate circumstances, and the immediate need for the presence of an able spiritual leader there, the Mixed Assembly‡ of the National Central Administration has appointed Your Reverence to the position of locum

*Raiders, brigands, irregulars.—G.B.

†See Biographical Glossary.

‡National Religious Assembly and the Political Assemblies combined, with responsibility for the administration of mixed affairs. See also Glossary.—trans.

tenens of the diocese of said province. We trust as to your feelings of love for your nation and are aware of your competence and administrative proficiency in diocesan affairs.

In conveying our worthy selection of Your reverence, we are sure that, given the demands of the present situation, you will willingly accept this important position, and inform us of your agreement immediately, in order for the proper plans to be made.

Prayerfully
Patriarch of the Armenians in Turkey
Archbishop Zaven Der Yeghiayan

....

Scutari, October 28, 1914.

Most Reverend
Your Eminence Archbishop Zaven Der Yeghiayan
Patriarch of the Armenians in Turkey
In Constantinople.

I had the honor of receiving the official letter of October 22 from your High Holiness, informing me that I have been chosen to be the locum tenens of the diocese of Erzinjan.

Your patriarchate has left such heavily Armenian areas and historically the most important dioceses like Van, Diyarbekir, Sivas, and Erzinjan without shepherds for more than two and, in the case of the latter, three years, during this historic period of radical transformation of the Ottoman fatherland. And this, despite the fact that there were half a dozen newly consecrated archbishops and experienced archimandrites in the capital city, who were suited for provincial pastorships, yet were unemployed.

But now at the last minute, with the Ottoman fatherland having entered the war just a few weeks ago, the first and last dioceses, particularly Van and Erzinjan, are provinces that border Russia and are subject to imminent danger. By appointing spiritual shepherds in such untimely circumstances, [the Mixed Assembly] puts the weighty responsibility of its shortsighted course of action upon shepherds who will not be able to travel in the present conditions.

I will await a tranquil moment to determine who is responsible for this decision, but meanwhile for the first time in my fifteen years of ecclesiastical ministry, I am obliged absolutely to decline this appointment. And, I don't want to encourage your modern spiritual authority in its erroneous and shortsighted actions, with passive obedience.

Despite the fact of my having been permitted by the spiritual authority (1913) to study in Germany, now finding myself temporarily returned to Constantinople as a guest only because of the European war, please do not be surprised, Your Holiness, if I state my deep regret at this plan made deliberately at the eleventh hour.

I remain the humble servant of my nation
Very Rev. G. Balakian.

I don't know how, but an inexplicable obsession was tormenting my mind and soul and a voice was saying to me, "Don't go; you will be killed."

Precisely because of my fear, I wrote my brother-in-law in Trebizond (he was the general agricultural government inspector of three provinces: Trebizond, Erzerum, and Bitlis) and informed him that "the Armenians in the provinces are going to be annihilated. Come to Constantinople immediately, and bring your son with you." But when I saw that it was a matter of days before war would break out between Russia and Turkey, and that my brother-in-law, because of his official position, was unwilling or unable to come to Constantinople, I sent him a telegram that stated: MY SISTER IS DEATHLY ILL. COME TO CONSTANTINOPLE QUICKLY.

When he received this message, he hastened to come to Constantinople with my nephew. He arrived extremely worried, but I calmed him down on the quay, telling him, "No one is ill; but I had no other way of getting you to come to Constantinople. The situation is much worse than it is thought to be."

Ten days later in the Black Sea, the Russian fleet attacked the German *Goeben* and *Breslau* men-of-war, and entry to the Black Sea from the Bosphorus was altogether shut down by mines, henceforth putting an end to all steamship traffic. Seeing that it would be impossible to send me even by force to Erzinjan, a few days later [the patriarchate] summoned to the same post the Very Rev. Sahag Odabashian,* prelate of Bursa, who had been ordained archimandrite at the same time I was.

Consumed by the prevailing enthusiasm, and despite my fraternal cautions, Archimandrite Sahag accepted the applause and praise lavished upon him by the Armenian daily newspapers, and he departed for Sivas. He lacked the courage to resist, and only as he was leaving did he send me

*See Biographical Glossary.

a message saying: "Although I don't want to go, I have no choice, since I am afraid that the patriarchate will persecute me, as they have persecuted you."

After resting for a few days in Sivas, his birthplace, Archimandrite Sahag got on the road toward Erzinjan. When he was near Sooshehir, about ten hours from Sivas, the *chete* horsemen, organized by the Ittihad Special Organization and commissioned by Minister of the Interior Talaat,* put nine bullets in him, brutally murdering and dismembering Archimandrite Sahag instead of me. He was the innocent victim of the imprudent arrangement of his shortsighted superiors.

Subsequently a grand memorial service was held in the Mother Church, and the deceased was praised as one fallen in the line of duty, by individuals who took every means to ensure that they themselves would not end up on that very same road of duty they so extolled.

I was present at this heartrending memorial to my colleague, which, had I been the kind to resign myself to blind obedience, would have been sung for me. But the killing of Archimandrite Sahag was only the beginning of a long chain of events.

Talaat, the interior minister, had committed this first crime immediately after the start of the Russo-Turkish War, on the belief that the Armenian Partriarchate would use the pretext of sending a prelate to Erzinjan to send a special legate to the Russian borders in order to pass secret instructions to the Armenian generals of the Russian army, and the head of the Armenian volunteer army, Antranig.* So it had happened in the 1877–78 Russo-Turkish War, when Archimandrite Vahan of Bardizag was sent, on behalf of Patriarch Nerses of blessed memory, as an envoy to General Mikhail Loris-Melikov.* Eight Turkish officers, disguised in Circassian dress, had murdered the unfortunate archimandrite with government-issue Mausers and taken only his official papers, leaving his gold watch and a large sum of money next to the victim in the carriage. This latter circumstance confirmed, in and of itself, that the purpose of the killing was not robbery: no doubt remained as to the political nature of the crime.

During these historic days, owing to the passivity of the Armenian political leaders, the patriarchate in Constantinople, though in charge of the fate of the nation, was also in a state of confusion and was incapable of assessing the increasingly grave situation. The patriarch, who had been brought to Constantinople from Diyarbekir and had held his post for hardly a year, could not comprehend the crisis. He was unfamiliar with Armenian governmental and civic figures and events, and to make matters worse, his advisers were far from wise mentors.

*See Biographical Glossary.

The political assembly,* made up of ordinary individuals who had been elected six months earlier, was just as unfamiliar with the nature of events happening around them. As such, the official leaders of the Armenian nation were subjected, unwittingly, to the Machiavellian frauds and deceptions of Armenian traitors lurking outside and especially inside the patriarchate.

The most dangerous of these Armenian traitors were Artin Megerdichian, *muhtar*† of Beshiktash and the main author of the blacklist of arrested Armenian intellectuals, and Kamer Shirinian, an employee of the patriarchate, whom Talaat skillfully used to stay informed about its goings-on.

Among this pack of wolves in sheep's clothing, there was no lack of adventurers seeking the title of revolutionary. Like Hmayag Aramiantz, they were engaged in feverish activity, as moles, and brought reassuring *selams* [greetings] from Talaat. They made every effort to convince the patriarch that there was not any danger to the Armenians.

The all-powerful Talaat had created a secret army of practiced Armenian and Turkish traitors and spies to furnish daily intelligence on all private and public aspects of Armenian life in the capital city, so that, under cover of darkness, he might use his power to achieve his previously determined goal of annihilating the Armenian race.

Meanwhile the heads of the Armenian political organizations were also in a state of confusion,though in truth they were more optimistic than pessimistic. In July 1914, when the war started, during their annual assembly in Erzerum, the Dashnak‡ Party had decided to remain neutral with respect to the question of Turkey's participation. At the same time they had made every effort with their Ittihad Turkish friends, and especially with Talaat, to get Turkey to shy away from this great war.

But after Turkey did enter the war, the Dashnaks refused the Ittihads' invitation to help the government, despite the promises lavished on them. Still, the conduct of the Armenian political parties toward the Turkish government was always friendly and never conspiratorial, as the major criminal Ittihad fugitives responsible for shedding Armenian blood[3] are now endeavoring to show, of course in the hope of gaining exoneration for their great crime.

During the first days following my arrival in Constantinople, I hastened to call on the present patriarch, the previous patriarchs, national representatives, members of the political assembly, and heads of the

*A group of twenty laymen who oversaw the political affairs of the Armenian nation—trans.

†Alderman; headman of the Armenian community *(millet)*.—trans.

‡The Armenian Revolutionary Federation, political party founded in 1890, devoted to civil rights and reform.—trans.

Armenian political parties, whom I had known for a long time and who were friends of mine. My general impression was this: no one grasped the gravity of the situation, and no one was worried about tomorrow.

Many of them insisted that Turkey would not enter the war; when it began, they said the mobilization was simply a precaution. They were simple-minded people, convinced that as long as the government was in the hands of the Ittihad, and the Armenians' beloved Talaat was interior minister, no danger faced them.

I met with the heads of the Armenian political parties. With a happy and self-satisfied smile, they would whisper in my ear: "The Ittihad Committee has promised a broader implementation of the reform plan for the six Armenian provinces, inaugurated at the time of the Balkan War of 1913 to satisfy the Armenians, as long as we help the Turkish government in the event of war." The conjectures that abounded were ill-founded and even contradictory; thus it seemed clear that our leaders were lacking in foresight and clarity, insofar as to govern means to be farsighted.

Yet the horrific massacre carried out by the Ittihad Committee on April 13, 1909, in Adana[4] was still fresh in everyone's mind, and the official published report of the joint Turkish-Armenian investigative committee left no doubt about the Ittihad's criminal involvement in and responsibility for it.

But when Turkey declared war on the Entente powers, the leaders of our political parties maintained their promised neutrality with perfect rectitude and were careful not to cause any difficulty for the Ittihad government.

The intellectual leaders of the Armenian political parties fell prey to the temptation of believing that the Turkish Itthadists were noble ideological comrades. In reality, they were street thugs who, by their audacity and with one unexpected fateful blow, had been elevated to the most responsible posts of minister and prime minister.

Assuredly these Young Turks,* who were thought to have brought the ideal of freedom from Salonica in 1908, were the most ferocious and most savage of tigers, hiding behind the mask of idealistic liberalism. But alas, the Armenian leaders came to understand this only when they were already walking on the road to death. So deceived were they by the flattery and mellifluous promises lavished upon them by Talaat and his comrades that when a chief of police and several policemen came from Galata-seray to Pera to find Agnouni,† one of the Dashnak Party leaders and a brilliant Russian-Armenian writer, and placed him under arrest, the stupefied

* Political reform movement that led to the overthrow of the sultan.—trans.

†See Biographical Glossary.

Agnouni asked if Talaat knew about this. And when the police chief showed him the arrest warrant bearing Talaat's signature, Agnouni was even more stunned and replied that he had been at Talaat's for dinner a short while before and wanted to know why Talaat hadn't said anything about it.

The unfortunate Agnouni, being an idealistic and honorable man, could not comprehend how Talaat could plot against him so cynically—the same Talaat whom he had sheltered in order to save Talaat's life while risking his own during the counterrevolution following March 31,1909.

Along with his five comrades, Agnouni was taken from Ayash, under the pretext of being brought before the court-martial in Diyarbekir. At Osmaniye, four-fifths of the way, he realized that he was going to be murdered and said, overcome with emotion: "I am not sorry for my death since one day death will find us all, but I am sorry that we were deceived by these Turkish criminals."

And when Vahak, the well-known leader of the Dashnaks in Cilicia, was warned by his bosom friends in Adana, "Vahak, they arrested and killed all your comrades. Don't be too visible; cover your tracks," he answered calmly and with deep conviction: "As long as Jemal Pasha* [chief commander of the Turkish army in Syria and Palestine] is alive, no one can touch a hair on my head." Then, pointing to the large portrait of Jemal Pasha in a gilt frame prominently displayed in his room, he said, "Long live my good friend and friend of the Armenians—Jemal Pasha." I recall in detail the circumstances of Vahak's hanging, ordered by Jemal Pasha. This fellow too fell victim to blind faith in the Turks, which, along with their own lives, also cost the lives of millions of their innocent countrymen.

In the midst of this combination of optimism and bewildered submission on the part of the Armenians, the Ittihad camarilla day by day secretly recorded the movements of the Armenian volunteers working abroad, particularly on the Russo-Turkish borders of the Caucasus—recorded them on the debit column of the Armenian account. These political and military movements, which took place against the will of the responsible leaders of the Armenian political parties in Turkey, plunged the Armenian people into chaos.

Meanwhile the Ittihad government and the Turkish dailies were extremely irritated at seeing Karekin Pastermajian,* deputy of the Ottoman Parliament from Erzerum, at the head of an Armenian volunteer regiment approaching their borders. Having no military qualification or experience, never having been in any military action, he had his photo-

*See Biographical Glossary.

graph taken in Tiflis with a few well-armed comrades, bearing Mosin guns. He placed the photograph as an "advertisement" in the *London Daily Graphic*, needlessly provoking Turkish government officials and a public already aflame with hate and longing for vengeance against an unarmed, confused—and doomed—Armenian population.

As the sun was setting on the Ottoman Empire, the Young Turks [Ittihadists] were desperately consumed by a pan-Turkic and pan-Islamic dream of creating an empire from the Ottoman territories in Egypt, Transcaucasia, Persia, Afghanistan, and Pakistan, reaching right through to India. Had they really forgotten that the Muslims already living in the empire—the Albanians, Arabs, Circassians, and Kurds—had suffered deeply under Turkish rule, had for a long time wanted to break free of the oppression, and in some cases had succeeded? And if these Islamic peoples couldn't take Turkish oppression, imagine what the Christians—Armenians, Greeks, Assyrians, Chaldeans, and Nestorians—had to suffer. And it so happened that of the Christian peoples, only the Armenians, with their protests and calls for reform, provoked the Turks—in part, because those calls aroused the concern of the European powers. This was why the Ittihad government was awaiting the opportunity that the world war provided, to exterminate the Armenian race.

Throughout the nineteenth century the Russian government had helped dismember Turkey, having encouraged rebellion by the Greeks in 1826, the Romanians and Serbs in 1854, and the Bulgarians in 1878. Now, with Russia pursuing the reform plan[5] for the six provinces (Erzerum, Van, Bitlis, Sivas, Harput, and Diyarbekir) that were populated mainly by the Armenians (the only slaves left) during the 1913 Balkan War, the Turkish government could see that the Russians were again trying to carve up the Ottoman state. Moreover, in order to prevent what the Turks feared could have led to further dismemberment of the empire in eastern Anatolia, the Armenian heartland, they decided to completely eliminate the Armenian race.

To carry out this plan, the Turkish government took the following secret measures:

A. First and foremost, under the lawful pretext of general mobilization effected immediately after the declaration of world war, the government conscripted all Armenian youths and adult males between the ages of twenty and forty-six. By this measure, the Armenians would be deprived of their strength and potential for self-defense. They would also be deprived of their workforce and be subject to material and financial hardship for the duration of the war. And although the approximately fifty thousand Armenian conscripts initially received weapons, by the third or fourth month of the war, after the desertion of a few dozen Armenian soldiers during the intense fighting near the Russo-Turkish border area of Koprukoy, all Armenian soldiers were completely disarmed and sent to the depths of Asia Minor on the pretext of building roads.

However, purposely deprived of adequate food, clothing, medicines, and medical care, the Armenian labor battalions [*amele taburi*] were decimated by hunger and the cold. This went on until the months of July and August 1915, by which time the remaining soldiers were ruthlessly massacred by their fellow Turkish soldiers at the command of Minister of War Enver.*

B. In order to neutralize from the start any possible attempt at resistance, in one blow the Turks arrested all well-known Armenian intellectuals and principal activists in the capital, regardless of whether they belonged to a political party or were apolitical, liberal, or conservative, irrespective of profession—any who were perceived as potential influences in an eventual Armenian movement.

C. Then the government disarmed the entire Armenian population left in the capital and all the Armenians in the interior provinces, who had already paid their war taxes.

D. But before undertaking the general disarmament, they first disarmed invincible Zeytoun, in order to destroy this centuries-old mountain lions' den, which they thought would cause major difficulties once they began the general deportation of the Cilician Armenians.

E. Likewise, prior to the deportation and slaughter of the Armenians in Northern Armenia, near the Russo-Turkish border, the government first disarmed the Armenians in Van and immediately deported them. Since Van was located in the northeastern corner of the Russo-Turkish and Persian borders and was the province with the greatest population (according to the last census, taken by the patriarchate in 1914, more than 200,000 Armenians lived in Van), the province could indeed have caused major political and military complications if strengthened by the Russian forces and the Armenian volunteer army.

Thus, with all of Asia Minor encompassed in a large triangle, with Constantinople in the west, Van in the northeast, and Zeytoun in the south, the Ittihad leaders had achieved their aim: to disarm and render impotent these three vital sectors of the Armenian cultural landscape in advance of the full-scale massacre.

And by the end of March 1915, the central government in Constantinople officially demanded that Constantinople's entire population, irrespective of race or religion, turn in their guns. The veiled purpose of this general order was to disarm the 120,000 Armenians in the capital.

*See Biographical Glossary.

During this same time the disarmament of the Armenian population—under threat of immediate execution for all who disobeyed—was also taking place in Van and Zeytoun. But if there was an escalation of events in Van, it was because of the anti-Armenian fanaticism of the provincial governor, Jevdet Bey, who was Enver's brother-in-law. As he and his Ittihad followers resorted to extraordinary, draconian measures, the disarmament gave rise to powerful resistance.

The Armenians of Van clearly had no premeditated intention or special preparation for revolt. This is evident from the prudent precautions of the entire Armenian constituency of Van, under their leader, Arshak Vramian [Vahab Onnig Tertsagian], an Ottoman Parliament member and Dashnak leader. He and his constituents were sending secret emissaries to His Holiness the Catholicos in Holy Etchmiadzin[6] and to the [Armenian] National Bureau in Tiflis, asking them to put an end to the Caucasus-Armenian volunteer movement; they urged them to take a cautious, wait-and-see position so as not to provoke the Ittihad government, which was ready to murder the Armenians en masse; they urged them not to jeopardize the lives of the hundreds of thousands of Armenians living along the Russo-Turkish border.

On the one hand, Arshak Vramian* was trying to break the alarming momentum of the impetuous course taken by Van's governor, while making an effort to continue the friendliest of relations with Jevdet and the local military authorities. At the same time he sent a petition to the Sublime Porte regarding this increasingly complicated and critical situation and pleading for a solution.

Meanwhile Jevdet Bey* had Arshak Vramian arrested in Van without warning, in order to suppress the spirit of self-defense that was fermenting among the Armenians and to facilitate the central government's annihilation plan. In a related development, the well-known Dashnak activist Ishkhan had been sent from Van to the surrounding Armenian villages, presumably to check out the situation and calm people down. Jevdet had him murdered in the night by the police chief accompanied by police soldiers.† In so doing, he drove the Armenian population of Van to seek a quick means of self-defense; they were backed into a corner with no choice, as the plan to annihilate them was in motion. The Ittihad leaders and the government in Van had charted a course of destruction, and so it was not surprising when the bloody storm broke in early April.

The Armenian popular movement at Van, which began on April 21, 1915, coincided with the British navy's attack at the Dardanelles. How-

*See Biographical Glossary.

†Police soldiers (also "gendarmes"), a type of military police.—trans.

ever, this movement, which Talaat and his government tried to portray as revolutionary, was never a preplanned revolution at all. In fact, the disturbances in Van were an indictment of the Ittihad government.

The heavy military assault against the brave military deserters of Zeytoun, who had retreated into the mountains, also began in April. The central government and the regional government in Aleppo had spread the rumor that the Armenians of Zeytoun had revolted, and so a military force under the leadership of Major Suleyman was sent to Zeytoun to suppress the so-called uprising. Having climbed to an inaccessible site called Teke, the highest point in the region, about seven or eight hundred of Zeytoun's warriors had to resort to self-defense. And when Suleyman was killed in the ensuing fighting, news went out to the governments of Marash and Aleppo that the Armenians of Zeytoun were indeed in rebellion.

But if Zeytoun had revolted, could a few thousand Turkish soldiers have disarmed 20,000 tough mountaineers who had been able to resist for months Edhem Pasha's army of 50,000, which had defeated the Greeks in Thessaly in 1898?* On the contrary, as many times as the Zeytountsis sent messengers to the catholicos of Cilicia in Adana and the prominent local Armenians in Marash, they always received the same reply: Do nothing extreme that would endanger the lives of the entire Armenian population of Cilicia. And this is why the Armenians of Zeytoun would come back from exile in 1919 absolutely outraged that the catholicos of Cilicia had opposed their need for self-defense in 1915.

If the Armenians of Zeytoun had indeed revolted, how would they have stood like a flock of sheep before a few hundred policemen and allowed themselves to be deported to the swampy, purely Muslim province of Soultaniye, adjacent to Konya?

The Turkish government was putting into effect its secret plan of annihilating the Armenians, while at the same time inventing rationalizations to exonerate itself, very much in keeping with the Turkish proverb that the person stealing the minaret always prepares its sheath as well.

As with the Armenians of the interior provinces, so too with the Armenian populace of Constantinople: all its official bodies were completely unaware of the escalating events of Easter 1915. Indeed, preoccupied with concerts, dances, and parties, they were lost in mirth and exultation, each day expecting to hear of the capture of Constantinople by the European powers.

*Balakian's reference to 700 or 800 Zeytoun warriors is inaccurate. There were about 35 to 40 young Armenian men who defected from the army and were fighting back in late March, and at times the number grew to a few hundred. His reference to 20,000 Armenians in the next paragraph refers to events that took place in 1894–96 during the Hamidian Massacres.

However, across from the Persian embassy, upstairs in the main Ittihad club, Talaat, the minister of the interior, along with his government's two pillars, Dr. Nazim* and Behaeddin Shakir,* as well as the general secretary of the party, Midhat Shukri,* were deciding that the time had come to put into effect the plan they had been hatching—a plan that had not even occurred to their ancestors, a plan that would subject them to the eternal curses of their Turkish decendants. Within a few months, in this enlightened century, right before the eyes of Christian Europe, the Ittihad government succeeded in doing what their forefathers never could have imagined doing.

The responsible and irresponsible leaders of the Turkish government believed that the world war was their sole opportunity, one unprecedented in the course of history, to destroy the Armenian people—the cancer destroying the Turkish empire. The countries of civilized Christian Europe were busy ripping one another apart, and Turkey's ally, Germany, was passive and silent in the matter. The Ittihad government, in keeping with the prevailing view at the beginning of the war, saw Germany as having a 90 percent chance of success. As a victor and Germany's ally, they would not be held responsible for shedding the blood of more than one million innocent and defenseless Armenians. And even if the Germans should lose, against all odds, the Turks realized they would give up everything; but inasmuch as an Armenia formed anew on the ruins of Turkey by a small number of Armenian survivors would make an extremely weak state, at least it was possible, at an appropriate time, to eliminate it in one blow and kill the newborn Armenian lion in its cradle.

During these days General Otto Liman von Sanders came to Constantinople to replace von der Goltz as drillmaster of the Turkish army. At the outbreak of the war he had been the German military commander in the Turkish defense of the Dardanelles. Von Sanders, in agreement with Enver Pasha—the minister of war and the real commander and generalissimo of the Ottoman army, after the sultan—decided to deport the Christian peoples living along the Russo-Turkish border (meaning the Armenians) and move them south, far from the war zone, as a putative means of protecting the army's rear.

Under the pretext of being in a war zone, the entire Armenian population was then to be deported, even from the neutral province of Kastemouni, which had very few Armenians and was far removed from both the northern and the southern war zones. As I noted earlier, this was the plan proposed by von der Goltz, president of the German-Turkish Society, at its opening meeting in Berlin in February 1914, and it was being put into

*See Biographical Glossary.

effect now because of the opportune circumstances brought on unexpectedly by the war.

Talaat and his three cohorts favored this radical plan of deportation, and he spared no effort to conceal his actions behind Enver's name; this way it would appear that Enver was responsible for the crimes against the Armenians and that there were military reasons for commiting them. Meanwhile Enver was so overburdened by actual military matters of increasing complexity on so many fronts that he had little time to attend to the details of the policy regarding the annihilation of the Armenians. He left all this completely to Talaat, with his full endorsement. But Talaat, as the interior minister, though focused intently on the secret plan, was at the same time doing everything possible to cover his bloody tracks.

Meanwhile the German Hohenzollern government saw the war as its best opportunity to turn all of Asia Minor into a German colony, making Turkey a vassal state. Why go all the way to their African colonies like the Cameroons, or all the way to Togo and Kiaochow in the Far East, when Asia Minor, with its rich lands and abundant water sources and its wealth of natural resources so close to Europe, was at hand to be colonized?

Vice Admiral Pashich, the commander of the German cruiser *Strassburg*, which had laid anchor for the protection of the Armenians in the port of Mersin, said these very things to me on my shipboard visit on behalf of the catholicos, during my trip to Cilicia on official business in 1913 at the end of the Balkan War. Admiring the fertile and expansive fields of Cilicia, as a military man not accustomed to diplomatic reserve, he told me rather pointedly: "Under proper administration, Cilicia could be a richer land than Egypt; since Egypt has only one Nile, while Cilicia has two larger rivers, and the Taurus mountain range is an inexhaustible source of water for its the fertile plains, which are vast and flat and level like the surface of the sea and which produce a variety of crops several times a year."

The Germans had constructed the Baghdad railway with such a vision in mind. The Berlin-Constantinople-Balkan express took only three days to make the three-thousand-kilometer trip, and it would soon be possible to go from Constantinople to Baghdad (a distance of three thousand kilometers) in three to five days. And soon there would be express service there, too.

Following their imperial plan, the Germans posted railway officials at every important station from the central station of Haydar Pasha in Constantinople all the way to the Taurus mountain tunnels. They had in this way imperceptibly established small German colonies all along the route with the hub at Eskishehir, where the Baghdad railway's central factories were located.

Like the sun setting on the far-off horizon on the sea, the Ottoman Empire was gradually sinking into the eternal abyss of history, and Germany was appointing itself heir. Having no will in hand, the German government nevertheless hoped to seize the lion's share of the dissolving empire by virtue of military might.

There were, however, two ancient nations rivaling the Germans in Asia Minor, as true heirs to these historic lands: the Armenian and the Greek, the former in the interior provinces, the latter in the coastal cities. Hence the Germans found it necessary, if not by active assistance then at least by passive and silent compliance, to allow the Turks to do away with these two races, in particular the Armenians, since the king of Greece was the son-in-law of the German emperor.

By so doing, the Germans would cut the Gordian knot of the dangerous Eastern Question, and they would have no further competition among the European powers. Never mind that this criminal plan in service of an imperialistic policy would be achieved over the bodies of millions of innocent victims piled as high as small mountains. After all, hadn't the former Russian foreign minister Lobanov[7] considered the policy of "Armenia without Armenians" a possibility and said so years ago? Certainly the time was unprecedentedly ripe. And so Turkish government officials, with the tacit agreement and indirect encouragement of the militaristic and imperialistic Hohenzollern government, hastened to execute the grand plan, the likes of which had never before been recorded in even the bloodiest pages of history.

5

The First Bad News from Cilicia: The Secret Messenger

The Ittihad officials could not have more falsely portrayed the Armenians as a people in revolt, even though the Armenian leaders had done everything possible to gain their trust and goodwill. Patriarch Zaven Der Yeghiayan, for example, in response to Enver's complaint regarding Armenian soldiers deserting, issued an encyclical that was circulated everywhere, recommending that the Armenian people extend all manner of material and moral assistance to the governmental committees raising money for the army and the fleet, and facilitate the task of protecting the Ottoman fatherland.

In special divisions of the Armenian hospitals of Constantinople and Smyrna, hundreds of beds were made available for the thousands of wounded Turkish soldiers who were brought there daily from the Dardanelles. The Armenians generously donated to the Turkish Red Crescent, even while living under fearful constraints. In Constantinople and in the provinces, the government had held charity bazaars, and their best customers were Armenians. By strictly enforcing martial laws, especially for the Armenians, Armenian soldiers, doctors, pharmacists, nurses, and artisans actively supported the Turkish military.

In short, with the encouragement of their patriarchate and the political parties, the Armenian community surpassed all the others in the capital, many of them much richer, in material support of the Ottoman troops. I recall that during the first months of my exile, when I was living among many Armenian political leaders from Constantinople, they never voiced, even in our most candid and intimate conversations, any ideas about revolt. They came to deeply regret that they had been gullible enough to believe the Ittihad government's promises and assurances. Later they were all killed.

But for now all the Armenian political leaders in Constantinople and the provinces remained peacefully in place, taking a wait-and-see attitude. No one considered leaving the country because, unfortunately, no one anticipated any immediate danger.

During my four-year exile, which began in April 1915, I would meet young Armenian party members who bitterly and scornfully recalled that their leaders had criticized them for avoiding enlistment in the army and for not hurrying to do their patriotic duty for the Ottoman fatherland. This is how far our inexperienced dogmatists of "socialism" had taken their impractical idealism.

Then the [Russian] viceroy Count Vorontsov-Dashkov announced that "the Turkish territories seized by the Armenian volunteers* shall be theirs," which was completely erroneous but caused extraordinary excitement among the Armenians abroad and especially in the Caucasus. Despite the volunteer movements, the two million Armenians living within the borders of Turkey were totally unaware of any imminent danger of annihilation.

On the contrary, it was because Minister Talaat and German ambassador von Wangenheim frequently made reassuring guarantees that the Armenians had nothing to fear and they should trust the government's goodwill that they were caught off-guard and were celebrating without worrying about tomorrow.

However, despite this internal calm, the death sentence of the Armenian people had been passed months before. And as I have noted, the people of Van had not revolted; nor was the rear of the Ottoman army in danger; nor were there any threatening internal Armenian movements, just a couple of groups of army deserters in Zeytoun and Moush.

In addition, I learned of an encounter that will convince even the most stubborn doubters of the Armenians' loyalty. It has until now had to remain a secret. Three months before the alleged revolt at Van on April 21, 1915, the Turkish government had already decided to exterminate the Armenian people under the pretext of deporting them into exile.

A high-ranking Turkish official in Adana had a close relationship with a wealthy Armenian who held an official position in that city[1] and enjoyed respect and influence in local European circles. One day in the beginning of February 1915 the former invited the latter to meet with him, and said to him in confidence: "A new storm is about to break upon the Armenians, and it will exceed anything that has happened before. You know I like you, so I hope that you will save yourself." The horrified Armenian merchant asked, "What can I do to save myself?" The Turkish official answered tersely, "Go to Mersin, get on a steamship, and escape to Europe . . . don't waste time by saying, 'Let me save my wealth.' Believe me, later you will be sorry."

*Armenian volunteers who joined the tsarist Russian army to fight against Ottoman Turkey.—trans.

Naturally on hearing such dreadful, unexpected news, the Armenian asked for more details. The official made him take an oath on his children, then said: "All the Armenians of Zeytoun, Hajin, and Deort-Yol, as well as Adana, will be deported, and their wealth will be confiscated. Not even your wives and daughters will be left to you . . . I say little; you must understand a lot. Do what you have to do and get away from here as soon as possible so that you also will not drown in the coming storm."

Deeply shaken, the merchant hurried to make preparations for his departure. But before he left, he went to inform the catholicos of Cilicia of what he had been told. A few days later he accomplished the impossible, taking advantage of his closeness to the governor of Adana to receive exceptional permission to leave Cilicia. And so in mid-February 1915 he and his entire family went to Mersin and boarded an Italian steamship* for Europe.

Sahag II, the elderly catholicos of Cilicia, was deeply disturbed by this news and spent sleepless nights trying to figure out a way to verify it. At this time Jemal, high commander of the Syrian and Palestinian front and minister of the marine, was passing through Cilicia, returning to Syria from Constantinople. Hoping to take advantage of this unusual opportunity, the catholicos hurried to meet with Jemal and privately asked for clarification of what he had heard.

Jemal would tell him only this much: "During the deliberation over this matter in the council of ministers, I tried very hard to argue that instead of deporting and exiling the entire Armenian population, only the writers, intellectuals, and Armenian political party leaders—say fifteen or twenty people from each town—should be exiled. I felt that the helpless common people should be spared, but I am sorry to say that I was not able to make my voice heard."

An indirect but authentic source tells me that the chief executioners of the Armenians—Talaat, Behaeddin Shakir, and Dr. Nazim—were consistently opposed to those who spoke in favor of a more moderate policy, be they within the Ittihad government or in ministerial meetings or any other secret discussions of this question.

One night in the beginning of March the catholicos invited to his residence a very trustworthy friend, a merchant known for his patriotism. He told him the news, then instructed him to depart for Constantinople and confidentially report it to the patriarch of Constantinople.

But in these days, for an Armenian, even the exchange of letters and telegrams with Constantinople was subject to certain formalities of censorship and military and police constraints, such that travel was very difficult

*Italy at this time had not yet entered the war.—GB

and dangerous. Nonetheless this Armenian merchant, thanks to Turkish officials who were his friends, feigned illness and succeeded in obtaining a special travel visa to depart March 2 by train for Constantinople.

In Konya, however, the Turkish chief of police confiscated his visa, and he was stalled until a high-ranking Armenian official who happened to be in the city on examiner's business got the visa returned. He continued on to Constantinople safely.

On the day after his arrival, the evening of March 8, he met with Patriarch Zaven Der Yeghiayan and presented the calling card of the catholicos, which noted that its bearer would deliver his message orally and in confidence. At first the patriarch did not want to accept the news and told him that the catholicos of Cilicia was being an alarmist. But then Zaven Der Yeghiayan asked the merchant to delay his departure by a day or two so that he could look into the matter before replying to Sahag.

Two days later, the messenger reappeared before the patriarch alone. The patriarch, responding to the catholicos's message, said nonchalantly, among other things, "The German ambassador [Wangenheim], in the name of his government, assures us that neither will there be a massacre, nor will the Armenians be deported. Minister of the Interior Talaat Pasha also gives us assurances that all that is possible will be done to let the Armenian people live comfortably where they are. Only people whom the government considers suspicious, or criminals, will be rounded up."

On this occasion Zaven Der Yeghiayan recommended that the Armenian people, particularly in Cilicia, be on their good behavior insofar as the local government officials were concerned: steer clear of provocative actions, busy themselves with their daily work, and obey government orders and instructions. The patriarch added that he was sorry that he could do nothing more.

The messenger's impression was that Zaven Der Yeghiayan had not acknowledged with due seriousness the danger pointed out to him, attributing it to the alarmism of the catholicos. The messenger hurried back to Adana and hastened to give an account of his secret mission to the catholicos. Thus the catholicos was satisfied to have fulfilled the obligation that weighed on him by the disclosure, and the patriarch was likewise satisfied, having conveyed to the catholicos the assurances Talaat had given him!

Unfortunately the grave news was kept secret until the end; no one, not even the Armenian leaders, found out about these critical developments, which meant life or death to the Armenian people, until the night of terror, Saturday, April 24, 1915.* On that evening none of our intellectuals

*G.B. recorded dates by the Julian calendar used in the Ottoman Empire. April 11 is April 24 by the Gregorian calendar. Because April 24 is the worldwide day the Armenian Genocide is commemorated, we note both dates for the events of April 1915. See Translator's Note.

and political leaders in Constantinople were aware of what the Ittihad leaders had planned for them, and they fell into their trap. In a single night they were all exiled and, except for a few, later martyred by unspeakably torturous means.

I became aware of these events, which had taken place months before the mass arrest of all of us, when I met this very same messenger, Vartan Prenian, in England in 1922. We told everyone because none of us, none of the many Armenian political party leaders from the capital who were arrested and exiled, among whom were many members of the Central National Administration,* had had a clue about what was going to happen. If even one person among us, while we were in prison or on the roads to exile, had known about this secret messenger sent from Cilicia to Constantinople, no one would have continued to ask why we were being arrested.

*The executive office of the president of all the national assemblies, who was the patriarch of Constantinople. He was elected by the General Assembly to uphold the Armenian National Constitution, and serve as mediator with the Ottoman government when needed.—trans.

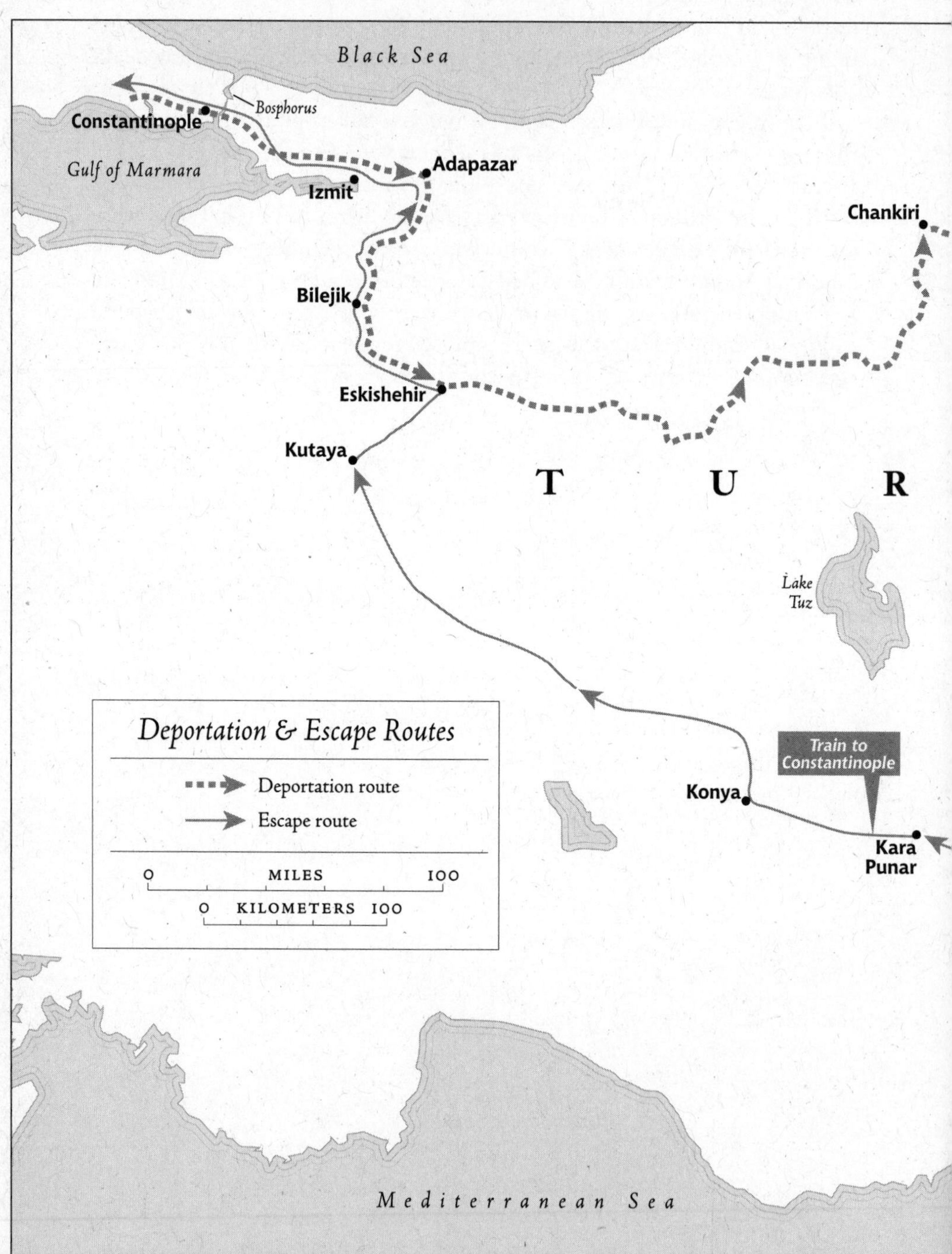

Black Sea
Bosphorus
Constantinople
Gulf of Marmara
Izmit
Adapazar
Chankiri
Bilejik
Eskishehir
Kutaya
T U R
Lake Tuz
Deportation & Escape Routes
Deportation route
Escape route
0 MILES 100
0 KILOMETERS 100
Train to Constantinople
Konya
Kara Punar
Mediterranean Sea

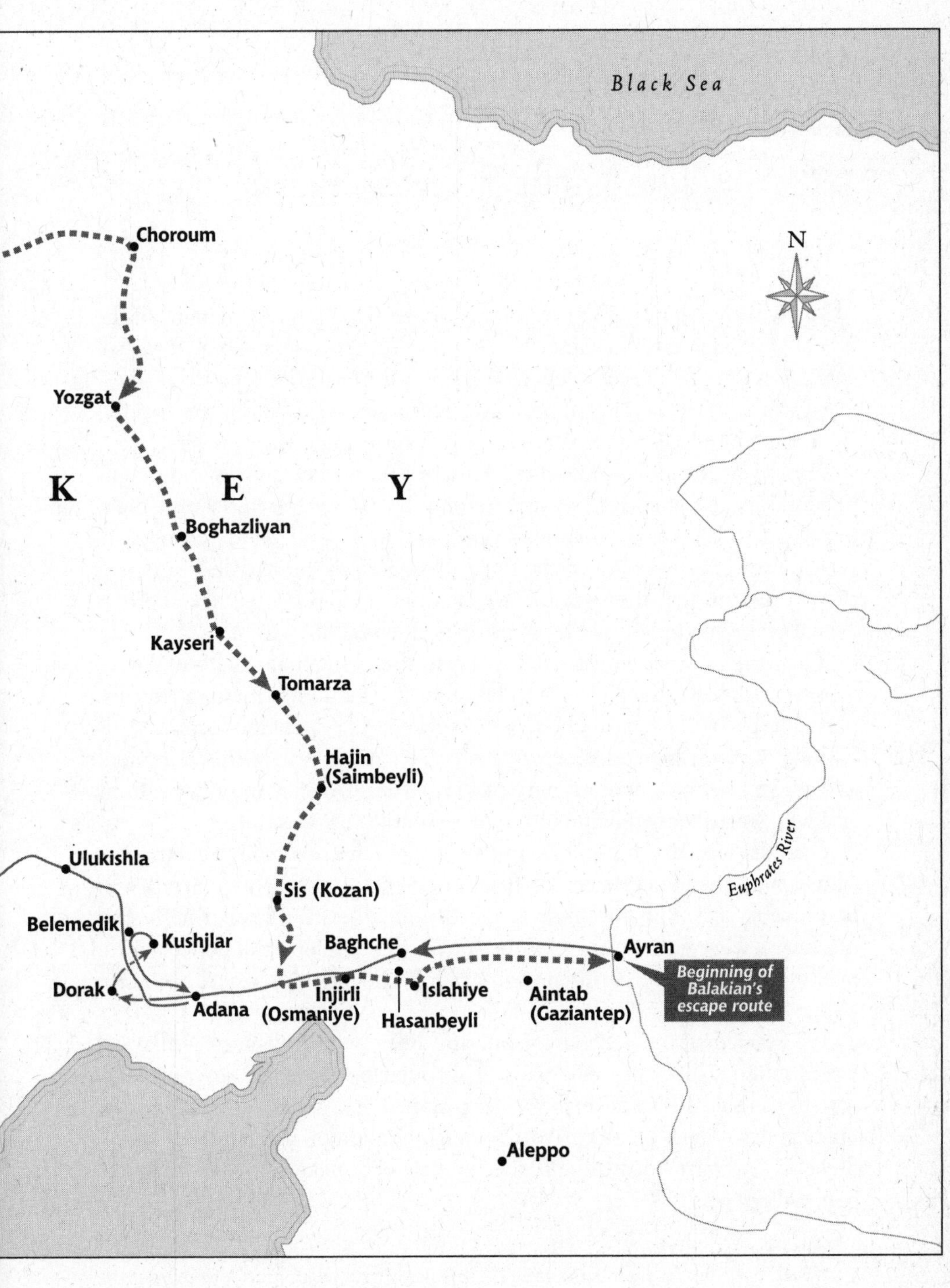
Black Sea
N
Choroum
Yozgat
K
E
Y
Boghazliyan
Kayseri
Tomarza
Hajin
(Saimbeyli)
Ulukishla
Euphrates River
Sis (Kozan)
Belemedik
Kushjlar
Baghche
Ayran
Dorak
Adana
Injirli
(Osmaniye)
Islahiye
Hasanbeyli
Aintab
(Gaziantep)
Beginning of
Balakian's
escape route
Aleppo

6

The Night of Gethsemane

On the night of Saturday, April 11/24, 1915, the Armenians of the capital city, exhausted from the Easter celebrations that had come to an end a few days earlier, were snoring in a calm sleep. Meanwhile on the heights of Stambul, near Ayesofia, a highly secret activity was taking place in the palatial central police station.

Groups of Armenians had just been arrested in the suburbs and neighborhoods of the capital; blood-colored military buses were now transporting them to the central prison. Weeks earlier Bedri,* chief of police in Constantinople, had sent official sealed orders to all the guardhouses, with the instruction that they not be opened until the designated day and that they then be carried out with precision and in secrecy.

The orders were warrants to arrest the Armenians whose names were on the blacklist, a list compiled with the help of Armenian traitors, particularly Artin Megerdichian, who worked with the neighborhood Ittihad clubs.† Condemned to death were Armenians who were prominent and active in either revolutionary or nonpartisan Armenian organizations and who were deemed liable to incite revolution or resistance.‡

On this Saturday night I, along with eight friends from Scutari, was transported by a small steamboat from the quay of the huge armory of Selimiye to Sirkedji. The night smelled of death; the sea was rough, and our hearts were full of terror. We prisoners were under strict police guard, not allowed to speak to one another. We had no idea where we were going.

We arrived at the central prison, and here behind gigantic walls and large bolted gates, they put us in a wooden pavilion in the courtyard, which was said by some to have once served as a school. We sat there, quiet and somber, on the bare wooden floor under the faint light of a flickering lantern, too stunned and confused to make sense of what was happening.

*See Biographical Glossary.

†Meeting places for members of the local Ittihad Party committees throughout the empire.—trans.

‡*Revolutionary* here refers to reform-oriented political workers.—trans.

We had barely begun to sink into fear and despair when the giant iron gates of the prison creaked open again and a multitude of new faces were pushed inside. They were all familiar faces—revolutionary and political leaders, public figures, and nonpartisan and even antipartisan intellectuals.

From the deep silence of the night until morning, every few hours Armenians were brought to the prison. And so behind these high walls, the jostling and commotion increased as the crowd of prisoners became denser. It was as if all the prominent Armenian public figures—assemblymen, representatives, revolutionaries, editors, teachers, doctors, pharmacists, dentists, merchants, bankers, and others in the capital city—had made an appointment to meet in these dim prison cells. Some even appeared in their nightclothes and slippers. The more those familiar faces kept appearing, the more the chatter abated and our anxiety grew.

Before long everyone looked solemn, our hearts heavy and full of worry about an impending storm. Not one of us understood why we had been arrested, and no one could assess the consequences. As the night's hours slipped by, our distress mounted. Except for a few rare stoics, we were in a state of spiritual anguish, terrified of the unknown and longing for comfort.

Right through till morning new Armenian prisoners arrived, and each time we heard the roar of the military cars, we hurried to the windows to see who they were. The new arrivals had contemptuous smiles on their faces, but when they saw hundreds of other well-known Armenians old and young around them, they too sank into fear. We were all searching for answers, asking what all of this meant, and pondering our fate.

7

Red Sunday

We, the majority of Constantinople's Armenian intellectuals and public figures, spent Red Sunday, April 12/25, which followed Easter 1915, in the central prison, sad and worried and hoping for some unexpected help from somewhere.

Having no choice but to conform to the ways of prison life and knowing that our leaders had been in and out of Turkish prisons many times, many of us, as morning approached, began to think about eating something. Meanwhile others were offering sizable sums to anyone who could carry secret notes to their families and influential friends, begging them to come to the rescue.

Our Red Sunday passed without any further unusual incident except for hearing intermittent dull thunder from the huge English and Russian naval cannons. Some naïve prisoners thought that the loud explosions were from battleships coming to our aid.

Indeed on that very day the fortress gates of Constantinople were being charged by British battleships from the Dardanelles and by Russian ones from the Black Sea. Some of us even conjectured that with Constantinople in danger of capture by the British, and with the Turkish government not yet transferred from Constantinople to Konya, the authorities had hastened to arrest us in order to ransom us for the safety of the capital. So we spent Red Sunday this way in the Mehderhane [formerly military barracks] *mektep*, the school of the central prison of Constantinople, terrified and confused.

At evening the prison muezzin finished calling out *Allah akhbar* from the nearby minaret. When dusk fell, the guards ordered us all to assemble in front of the main iron gate. Finally, after twenty-four hours of soul-destroying uncertainty, our fate was to be determined; meanwhile the stern head warden, with all the high- and low-ranking police officers around him, began to ceremoniously read the blacklist, the names of those condemned to death.

They verified that we were all present. Then hundreds of military police with bayonets and other police officers took us to the police administration building a little ways from the central prison. They searched us one by one, confiscating all our personal effects: money, insignificant pieces of paper, pocketknives, pencils, diaries, even our umbrellas and canes. They told us we would get them back.

When they completed their searches, they escorted us in small groups of twenty or more to the red military buses waiting in front of the central police administration building. At last the mystery of the past twenty-four hours was partly solved. The second act of our tragedy began when it became clear that they were going to take us out of Constantinople. But where? No one knew.

There were twenty of us in our bus, and more than ten soldiers armed with bayonets, ready to fire if anyone tried to escape. Led by Police Chief Bedri in his special car, the convoy of buses departed, rumbling in clouds of dust from Ayasofia Boulevard toward the seashore in the direction of Sirkedji. From the buses sobbing could be heard, which naturally attracted the attention of passersby who seemed bewildered at this caravan moving by so rapidly.

More than ten buses entered the Saray-Bournou, or Gulhane, grove, and our collective emotions peaked. Fear of death was pervasive, as memories of those black days of tyranny under the great executioner of the Armenians, the Red Sultan [Abdul Hamid II],* were still fresh in our minds. As we all knew, hundreds of innocent young Armenian and Turkish intellectuals had been drowned in the sea, with rocks tied to their legs or necks.

Making our nightmare even worse, the thick darkness and a storm at sea coincided with the vernal equinox. Saray-Bournou squarely faced the north wind, and its waters were always turbulent, but on this night foaming waves were hitting the quay and sending the spray of salt water tens of meters inland.

Even the bravest were trembling, because we instinctively felt that we were headed to the grave. For in a clandestine way that was typically criminal, the Ittihad government had caught us all in one net in a single night. After assembling on the grounds of Saray-Bournou, we formed a procession in pairs and were led to the Shirket No. 67 steamship, which was waiting at the quay, its engines already fired.

The steamship was filled with more than 220 of us but also with a larger number of police soldiers armed with bayonets, as well as young soldiers sent by Enver, commissars, army officers, and police officials of all ranks. For an instant all of us were convinced that we were being taken to the Sea

*See Biographical Glossary. The Hamidian Massacres of 200,000 to 250,000 Armenians took place during 1894–96.—trans.

of Marmara to be drowned. Many were crying, remembering their loved ones, and in this state of emotion we set out for the open sea.

But amid blacker days a few months later, many of us would sorely wish we had been drowned that night. For death at sea would have been less cruel than torture and martyrdom under the ax and the hatchet. Back in the sultan's capital, under its shroud of secrecy, new criminal plans were being forged, encouraged by this initial success.

Finally our steamship approached the Haydar Pasha wharf, and we were marched out in pairs encircled by hundreds of bayonets. Then we were taken to waiting halls A and B, normally assigned to travelers, in the huge and magnificent Haydar Pasha station. Here we waited impatiently for new surprises.

None of us had any appetite, or even the presence of mind to think about our hunger and thirst. A young Armenian military pharmacist among us, who was eating a piece of sausage that he had ordered, was approached by a police chief, who grabbed his plate and threw the sausage and the plate away. Then, stripping the gold buttons from the Armenian's uniform, he yelled: "From now on, you enemies of the state are not worthy of this honor."

After more than two hours in silence and spiritual torture, we were taken under the strictest of military supervision to a special train that was waiting to take us to the recesses of Asia Minor.

The lights went out, the car doors closed, and with the policemen and police soldiers around us, the train started. Slowly we left behind the places where we all had grieving and defenseless mothers, sisters, wives, children, as well as worldly goods. We moved toward our graves, nameless and unknown, to be buried forever.

8

Toward a Place of Exile: The Names of the Exiles in Ayash

Our mysterious train passed through stations in the dark without stopping. By and by the shining Prince Islands disappeared from view, and we skirted the edge of Marmara toward Izmit, past the renowned center of the sultans' debauchery and political crimes. It was dark outside and inside the train, and our hearts were just as dark, as the specter of death stood before us. No one on the train was in the mood to talk; we were all silent, absorbed with torment and worry.

After midnight the chief of the train, a noble and selfless Armenian official, approached me and said softly: "Reverend Father, please write the names of your arrested friends on this piece of paper and give it to me." With a surreptitious motion of his hand, he slipped a pencil and a piece of paper into my hand and, leaving the lamp with me, went to distract the police officials supervising us. With a trembling heart, under the flickering rays of the dim light, I hastily wrote the names of all the friends that I could remember. Then I secretly gave this list to the official without saying a word.

At dawn our train passed through the town of Izmit without stopping. A few passersby, mostly Armenian women who worked in the spinning mills, stared as we went by, seeming suspicious and surprised, but they had no idea what was going on.

Our train sped along, and by and by, along with the Sea of Marmara, we left behind the beautiful gulf with its wavy ripples; Izmit [Nicomedia], Bardizag, perched on the summit of the mountains on the facing shore, and known for its thriving Armenian life; the brave Aslanbeg, the beautiful verdant and fertile fields; the numerous Armenian villages of Bursa; the glimmering lake of Sabanja; and orchards in spring flower. At dusk we reached Eskishehir.

It had been about twenty-four hours since we left the prison; now on the edge of this old town of volcanic rocks, some of us began to feel hunger and thirst. Our train's kind Armenian officials, ignoring the risk and refusing pay, eagerly got us something to eat, and we had a light repast that momentarily satisfied our stomachs. Because Eskishehir was the separation point of the Ankara and Konya railway lines, it was here that our fate would be decided, or in whichever direction lay our deaths. While we were all waiting, tensely consumed with curiosity, our train began to move toward Ankara.

Having departed from Constantinople on Sunday night, April 12/25, 1915, we arrived at around noon Tuesday at the railway station of Senjan Keoy, near Ankara on the way to Ayash. Here such a horrible scene unfolded that those of us who miraculously survived recall it with no less a shudder than when we lived it.

When the train reached the Senjan Keoy station, Ibrahim, the detested head of the central prison, who had accompanied us from Constantinople, came forward. Surrounded by police chiefs and police soldiers, he had the blacklist of our names in hand and started to read aloud: "Silvoyrichi, Agnouni, Zartarian, Khajag, Shahrigian, Jihangulian, Dr. Daghavarian, Sarkis Minasian," and so on. A hodgepodge of names of prominent revolutionaries, nonparty members, and conservatives, nearly seventy-five persons in all.

Those whose names were read disembarked from the train and lined up one behind the other, within a cordon of military personnel. We shuddered down to our bones, even though none of us knew why we were being divided up this way. Still, the names of those called, one after another, were notable. We exchanged kisses with those who were leaving us, and in a fleeting moment, we cried and made one another cry, feeling instinctively that we were being separated forever.

Below are the names of those noble comrades who, having left us in front of the Senjan Keoy station, went on toward Ayash. A few months later, in the valleys near Ankara, they were martyred in torturous deaths.

The Roster of Names of Those Deported to Ayash

[*See the Biographical Glossary for additional information.]

1. Khachadour Maloumian (Agnouni):* famous writer and Dashnak leader, martyred on the road to Ourfa.
2. Karekin Khajag:* teacher-writer and Dashnak worker, martyred on the road to Ourfa.
3. Rupen Zartarian:* teacher, writer, representative in the National Assembly, Dashnak worker, and editor of Dashnak organ *Azadamard*, martyred on the road to Ourfa.
4. Sarkis Minasian: editor of *Droshak*, teacher, and Dashnak worker, martyred on the road to Ourfa.
5. Haroutiun Jangoulian: Hunchak leader, representative in the National Assembly, martyred on the road to Ourfa.

6. Dr. Nazareth Daghavarian:* active public figure, representative in the National Assembly, author/publisher of medical treatises, martyred on the road to Ourfa.
7. Hampartsoum Boyadjian (Mourad): famous Hunchak leader, representative in the National Assembly, martyred in Kayseri.
8. Haroutiun Shahrigian:* lawyer, public figure, representative in the National Assembly, and prominent Dashnak, martyred in Ankara.
9. Adom Yarjanian (Siamanto):* poet, Dashnak, representative in the National Assembly, martyred in Ankara.
10. Haig Tiryakian (Hrach): Dashnak worker, representative in the National Assembly, martyred in Ankara.
11. Nerses Zakarian: teacher and Hunchak worker, representative in the National Assembly, and member of the National Central Administration, martyred in Ankara.
12. Parsegh Shahbaz: lawyer, Dashnak worker, martyred on the road between Harput and Malatya.
13. Shavarsh Chrisian: teacher and Dashnak worker, martyred in Ankara.
14. Yenovk Shahen: actor, martyred in Ankara.
15. Chris Fenerdjian (Silviorichi): a Bulgarian citizen, saved and returned to Bulgaria.
16. Jack Sayabalian (Paylak):* active public worker and representative in the National Assembly, martyred in Ankara.
17. Dr. Avedis Nakashian: public figure, returned to Constantinople.
18. Dr. Khachig Bardizbanian: public figure, martyred in Ankara.
19. Dr. G. [*sic*] [Khachig] Boghosian: well-known psychiatrist, representative in the National Assembly, saved and, after the Armistice, returned to Constantinople.
20. Dr. Melkon Gulisdanian: returned to Constantinople.
21. Dr. Garabed Pashaian: former member of Ottoman parliament, representative in the National Assembly, Dashnak worker, martyred in Ankara.
22. Dr. Dickran Alaverdi: member of patriarchal councils, returned to Constantinople.
23. Arisdages Kasbarian: lawyer, active public figure and representative in the National Assembly, martyred in Ankara.
24. Nerses Papazian (formerly Archimandrite Mashdotz): editor of Dashnak organ *Azadamard* and Dashnak worker, martyred in Ankara.
25. Hampartsoum Hampartsoumian: editor, martyred in Ankara.
26. Krikor Torosian (Gigo): editor of the satirical paper of the same name and public figure, martyred in Ankara.
27. Rosdom Rosdomian: merchant and public figure, martyred in Ankara.
28. Sempad Piurad: novelist, public figure, representative in the National Assembly, martyred in Ankara.

29. Melkon Gurdjian (known by pen name Hrant): representative in the National Assembly, Armenist, Dashnak worker, martyred in Ankara.
30. Theodore Medzigian: merchant, martyred in Ankara.
31. Kevork Terdjimanian: merchant, martyred in Ankara.
32. Haig Tiryakian: arrested instead of the Dashnak leader Haig Tiryakian, later returned to Constantinople.
33. Khachig Idaredjian: teacher, martyred in Ankara.
34. Megerdich Hovhannesian: teacher, Dashnak worker, martyred in Ankara.
35. Megerdich Hovhannesian:† arrested instead of the aforementioned person and later returned to Constantinople.
36. Sarkis Apo: Caucasus Armenian teacher, Dashnak worker, martyred in Ankara.
37. Abraham Hayrigian: Turkish scholar and principal of Arti Academy, representative in the National Assembly, martyred in Ankara.
38. Levon Shamdandjian: arrested instead of Mikayel Shamdandjian and returned to Constantinople.
39. Puzant Boyadjian: representative in the National Assembly, returned to Constantinople.
40. Kegham Parseghian: editor, teacher, and Dashnak worker, martyred in Ankara.
41. Hovhannes Keledjian: bookseller, martyred in Ankara.
42. Onnig-Jirair: teacher, martyred in Ankara.
43. Levon Larents: Reformed Hunchak leader, writer, teacher, martyred in Ankara.
44. Dickran Cheogurian: scholar, teacher, chief editor of *Vosdan* periodical in Constantinople, public figure, martyred in Ankara.
45. Ghazar Ghazarian (Marzbed): old Dashnak worker and teacher; acted as a Turkish undercover agent for the Germans, employed on the Intilli side of the Amanos tunnels; later went to Nisibin; fell off a horse and died in Nisibin just before the Armistice.
46. Haroutiun Konyalian: tailor, martyred in Ankara.
47. Mihrtad Haikazn: umbrella salesman, longtime exile, Dashnak worker, representative in the National Assembly, martyred in Ankara.
48. Bedros Kalfaian: president of the Makrkiugh [Makr Koy] municipality, martyred in Ankara.
49. Bedros Kalfaian:† exiled instead of the aforementioned one, merchant, martyred in Ankara.
50. Garabed Tashjian: martyred in Ankara.
51. Haroutiun Asdourian: martyred in Ankara.

†Mistaken identity.

52. Garabed Sarafian: official of Reji [former Turkish tobacco monopoly], martyred in Ankara.
53. Vramshabouh Samuelof: Russian-Armenian banker, active public figure, martyred in Ankara.
54. Sarkis Armdantsi: martyred in Ankara.
55. Khachig Berberian: teacher, returned to Constantinople.
56. Vrtanes Mardigian: returned to Constantinople.
57. Mihran Aghadjanian: banker, returned to Constantinople and hanged.
58. Nshan: enamelist from Kum Kapu, martyred in Ankara.
59. Dickran Adjemian: returned to Constantinople.
60. Margos Sefer: lawyer, exiled instead of Margos Nathanian, returned to Constantinople.
61. Serope Noradoungian: teacher at Sanassarian School, Dashnak worker, and representative in the National Assembly, martyred in Ankara.
62. Partogh Zorian (Jirair): publisher, Dashnak worker, martyred in Ankara.

    (Note: Regrettably, it was not possible to record the names of the remaining thirteen exiled companions, despite all my inquiries.)

In front of the station in Ayash, more than twenty carriages were waiting, with a multitude of mounted police. Those listed above boarded after a few minutes, under strict guard, and the caravan of carriages was on the road to Ayash, only a few hours from the Senjan Keoy station.

Emotions were running high, and our feelings were hard to bear. With tearful eyes we watched our comrades' carriages disappear in clouds of dust. Today, five years later, with tears in my eyes, I feel a sacred duty to say a few words of farewell, which I was unable to say then during our hasty separation.

> *Depart in peace, greatly admired friends, selfless apostles of our much-tortured fatherland, who waged the struggle in spoken and written word as well as deed. Not for a day, not even for an hour, did you stray from the thorny road of idealism, all the time knowing that, sooner or later, you would be climbing toward Calvary. Future Armenian generations will fall to their knees before your memory perfumed with incense, and tomorrow's free Armenians will erect a monument in honor of your eternal memory.*
>
> *With your torturous martyrdom you opened a new era and brought to the Armenian people new life, new sun, and glorious new careers. May your saintly memory be blessed for centuries hence, and your gold-carved*

names be blessed by grateful generations of Armenians for ages to come. May you go in peace.

At last our train moved toward Ankara. None of us had the heart to speak; no one dared to break the deathly silence. Our minds did not want to work or ponder, would not venture to analyze the events of the day. Meanwhile our hearts were already graves, without corpses or tombstones.

A few hours later, toward noon, our train stopped once and for all in Ankara. The police chief of this city (which was the seat of the governor-general), along with numerous policemen and police soldiers and carriages, apparently had been awaiting our arrival since morning.

We had hardly disembarked and set foot in the Ankara station when the police chief, allowing us not a moment's rest, handed each of us a piece of bread and ordered us, in groups of five, to sit in the waiting horse-drawn open freight carriages. There was no chance to hesitate and we all took our places, the five of us clergymen sharing a carriage with springs. With a police soldier in each of the forty-four carriages, we began to move toward Kastemouni.

Now in place of the velvet-covered seats of the railway cars, we were sitting on hard wooden planks. Moving along at a hasty clip, the carriages made a clatter and raised clouds of dust. We left with Ankara on our right and entered the rough winding roads of the mountains and valleys.

The more we moved away from civilization, the more agitated were our souls and the more our minds were racked with fear. We thought we saw bandits behind every boulder; the hammocks or cradles hanging from every tree seemed like gallows ropes. The expert on Armenian peasant songs, the peerless archimandrite Father Komitas, who was in our carriage, seemed mentally unstable. He thought the trees were bandits on the attack and continually hid his head under the hem of my overcoat, like a fearful partridge. He begged me to say a blessing for him ("The Savior") in the hope that it would calm him. Elsewhere another acquaintance, an elderly lawyer, gave his gold watch and money to the carriage driver, asking him to deliver them to his wife as a remembrance upon his return to Constantinople.

Our carriages rolled along at reckless speed, to the ceaseless crack of the coachmen's whips and the curses of the police soldiers. Many times our comrades, unable to endure the jolts on the hard planks caused by the breakneck speed, fell out, barely to escape being run over.

It was forbidden for the carriages to stop, even for the most urgent of needs. Without bread, without water, our bones throbbing in pain, we advanced as if enemies were in pursuit; but of course they had already caught us. At dusk we reached the country town of Kalayjek, the seat of the district governor. Our guards led us to a Turkish coffeehouse-inn [*khan*].

As soon as we got inside, some of our friends, exhausted, fainted and fell to the floor, unable to withstand the foul stench of the *khan*. Revived by the handful of skillful doctors among us, they looked up as if they were awakening from a dream and expected to see their loved ones.

No one thought about bread or water, only of resting his weary bones. Everyone fell down randomly on any free spot on the hard wooden floor. After an awful night amid dirt, bedbugs, dust, lice, and the unbearable stench (made all the worse by our crowd of more than 150), we awoke at dawn, numbed and dazed, and departed Kalayjek for Chankiri.

After a nonstop journey of more than ten hours at the previous day's breakneck speed, we at last saw Chankiri's dim lights. Strengthened by hope for an imminent rest and with restrained impatience, we counted the minutes until our arrival. But when the lights seemed to draw no closer, our fatigue redoubled. Instead of taking us to the city, the carriages suddenly took a different road, turned right, and stopped before the large gates of a gigantic building that was hidden in the dark of night.

The first carriage was ours, and I was the first to alight, casting a fearful glance all around me. Passing by guard soldiers armed with bayonets, a captain in the reserve corps of the regular army approached us and said, in a less harsh voice: "*Effendis*, welcome."

When everyone had disembarked, the captain led us through the large arched door into the interior of the gigantic building, a stone armory that could quarter five thousand soldiers; it was surrounded by rectangular buildings connected to one another, with a training ground in the middle.

Here another black curtain fell.

9

Life in Chankiri Armory: The Names of the Deportees in Chankiri

On the fourth day after our arrest, late on the night of April 14/27, 1915, we were settling into one of the large basement halls of this colossal armory. The hall was dirty and dusty, but none of us cared and we all fell onto the boards to sleep.

But how was it possible to fall asleep on dry boards when the freezing northern wind was blowing through the broken windows? Whatever torments our keepers omitted, nature supplied; for on this spring night it was snowing, and we were freezing in our bones and in constant pain from the jolts of the carriage ride.

We were human flotsam and jetsam, snatched from the bosom of family and society and thrown suddenly into a remote corner of Asia Minor. Deprived of life's basic necessities, we lay on hard boards, head to head, foot to foot, yearning for our loved ones and terrified in our souls of tomorrow's uncertainty. On the following day, however, in response to our special petitions, we were granted permission to walk about the armory yard and breathe some fresh air.

List of Those Exiled to Chankiri

[*See the Biographical Glossary for additional information.]

1. Archimandrite Rev. Komitas Soghomonian:* confined in a Paris home for the mentally ill.
2. Very Rev. Grigoris Balakian: survivor.
3. Archimandrite Hovhan Garabedian: survivor, currently an apostate.
4. Fr. Housig Kachouni: died of an illness in a village near Meskene.
5. Fr. Vartan of Ferikoy: survivor.
6. Rev. Grigorian: editor of *Avedaper* [*Good News*] in Constantinople, survivor.
7. Dr. Rupen Chilingirian (Sevag):* intellectual and public figure, martyred on the road between Chankiri and Kalayjek.

8. Daniel Varoujan:* poet and Dashnak worker, martyred with Dr. Chilingirian on the same road in Tiuna.
9. Kaspar Cheraz: lawyer, exiled instead of his eminent brother, survivor.
10. Diran Kelegian:* editor in chief of *Sabah* newspaper, and Ramgavar Party leader, martyred near the bridge over the Halys River in Sivas.
11. Dr. V. Torkomian: writer and public figure, survivor.
12. Puzant Kechian: owner and chief editor of *Puzantion* newspaper, now no longer in print, survivor.
13. Dr. Armenag Parseghian:* teacher and Dashnak worker, survivor.
14. Dr. Krikor Jelal: old Hunchak worker, survivor.
15. Dr. Misak Jevahirjian: member of the judiciary committee, survivor.
16. Dr. Parsegh Dinanian: public figure, survivor.
17. Dr. Levon Bardizbanian: public figure, survivor.
18. Dr. Arshag Kazazian: public figure, survivor.
19. Dr. Mirza Ketenjian: Dashnak worker, survivor.
20. Dr. Stepan Miskjian: martyred near Ankara.
21. Nshan Kalfayian: engineer-agriculturalist, teacher-official, and public figure, survivor.
22. Yervant Chavoushian: worker of the Reorganized Hunchak Party, teacher, perished due to illness, with Fr. Kachouni, and under the same tent.
23. Mikayel Shamdanjian: teacher, writer, editor of *Vostan*, and public figure, survivor.
24. Haig Khojasarian: veteran teacher and public figure, survivor.
25. Sarkis Kuljian (Srents): writer-teacher, editor, Dashnak worker, survivor.
26. Yervand Tolayian: editor of *Gavrosh* satirical paper, survivor.
27. Aram Andonian:* editor, writer, survivor.
28. H. Topjian Ramgavar: public figure and editor, survivor.
29. Movses Bedrosian: teacher and Dashnak worker; being a Bulgarian-Armenian, he was released and sent to Sofia.
30. Aris Israelian: teacher and Dashnak worker, cause of death unknown.
31. Samvel Tomajanian: Hunchak worker, cause of death unknown.
32. Hiusian (surnamed Dorian): teacher, editor, martyred near Ankara.
33. Boghos Danielian: lawyer, Dashnak worker, martyred around Der Zor.
34. Vahram Asdourian: pharmacist and public figure, survivor.
35. Avedis Zarifian: pharmacist and public figure, survivor.
36. Bedros Manigian: pharmacist and public figure, survivor.
37. Azarig: pharmacist, martyred around Der Zor.
38. Asadour Arsenian: pharmacist, martyred around Der Zor.
39. Hagop Nargilejian: pharmacist and public figure, survivor.

40. Krikor Miskjian: pharmacist, martyred with his doctor brother near Ankara.
41. Hagop Terzian: pharmacist and Hunchak worker from Hajin, martyred near Ankara.
42. Gulustanian: dentist, survivor.
43. Vahan Altounian: dentist, survivor.
44. Simon Melkonian: from Ortakoy, architect, survivor.
45. Manoug Basmajian: architect, intellectual, and public figure, survivor.
46. Hagop Korian: seventy-year-old patriotic merchant from Agn, occasionally a teacher, returned to Constantinople and died of natural causes.
47. Karnig Injijian: merchant and public figure, survivor.
48. Terlemezian: banker from Van, survivor.
49. Asdvadzadour Maneasian: merchant, survivor.
50. Ardashes Parisian: merchant, survivor.
51. Megerdich Barsamian: arms salesman, public figure, survivor.
52. Hagop Beylerian: merchant, public figure, survivor.
53. Noyig D. Stepanian: merchant from Erzinjan, survivor.
54. Danielian: tailor from Bandirma in Constantinople and well-known Hunchak worker, survivor.
55. Krikor Ohnigian: father of three sons, seventy-five years old, died due to illness in Chankiri.
56. Aram Ohnigian: chemist, survivor.
57. Hovhannes Ohnigian: died due to illness in Hajkri, near Belemedik.
58. Megerdich Ohnigian: martyred in Der Zor.
59. Kevork Keoleian: martyred near Ankara.
60. Khonjegulian: merchant from Agn, died around Meskene.
61. Onnig Maghazajian: martyred with Varoujan and Sevag in Tiuna, six hours from Chankiri.
62. Garabed Deovletian: mint official and public figure, survivor.
63. Aram Kalenderian: official of the Ottoman Bank and active public figure, survivor.
64. Vaghinag Bardizbanian: official of Shirket Khayriye [charitable association] and public figure, survivor.
65. Parounag Saroukhan: municipal official, cause of death unknown.
66. Momjian: translator for the Russian consulate, martyred near Ankara.
67. Mihran Kayekjian: martyred in Ankara along with two brothers listed below.
68. Levon Kayekjian.
69. Kevork Kayekjian.

Unfortunately, it was possible to obtain only half the names of our comrades exiled to Chankiri, and that with great difficulty; there were, besides these, noble and self-sacrificing youths from the humble class of society, and I so wish I could remember all of them here.

All these individuals were worthy of being recorded, one by one, in this journal of mine. Because they came from a very humble class, they were much more patriotic, always saying, "If we are going to die for the liberty of our people, may our blood be worthy." Or they would console themselves, saying, "At least this will be the last time Armenian blood is shed." These too are to be added to the roll of those myriad unknown martyrs who with their precious blood bought the freedom of the fatherland, and before whose eternal memory all future free Armenian generations must kneel with reverence.

How can I ever forget those nights when hundreds of intellectuals, clergymen, doctors, editors, teachers, wealthy merchants, and bankers lay piled next to one another on the hard boards of the armory, dozing because it was impossible to sleep? But when blacker days came, we would think of these times as pleasant ones. Still, these conditions were truly unbearable; and so everyone tried his best to make do and, thanks to the power of money, to get some food. But the majority, who had no money, appealed to me as a spiritual father. Alas, sharing their penury as well as their fate, I was of scarcely any service to them. As the former prelate of Kastemouni and Chankiri, however, I had some influence with old friends, and so it was possible to get some bedding, blankets, and carpets from fellow Armenians in the region, so that at least we were spared sleeping on the hard boards.

Thus gradually we regained some sense of normalcy and helped the needier among us by taking up a collection and surreptitiously corresponding with our relatives in Constantinople to obtain money. As our financial means grew, thanks to generous gifts, the restrictions placed on us by the military and police officials eased.

I was able to secure a prayer book from the Armenian chapel, and on our fourth evening, with the permission of the captain (who was the inspector of the armory), we began the compline service [vespers]. In my twenty years as a clergyman, only three times have I felt such torment in the depths of my soul.

The first time was when, on behalf of the Turkish-Armenian clergy, I accompanied the late Catholicos [Matheos] Izmirlian* on a historic journey to St. Petersburg, Moscow, Tiflis, and Holy Etchmiadzin, with a stop at Ani on the way. It was the first time in several hundred years that the Catholicos of All Armenians had made a pilgrimage to Ani—this magnificent capital city of the Pakradouni kings—in order to pay respects to these sacred ruins, anointed by holiness and such history. For this occasion a

*Matheos Izmirlian (1848–1911), the "Iron Patriarch," was Patriarch of Constantinople (1894–96 and 1908–09) before becoming catholicos in Etchmiadzin, occupying the throne until 1910. See Biographical Glossary.

great throng of Armenians from Alexandropol and its environs made a pilgrimage to Ani in large caravans to meet their newly elected supreme patriarch.

When His Holiness, the pontiff of blessed memory—surrounded by more than twenty archbishops, bishops, archimandrites, and priests, as well as the large numbers of pilgrims, singing the sublime hymn "Hrashapar Asdvadz" [Magnificent God]—was escorted to the cathedral of Ani, those centuries-old arches and pillars reverberated with the impassioned voices of the singers, and we all felt a shiver of emotion. For we were disturbing the deathly silence of the magnificent thousand-year-old, half-demolished cathedral with our alleluias inspired by the Holy Spirit, and with the sweet melodies, hymns of repentance, and fragrances of incense and smoke.

With our heartfelt prayers we recalled our blessed patriarchs and kings who had performed royal and patriarchal consecrations in this holy temple between the years AD 850 and 1000,* sacred rituals whose participants included the Armenian princes, *nakharars* [nobles], generals, soldiers, and the free and independent people of our nation. It was indeed impossible to see and feel all of this and not be moved; even an unbeliever would be moved by a religious celebration anointed with such sanctity.

The second time was at the end of July 1909. Again with the late Catholicos Izmirlian, I visited Tiflis, in particular the historic Metekh prison on the banks of the Kura River. This is where Shoushanig—the granddaughter of the noble patriarch Sahag Bartev, daughter of the immortal general Vartan Mamigonian, and bride of the Georgian king—rests in eternal sleep.

When His Holiness, surrounded by archbishops, bishops, and archimandrites, entered this historic fortress that stood out on the precipice over the banks of the Kura River, all the famous contemporary Caucasus-Armenian intellectuals (writers, poets, educators, teachers, and editors, who had been imprisoned here for months by order of the tsarist government, some of whom would end up in our caravan of exiles to be martyred in the vicinity of Ankara) came to the iron main gate of the fortress to meet him. All of them, believers and skeptics alike, the freethinkers and the pious, proceeded in pairs with lit candles, singing the inspirational hymn "Ourakh ler S. Yegeghetsi" [Happily Come Holy Church].

And behold, sobbing, lamenting, and wailing began; we were crying, all of us, from the pontiff and his retinue right down to the prisoners: revolutionary political workers, veterans of the Armenian struggle who had all been confined here in dark cells underground for many months because

*Balakian's dates are inaccurate here. The Cathedral was completed in either 1001 or 1010. The Pakradouni nobles participated in its consecration and in ceremonies thereafter until 1045, when Ani fell to the Byzantines.

they had preached freedom for the Armenian population in word, written and spoken, and in deed. We felt shivers down to our bones, as the black fate of the Armenians haunted the pontiff, the intellectuals, and the common folk alike.

Although the late Holy Catholicos comforted everyone, it was difficult to console these unfortunate intellectuals, who, without a trial, faced an uncertain end in these dark cellars. There they sat mournfully longing for their loved ones, as the vision of the frozen roads of Siberia haunted them; from one day to the next, they waited, abject and disoriented, for the tsar's orders, which could mean life or death.

And now we, the more than 150 intellectuals and comrades exiled from Constantinople, assembled—irrespective of political party or class, of piety or skepticism—to hold evening service at dusk, by dim candlelight, behind the high walls of the huge armory of Chankiri, with the icy spring gale blowing through the broken windows. When Archimandrite Komitas began his melancholy and heart-wrenching "Lord Have Mercy" [*Der Voghormia*], the sobbing was impossible to contain. We all cried like boys, cried over loved ones left behind, cried over our black fate, our nation's misfortune; we cried over the bloody days we had just passed, even without knowing that we were on the brink of unprecedented storms of blood.

Perhaps Archimandrite Komitas had never in his life sung "Lord Have Mercy" with such emotion. Normally he would sing it ex officio, as solace for the pain, grief, and mourning of others; this time he sang out of his own grief and emotional turmoil, asking the eternal God for comfort and solace. God, however, remained silent.

In these oppressive circumstances in the armory we passed our days monotonously, consumed with worries about tomorrow, our eyes always fixed on the main gate, at which we hoped would come the good news of our deliverance. With special and exclusive permission, our friends went to town in turns under strict guard to buy things. They brought back various bits of news and information as well; however outdated it was, we listened to it joyfully, so cut off were we from the outside world.

Finally, two weeks later, we were allowed to leave the armory. Everyone hurried to find a place to stay with friends or else elected to remain in the intimate circle of compatriots to pass these tedious days of waiting for our fate to be decided. There were among us even some optimists who were prepared to discount the past two weeks as spring vacation, courtesy of the Ittihad government.

10

Life of the Deportees in the City

We had barely settled in Chankiri when many of us forgot our exiled state and began to display the vulgar manners of Constantinople in this clean, peaceful rural town. Small groups went into the gardens and orchards for picnics; others, supposedly intellectuals, sat all day long at gaming tables, playing poker and cribbage as if they were on some kind of vacation. Daily amusements and pleasures assumed such a remarkable dimension that the Turks questioned the elderly among us: "Don't you know that this is a delicate moment? Why have your compatriots given themselves over to eating and drinking? This is hardly the time for such things." For their part, the Armenian population of this little rural town, having had the opportunity to closely examine the "weaknesses" of their leaders from Constantinople, felt shame and disgust.

At about this time small sums occasionally arrived from the patriarchate, though never exceeding 150 gold liras. Still, small internal quarrels arose over this money, particularly when I was bedridden for about six weeks. Thanks to the able doctors exiled with us, I had gotten back on my feet. Afterward I withdrew to an orchard near the town and busied myself with literary work; it was the only way I could forget our worrisome condition.

Everyone expended much effort petitioning the all-powerful Interior Minister and Armenophile Talaat, demanding justice by telegram. Some appealed to influential friends of various nationalities, requesting intervention. Meanwhile still others secretly appealed to their close or distant relatives, asking that they buy their freedom with small or large bribes. About a week after leaving the armory, thanks to the American ambassador Henry Morgenthau* and some others, five exiled friends [Dr. V. Torkomian, Rev. Krikorian, Puzant Kechian, Yervant Tolayian, and the pharmacist Hagop Nargilejian] succeeded in returning to Constantinople. After the departure of this first fortunate group, our hope of imminent salvation grew, and the secret bargaining efforts were redoubled. But months on, none of our other friends had gained release.

*Morgenthau was ambassador to Turkey, 1913–16 (see Biographical Glossary).—trans.

None of us who survived can forget that black day, on the very Sunday of Vartevar [Transfiguration of Our Lord],* 1915. I was in the garden preparing to celebrate the liturgy in the small Armenian church in Chankiri. Barely had dawn broken when a few young men brought me the bad news that police guards had circled their houses all night.

After we had been released from the armory, each of us exiles had been obliged to go to the guardhouse once every twenty-four hours to appear before the police and sign a special logbook. Soon another young man approached us, out of breath, saying, "Holy Father, the police chief has ordered that all of us exiles from Constantinople gather in front of the government building. He has something official to tell us."

About 135 to 140 of us, depressed and feeling like condemned criminals, stood there waiting. The police chief, accompanied by the commander of the police soldiers and police attendants, proceeded to the top step in front of the outer door and, in a harsh voice, read out the new blacklist. He ordered those named to one side of the door, as if he were separating the goats from the sheep. And so fifty-six of our comrades went there and we remained on the other side. Although we knew nothing specific, we all felt horror and a deathly shiver in our bones.

The chief of police ordered those named into the waiting carriages. Everyone was pleading with me to intercede, to ask for a few hours' time so that they could go to their rooms, prepare for departure, and at least collect their underwear.

There was no time to think; I had to see the chief of police immediately. Of course I had no official authority, but still, I wanted to ask for a few hours for my comrades to get ready. Despite our pessimism, they were granted an hour.

It's impossible to describe the panic prevailing among us; we were all confused and did not know how to prioritize our needs. Thanks to a few selfless party members who were teachers, we were able to collect almost sixty gold liras for the road expenses of our friends, or about one gold lira for each of them. Luckily, some didn't need any monetary assistance.

As the eleven carriages made ready to go, we kissed our friends for what would be the last time. Then the caravan set out, escorted by more than ten mounted police soldiers, and as thick clouds of dust rose, they gradually disappeared from view. By now none of us could remain standing; as if we had just returned from a long journey, we desperately needed rest.

We were all overwrought, especially because some of the policemen had whispered in our ears that the caravan was going to Der Zor. Those

*June 29.

who had departed were told that they were being taken to Ankara, to remain there till the end of the war.

At the beginning of June some of our exiled friends who were in contact with relatives in Ankara province received telegrams from them announcing they had picked up their entire family and departed Erzinjan for Agn, leaving all their movable and immovable goods with their Turkish friends. A few days later came telegrams from Agn that the same relatives were departing for Harput in a large caravan. After that no further news ever came.

None of us had been contemplating a large-scale Armenian massacre. We continued to appeal by telegram to Talaat, the Armenians' dear and friendly minister of the interior, as well as to the police chief, Jan-Bolat, demanding trials and sentencing and justice in the name of the Ottoman Constitution. My fellow exiles would send regular telegrams to the central government in Constantinople demanding justice, and as the spiritual leader of the exiles, I was asked to sign them. But I myself never personally petitioned anyone, because I felt my only chance to be saved lay in escaping attention.

But when we put our fifty-six friends on the road to Der Zor on the day of the Transfiguration of Our Lord, at least some of us came to our senses and, realizing the imminent danger, decided to do everything possible to save ourselves from the trap into which we had fallen. Still, once again, no one could judge the magnitude of the danger or its precipitate depth.

I want to mention, for the sake of history, the noble and heroic action performed by one of our unfortunate exiled friends, the martyred Dashnak Haig Tiryakian (Hrach). Seeing that his namesake, a sixty-year-old Armenian grocer, had been mistakenly exiled to Ayash in his place, Hrach petitioned the police administration in Constantinople to relieve the poor innocent elderly man and take Hrach to Ayash from Chankiri. When Hrach was making this petition, the bloody storm had already begun, and so like the rest of us he knew very well that he was asking for his own death. But he did not want an innocent person to perish in his stead. Thus the fatal order came, and Hrach was transported to Ayash, to be martyred a short time later with his unfortunate friends during the horrendous massacre carried out in Ankara province.

But during the early days our exiled friends, unable to see the major criminal plot entangling them, remained largely indifferent. The police chief from Salonica and the police escorting us from Constantinople would enter our ranks daily and eat in the special restaurant we had on the riverbank and even play backgammon with us. But all the while they were spying on us and reporting back to Constantinople. It was from these secret reports that the blacklists were prepared in Constantinople and sent to Chankiri; thus were our ranks gradually thinned following the dispatch of our friends toward Der Zor.

By and by, the fortunate ones among us, thanks to large bribes or powerful and influential connections, succeeded in returning to Constantinople and were saved.

11

Plan for the Extinction of the Armenians in Turkey

According to the decision of the 1915 general assembly of the Turkish nationalist party Ittihad ve Terakki (Union and Progress), the Armenian people were secretly sentenced to death according to the following plan.

A. First, under the new martial laws, the Armenians of Turkey were absolutely forbidden to travel. Even travel between the closest towns and villages was unconditionally forbidden. The official order of the Ittihad government imposed on the Armenians was: "All Armenians Must Stay Put Where They Are."

B. In every town with an Armenian population, the influential Armenians—clergy and laypeople, party members and nonparty members, liberals and conservatives—and those thought to have influence were arrested and imprisoned to prevent their organizing the people in resistance. It was just as it had happened in Constantinople.

C. The Armenian people were generally disarmed, even to the point of confiscating their large kitchen knives, in order to make impossible any potential seditious movement.

D. The entire Armenian population of Asia Minor, including all families, were to be deported or put on the road to Der Zor, on the pretense of exile, with the intent that they all be mercilessly massacred, from the innocent babe in the cradle to the ninety-year-old. Those not from the six Armenian provinces (Karin [Erzerum], Van, Baghesh [Bitlis], Kharpert [Harput], Sepastia [Sivas], and Dikranagerd [Diyarbekir]) were by thirst and hunger to be annihilated in the deserts of Der Zor.

E. Permission was given to take the beautiful Armenian brides and virgins to the Turkish harems.

F. Any conversion to Islam was disallowed because the events of 1895–96 showed that Armenians were not able to sincerely abandon their religion.

G. The entire wealth of the Armenian people and their cultural institutions was to be confiscated. The movable and immovable wealth of individual Armenians, including all the money and gold and silver jewelry deposited in local banks, was to be confiscated by the specially organized Commission on Abandoned Goods and Estates.

H. Special blacklists of the Armenians to be massacred, irrespective of sex or age, were prepared by the provincial police authorities; a copy of each list was sent to the Ministry of the Interior in Constantinople so that Talaat and the Ittihad Committee would know on a daily basis how many Armenians had been killed and how many were still left. One copy of these blacklists was transmitted to the Ministry of War so that it could maintain control and know on a daily basis the overall number of dead Armenians, compared to that of the Turkish and other Muslim soldiers being killed on the war fronts.

In order to carry out this plan to exterminate an entire people, the following criminal means were used:

1. All the prisoners on death row, and all the convicts and criminals in the prisons of all the towns in Turkey, were to be pardoned and organized into bandit groups (*chetes*) to plunder and massacre the Armenian population without mercy, on the pretext of protecting the rear of the Ottoman army.

2. All governors *vali* [governor-general], *mutasarrif* [vice governor-general or provincial governor], *kaymakam* [district governor], mayors, and supervisors who refused to carry out the orders from central headquarters to exterminate the Armenians would be immediately removed from office and replaced by obedient bureaucrats.

3. Overall supervision for the execution of these plans of the Ittihad General Assembly was assigned to the provincial chapters of the Ittihad Committee in Asia Minor. At the same time those chapters were granted authority to act with greater severity if they deemed it necessary.

One day one of our friends in exile (who is still alive) visited the office of Yunuz, the responsible secretary* of the Chankiri Ittihad Committee. In

*An official who functioned locally as the eyes and ears of the Ittihad Central Committee in Constantinople.—trans.

the course of their meeting, Yunuz left the room for a minute. Prior to his return, our exile friend felt compelled to read an official document that had been left on the table. It had the following text verbatim.

> WITHOUT MERCY AND WITHOUT PITY, KILL ALL FROM THE ONE-MONTH-OLD TO THE NINETY-YEAR-OLD, BUT SEE TO IT THAT THIS MASSACRE IS NOT CONDUCTED IN THE TOWNS AND IN THE PRESENCE OF THE PEOPLE.
>
> BILA TEREDDEUT VE MERHABET BIT AYLUGDAN DOKSAN YASHENA KADAR ITLAFE, SHEHIR DEROUNINDE, EHALI HOUZOURENDA OLMAMASENA DUKKAT.

In order to give this criminal plan of the Ittihad Committee, a plan unprecedented in human history, a "legitimate" facade, [in May 1915] the Ittihad ministry introduced a bill into the Ottoman Parliament calling for the deportation of the Armenians as well as the confiscation of their movable and immovable wealth. Needless to say, the bill passed after one reading and became law, whereupon Sultan Reshad was ordered to carry it out.

The overall plan to exterminate the Armenians, outlined at the beginning of this chapter, was published officially in the newspapers, and when at the beginning of June it reached us in Chankiri, we all said the same thing: This is the epitaph of the Armenian nation. Suddenly the secret plan, which had been devised by Talaat, Behaeddin Shakir, and Dr. Nazim, was being revealed, having assumed legal form in the Ottoman Parliament.*

In the end the holy war, or *jihad* [the Sheikh-ul-Islam had], declared against the Entente powers was carried out only against the unarmed and defenseless Armenian population by the most savage of means. Not one of the Ittihad's projected 400 million Muslims heeded the cry of *jihad;* on the contrary, the king of Arabia, Hussein, at the suggestion of the British, issued a counter *fatwa.* Thus Talaat, after having Behaeddin Shakir's

*Balakian is referring to the publication in the Ottoman *Parliamentary Gazette*, and then in local papers, of the news of the Temporary Law of Deportation, which was approved by the Ittihad government (not by the Ottoman Parliament) in May 1915. This law formalized the arrest and deportation of the Armenian population of turkey. Although the law appeared to be a security measure aimed at removing the Armenians during wartime, those like Balakian who were beginning to see what was happening realized that deportation meant massacre and other atrocities.

Armenian extermination plan approved by the Ottoman Parliament, had the Sheikh-ul-Islam issue a *fatwa* declaring the Armenians to be enemies of Islam and of the fatherland. Then the sultan as well [officially] ordered the execution of the plan to exterminate the Armenians.*

The execution of this plan had started with the collective arrest and exile of us intellectuals on April 11/24, 1915. It then spread to the Armenian populations of all the towns and small villages throughout Turkey, except for the few Armenian towns that could be found, by the fall, anywhere.

To facilitate implementing the plan, Talaat successively dismissed all the governors-general, provincial governors, and district governors of Kastemouni, Ankara, Yozgat, and Erzinjan and others who opposed the deportations and massacres. In their place, he appointed young and fiercely Armenophobic officials.

Owing to the extraordinary secrecy ordered from above, we were uninformed about any of these actions happening around us. Only after we met Asaf, who had been the governor of Osmaniye during the Armenian massacres of 1909 in Adana, were we able to comprehend a little bit of the plan to annihilate a nation. During the massacres Asaf† had committed barbaric acts against the Armenians, for which he was indicted and barely escaped hanging. Later he was appointed *mutasarrif* of Chankiri.

Asaf had been a student of Diran Kelegian's† at the Ottoman University and had great respect for Kelegian, who was also editor in chief of the newspaper *Sabah*. Kelegian would go to visit Asaf once in a while. One day Kelegian, who was also the head of the Armenian Ramgavar Party [Armenian Democratic Liberal Party], invited me to join him on a visit to *Mutasarrif* Asaf. "Let's see," he said, "what advice he can give us about getting free from this trap that we have fallen into."

I objected, saying that the less we were seen by officials, the more prudent it would be for us. But Kelegian insisted, assuring me that because Asaf had been his student and was very amicably disposed toward him, and since he had not visited Asaf in more than two weeks, it would be good to go and confer with him. To encourage me, he recalled that Asaf as his grateful student used to kiss his hand. Almost involuntarily, then, I went with Kelegian to visit Asaf in his office. He received us with great respect, as if we were not exiles. He had us sit down in the two armchairs that were for dignitaries and ordered Turkish coffee for us, which during those days was offered only to the highest of officials because of wartime frugality.

Kelegian asked Asaf what new means he would recommend for our

*The creation of mobile killing squads had begun as early as February 1915. The Sheikh-ul-Islam issued his *fatwa* in November 1914.—trans.

†See Biographical Glossary.

returning to Constantinople, since thus far nothing had worked. Asaf answered, "Kelegian *Effendi*, do whatever you can and get back to Constantinople as soon as possible, because soon it will be too late for you." Naturally we asked anxiously, "Why will it be too late for us? What will happen?" We were hardly aware that a secret plan was unfolding around us. Asaf answered, "I don't see the government policy toward the Armenians being good. Again, some things are going to happen; see that you get to Constantinople, the earlier the better. I see signs of new storms."

Curious, and distraught at this reply, Kelegian asked for elaboration. Asaf was at first evasive, then finally said: "From the little I've said, you can understand much. You are intellectual people—certainly you understand what I am trying to say." But we really didn't understand what he meant, other than that some bad things would happen to us. In response to our urgent insistence, Asaf said, "You are a clergyman, and it is your duty to keep a confession to yourself. And Kelegian *Effendi*, you are my teacher, I love you. Take this telegram and read it quickly!" He took out of his desk drawer an encoded telegram on official letterhead, the decoded text of which was on a separate piece of paper:

TELEGRAPH US IMMEDIATELY AS TO HOW MANY ARMENIANS HAVE ALREADY DIED AND HOW MANY ARE LEFT ALIVE—TALAAT.

It was impossible to comprehend. Kelegian asked, "What does this mean? I don't understand." Asaf, with a sarcastic laugh, said: "You are such an intelligent man, and you don't understand?" I answered, "They put us in such a state that we have neither brainpower nor moral vigor." Asaf said, "This simply means, 'How many have you already massacred and how many are still alive?' Because there has been neither earthquake nor flood, nor any other natural disaster by which people would die en masse."*

Kelegian began to weep and said, "It is a shame that I will die without having secured my children's future." Asaf offered a few comforting and encouraging words and then went on:

> I am going to resign my office in fifteen days. The officials who sit in Constantinople have us do all the dirty work, but if their backs are ever against the wall one day and there is a day of reckoning, they will escape and we minor officials will be trampled. During the Adana massacres in 1909, I was the governor of Osmaniye; I was almost sentenced to be hanged and just barely saved my neck.
>
> I don't see this as a good situation, and I don't want to become

*Although Balakian notes previously that the Turkish government's plan to annihilate the Armenians was becoming clear from what was published in the papers, it is obvious that he is in a characteristic state of "dissociation," in which he knows horrible things are about to happen but is not able to fully accept such knowledge (see Introduction).

a tool in the hands of others. In a week or two I shall be going to Constantinople, leaving government service once and for all and going back to practice my old profession of law.

Indeed, fifteen days later Asaf resigned, returning to Constantinople.

After the 1918 Armistice, just as he had predicted, the Ittihad camarilla escaped abroad, leaving all the officials big and small who had been accomplices in this crime to their own fate.

I must tell you emphatically that still we were unable to see this secret plan for what it was. For the extermination of a historic nation of four thousand years was unimaginable. Even in the bloodiest periods of history, such a thing had never happened. Never had the Turkish sultans, who had conquered the world, thought of wiping out a nation all at once; even in six centuries of bloody rule, it had not crossed their minds.

But Talaat's camarilla was convinced that, against all odds, with the world war winding down, even if a punishment was to be administered, the punishment for killing one or one million Armenians would still be death. And in the event that despite their belief in certain victory, the Turks and the Germans were to lose the war, Talaat and company had already made arrangements to escape to Germany. No matter that a few high-ranking officials would be hanged; it was worth the price of their heads to get rid of the Armenians.

12

The Armenian Carnage in Ankara

Just as everywhere else, orders arrived in Ankara from the Ittihad center and Talaat in Constantinople to deport the Armenian population, caravan by caravan, and to massacre them without mercy.

However, the governor-general of Ankara, Mazhar, did not want to obey the orders. On the contrary, he did everything possible to prevent the deportation, knowing that it would mean the massacre of an unarmed, defenseless, and peaceful population. He invited prominent Turks of Ankara to his office and, informing them of Talaat's order, asked them if the Armenians of Ankara were untrustworthy. They all responded, in turn, that they had no suspicions about any of the Armenians of Ankara. Governor Mazhar then had these prominent Turks [*eshraf*] sign a petition affirming this fact and sent it to the Ministry of the Interior.

When Talaat received this petition, he was furious and started circulating rumors that the governor of Ankara was involved in questionable business dealings. Eventually Mazhar grew fed up with the deception set in motion around him and finally resigned on July 25, 1915, and departed for Constantinople.

To replace him, Talaat sent the fanatical young Ittihadist Atif to be vice governor of Ankara. He was a thirty-year-old native of Salonica and deputy director of personnel at the Sublime Porte; the word was that he was Talaat's secret personal secretary. The Armenophobic Atif brought with him from Constantinople a new police chief named Behaeddin, a young and equally fanatical Ittihadist. Barely had the two arrived in Ankara than they went to work, carrying out the secret and urgent verbal orders from headquarters.

First, they issued an official decree requiring the population, without regard to religion or race, to turn in their weapons at a designated site. Whatever weapons Muslims brought during the day were returned at night. Obviously this decree was aimed at the Armenians, all of whom, irrespective of denomination, fearing the threat of severe punishment, turned in whatever kinds of weapons they had, and did not receive them back.

Second, after releasing all the criminals from the Ankara prison, Atif and Behaeddin formed *chetes* or bandit groups, each under the leadership of a Circassian.

Then Vice-Governor Atif convened a secret meeting with all the members of the local Ittihad committee and all the main government officials, led by Police Chief Behaeddin. They decided* to massacre all the Armenians in Ankara province, irrespective of age or sex.

Under a third measure, Atif and Behaeddin arrested the city's prominent Armenians, regardless of denomination. And on the night of August 11, 1915, the local military commander and the police chief, having previously taken all "restrictive," precautionary measures, arrested all the remaining Armenians. Telling them, "The police department wants you," they filled up the prisons and various buildings that had been converted into prisons with Armenians.

The prominent prisoners—lawyers, bankers, merchants, and Armenian government officials—were taken out on the road in the first caravan, under the supervision of the police commissioner, the prison warden,

*Talaat issued all orders for the massacres, but local Ittihad committees planned them and carried them out.—trans.

police soldiers, and officers. Overall superintendence was assigned to Shemseddin, the son of Tabib, a member of the Ottoman Parliament from Ankara. Although those in the caravan were the distinguished people of this city, a mark was put on their arms and their fezes, shoes, and coats were taken from them before they left the prison; then these 150 or so were taken out of town on foot and tied together with a rope.

The tools that would be used to kill these Armenians—axes, cleavers, paddles, large knives, and other weapons—were transported in four or five carriages directly behind the caravan,* and following them were a few carriages filled with lime.

To make sure that the crying and screaming of the people in this caravan would not be heard, some of the soldiers were ordered to play trumpets and drums as they left Ankara via the town's famous Tash Khan section.

Seven hours from the town, this dust-covered caravan reached the forest known as Kouroukjeoghlu, near the village of Buknam. There they were met by the *chetes*, who possessed all kinds of weapons.

A well-known lawyer, Armenag, pleaded with the chief of the bandit group to be given, as the sacred last right of one condemned to death, permission to say a few words. He received permission. Then he said, with unusual coldheartedness and a cavalier indifference to death that surprised even the *chetes:* "It's no longer a secret that you have brought us here to be killed. But I want to ask you if you know why you are going to kill us." The leader of the bandits answered that he didn't know why. Armenag continued: "You should know that the high-ranking officials and the Ittihad committee who gave you the orders to kill us did so solely to secure their personal gain, and they are leaving a stain on your history and laying waste to the fatherland. The Koran demands that you act with compassion toward non-Muslims, like brothers. But those who ordered you to kill us haven't read the Koran and don't even want to read it. Those who ordered us killed and those who kill us will suffer the deserved punishment for our innocent blood, answering for their crime with the same kind of death, and right here. Since we are incapable of resisting you, do what you will."

Barely had he spoken these prophetic words when hundreds of *chetes* attacked from all sides, cutting and hacking off legs and arms and necks with axes and hatchets, ripping them off partly or entirely, and crushing heads with rocks. Then the bodies were thrown half alive, dead, or in the throes of death into prepared ditches and covered with lime. Those who were partly sticking out of the dirt and the lime made the heavenly arches

**Caravan:* broad term that covered the movement of a group by any means, usually on foot.—trans.

resound with their cries of agony; more dirt was poured on them until they were buried alive.

When the massacre of the first caravan was finished, the second caravan of more than 320 people was sent forward. Transported to the park known as Kayash, six hours from town, these people were massacred in the same merciless manner. The dismembered bodies of the martyrs were left unburied for fifteen days. Turkish officers then oversaw their burial by Armenian laborer-soldiers. After massacring all these people, the *chetes* came back to town wearing clothes, shoes, and other items they had taken from them. Everywhere they boasted about how many Armenians they had killed and how in unheard-of ways they had tortured and dismembered those who were still alive and even mutilated the corpses.

For one hundred years, since the official inception of Catholicism in Asia Minor, Ankara had been a center for Armenian Catholics. Having remained aloof from all nationalistic movements, the local Catholics had always been exempt from violence, even during the bloodiest periods of Armenian persecution. Ankara had more than two thousand Armenian Catholic households, and thanks to their neutrality, they had been able to amass great wealth and make great progress.

Having destroyed more than 1,000 Armenian households in Ankara and nearby regions, Vice-Governor Atif and Police Chief Behaeddin wanted to exterminate Ankara's Armenian Catholics at the first opportunity, before beginning the liquidation of more than 50,000 Armenians in the more remote regions of the province. They couldn't confiscate the immense wealth of the Armenian Catholics fast enough, and they couldn't wait to abduct the beautiful brides and virgin girls.

The police chief went to Constantinople to make sure the extermination of the Catholic Armenians was at the top of the agenda. Talaat, who had acceded to the frequent appeals of the ambassador of Austria-Hungary not to massacre the Armenian Catholics of Ankara, now went back on his promise. With the unanimous approval of the Ittihad Central Committee, he gave the verbal order to exterminate Ankara's Armenian Catholics.

Thus, on August 26, 1915, Police Chief Behaeddin returned to Ankara with the order he had sought. The next day the prominent Armenian Catholics were arrested, using the same warrant: "The governor wants to see you." They remained in prison for a few days, and then their arms were tied together, just as had been done to their conationals. Along with their monsignor, this pitiful caravan was taken out of the city by night, under supervision, and brought to the village of Kara-gedig.

The torture of these people was increased by forcing them to pull the carriages that contained the instruments of their death. When they reached Kara-gedig, they found themselves surrounded by hundreds of Turkish bandits, who, at the government's behest, had rushed to this orgy of blood. Then, however, like a miracle, a mounted messenger from Ankara suddenly appeared with orders from Atif not to kill these deportees.

The commander of the deportation [*sevkiyat*], issued the following statement:

> The Ottoman government, in declaring war against Russia, England, France and other great powers, has emerged victorious, lest you think that one day we shall be required to account for our actions. No one can demand you from us; since they did not give you to us by count, they cannot ask you back by count! [*sic*] However, you are not going to be killed like the other Armenians.* Don't be afraid for your life, but pray for the nation and the government.

The next day this caravan of more than 120 souls was put on the road toward Der Zor via Kayseri. A week later a second caravan of 200 Armenian Catholics was taken toward Der Zor via the same route. I met some of them in the vicinity of Amanos.

Once the majority of Armenian Catholic males had been taken, caravan by caravan, out of the city on the dangerous mountainous roads toward Der Zor, the women's turn came. On August 27, by government order, a Turkish town crier announced, "Let the Catholics go to the railway station. They are going to depart this afternoon." The Armenian Catholics apprehensively hurried to the station, and those who would not go voluntarily were taken by force.

Ankara's Ittihad club members went to the railway station and demanded the beautiful virgin daughters from their mothers. But the mothers and daughters declared, without exception, that they preferred death to life in these degrading and infernal conditions. Then they were offered the possibility of saving their lives by converting to Islam. Among the thousands of people, nine-tenths of whom were women and girls, only about ten or fifteen agreed to this and were separated from the caravan and returned to the town. The others took it upon themselves to go where the government dictated; even knowing that death was waiting for them, they said, "Whatever they're doing to our nation, let it happen to us too" [*Oumoum millet ne olouyersa, bizde beraber olourouz.*] These thousands of Armenians were forced to stay in the grain warehouses of the railway station for more than two weeks, until one group was sent to Konya, one to

*Meaning Armenian Apostolics and Protestants.—trans.

Eskishehir, and one to Eregli, in a miserable state; the majority were robbed of their silver and gold jewelry, while their houses and all they contained were left as spoils for the local Ittihad committee.

The hundreds of orphaned children of those who had been killed were converted to Islam. Days of grand circumcision ceremonies were held for boys between the ages of five and twelve; these newly converted Muslims were paraded around the town in carriages, unaware of what had happened to them.

The *hoja** of the village of Kayal, Mehmed, bragged about having killed the 350 Armenians of the village of Stanos, near Ankara, without regard to sex or age. After this horrendous carnage, the plunder began. One by one, the stores filled with all kinds of looted merchandise. The homes of all the wealthy Armenians were opened, and for days on end their contents were carried off to the homes of high government officials and the members of the Ittihad club.

After this general pillage the Commission on Abandoned Goods and Estates was formed; its sole purpose was to distribute the remaining booty among its members. In the entire city there were at most a few old Turks who did not participate in this pillage, saying compunctiously, "The merchandise of the person crying does not bring happiness to the buyer" [*Aghlayanun maluh, alana khair getirmez*].

Ankara, being close to Constantinople and connected with Europe by the railroad, was a rich commercial center of Asia Minor; the wealth of its Armenians, worth millions of gold pounds, passed by such means into the hands of plunderers, who became the "legal" heirs of all the Armenians whom they had led to the slaughter.

The Turks of Ankara would brag about their bloody conquests in detail to their countrymen and coreligionists, and despite government attempts to keep it secret, news of this bloodbath reached our ears far away in Chankiri, pitching us into a state of grief.

And the blood spread, step-by-step, from Ankara to distant cities, towns, and villages. Similar massacres took place in Denek-Maden, Isgilib, and Sungurlu, and with even greater cruelty in Yozgat. First, all the Armenian males of a city or town, and then the women and girls, were bound together and taken on foot to deep valleys a few hours away, accompanied by a Turkish mob armed with axes. There they were slaughtered like sheep, pregnant women and suckling babies included.

At the end of August 1915, a girl barely thirteen years old, who was a native of Sungurlu, told me of the following, to which she had been an eyewitness and which she only by some miracle had survived.

In mid-August, just as in Ankara (from whence the order issued), all

**Hoja:* wise one.—trans.

Armenian males from twelve to eighty in Sungurlu were arrested, taken out of town, and killed by unheard-of tortures. Next it was the turn of the girls and women. On August 20, all the Armenian women, girls, and small boys were taken out of Sungurlu in more than seventy carriages and brought to a valley by a bridge an hour and a half away. Following these carriages from town was an armed mob of Turks, each of whom on the way, chose a sheep or lamb to slaughter.

When they reached the area under the bridge, police and police soldiers, having joined the savage mob, set upon these poor, defenseless women—mothers, brides, virgins—and children. Just as spring trees are cut down with bill-hooked hedge knives, the bloodthirsty mob attacked this group of more than four hundred with axes, hatchets, shovels, and pitchforks, hacking off their appendages: noses, ears, legs, arms, fingers, shoulders . . . They dashed the little children against the rocks before the eyes of their mothers while shouting, "Allah, Allah."

The screams of the mothers and virgins and little children echoed across the valley and the surrounding rocky hills and caves. The children screamed, "*Mayrig, Mayrig* [Mother, Mother], help us, please!" But the mob, indifferent, continued to rip apart the bodies so that even the stones cried out. Finally, after four to five hours of carnage and plunder, night's black blanket covered this scene of blood, which would stir the envy of wild animals.

With the fall of night, the Turkish mob, police, and police soldiers returned to town with their bundles of loot. Whatever they had left, hyenas, wolves, jackals, and other scavengers came to finish off. The precipices of the valley were strewn with corpses, naked or half-naked. It was a scene beyond all human imagination. Now and then, in the darkness of the night, the moans and groans of the badly wounded and the raspy drone of those giving up the ghost could be heard.

After midnight, in the thick darkness, a refreshing dew began to fall, and behold, a slightly wounded, numb little girl, invigorated by the dew, woke up. Half alive, she began to rove in search of her mother and two sisters. In vain she called them by name, but alas they were gone to eternal sleep. At last she found their crushed bodies, which had fallen one beside the other.

In shock, the girl began to shake and sob uncontrollably; her teeth chattering, she did not move from that spot until morning, as if the bodies of her mother and older sisters compelled her to stay there.

At dawn a few Kurdish cowherds crossing the bridge in the vicinity of this carnage saw one of the corpses moving in the distance. They approached her, took pity on her, and brought her home to their father's care. Being a *kizilbash*,* he secretly turned her over to his longtime friend in Chankiri.

*Turcophobic Muslim sectarian friendly to the Christians.—trans.

It was with the arrival of this little girl in the town where we were staying that, for the first time, we became aware of the extent of the killing being carried out around us without a sound or a whisper. We too were now tortured by the nightmare of impending death.

Meanwhile, throughout June–August 1915, the widespread slaughter of the Armenians continued day and night in the interior provinces, but the singed smell of innocent blood had not reached Constantinople. However, because Ankara was close to the center, and there were Armenians among the railway officials, news of the Armenian massacre of Ankara soon made its way to Constantinople. It stirred all the European and local Christians in the capital. In particular, it propelled the papal nuncio and, through his influence, the Austro-Hungarian consul into a flurry of activity, and they lodged an eleventh-hour protest.

The German consulate as well was unable to remain indifferent; at least for appearances' sake, and to save Germany from any future accountability, the consulate lost no time in sending investigators to Ankara for a pro forma investigation.

Even before that, however, the man ordering the massacres, Talaat himself, had gone all the way to Ankara. He ordered that the 42,000 Armenian bodies left unburied in the valleys throughout the provinces, and torn to pieces by animals, be moved to large mass graves. For his token investigation, the inspector from the German consulate met with high-ranking Turkish officials and questioned them, then went back to Constantinople and reported to the coldhearted German ambassador, von Wangenheim, that he had "not run into any evidence bearing the trace of massacres committed against the Armenians, and that this was all the result of rumors."

To the many stinging protests made to the German consulate, von Wangenheim responded matter-of-factly, saying that he had no right to interfere with Turkish internal affairs or to violate Turkish sovereignty. He added that no European government would remain indifferent toward a similar seditious movement within its own borders, and would find a way to suppress it. And so the German ambassador brushed aside the massacres organized to exterminate the Armenian people as merely a means of control.

13

The Tragic End of Deportee Friends in Ayash

While the rivers and tributaries of Ankara province were filling with blood, and the valleys with unburied corpses, eight hours away in Ayash—a small country town and district center—the condition of our exiled comrades was no less tragic. After being transported to Ayash, these seventy-five were locked up in an old armory called Sare-Kushla [Yellow Barracks], at the far end of town; its shattered windows were boarded up.

Over the course of one month, as in Chankiri, thirteen lucky ones succeeded in returning to Constantinople, thanks to powerful interventions and generous bribes. Our comrades sent telegrams and letters to the minister of the interior and to influential Turkish friends, demanding justice in the name of the Ottoman Constitution. A special commission of able lawyers and linguists was formed to polish the language of these telegrams and petitions, in the hope of pressuring the central government to negotiate.

For the most part Haroutiun Shahrigian edited these telegrams and petitions. And with the assent of friends with him in prison, he mustered heroic courage worthy of the esteem of future generations, writing to Talaat in a telegram, "If it was party members that you were after, what right did you have to put nonparty members in prison?"

Of course, all the petitions went unanswered. And even though all [the writers] were distinguished and prolific intellectuals of the Armenian nation with many years of experience in political life, none of them could comprehend the magnitude of the danger facing them.

With the corner of the envelope only just newly opened, one of those still ignorant of the entire tragedy was Agnouni (Khachadour Maloumian). He was simply stupefied, unable to explain these mass arrests and this reign of terror. Agnouni kept sending personal telegrams to Talaat, demanding trials and and justice.

A survivor later told us that Agnouni would say to comrades:

> I wonder why Talaat Bey does not deign to reply to my personal telegrams. In the midst of the confrontation between the two Turkish political parties, Ittihad and Itilaf, in Constantinople during the Balkan War of 1912–1913, I hid Talaat in my house, and saved him from most certain death. Can he have forgotten the kindness I showed him? Why doesn't he reply to me?

With such conviction, Agnouni waited at Ayash from day to day for his freedom and his return to Constantinople.

So well had the Ittihad Committee leaders played their role, and so successfully had they gained the blind trust of the Armenian revolutionary leaders, that the latter found themselves facing a great riddle that they were unable to solve. Alas, such blind faith cost the precious lives of one million innocent people.

These Armenian leaders had thought of the Ittihad leaders as their ideological comrades. In fact, they were no more than common criminals; only through audacity had they gotten their hands on the helm of the country—not to save the fatherland but to satisfy their personal ambitions and greed.

For the most part, those exiled to Ayash spent their last days in material privation. Of these, poor Shahrigian cried like a boy when he received five gold pieces in the mail from Constantinople. When his friends asked why he was so emotional, he said, "The person who sent me this money is the poor Greek washerwoman who lives in my house in Constantinople. What sacrifice has she made? Where did she find this sum, when she is so needy herself? The poor woman must have wanted to ease my grief." All our intellectuals, who would do any nation proud, not only suffered unspeakable mental anguish and emotional turmoil but had begun to wash their own laundry in order to save money.*

For the sake of caution and appearances, the clergy and lay leaders in the official center of Armenian life—Constantinople—took a circumspect attitude. Thus the patriarchate sent those of us in Chankiri insufficient money for bread, amounting to only a few hundred gold pieces, when more than half of the 150 of us were in need. Thus we exiles covered our own traveling and food expenses with internal loans and other contributions. To the twenty-six young intellectuals who were being separated from us for the last time, we were unable to give money for bread, let alone pay for their transport by carriage.

In the end, the fossilized formula of perpetual apology was always on

*At this time, it was highly unusual for men in the Near East to do domestic chores.—trans.

the tip of the tongues of our Armenian officials: "Brother, we can't do anything, we don't have an army, we don't have a navy, we are a poor nationality, we aren't able to do anything . . . We always do all that we can, the necessary appeals are always made, but nobody listens."

A month after our unfortunate friends were interned in the armory at Ayash, the Hunchak Party's distinguished and conscientious leader, Hampartsoum Boyadjian (Mourad), was bound in chains and transported under strict police surveillance to Kayseri. There he was sentenced to death by court-martial. As self-sacrificing and brave an old revolutionary as Mourad was, he was an equally kind and noble friend. It was impossible to know him and not to like him, to not feel an affinity with him, even if one did not agree with all of his ideas.

Mourad had not been involved in any acts of treachery against the government after the adoption of the Ottoman Constitution, and he had taken a reserved, wait-and-see attitude during the war. Yet the court-martial in Kayseri accused him of inciting the people to rebel—a basic device for falsely accusing innocent individuals that was used everywhere to justify the annihilation of the Armenians. This devoted servant of the Armenian people, giving his life for his idealism, also rose to the summit of the thorny Armenian Golgotha.

In Ayash, our friends often sang religious hymns and patriotic songs, led by Melkon Gurdjian (Hrant). They hoped the songs would transport them back to the good old days, when we were free and inflamed by our idealism and love of liberty. With the removal of Mourad, however, even the most indifferent grew pessimistic, especially when six more of our comrades were taken away.

One black day Agnouni, Rupen Zartarian, Khajag, Minasian, Dr. Daghavarian,* and Haroutiun Jangoulian were ordered out of the armory at Ayash. The first four were distinguished Dashnak intellectuals; Daghavarian was a former Hunchak and more recently an ardent Ramgavar [Democratic Liberal]; and Jangoulian was one of the old chiefs of the Hunchak Party, as well as the hero of the first civic protest at Kum Kapu in 1891.

Under the strictest police supervision, these six were transported by rail toward Adana-Aleppo, supposedly to be tried before the court-martial in Diyarbekir. When they arrived in Adana, the six wished to establish contact with local Armenian officials whose deportation had not yet begun, but they had no means of doing so. On the contrary, when local government officials heard that Krikor Zohrab and Vartkes Serengulian* had also been brought to Adana, they hurried to put the new arrivals on the road to

*See Biographical Glossary for these.

Aleppo in order to prevent them from having any contact with the local Armenians.

In July 1915 the tunnels of Ayran in Mount Amanos had not yet opened, nor had the railway reached as far as Osmaniye. So the police arranged for these exiles to remain in the Osmaniye prison for one day while arrangements were made for a carriage. Osmaniye was the last station on the line extending from Adana to Aleppo, and from there on it was invariably necessary to travel by carriage up to Islahiye, passing through Hasanbeyli. At that time Osmaniye and Islahiye were the western and eastern railroad stations respectively of the Amanos mountains.

A well-known merchant in Osmaniye, a native of Sivas, was one of Dr. Daghavarian's relatives. He was also the manager of the Adana branch of a large and famous store, and having been established in Adana for a long time, he had a close business relationship with the governor-general, who gave him some advice: "In these days, in order not to attract attention in Adana, go to Osmaniye."

So when Dr. Daghavarian and his five comrades arrived in Osmaniye and were escorted to prison, this merchant hurried to the commander of the police soldiers, a friend of his, and asked that he be allowed to take the six prisoners home with him for supper. He received permission to do so, on the condition that he also take the policeman who was guarding them.

The policeman delivered the prisoners to the house and obtained the necessary signature, then went off to the market on personal business. At that point the merchant promised to arrange for their escape by bribing the captain of the police troops.

But Agnouni and his comrades refused, saying that they didn't want others to be put in danger on their account; they also expressed their belief that they would be acquitted before the court-martial in Diyarbekir. These comrades, who were later to perish, had traversed nine-tenths of the way to their death and yet they were still optimistic.

At this point the policeman returned to the house and, being tired, went to another room and fell asleep. With extreme temerity, the merchant removed the official document pertaining to the prisoners from the policeman's pocket. Only then did he realize the horrible reality that—on the pretext of going to the court-martial in Diyarbekir—the six were being taken to be massacred. (The merchant, who personally told me all these details, also had a copy of this document, but during my escape in 1918, I destroyed it as a precautionary measure.)

Naturally everyone was greatly distressed. No one felt like eating any of the various dishes of the nice supper set before them. Everyone fell into a state of mourning, knowing they were to face the Grim Reaper. They had no hope of being saved, for the government in Constantinople was accusing these six of being revolutionaries who were inciting rebellion and helping foreign enemies take over Turkish lands.

After the initial shock subsided a little, Agnouni said: "I am not sorry for my death since one day death will find us all, but I am sorry that we were deceived by these Turkish criminals."

At this point, at the order of the commander of the police soldiers, they were transported back to prison, along with their police escort, into whose pocket they had returned the official document. The next day they were taken by carriage toward Aleppo with four mounted soldiers. After being held in prison there for two days under strict guard, they were taken on the road, supposedly heading for Diyarbekir, via Ourfa.

On the road to Diyarbekir, a day's journey from Ourfa, *chetes* that had been sent by the governor of Diyarbekir, Dr. Reshid,* suddenly surrounded them. They were subjected to unspeakable tortures, then killed. Under such criminal circumstances were the lives of six talented and productive intellectuals and public servants put to an end.

Unfortunately, those who remained in Ayash were no luckier. During the horrible massacre of the Ankara Armenians in mid-August 1915, some of the exiles in Ayash were transported to the Ankara prison. One black day, together with a twelve-hundred-person caravan of native Ankaran Armenians, they were all killed in gruesome ways in a valley about four or five hours from town.

Meanwhile the rest of our exiled comrades in Ayash were martyred a few hours from there, on the famous mountain Kable Bel, under the following circumstances. By order of the vice-governor of Ankara, Atif, the remaining twenty-seven were turned over to the Cretan commissar Zeki. Accompanied by police soldiers, he brought these scapegoats to Kable Bel and ordered them to rest.

Suddenly the commissar gave the order to open fire. Corporal Fashil Oghlou Refik, a native of Ayash, disobeyed, refusing to fire on innocent people. At that point the commissar aimed his own pistol at the heads of a few of the exiles and fired, whereupon the battalion commander, Hassan, and Khourshid† *chavush* also opened fire on our friends. But their thirst for blood was unquenched by the shooting, so they attached bayonets to their guns and fell upon the victims, tearing their bodies apart. Some of our comrades, although their bodies were torn or dismembered, had not yet died, and in heartrending voices they pleaded with the police soldiers: "For the love of God, shoot us so we can be delivered."

The local Turkish villagers, having come from the surrounding areas at dawn, also took part in the massacre, using axes, hatchets [*satr*], hoes,

*See Biographical Glossary.
†Sergeant, petty officer.—trans.

rocks, and iron rods. Khourshid *chavush* himself boasted about these very details in Ankara to an Armenian doctor, a survivor, adding: "When we started the massacre, the valley and the mountain resounded with the screams and cries of those being killed. First I dug out the eyes of Dr. Pashaian, then I broke his neck. Here is his gold watch and chain." And after relating this with a diabolical smile, Khourshid said that he gave praise to Allah that, having been fortunate enough to participate in the *jihad*, he had now become worthy of the *jennet* of their holy prophet, meaning he had become worthy of paradise.

Eyewitnesses who miraculously survived recounted that the Turkish villagers from the vicinity of Ankara were wearing redingotes [frock coats], overcoats, jackets, and shoes taken from those they had killed, sporting the undeniable evidence of their participation in the blood fest.

Khourshid *chavush* also told the Armenian doctor with satisfaction that the Turkish villagers poked at the mangled bodies for hours, as if for amusement, as they further dismembered the dead remains. This went on until the coming of darkness, when out of their dens came the corpse-eating hyenas and other wild animals to finish what was left.

14

The Tragic End of the Chankiri Deportees

While a whirlwind of blood was reducing the prosperous towns and villages of Asia Minor to ruins, and the sickle of death was cutting down hundreds of thousands of innocent lives in the course of a few months, filling the mountains and valleys of Armenia with masses of martyred bodies, we exiles in Chankiri were living through our last days. The nightmare of impending death was weighing heavily on our minds and souls, as we awaited our turn.

During this time, as Armenian newspapers reached us from Constantinople, we learned with astonishment about the ceremonies in the garden of the Armenian National Hospital—the dances, banquets, and toasts on the occasion of the May 1915 anniversary of the Armenian National Constitution. (These papers reached us only by chance and months later.)

As in the past, the commencement exercises of the schools in Constantinople took place with the patriarch presiding, as did the Armenian community's Olympic games, soccer matches, swimming and cycling races, and summer pilgrimages via steamship to the famous vacation spots of Constantinople.[1] No one in the city was yet aware of the agony of a people dying in the provinces.

The patriarchate, having sent a few hundred gold pieces from Constantinople to the exiled intellectuals, thought it had fulfilled its duty. But our fortunate friends who returned to Constantinople carried reports to the patriarch, sounding the alarm about the extermination of the Armenians. Even so, no one comprehended the gravity of the overall situation; everybody remained unmoved, like calm observers, repeating over and over again the ready phrase, "What can we do?" as if it were chewing gum.

Our fifty-six comrades, who were transported from Chankiri to Ankara on the day of the Transfiguration of Our Lord, were all escorted to prison. Thanks to the tireless and noble efforts of American ambassador Morgenthau, five had been able to return to Constantinople.* Meanwhile the rest were requesting financial help from me via telegram. We were able to raise sixty gold pieces among ourselves, which we sent to our ill-fated comrades through the Ipranosian store of Ankara; it came to one gold piece per person, and this had to last them till Der Zor, for they had mentioned in their telegram that they had been given two days to get ready for the trip to Der Zor. They were given this advance notice on purpose so that they would start their journey with as much money as possible—making the spoils richer for those who held the exiles' fate in their hands.

But in mid-August, as the massacre of the Armenians of Ankara started, these exiles who had been kept in prison for a month were not transported to Der Zor; rather, they were taken to join the caravans being led to carnage. They suffered the torment of martyrs' deaths, as did the first Armenian caravan of Ankara.

A month after the departure of the first caravan of fifty-six from Chankiri, a second caravan—this one carrying twenty-six of us—was dispatched. While we had been optimistic that the first caravan might reach Der Zor alive, by the day the second caravan departed from Chankiri, we knew we were simply accompanying our comrades in a funeral procession.

We had to hold back the tears that were burning our hearts and our eyes. Even knowing that we were escorting our comrades to their death,

*The late Shmavonian, the legal adviser and interpreter at the American embassy in Constantinople, who died recently in New York, had the greatest share in these efforts.—G.B.

we were careful not to express our feelings, so as not to distress them. We went with them as far as the armory where we had previously been imprisoned, about half an hour from town, without exchanging a word. And how young they were! . . . They were all eighteen- to twenty-five-year-old college students or graduates of the University of Constantinople in a variety of disciplines; they were intellectual, patriotic, gallant young men, each exceeding the one before in honor, self-sacrifice, patriotism, hopefulness, and enthusiasm for the future glory of the Armenians. We were seeing these young men off with only seven hundred piasters, which wouldn't even cover a day's expenses, for we had not yet been able to pay back our previous internal loan of sixty gold pieces.

Immediately upon reaching Ankara, these exiles were escorted to prison, and a few days later they too were taken to slaughter, along with the second or third caravan from Ankara. Only one of them—Aram Andonian—was miraculously saved after having fallen from the carriage on the way and broken his leg, whereupon he was taken directly to the hospital.

Also among this second group were six lucky friends going to Ankara who, as rich merchants, had been able to buy their freedom with substantial bribes. The Ministry of the Interior explicitly ordered them to be returned to Constantinople, but Atif had them depart by train for Aleppo. Fortunately, with the aid of further material and moral sacrifice, they were able to get another order from Constantinople, and they finally succeeded in returning there from Tarsus, thus having tasted all the bitterness of the road of exile.

At the beginning of August on the very same day of the the departure of our twenty-six comrades, the rest of us exiles from Constantinople were ordered to the government building, where the *mutasarrif* officially told us, "An order of pardon has arrived from the Interior Ministry, and you can go wherever you want, except for Constantinople; so, go and pray for the king."

We came out of the government building abject, our heads hanging low; we were confused, not knowing whether we were saved or doomed. Blood was flowing everywhere, and we didn't know whether it was even possible to travel. Our only consolation was that, unlike our comrades who had already departed, death was no longer the issue of the day for us but rather an item on a longer agenda, and we could still think about being saved.

Even though we were now free to remain in Chankiri or go to a provincial town, we were troubled that the police chief, a native of Salonica, and the rest of the police who had escorted us from Constantinople were pushing us to leave Chankiri in two days without fail.

At the same time, we were feeling panic because five of our comrades, among them Daniel Varoujan* and Dr. Chilingirian (Sevag),* were ordered by the government to depart immediately for Ayash via Ankara. By now we knew what it meant to be sent to Ayash.

Despite the whispers about the massacres that had reached our ears, the eleven of us, myself included, wished to take advantage of the government's permission to go, and we readied ourselves to leave for Smyrna. We were uneasy about having to pass through Ankara, but there was no other road to the railway. Bearing in mind the Oriental proverb "He who falls into the sea will hold on to a snake," we wanted to afford ourselves the protection of the police and police soldiers escorting our five comrades to Ayash. Our comrades, however, pleaded with us to save them somehow from being transported to Ayash via Ankara.

In a last effort to save them and with no time to lose, Diran Kelegian and I visited the deputy *mutasarrif* of Chankiri. He was interim commander of the police soldiers of the province of Kastemouni, pending the arrival of the new governor-general. The previous governor, Asaf, as I noted earlier, had left the post because he did not want to be held accountable for a repeat of the disasters that had befallen him after the Armenian massacres at Adana. He had said: "One day . . . the officers who sit in Constantinople [who are actually responsible] will escape, and we minor officials will be trampled underfoot."

The vice-governor of Chankiri, a Circassian and a sensible and kind man, greeted us warmly and inquired about our condition. Noting his friendliness, I asked him whether he thought it a good idea to take advantage of the unusual permission granted us to go to Armash and wait there until the end of the war. I asked too whether he would be willing to furnish a police-soldier escort to ensure my safe journey to Ankara.

And this was his answer, word for word: "I do not advise you, *murahhasa*† *effendi*, to go to Armash, since who knows if even the monastery in Armash is still standing."

I then asked whether he thought it made sense for me to go to Kastemouni, where the storm of blood had not yet reached. And he answered:

> For a time, you served as prelate there; it is not prudent that you should go there, for you may very well disturb your peace and that of the local Armenians . . . I advise you to stay right where you are . . . I am sorry that I can't give you any further explanation . . . you are intelligent men; from my little, understand much.

*See Biographical Glossary.

†Turkish form of address for Armenian bishop or prelate.—trans.

And when we asked whether he could postpone the departure of our five comrades until we could get the order rescinded, he answered:

"I cannot disregard an order from Constantinople; however, you may be sure—and I swear on my children—I have done everything possible to ensure that these five friends of yours reach Ankara safely." Having understood the profound value of these words coming from the mouth of an official, we left the vice-governor, more than ever realizing that we were on the edge of a very steep precipice . . . and facing the immediate probability of being ripped apart by death's claws.

The very same night a Turk came to visit the garden where I was then residing. He was someone to whom I had often sent doctors, free medication, and remedies, and I had also repaired an old water fountain in his garden at my own expense, thus gaining his gratitude; in fact, I had been generous to him, knowing that I would need his help in the difficult days to come. Withdrawing to one corner of the garden, he told me confidentially: "I heard that you are getting ready to go to Smyrna via Ankara a day from now. I have come to advise you not to go to Ankara . . . I have seen much kindness from you . . . I have come to beseech you not to put yourself in harm's way." Upon my insisting to know the reason for his advice, he said:

> Blood is flowing in the province of Ankara. Where will you be able to go? . . . I can't say more than this. My son is a corporal in the police soldiers; if I tell you what my son has seen and told me about what is happening in Ankara, you will simply lose your mind . . . I can only say this much, for God's sake . . . don't go.

Based on what we had heard, it was obvious that to leave Chankiri at this time would be foolish. For death's shadow had knocked on our doors as well, during these days of blood and tears, and horror prevailed everywhere; it was not the time to budge from one's place. Thus the next day, Tuesday, I hurried to the café by the river, which had been frequented by our comrades and was now deserted, to convince our friends not to leave Chankiri. Among our eleven traveling friends, however, were some stubborn ones who wanted to depart at any cost, and had already bribed the carriage drivers. So I could only do my best to convince the drivers to arrive late the next morning and thus prevent our stubborn friends from going.

It was at dawn on that unforgettable black day, Thursday, August 19, 1915, that we, the remaining eighteen Armenian exiles in Chankiri, assembled in front of the two carriages waiting near the bridge by the riverside café. This was the bridge that those traveling from Chankiri to

Ankara had to cross, because the causeway stretched from here to Kalayjek via Ankara.

We were all very emotional, and despite our best efforts, we were unable to suppress our tears. A deathly shudder enveloped us, tormented our minds and souls, as we witnessed the lamentations of our soon-to-depart Varoujan, Sevag, Onnig Maghazajian, and two [other] friends.

I had never encountered such instinctual emotion. They said to us, "Goodbye; we are going off to die. Reverend Fathers, pray for us." Varoujan and Sevag turned to us and said, "Take care of our orphans." And then Varoujan said, "I've just had a new boy; let them name him Varoujan." Our emotions overflowed, and our minds were in such shock that we could not even offer a few comforting words.

Oh, I cannot remember such a heart-wrenching separation at any point in my life, and it was all the more unbearable that we were seeing these five friends off to imminent death and we were powerless to save them. One of the carriages of our other friends was coming, and the two carriages already there seemed to linger in a mysterious way, while our friends who had insisted on departing at all costs were staying because the carriages did not come to get them.

We embraced our five friends once more, and the two carriages, under the watch of one policeman, a native of Salonica, and one police soldier, finally disappeared from view. With the dawn still unable to dissipate the darkness, we kept gazing at one another, knowing that it was the last time we would meet. We were crushed mentally and spiritually, as well as physically, and with tears in our eyes and the blood frozen in our hearts, we returned to our homes and waited for the bad news, hour by hour. Unable to bear this unceasing grief, and having barely reached the garden and my room, I fell on my bed and lay there staring at the big garden door.

At noon the next day, August 20, 1915, Hovan Vartabed and Diran Kelegian came to see me; they sat on the sofa facing my bed and said nothing. But their grim countenances betrayed their anguish, and I finally broke the silence by asking them why they had come. The words poured forth from their mouths: "May God give you days."

Oh, our grief was boundless and inexpressible; we were overwhelmed by grief for the martyrs who had already died and for ourselves, who were waiting our turn.

Here are the details of this criminal event.

For a long time the members of the Ittihad club in Chankiri had wanted to participate in the *jihad* and become worthy of the reward of the Prophet of Islam. And so, taking advantage of the transfer to Ankara of Dr. Chilingirian, Varoujan, and the three [other] friends, they had sent a Kurdish criminal named Halo on ahead, with a few of his friends, to a place called Tiuna, six hours away, to lie in wait for them.

On Thursday, August 19, when our friends were departing Chankiri, the responsible secretary of the local Ittihad committee, Yunuz, phoned the police guardposts along the Chankiri-Kalayjek road to inform them of the departure of our comrades. The next day, Friday, he called the guard office in Tiuna, asking, "Have those arriving been killed yet?" But as it was Friday, the police soldiers were having a picnic under a tree a little ways from the guard office, and in the guardhouse there was only an Armenian workman who was busy coating the walls with lime; thus he was privy to these incriminating words.

When the two carriages bearing our five comrades reached the summit in Tiuna, where the Kalayjek headland begins, the four Kurds waiting in ambush came to meet them. The Kurds advanced toward the first carriage and ordered the driver to halt its horses, to which the police soldier ordered the criminals to leave the horses alone or he would shoot them. But the young policeman from Salonica told the police soldier [whom he outranked] not to resist. He didn't want the police soldier to know in advance that the crime he had been commissioned to expedite was about to be committed, and by some accidental indiscretion undermine the plan. And so with the compliance of the policeman and the police soldier, the Kurd Halo ordered those in the carriages to disembark.

Having stepped down, Dr. Chilingirian earnestly pleaded with the four Kurds to spare their lives; he promised that he and his friends would give them all their riches and belongings. But despite these heart-wrenching pleas, the Kurds took our five friends to the edge of a brook that runs through the nearby valley and stripped them, so as not to damage their clothing. Then they drew their daggers and attacked them, ripping their bodies apart and slashing their legs and arms and other sensitive parts. Only Varoujan defended himself, and as a punishment, after gutting him, the criminals dug out the eyes of the patriotic poet.

More than 450 Ottoman gold pieces had been sewn into the hems of the clothing of Dr. Chilingirian and Onnig Maghazajian. The Kurds gave some to the policeman and the police soldier, dividing the rest among themselves. They likewise divided the baggage in the carriages, ordering the two Turkish drivers to return immediately to Chankiri.

The Turkish carriage drivers returned to Chankiri with their heads down, and one of them, who was about twenty years old and the son of the local bathhouse keeper, told me all this in detail, saying with tears: "To hell with a business like this, I don't need to make money this way . . . tomorrow I am going to sell my horses and carriage and get out of this town."

These atrocities had a profound effect on this young man, who also insisted that if the policeman from Salonica had not opposed the soldier, it would have been possible to resist and save our friends. Barely had the two carriages returned empty to Chankiri at noon on Friday when word about what had happened reached us and the fifty Armenian households in Chankiri, terrifying us all.

The vice-governor—who had sworn on his children's lives that our friends would reach Ankara unharmed—along with some investigating judges and policemen and the commander of the police soldiers of Kastemouni province, mounted their horses and hurried to Tiuna, to the scene of the crime.

They found the five in unrecognizable condition, thrown into the creek. After their bodies were buried and the criminals were apprehended, the latter, along with the policeman and the police soldier, were put in the Ankara prison to await trial before a military tribunal. At the courthouse the four Kurds were emphatic in stating that they had carried out an explicit order and commission of the Ittihad Committee of Chankiri, which body it was therefore necessary to summon to court as well.

> The leader of the group, the Kurd Halo, whose sick daughter Dr. Chilingirian had saved from death a month earlier, had told Sevag, "I pity you; trouble is going to befall you; none of you is going to be saved; convert to Islam; let me give you my daughter, and save your young life. Listen, they want to kill you as it is, and if you refuse me, when the time comes I will personally cut you up into pieces.

Another obvious proof that the crime had been premeditated.

Prior to his death, Sevag had related his conversation with Halo confidentially to a few close friends, and then, after this threat, he had moved his residence from the orchard to the city as a precaution.

In this manner our nation, in the course of being exterminated, lost two talented poets and writers, as well as five devoted loving fathers of young children. But unfortunately, we did not have much time to mourn, as new carnage and torrents of blood came with each day.

15

The Deportation and Killing of Zohrab and Vartkes

During those black days of August 1915, when the Armenians of Asia Minor—the toddlers, the elderly, the virgins, the brides, and the grandmothers—were being massacred under the guise of "deportation" or "exile," and when the fate of those exiled to Chankiri and Ayash had already been settled, the eighteen to twenty of us who remained in Chankiri were awaiting ours. The Ottoman Parliament members Krikor Zohrab and Vartkes Serengulian had been arrested in Constantinople during this time, and after being held in prison briefly, they had been put on a train to Diyarbekir on the pretext of being tried before the court-martial there.

We had the continual misfortune of remembering the special significance of an Armenian exile's being sent before the court-martial in Diyarbekir. At the same time Agnouni and five friends from Ayash were sent to exile in Diyarbekir on the same pretext.

These two brave deputies, who had always struggled in the Ottoman Parliament on behalf of Armenian interests, had the opportunity to meet with a few Armenians in Konya and refused the material help offered them. At the railway station of Eregli, near Konya, an [Armenian] railroad official who belonged to the Dashnak Party was brave enough to meet secretly with Zohrab and Vartkes and offer them help to escape. But they replied that being deputies of the Ottoman Parliament, they had no fear for their lives and no doubt that they would be acquitted by the court-martial in Diyarbekir.

When Zohrab and Vartkes arrived in Adana the next day, a few influential Armenians got special permission to meet with them, and they also offered help. But they again replied that they didn't need any; they asked only that word be sent to their families in Constantinople that they had passed through Adana alive.

Under the strict guard of the police chief and officers who had accompanied them from Constantinople, they finally reached Aleppo. At that time the governor was a man named Jelal,* formerly governor of Erzerum and later minister of the interior, who was known to be friendly to the Armenians. Being friends with both these men, he did all that was possible to save their lives. Instead of sending them to prison, he had them taken to an inn, and he gave permission for friends and admirers to come and see these famous exiles. He also petitioned their "personal friend," Interior Minister Talaat, requesting that he be allowed to keep them in Aleppo.

A few other influential Turkish friends in Aleppo also petitioned the commander of the Turkish army in Syria and the minister of the marine, Jemal, requesting that the two exiles be set free in Aleppo. Everyone knew what would otherwise happen. The bandit groups organized by Dr. Reshid, the governor of Diyarbekir province, had left no Armenians alive along the roads between Ourfa and the city of Diyarbekir.† As it was impossible for an Armenian to reach Diyarbekir from Ourfa safely, all these friends were trying to do whatever they could to prevent a tragedy. Zohrab and Vartkes, now comprehending their situation, also petitioned their old Turkish friends, pleading with them to save their lives.

As Talaat could perceive that Jelal was trying to protect Zohrab and Vartkes, he immediately sent an order terminating Jelal as governor and replacing him with "Hakim." The day after Jelal's departure from Aleppo, Zohrab and Vartkes were put on the road to Ourfa in a two-horse carriage, and as soon as they reached the town, they were taken to prison. At the same time the Very Rev. Ardavazt Kalenderian,* the prelate of Ourfa, who had been ordained an archimandrite along with me, and two prominent natives of Ourfa were also thrown into prison as a prelude to the deportation of the Armenians.

In Ourfa, Zohrab and Vartkes were invited to the home of Mahmoud Nedim, deputy from Ourfa in the Ottoman Parliament and therefore their colleague—but it was a trap. Barely had they finished the evening meal when four policemen appeared, demanding that the Turkish landlord hand over the two exiles, saying: "The carriage is waiting. They are going to Harput."

Sensing that their hours were numbered, Zohrab appealed to Mahmoud Nedim for mercy, saying, "They are taking us to be killed; I beg of you to intervene." But Vartkes, with the stoicism befitting a revolutionary,

*See Biographical Glossary.

†After Diyarbekir's bloodthirsty governor, Dr. Reshid, the most influential people in the region were the Circassian Ahmed, who later killed Zeki in Constantinople, and the war minister Khalil, Enver's paternal uncle. Leading hundreds of *chetes* over all the roads stretching through the deserts from north to south, these two mercilessly massacred the remnants of all the caravans of deported Armenians that had been driven down there like sheep, thus making a slaughterhouse of the Malatya-Ourfa-Diyarbekir region and its roads.—G.B.

had long since become accustomed to the idea of death, and so considered whatever life he was able to live a bonus. Mahmoud Nedim promised to intervene, but in the end no one could interfere with the plan that was in motion.

Finally, under mounted police soldiers' surveillance, Zohrab and Vartkes were put in one carriage, the Very Rev. Kalenderian, along with the two prominent local Armenians, were put in another, and both were dispatched to Diyarbekir. When they reached a place called Karakopru, an hour from Ourfa, they were surrounded. The Circassians Mehmed and Khalil, with their armed and mounted *chetes*, halted the small caravan and ordered the police soldiers to leave the victims and return [to Ourfa], as their job was done.

Then the bandit chief took the doomed exiles from the carriages and nailed them to the ground with iron stakes that were a meter long. They proceeded to pluck all the hairs out of Archimandrite Ardavazt's beard, and after administering various tortures, they cut off his head. Then they beheaded everyone else. Finally they stripped them naked and cut off their limbs.

The mayor of Ourfa telegraphed the news to Constantinople, where Talaat and the Ittihad Central Committee were awaiting his report. Having received the news of the killings, Zohrab's supposed friend Talaat sent word to Zohrab's wife that her husband, who had a heart condition, had suffered a stroke on the road to Diyarbekir. In the meantime Talaat had given Vartkes's wife permission to go to Bulgaria; he had declined Vartkes's own petitions by saying to him: "Vartkes, I cannot give you permission to go to Bulgaria. I know you want to save yourself, but we have no alternative. Whatever happens to us, must happen to you too." Those who later lost their lives understood the meaning of these mysterious words only after it was too late. Eight days earlier the four thousand Armenian soldiers who comprised the labor battalions [*amele taburi*] of Ourfa and Diyarbekir were tortured and massacred in the exact same place.

Thus did Zohrab and Vartkes, the eloquent advocates of the Armenian people, having been elected to Parliament during the Ottoman Representatives Assembly (held following the adoption of the Ottoman Constitution of 1908), come to such criminal deaths. Vartkes, a native of Erzerum, had been a courageous veteran of the Armenian cause for justice since his twenties; he had been repeatedly imprisoned, persecuted, and tormented for many years and had been released from prison only under the Ottoman Constitution's general pardon of all political prisoners.

It is worth noting that among these martyrs was the late Archimandrite Ardavazt, prelate of Ourfa. Having been ordained together, we were close friends. He was a patriotic clergyman and a renowned musicologist, equally expert in the music of the Armenian Church and of Europe.

Meanwhile the central government in Constantinople rewarded the man who had played the lead role in this crime, Enver's relative Khalil: he received the rank of pasha and was named commander in chief of the Turkish army in Baghdad, affording him a more extensive field for new criminal deeds.

This same Khalil later fought on the Caucasus front for the newly formed Tatar Republic of Azerbaijan, with the hope of exterminating the Caucasus Armenians as well. And if that couldn't be done, then the goal was to make Armenia so weak that it could be dismembered at the first opportunity.[1]

16

The Armenians of Chankiri in the Days of Horror

By the end of 1915 three-quarters of the Armenian population that had been living within the boundaries of historic Armenia in the Ottoman Turkish Empire, except for Constantinople and Smyrna, was already extinct.*

In July, the central government issued an urgent order to deport to the deserts of Der Zor the entire Armenian population of the province of Kastemouni† as well, where there were about 1,800 households, or 10,000 people, including the thousand-plus households of Armenian Gypsies.

Governor Reshid Pasha, however, a kind and thoughtful man of the old Turkish school, was privately opposed to the criminal behavior of the Ittihad Committee and did not act on this order upon its arrival from Constantinople. He invited the important members of the Turkish community of Kastemouni's provincial capital for a discussion, to ask them whether

*Although the Ittihad government tried to avoid killing Armenians in Constantinople and Smyrna because of the prominence of European diplomats there, in the end significant portions of the Armenian populations in those cities were killed.

†Not one of the historically Armenian provinces: Bitlis, Diyarbekir, Erzerum, Harput, Sivas, and Van.

they had any cause for complaint with their Armenian neighbors. First verbally, and then in writing through Reshid Pasha, the prominent Turks informed Constantinople that they had had good neighborly and commercial relations with the Armenians for centuries, and far from feeling dissatisfaction, they would suffer great material losses if the Armenians were deported.

For his part, Governor Reshid Pasha openly asserted that the Armenians were pillars of the Ottoman state, that without them the country would be subject to extreme poverty, and that by seeking the extermination of the Armenians, the Ittihad Committee was pursuing an extremely shortsighted policy, one contrary to the interests of the fatherland. That policy, moreover, could subject the Ottoman government to grave consequential accountability down the road.

So adament was Governor Reshid's opposition to the Ittihad government's plan for the Armenians that Interior Minister Talaat sent word verbally, through the deputy of Kastemouni in the Ottoman Parliament, that if Reshid Pasha wished to avoid dismissal, he should immediately resign from his position as governor-general. And so Reshid Pasha, being a noble and principled public servant, resigned from his post and went to Constantinople, intending to fight the policy against the Armenians while there was still time.

The judge [*kadi*] who replaced Reshid Pasha immediately ordered Chankiri's newly arrived governor to have all the homes of the local Armenians searched and to confiscate whatever weapons they discovered. So one day at the beginning of September we found all the Armenian neighborhoods of Chankiri surrounded by police and police soldiers, sowing fear and dread. Despite the painstaking searches, however, not one weapon was found in an Armenian home. This fact was communicated to Kastemouni in a report that was favorable to the Armenians. But the Ittihad committee of Chankiri was not at all satisfied at coming up empty-handed and without the pretext that they needed to deport the Armenians. So the next day Yunuz, the responsible secretary of the Ittihad committee who had organized the killing of the late Sevag and Varoujan, reprimanded the police chief of Chankiri:

> If you cannot find weapons in the Armenian households, can you at least take some weapons with you and plant them in the Armenian homes, and then make an official police report saying so. Aren't you aware of the official policy?

It is worth mentioning here that they had planted a hundred weapons in Armenian homes for every five they may have found, and yet this was a big part of how they would justify their great crime.

Furthermore, numerous eyewitness survivors and Armenian photographers testified that in many places such as in Adana, officials collected the weapons of police soldiers and piled them up haphazardly, placing a few government-issue hand grenades on top; those piles were photographed and published in books and newspapers as so-called evidence, in order to fend off criticism of what was happening to the Armenians.

At the insistence of the local Ittihad committee, the police soldiers came again one month later and, with utmost thoroughness, searched all the Armenian households in Chankiri, only to depart again empty-handed and dejected. Still, the tenacious Ittihad committee (or bureau) of Chankiri gave the order to the Chankiri government to deport the local Armenians, and its execution was not delayed.

By an evil coincidence—as it had been on the day of the Transfiguration of Our Lord in 1915—Chankiri's Armenian population of only a handful spent the holy day of the Birth of the Holy Mother of God in mourning and in horror, under the following circumstances. While the majority of Armenians of both sexes were in church, the following order from the military commander of Chankiri was suddenly relayed to me through the Armenian headman [*muhtar*], so that I might inform the congregation before me:

> Three days' time is being given to the Armenian population of Chankiri to get ready for the journey toward Der Zor. Each person is free to take his wife and children with him, or to leave them in the city. Those who run or hide will be punished by death.

Barely had I spoken these words when the temple of prayer turned into a place of wailing and crying and commotion. The mourning was universal, because everyone knew what it meant to go to Der Zor. Everyone from the children to the eighty-year-olds rushed to the altar, begging us to prepare them for their deaths with the final holy sacrament. By the time we were singing the Lord's Prayer, fifty-eight men knowing their fate were waiting before the altar, in tears, sobbing, unable to control their emotions. But even more heart-wrenching was the crying of the women, children, and grandmothers, whose sighs, lamentations, and curses echoed over the low arches of the church.

We all cried, shepherd and flock alike; we cried for those who were leaving and for those who were staying. The order was strict—the Ittihad's sickle of death did not discriminate between partisans and conservatives, toddlers and elderly, males and females.

My situation was all the more unbearable as I was the shepherd of a people sentenced to death, the one to whom everyone ran for help, for salvation, for a word of encouragement or hope. But alas, I myself was one of the first among the condemned and powerless to help.

We were living through days of such unheard-of horror, it was impossible for the mind to fully comprehend. Those of us still alive envied those who had already paid their inevitable dues of bloody torture and death. And so we survivors became living martyrs, every day dying a few deaths and returning to life again.

Notwithstanding it all, we still had the will to make a final attempt at staying alive; we thought, who knew, maybe we would succeed despite our despair—after all, the Turks were always willing to be bribed. Thus I invited two of the town's most prominent Armenians to my apartment, and we explored all the favorable and unfavorable probabilities.

After consulting with one another, we decided that on the next day, the Monday of All Souls', we would enter into secret bargaining with Yunuz, the Ittihad committee's responsible secretary from Constantinople and the central organizer of the killing plan here. We were hopeful because one of the prominent local Armenians—with whom we had consulted and discussed our small population's tight financial straits—had promised to deliver that day five hundred gold pieces on our behalf, and to make still further financial sacrifices if there was hope of saving the people from certain death.

Moreover, to save the worldly goods of the Armenians of Chankiri, valued in the hundreds of thousands of gold pieces, we decided to pay a ransom of a few thousand gold pieces, even though of course no price could be put on the hundreds of lives that might be saved with further contributions from prominent Chankiri Armenians. We concluded these discussions and agreed to make the payment in three days. We had to conduct all aspects of the process in utmost secrecy, because if we failed, we would have expedited the death awaiting us.

The Ittihad Central Committee had sent investigators with the title "responsible secretary" to all the large and small towns. These responsible secretaries were to report to Constantinople on anyone who went against Ittihad policy, and any disobedient local official, be he a district governor, or a provincial governor, or even a governor-general, would be relieved. And so the helm of the government was actually in the hands of these Ittihad Central Committee members.

The next night, two individuals appeared for a secret nighttime appointment at the home of Yunuz, the responsible secretary. After long conversations and bargaining, Yunuz demanded, as his final price, fifteen hundred gold pieces, to be paid in twenty-four hours, failing which he would put into effect the order to deport us to Der Zor.

The responsible secretary also imposed two special conditions: one, that this blood bargain, which if revealed would jeopardize both sides, be kept in the strictest confidence, and two, that no receipt be demanded for the fifteen hundred gold pieces; rather, it was to be given as a gift toward the cost of purchasing land and constructing an Ittihad club in Chankiri. In return, the secretary, with the consent of the most influential member of the Ittihad club of Chankiri, promised not to deport the Armenians of Chankiri and to take measures to protect the small local Armenian population of about fifty households.

The next day, before the time was up, one thousand gold pieces were paid to the responsible secretary. Half of this sum was paid personally by *haji* Setrag Shakhian, an honest and honorable elderly man. We knew this action could not save the Chankiri Armenians from ultimate exile and death, but we were able at least to buy [what turned out to be] a seven-month reprieve in the midst of the widespread storm of blood passing over us. Had our exile coincided with the days of the general massacres there, not one of us would have been saved from death, as not one exile caravan was to survive those roads we later passed—to Yozgat, Boghazliyan, and Kayseri.

Still, in paying the bribe, we knew we had only temporarily avoided the whirlwind. Our only hopes were that the people of Constantinople would rise up against the Ittihad or that the British navy would seize the Dardanelles and capture Constantinople.

In the last days of September six of the exiles remaining in Chankiri, two of them clergymen, took advantage of the order from Constantinople to depart to wherever we wished to, any place other than Constantinople. They mustered the courage to leave Chankiri for Smyrna via Ankara.

We remained full of apprehension because after so many bloody attempts and losses, it was audacious to go anywhere via Ankara. But fortunately our comrades let us know by letter that after being kept in prison in Smyrna for one night, they had been sent to Oushak with permission to live there.*

Having massacred 90 percent of the 85,000 Armenians in the province of Ankara, Atif, the provincial chief executioner and vice-governor, had no tasks left to perform there. To reward him for his "good" service, Talaat elevated him to the rank of governor and called him to Kastemouni to replace Reshid Pasha, who had been forced to resign from his post for refusing to deport the Armenians.

The news that Atif had been appointed governor of Kastemouni, and that he would be going there in a few days via Chankiri, plunged the

*After the Armistice, all six of them would return to Constantinople and devote themselves to public service, as courageous intellectuals.—G.B.

Chankiri Armenians into a state of horror. We instinctively guessed that he had been appointed governor for the sole purpose of wiping out those of us who were still alive in the province but had not yet been deported.

Having just heard the distressing news, Diran Kelegian came to my apartment, greatly disturbed, and said to me:

> Reverend Father, we are finished . . . Atif has been appointed governor of Kastemouni . . . in a few days he will assume his post, after passing through our town. Our days are numbered . . . I beg you, let's go to church, and I ask you to give me holy communion; it is time to get ready for death, because it will be impossible to be saved from the hands of this monster.
>
> I tried to console and encourage him and convince him that all hope was not yet lost and that we could still think of ways to survive. But he replied, Reverend Father, you don't know the Turks; I've been among them for thirty years, and I have been a teacher of Turkish history for many years in the Ottoman University. These people are criminals. They have had thirty-six sultans, and they have killed fourteen of them. Will a people that does not spare its own kings possibly spare us? It is a shame that, for thirty years, I have been pushing my pen and tiring my mind. I wish that they had broken my hands, now that I know my end has come to this. At least you can console yourself with the knowledge that you were deported and will die for your nation, but was it worth it for me to have worked diligently for thirty years for such an ungrateful people?

I told him then and there with great conviction that *at whatever cost I had decided to not die*, so that I could see the emancipated dawn of a reborn Armenia.

Actually, Kelegian was not mistaken. We would remember these significant words he had spoken when his death was a fait accompli.

Even in contemporary Turkish history, the Turkish people had killed Sultan Abdul Aziz in 1876. His successor, Mourad, after being sultan for barely three months, was declared crazy, forced from the throne, and imprisoned for twenty-eight years in one of the isolated palaces in the Yildiz gardens, until his death in 1904.

The "Red Sultan," Abdul Hamid II, succeeded Sultan Mourad in late 1876, having ascended the throne with blood; and he ruled for thirty-three years in seas of more blood. Then he himself was dethroned in April 1909 by the Turkish freedom army from Salonica. During the Balkan War of 1912, after being imprisoned in the Alatin fortress of Salonica, he was transferred to a marble-covered palace in Beylerbey, where he remained a king dethroned until 1918. One day he was poisoned after eating oysters [so it was said]; thus he bade farewell to his blood-soaked life, leaving behind the remains of a once-great empire that now resembled a huge pile of ruins; the millions of crying and mourning people, Muslims and Christians whom he had so fiercely persecuted, cursed him eternally.

Immediately after the dethroning of Sultan Abdul Hamid in 1909, the Ittihad Committee elevated Sultan Reshad to the throne. Having been imprisoned for thirty years and dazed from alcoholism, he served as the willing tool for all their criminal plans.* It was during his reign (1915–18) that the widespread massacre of the Armenian people took place.

At the beginning of 1916 Prince Yusuf Izzedin, heir to the throne, was killed by Enver and Talaat's criminal clique, under precisely the same criminal circumstances that had attended the killing of the heir's father, Sultan Abdul Aziz. Enver himself killed Yusuf Izzedin at the imperial farm of Balmomji, an isolated site only about a half hour from the palace of Yildiz. Afterward an official announcement to the newspapers stated that "in a fit of madness, the crown prince committed suicide by cutting his right wrist with a razor." History had repeated itself, since the same explanation was used after the murder of Sultan Abdul Aziz in 1876.

Enver had committed the murder personally for a reason. The crown prince had visited the Dardanelles in the spring of 1915, just as the combined English and French armada was making its fiercest attacks on the strongholds of the straits. The sight of thousands of Turkish soldiers' dead bodies caused the prince to cry: "The Dardanelles is the grave of the Turkish army." During a disagreement sometime afterward, the crown prince threatened War Minister Enver with a pistol. He was murdered a few months later.

Thus during a short period of forty years, only one of five successive sultans, Sultan Mehmed V (Reshad), died a natural death. The others had become the victims of the criminal inclinations of their society. I don't think the current sultan will be any more fortunate than his ill-fated predecessors.†

Yes, Kelegian instinctively predicted his own imminent death . . . and always repeated, "It is futile to attempt saving oneself anymore . . . because Atif is coming to Kastemouni, we are all lost." He bitterly regretted not having accompanied our six brave friends who had left Chankiri a few

*Mehmet Reshad Effendi (1844–1918) became Sultan Mehmet V. A son of Abdul Mejid, he succeeded his brother Abdul Hamid in April–May 1909. Having spent his life in seclusion and coming to the throne in old age, he was no match for the Young Turks. He fell under their control and was content to play the role of figurehead.—trans.

†Sultan Mehmed VI (Vahideddin) reigned from 1918 to 1922, when the sultanate was abolished. He spent the rest of his life on the Italian Riviera.—trans.

weeks earlier, because he had hoped that his wife would be able to save him and have him sent back to Constantinople.

Diran Kelegian had arrived in Chankiri with the six who had returned to Constantinople by order from headquarters. He, like the rest of us, had received an order from the Interior Ministry that he could go anywhere to live except for Constantinople. But he had refused the opportunity, hoping that there would be some way for him to return to the capital. So he had insisted on staying in Chankiri, expecting to receive a further order, the fruit of his wife's efforts, to return there.

Unfortunately, Kelegian's fears were realized a few weeks later. When Atif was passing through Chankiri on the way to his post in Kastemouni, Kelegian, against my advice, hurried to visit him. Atif, seeing Kelegian, cried out, "Kelegian *Effendi*, are you still here?" By this he meant, of course: "Everyone else has been killed, so how have you managed to stay alive?" or "How did they miss you?"

Having just assumed the post of governor-general, Atif ordered the governor of Chankiri to arrest Kelegian and send him to be tried before the court-martial in Diyarbekir. We now knew, many times over, what such an order really meant.

On Saturday, October 12, 1915, we, the remaining exiles, were taking advantage of the beautiful fall weather to gather at the coffeehouse on the bank of the river and lament the murder of our nation and our hopeless condition. Suddenly two policemen came by, asking us, "Who is Kelegian *Effendi*? He is wanted at the police station. We have come for him." Kelegian, turning pale, said: "I'll go and be right back." He departed from us with the two policemen. We had no doubt that he was never to return.

Barely had Kelegian reached the guard station when the chief of police told him in official terms: "Kelegian *Effendi*, a horse has been prepared, and two police soldiers are waiting to escort you because we have received orders from Constantinople to send you."

After making exceptional efforts, Kelegian obtained a half hour to go to the telegraph office and send a message to his wife in Constantinople, and to fetch fresh underwear for the trip. After exchanging farewell kisses with all those who had gone to the government building to see him off, he said with tears in his eyes, "Like our murdered friends, I too am going to eternity. Pray for me, and I beg of you, inform my wife and children of my departure." Only at the last moment before he departed had he realized he was going to his grave.

A final glance, and the three riders disappeared from view, immersing us again in thoughts of death. A half hour after his departure, the Turkish official who had been Kelegian's student at the University of Constantinople told us, "Kelegian *Effendi*, too, was sent to the court-martial in Diyarbekir."

Two weeks later the Turkish manager of the *reji* in Chankiri, who had been Kelegian's student, ran into one of our fellow exiles and said with a sarcastic grin: "May God give you days . . . when poor Kelegian *Effendi* was crossing the Halys River bridge near Sivas, he suddenly lost his mind and jumped into the river. Despite the efforts of the two police soldiers escorting him, he disappeared in the eddying waters."

By order of Sivas's governor, Muammer, who had also been Kelegian's student and friend, they had killed Kelegian on the bridge over the Halys. For thirty years he had written to promote the advancement of Turkish culture. Why was this Ramgavar Party leader murdered? Because his name appeared on a few lists?

After the news of the killing spread, the son of Chankiri's governor quite boldly told a few Armenians in private:

> The Central Committee of Ittihad had Kelegian killed because if he had been allowed to live, he would have become an implacable enemy of the Ittihad [Central] Committee after the war, and certainly would have used his extremely poisonous pen against them . . . we got rid of this evil once and for all.

None of us was able to sleep or eat, our appetite extinguished by the continuous nightmare of death; we were smoldering without a flame, consumed without burning.

In these days a young Turkish Ittihadist captain going from Erzerum to Constantinople suddenly had a chance encounter with one of our exiled friends in Chankiri, a longtime acquaintance of his from Constantinople. Our friend asked him questions out of simple curiosity. In response the captain said, among other things: "Look, we exterminated an ancient nation in a matter of two months" [*Ishde bir esgi millet iki ay zarfnda maf idik*].

Our grief and panic redoubled when we heard details of the massacres of the Armenians in the areas, towns, and villages near Chankiri. We heard about them from the perpetrators themselves, who were boasting about the unspeakable crimes they had committed.

One of these perpetrators, a Turkish youth from Sungurlu, told a longtime Chankiri Armenian friend that he had joined the Turkish mob that was following a caravan of Armenian women and girls being taken to slaughter. A young unmarried Armenian girl of school age caught his eye, and wanting to save her from certain death, he proposed that she accept Islam and be *nikeah* [Turkish *nikah*] with him; that is, marry him according to the Muslim tradition. The Armenian girl replied insolently, "Instead of my becoming a Muslim, you become an Armenian and I will marry you." The Turk tried again to convince the beautiful Armenian lass [to leave the caravan], but finding it impossible, he walked away. The Turkish butchers made her lie down on the ground, and after crushing the girl's virgin chest

Grigoris Balakian as a theology student at the University of Berlin in 1914, where the narrative of *Armenian Golgotha* begins

The Sheikh-ul-Islam, the spiritual leader of all Sunni Muslims, announcing on November 14, 1914, before the Fathi Mosque in Constantinople the *jihad* (holy war) against the "infidels" and "enemies of the faith"

Armenians were drafted into *amele taburlari*—unarmed labor battalions—of the Ottoman army; stripped of weapons, they were massacred while on their labor assignments.

Execution of Armenians in a public square

Armenians being marched out of Harput under armed guard, May 1915. A German businessman took this photograph from his window.

Armenian deportees walking, 1915

Massacred Armenians in Ankara province, summer 1915 (Balakian describes the Ankara massacres in chapter 12.)

Armenians deported by Baghdad Railway, October 1915. From a report by Franz Günther, vice president of the Anatolian Railway Society.

CUP (Ittihad) leaders at social gathering, summer 1918: (1) Talaat, (2) Enver, (3) Sayid Halim, (4) Jemal Pasha.

Ismail Enver Pasha, Ottoman minister of war and a leading force in the plan to exterminate the Armenians

Mehmet Talaat Pasha, Ottoman minister of the interior in 1915 and chief director of the Armenian Genocide

Ottoman killers pose with the heads of their victims; Bishop Smbat Saatetjan (left) and an Armenian Protestant minister (right).

Daniel Varoujan (Taniel Tchiboukkearian), one of the leading poets of his generation, arrested on April 24, 1915. Grigoris Balakian bade farewell as Varoujan and a few others were taken on the Chankiri-Kalayjek road, where they were tortured and killed (see chapter 14).

Bridge over the Halys River on the road from Tokat to Amasia: "the grave of numerous deportees as well as the site of Diran Kelegian's death."

Krikor Zohrab: fiction writer, editor, attorney, Ottoman Parliament member. Arrested in June 1915, he continued to think he would be released, right up until the eve of his murder (see chapter 15).

Siamanto (Adom Yarjanian): prominent poet and editor. He was arrested in Constantinople on April 24, 1915, and deported to Ayash, where he was murdered.

Komitas (Soghomon Soghomonian): *vartabed* (celibate clergyman) in the Armenian Church; renowned composer, musicologist, and scholar. He was arrested in Constantinople on April 24, 1915, suffered a permanent mental breakdown from his deportation experience and spent the final decades of his life in various French mental hospitals. He died in Paris in 1935. (Balakian describes Komitas's first breakdown in chapter 8.)

under their knees and inflicting various tortures and abuses, they cut off her head like a sheep's. Then they ravaged the lifeless body, cutting it to pieces. They couldn't satisfy their vengefulness, provoked as they were by her courage in answering with such bold disrespect for the Muslim religion.

I think of this as an immortal episode in the martyrology of Armenian virgins; it even surpasses the martyrdom of the virgins Hripsime and Gayane, which are celebrated by the Armenian Church.* The killing of this girl is worthy of eternal commemoration and blessing, consecrated with sainthood by all future Armenian generations.

With supreme determination, I wished to make one final try with three friends—the teacher S., Dr. M. K., and a brave youth by the name of Mgrdich (all three Dashnaks)—to secretly flee Chankiri. In Inebolu, the seaport of Kastemouni on the Black Sea, we would board a sailboat manned by a Laz in the hope of reaching Batum, or Varna, or wherever the currents of sea and wind might take us.

Having paid off Chankiri's Turkish postmaster, we sent the daring Dr. M. K. on a horse carrying the mail to Kastemouni, a twenty-four-hour ride, and from there to Inebolu, another twenty-four hours away. As a former prelate of the Kastemouni diocese, I had also sent recommendations to my longtime and trusted acquaintances. Unfortunately, however, Dr. M. K. was arrested a few days after arriving in Kastemouni, though the kind intervention of the commander of the local police soldiers saved him from being conscripted into service as a doctor in the Ottoman army with the rank of captain. Dr. M. K. passed through Chankiri on his way to Ankara and Konya, and so our bold plan was defeated virtually at its inception.

Thereafter one of our cohorts intent on flight, S., along with another exile friend who was a pharmacist, managed to bribe the local police chief and obtain an official travel document. It was supposed to say, "They can go anywhere they wish except for Constantinople," but the words "except for Constantinople" were omitted, and so they set out for Constantinople. But both were arrested a while later. One was deported to Der Zor, but he obtained permission to stay in Konya and, following the Armistice, had the good fortune of returning to the capital.

Despite our shared pessimism, the days and months passed, and Atif, the bloodthirsty governor-general of Kastemouni, wasn't much thinking of us. Rather, in order to prepare the ground for the unhindered deportation of all Kastemouni's Armenians, Atif had gradually removed, on various pretexts, the high-ranking and influential government officials around him who wouldn't cooperate.

*The martyrdom of two pious, evangelizing women, Hripsime and Gayane, and others in the late third century helped to bring Christianity to Armenia.—trans.

The first was the Circassian commander of the central police soldiers of Kastemouni, who openly opposed the deportation. Unknown to this commander, Atif had ordered the deportation to Der Zor of the 150 Armenian households engaged in the hair business [artisans who made rope, thread, and other items from hair] in Tashkopru, six hours from Kastemouni. On discovering that such an important arrangement had been made without his knowledge, this noble Circassian commander became irate. He objected that the police soldiers accompanying the exiled Armenians to prevent their escape could do nothing except by his command. So he immediately ordered the Armenians, who were already on the road, to return to their homes. By special mounted police soldiers, he sent word to the huge, dust-covered caravan of 850 deportees of both sexes, after they had been on the road for four hours.

The joy that the Armenians felt at their sudden and miraculous return to their homes was indescribable. This commander had also succeeded in returning about forty other Armenians to their homes; with their families, they had been exiled in eight carriages to Ankara, from there to be taken to Der Zor.

We, the few remaining exiles of Chankiri, shall never forget that black day when the carriages of exiles returning to their homes from Ankara suddenly stopped in front of the church in Chankiri. In two weeks they had lost fourteen persons to spotted typhus fever in the prison, and a few more fell sick and died in Chankiri. The local priest, Father Simon, caught the disease from them and also died. And when we, without a sound or whisper, were transporting the priest's coffin to the Armenian cemetery near the orchards outside of town, Turkish boys stoned our procession. So bereft were we of means to defend ourselves or seek justice that we envied the dead priest, who had died a natural death and was free, having at least earned a burial mound. We knew that, like our comrades martyred before us, we wouldn't get even a mound of soil.

We, Chankiri's surviving handful of Armenians, awaiting our turn to be deported and die, watched in horror the decimation of the Armenians sent on a forty-eight-hour journey into exile by carriage, only to return. We were always wondering when we would leave for Der Zor and under what conditions. How many would endure such a journey of many months? Who among us would survive—assuming they did not put us to a torturous death by ax on the way, as they had so many of our compatriots?

Indeed, we had long since gotten accustomed to the idea of merciless death. Yes, we had thought so much about it, day and night, that it did not frighten us anymore. Our only wish was to not die in the manner in which Turkish executioners, young and old, official and unofficial, killed Armenians—by brutally torturing them as they writhed in the throes of death.

As for the police-soldier commander who had protected the Armenians, Governor-General Atif had the Central Committee in Constantinople send him to Diyarbekir, where he would be the inspector-general of the police soldiers there, also overseeing Harput and Mosul.

By exiling this fair-minded Circassian commander to such a remote province, Atif removed the main obstacle to the annihilation of the Armenians of Kastemouni. His removal left us with no doubt that our days were numbered . . . and from one day to the next we waited to hear the bell toll for us, which, alas, was not late in coming.

17

The General Condition of the Armenians at the Beginning of 1916

Finally, the horrible year of 1915 passed, leaving in its wake mourning and wailing, blood and tears. In all the prosperous and lively towns and villages where Armenians had once lived, only smoking ruins were left and, on the thousands of Armenian churches and monasteries, only hooting owls.

The industrious Armenian people, who as tradesmen, artists, and merchants had been the backbone of the Turkish empire for five continuous centuries, had been condemned to death, and the sentence had been carried out. By contrast, the governments of Russia, Iran, Hungary, Romania, Bulgaria, and Ethiopia, as well as the British rulers in India and Egypt, had allowed the Armenians, as a creative and productive people, to engage in private enterprise and enjoy all kinds of privileges. Armenians rose to be government ministers in Egypt and Hungary and senators in Romania. In the case of the Russian empire, one rose all the way up to a rank of supreme power in the person of Count Mikhail Tarielovich Loris-Melikov,* who, as minister of the interior under Tsar Alexander II, enjoyed exceptional powers.

The wiser Turkish sultans had commissioned Armenians to build

*See Biographical Glossary.

almost all the imperial palaces, castles, and famous mosques on the Bosphorus. Even the distrustful Turkish sultans of the last century had entrusted their entire state and personal wealth, as well as the government mint, only to Armenians.

But in 1915 in a matter of six months the Turkish people—almost all the official and unofficial leaders from the sultan to the ministers, to members of the Turkish Parliament and senators, and all the way to the provincial governors-general, district governors, and village chiefs, in concert with the Turkish mob—had carried out the monstrous plan that none before had dared to execute or even consider.

Carried away by pan-Islamic and pan-Turkic dreams, the Turkish leaders thought that by eliminating the Armenians, they could turn the Ottoman Empire into a huge Islamic state, stretching from the Mediterranean all the way to the Ural mountains or the Caucasus. In reality, however, they were cutting the branch on which they were sitting; by exterminating the Armenians, they were destroying the foundation of the Ottoman Empire. Each time they killed an Armenian, they wrenched a polished stone from its huge but shaky edifice.

The bloody pages of Armenian history, stretching back over fifteen hundred years, were already filled with massacres. Bugha;* Chormagan,† who destroyed Ani; Genghis Khan; and especially Tamerlane used fire and the sword to spread Islam. Armenian historians recorded that hundreds of thousands more Armenians were lost in the days of Shah Abbas at the end of the Middle Ages.

But in the case of Shah Abbas, the Persian king, the purpose was not massacre and annihilation per se. Rather, valuing the reputation of the Armenian people as creative, constructive, hardworking, and talented, he wanted to transport them to his somewhat backward and poor kingdom to colonize it. He even decided to carry the stones of Holy Etchmiadzin there and construct a new sanctuary for the Armenians in his capital, so that their hearts and eyes would not look back.

And when the Turkish army appeared and stood in front of him, even in the confusion of retreat, Shah Abbas would not give up his treasure, the Armenians, and so he had his army drive some 400,000 of them, men and women, like a flock of sheep toward the borders of his country at Salmasd. But as they were crossing the Arax River, pursued by the Turkish army,

*General Bugha al-Kabir al-Shabi (aka Bugha the Turk) led the caliph of Baghdad's Turkish forces to the Tblisi Emirate (now part of Georgia) in 853 to subdue rebellious princes, including Armenian Pakratounis. He burned the prosperous city of Tblisi to the ground and killed its large population.—trans.

†A Mongol general who took part in the invasions of Armenian lands, which may have included Ani, in the early thirteenth century.—trans.

thousands in the vanguard fell. The river became clogged with the corpses, creating a natural bridge for those who were coming up from the rear, and half of the Armenians perished in this manner.

I mention this only briefly so that the reader will have a comparative understanding that this Turkish massacre of 1915 surpasses all the massacres of all the previous ages combined.

Even if one were to suddenly forget all the voluntary services rendered by the Armenian people over many centuries, one would have to be blind not to see that the forced labor of the Armenians, even during the four years of the world war, was irreplaceable. As soldiers, as craftsmen (ironworkers, shoemakers, carpenters, tailors, tin workers), as doctors, veterinarians, pharmacists, procurers, as workers and officials of the railroad, the telegraph, and the telephone, they toiled with no payment but a piece of dry bread and the hope of saving their lives. Nevertheless, these soldiers, doctors, and pharmacists too were mercilessly massacred, along with the rest of the Armenian people, as soon as it seemed that they were no longer needed. No craftsmen were left in the cities, and just to have a pair of shoes repaired the Turks had to travel from city to city to find a Turkish shoemaker.

At the beginning of winter, Armenian craftsmen installed stoves in the army hospitals. On orders from Constantinople, the craftsmen involved were then taken, along with the rest, to the valleys outside of town and murdered. Many Turkish soldiers died from the cold in the hospitals in Soma, but that did not matter. All that counted was that no Armenian should be allowed to live: this was the Turkish national rallying cry, handed down from the highest levels of government. The chief executioner, Talaat, openly declared:

> It is necessary to eradicate the Armenians . . . For, if 1000 Armenians are left alive by some misfortune, before long they will become 100,000 and again they will be trouble for the Turkish government.

Thus the Turkish people, with the participation of all classes, including the women, with whatever tools were at hand—axes, hatchets, saws, spades, hoes, clubs—struck, massacred, butchered, burned, and violated the Armenians. They converted them by force [the other option being death] to Islam. They threw them into seas, rivers, and wells and drowned them. They buried them alive. They tortured them to death on the roads and in the valleys, all in the name of exile. They plundered the immense wealth of the Armenian churches and monasteries, the thousands of Armenian-owned stores and shops, taking home all European and domestic goods, imports and intended exports, worth millions of gold pounds, reducing the country to ruins.

While the Turkish people were welcoming the New Year of 1916 with gaiety and rapture, feasting and celebrating the successful implementation of the monstrous plan, the remaining ill-fated flotsam and jetsam of the shipwrecked Armenian people were enveloped in a shroud of unspeakable grief, filled with nightmares of imminent deportation and impending death.

Of the 2.15 million Armenians in Turkey, only a few hundred thousand were left—those of Constantinople and Smyrna, and those along the railway line stretching to Cilicia. Another few hundred thousand more—naked, hungry, and emaciated half-dead survivors—remained in the deserts of Der Zor and in various towns, villages, and regions of Syria. Another few hundred thousand, taking advantage of the proximity of the border, had succeeded in crossing into Russia, and after traveling the road to Igdir and Sarikamish, they found refuge in Yerevan, Etchmiadzin, and the surrounding areas.

Of course, amid this general chaos, it was impossible to ascertain definite numbers, especially since the Turks were still in the process of cleansing the country of its Armenians.

The Turkish people, particularly the government officials, who had filled their storerooms with goods plundered from the homes and shops of annihilated Armenians, now ate, drank, and got drunk. With unheard-of debauchery, they savagely delighted in the virgin Armenian girls ten to twenty years old, whom they forced into their harems. They blessed the Ittihad Central Committee and the Ittihad government, which almost overnight had bestowed upon them such inexhaustible wealth and loveliness.

In the fall of 1915, after the widespread carnage, *hoja* Said, deputy from Harput, had traveled over the corpses of Armenians for three days on his way to Constantinople. There he officially announced in the Ottoman Parliament that he brought with him the boundless thanks of the Turkish people in the provinces. This is what he said, word for word:

> The country has been transformed into a paradise. On behalf of the people, we express our gratitude to the wise leaders of the nation who understood the people's longing for progress . . . and granted them opportunities.

By "the people," he was refering to the Turks and other Muslims, since there were no Armenians left; and by "progress," he had in mind the immense wealth that the Turkish people had acquired in just a few months' time. No one feared any serious consequences in the future. And so all the Turkish intellectuals and editors praised the plan to exterminate the Armenian race.

We remnants of the Armenians scattered here and there kept our eyes fixed firmly on the north. We hoped to be saved by the Russian armies of the Caucasus and by our volunteers. Meanwhile the Russian armies, making harried advances and mysterious retreats . . . were coming and going, using up the Armenian volunteer regiments on the front lines. In vain we waited . . . for the almighty British navy to break through the straits of the Dardanelles and reach Constantinople. But unfortunately on the Western Front, on the German-French borders, destiny smiled more on Germany than on the Entente powers.

The Entente powers had declared this world war a fight for the liberation of small nations and peoples who were groaning under the chains of slavery. They saw it as a struggle for justice against Germany's brute force. The big and small nations rallied, one by one, to their side. But at the beginning of 1916 the Entente powers, fighting for freedom and justice, started to divide among themselves, piece by piece, western Armenia, or Turkey, as if it were a country without a people. Had not the people whose land this had been for four thousand years died and been buried? Who would then stand in the way of the Turks, protesting in the name of right and justice? We lived in a time of such cyclopean crimes that killing a single person, even a sultan, was of no significance; nor was killing a few hundred thousand persons.

If, thanks to the Germans, the Turks were to emerge victorious and thus be absolved of all responsibility, they would impose costly terms of surrender on their defeated enemies. But if they lost, naturally, punishment for the perpetrators could only be death, whether the crime involved the loss of one hundred thousand more or less, or one million more or less.

Upon my return from Berlin, my spiritual parent, His Grace Archbishop Yeghishe Tourian, had asked me why I had been so imprudent as to come back to Constantinople. I had said, "I returned to Constantinople in order to be present for the funeral of the Turkish government."

But alas, the opposite occurred: I had witnessed and would continue to witness the funeral of my unfortunate nation, from Constantinople all the way to the deserts of the south. And every day I was ready and waiting for my own funeral, with resignation, willing or unwilling. I was facing, as I thought, the inevitable, since the organizers of the Armenian annihilation, with their circumspect surveillance and their German methods, had up until this time ensured that my every daring attempt to escape had failed.

Thus we spent the New Year of 1916 without celebrations or festivities.

Like all other surviving Armenians, we too, the sixteen exiles remaining in Chankiri, retreated to our small unfurnished cells enclosed with dry wooden planks, recalling New Year's Eves past that we had spent joyfully with our loved ones, the tables decorated with fruit. And we cried like children, regretting that we had not fully appreciated those occasions.

We envied those who, a year from now, would be able to greet the new year of 1917, for though we were without a home or a protector, persecuted and exiled, in the deep recesses of our hearts, we had yet a secret altar.

18

Second Arrest and Imprisonment

Finally, after repeated delays, the dreadful day came when the remaining Armenians of Chankiri were ordered to depart for Der Zor. This time, however, we had no escape route; we had to resign ourselves to the black fate that was sweeping away the entire Armenian population of Asia Minor. We had bought only six or seven months' time with the ransom we had paid to the Ittihad [committee]. This time, however, Atif, the governor-general of Kastemouni, had sent such a strict order for our deportation that delay was impossible.

February 12, 1916, was another of the darkest days of our lives: word came that the local Armenians were being rounded up and jailed, while the police sealed all the Armenians' shops. There was no more doubt that it was the Chankiri Armenians' turn to be deported. But among those of us exiled here from Constantinople, there were still optimists who hoped that we would be able to escape this second deportation, because we had permission from the Ministry of the Interior to go to the destination of our choice. Nevertheless I was pessimistic. During the various stages of my ministry—as a provincial prelate, as a member of the Central National Administration in Constantinople, and especially as a member of the Political Committee during the Balkan War of 1912–1913—I had learned through bitter experience that there was nothing more fickle than the written promises of the Turks. The Turkish sultan might issue an edict, or some minister or governor-general might swear on the names of his own children, but it would turn out to mean nothing.

Therefore, at this grave news, I was convinced that we would be arrested soon. I wasted no time in preparing my last will and placed my work *Hai Endanik [Armenian Family]*, which I had been writing in my exile, in a tin box, entrusting it to the family that had extended me hospitality, to deliver it to my older brother in Melbourne, whom I had designated as executor.*

The local Armenians were arrested in the morning. The deportees brought from Constantinople were arrested throughout the afternoon. Two policemen came to arrest me too. One of them, who was elderly and had months earlier arrested the late Kelegian, told me discreetly when we had barely gotten outside the house, "The police commissioner wishes to see you privately, so please let's go to the government headquarters." Indeed, the meaning of these words, uttered in a confidential, friendly tone, was lost on me. But there was no time to think; and so with my head down, I followed the policeman, who escorted me directly to the first police commissioner's office, where he carefully closed the door behind me.

The police commissioner, who was also police chief for the local government of Chankiri, stated that he could exempt me from deportation if I were to reward him in accordance with the gravity of the action. This sour commissioner had been bribed to facilitate the escape of two of our comrades to Constantinople. But I couldn't accept his offer. All the money I had barely amounted to three silver *mecidiye* (twelve francs, according to the old rate of exchange), whereas he was expecting a hundred gold pounds at least. He had already received a hundred gold pounds from the elderly Krikor Ohnigian, the well-known tobacconist whose shop was in Galata-seray and who, on the pretext of illness, had left his house and was saved from the second deportation, although he would subsequently die in Chankiri. Furthermore, it wasn't safe for me to remain in Chankiri, because if the monster Atif were to learn that I was still there, he would see to it that I suffered the same fate as Kelegian.

Only by going beyond the limits of his authority could I perhaps find an escape route, and I had long since planned it, knowing that my only salvation lay in fleeing and covering my tracks. So I responded to the commissioner with a Turkish phrase, "*Kadir ne' ise o olur*," which means "Whatever fate has in store, will be." Of course, I was never a believer in this passivity preached by the Koran. On the contrary, believing that wishing for something could make it happen, I used to repeat over and over to those around me, "I have decided not to die."

I was then taken to the jail, where I found my remaining comrades from

*His brother Haroutiun Balakian was imprisoned during the Hamidian Massacres and later fled Turkey, arriving in 1896 in Melbourne, where he became a leader of the Armenian community in Australia and a prosperous merchant.

Constantinople suffering, along with all the Armenians of Chankiri. We were straightaway informed that eight or ten of the prominent Chankiri Armenians, hoping to be saved, had petitioned the governor, pledging to convert to Islam. That group was assembled in a separate corner, while those who considered deportation and death preferable to religious conversion—about nine-tenths of those in prison—were gathered around me. Perhaps some might justify this petition for religious conversion as a means of escaping death in the deserts of Der Zor. But my fond admiration was for the people I was among. They stood like granite, facing imminent catastrophe, mocking death, unwilling to become coreligionists of those who had ravaged the Armenian race. Some of them said quietly to me: "Reverend Father, we know that we are on our way to die, but to die is better than to pray together with these dogs." It was no matter; by evening, the governor had sent word to the petitioners that the governor-general had refused their request.

Depressed, ashamed of their failed gesture, and now scorned by the others, these prominent Armenians prepared for deportation. That night the petty officer of the police soldiers, who the next day was to lead the caravan of us deportees toward the hinterland of Asia Minor, came to us and announced that we were permitted to rent horses for the trip. Practically all of the local Chankiri Armenians were able to do so, but the exiles from Constantinople, myself included, had long since exhausted our financial means and had no money to even buy bread.

Furthermore, the local government had confiscated whatever money my family had managed to send me. Fortunately, the venerable *haji* Setrag Shakhian again came to my aid: "Reverend Father, don't worry. My resources will suffice for you too. We're going to our death anyway, so what are we going to do with wealth from this point on, and for whom are we going to keep it?" This same man had paid the largest ransom to the responsible secretary of the Ittihad committee in Chankiri, making it possible for us to prolong our existence until now.

I suggested in confidence to Mr. Shakhian that if he was keeping a hoard of gold pieces in his house, he should take it with him, because in tight moments we might be able to bargain for our lives. Through the commissioner, the local government announced that "whoever wished could take his family and children with him, but if the children were left in town, they would be protected." After deliberations, we decided that the families should remain in Chankiri, at least to be spared the debilitating tribulations of a trip lasting months. And we deportees would at least be spared seeing the agonizing tortures and perverse deaths of our loved ones. The suffering to be borne by us was already too much. That notwithstanding, few believed the Turks' promises that the Armenian families, women and girls, left in town would be protected.

Such protection couldn't amount to more than that shown by the wolf to the lamb. For this reason all the local Armenians, expecting to be put on the road of exile the next day, paid bribes so that their wives and children could be brought to the jail for their final instructions, to receive last wills, and to be prepared for the next day's ultimate separation. Meanwhile we spent a miserable sleepless night in the jail, tormented by parasites feeding on the filth, and crushed in mind and spirit.

The following morning, about thirty horses were brought to the jail, their price four times the regular rate, as determined by the muleteers. A fifth of the fee went to the muleteers, and the balance went into the pocket of the petty officer in charge of the ten to twelve mounted police soldiers. We were in such an agitated, emotional state, however, that nobody gave a thought to the fee. Our only concern was: For this second time, would we be able to survive the climb up the thorny and bloody Golgotha of the Armenian people?

19

Departure from Chankiri to Choroum

It was a cold winter, and all the mountains close to the city were covered with snow. A bitter wind muted the effect of the weak sun. Early on February 13, 1916, we were ordered to leave the Chankiri jail in line, in pairs, through the large iron gate, where we were to wait for final instructions from the chief of police. It is impossible to describe the heartrending scene as we emerged from the jail. Children were wailing and crying, mobbing their fathers as they appeared. They were followed by the elderly mothers and other women grieving over those going into exile. No one could stand to hear the policemen and police soldiers shouting orders. Everybody knew by now that exile to Der Zor meant death. Even if we escaped massacre by a bloodthirsty mob en route, and even if some of us reached the deserts of Zor after a grueling journey of months, we would still die emaciated and exhausted in the sun-baked stretches of sand.

Therefore the Chankiri Armenian families hastened to say their final goodbyes to loved ones being deported. The mothers hanging on to their sons were crying out in Turkish (because the Armenians of Chankiri are

Turkish-speaking): "We gave birth to our children in pain and raised them through tears, only for them to be scattered and killed . . . woe, my darling child [*yavrum*], woe! . . . what black days have come upon us! . . . oh, if only we hadn't given birth to you!" Such doleful words, such poignant lamentation and wailing as if to bring down the deaf canopies of heaven . . . Wretched Armenian mothers—among all the nations of the world, are there any mothers who have suffered more, whose hearts have bled more from their children's affliction? As for the young wives, dispensing with all customary modesty they embraced their young husbands headed for death and cried out with tears streaming down their faces: "Where are you going, leaving us at the mercy of our enemies?"

Then there were the hapless children, the more tragic grown and underage girls, and the unaware little ones, who, sensing disaster, clung to the legs of their fathers, crying: "Father, why are you leaving us here, and where are you going? . . . I'll come along with you . . . take me with you." Their wailing was so powerful, it could have split open rocks. Then the mothers and the white-haired, hunchbacked grandmothers scurried over to me and, smothering my hands with tearful kisses, beseeched me: "We are entrusting our husbands and sons first to God and then to you. Take care of them . . . they no longer have a master and protector; there's just God in heaven and you on earth." Oh, my tribulation was unbearable, for I was the only surviving shepherd of a banished flock.

But I too was a deportee and a wanderer. I could do nothing but witness firsthand the martyrdom of my race and, if by God's grace I managed to survive, attest to this great crime to future generations. If it were only possible to say something to comfort the mothers and other women enveloped in their indescribable grief. And who would console me in my silent grief and anguish? I too stood at the threshold of death.

Seeing the anguish caused by this final separation, the Turkish officials at the windows of the government building above the jail looked down with diabolical grins. Some even jeered, guffawing and cackling at our misery. On the ground a rabble of local Turks, men and women, surrounded us, seeming no less happy that the Armenians were going to their deaths. As they spoke among themselves, they made sure we heard them: "Of course, this had to be the final end of the enemies of the state and people" [*Dovlet, millet dushmanlarin sone helbet bu olajaghede*]. Some of them explicitly praised the Ittihad government for having had the courage to liberate the Turkish state and people from the "Armenian Menace" with one decisive blow.

Many Turks unashamedly exploited this unique opportunity to revive old, disputed monetary claims against the local Armenians going into exile. They were indifferent and merciless in the face of the deportees' pleas and entreaties—the fact that the Armenians headed for the deserts would need all the money they had to try to save themselves meant nothing. Some of the Turks' financial demands had already been properly settled through arbitration, yet they would not relent. As business partners or in business dealings, they had always exploited their Armenian friends, enriching themselves by the honest sweat of the Armenians' brows. Now in one day they had become openly ungrateful enemies.

On the other hand, when the Armenian exiles presented Turks with their legitimate promissory notes and made numerous pleas to be paid, not a single Turk had any qualms about shirking his debt, saying that, by government decree, they could pay their debts to Armenian deportees only to the recently established state committees of abandoned goods. All the pleas that the deportees made to their Turkish debtors in the name of longstanding friendship proved futile.

Our caravan of forty-five to fifty people moved forward, accompanied by about a dozen mounted police soldiers as well as a Turkish petty officer. Some of us were riding horses; others were on donkeys; while still others were on foot. We headed toward Der Zor, leaving behind wailing and lamentation, shrieks, grief, tears, and an eternal curse.

Our dread and anxiety became even greater when the police soldier who acted as the guide suddenly took the deserted mountainous route toward Choroum, via Isgilib, instead of leading us to the Ankara station, which was only twenty-four hours away, and then by train to Aleppo via Konya—a five- to six-day journey. As we were passing by the last vegetable gardens on the edge of town, we saw an elderly hunchbacked Turkish woman with disheveled hair, dressed in rags. She stood like a statue, sometimes raising her hands to the sky and then striking her knees, and shouting:

> Cursed be they, it's a world of doers and finders; they're taking these innocent people away to murder them; the enemy to come, in turn, will treat us this way in the future . . . Look here, those who remain alive won't enjoy the spoils . . . may God be with you, my children.
>
> *Kahe olsunlar, iden bulur dunyase der, mahsumahalii yoldurmeye goturiyorlar; gelen dushman de yarenbizi boyle idejek . . . Ey yapanlarada kalmaz ishallah . . . evladlarem Allah sizin ile beraber olsun.*

This solitary compassionate Turkish woman, prophetically cursing the Ittihad government at the top of her lungs, made a deep impression on us all. The police soldiers jeered at her, calling her demented! Two hours later we had ascended snow-covered mountains, where, as evening came, the blustery winter wind began to freeze our fingers and ears.

The ten or fifteen of us on foot found walking on the now-crusty snow difficult, and the police soldiers grew impatient. After eight hours, at twilight, we finally arrived at a Turkish village.

By arrangement of the petty officer in charge, we spent the night at the Muslim house of prayer in the village, in the absence of more suitable quarters. Since all its windows were broken, the night cold bit into our limbs, which were as yet unaccustomed to the journey. The indelible emotions of the morning and the day's journey robbed us of heart and soul; and so stretching our weary bodies on the few dirty and lice-infested mats, we curled up and lay, half asleep and half awake, until dawn, awaiting the surprises of the next day. At sunrise, with the horizon tinged red, we set out again in dread. After deliberating among ourselves, we bribed the supervising petty officer with thirty gold pieces not to take us to Choroum by way of Sungurlu. We knew that the Turks of Sungurlu had killed the Armenians there—both men and women—with such barbarity that even the thought of it terrified us. By taking a circuitous route, therefore, and avoiding the Halys River as much as possible, we moved slowly toward the massive new Halys bridge, which was just a few hours from Isgilib.

After walking for hours, we reached the banks of the Halys, which even in winter had overflowed. It roared and rushed in torrents, churning with tree trunks, branches, and even whole uprooted trees. The water was murky, but we were slowly leaving behind human custom, and like animals, we found ourselves drinking from it.

By the second day we had become friendly—thanks to the bribe—with the young Turkish petty officer in charge of us. As a result, he showed us the official document with the orders about us. Although it was addressed to the governor-general of Aleppo, it was in an open envelope so that the local government officials along the roads would know how to deal with us. The document said the following:

> According to the official document of the Ministry of the Interior dated . . . and numbered . . . , these 48 Armenians are being exiled, under surveillance and protection, to Zor via Aleppo. And when they arrive in Kayseri, the government in Chankiri and the ministry of the interior must be notified by telegram.

> *Dakhiliye Nezarete jelilesinin . . . tarikhli ve . . . nomerolu emir mujib. Chankiri Ermeni Jumaate olub 48 ferd, muhafaza tahtenda Haleb tariri ile Der Zora sefke, ve selameten Kayseriye avdetlerinde, ba telegraf gerek merkez hokumetine, ve gerek Dakhiliye Nezaretine ishare.*

The governor of Chankiri had written this official order to the governor-general of Aleppo, on the order of Atif, governor-general of Kastemouni. The petty officer was trying to encourage me by saying that the order was very well written and that we mustn't fear or worry about being killed. He told me that in many deportation orders the words "under surveillance and protection" were not to be found, and that the request to telegraph upon their safe arrival in Kayseri was also a good sign. So for the moment, we took solace (after all, this was a Turkish document), and we hastened to spread the word among ourselves in order to ease the obsessive nightmare of death.

On the next day, we set out at dawn. The road was more like a footpath, on which it was difficult to proceed except on horseback, since the snow, having softened, had partially melted in places and was crumbly. Those forced to walk were having a difficult time trudging through snow for six- to eight-hour days, and their feet swelled. Those of us on horseback would lend them our horses for a while to give them a rest. At sunset we stopped at a village of *kizilbashes*. These Muslim sectarians, who had retained certain ancient Christian customs, never liked the Turks, and the animosity was mutual. Often when Armenians had been cruelly persecuted, the *kizilbashes* protected them.

Thus they received us with great compassion, refusing to accept payment for the yogurt and eggs they gave us. On the other hand, in all the Turkish villages we subsequently passed through, we were robbed blind; no regard at all was shown for our circumstances. A few of the Chankiri natives accompanying us had longtime friends among the *kizilbashes*, and, unbeknownst to the police soldiers, they invited their exiled Armenian friends to their houses; sympathizing with us, they wept bitterly and advised us to flee.

At the crack of dawn we set out, because we had a lot of ground to cover to reach the Halys bridge. A few hours later, when we came upon the Halys River valley, the air turned warm, and we left the snow-covered mountains. On the distant horizon was the famous Mount Argeos, or as the Turks call it, Ergias, its snowcapped peak enveloped in clouds and rising 4,000 meters [13,123 feet] above sea level. In order to avoid the road to Sungurlu, we wandered along oblique paths, and after a tortuous eleven hours in the pitch-black winter darkness, we finally reached the marvelous stone bridge over the Halys River, called Koyun-baba. The river was surging with a tumultuous uproar as it flowed under the huge, well-shaped arches of the bridge, creating a vortex with clay-colored waves that pushed toward the Black Sea.

On the Isgilib side of this bridge stood an Oriental *khan* with only one room, in which we were to spend the night. Upon entering the room, however, we discovered already ensconced there a group of bandits armed with old bow-shaped Persian sabers, daggers, and other weapons, as well as cartridge belts strapped around their shoulders and under their arms. With a kind of scrutiny peculiar to bandits, they examined us one by one, from head to toe.

We were terrified at the sight of these thugs, whose sunburned faces and ferocious looks bespoke their bloodthirsty exploits, in recent days no doubt involving the slaughter of Armenians. Forced to sit among them, full of terror, we expected them to attack us at any moment. The police soldiers, and especially the petty officer in charge of us, urged us not to be afraid, but needless to say, none of us slept that night, between the bandits and the surging Halys River.

Our situation particularly affected those with weak hearts, and about ten prominent Chankiri natives decided to commit suicide, not wishing to lose the opportunity afforded by the Halys. They truly believed that it was impossible to reach Der Zor alive. At the last minute one of them lost the courage to jump into the river. Just past midnight he ran to inform me that I should intervene with the others while there was still time.

I ran out of the *khan* and found our companions preparing to jump from the high wall on the riverbank. Some of them had already written their last wills on pieces of paper. I pleaded with them to desist; they begged me to leave them alone and not interfere as they took their only chance. Moreover they called on the rest of us to jump into the river with them and escape our fate. Seeing that no one was heeding my pleas and religious counsel and exhortations, I tried to convince them that our money might yet keep us alive. Our most sacred act of patriotism, I declared, was to remain alive in order to witness the rebirth and resurrection of the Armenian nation and the new dawning of Armenian freedom.

Finally, my pleas and arguments overcame their determination and brought them all back to the inn. There I kept watch over them all until morning, to prevent any rash reconsideration. At dawn, on horses and donkeys or on foot, we began to ascend the deserted mountains, leaving behind for good the muddy waters of the Halys River, the inn in which we had shuddered, and the huge, deathly Koyun-baba bridge with its mysterious solitude. Again our journey was exhausting as we climbed up snow-capped mountains, the cold wind lashing our bodies. After about seven hours, we reached an isolated *khan* built of stone, surrounded by high hills. It was, actually, more a den of thieves than an inn; it consisted of a single room [*ghovush*], where again, supposedly by chance, more than twenty armed Turkish robbers were to spend the night with us. Actually they had come explicitly to claim our "unlimited" wealth and then lay out our corpses.

Once again it was impossible to sleep through the night, with the bandits plotting among themselves. But thanks to our petty officer, whom we paid in advance for his vigilance, they were not able to assault us. Barely had dawn broken when we asked to get an early start so we could reach a Turkish village that was remote and peaceful. There, with our petty officer's influence, we hoped to find food and spend a safe night. By sunset he got us to a small Turkish village, where, after four wakeful nights, we were finally able to sleep a little and get some food. Though the days were passing, the tormenting idea of impending death prevented us from thinking about eating. Rather, we were thinking about how to keep from becoming the victims of these two-legged marauding wolves.

Yervant Chavusian, a reformed Hunchak Party worker and a teacher for many years, had prominent friends and pupils but had had no money in Chankiri to rent a horse or a donkey. He became ill, and on the fifth day of our journey he was unable to walk any farther. So I rented a donkey from the villagers, took him with me, and continued to help him throughout the journey with money borrowed from others. Shortly after noon on the fifth day, we reached the city of Choroum, which was a government seat built in a field and surrounded by extensive gardens and vegetable plots. Having wandered over desolate mountain roads for five days, we had come to look truly wild. We were overjoyed at our good fortune to be entering a city that gave evidence of traces of civilization, but our solace lasted only a few moments.

20

From Choroum to Yozgat

Numerous policemen came to meet us and then escorted us to a half-destroyed *khan* on the western edge of the city. There all forty-eight of us were stuffed into a small room on the ground floor, in which no more than twenty could sit. As if this weren't bad enough, a nasty police-soldier captain appeared and bolted the door shut on us. Stationing a police soldier at the door with a bayonet rifle, he ordered him loudly enough for us all to hear: "Don't bring bread or water to these dogs. Let them starve so they will understand what it means to rebel." So we gave up on any hope of finding bread and water. During our five-day trek through the mountains, we had used up the food we had brought from Chankiri, so we were now starving. We could get nothing from the village either, since most of the villagers had been sent to the front, and the peasants left behind were without food themselves.

We were practically sitting on top of one another, so it was impossible to lie down or, even if we'd had food, eat. The exhaustion of the journey and our hunger made us think that death was a thousand times better than living like this. Those whose suicide I had prevented were vexed by this suffering and asked me why I had interfered. They kept saying that it would have been better to drown in that river than to suffer like this, only to die in a cruel and ghastly way.

We were even prevented from leaving to answer nature's call. So we struck a bargain with the captain, and for five silver piasters each, we were allowed to take care of our urgent needs under surveillance. After spending an uncomfortable and sleepless night in that fetid atmosphere, we tried everything, including a bribe, to induce the hard-hearted captain to ease up on these restrictions. But the more we tried to win his favor, the more inflexible he became; then he told us that our horses had been taken away from us and we should be prepared to go to Yozgat on foot.

At this news our grief became indescribable. Our comrades from Chankiri had brought rugs, carpets, light bedding, and other things, but the sixteen of us from Constantinople had nothing but our souls. As it was, some of us were growing steadily weaker, and some had been ill when the deportation began. The question was, how were we going to take these individuals with us? The captain told us that there were not enough carriages, so we had to go on foot. Then Turkish coachmen came to the iron-barred and broken windows of our ground-floor room to bargain with us, on the condition that we take care of the captain financially. The coachmen were obviously approaching us at his suggestion, so we had no choice but to make a final attempt. After liberally paying off the police soldier who was guarding our room, I got permission to go see the captain. After scornfully listening to my pleading, he said he would allow us to bargain with the coachmen as long as the deal was satisfactory to him.

After we had satisfied his greed, he allowed us to rent carriages—but only on condition that, in addition to the bribe we had paid him, we pay him another bribe equivalent to the total fee for each carriage from Choroum to Yozgat. Thus he would quietly receive more than fifty gold pounds from us. And since we had no other means of saving ourselves, we accepted. We were being fleeced, but we didn't give it a second thought and rented ten or twelve carriages; we were ordered to be ready in a half hour.

Before we set out, we had the pleasure of receiving a visit from a few

Armenian youths—Russian citizens who had been exiled from Constantinople. They encouraged us, saying that the commander of the local police force, with whom they had a close relationship, had given them special permission to enter our jail-*khan*. He supposedly had said to them in a friendly manner:

> The official document regarding these deportees is written in a benign style; they should not fear being killed. The only thing is, they should always be on the alert . . . they should keep the sergeant (petty officer) accompanying them content and not get scattered along the way. They have nothing to fear, should they be able to make the very dangerous journey from Yozgat to Boghazliyan and then on to Kayseri.

Still we remained apprehensive about the journey from Yozgat to Boghazliyan because thus far not a single caravan had managed to complete this bloody trek alive. Thus, the closer we got to these roads reeking of death, the more we shuddered. The Turkish police soldiers, in turn, were fueling our fears, so that we were on the verge of losing our composure. Finally at midday, with some in carriages and others on foot, we set out, and at sunset we reached the Turkish village of Mejid-Ozu without incident. There we spent a night in much more comfortable conditions than at Choroum, and we were also able to satisfy our hunger and thirst in exchange for liberal payments.

The second day, at dawn, our caravan set out toward desolate mountains and valleys; our only consolation was that our carriages allowed us to travel along carriage routes this time. Our companions traveling on foot, whose number gradually increased with the depletion of funds, could also now proceed more easily without constantly stumbling over rocks that had fallen on the paths, as they had before.

On the third day, after traveling along deserted and desolate roads, we were lucky to arrive at another oasis of Oriental civilization, the town of Alaja, whose deputy mayor [*kaymakam*] showed some compassion for our wretched condition.

He, along with a few others, called at the coffeehouse we had found, asking how we were and allowing us to purchase whatever we needed and could afford. This was something usually denied to us. Upon our request, he also permitted us to send telegrams to relatives to ask for money.

Taking advantage of this special permission, we sent a telegram to the Ministry of the Interior, protesting that we were being exiled to Der Zor despite having been granted "permission to go to the places we desired." (Astonishingly, even now some among us still insisted that "Talaat is a end of the Armenians and he's against the massacres.") We departed from Alaja sufficiently invigorated and comforted and slowly approached Yozgat. But no matter how we tried to keep our spirits up, we could not drive away the specter of death. In my mind's eye, I kept seeing a skeleton holding a sickle, as in the Swiss painter Arnold Böcklin's print *Der Totentanz* (Dance of Death).

On the fourth day we left Alaja, and at twilight we reached a stone *khan* in the deserted mountains. Drawn by the news that our caravan was passing through, eight or ten bandits had gathered there, posing as travelers. They were scrutinizing us and our goods, already imagining the division of booty. All night they sat opposite us and deliberated among themselves, but because of the police soldiers, they didn't dare act. Then on the fifth day our caravan set out toward Yozgat. All of us spent this day in fear and dread. Some wrote letters as their last wills to family members in Chankiri. Again, our comrades bribed the police soldiers to see that these letters reached their wives.

No matter how unavoidable death seemed, we could do nothing but move forward. As for the police soldiers, seeing our dread as we approached Yozgat, they would say: "Don't be afraid; whatever destiny has in store for you will be" [*Korkmayiniz kadir neise o olur*]. But it was through bribes, not destiny, that we were able to continue on to Yozgat without any losses.

21

From Yozgat to Boghazliyan: The Skulls

There is a Turkish village on the road to Boghazliyan, two hours from Yozgat. Before it there is a bridge. There Shukri, the captain of the Yozgat police soldiers, a sixty-five-year-old man, had been waiting for us since morning with eleven mounted police soldiers. Our carriage drivers, who assumed that we were going to be killed under this bridge, ordered those of us in carriages to get out and remove our goods. Having collected double their fees in advance, they then lashed their horses and galloped off in the opposite direction. All of us were stupefied at this inexplicable action. We then gathered up our goods, which had been dumped from the carriages, and after much hardship, we arrived, covered in mud, at the village, where the captain and his police soldiers were waiting for us. Captain Shukri took command of our caravan from the police soldiers who had accompanied us from Choroum, and received the blacklist of our names and other official documents.

After checking to make sure that no one on the list was missing, Captain Shukri made us set out without giving us the least respite. Instead of escorting us to Boghazliyan, as we had hoped, he and his men took us to a Turkish village where no one would sell us any milk, yogurt, eggs, or bread, not even at a premium. Anxious about the hostility of the villagers, we spent a sleepless night. At dawn eight or ten horsemen arrived from Yozgat and burst into our rooms. As if they were customs officials, they searched our Turkish saddlebags made of leather or rugs [*heybe*]. The police soldiers accompanying us confirmed that these horsemen were bandit chieftains who had come to kill us and divide the spoils. But Captain Shukri ordered them out and forced them to leave empty-handed.

Nevertheless, we were now proceeding along the bloodstained roads from Yozgat to Boghazliyan, from which not a single caravan before us had emerged alive. And Turkish peasants we met gave us shocking accounts of the massacres, without regard to sex or age, of the Armenians of Yozgat and the vicinity.

We had no time to think; we had to march. The interior minister and chief executioner, Talaat, had given orders by telegram throughout the disintegrating Ottoman Empire, even as far as the most remote villages, to take the Armenians outside of the cities and towns, into the mountains and valleys, and mercilessly massacre them. He had also ordered that the remaining old women and children be marched along routes deliberately made longer, then annihilated by being left in the deserts of Der Zor without bread, water, or even a final resting place.

More than one million Armenian city dwellers and peasants were savagely slaughtered and made to choke quietly on their own blood. Tens of thousands of Armenian males, lashed together with string or rope, were mercilessly butchered along all the roads of Asia Minor, or massacred with axes, like tree branches being pruned. The executioners were deaf to the crying and weeping of these wretched victims, even to their pleas to shoot them so that they might escape torment: the order had come from on high, and the *jihad* against the Armenians truly had been proclaimed. Yes, it was necessary to mercilessly slaughter them until not a single Armenian was left within the confines of the Ottoman Empire. The order for this wholesale massacre was executed with exceptional ferocity throughout the district of Yozgat because of Atif, the vice-governor of Ankara.

In July 1915 the governor of the Yozgat region had been unwilling to execute the order to massacre the Armenians, and was quickly dismissed; Mehmet Kemal, the *kaymakam* of Boghazliyan, was temporarily made vice-governor. Barely had he assumed his post when he ordered the massacre of 42,000 Armenians throughout the Yozgat region. The order was carried out at a monstrous pace and included the suckling infants, the heartrending details of which I will get to.

On our second day along the Yozgat-Boghazliyan route, we saw, in the fields on both sides of the road, the first decomposed human skeletons and even more skulls; long hair was still attached to them, leaving no doubt that they belonged to females.

Among our companions were young Armenian intellectuals of Constantinople. They often bent down to pick up these skulls and kiss them tearfully. After all, these were the sacred remains of our mothers and sisters who had been martyred. Captain Shukri of the Yozgat police soldiers, who personally escorted us along these most dangerous and bloody roads, rode beside me for a few hours, during which time I became rather friendly with him (to the extent that the wolf and the lamb can be friendly). He exhorted me, "*Murahhasa effendi*, tell your people not to give way to emotion—picking up skulls they come across and kissing them. They don't know that the same fate awaits them a little farther on."

Naturally I warned my companions to refrain from such imprudent acts. Although our days were numbered, we endeavored as much as possible, with trust in God, to drive away thoughts of death. We were proceeding along roads where the slightest ill-advised or careless step could become the cause of our instant death. Shukri was so cruel that he wouldn't deign to speak to any other member of our caravan. It was just by good fortune that I had been able in a few hours to win his favor, and so we kept riding together, conversing about various topics. From him I learned that at the beginning of 1916, as we were traveling through there, the vice-governor of Yozgat, Mehmet Kemal, had been reappointed to his previous post, *kaymakam* of Boghazliyan.[1]

PART III

The Second Deportation: The Caravan of Death to Der Zor

FEBRUARY–APRIL 1916

22

The Confessions of a Slayer Captain

I wished to take advantage of the rare goodwill that was shown to me by Captain Shukri, to learn more about the major uncertainties facing us. Trying to be discreet, I asked him, "Bey, where have all these human bones along this road come from?"

The captain pointed to the deep valley before us and answered, "These are the bones of Armenians who were killed in August and September. The order had come from Constantinople. Even though the minister of the interior had huge ditches dug for the corpses, the winter floods washed the dirt away, and now the bones are everywhere, as you see."

"Are these the bones of the Armenian deportees who came from far-off places and passed this way," I asked, "or are they the bones of Armenians from this area?"

"Do you see this road? Aside from the first caravan of Armenians from Choroum, in July, no other caravans have traversed this road and survived."

"Shukri Bey, in your opinion, how many Armenians were massacred along these roads that we have traveled? As captain of the Yozgat police soldiers, you must know." He replied:

> Now it's not secret anymore; about 86,000 Armenians were massacred. We too were surprised, because the government didn't know that there was such a great Armenian population in the province of Ankara. However this includes a few thousand other Armenians from surrounding provinces who were deported on these roads. They were put on this road so that we could cleanse them.

Paklayalum was the word he used for "cleanse"; the Turks always used this term, especially the government officials, when referring to the massacres of Armenians.

"Upon whose orders were the massacres of Armenians committed?"

"The orders came from the Ittihad Central Committee and the Interior Ministry in Constantinople. This order was carried out most severely by Kemal, *kaymakam* of Boghazliyan and vice-governor of Yozgat. When Kemal, a native of Van, heard that the Armenians had massacred all his family members at the time of the Van revolt, he sought revenge and massacred the women and children, together with the men."

"So were the women in these areas of Yozgat also massacred? I ask this because we had heard that while the men were massacred, the women were spared. We heard that the beautiful virgins and young brides were taken by those who desired them for their harems, while the elderly women were driven to Der Zor. Did it happen this way in your *sanjak* [province] too?"

"It didn't, because as I said, the *kaymakam* of Boghazliyan was so enraged over the murder of his family during the Van rebellion in April 1915 that he had no concern for appearances and had the women and children, even the suckling infants, massacred. He was said to have said: 'I have made a vow on the honor of the Prophet: I shall not leave a single Armenian alive in the *sanjak* of Yozgat.' "

I asked Shukri Bey how the women and girls of Yozgat were massacred, but just then one of the police soldiers, a corporal, having noticed something down the road, came over to ask the captain for instructions, and our conversation was interrupted. While traveling this road to death, I was intent on learning everything I could about the martyrdom of my race. I was thinking, too, that if it was possible somehow to survive, I might shed light on these criminal events. A piece of testimony like this—from the actual place of killing and from a killer who had overseen the deaths of 42,000 Armenians in the *sanjak* of Yozgat—could be valuable.

It was riding on horseback that had given me this unique opportunity. All those who have traveled long days by horseback know that a horseman on a long journey always seeks out a fellow rider to relieve the boredom. At times when I separated from him, he would invite me back over so that we could continue talking and riding together.

He was candid with me, as he himself stated, because he was convinced that none of us would survive. He treated me respectfully, not out of sincerity or respect for my position as prelate, but because he was trying to extort us without resorting to violence. In order to win his favor, I told him I had always been a Turcophile and that I had been exiled from Constantinople because I had been mistaken for a revolutionary with the same name. I even told him I had been decorated by Sultan Hamid himself. I criticized the extremist acts of the Armenian revolutionary committees and told him that the Armenian revolutionaries were the sole cause of our misfortunes.

I seem to have succeeded in winning Captain Shukri over, because he said to me, using the Armenian word *khosdovanapar* [confidentially], "*Murahhasa effendi*, even if I am not able to rescue your companions from the murderous mob, I'll save you, as long as you convert to Islam. I want this to be understood." Whatever proposal he made, I responded affirmatively; I even demonstrated my knowledge of the Koran, which delighted him.

I want to underscore that I made every effort to remain alive, but with the hope that I would emerge from all of this with my honor intact and not as an apostate. However, I did not want to judge all of the other surviving Armenians. It was enough that they should save themselves any way they could.

A half hour later, when we started riding together again, I resumed our conversation, "Bey, why did you commit massacres on the main roads? Wouldn't it have been prudent to have done it in the hidden valleys?"

He replied, "The massacres weren't committed on these roads. As I mentioned, it was the winter floods that scattered these bones and skulls all over the roads. Do you see the mill in this valley facing us?" He pointed to it. "There's a story I'll tell you about it." In a half hour our caravan reached the mill, and I spurred my horse on to catch up to the captain and asked him to tell his story.

"It was precisely here," the captain continued, "that the search of the women of Yozgat took place."

"Bey, tell me all about it so we might pass the time." He did so:

> There's no reason to hide it . . . it was eight months ago, after all, and these stories are getting around . . . the news has even reached Europe. The German embassy was so upset that they rebuked our government, and orders then came from Constantinople telling us to cease the massacres.[1] Nevertheless, after we had massacred all the males of the city of Yozgat—about eight thousand to nine thousand of them* in the valleys near these sites, it was the women's turn. So two months later Governor [Mehmet] Kemal summoned town criers and had them make the following announcement:
>
> "Inasmuch as your husbands have arrived safely in Aleppo and presented a petition to the local governor-general, requesting that their families be brought to Aleppo too, the *mutasarrif* is giving you a three-day period to make the necessary preparations for a long journey and then wait for the signal to depart. Whoever can afford the fee can have a horse- or ox-drawn cart and take with her whatever she likes; the government has already made all the

*And their prelate, Bishop Nerses Tanielian, and his fellow priests—G.B.

> arrangements. There is no reason to be afraid. The *mutasarrif* has undertaken all precautionary measures to see to it that you are taken safely to your husbands in Aleppo. Those who disobey this government order and those who go into hiding will be subjected to the strictest of punishments; this is being communicated to the Armenian families."
>
> Upon this official announcement, made by Turkish town criers throughout the city, the Armenian women rejoiced and briskly made preparations for the road. Many of them, as though going on a pilgrimage to Jerusalem, even made sweets—*gata*s and *paklava*s—and arranged them in tin boxes to take to their husbands in Aleppo. Then after the three days had passed, we had them all depart at once, some by carriage, some by cart, and the poor ones on foot.

"Do you perhaps remember what the number of carriages and carts was?"

"I would say that there were 280 horse-drawn carriages, 550 ox-drawn carts; so altogether we had about 830 carriages and carts."

"But," I asked, "was it possible to find so many carriages and carts in town?"

"Well," the captain said, "the Yozgat government sent police soldiers to all the regional village centers and had them bring back all available carriages and carts."

"Bey," I asked, "do you have any idea how many women and children were involved?"

"I believe the total number of women, girls, and children was about 6,400. This included boys under the age of twelve who hadn't been sent with the caravans of men."

"How many of these women went on foot?"

"To the best of my recollection, about four thousand were able to find room in the carriages and carts; the rest, being unable to pay the rental fee, were forced to follow the caravan on foot."

"To whom was this caravan assigned for transport to Aleppo?"

> The caravans were always assigned to me because I was the police soldiers' commander and familiar with this region. When this large caravan with about eighty police soldiers reached the three mills, in this valley four to five hours from town,* I gave the order

*It is impossible to accurately remember here such details as the names of places and hours' distances.—G.B.

> to the police-soldier officers to rest at this spot. I then ordered all the carriage and cart drivers to leave the families there and return to their villages. Then I had twenty-five to thirty midwives come in from town to begin a rigorous inspection. Every woman, girl, and boy was searched down to their underwear. We collected all the gold, silver, diamond jewelry, and other valuables, as well as the gold pieces sewn into the hems of their clothes. All these women, duped into thinking that they were going to join their husbands in Aleppo, had taken with them all their valuable and movable possessions, including their valuable rugs and carpets. The government's pretense had worked beautifully.
>
> Before long we had made piles of hundreds if not thousands of gold chains, gold watches, necklaces, bracelets, earrings, and rings with diamonds and other precious stones.* We found thousands of gold pieces sewn into the women's clothes. For this reason too, the search took so long and created such difficulty that we had to bring in new women from town to continue the effort. They found even more pieces of jewelry and gold hidden or sewn into the folds of clothes and linens.

"Shukri Bey, how many pounds of gold do you think you collected from these women and children?"

"It's difficult to say because we didn't keep a record. Whoever got hold of something kept it. If I say thirty thousand gold pounds, understand it to be sixty thousand gold pounds."

"I understand that the wealth remained in the hands of those who snatched it, but who took the largest amounts?"

"It ran the gamut, from the common police soldier to the highest government official."

"Shukri Bey, as long as we are talking so candidly and confidentially, forgive me for asking another question. But how much wealth were you able to obtain as a result of these massacres? After all, as police-soldier captain, you had the greatest opportunities."

> If all of it had been left to me, that would have been nice, but I sent the leather bags, filled and sealed, to the *mutasarrif* in town, and there was a lot of stealing; barely half of these goods reached the government. We collected thousands of rugs and carpets and piled them up near these mills, but the police soldiers stole some of

*Armenian people living in the provinces, in the absence of savings banks, put all their savings in this type of jewelry, in accordance with an old Oriental custom with the force of law.—G.B.

> them . . . To be accurate, I barely got ten thousand pieces of gold or jewelry from the booty of the Armenians.
>
> I've been serving in Yozgat for thirty years, and although I've been offered higher positions, I didn't want to leave my birthplace and home. I'm a landowner in Yozgat and have a big family here. I'm over sixty-five now, and where am I going to go after this? I have houses, shops, and two mills in Yozgat, and I'm a Muslim, thank God [*Erhamdullah islamum*]. I won't lie—I amassed great wealth from this last deportation and the massacres of the Armenians. But I'm old—what can I do with the wealth? My only son will enjoy it. Presently he's in Germany pursuing a military education; he will enjoy it. Let him do so.

"Bey," I said, "we wandered from your story. Can you tell me what happened to these sixty-four hundred women, girls, and children?"

> Yes, you're right, I was talking about one thing and got on to something else. We continued to search the women's bodies and clothes for four days and four nights. After stripping them all of their possessions and leaving them only what they were wearing, we made them all turn back on foot to the broad promontory located near the city of Yozgat. We told them that a new government order had come to have them return to town, and they followed willingly. When we reached the promontory I pointed out yesterday, ten to twelve thousand Muslims were waiting there. They had been waiting for a day.

"Bey, may I ask—how did these common people know about the government's plan for the Armenians?"

> During the time we were searching the women, the government officials of Yozgat sent police soldiers to all the surrounding Turkish villages and in the name of holy *jihad* invited the Muslim population to participate in this sacred religious obligation . . .
>
> Thus, when we arrived at the designated site, this mass of people was waiting. The government order was clear: all were to be massacred, and nobody was to be spared. Therefore, in order to prevent any escape attempt, and to thwart any secret attempts of sympathizers intent on freeing them, I had the eighty police soldiers encircle this hill, and I stationed guards at every probable site of escape or hiding.
>
> Then I had the police soldiers announce to the people that

> whoever wished to select a virgin girl or young bride could do so immediately, on the condition of taking them as wives and not with the intention of rescuing them. Making a selection during the massacre was forbidden. Thus about two hundred-fifty girls and young brides were selected by the people and the police soldiers.

Then the captain did something striking. Before continuing to tell his story of the actual massacre, he closed his eyes; in the special manner of performing ablutions [*aptes*], he raised his hands to his face and ran them down to his white beard as if washing up. And muttering a few prayers, he turned and said to me, "May God not show such death as this to anybody," or in his words, "*Allah beoyle eolium kimseyegostermesin.*"

"Did you shoot them dead or bayonet them to death?" I asked.

"It's wartime, and bullets are expensive. So people grabbed whatever they could from their villages—axes, hatchets, scythes, sickles, clubs, hoes, pickaxes, shovels—and they did the killing accordingly."

It is impossible for me to convey what happened to those 6,400 defenseless women, virgins, and brides, as well as children and suckling infants. Their heartrending cries and doleful pleas brought down the deaf canopies of heaven. The police soldiers in Yozgat and Boghazliyan who accompanied us would even boast to some of us about how they had committed tortures and decapitations, cut off and chopped up body parts with axes, and how they had dismembered suckling infants and children by pulling apart their legs, or dashing them on rocks.

Oh, it is useless to try to depict such carnage. Neither [the Mongol] Chormagan nor [the Seljuk Sultan] Alp Arslan, neither Genghis Khan, nor even Tamerlane, would treat the peoples he conquered, especially the women, girls, and innocent children, in such a savage manner. The conquering Tatars, Seljuks, and Mamluks, who brought Islam to this part of the world, had not committed as much violence a thousand years ago as the savage leaders of the Ittihad ve Terakki [Union and Progress] who now ruled Turkey. And everyone was involved—high-ranking and subordinate civil and military officials in the provinces, as well as the Turkish populace. Everyone seemed to be trying to outdo everyone else. And as if that weren't enough, they were not ashamed to brag about these criminal exploits in front of the Armenians on the death marches.

As we rode our horses side by side, our conversation about the deportations and massacres finally reached a point where I was no longer able to restrain myself. Stiffened by this unfathomable and crushing story, I turned to Shukri, who was relating all this as if it were a children's fairy tale, and said, "But bey, you are an elderly Muslim. How did you have this many thousands of innocent women, girls, and children massacred without feeling any remorse or guilt, when they were neither conspirators nor rebels? Won't you remain accountable for this innocent blood spilled, before God, the Prophet [Muhammad], and your conscience?"

"Not at all," he replied. "On the contrary, I carried out my sacred and holy obligation before God, my Prophet, and my caliph. . . . A *jihad* was proclaimed . . . The Sheikh-ul-Islam* had issued a *fatwa* to annihilate the Armenians as traitors to our state, and the caliph, in turn, ratifying this *fatwa*, had ordered its execution . . . And I, as a military officer, carried out the order of my king . . . Killing people during war is not considered a crime now, is it?"

Following this shameless and abhorrent statement, I fell silent, because there was nothing I could say in reply to an executioner who had likened the merciless massacre of unarmed, defenseless women and infants to killing people in war. In total, he was responsible for the murder of 42,000 innocent people.

Since our journey had entered a stage when we were laden with the frightful necessity of facing death at any moment, I did not want to anger our captain and tried to mask my contempt with humor. So I asked, "Bey, you know that we clergymen frighten people with punishments in the other world . . . how are you going to atone for these sins of yours in the other world?"

"Oh, very easily. I already atoned for them and didn't leave anything unsettled for the other world. As I've always done, after this massacre as well, I spread out my prayer rug and said my prayers [*namaz*], giving glory to Allah and the Prophet who made me worthy of personally participating in the holy *jihad* in these days of my old age. Many, many times a few years ago, they wanted me to retire on account of my age; it's a good thing that I didn't."

I wanted to continue to take advantage of the captain's candor, so to shift our conversation slightly, I asked, "But if Germany was aware of all this, didn't she protest the slaughter of more than a million Christians?" I was interested in determining the extent and degree of German culpability in these massacres, and I wanted to hear it from a high-level government and military official who, in a province of such notorious massacres, would know the secret external and internal developments of the state. He told me:

> When news of the Ankara massacres reached Constantinople last year, she [Germany] issued a protest as a formality, and sent an inspector to Ankara in order to deceive Europe. But we knew well

*Appointed by the Ittihad leaders as the highest Sunni religious authority, his role was merely ceremonial. The position of Sheikh-ul-Islam was abolished in 1924.—trans.

that the real reason for this protest was to protect Germany from any claim that she had a role in the massacres.

After the Germans protested, the massacres stopped for a short time, and when they resumed, they were done with a bit more discretion, so that the corpses were not simply left on the roads. The government in Constantinople did everything it could to keep knowledge of the massacres that were being carried out in the remote areas of Anatolia from the American missionaries.

"Bey, the general opinion is that Germany has played a role in these massacres. How accurate is this?" He replied:

> Is there any doubt about it? What the conquering and all-powerful sultans couldn't do over the centuries had become the mission of the Ittihad Committee, or of Talaat and Enver—to do it and finish it this way in a few months' time. Germany made us understand that unless we reduced the population of subject races within the Ottoman Empire to twenty percent of our population [of Turks], we would not be free of the troubles continually affecting us. But don't think that the Ittihad will be content with massacring just the Armenians; in a short while, they will get rid of the other races, particularly the Arabs.* As it was, it had the local Circassians massacre the Armenians of Sivas; then the government besieged the Circassians and massacred them, in turn, for having massacred Armenians without the government's knowledge!
>
> Surely you are aware of the intrigues of the Turkish government, as you have served for so long as prelate in the provinces. How can the Germans pretend to be innocent about the Armenian massacres? I oversaw the shipment of the copperware from the kitchens of the hundreds of thousands of Armenians deported and massacred in Anatolia. The copperware was transported by hundreds of carriages and carts, then was put on the train from Yozgat to Ankara, then was sent to Germany for the making of weapons. And we sent all the bells—large and small from the hundreds of abandoned and plundered Armenian churches and monasteries—to Germany, where they were melted down and made into cannons in the Krupp factory. From this alone, didn't the Germans understand what was happening to the Christians in Anatolia?

*Truly, a few months later, in the summer of 1916, the supreme commander of the army in Syria, Jemal, began persecution against the Arabs too, hanging Arab bigwigs in Damascus.—G.B.

After we had talked for two or three hours, almost without interruption, Shukri and the police soldier *chavush* moved ahead. The lawyer Boghos Tanielian, one of the Constantinople intellectuals who was on foot, had been listening closely to our conversation, along with a few of his companions. After I was left alone, he said, "If you were an official of great authority from Constantinople, you couldn't have gotten such a confession from this criminal. I hope someday the world will hear this—this man who massacred forty thousand Armenians."

As I mentioned before, the captain often repeated: "There is no salvation for you either; all of you will die. The only difference is that I have instructions from the government to do what is possible to have your caravan, and the caravan of Armenians of Kastemouni following yours, come through safe and sound."

Likewise, he often said to me, "Don't be a fool, thinking that the Armenians exiled to Der Zor and the surrounding deserts will be left alive. They too will eventually *be killed.*" The words he used [*paklamak* or *harjarik*] became kind of a refrain, as in, "We shall get rid of or gradually *do away with* the remaining ones."

If there was one point in which this elderly criminal erred, it was in constantly repeating that the Armenians of Constantinople and Smyrna would be deported and "cleansed." I would respond that the Armenians of these two places were still there. He would shake his head and express surprise, since the Ittihad Committee had decided to deport them as well.

A little later the Yozgat police soldiers accompanying us provided the details of the final moments before the carnage that Captain Shukri had described. They had been eyewitnesses to the wholesale massacre. Because I was with the captain, however, I did not hear their account. These police soldiers recounted how the Turkish mob, having been assembled from the surrounding areas and numbering over 10,000, attacked the more than 6,400 defenseless women, girls, and children, wildly shouting, *Allah, Allah.* Using axes, hatchets, and other such weapons, this mob attacked the victims so savagely that the horrendous commotion of their wailing and screaming was heard in the surrounding villages an hour and a half away. Under government orders, nobody dared to spare the residents of their city or the families they knew, for those who did would be put to death.

Thus, remaining indifferent to all pleas, the mob massacred mercilessly. It is impossible to imagine, let alone write about, such a crime or drama in full detail; to have an imagination that powerful requires the special inner capacities of criminals. When the carnage was over, the mob stripped the murdered and dismembered thousands in order to take their clothes. To participate in this "body snatching," Turkish women arrived at the site of the crime from the neighboring villages. Many came carrying their suckling infants, or one- or two-year-olds, since there was nobody at home to take care of them.

The plunder of the clothes of these thousands of older and younger female martyrs (who are consecrated with eternal divinity) lasted four to five days. Then it was the turn of the dogs, wolves, and jackals, which picked up the scent of blood and came from all directions to complete the job started by the Turks. Left in the open air, the bodies then began to swell, rot, and decompose. When Interior Minister Talaat himself suddenly arrived in Ankara (on the pretext of transporting cereals and legumes stored there to Constantinople, no less), he secretly visited Yozgat. Wishing to inspect the site to see how well his orders had been carried out, then to remove the traces of the crime, he had large ditches dug, and had the scattered, by now partially skeletonized remains of the wretched female martyrs collected and buried, imagining he could thereby also bury the black and bloody story of this great tragedy.

Not long afterward, when Talaat visited Berlin, the German Kaiser Wilhelm honored him with the black eagle insignia, an honor very rarely given to non-Germans. With this decoration, Talaat was elevated to the ranks of German nobility, as the Gambetta, Cavour, or Bismarck of the Ottoman Empire.

Perhaps this Turkish captain was accusing the Germans of complicity in this crime with an eye toward mitigating the guilt of his own people. But the German civilian and military officials, like Pilate, could not wash their hands of innocent Armenian blood.

On all the roads we traversed between Yozgat and Kayseri, about 80 percent of the Muslims we encountered (there were no Christians left in these parts) were wearing European clothes, bearing on their persons proof of the crimes they had committed. Indeed, it was an absurd sight: overcoats, frock coats, jackets—various men's and women's European garments of the finest materials—on villagers who were also wearing sandals and traditional baggy pants [*shalvars*]. Barefoot Turkish peasant boys wore formal clothes; men sported gold chains and watches. It was reported that the women had confiscated many pieces of diamond jewelry, but [as they were sequestered] we had no way of encountering them.

Although Captain Shukri carried out the criminal orders of the Ittihad Committee with gusto, as national policy, he generally spoke disparagingly of the Ittihad leaders, especially Talaat and Enver. He often said,

"These are adventurers descended from Gypsies or converts to Islam from Judaism [*donme*];* they do whatever crosses their minds; they don't consider the long run." In referring to the Armenian massacres, he said, "Let's see how we are going to escape the consequences of what we have done." However, these final apprehensive words he said out of fear of punishment, not contrition.

23

Encountering Another Caravan of the Condemned

My conversation with the captain unnerved me, particularly because I had to keep my rage to myself. Worse, in order to remain on friendly terms with him, I had to be ingratiating and affable, even to defend him and the criminal actions of the Turkish government. Nevertheless, I expended all my effort and energy in a process of harrowing mental record-keeping, classifying and rooting firmly in my memory, one by one, the frightful episodes I had just heard described. If, by the grace of God, I managed to survive, I would one day be able to make good use of all that I had seen and heard. Of this I was deeply convinced.

Near noon on our second day on the road from Yozgat to Boghazliyan, we witnessed something in a narrow valley near a water mill. This time it was not a bloody incident that would make for a painful recollection, but a bitter reality that had frozen before our eyes. Our caravan, as usual, was scattered along the road, with almost a quarter of an hour's distance separating one end from the other, when it suddenly came to a halt.

Gradually the deportees drew closer together in tight rows. The captain and I, as usual, were proceeding on horseback at the very rear when we saw another caravan of fifty-four individuals tightly bound to one another with thick ropes. They were either men over sixty or youths between the ages of thirteen and sixteen, their clothes totally worn and

**Donme:* Jewish converts to Islam in Turkey, often originating in Salonica.—trans.

tattered; some of them were clad in rags. These deportees were the sole male survivors of the three thousand Armenian families of Yozgat. Since the fall of 1915 they had been in hiding, somehow, with a few dozen families of soldiers who had miraculously remained in town. After some months, however, thinking that the danger had passed, and encouraged by the deliberate false news of a general pardon granted to Armenians, they had gradually emerged and begun to look for jobs.

One day, suddenly, all those who had come out into the open, and whose names were on a well-kept list, were arrested. They were held in jail for a few days. Then, supposedly being exiled, these hapless individuals were bound together and brought to this desolate valley to be murdered. The eight police soldiers traveling on foot, allegedly assigned for their security, had killed four of the deportees that very morning, starting with the bravest and most educated youths. Their plan was to turn over the remaining ones to the mob of villagers who had come from all over to get rid of or "cleanse" them, as the Turks were wont to say.

Oh, it is impossible to forget that heartrending scene. Having noticed our caravan, they hastened to cross our path, encouraged especially by seeing an Armenian clergyman on horseback engaged in friendly conversation with their old acquaintance, Captain Shukri. Resembling fearful chicks running under the wings of their mother with a buzzard in pursuit, they paid no attention to the threats of the police soldiers marching them. Tearfully they pleaded with me to save them; in Turkish they begged both the captain and me to spare their lives. The schoolboys, speaking to me in Armenian, let me know that four among them had already been killed and that the rest of them would be dealt with when the mob of Turkish villagers being assembled from the surrounding areas got large enough.

"For the love of God," they said, "take us with you. If you leave us here, they'll murder us as they did our companions."

With all of them lashed together above the elbow, the movement of a few forced the whole caravan to move. These emaciated survivors came forth to beg that one favor—their life—of their own clergyman, who was himself a deportee bound for death just like them, except that the hour of his death had not yet been determined. There are indeed moments when even the most fainthearted become heroes, and even the most timid and subdued speakers are miraculously made orators.

Oh, it was impossible for us not to be moved by this tearful supplication, even if at the cost of our lives. Captain Shukri watched this scene silently and indifferently, listening to what the schoolboys were saying. As he showed no mercy, I implored him to let them join our caravan, but, with the practiced composure of a professional criminal, he said, "How can I defy the government order?" I told him that at this moment our lives were in his hands alone; that he was not only our commander and marshal but our sultan as well; that our treatment was up to his conscience; and that if perchance anyone were to ask him about his actions, it was for him to explain them as he saw fit.

Amid all these mollifying words, all the elderly men bound together approached our horses to kiss the captain's feet and dolefully beg for their lives. Finally he deigned to address me, saying, "This kind of thing doesn't come free." I promised to satisfy all his wishes. Thus he ordered the police soldiers, the ones standing guard over the caravan of Yozgat natives, to return to their city, saying their job was done. As for the police soldiers overseeing our caravan, he ordered them to incorporate the caravan of Yozgat natives. Barely had he issued this order when all of them together threw themselves upon the captain and me, tearfully kissing his feet and my hands. Indeed, all of us were deeply moved.

Our destinies now linked, we bolstered one another's hope of rescue; in actuality, we were trying to drive away our death, only temporarily of course. We had hardly set out when our new companions begged me to have their arms unbound. The ropes had been tied so tightly that the blood in their right arms had ceased to circulate. Their oppressors, they said, had deliberately done it to cause their arms to become numb, rendering them incapable of self-defense during the eventual massacre. This was the general procedure for those being taken to slaughter. I tried to petition Shukri in this matter too, and after raising some objections, he said the caravan could rest by the edge of a stream in an hour, and he promised to untie them at that time. He did not fail to repeat that he expected monetary compensation. Shortly thereafter, when we reached the indicated spot, he had all of them freed from their bonds.

Twenty-four hours had passed since their departure from Yozgat, during which they had not eaten or drunk anything, but the unbound were so overwhelmed with emotion and confusion that none could savor the morsels offered them. Our two caravans having been joined together, we had become a crowd of approximately one hundred deportees. We continued on our way until sunset, when we stopped at a Turkish village. Owing to the exceptional license granted me by Captain Shukri, the police soldiers, along with the captain, found suitable rooms for rent, ten of us, along with a police soldier, to each room. I had already given my personal guarantee that no one would escape and assured the captain that if any did, I was prepared to forfeit my life.

We took this opportunity to provide our new companions with a piece of dry bread. The following morning, the third day since leaving Yozgat, we were just about to cross a narrow valley, thinking that the figures on the distant mountains were grazing sheep, when again we found ourselves surrounded by a mob. The mountains on both sides of the valley, particularly those to our left, were covered with hundreds of people from the surrounding villages. Having caught the scent of blood and booty, they had hastened there like a pack of hunting dogs. It is very difficult to specify an exact number, but there were probably seven hundred to eight hundred, among them women and girls. Based on the assurances given to us, such an attack hadn't crossed our minds.

As usual, the captain and I had been riding together in the rear, conversing, when a few youths came to report that we were surrounded. Finding ourselves suddenly besieged, we all lost our composure, and many of our caravan began crying; some, bewildered, fell on their knees, and a few old men were slapping their knees, saying, "We're done for." In an instant, instinctively, the ranks of our dispersed caravan tightened up.

About ten horsemen rode up to greet us. When the captain asked them where they were coming from, they addressed him with great respect, explaining that they had come from collecting the "sheep tax" . . . Captain Shukri whispered to me that he knew these horsemen well, adding that they were the leaders of the assembled mob; posing as random travelers, they were eyeing the caravan to determine the number of deportees and thus the prospects for booty. We had no time to lose. I pleaded with Captain Shukri to save us from this imminent danger.

In the heat of the moment, I would have promised him anything. All were in such confusion that if an attack had ensued, the mob could have slaughtered us like sheep. For a moment our blood froze, death rising up like a pillar before us. But then our dread seemed to wane. Perhaps having experienced the continuous nightmare of death for a year now, we had become inured to it.

As long as we remained alive, we considered it a boon. We had no time; our minds were incapable of reasoning out any course of action whatsoever. Everybody's hopes were pinned on me, with the expectation that I might find a way out through the friendship I had cultivated with the captain. Finally, Captain Shukri—with the ingenuity peculiar to hagglers—cited certain difficulties and demanded one hundred gold pounds, to be paid that very evening. For this he promised to disperse the mob. He further stipulated that he would hold me personally responsible for the ransom, as he did not wish to deal with the others. Obviously I accepted his terms. At the same time, through a second person, we promised the corporal of the police soldiers a tip of ten gold pounds to ensure that he would carry out the order of his commander.

As police-soldier commander in the Yozgat region for thirty years, Captain Shukri was known throughout the *sanjak* as an old fox who got his way; and as the police soldiers accompanying us attested, he struck terror in everyone's heart. At whatever Turkish village we stopped, the residents knew him personally and treated him with great respect and fearful reverence.

We had hardly struck this bargain when Shukri ordered the corporal to take a few of his men and disperse the mob. The corporal turned and asked the commander what to do in the event that the mob refused to disperse. The commander told him to fire upon them. On this order, four or five mounted police soldiers, led by the corporal, galloped off and assaulted the mob that had gathered on the mountainsides awaiting the signal to attack us.

Accustomed by now to butchery, and driven by an insatiable desire for plunder, the mob refused to retreat. Its eight to ten mounted leaders, whom we had encountered earlier, started to attack. In horror we stood watching this comedy of death being performed a few hundred meters from us, fearing it could end in carnage. Suddenly the whistle of Mauser bullets roused us from morbid bewilderment. One of the most impetuous leaders of the rabble was shot in the foot and fell to the ground. To our astonishment, the mob, packed in ranks of hundreds, inflamed by bestial passions only a moment before, now ran frightened and panting up the mountain, leaving behind the horses and donkeys that they had brought to transport the booty.

On hearing the gunfire, they understood that this was not a game or a pretense of resistance, as was often the case. How effectively a crowd of hundreds could be dispersed with just a few police soldiers—if the government really wished to do it! There could be no more indisputable and practical proof that the government was responsible for massacring the Armenians.

Behind the mob fleeing up the slopes, we saw another mob of hundreds waiting in ambush on the opposite side of the mountain. They were sealing off the valley, so that in the event of a successful attack, they could join their comrades who were in the vanguard. But that danger had now passed. We took the horses and donkeys left by the fleeing mob with us and resumed our journey, ever fearful of new attacks.

Following this triumph, Captain Shukri boasted of his powerful influence on the population of the province. I responded with a bit of flattering prattle designed to make him elaborate, then asked him whether he would in any way be held accountable for the injured man. He replied, "In what way should I be held accountable? After all, he's not a numbered sheep."

> I will have a police report [*zabit varakase*] written up, stating that they attacked the caravan of deportees [*sevkiyat*] and when I wished to disperse them, they resisted, and for this reason, they

> were wounded . . . that's all there is to it. Now it's wartime [*seferberlik*]—who's accountable to whom? We have done many worse things, yet nobody sought an explanation. There's nothing left for one to say to another . . . do you understand, *murahhasa*? . . . you should just worry about collecting the hundred gold pounds from your rich *agas* and putting them in my hand; never mind about this incident.

I knew, after working in the provinces and in Constantinople for fifteen years—with ministers, governors-general, and high-level as well as low-ranking government officials—that this was the way of things. I just wanted to take advantage of this moment to probe this captain's attitude.

My success with the offer of a hundred gold pounds reminded me of an incident in Roman history. General Jugurtha, a descendant of King Masinissa of Numidia in Africa, after continuous battle with Rome, observed the pronounced avarice of the Roman generals and the internal corruption among the Romans. Upon his departure from Rome he declared: "Mercenary city, you would be for sale too if there were a buyer." We could likewise rightfully shout, "Venal Turkey, all that is needed is a buyer."[1]

We lost no time in continuing on our way. On average we could travel only six or seven hours per day on account of those on foot, who made up about four-fifths of us; on this day we had gone some eight hours when, at sunset, covered with mud and exhausted, we stopped at a Turkish village. None of us had any appetite to eat, and crouched together in various little rooms, we passed another sleepless night under vigilant watch. There were only dirty mats to lie on, and we became covered with lice, though by now we had grown accustomed to them. Yes, sleep was impossible, because not only had we come close to our graves, we felt as if we had entered them, and we didn't know in what ways death might be waiting for us at dawn.

We wanted the night to pass as quickly as possible, mindful that all crimes are plotted in that darkness, though actually, where professional criminals are concerned, any hour of the day is suitable for both their conception and execution. Fortunately, we passed that night without incident.

Prior to the departure of the caravan, I hastened to carry out my obligation, which none of us had had the energy to think about during the night. Collecting the hundred gold pounds turned out to be very easy, with contributions coming even from those with barely a few weeks' bread money; they saw that this was no time to haggle, particularly as we still had to pass through desolate mountains and valleys, and our lives would depend solely on the goodwill of the criminal and corrupt Captain Shukri.

A few Chankiri merchants among us counted the hundred gold pieces one by one into Shukri's palms. The sight of these gold pieces whetted his avarice, and glad for the clear understanding between us, he became even friendlier toward us all. He began to do special favors and invited me to his mess.

Fortunately, the rest of the day passed without worrisome incident. We were at liberty to think a bit about our nourishment, to stock up on provisions, and also to provide for the fifty-some indigent deportees from Yozgat. Obtaining food was difficult because, out of the more than one hundred of us, barely thirty natives of Chankiri had money in reserve, while the rest were destitute in the full sense of the word. In particular, fifty-four Yozgat natives were now without clothes, completely naked, and it was necessary to feed these wretched, hungry souls. Likewise, ten of our sixteen old companions from Constantinople were in need of assistance. Inasmuch as it was not possible to beg for bread money all the time, I was obliged to take out personal loans, thereby managing to provide for some of our companions in need.

Another difficulty was this: between Yozgat and Kayseri, the Turkish villagers were so vengeful that only the intervention of the police soldiers could induce them to sell us bread, onions, eggs, and yogurt in exchange for gold pieces. These were our only foods. Subsequently we would find no eggs or yogurt or even bread to buy; never mind that the bread, when available, was a dull mixture of rye and millet; it was still a source of nourishment for us who were starving. Still, the daily nightmare of impending death had made us too uneasy to think much of food or drink; we aimed only to avoid sudden massacre. In actuality, however, we had little hope because we were Armenians, and calamity had already befallen our nation. As it had all the Armenian people, an unexpected blow of fate had dispossessed, deported, and dispersed us. Would we not all end the same way, sooner or later—dead from hunger and thirst in the deserts of Der Zor?

We set out at dawn on the fourth day, anxious and depressed as usual, trusting solely in God. We had already given up all hope for our relatives, even if they had managed to survive, for those who might rescue them—the British, French, and Russians—were still too far away.

As Shukri and I were riding and conversing together, we passed through a narrow valley, where behind a few hills we saw the heads of some men who were hiding. As they were few, I thought they must be vanguard scouts, not bold enough to attack, but I wondered, Was this rabble appearing spontaneously for us, or had Captain Shukri secretly sent his men to bring them here to rob us? So I asked, "Shukri Bey, who is sending these men toward us? How do they know that a caravan of Armenian deportees is passing through here? Obviously, they are making their way hastily from distant villages in this cold weather to come and lie in wait for us, and then murder and rob us."

He replied, "To tell the truth, they're not to blame; we got them accustomed to this." Although Captain Shukri was a well-known criminal and executioner, I must say that he was also a fanatical old Turk, truthful and sincere in his convictions, offering his opinions with a bluntness that amazed me. So, I interrogated tactfully, "Shukri Bey, why did the Young Turks not have the Armenians massacred in the cities they lived in, as happened under Sultan Hamid? Couldn't you have easily annihilated the Armenian women of Yozgat without removing them from the city?" And he answered:

> The course taken by the Ittihadists is more prudent than that taken by their predecessor, for if we had wished to massacre the Armenians the way the sultan did, then we would have suffered many losses too.
>
> Just as in Adana in 1909, the Armenians would not have surrendered easily, and they would have fortified themselves behind barricades set up in the streets and in their stone houses and would have resisted with weapons. The Armenians in Shabin Karahisar and Ourfa, for example, engaged the government for months. Now, wasn't this way more practical?
>
> In telling the Armenians that they were going to be exiled, first we disarmed them, and then, after having deported them, we eliminated them without even the slightest resistance. As for the women of Yozgat, if we had wished to get rid of them in town, they would have thrown all their jewelry of gold, silver, and precious gems into the sewers or destroyed it, to prevent us from getting our hands on it. This way was more effective. Once they were deceived into thinking that we were going to send them to their husbands, they took all their jewelry and precious gems, as well as their rugs and carpets, with them.
>
> Thus it was very easy for us to assemble them all in a few days and strip them naked. By the way, you know that they had swallowed many pieces of diamond jewelry during the course of our searches. But the Turkish villagers, particularly the women, roamed for days among these thousands of stinking corpses, slitting their intestines and finding a considerable amount of jewelry, which they subsequently brought to town and sold. All of us government officials were amazed at the immense wealth that came from the homes of the Armenians of Yozgat. Despite the fact that the government is in the hands of our race [the Turks], the Turk-

> ish people, with the exception of a few notables [*eshraf*], are poor and don't have a single carpet in their homes. We were astonished that, despite governmental restrictions, the Armenians had accumulated this much wealth during the old regime—the regime about which they used to complain so much. The constitution took effect only a few years ago, and this wealth was accumulated long before.

I should mention that scattered on all the roads and in all the valleys and fields we traversed we saw tattered pieces of clothing and underwear, worn-out pieces of shoes, and pages of prayer books and Bibles torn to pieces. Evidently large caravans of Armenian deportees had passed along these roads and were subsequently massacred.

The police soldiers accompanying us told us how, up in the wooded mountains called Chat near Yozgat, a handful of Armenian fighters had been holding out against Turkish troops and police soldiers for almost a year now, attracting the local government's attention.

The Armenian villagers from around Chat realized that they were next and they anticipated the Turkish government's move. When a slew of police soldiers from Yozgat entered this Armenian village at dawn to deport its population, they were surprised to find only a few dogs and roosters left behind; their barking and crowing had made the peasants' quiet departure imperceptible.

The government realized what was going on and sent about a thousand irregulars [*bashibozuk*] and a hundred police soldiers with rough-terrain cannons to force the handful of Armenian fighters to surrender. The latter, however, led by Sergeant Samuel, took cover in the dense woods of Mount Chat and began a heroic struggle. They made their abode in a large, deep cave in the Chat mountains. When their food supply ran out, they invaded the nearby Turkish villages and forced the residents to give them provisions. The government of Yozgat despaired at the losses suffered in those frequent attacks and saw that it would be impossible to subdue the brave fighters and force them to surrender. So it punished the local Turkish peasants, branding them enemies of the state for giving provisions to Samuel and his comrades. This has always been the modus operandi of the Turkish government: when it is unable to punish the guilty, it seeks retaliation against the innocent.

The police soldiers who told us this story remarked with astonishment that some of them who had participated in these skirmishes around Chat had even seen cannons in the possession of the Armenian resisters there; they were filled with rocks mixed with gunpowder, effective enough to prevent the attacking forces' advance. We listened to the romantic details of these stories with disappointment, but inside we felt some hope for our own freedom. Then, remembering that we had been arrested, and that release was almost impossible on these horrible roads of blood, we were quickly demoralized again. The Armenians at Chat had resisted from August 1915 to March 1916, and the police soldiers asserted that it was impossible to defeat them. Indeed, this handful of young Armenian men continued their triumphant struggle at Chat until the salutary armistice ending the world war in October 1918. At that time they took their weapons and surrendered to General Allenby, supreme commander of the British troops in Aleppo. Holding them in high esteem and praising them, the British commander hesitated to accept the weapons of these men who had brought honor to the Armenian race with their heroic resistance.

At sunset we stopped at a Turkish village called Keller, barely five hours from Boghazliyan. This turned out to be one of the most frightful episodes of our years of tribulation.

As was the custom, the members of our hundred-person caravan, together with a corporal, were assigned, for a fee, to spend the night in small rooms belonging to eight or ten villagers. As everybody was finding a niche to squat in, the corporal came and said to me, "Shukri *Effendi* wishes to see you. He has something to tell you in private." At first I didn't want to go, fearing imminent danger. When the invitation was repeated, however, I had no choice but to find the captain, who was waiting for me at the edge of the village. While preparing to find him, I had not neglected to recommend to a few of the intrepid youths sharing our hut that they follow me in stealth with watchful eyes. When I reached the captain's side, he said to me in a mysterious tone, "*Murahhasa effendi*, I've got bad news for you. Hearing that a *sevkiyat** will pass through here, hundreds of residents of the surrounding villages have assembled in the vicinity and are ready to attack us. We are in great danger."

"Shukri Bey," I replied, "you vowed in your child's name that you would take us safely to Boghazliyan. For the love of God, please use all your influence to drive this mob away. I'm certain that they will fear you if you threaten them, and they will disperse. You must save us." At the same time I was thinking that this could be a new plot to rob us. Seeing my hesitation, he suggested that we take a little walk, and he accompanied me to a small valley near the spring above the village, about 150 steps away.

There, my God, before my eyes were the swollen and dismembered bodies of murdered men and women; many of their heads were detached from the bodies, and in some cases, their bowels were spilled out. All these bodies had been stripped bare, and hands and feet or legs were thrown far from the torsos.

It is difficult to describe the shocking sight of these martyred compatri-

*Another caravan of Armenian deportees.—trans.

ots, and I don't remember ever having found myself this close to my grave. Such proximity to death made me feel weak, and as my already tired legs became wobbly, I fell to the ground. I did not, however, lose consciousness. In the wink of an eye, all the notable events of my life flashed before me like a motion picture, and I became bewildered, imagining that from one minute to the next we could be subjected to the same black fate. The captain rushed over to pick me up from the ground and said in an encouraging tone:

> Don't be afraid, *murahhasa effendi;* there's no danger for our caravan. Kemal, the *kaymakam* of Boghazliyan, came to this village last night and had the mob murder all the men in the labor battalion here, plus the women, twenty-eight persons all together. Then he picked up and left. He committed this carnage, hearing of course that a new caravan was coming, and then incited the villagers to carry out a new round of slaughter.
>
> However, after having been dismissed by the vice-governor of Yozgat, his previous influence has waned, and his power has been broken since his return to Boghazliyan. Don't be afraid; he can't do anything to us. Don't worry; I will immediately disperse the mob assembled here before it gets totally dark. Just tell me, what are you going to give me?

My sole immediate response was: "Shukri Bey, we'll give you whatever you want. Just save us from this peril too." He replied, "Give me the rugs in your possession this very night, and I will arm my police soldiers right away and disperse the mob."

It was no time to bargain, so I asked him to proceed without delay while I went to find a few of our well-to-do merchants and figure out a way to satisfy him. Accompanied by the corporal, I rushed to get four or five wealthy men out of their rooms to impress upon them the necessity of satisfying the captain's demand. So beset were we by the fear of death that, despite the mistrustful attitude of a few, without delay we sent fifty gold pieces, along with a few rugs, to the captain. The captain, in accordance with his promise, personally led all the police soldiers to where the mob was lying in wait. Summoning their leaders, he ordered them to disperse immediately and return to their villages; otherwise he threatened to fire upon them. Seeing that the government was against the carnage to be committed by them, the mob left, dejected, unable to explain this riddle.

I received the reassuring news through the corporal, but none of us was yet able to sleep. We who had made the bargain had wished to keep the matter secret so as not to arouse more fear among our companions. However, our mysterious comings and goings, and particularly our pale countenances, led our fellow deportees to conjecture that we were facing a new danger, and they were impatient for dawn to break. At dawn we hastened to depart from this gloomy village.

Walking briskly, we began our descent toward Boghazliyan. Barely an hour from Keller, we encountered Ali Kemal, a member of the Ottoman Parliament from Kayseri, who was traveling from Yozgat by carriage to Constantinople via Ankara. After passing through our drawn-out caravan, his carriage approached me, and he abruptly stopped it. He asked me where we were coming from and where we were headed. I said that we were coming from Chankiri but didn't know where we were going, only God knew. Ali Kemal said, "May God be with you." This laconic response naturally meant that God alone could help us.

It was a six-hour trip from Keller to Boghazliyan. When we were within two hours of town, we encountered Turkish villagers who blurted out the good news that *afushahane*, namely, an imperial general pardon, had been granted to the Armenians, and that all deportees were to return to their birthplaces. At the same time they informed us that notices of the general pardon papers were posted on walls in the villages and that they had read them with their own eyes. All of us asked one another why, given the general pardon, we were still being taken to Zor instead of summarily returned to our homes. I again got ahold of our captain and asked him for the meaning of this riddle.

He replied, "*Murahhasa effendi*, don't you know by now that all dealings in these strategies of ours are done with deceit? The *kaymakam* of Boghazliyan deliberately issued this false proclamation so that any Armenians who are hiding here and there will emerge, believing that a general imperial pardon has been granted, and be easily apprehended and done away with." Captain Shukri was quite truthful. As we had seen, all the orders for the annihilation of the Armenians were executed with duplicity and deception.

Finally, on the sixth day following our departure from the bridge near Yozgat, we apprehensively reached Boghazliyan several hours before sunset. Yes, we were filled with dread as we entered this seat of bloodshed and massacre, because an authoritative source had told us that the bloodthirsty [Mehmet] Kemal, overall organizer of the massacres of the Armenians of Yozgat and temporary vice-governor, had been returned to his post of *kaymakam* of Boghazliyan, having completed his former assignment.

24

From Boghazliyan to Kayseri: The Halys River Bridge and the Bandits of the Ittihad

With about four-fifths of our caravan on foot and able to tread at most six or seven hours a day, after six days we had barely been able to get from Yozgat to Boghazliyan (a three-day journey by carriage). We felt great consolation when we considered the inevitable fatal consequences if, having taken advantage of the government's permission, we had brought with us the Chankiri Armenians' families. What would have been our lot traveling with three or four times our present number, with women, girls, and infants, making our way along these bloody roads?

Like the Armenians of Chankiri, the deportees of Kastemouni—some four hundred who followed a couple of days later—had not brought their women, girls, and children. But their families were then driven out and transported to the surrounding Turkish villages by the local government, as the families of Chankiri had been. However, the Turks of the Kastemouni provincial government hated Armenians less than other Turks did, having fewer Armenian neighbors, who were also Turkish speaking. And so they did not subject the Armenian families scattered among the villages to forced Islamization, as was done in all other places, or otherwise treat them horribly.[1]

When our caravan entered Boghazliyan, they marched us in front of the government building, where officials standing on the balcony could see us. Kemal, the *kaymakam*, who had directed the massacres of Yozgat, was ill, according to the police soldiers, and therefore absent.

Our caravan was then escorted to one side of town, to a stone building with no glass in its windows that served as a barracks. As soon as we arrived there, Captain Shukri took leave of us. As we had asked, he entrusted the leadership of our caravan to a reliable *chavush*, who would take us to Kayseri.

Barely had word gotten out in Boghazliyan that a caravan of Armenian deportees had arrived than some emaciated Armenian orphan girls in rags, aged six to twelve, came to linger around our building. These wretched remnants of an ancient noble race came up to the windows of our cell, held out their hands, and sobbed, "*Der baba* [Reverend Father], we're hungry . . . we're cold . . . give us bread money . . . we'll kiss your feet; take us with you."

Oh! The tragedy of being unable to help these little orphans, snatched from the warm bosoms of their mothers, who had suffered abysmal death in the course of the Armenian martyrdom—it was a thousandfold more unbearable than the imminence of our death, which caused us all such terror. As the exiled shepherd of a scattered flock, I was unable to offer these unfortunate orphans even a piece of bread, having none myself. What could I do? Nothing—except try to firmly hold all these criminal and tragic events in the black folds of my memory and, in the event of my survival, bequeath them to future other generations. These orphans were not Turkish-speaking. If—like the natives of Yozgat, the Armenian population of Boghazliyan, and the other villages in the vicinity—they were Armenian-speaking, as the police soldiers assured us, were they from this region? Or were these the sole survivors of caravans of deportees from the interior provinces who had traveled these roads?

For the first time since our departure from Chankiri, in Boghazliyan we were encountering survivors of the massacres. In addition to feeling pity, we were filled with mortal dread when we imagined the scenes whose irrefutable proof were these unfortunate souls, human flotsam and jetsam. We spent an anxious night here in the province of the bloodthirsty governor Kemal, then at dawn departed Boghazliyan for Kayseri. Everybody—Captain Shukri and all the police soldiers accompanying us—had said to us, "If you can survive the trek from Boghazliyan to Kayseri, don't be afraid from there on."

Almost immediately after setting forth, as was my custom, I began to cultivate the new police soldiers accompanying us and especially their captain, an educated young man from Constantinople named Osman, who had worked in the central telegraph office there. To avoid being sent to the front as a soldier, he had taken this job as petty police-soldier officer and had just arrived in this most bloody district of Boghazliyan. Fortunately, our first day passed without incident, and we stopped for the night at a small Turkish village called Chanter.

On the second day we crossed an extensive plateau. Oh, it was something to behold the beauty of nature reawakening at the start of spring. Having departed Chankiri on February 12, in the dead of winter, we had traveled on roads steeped in snow, and now the second week of March had almost passed. The majority of the deportees in our caravan no longer had shoes, having worn them out; they had subsequently got hold of domestic leather from the Turkish villagers and made sandals, which they were all now wearing.

The charm of greening spring, dotted with yellow, red, and white flowers, was our only comfort. Indeed our hearts bled at the thought of being killed amid the vivid beauties of nature's reawakening. Dying in winter and in such a harrowing way would not have been so distressing—such death would coincide with nature's dormancy. But death in spring was a bitter contradiction, in this season of nature's resurrection. The surrounding green meadows were decorated with meadow saffron (also called spring snowflake), the first fruits of spring. Alongside their white hoods were blue violets sparkling like the eyes of the martyred virgins against the green and white fields. But the beauty of verdant nature was small solace, and we couldn't smell the trees or flowers. These meadows were enchanting, but our minds were filled with images of the dismembered bodies of our compatriots. Our senses were not working right with our hearts in grief, our souls in anguish. Of what benefit to us was spring with its marvelous wonders of providence? What remedy did it offer our troubled hearts?

The bloody specter of the Turk pursued us relentlessly as we crossed mountain and valley like the wind . . . never in one place for more than one night. That specter kept saying, *Doomed Armenian, walk, walk! . . . There's no looking back for you . . . Walk on! . . . Your only salvation is the desert . . . Your only solace is death . . . Just pray that your death won't be harrowing, and never mind that you won't have a grave.*

We remained unmoved by the budding of spring all around us, and passed the first and second day without incident worthy of mention. On the third day, however, just as we were thinking that we had already passed through the frightful parts of the region, we found ourselves facing a real and organized danger that threatened our lives.

We were approaching the stone bridge called Many Eyes [Chok Goz] that spanned the Halys River a half hour away, when suddenly we heard the successive blasts of Mauser guns. Their echoes shook the nearby valleys and hollows, then gradually weakened.

The captain dispatched one of the police soldiers to investigate. We thought that we would turn back and seek refuge in a Turkish village off the road until the danger passed. But when the dispatched police soldier didn't return, the captain sent a second one in the same direction. He did not return either.

Using a secret signal, we instructed Mgrdich, an intrepid and patriotic youth always in the vanguard of our caravan, not to proceed. Seeing that the police-soldier chief was pressing our caravan to advance, we bribed him to delay for about half an hour. But after waiting in vain for the return of the two police soldiers, we had no choice but to continue at an apprehensively slow pace.

We had hardly begun to descend the humped slope extending toward the river when we saw that we had fallen into a trap. Kemal, the bloodthirsty *kaymakam* of Boghazliyan, who had feigned illness when we passed through the town, had informed the Ittihad club of Kayseri by telephone that a caravan of Armenian deportees had set out in their direction. On receiving this news, the Ittihad club immediately rallied its hundred-plus mounted *chetes*, who came to take up their positions along the way to the bridge across the Halys, which every caravan headed for Kayseri had to cross.

Indeed, this bridge was a most suitable site for the execution of crimes . . . The swift river was actually a gorge, formed of gigantic, precipitous rocks on both sides, particularly on the Kayseri side. On the side from which we were coming, there was a plain with numerous caves, and a few half-destroyed stone buildings, as well as an enclosure where the muleteers' animals could rest, or in local parlance, a *khan*.

Most of the mounted *chetes* stabled their horses in these caves, while the horses of the leaders, with their Circassian silver-plated bridles and saddles, were tied up outside. The wandering *chetes* were in Circassian costume; on their heads were black *papakhs* with red tops of newborn lambskin.

In the summer of 1915 thousands of Armenians had been murdered in the most barbarous ways in this gorge, right in front of this bridge, their bodies thrown into the river. But for the past eight or nine months, not a single caravan had passed through. That was because there were no Armenians left in the interior provinces; they had all been "cleansed."

Now this band, thirsty for the blood of innocents, had rushed to greet us at this narrow gorge, its appetite whetted for a fresh bloody feast.

All the *chete* leaders were young Ittihadist officers who had been selected for their ferocity from the regular army. The leader or commander of these brigands, who was most infamous for the massacres committed in Kayseri, was the leader of the local Ittihad club and the municipality as well.

Although the presidents of municipalities, by law, had to be local landowners, the Ittihad Central Committee in Constantinople, to relieve its financial difficulty during the world war, had arranged to replace all the local presidents of the provincial clubs with Ittihad members from Constantinople so they would be paid their monthly salaries out of the town treasuries.

When our hundred-member caravan reached the bridge, five men were waiting in a carriage. I was called over to the carriage and asked where we had come from and why we had been deported so late.

By now eight months had passed since we had been deported from Chankiri and there were no Armenians left in Asia Minor, except those who worked on the railway line. They were the only survivors of the caravans sent to Der Zor; through bribery or other means, they had managed to remain in Eskishehir, Kutahya, Konya, Eregli, Bozanti, Belemedik, or Adana, as laborers and officials in the construction of the Amanos tunnels.

After I gave the required explanation, the men departed in the direction of Boghazliyan. When the carriage reached the top of the nearby hill, overlooking the bridge, it stopped and the men got out. Then they wandered around, smoking, as if they were waiting for something.

All of us had taken them for ordinary travelers, but the police soldiers guarding us and our petty officer told us that in the carriage were the mayor and four members of the Ittihad club of Kayseri. We also learned of the diabolical plan that had brought them here, and of the bloody roles they had played in the deportations during the summer of 1915.

Standing before the bridge was the leader of the *chetes*, a major in the regular army who was wearing a civilian jacket [*sivil*] and military pants with a red stripe. The first police soldier we had sent was with the *chete* leader, who began to beat him with the man's own Martin rifle. The police soldier, not knowing the identity of the band he had discovered, had dared to ask these men firing their Mausers who they were. He had been about to record their names when the *chete* leader grabbed him and beat him severely, cursing the local government for "having made police soldiers out of pieces of wood like this."

Out of the caves facing us, about a hundred feet away, came four or five huge brigands in Circassian dress, exchanging signs and glances. It was a frightening moment. We were a handful of helpless Armenians, hungry, exhausted, and emaciated after weeks of deportation. To massacre us all, they had no need for such a multitude; just ten of these bandits, who had been trained to kill, would have sufficed.

The mounted brigands were stationed on all the escape routes. Our blood froze; our minds weren't working; our consciousness and judgment were drained; we were truly a flock of sheep. If they had attacked us then, we would just have extended our necks to meet the rising and falling knives.

At this point a brigand came and ordered all of us into the walled, uncovered stable, an abandoned sheepfold a few steps away. Many of us began to move toward the fold, and a few entered. It was a critical moment, with death staring us in the face.

We had previously reached an agreement among ourselves that in the event of inescapable disaster, we would run onto the bridge, ten steps away, and jump into the river. With the spring thaw, the Halys had swelled and overflowed until it had become like a vast sea. Surely this deep grave of tens of thousands of Armenians would not refuse to take us too into its flowing turbid currents . . . and save us from harrowing and cruel deaths, at the hands of these Turkish criminals.

Preparing to jump with my mount into the river, my feet still in the stirrups, I was panting, my heart pounding. But just then the attorney Tanielian, one of our original group of intellectuals from Constantinople, came to rouse me from my stuporous terror and exhort me to act. He said, "Reverend Father, don't you see that they're taking us to the stable to kill us? . . . Don't let the people enter it . . . call them out." All this had transpired before my eyes, but so bewildered was I that, for the first time, I had lost my presence of mind. I hadn't noticed that the deportees had begun to enter the stable; my eyes had been steadily fixed on the leader of the brigands.

I immediately told a few brave youths standing near me to go and bring back those who were entering the stable. And I urged everyone else to proceed discreetly toward the river. Asdvadzadour, one of the Chankiri merchants and an extremely popular and kind man, approached the *chete* leader and, as he caressed and kissed his hands, pleaded with him to stop beating our police soldier, and forgive him. The petty police-soldier officer accompanying us also pleaded with the leader on behalf of his fellow police soldier.

Encouraged by the intercessions of these two, I got down from my horse and rushed over to the brigand leader, to join in the pleading for the police soldier. At the same time, I beseeched him to allow us to continue on our way. Releasing the police soldier, the *chete* leader began to question me about our caravan. I hastened to answer all his questions as well and obligingly as I could.

Among other things, I gave him to understand that the forty Armenian families of Chankiri were devoid of political and national consciousness, that they were wretched, innocent Turkish-speaking people. For this reason, I further explained, [the government] had not wished to deport them; they had been sent from their homes only because of a misunderstanding . . . arising from a personal antagonism. I informed him that we were in possession of an official document that in a very beneficial tone confirmed my claims, and I requested that he be kind enough to read it through. I was certain that the tone would make an extremely positive impression on him, as it had on other Turkish civilian and military officials throughout the period of our exile.

We all took a deep breath when, mollified, he turned to the petty officer and demanded the official document. He read it twice; the second time he read aloud the lines "Inform the Minister of the Interior and the government in Chankiri by telegram upon their safe arrival in Kayseri." Then, giving a signal to the Turkish officers around him, who were likewise disguised in civilian dress, he said to me laconically, "You can go" [*Gide bilirsiniz*]. The wrinkled and strained sunburned face of this bloodthirsty ringleader expressed a hunter's anger at the prey's having slipped through his fingers.

We were saved. Our lives had been granted to us. And this whole episode had lasted only twenty minutes at most. After a series of reverential—or rather, servile—Turkish thank-yous [*temmanah*] with the requisite wishes for a long life, which I forced myself to express, I signaled my hapless companions to be on our way.

To our poor caravan, already worn out from walking for six or seven hours, these last minutes had seemed like years. We tried hard to contain our panic until we could get out of this place. None of us dared look back, afraid of turning into pillars of salt. It was a sight to see, these emaciated men in their seventies and eighties, rushing with youthful steps away from that bloody river, that bridge, and those mysterious caves. As we began to ascend the precipice directly opposite the bridge, a few brigands on horseback approached. Fortunately, however, after a few hushed words with our petty officer, they left and headed toward the bridge to join their group—and no doubt report to their bloodthirsty leader on some assignment he had given them.

After a hectic few hours of climbing, we reached a promontory with a new stone *khan*, and it was decided that we would spend the night there. There was the possibility of preparing a supper, but we were all still unnerved by our brush with death near the Halys bridge, and so none of us had any appetite. Rather, we washed up quickly and then lay down on the floor of the spacious coffeehouse.

None of us could sleep or even doze; with our eyes closed, we recalled the terror we had just survived, down to the most minute detail. Many of us raved during the night, letting out terrifying shrieks; some opened their eyes with a start and dashed outside, imagining they were being attacked in the dark. Some too were sobbing quietly, recalling their wives, children, and other loved ones, and all the sweet memories of their former lives. I think we all felt that we had never come so close to the grave.

In the morning, before the sun had fully risen, we hastened to depart these places and their memories. When, as was the custom, I asked the elderly Turkish innkeeper how much we owed for the night's lodging in his *khan*, to our great surprise he answered, "How could it be acceptable to God for me to charge such wretched persons, who, having left behind house and home, family and wealth, are being taken into exile like a flock of sheep?" When I said that every other innkeeper had collected tenfold what was due from us, as much as five silver piasters, he replied, "Those who act thus are godless; this world is one of doers and finders [*iden bulur dunyase dur*; *yah*]. God shall punish those who are bringing these misfortunes upon us; it's too bad that the country is being destroyed at the hands of a few rogues."

After thanking him, we left so we might reach Kayseri the same day without fail. Near the Turkish village of Ekrek we began the ponderous descent of a twisting slope across a series of desolate hills, which took us toward the spacious Kayseri plain.

Barely had we reached the vast sandy plain when a tremendous whirlwind raised clouds and columns of sand around us, burying us where we stood. It was impossible to see. We lay down on the ground, intertwined with one another, our faces down to protect them from the sting of the swirling sands.

Our police-soldier guards were indifferent to our supplications to take us away from here at once, saying only that they had telephoned Kayseri and were awaiting instructions. When the sandstorm grew fiercer, they left us and took refuge in a ruined hut a few hundred meters away. When the sandstorm finally ceased a few hours later, I realized that my groom had taken my horse, together with my bundle, and fled. Outside Yozgat, he had already collected fivefold the usual fee for the horse rental from there to Kayseri.

After sunset police soldiers from Kayseri read the official roll, then received us into their legal custody. The mounted police soldiers, having been abundantly compensated by us, returned to Boghazliyan. We then set out for Kayseri with our new masters.

We were all consoling ourselves that we would finally see a city again, when we realized that instead of taking us into Kayseri, they were escorting us to Talas, a town built on a hill on the edge of the city, an hour away. As we were proceeding along the outskirts of Kayseri, a crowd of curious Turks formed to gawk at us; they were surprised that there were still Armenians left in Anatolia. Some of these Turks furtively approached us and asked whether our late deportation indicated that we had converted to Islam.

Groping along in the evening darkness, we ascended to Talas. When our caravan was passing through the streets of that town, we saw in the windows of the two-story stone houses women clutching handkerchiefs, apparently crying. Subsequently we heard that these were Islamized Armenian families who had been moved at the sight of new caravans of exiled compatriots. No doubt they thought that we too were being taken to Der Zor, that Armenian graveyard without tombstones.

25

Kayseri to Tomarza

When we arrived in Talas, we were taken to the stone *khan* adjoining the Armenian church. Following the deportation of the local Armenians, the Turks were using it for their incidental needs; in the process they had smashed the windows, window frames, and doors of the *khan*, making it a stable. They herded us inside like animals and stationed two soldiers armed with bayonets in front of the huge doors, thus preventing any communication between us and the townspeople.

The solid one-story *khan* had about twelve rooms, some with stone floors, and a few with wooden ones. Pieces of dirty ripped mats still partially covered some of the floors. Our grievance, though, did not concern the unsuitable aspects of this or that *khan*. We had long since gotten used to dirty stables, many times having been forced to spend the night outdoors, subjected to the cold, sleet, snow, and frost, though the Lord had protected us. Whereas earlier, before these years of tribulation, we had been prone to illness caused by a draft coming from an imperceptible opening in a bedroom window, more extreme conditions had since become so ordinary that they no longer affected us; now with the nightmare of death dogging us every hour of every day, we paid them no attention.

Our greatest anxiety, and our rage, which grew as we had to repress it, had to do with being forbidden to buy even dry bread with our own money. Many Islamized Armenian women, now wearing a double veil, and their children, aged about eight to ten, came to the door of the *khan* to offer us bread, cheese, salted and spiced beef, dried fruits, and jugs of water. But the police soldiers kept repeating: "*Yasaktir.*"*

Having walked for more than eight hours that day, we were hungry, and

**Yasaktir*: It's forbidden.—trans.

the sandstorm had parched us, inside and out. Whenever we heard "*Yasaktir,*" mixed with curses, our souls suffered no less than they had the day before when we had been under the threat of death from the *chetes* at the Halys bridge. Unable to express rage in any way, many of us cried and sobbed like little boys.

We had walked continuously for days and weeks, like a flock of migrating birds driven by the autumn winds, entertaining hopes of entering Kayseri, but now we were in Talas and denied our most basic needs. Some dared to buy a few loaves of bread when the police-soldier guards were momentarily distracted; the guards subsequently snatched those loaves from their hands and gave them a severe drubbing for their disobedience.

We resembled Tantalus, the Phrygian king of classical mythology who, for his crimes, was condemned to remain in hell [Tartarus], chin deep in water with fruit-laden branches hanging above his head, unable to drink or eat. We could see the bread but we couldn't eat it; when water spilled from the pails people were carrying, we would envy the dirt on which it spilled.

As our stomachs churned from hunger, we withdrew in small groups to crouch in the small rooms, or to take brief interrupted naps to relieve our fatigue. We tried to console ourselves with the next day's prospects.

This *khan*, which had been a center of Armenian-owned businesses prior to the deportations, adjoined the St. Asdvadzadzin (Holy Mother of God) Armenian mother (main) church. The room in which about ten of us were napping, curled up next to one another for warmth, had two windows that looked out on the courtyard of the church, from which, in the heavy nocturnal darkness we heard a soft voice repeating, "Reverend Father, Reverend Father." One of us arose and went to the window to see where the voice was coming from and what the person wanted. Standing there he saw a group of veiled Armenian women with a boy of about thirteen calling for me. I rushed to climb up to the rather high window.

These Armenian women were Turkish speakers and so had brought an Armenian lad with them to speak to me in Armenian so that no passing night watchman or police soldier would understand us. In a barely audible voice, in his mother tongue, he spoke for the women:

> Reverend Father, as soon as we heard of your arrival, we came with our heads covered with the double veil to the door of your *khan* to bring you bread, water, and food, on the pretext of selling you these things. But the police soldiers drove us away, beating us with whips. Thus, we have to resort to this. Don't worry; the church is in ruins and the surrounding houses are uninhabited;

> just lower a rope from the window so we can give you and the rest bread and other food.

This noble initiative on the part of our mothers and sisters of Kayseri was so unexpected and so providential that our pent-up emotion burst forth, and we began to cry. For the first time since the deportation we were receiving help and compassion from those who themselves were just managing to survive—for these people had been forcibly Islamized, their bodies and souls subjected to unthinkable trials and tribulations. They were Armenian mothers and sisters risking their lives to come to our aid.

If their selfless act had been observed by the police soldiers, the consequences would have been disastrous for them. We were already lost souls bound for Zor, where we would walk into our own graves. But the risk these women took by helping us was that the deceit and sham of their Islamization would become apparent to the Turks.

Taking advantage of the dark, we positioned ourselves to haul up the food. Since we didn't have a long enough rope, the youths among us tied their belts together and lowered them toward the moving shadows. When the signal was given, they pulled up the heavy basket. But it was impossible to bring the basket inside through the iron gates of the windows. Thus we reached outside to empty the basket, and soon there was a pile of bread, cheese, salted and spiced beef, raisins, figs, and dried curds on the floor before our famished eyes. We lowered the empty basket and brought it back up, again full of all kinds of good things to eat. Then we quietly distributed the food to our companions in the adjoining rooms, taking care to avoid being seen by the police soldiers, who fortunately were sleeping.

Despite the darkness, by faint candlelight we could see that there was activity in the Armenian homes near the church; girls and young brides were going from house to house to gather gifts of food. Although we asked for water too, it was impossible to bring the pitcher inside through the iron grates. Nor did we have any sort of vessel into which to empty the pitcher from the outside so we could wet our dried lips and slake our burning thirst. As the pitcher was lowered with a rope again and again you can imagine our anguish after each disheartening result. And our thirst was now exacerbated by the beef spiced with Kayseri garlic that we had just eaten, and the cheese that had been soaking in brine.

When our hunger was satisfied, the women—who had learned by bribing our police soldiers that we had been deported from Constantinople—prodded us for information, especially about Constantinople's Armenians. Believing that city's Armenians had also been deported, they greatly rejoiced at learning that this was not the case, for many of them had relatives there who represented their only hope for salvation and future support.

I had joined in the conversation with them, hoping to gather information about their circumstances, when a young Armenian woman arrived and, speaking in Armenian, said,

> Oh, Reverend Father, we're finished. There's no pain that we haven't suffered; there's no misfortune that hasn't befallen us. They deceived us, saying that if we converted to Islam, we would be saved from all manner of adversity; we became Islamized with the hope of at least rescuing the remnants [of our families]. But our situation worsened; our young brides and girls were forcibly taken in marriage [*nikah*] to the harems. There is no cruelty that they didn't commit, there is no torture that they didn't administer to us. We would have been better off if we had gone into exile and died; that way we would have been freed at last, and we wouldn't have stained our consciences. Oh, where is the God proclaimed by us? Doesn't he see the infinite suffering we have endured?

Then the youth, still standing beneath our window near the women, asked, "Reverend Father, are the Russians near? . . . The Turks of our city are telling us that there are no longer any Armenians left in Turkey; is that true? . . . Where are they taking you?"

"Poor boy," I answered. "How should I know where they are taking us? . . . And why the God of the Armenians is unmerciful in the face of our boundless woes and innocent blood—how should I know, while I'm in such misery?

"Yes, good days will come . . . This time, of course, spring will finally come for the Armenians . . . but only the survivors will see it . . . How lucky, so very lucky will be the eyes of those who will be able to hail the dawn of Armenian independence!"

After spending a turbulent yet comforting night, in the morning we bore witness to a scene even more comforting, which moved us all very much. This time it was the girls of Kayseri, who were striving to surpass their self-sacrificing mothers.

For many years now Talas had been one of the provincial centers of enlightenment, where selfless and noble American women, pioneers of civilization in the Orient, had come and established residence. Assembled at the American girls' college of Talas* were not only the girls of most of the Armenian families that had gone into exile rather than accept Islam, but also the girls of the few Armenian families that had converted and remained. Permanently separated from their martyred parents, these

*U.S. Protestant missionary college, and later boarding school, established in Talas near Kayseri in 1871.—trans.

homeless, defenseless birds were without nests or wings and, having been chased by ravenous hawks and buzzards, had taken refuge under the star-spangled, disinterested American flag.

When the dainty Armenian girls at this college heard that a large new caravan of deportees with a *vartabed*, priest, and laymen from far away had arrived in town and that they would be walking for months toward Zor, these girls spent the whole night crying and praying. Seeing this muted mourning, their noble American headmistress was moved to allow them to offer us the full portion of their next day's meals.

As soon as she heard of our arrival that night, the gracious director, Mrs. [Jane S.] Wingate, had rushed to Kayseri (an hour away) and requested permission from the Turkish governor to assist us. Wary of assuming sole responsibility in this regard, the governor sent her to the commander of the police soldiers. After coming and going thus in the dark of night, she succeeded in obtaining written permission to come and feed us the following day.

Having made all the preparations the night before, early the next morning she brought us enough milk, cheese, pilaf, soup, pastry, bread, and apples, along with a full array of utensils, to satisfy a hundred persons. She also brought the most suitable of the Armenian college girls to serve us.

When the main door of our *khan*-jail opened and these angels of mercy entered carrying baskets of food, an indescribable excitement gripped us all. More indispensable than nourishment for our tormented souls was the word or two of compassion and pity that the headmistress spoke to cool our hearts. This noble and selfless American woman asked me to sit next to her and tell her about our journey, and when the command was given, the deportees sat in groups and began to eat insatiably. We had long since forgotten milk, cheese, pastry, and apples, because until we arrived in Talas, our only sustenance had been dry bread, onions, garlic, and sometimes wheat pilaf and *tarhana* soup [made of dried curds and pearled wheat]. The Armenian girls served these delicacies to the emaciated remnants of their ill-starred nation.

Many of the young Armenian intellectuals in the caravan were so moved that despite their hunger, they didn't eat at all but were consumed with voicing their thoughts about why these orphaned sisters had come to our rescue with their compassion and assistance, when instead we should have been helping them. It was an eruption of our wounded male dignity, which hadn't yet disappeared from our worn bodies.

In addition to the food, the female teachers and girls of the college, having taken up a collection among themselves, handed me a knotted handkerchief containing 420 silver piasters. They requested that we bless the coins and distribute them to the neediest among us. Not only did we bless—and will forever bless—them, we also record their noble gesture in this enduring memoir of Armenian tribulation, so that all future Armenian generations, from year to year and from century to century, will likewise bless you, self-sacrificing and compassionate Armenian girls, together with your mothers and your female teachers.

I asked the benevolent Mrs. Wingate for a loan of gold pounds, which we absolutely required to help our destitute comrades. This noble director recommended that I prepare a receipt for a twenty-five-gold-pound loan; meanwhile she rushed back to the college to get the money.

While this benevolent American woman was running to fetch the money, the captain who was the commander of the police soldiers in Talas suddenly entered and severely drubbed our police soldiers, loudly reprimanding them for letting the American teachers and girls talk to us about our plight and what we had seen along the way. This was the reason the police soldiers didn't take us into cities; they didn't want us to communicate to anybody the truth about the horrible massacres.

As punishment, the police-soldier captain ordered that we prepare to depart in a few hours; he absolutely forbade us even to rent beasts of burden to transport our possessions. Seeing that all appeals in this regard were fruitless, we had no choice but to divide up our small bundles among ourselves and then set out toward evening for Tomarza.

All of us were agitated, as our cup of misery and bitterness had long since overflowed. The food we had eaten in the morning, and the care and attention we had enjoyed, soon gave way to sighs and tears. Yes, we'd been abandoned by both God and mankind; our only salvation was the grave, but we couldn't even count on that. No spadeful of earth would cover us—we would be food for vultures and wild beasts.

As our caravan of one hundred proceeded on foot, we went through the narrow muddy streets of Talas, passing in front of the American college. The Armenian girls, the Armenian women teachers, and the kind director all stood at the windows or on the roof, crying into their handkerchiefs. The Islamized Armenian women, concealed behind the windows of the neighboring houses, also cried. Our caravan of deportees was like a funeral procession, in which we were both the deceased and the mourners, walking toward an uncertain end.

By inexplicable coincidence, at that moment the bells of the Greek church began to peal. The ringing of the church bell, the hundred-man procession, the *vartabed* and priest at its head, the crying women and girls at the windows—it was a perfect illusion, missing only wax candles and a black cross. Alas! Even without a cross, we were all climbing the thorny Armenian Golgotha.

When we first heard the pealing bell, the sound echoing from the nearby valleys, we shuddered to the depths of our souls, because we had not heard the bell of any Christian church for a year now. Yes, it was announcing that the Armenian race had died—and we were the last funeral procession, bound for Der Zor to disappear in its arid plains.

Out of Kayseri's once-large Armenian population of some 3,000 households, we left behind only 260 Islamized Armenian houses. The rest were deported, under the guise of exile, and massacred; the young brides and girls were taken to harems and forced into concubinage. The famous St. Garabed monastery was plundered and converted into a Turkish orphanage, while its surrounding properties were distributed among the newly arrived Turkish refugees.

The exquisite church of Talas, which had been the prelate's headquarters, was now the roost of hooting owls. The right side of the church, as well as the marble slabs of the tombs of former prelates located beneath the *khan* where we had stayed, had been shattered to pieces. The vacant houses of Armenian deportees who had been slaughtered on the roads were taken over by Turkish refugees from the interior provinces. During the winter that had just passed, they had smashed to pieces and used for firewood all the furnishings of the Armenian houses in which they now resided.

Whereas the chaste Armenian college girls were crying over us, we in turn were crying over the black fate awaiting them. It was still only the second year of the war, and many dark days, bringing new bloody surprises, were still to come before the Armistice. Indeed, when America declared war against Germany, and Turkey hastened to sever its relations with America, the American women of the Talas college were sent back home. The Armenian college girls, in turn, were taken to the harems of Turkish notables, to be made victims of unimaginable debauchery.

Climbing up the side of the mountain named Kohanam or St. Parsegh (after the patriarch), located precisely behind Talas on the road from Talas to Tomarza, our caravan reached a spacious plateau; we then began to walk swiftly, as the police soldiers goaded us with their clubs.

By the time we reached a village populated by *kizilbash*—two hours from Talas—to spend the night, the sun had long since set. We had barely gotten settled, however, when the police soldiers ordered us to continue on our way. We were overcome with dread at this inexplicable command, but having no choice, we again set out and began to descend a deep rocky valley. Then the few young Armenian fighters who were always in the vanguard of our caravan suddenly ran up to me in dismay and said, "Reverend Father, moving shadows and heads are visible behind those rocks. For God's sake, let's turn back; we're in danger."

Immediately locating our *chavush*, I informed him of the imminent danger and promised a generous tip, provided he would save us. The *chavush*, taken by surprise as well, ordered us to turn back at once and get out of the valley. We subsequently found out that the Turkish villagers had objected to our spending the night in their village; furthermore, the villager whom they had given us as a guide had been instructed to lead us to this valley. Here the villagers, having taken a shortcut, lay in wait for us, in order to kill us and seize our possessions.

Because our police soldiers and especially our *chavush* had had no part in this plot, they did what they could to rescue us from certain mortal danger. After groping along in the darkness for two or three hours, we arrived at a broken-down *khan* in a desolate location. This *khan* was a large one-room stable, in which there were about twenty-five or thirty horses, mules, and donkeys. It could not accommodate a caravan of a hundred people as well; therefore we promised to pay if the animals were removed to make room for us. But the Turkish muleteers responded that their animals were more valuable than us, or in their word, *kismetli.**

By paying a generous reward in advance, we secured from the *khan*'s owner the right to remain with the animals. But inasmuch as they had wet the floor, we were forced to buy straw, for five to ten piasters, to spread over it. Indeed, our situation was deplorable; we were downright envious of the animals next to us, which were so well cared for, while we were being chased away like lepers.

That evening I found a corner for myself and, scattering some straw there, lay down, using a stone covered with straw as my pillow. We consoled ourselves, recalling the certain fatal danger of a few hours earlier, and were glad to be worthy of a stable like this, which for us was a palace. It was so bitterly cold outside, thanks to the huge snowcapped Mount Argeos not far from here, that we were shivering. Still, inside the stable there was quite a bit of heat, as our breath mingled with the hot breath of the animals.

Throughout our journey, but especially along the Yozgat–Boghazliyan–Kayseri route, we had noticed that the majority of the police soldiers guarding us passed their nights on horseback, without sleeping. Seeing the sentry right next to me in this position now, I asked why he wasn't sleeping. He replied:

> *Papaz,*† I killed so many people in this past year that my victims won't let me sleep peacefully. I can't even close my eyes because

**Kismetli:* lucky.—trans.

†Turkish for priest, clergyman, monk, friar.—trans.

> those I dismembered appear before me. In particular, the souls of the more than twenty virgin girls whom I violated and then killed won't let go of me.

Was this perhaps remorse? If so, why were they always perpetrating new massacres? Why did they seem to have an insatiable thirst for innocent blood?

At dawn the following day we departed this den of thieves. Fortunately, the second day passed without incident; the nightmare of death, however, had become flesh and bone for us, and we proceeded with constant apprehension. All of us were on foot now, and because many were weighed down with bundles, we walked slowly and were often subjected to the blows of our guards' cudgels. At sunrise on the third day, as we entered the plain of Tomarza, we encountered flocks of migrating birds heading north, toward Armenia. It was already the end of March 1916: spring was all around us; nature had begun to revive; the trees and flowers, wearing green and many other colors, were glorifying the Creator with their resurrected beauty. Flocks of swallows were going toward Armenia to rebuild their old nests under the roofs of their paternal homes and start a new life.

Oh, how touching was the immortal Totokhian's song:

Far yonder I have a father,
White-haired and in mourning,
Who is waiting daily
For the return of his only son.

Oh, sweet blissful days when there was just one grieving father waiting in the homeland. Today, with the entire fatherland bathed in blood and all the Armenian survivors in mourning, we were lamenting the myriad victims slaughtered like a million sheep, and we knew that even blacker days awaited us. Yes, black days, when we would be longing for all black days past . . . because the closer we drew to the summit, the thornier became the Armenian Golgotha.

Sweet young birds of spring, where are you going oh so fast? The fatherland is in ruins, owls are hooting under the roofs, the bloody plains are covered with corpses, and the deep valleys and caves are full of them. Return, return to your old haunts, go back to where you came from, and tell about what you saw and heard of the widespread woes and deathly happenings, salty, bitter tears of the Armenians. Flee, flee, sprightly swallows; flee, young birds, harbingers of spring; your nests, your place, is not here, where there is grief and mourning, blood and tears. In your place let the corpse-pecking birds, the buzzards, hawks, and vultures, come.

If they come this year, however, these birds will not find torn-apart corpses, which last year made feasts for lions. You black vultures, go down toward Mesopotamia, where feasts of justice are awaiting you in Kut-al-Amara, or up to the Dardanelles. One stronger than the other, the Turks too fell wounded; the Turks, who crucified justice, were killed in myriad number, and justice was partially fulfilled.

With a half hour remaining in our journey to Tomarza, eight or ten men on horseback greeted us, making us all apprehensive. The *kaymakam* of Tomarza had come with his mounted policemen to escort our caravan of emaciated deportees to the town. When we passed through Tomarza, we saw that all the stores were closed, and all the houses were filled with Turkish refugees: there were no traces of Armenians, those who had previously been the only industrious cultivators of these spacious fertile plains.

26

Tomarza to Gazbel

Located on a fertile plateau, Tomarza is the seat of a small district government (*kaymakamlik*), barely two days from Kayseri; it is approximately 1,200 meters high. Prior to the deportations of 1915, 60 percent of the villages in the Tomarza district and 80 percent of the town's population were Armenian. Since then, however, the Armenian houses and lands had been turned over to Turkish refugees.* Only a few butcher shops and grocery stores remained open, along with a few small, dirty Turkish coffeehouses.

During the winter the houses not occupied by refugees had been demolished for firewood. The roof of the St. Toros church had been torn down; the St. Asdvadzadzin (Holy Mother of God) monastery, just a half hour away, was largely destroyed. Only two of the town's numerous free-flowing fountains were still working; the others had dried up.

We visited with a few local Turks, who were pained to tell us that the

*Many of these Turkish refugees were from the Balkans and Crimea following recent wars there.—trans.

town had neither a shoemaker nor a smith to repair a broken plowshare; all the artisans in their district had been Armenians and were deported. Thus the Turks were forced to make a two-day trip all the way to Kayseri to have their shoes repaired—again, by Armenians who had managed to remain there by converting to Islam. But it must be stressed that only 10 percent of the Armenians of Kayseri and the surrounding regions wished to save themselves by Islamization. The rest willingly submitted to deportation and set out for Zor, knowing that they were headed for annihilation in the desert from which there was no salvation.

Being deprived, once and for all, of centuries of Armenian skill and talent, the Turks had realized, for the first time, that they could do nothing without the constructive and creative work of the Armenians; that indeed the Armenians had been a pillar of the Ottoman Empire, as farmers, artisans, merchants, bankers, doctors, pharmacists, financiers, artists, architects, engineers, and politicians.

Now that the Armenian people were gone, the Turks had begun to admit that the country's blessings and abundance had gone with them. For centuries Tomarza, thanks to the industrious Armenian peasantry, had been the granary of the surrounding regions. Now not only couldn't we find wheat bread but we were barely able to get black bread made of wild oats [*delije*], which was extremely hard to digest and of which we could buy hardly one hundred drams for five silver piasters.

The fields of Tomarza, once full of ears of wheat, and the surrounding lands that had belonged to the Armenians now lay fallow and abandoned. There was neither plow handle nor plowman; there was neither plow nor ox fit for harness.

The night we spent in Tomarza was rather restless, this time for internal reasons. Of the hundred members of our caravan, about twenty-five or thirty had means of subsistence; the remaining ones, particularly the fifty natives of Yozgat, lacked two necessities—bread and sandals. A few of our wealthy deportees from Chankiri no longer wished to help them, objecting that they too had now become poor and that the poverty of the coming days terrified them. The needy ones made threats, but the dissension was curtailed when a little bread money was solicited for them. In addition, by securing another personal loan from *haji* Setrag Shakhian, I was able to take care of my companions' extremely urgent needs and mine as well. In Tomarza all whose sandals were worn out either had them repaired or bought new ones before we set out the following day for Gazbel.

We had barely gotten out of town and entered the plain when an extraordinary scene appeared before our eyes. The entire spacious plain was covered with yellowish fields; it was autumn in spring. In fact, the plain was yellow because of the hundreds of unharvested wheat fields. The deportation of the Armenians had coincided with autumn, thus the departing Armenians had been forbidden to reap the harvest. Seeing around us sheaves that had been tied and piled in the yellowish wheat fields made the illusion of autumn complete. Although a winter had passed, only the ears of wheat had fallen to the ground while the stalks still stood tall and strong, waving in the wind.

Yes, it was autumn in spring. Curiosity moved me to ask the police soldiers why these fields hadn't been harvested. One of them replied:

> The *kaymakam* of Tomarza was such an Armenian-hater that when the deportation order came from Constantinople in August 1915, he did not let the Armenian peasants make the harvest. If he had permitted it, their deportation would have been postponed for at least a month. Our *kaymakam*, in turn, said, "Neither is their wheat necessary, nor do we need to see their faces for an extra month. Let them go and get lost."

Naturally, I yielded to temptation and asked why, after the Armenians were deported, the *kaymakam* had not allowed the neighboring Turkish peasants to make the harvest; the wheat and barley had long since matured, and the crop was so abundant. I pointed out further that in time of war, every government endeavored to store as much grain as possible in order to prevent a highly probable famine.

The same police soldier responded, "*Effendi*, after the Armenians were deported, the *bereket*, namely the blessing and the abundance, disappeared from our land. That was the reason, wasn't it?"

Rightly so. In subsequent years we found out from those who came to Belemedik from Kayseri that with the fertile fields of Tomarza remaining unplowed and untilled, bread had become so scarce and so expensive that the Turkish people had begun to die of starvation.

We passed through these abundant wheat fields of Tomarza moved to tears. The Armenian people had departed eight or nine months before from their paternal hearths of thousands of years, never to return, yet the golden result of their creative labor was still there as a silent protest against the injustice they had suffered. Everywhere, all around us on a vast expanse to the distant horizons, was an immense sea of yellowish wheat fields, often dotted with sheaves, piles, and ricks. And here and there herbivorous domesticated animals had come to graze.

It was impossible to grasp what kind of madness, what maniacal frenzy had gripped the government officials, to the point where they would destroy so many working hands and so much productivity. The Ottoman government had committed suicide—and the day was not far off when it would suffer the disastrous and unavoidable consequences of its crimes, when the frightful day of justice would finally arrive.

On the second day after our departure from Tomarza, we spent the night in a large village of about 130 households; 90 of them had belonged to Armenian deportees, and so the town was almost completely in ruins. We enjoyed a very good reception in this village and went about acquiring basic foodstuffs at rather modest prices. The local Turkish alderman [*muhtar*] and chaplain [*imam*], along with a few elderly Turkish villagers, hearing that there was a prelate in the arriving caravan, hastened to pay us a visit. This was the first time throughout our lengthy journey that we had merited such an honor, to the great surprise of us all.

Because the Turks with whom we were engaged in conversation were naïve villagers, ignorant of the official formalities, they expressed themselves without reserve. Here an opportunity presented itself to get a sense of the psychology of these people, particularly since the *imam*, a credible individual who had been to Constantinople, seemed to be a bright man. He even understood rudimentary Armenian (having learned some from his villagers) and often used Armenian words in his conversation.

After the usual Oriental courtesies of welcome, the Turks asked me, "*Murahhasa effendi*, when will our Armenian neighbors return from exile? Why are our neighbors so late in coming back? When Sultan Hamid used to punish the Armenians, he would pardon them. Why haven't the Young Turks ended this persecution that they started against the Armenians? The country has become desolate. What are they waiting for?"

In reply, I asked them whether perhaps they weren't content that the area was left solely to them, without a competitor, by the exile of their neighbors for centuries, the Armenians. After all, they had come to own the deported Armenians' homes, gardens, orchards, lands, flocks of sheep, and movable and immovable goods—ultimately their entire wealth. What more could they want? Weren't they grateful to the Ittihad government for having, overnight, brought them such immense wealth, such as they couldn't have imagined in their wildest dreams?

On behalf of his friends, the *imam* replied:

> *Murahhasa effendi*, what are you saying? Do you think that we are content over the deportation of the Armenians? . . . There were 130 households in our village and 90 of them were Armenian; our 40 Turkish households made a living thanks to our Armenian neighbors, as agriculture and the trades were in their hands. We worked on their lands as partners [*ortak*], and we lived well and were prosperous. Talaat and Enver deserve to die for deporting

> the Armenians, whereby they ravaged the country and impoverished us as well. Until now, we used to pay 20 to 30 *paras* for an *oke* of soft, cottonlike white bread;* now we've started paying 20 to 30 piasters, and tomorrow who knows how much it will cost! *Effendi*, tell us, is there no hope at all then that our Armenian neighbors will return to their homes?

Our conversation was extremely interesting, and their concern was sincere and candid; therefore, we too began to express ourselves unreservedly, especially since none of the police soldiers had remained with us, having gone to rest their horses.

I replied, "*Hoja effendi*, you await the return of your Armenian neighbors in vain. It's been a year now since their annihilation on the roads began. If a scarce few have made it to Der Zor, they too are dead of starvation and thirst in the desert." Incidentally, inasmuch as the Armenians of Tomarza had been deported quite early on, the majority managed to reach Der Zor alive. There, however, some of them died of hunger, while most of them were mercilessly slaughtered in the general massacre of July 1916 in Ras-ul-Ain and Der Zor.

"But tell us, *hoja effendi*," I continued, "tell us. What's the news from Constantinople? We've been on the road for more than a month, and we're out of touch. What's new? . . . Is it calm in Constantinople?"

He replied:

> Oh, *murahhasa effendi*, there's no hope whatsoever of imminent peace. We gave our collar to the Germans; whether we like it or not, we shall go in whatever direction they pull us. Enver is said to have fled, but we've heard that a thousand times, and it's turned out to be false a thousand times. Oh, when will we hear, Allah, that Talaat and Enver have been killed like dogs? . . . There hasn't been a misfortune that they haven't brought upon this poor nation . . . Cursed be they—if only the Young Turks didn't exist . . . they have neither faith nor religion; they're all Masons . . .
>
> Previously, in the old regime, there was one Sultan Hamid. Now we've got a hundred Sultan Hamids over our heads . . . We have long since begun to seek Sultan Hamid again . . . *murahhasa effendi*, don't think that we Turks have been or will be happy [*ihya*] . . . the weeper's goods [*mal*] and property [*mulk*] do not bring happiness to the buyer or taker . . .
>
> The Armenians were the salt of our land. They left . . . that

*One para = 1/40 of a piaster; one oke = 400 drams, or 2.83 pounds.—G.B.

> which gave us taste and aroma is gone . . . may God look after us all.

Meanwhile the others said twice and thrice "Amen, amen" [*Amin, amin*] . . .

Several times they mentioned that inasmuch as I was a clergyman, they would "confess" to me, using the Armenian word for it—*khosdovanank*. They added that if the government officials were to hear that they had spoken to me this way, they too would be deported and subjected to *tarmar*; that is, they would be destroyed . . . The unreserved utterances of these sincere villagers brought solace to our grieving hearts. During the five years of our suffering, I can recall only one or two such instances of repentance . . .

We hastened to depart at dawn the next day, having a wearisome ten-hour distance to cover. At sunset, we finally arrived at Gazbel, one of the highest passes in the Taurus mountain chain, and spent the night in a small Avshar village called Keoseler.

27

Gazbel to Hajin

Located at the mouth of the gorge called Gazbel [Goose waist], this village called Keoseler had barely twenty-five households. The gorge is the only natural passage connecting the plateau of Tomarza with the Cilician plain, via the neck-shaped valley stretching from Hajin to Sis.

The Taurus mountain chain rises from the edge of the Mediterranean Sea at Mersin and Seleucia, then gradually gains elevation as it proceeds eastward toward the Armenian chain and then on to the Caucasus. The Taurus mountains have only two natural gates from the north: the first is the Gulek Bogazi pass in Bozanti-Belemedik, through which the railroad goes to Aleppo via long tunnels; the second is the Gazbel pass, through which we went. These are the natural gateways to Cilicia, where under the Rubenid kings [1080–1226] so many fortresses had been successively built as bulwarks against the attacks of the sultans of Konya.

The Taurus mountain chain has snowcapped peaks and is surrounded by virgin cedar forests. It is the perpetually flowing basin of the turbulent rivers of Cilicia: Saros (Sihun) and Brimos (Jihun), Gitnos (Tarsus irmaghe) and Galigatnos (Zilifge irmaghe), the source of the famous fertility of the ample Cilician plain.

One coming from Tomarza must descend a 200-meter wooded slope to get to this Keoseler village, where there was a police guardhouse with a telephone connection to Tomarza and Hajin. This natural gorge, dug out of these mountains standing 2,000 to 3,000 meters high (the only pass to the Cilician plain), is a marvel of nature.

When we reached this pass at the end of March, it was entirely covered with thick layers of snow. For a few weeks now all travel had come to a complete halt, even between villages an hour from each other, inside the pass.

The petty officer of the guardhouse was a polite young man from Constantinople who, having many Armenian friends, appeared to feel bad about the great disaster that had befallen the Armenians. I must confess that he received us with compassion and respect, which was an exceptional honor for us. He took me to his private room, and after personally preparing Turkish coffee, he brought and served it to me, despite the readiness of the police soldiers under his command to be of service. Likewise, instead of confining the hundred of us, he permitted us the freedom to find places in the huts of the Avshars.

The Avshar villagers likewise received us with respect in their rustic homes. It is widely thought that the Avshars were Armenians who had been forcibly Islamized, and generally speaking, they are very friendly to Christians, particularly Armenians. They don't know the meaning of "stranger," and their women did not shy away from us at all.

Their houses were one-room huts with very small windows, four low walls, and a sod roof. The interior was divided into two sections with nothing more than poles nailed to the floor: the inner section was occupied by the animals, and the family lived in the section near the door. Nevertheless, the inhabitants of both sections could see each other. The advantage of this cohabitation was that the heat generated in the inner section of the hut helped to offset the bitter winter cold, especially at dawn and dusk, when it is most severe. The villagers also warmed themselves with fires, which were always going, inasmuch as firewood was available in the forests adjoining their settlement. Still, they valued their animals more than themselves and were more solicitous toward them.

In this small village we encountered another Armenian caravan of fifteen or twenty individuals. They had arrived several days before us and had gotten stuck here because of the snow. They too had come from Kayseri, except for two brothers from Adapazar, who had been brought here from Constantinople via Konya and Kayseri. All of them, in turn, had become Islamized, including two priests who now wore green turbans.

I was drinking my coffee and carrying on a friendly conversation with the petty officer when a man with an unmistakably Turkish appearance, wearing a white turban, came into the room and invited me to join him for supper. I momentarily hesitated, not sure whether this was a trap.

When the petty officer turned to giving orders to the police soldiers, the Turk approached me and whispered, "Reverend Father, don't be afraid. I'm Armenian. Come with me, I've got something to tell you" [*Hayr surpum, korkma hayem, hai, gel taame beraber idelim, deyejeyim var*]. I was surprised to suddenly find out that the individual I had thought was a Turk, which had caused me so much alarm, was Armenian. For appearances' sake, however, I said out loud, "Since I'm a guest of the guardhouse petty officer, I can't accept another invitation. Only if the officer comes with me would I be willing to go."

The young petty officer understood immediately that I was asking permission and quickly replied that I could accept the invitation, adding that he would come to visit us deportees after supper. Thus, I followed the turbaned Armenian toward his hut, a well-built home belonging to one of the village notables and better than the other huts. Inside I had barely stretched out on one of the beds when the wife of our Armenian host entered with their four children. She fell at my feet crying, and because she was not from Kayseri, in Armenian she said, "Reverend Father, I respect your office, you're a servant of God, we were forcibly Islamized . . . Grant us pardon for God's sake so that we can at least die in peace."

My emotion was overflowing too, because at this point, father, mother, grown-up daughter, and three little boys had fallen to their knees, clinging to and kissing the hem of my coat, crying, and begging for forgiveness.

My God, this was a grievous and tragic scene for the pastor of a people. With my own eyes I had seen my flock scattered and devoured by wolves, the unburied bodies of martyrs become food for grave-robbing hyenas. As for the survivors, they had been forcibly Islamized. Now, by mere coincidence, pastor and flock had met on these historic Armenian mountains of the Taurus range, and inside, I was shedding tears for those already dead and for those of us who would be dying soon.

The poor woman said, "Thank God that the Lord deemed us worthy of seeing with our own eyes for one more time a religious leader of our nation." Indeed, Armenian clergymen had become so scarce that the only surviving ones in all these interior provinces of Asia Minor were the elderly Father Housig Kachouni and I.

Finally, through questioning them, I found out that despite having become Islamized, they had been exiled anew from Kayseri during this bitterly cold winter for the following reason. The lively and vivacious eight-year-old son of this family used to get into arguments and fights with the neighborhood Muslim boys his age. One day, angry after getting beaten up, he threatened the Muslim boys, saying, "When the Russians come, we shall beat and kill you" [*Mosgof geise, bizde sizi doyejeyiz ve oldurejeyiz*].

The parents of the Turkish boys informed the governor of Kayseri of this comment. Though the boy had made it in naïveté, during a fit of anger, nevertheless they ascribed grave significance to it. Officials in both the upper and lower ranks of the local government added fuel to the fire by explaining that if the Islamized Armenians hadn't secretly discussed such matters and expressed such opinions in their homes, their children wouldn't be making such "serious" threats against Turkish children.

So without investigation, the government decided to exile this family, claiming that no matter how Islamized, an Armenian was still an enemy of the Turkish state [*dovlet, millet dushmane*]. The entire family, its near and distant relatives, including two elderly Islamized priests—sixteen persons in all—were put on the road to Der Zor in the freezing winter.

When they reached Gazbel, however, they found the pass buried under weeks of snow. They were unable to cross it, particularly with all their baggage and several horses. By bribing the petty police-soldier officer, they received permission to remain in this Avshar village until the road was open. In this way, they were able to extend their stay and rest.

At this point supper was served, but none of us had any appetite left. We were full of emotion from telling one another about the adversities we had experienced . . . and from our fears of what was yet to come. Nevertheless, we were attempting to eat something when the poor Armenian woman, feeling such deep remorse over her apostasy, begged me to consider the table before me a Christian and not a Muslim one and to bless it accordingly. Behold, the sobbing began anew; everybody was crying, husband and wife, daughter and innocent little sons. The Lord's Prayer ended with sobbing.

I had barely sat down again when mother and daughter earnestly beseeched me to hear their confessions and give them communion.

How could an exiled clergyman have carried the elements of Holy Communion or any ecclesiastical book while wandering for a year from one mountain to the next? Still, they were imploring me so ardently and plaintively that I had to find a way to do this for them. After all, the Holy Gospel recommends that forgiveness be given seven times seventy times. How could I ignore such tearful penitence, following forced Islamization? How could I deprive them of the ultimate solace of religion on this horrible road of death, when I myself with my hundred companions also stood on the threshold between life and death, my gaze fixed on eternity?

I heard their confessions and gave them a heartfelt and tearful blessing. Then, lacking wine, I dipped the bread in vinegar and gave it to them to relish as Holy Communion. After all, vinegar mixed with bitters was given to the crucified Jesus at the end. At the same time, the life we lived was more bitter and acerbic than the bitters offered to Christ. In the final analysis, the vinegar had come from wine . . . It was the commemoration not only of the innocent blood spilled drop by drop from Jesus' rib, but also of the oceans of innocent blood spilled by a million Armenian martyrs.

But such a collapse had occured in the deep secret folds of our souls that none of us had any desire to eat. Indeed, we had suffered hours of spiritual torture in which we wished for salvation in death—provided it didn't come from ax blows, which brought agonizing pain.

After this table of tears, I spoke with two young patriotic brothers from the other caravan, natives of Adapazar and residents of Constantinople, who had been accused of being Hunchaks and were exiled to Der Zor. After they reached Konya by train, police soldiers took them from there via Ulukishla to Kayseri, where they were to have continued by train toward Adana-Aleppo; instead in Kayseri they were exiled with the Islamized natives via Gazbel, en route to Aleppo.

The following was written in the official document pertaining to them: "As longtime activists of the Hunchak Party, these two brothers were working to have the sections of the Ottoman Empire divided among foreign powers; therefore, they are enemies of the Turkish state."

Having written such things, the authorities wished to subject them to the wrath of the vindictive police soldiers . . . But like us and many others, these two had spent large sums of money, and by giving bribes, they had been able to escape the plots and fatal traps the police soldiers set for them.

So it was that we scattered and wretched survivors had come together by chance in this snow-covered pass of the Taurus mountains, and we secretly consoled one another, each lulling the others into dreams of tomorrow's salvation . . . It was these two courageous brothers who first suggested that I escape, and tried to convince me that only those who ran away could be saved. I, however, refused to abandon my companions, particularly since I was already conjuring plans for a way for the entire caravan to flee.

At midnight the officer of the police guardhouse came to visit, as he had said he would. But when he saw eight or ten of us sitting, sad and dejected, consoling one another, he suspected that perhaps we were pondering plans of escape. He then asked me and the host to stay, and told the others to go back to their places to sleep.

For the first night since leaving Chankiri, I had a bed to sleep in, but none of us was able to sleep. Could we possibly sleep after so much emotional turmoil and physical pain? Shortly after dawn, at their invitation, I visited the remaining members of this caravan of Kayseri natives, among whom, as I have noted, were two Islamized priests wearing green turbans. I'm happy to say that during our deportation these were the only two clergymen we encountered who had renounced their faith. Naturally we comforted one another without dwelling on their Islamization; we even affected ignorance of the circumstance of the matter, especially since they were trying to conceal their previous clerical status.

The signal was given to depart, so we had to take leave of our companions from Kayseri; by using the snow as a pretext and paying substantial bribes, they would remain for another couple of weeks until the snows melted and the road opened. As for us, however, the police soldiers made us set forth, claiming that, as men, we could proceed on foot along the narrow ribbonlike path (about eighteen inches wide) over the thick layer of snow.

We were about to get going, and all the members of the caravan were lined up in pairs. As was customary, the police soldiers took count to verify that we were all there. Holding the official list of our names, the petty officer read them aloud, and we responded accordingly, saying "He's here" [*Burada der*]. An eighteen-year-old youth from Yozgat was missing, and his compatriots from Yozgat whispered that he had fled. We were all astonished by the temerity of his action; where could he flee in the snowy winter on these deserted mountains? Even if he eluded the two-legged tigers, he would fall prey to the hungry four-legged wolves. After almost an hour's delay for a search for him, we set out with great anxiety, because this was our first loss.

The petty officer said with a sarcastic laugh, "Don't worry; I'll find him and send him along. I'll make sure he catches up with you, without fail." When we finally got on the move, the police soldiers told us in confidence that they had the right to summarily execute deserters, and made clear that we shouldn't expect to see him again. Sure enough, not long after our departure, police soldiers coming from Gazbel reported that they had found the youth on the road to Tomarza and clubbed him to death on the spot. Despite great grief at our loss of an unlucky companion, who was the Benjamin* of our caravan, those of us who had been thinking of fleeing now lost all hope of doing so.

Truly, it is very difficult, if not impossible, to describe in true colors the

*Biblical founder of the Israelite tribe of Benjamin, he was said to be beloved of Yahweh and to never have sinned.—trans.

tortuous journey we made from the Avshar village of Keoseler to Saraijuk, where we spent the night. This small Kurdish village was in the pass, surrounded by inaccessible and untamed mountains. It consisted of about twenty-five huts that bowed under the snow burying them, as if on the verge of collapse.

In summertime, the trip on foot between these two villages took no more than an hour, but now it took about six hours because the snow was almost three meters deep, which had impeded all communication for weeks. We had contended with all sorts of human persecution, but now nature had become cruel too.

Stumbling along very slowly, our hundred-man caravan—which included boys of eighteen as well as emaciated eighty-year-old men, some barefoot no less—ascended and descended through the gorge. Many of us were carrying not only our own essential belongings but also those of our companions: a bread bag, a few pieces of old underwear, a strip of an old dirty blanket, shreds of clothing or worn-out shoes, a tin drinking cup, a worn-out European cover [*batania*], and so on. Parting with any one of them was impossible, as they all seemed indispensible, and they were the last remnants of our past glory and wealth.

Like a caravan of camels stretched out in single file, we proceeded with great caution, for if one stumbled or got stuck, those behind him would lose control and fall. With the gorge buried under snow for weeks, the villagers had opened a path two spans wide, upon which the snow had hardened. But one wrong step, and a man would fall off the path and find himself buried up to the neck in snow.

Although the weather was initially bright, these untamed peaks of the Taurus mountains gradually became enveloped in a cloudy mist. So we tried to climb this snow-covered Armenian Golgotha quickly, but in vain; the more we hurried, the more we stumbled, and the longer our journey became.

Among the elderly was the venerable priest Father Housig Kachouni, white-haired and over seventy. From 1880 to 1890, when the late Bishop Yeznig Abahouni was prelate of Arapkir, Father Housig had been the diocesan vicar. This self-sacrificing servant of God, one of the first victims of the repression that followed the early years of Armenian political activism, had been exiled to Constantinople, along with Bishop Abahouni. After many years in prison, he was freed, but the government ordered him to remain in Constantinople. This modest, provincial man was tossed by the curacy* from one unenviable parish church to another. Powerless to

*Office of a curate, typically a member of the clergy in charge of a parish, and those who serve in the curacy. Here the curacy referred to is the Patriarchate of Constantinople.—trans.

compete with his fellow clergymen of Constantinople, he bore his cross without complaint. The good priest had kept to himself, crying tears in his heart, and devoting himself to the education of his three sons, to whom he had been both father and mother, having become a widower early on. Suffering in great deprivation, if not hunger, he had sent his children to the Berberian School, from which they graduated.

Oh, what an irony, what an insult to justice, that these three sons, who bore a worthy resemblance to their father, should have served valiantly as trained officers of the Ottoman army and been awarded commendations in the Dardanelles campaign, only for their white-haired father to be arrested and sent in the first caravan of exiles and now endure the tribulations of our journey.

Along the way I had done my best to provide financial and moral support for this worthy old servant of God, bent down by the weight of more than seventy years; but he was unable to endure this thorny and bloody road of the Armenian cross until the end.

Emaciated, blinded by the whiteness of the snow, he could not keep his balance for hours on end along such a narrow path. Suddenly he stumbled and sank into the deep snow. We labored for a long time to rescue him, and when he was back on his feet, he pleaded with us to leave him and go on . . . and in a poignant tone he said, already mindful of eternity,

> Reverend Father, I can endure no longer . . . I've had enough . . . I'm going to die any minute now . . . I can't find a better, more tranquil death than this. Leave me here and go. Only don't forget to kiss the eyes of my three sons—Yeznig, Yeghishe, and Karekin . . . tell them about the misery of this journey . . . and don't forget to write about these unspeakable misfortunes that we suffered.

In the end we convinced Father Housig to remain with us, and we finally arrived at the Kurdish village of Saraijuk. Since firewood was abundant in this gorge surrounded by forests, we gathered around crackling bonfires to dry our wet clothes and thaw our frozen feet. It bears mentioning here that our caravan was so dispersed that those on one end were unaware of what had happened to those on the other. The cold aggravated our hunger, but many of us had no money to buy bread, and even those who did couldn't find enough of it in this small mountain village.

Only with great difficulty did we manage to provide dry bread to our fifty Yozgat natives in particular. How I marveled at the patience of these exiles, who bore their black cross without complaint, often saying, "We have no choice but to endure for the sake of the nation . . . let us give glory for this too" [*Ne yapalim millet ughuruna chekejeis . . . buizade . . . bin shukur*].

We set out from Saraijuk toward the steep southern slope of the gorge, and as the climate grew more moderate, the thick layers of snow gradually disappeared. Now we were walking along slippery paths of muddy clay, which stuck to our feet. In the end, whether snow or mud, rocks or sand, the harsh landscape made our journey all the more unbearable.

We exiled Armenians walked and walked, thinking that we were exhausting the road, but it was the road that was exhausting us. Expelled wanderers, we moved fast to get away from the bloody places wherein were scattered the limbs and skulls of hundreds of thousands of martyrs.

Yes, we were rushing to reach our beloved Cilicia as soon as possible, because we all believed that if we reached Cilicia alive, we were saved for good. Alas, what naïvete! . . . And what a shocking disappointment we would have!

We spent the third night in a small Kurdish village, where we were treated relatively well. The farther we got from the bloody regions and the terrible roads of Yozgat–Boghazliyan–Kayseri–Tomarza, and the closer we got to Cilicia, the less cruelly the Turkish and Kurdish villagers treated us, and the less they robbed us. At dawn on the fourth day we departed, in hope of reaching Hajin later that day. Gradually we left behind the Gazbel pass, with its numerous snow-covered mountains and skyscraping peaks, wooded valleys and black memories, and began our descent down a steep slope.

Finally we reached the source of the Hajin River, which is called Chatakh. The natural scenery here is indeed marvelous; steep mountains rose alongside us, covered sparsely with scattered cedar trees. Often visible on the summits were the narrow passages of concealed natural caves, which, like deep-set eyes, bore mute witness to our suffering.

Then, emerging mysteriously from beneath the bald rocks before us was the Hajin River, with clear, limpid cold water. It tasted so good that it whetted our negligible and forgotten appetite. Unfortunately few of us had slices of dry bread to chew, but we shared what we could and we gave thanks for that clear, sweet water. In days to come, no matter how hungry we became, our burning thirst was even worse. My companions would give anything to find a few drops of water, whether dirty, tainted, or bitter; the issue was finding it. For now, we sat for more than an hour by the river and then went on our way, feeling a bit invigorated.

Fifty steps below the source of this river, the Chatakh of Hajin, which originated in the rocks, was a mill. After the natives of Hajin were deported, the nearby Turkish villagers, instead of using it to grind flour, destroyed it.

Slowly we descended the valley, following the Hajin River. The farther we descended, the deeper the valley became, and the rampartlike mountains rose ever higher over us. The river, its waters high, churned impetuously along its winding course, crashing and resounding toward Hajin. Following the river's edge, we made our way down the length of this valley, often crossing stone bridges, sometimes on the left side, other times on the right.

When we got to within two hours of Hajin, the lush gardens of its people gradually came into view. The spring of 1916 was the first after the deportation of the Armenians; the gardens and vineyards had just begun to sprout and flower. Here and there the almond trees were decked out in white like brides, harbingers of spring, as were the red flowers of pomegranate and apple trees. But alas, their keepers were missing; they had been taken to the deserts, and here, survivors were scarce. Yes, the gardens and vineyards were untended, and the small cottages at the bottom of the valley, where the keepers had lived, had been unmercifully demolished, so that their beams could be used for firewood.

A little ways off, the cedar trees, corpulent and colossal, challenged their perpetual enemies, the ax and the hatchet. It was late March, and spring had already come. The charming greenery around and above us, the richly revived vegetation, tempered the natural wildness of the high, massive mountains. The scenery was indeed marvelous; the sweet spring fragrances of the flowering gardens and orchards, redolent of incense, filled us with energy and spirit. Industrious bees, buzzing about in swarms, came and went, preparing honey for abandoned beehives.

As we observed and reflected, we marveled at this creative work of the Hajin natives. They had transformed bald rocks into paradise and grown gardens on rocky mountains that even goats could hardly scale. They had planted seeds on those frightening, overhanging precipices, summits, and terraces, and made trees and flowers grow. These industrious people had changed rocks into bread.

We rejoiced at the resurrection of this enchanting natural world that animated us, relieving our daily torments and miseries. Distancing ourselves from the wearying fear of death that had hitherto enveloped us, we were filled with new hope at the sight of this colorful profusion of springtime verdure.

After we had wandered for weeks on end along deserted roads and across desolate mountains, the thought of spending a comfortable night in Hajin made us particularly glad. But the closer we got to the town, the more the black worm of grief came again to gnaw stealthily at our tormented souls, neutralizing the sweetness of the revival of nature. For although we had passed through hundreds of orchards on our way down the ever-widening valley, we had not come across a single living thing, be it human or animal; everywhere was silence and desolation.

Oh, how bitter it was to recall the blissful days when the youths and young brides, girls and boys of Hajin, dug and sowed, planted and harvested in these hundreds of scattered orchards, with regional songs on their lips and divine grace bestowed upon them! Oh, blessed, a thousand times blessed, were those days when the productive and sinewy arms of the industrious Armenian people had transformed these steep slopes and bare, rocky, untamed mountains—up to their practically inaccessible peaks—into a paradise. I wondered, would those blessed days ever come again? Who knows? *Oh, let them come . . . let them come . . . and let these cursed black days go . . . and not come back.*

In these myriad orchards left unattended by their owners, we saw apple trees, pear trees, plum trees, and grapevines that had begun to wither. The weeds had grown some forty-five inches high, suffocating the noble fructiferous trees and once-bunch-laden grapevines. It was as if the trees and flowers were asking, in a voice audible only to our hearts, *Where are our owners . . . our beloved? . . . When are they going to come? . . . When are they going to free us from these weeds that are choking us? . . . Let them come quickly while we still show signs of life . . . After that it will be too late.*

As for the cottages of the gardeners and orchard keepers and the vineyard huts, they had been dismantled* and the doors, windows, and large floorboards hauled away as firewood.

We saw scenes like this throughout our journey, particularly later in Adana, where in orchards everywhere we saw traces of the destructive Turks. They had even removed and carried off the beams of bridges along the roads, thinking of course that with the *giaours* [infidels] gone, never to return, nobody would again traverse these roads.

When we approached the outskirts of Hajin, we saw a few hunchbacked old Armenian women scattered in the nearby orchards, gathering bent grass. These wretched grandmothers and eight or ten others dressed in black—thin and emaciated—had originally been left in the city because they were related to Armenian soldiers; the young girls had long since been abducted and taken to the harems of the Turks. But these old women had been left behind, like owls perched on ruins. Dressed in rags, barefoot and bareheaded, they would boil and eat the bent grass they gathered. During the bitter-cold winter they had sold everything and were now reduced to this last means of survival.

When these wretched Armenian women saw us coming from afar, they

*There is a certain saying in Asia Minor: If you want to build something, hire a Christian worker, but if you want to have a house razed or demolished, then hire a Turkish worker.—G.B.

crossed themselves and ran toward our caravan. A few came over to me, piously kissed my hands, and said in the difficult-to-understand Hajin dialect, "Oh, thank God, there are still Armenians left in the world."

Our group was scattered, and the police soldiers were at the head and rear of the caravan, far removed from us. So the women, cut off from the outside world, were free to bombard us with questions. We too had come to look like wild creatures during the course of our journey of weeks and months, going from one mountain to the next, one province to the next. They related their endless woes, crying, as they accompanied us toward the town. They then promised that when we reached Hajin to spend the night there, they would give us a portion of their sparse meal and secure bread for us from the few rich Armenians left.

They cried over us, and we cried over them.

In Hajin, when the Armenian women saw the approach of our caravan, they came out into the valley to meet us, asking questions while they distributed oranges to us. By this time the police soldiers had noticed what was going on, and administered a drubbing both to the women handing out the oranges and to the men eating them.

After an eight-hour journey, we arrived at the government building in Hajin—and waited to be taken somewhere to rest and spend the night.

28

Hajin to Sis

Prior to the deportations, Hajin had been a purely Armenian town of about 5,000 homes and 28,000 inhabitants. It was now a heap of ruins.* In the fall of 1915, after the deportations, the Turks had burned it down to put an end to this mountain nest of Armenian eagles, near the famous fortress of Vahka, of the once-great Rubenid dynasty.

The marvelous three-story stone building of the Armenian school, located on the city's heights, remained, and there were still about two hundred houses of poor Armenians in the town's foothills. The government

*What remained of Hajin in 1916 was destroyed in 1920 by Kemalist forces. It was renamed Siambeyli, said to derive from Sayib Bey, a Kemalist who took part in its obliteration.—trans.

building in those foothills, on the road leading to Sis, was still standing. So were some fifty nearby houses with their wooden latticework [*kafes*] that belonged to Turkish government officials.

Hajin is situated in a valley through whose center flows the Hajin River. The grand boulevard toward Sis* runs along the river. On both sides of the valley rather huge mountains rise. The city had been built at the summit of the mountains on the side facing Sis. A historic monastery named after the pontiff St. Hagop of Mudzpin, whose architectural style is quite beautiful, was built of stone with thick high walls on a promontory on the west side of the river. Only this monastery, because of its location, had escaped the flames that had destroyed the town.

At a glance, an observer could picture this town, which had extended down the mountainsides in the configuration of an amphitheater. Now it was a frightening skeleton, its thousands of homes burned, only their bare walls still standing. Also still standing were the thick walls of a few burned-out churches and their stone vaulted altars and arches.

In the summer of 1915 a traitor named Aram, posing as a Hunchak, had told the Turkish police and the commander of the police soldiers where the Armenians had hidden their weapons. In so doing, he had thwarted any possibility of resistance, while also giving the government something to accuse the Armenians of. Nevertheless, whether they were armed or not, the Armenian people had already been living under a death sentence.

Prior to the general deportation of the Armenians in Cilicia, the population of Zeytoun had been deported, and shortly thereafter that of Hajin, so as to prevent resistance and internal complications. Now, of the Armenian population of Hajin and the surrounding twenty-two villages, perhaps 350 young children and decrepit old women remained. The rest had been driven into the desert. Just as Alexandropol had been the only purely Armenian city in the Caucasus, with a population of 30,000 (everything was Armenian there, with the exception of the huge barracks of Russian troops), so too Hajin had been the only city in Turkey with a purely Armenian population of as many as 28,000, according to Turkish statistics.

The Turks had wanted to raze this city so that the Armenians could not rebuild their impregnable eagles' nests in the remote mountains and passes and once again raise their heads against the despotic government. Yes, the city of Hajin was a skeleton that spoke wordlessly to us and opened new wounds in our already wounded hearts.

In April 1915, during the initial days of the deportation, Avni, the commander of the police soldiers of Adana province, had taken up a position

*Renamed Kozan.—trans.

in the monastery of St. Hagop of Mudzpin, on the slope facing the town. With two thousand regular army troops and hundreds of police soldiers, he had forced the Armenians of Hajin to surrender.

Having placed numerous mountain cannons around the monastery at night, he threatened to bombard the city if its residents put up the slightest resistance. Thanks to the traitor Aram, Avni was able to seize the weapons of the Hajin residents, thus preventing any serious resistance. The following summer this Adana police commander deported more than ten thousand Armenians working on the railway line in the Amanos mountains, ordering that they be massacred on the mountainous Baghche-Marash road.

We arrived at this skeleton of a city toward the end of March 1916 and waited in front of the government building for a place to spend the night. We did not care if our night's lodging was a basement buried under ruins or a stable for animals. Tired from almost nine hours of walking and deprived of even a dry crust of bread the whole day, we were hoping someone, out of compassion for our wretched condition, would give us a warm refuge for at least one night.

For more than an hour we waited in vain, as soldiers and government officials came and went. (Despite the city's ruined state, a *kaymakam* still resided in Hajin, and the old government structure continued to exist, as there were many Turkish villages in the surrounding area.)

Some elderly Armenian women of great compassion were waiting for us to be led to an inn, so they could give us a few morsels from their paltry table. Meanwhile a freezing wind from the snow-covered Gazbel pass chilled us. Dusk had already fallen when the *kaymakam*, a young Ittihadist Turk named Kemal—accompanied by the captain of the local police soldiers, two policemen, and a few municipal officials—came out of the government building and told us that we would have to continue on our way, because there was no suitable place in town to accommodate a hundred people.

It is impossible to describe our emotion; bewildered, we didn't know what to do. We had walked nine hours along uneven mountain roads, with only an hour's rest at Chatakh. We were powerless to resist; we stood there, some of us daring to plead with them to do us a favor [*merhamet*], for the love of their dear children . . . After a brief exchange between the captain and the *kaymakam*, the police soldiers began to attack us with whips and clubs. Blood flowed from the heads of us deportees as about a dozen police soldiers, amid the jeering of the government officials, pursued us toward the bridge that led to the road to Sis. And the elderly Armenian women were watching, lamenting our having come upon such black days.

Under a torrent of blows and curses, we walked fast to get out of this place. The darkness of night was weighing heavier, from the verdant mountain peaks to the emerald-green bottom of the deep valley, covering the monstrosities of human torture with a black shroud. Only in the nocturnal silence could one hear the confused echo of our steps, and the precipitous crashing sound of the fast-flowing, eddying river, along whose bank our road ran downward.

Groping along in the dark, we stumbled and picked ourselves up, muttering and cursing. After a strenuous hour and a half or so, we noticed pale lights on the slope of the mountain on the other side of the river. Excited at the prospect of an imminent rest, we walked frantically toward the lights, with the assent of the police soldiers.

Crossing the rickety wooden bridge over the river, we headed for the lights. The village was called Givoleshen, but the *hoja* there would not let us enter, saying: "There aren't any males left in the village; they have all been taken to war. The only men here are the *muhtar* and me, and we cannot accept such a large caravan of men with only women, girls, and children here."

We were greatly disappointed and offered him money to let us stay, telling him that we were tired from having walked eleven hours that day and could continue no longer in the depth of night. We would be happy to sleep in a stable or sheepfold at the far end of the village, we said, or even under a tree, if only a little bit of bread could be procured for us.

The townspeople, however, adamantly refused, saying they didn't have enough bread for a hundred-person caravan; they could barely find a piece for one or two people who would pass through the village now and then. There was no point in wasting any more time, and many of the deportees, especially the elderly who were totally exhausted, were lying stretched out on the ground, unable to move, heaving sighs as if in the throes of death.

In the thick darkness we made our way by groping along through the mountains and valleys, looking for shelter, even if only a pile of ruins. After another hour we noticed a faint light in the distance. Having no other recourse, we crossed the river again on another rickety bridge and reached the sizable Turkish village of Yardibi. I rushed to locate the village *muhtar* and *hoja;* then we bargained, paying three Ottoman gold pieces to be able to stay in a few stables at the lower end of the village . . . They insisted that we purchase bread, onions, yogurt, and *tarhana** at the prices they demanded; it was their way of robbing us. This was no time to deliberate; we were obliged to accept whatever conditions they dictated, without objection..

**Tarhana:* dried curds and pearled wheat.—trans.

Having now walked almost twelve hours with only short breaks, we plopped down on some dry dung in a corner of one of the stables, which had been emptied of animals, and pretended that we were at home in our soft beds. The good bit of bread we had bought silenced our growling stomachs.

The police soldiers allowed us to push off rather late in the morning, and once their malice was tempered with bribery, they treated us in a friendlier manner. On the second day, however, we moved forward at dawn. It was spring, and the weather was marvelous; we were still in the Taurus mountain chain, and the road from Hajin to Sis runs through a long winding valley whose mountains on both sides were covered with cedar forests. The Hajin River [Saran su] flows swiftly with a roar, resounding deep in the valley. Successively fed by secondary streams originating in mountains and valleys, it becomes a rather powerful river called the Geok su. Then, mingling with the Jihun River, it passes by Adana and empties into the Mediterranean, forming a large delta at Karatash.

For the first time since leaving Chankiri, at Chatakh, we had begun to pay attention to the lush greenery. Only after crossing into Cilicia were we gradually able to put distance between us and death, in whose bloody claws we had writhed for more than six weeks. Greenery was everywhere, punctuated by spring flowers of different colors and by thousands of ancient cedars that afforded us dense shade. And a perfume from the sap that flowed from the cedars, redolent of incense, gave us vitality, spiritually sick and grieving as we were.

A few days before, we had feared for our lives and were indifferent to nature; now, seeing the beauty of spring, we tried to put out of our minds the specter of the blood-soaked valleys, skeletons, and skulls; we thought, perhaps prematurely, that having entered the flowery domain of the Cilician Armenians, we were saved. After all, isn't it true that there is no resurrection without death?

On the evening of the second day after leaving Hajin, we stayed in a small village at the base of the historic Vahka fortress. There we were able to find food and shelter. The inhabitants of this village were Turks who apparently had not yet gotten the scent and taste of Armenian blood . . . and they treated our caravan kindly.

At dawn on the third day we departed from this hospitable village. The road took us through forested mountains and along a winding river valley. The resurrection of nature was so marvelous, we almost forgot that we were headed toward Zor, or death. Since the road gradually went downhill, it was less tiring on our exhausted legs, and inasmuch as we had been able to secure food for a few days, we had sufficiently regained our strength and, fortunately, had slept rather comfortably during the night.

Having recuperated a bit, a few of our most energetic and patriotic youths, thinking that the storks of spring flying northward, toward Armenia, were cranes, sang in trembling voices that betrayed their inner feeling:

Call crane, call, now that it's spring,
The heart of the émigrés is regiments of blood,
Dear crane, dear crane, it's spring!
Dear crane, dear crane, it's spring!
*Oh, my heart is blood!**

There, in the depths of black cedar forests and high up on the mountainside, we saw a few tents of black goatskin, belonging to Turks who made charcoal. Each of us wanted to become a member of that poor charcoal-making family. We were ready in earnest to be coal makers, provided we could live freely in those wild mountains and valleys until the blissful hour when international hostilities ceased, and those of us who were still alive could be saved.

We would have been so happy to withdraw into this peaceful solitude of nature, free from the persecutions of the Ittihad and out of human sight, free from the unbearable surveillance of police soldiers, just to live a simple life, to live free. We envied not only these coal makers but also the startled rabbits that sometimes jumped out from beneath the bushes and dashed away, and we envied the birds in the sky, free to go wherever they wanted. We were going toward burning deserts, to become handfuls of dust.

As the boys sang, the police soldiers reproached us: "What a carefree nation you are! We massacre you, we exile you, and yet you still sing songs" [*Ne arsuz milletsiniz, yolduruyoruz, suruyoruz, daha halen sharku seoyle yorsunuz*]. Yes, they were right, but if the Armenian nation had survived after five long centuries of persecution and massacre, the reason was this vitality, such that the more they massacred the hated hydra, the more new heads it grew . . .

Amazed that that song could spring from the hearts and lips of men so worn down, the deputy chief of the police soldiers said to me in jest, "Your nation is so shameless and opportunistic that if one Armenian remains, you'll be a source of trouble for us" [*Sizin millet eoyle arsuz millet dir ki, eyer yarun yeuz ermeni kalsa, yeine bashumuza bela olursunuz*].

Before the golden disk of the sun sank, we reached a small village with a Muslim population, where we got hold of a few pieces of dry bread. In

*The song "Groongner" has lyrics attributed to Nahabed Kuchag, musical transcription by Archimandrite Komitas.—trans.

some deserted huts we tried to get through the night while waging a full-scale war against armies of lice attacking us from all sides.

By the time our caravan set out in the morning in the extreme cold, our worn-out bodies were numb from the night wind. We had walked a few hours when a torrential downpour began, and while the rain was pouring down—or more accurately, spilling upon our heads—the muddy ground prevented our moving forward. Weary and emaciated from this never-ending trek, my fellow deportees urged me to pay off the police soldiers so that we could take refuge in a nearby hut.

I tried to convince the *chavush* to let us find shelter, telling him that we were soaked to our underwear and would all become sick. But the effort was in vain. In response to the pleading of an old man, one of the police soldiers said, "It's better if you get sick and die. As it is, the government wants to get you out of the way sooner rather than later; you'll be put out of your misery, and the government will be rid of you."

Having had no choice but to walk for more than half an hour in the rain, wind, storm, and mud, we finally reached another small village. There we found appropriate rooms that could hold about twenty individuals. But despite promises they had made to the contrary, the police soldiers and the *chavush* insisted that we continue in order to reach the village they had chosen for us to spend the night in.

As one of the police soldiers explained, they wanted to punish all of us because some of us had been singing. Our efforts were in vain. New torrents of rain poured down on us amid lightning and thunder, and the police soldiers kept prodding us on. The hotheaded youths of our caravan wanted to jump the police soldiers in a deserted valley, take their weapons, kill them, and flee to the mountains. Such was their bitterness.

Because I was in the most responsible position and knew that such acts would have disastrous consequences, I did what I could to prevent the boys from acting. Finally, after I convinced them and we encouraged one another, we set out again, and fortunately, the rain eased up. Still, in the drizzle and mud, it took us all of three hours to cover one hour's distance and reach the intended Turkish village.

Once we reached this village, we found out that it wasn't only because of the singers among us that we had been made to come here; the *chavush* reportedly had a mistress in the village, the young wife of a soldier who had gone off to battle.

Fortunately we found a good supply of firewood, though at tenfold the regular price; we made bonfires and sat around them in groups, hanging our clothes to dry. Indeed, it is shameful to confess that the crackle of thousands of lice falling off our underwear and clothes into the fire was like exploding gunpowder. We had long since grown accustomed to these parasites that were sucking the blood of our emaciated bodies; on this death march of ours, who had the heart to occupy himself with lice? Our overriding concern was to avoid being killed; aside from that, we had resigned ourselves to everything.

We departed from this little village rather late the following morning because the sergeant had spent the entire night in drunken debauchery and had instructed his subordinate corporal accordingly. Fortunately, after the previous day's rain, the weather was clear, and a strong southern Cilician sun warmed our bodies that so longed for heat. It was the fourth day since we had departed from Hajin, and we hoped we would reach Sis in about seven hours. When we emerged from the beautiful and verdant valley, we met a few camel drivers who were transporting oranges from Cilicia to the inner provinces, toward Kayseri. This was the first time over the entire course of our deportation that we had encountered a traveler or any moving creature, human or animal.

All the roads of Asia Minor were deserted; no one was traveling. No one was in a position to travel; the males had been forcibly sent off to the front, while the women and children had withdrawn to their villages, contenting themselves with what they had. Although it was spring, we hadn't come across any work being done in the fields. This was because the government, along with sending all the men to the front, had also seized, as war tax [*tekelife harbiye*], all the available animals—camels, horses, oxen, cows, and even donkeys—to replace the horses killed in battle, or for official transportation.

Very rarely while crossing the Tomarza plain did we see tilling and sowing in village fields. Otherwise, the plains were deserted, empty of all breathing creatures; the fields lay fallow, and weeds had taken the place of fine grains. There was hustle and bustle around the large cities, but life had stopped in the recesses of Asia Minor, in the provinces—particularly in the places we had passed through—where everybody was anxiously awaiting a quick end to the war.

The Hajin Valley, which extended from Hajin to Sis, was one of the most beautiful northern passes through the Taurus mountains. When we emerged from it we reached a promontory from which we could see the length and width of the fertile plains of Cilicia [Chukur Ovan], from Mersin to the foot of the Amanos mountains, as far as Osmaniye. This promontory was covered with vineyards belonging to the wealthy Armenian families of Sis, and lying two to three hundred meters above the plain, it was airy and subject to mountain breezes. We saw lovely walled-off vineyards and nicely constructed, painted houses suitable for vacations.

Down below, at the foot of a solitary wedge-shaped mountain on the lower plain, lay Sis, the famous capital city of the Rubenid kings. We found Sis to be the most beautiful of all the cities we had passed through; it was as if it were just built: a white city, with all the houses plastered with lime. And although its streets were dirty, it gave an external impression of cleanliness.

Because the houses had successively risen up the side of the mountain, the city had taken on the shape of an amphitheater. Some sixty or seventy meters above the city, at the summit of the mountain, stood the centuries-old monastery of the Catholicosate of Cilicia [established in 1058] with its high thick walls and gradually ascending structure, girding Sis like a wall from the northwest. The historic pontifical church was standing in silence—but the silence spoke loudly to us.

High above everything, on the mountaintop, there remained standing the ramparts and toothlike towers of the ruined fortress, which had been built by the Armenian kings of the Rubenid dynasty. Their very nakedness told the frightful tale.[1] These huge ramparts, two to four meters high, and the many towers standing five to eight meters high, surrounded the summit. The mountain itself, rocky, bald, and solitary, rose about three hundred meters above the open plain; detached from the Taurus mountain chain, it loomed over the city.

Sitting on the elevation that descended to the plain, we scrutinized our surroundings and enjoyed the marvelous natural beauty of this panorama of Cilicia. We looked far, far away, where no mountain was visible; there the sky and the earth blended together, oh, and there was the sea of our salvation . . . if only we could reach it . . .

Each of us, in turn, indicated to the others the way leading to the sea, and our souls vibrated with thoughts of flight and deliverance. We had been walking the road with a passivity characteristic of those resigned to their fate, without thinking about escape. Only one of us had been bold enough to attempt it, and he had been brutally killed; after that no one had entertained the thought of freedom. They were taking us to Der Zor, and many of us hoped to start a new life there that would last until the end of the world war, after which we would go to the new homeland of the Armenians. Our deportees thought that they would be allowed to live in Der Zor meanwhile . . . they were still expecting mercy from the Turks.

For now, the marvelous panorama of Cilicia opening before our eyes and the wide flat fertile plains, famous for their cereals and cotton, resurrected our worn-out souls and our extinguished hopes; we were facing the Gulf of Cilicia [Gulf of Alexandretta], which empties into the Mediterranean. A bit to the west was the Mediterranean's eastern queen, Cyprus. How we wanted to take wing and fly there and bring news of this unbelievable tragedy to our distant émigré brothers on that island.

After an hour's rest, we descended through the rocky, winding roads and, at last, set foot on the historic soil of Cilicia. Although spent and emaciated, many kneeled down to kiss the paternal earth, where reminders of past Armenian glories surrounded us. We were clothed in rags and had lost everything, but hope for a liberated Armenia still shined in our souls.

The widespread, uneven rows of vineyards that belonged to the Armenians of Sis reminded us of spring with their blooms in various colors; we turned to the west and, after about an hour, arrived in Sis. The local police escorted us to a rather clean two-story inn at one end of the city, a *khan* that had been the property of an Armenian but was now being used by the local government.

29

Sis to Garzbazar

Feeling no immediate fear of death, we spent a peaceful night, our only wish to find a way to stay in Sis a few more days. We had been walking for more than thirty-five days without stop, without spending more than one night in the same place. After leaving Chankiri, we had seen only two cities: Choroum, where we were confined and subjected to such deprivations that we longed for the stables of our villages, and Hajin, where they hadn't wanted to give us even one night's lodging and had driven us into the mountains with sticks.

Our bodies itched from the dirt and lice and constant scratching, and many of us were covered with sores. Still, the only time we reflected on our physical condition was after crossing into the region of Cilicia, when we found ourselves under a hot sun. Relieved from the immediate specter of death, during midday rest periods under the powerful southern sun we began to rid our bodies of these parasites. Now all of us felt the need to bathe, even more strongly than the need to eat. If only we could get cleaned up and be rid of this itching and the bloody sores!

Having traveled for a month, our faces were covered with hair, so that we were unrecognizable. None of us had had the chance or the means to get a haircut or shave, and with our faces buried in these dense thickets, our very expressions had been transformed; we looked half wild and savage . . . it was hard to differentiate us from boorish peasants. Only the tattered remnants of our European clothing might have indicated that we had once been human beings.

We all needed something that might serve as shoes, be they local slippers or sandals. Our own shoes were so worn out that many in our group had bound their bloody feet with pieces of *chul** while others walked barefoot. The most wretched were the natives of Yozgat.

I must confess here in the name of truth that in Sis the Turkish officials treated us with unreserved compassion. They even invited peddlers of bread and groceries to sell us their goods, and told them that if they asked too high a price, they would take their goods and give them to us for free. The inn was clean with rather newly built rooms and glass windows, and for once we spent a peaceful night. This friendliness gave us hope that we might be able to stay in Sis for a few more days.

We even received permission to send two people to the drugstore to get medicine for our sick. (Among us we had three well-known pharmacists from the Kum Kapu and Gedik-Pasha quarters of Constantinople, who had been our physicians throughout our journey.) Everybody was pleading with me to go and find the *mutasarrif* and get permission for a few days' rest.

I had long since lost my self-confidence. Gone were those blessed days when I used to visit ambassadors and provincial governors-general on behalf of the Armenian Patriarchate and speak with them on an equal footing. Several times I had even appeared before Sultan Reshad and with the then-patriarch. In July 1909 I had accompanied the entourage of the late Catholicos Matheos Izmirlian during his historic visit to St. Petersburg. I had appeared before Tsar Nicholas II of Russia and participated in his palatial banquet.

Yes, those days of glory and honor were irrevocably slipping from my memory like a dream, now that the black days of terrible pain and suffering had come, forcing us to drink and continue still to drink from the cup of bitterness until it was completely drained . . . saying, with Jesus, "If it be possible, let this cup pass from me: nevertheless not as I will, but as thou wilt" (Matthew 26:39).

But word came that we were to prepare for departure in two hours . . . and this was a friendly gesture, to give us two hours—though there was no time to think. Having no alternative but to yield to the earnest pleadings of my wretched traveling companions, I marshaled my remaining though scattered forces. After giving satisfactory baksheesh to the police soldier at the door to our inn, and making myself look as presentable as possible in my worn-out clothes, I left to go and find the *mutasarrif*.

A few old Turks on the road, in eager response to my questions, told me

**Chul:* Turkish horsecloth or haircloth.—trans.

that the governor would not have left his house yet so early in the day, so I should go directly there. I climbed quite a distance through the dirty winding streets, and the Turkish street children didn't insult me but pointed out the *mutasarrif*'s house, a surprisingly simple dwelling for the governor of the city and region of Kozan [Turkish name for Sis].

A police soldier at the house told me: "The governor is in the habit of taking a walk in the field on beautiful sunny days like this; go that way and you'll find him." I rushed off in the direction indicated, and indeed, outside of town I found him, a man of about fifty years, gray-bearded, whom I took to be the governor because he had a police soldier following him.

Seeing a clergyman in ecclesiastical garb, the *mutasarrif* stopped and asked me what I wanted. Speaking softly and with much emotion, I told him that we had been walking on the road for a month and a half, a caravan of one hundred, when we had reached Sis; we were worn out and had sick people in need of treatment. Because we had never been allowed to stay more than one night in any given place, we had not been able to purchase necessities, and we had had no nourishment, no change of underwear or clothes. We were wretched deportees being taken to Der Zor . . . and I earnestly pleaded in the name of his children that he take pity on us and permit us to remain in the city for at least three days in order to recuperate, get cleaned up, and get a change of clothes.

He listened compassionately to what I had to say, and replied:

> *Papaz Effendi*, there are very strict orders for us not to keep caravans of Armenian deportees for more than one night, but since you are beseeching that I take pity on your wretched people in the name of my children, very well, I'll make an exception and give you permission to stay one more day; go and see to it that you take care of your needs quickly. I'm sorry that I can't do any more than this. When I go to the government building, I'll summon the police commissioner and the commandant of the police soldiers and recommend that they put you back on the road not today but rather tomorrow afternoon, so that you'll have thirty to thirty-five hours. Get going. Don't worry, I'll take care of the rest.

An indescribable joy overtook my grieving heart; someone deemed me worthy of mercy and kind words, and remembered that I was a human being . . .

After Turkish formalities of gratitude, I rushed to give this good news to my comrades-in-suffering, who were anxiously waiting for me . . . so joyous were [these] miserable souls that they ran to give one another the good news as if it were tidings of our final salvation. Their exultation became even greater when I told them that, having assumed personal responsibility, I had obtained permission for all of us to move about the city freely and shop or bathe, on the condition that no one try to escape, which would subject me to punishment.

Reliable and influential persons were put in charge of the few suspicious youths who were always plotting escape; then everybody scattered across the town to shop or get medicine. Many hired a barber to rid themselves of bunches of hair and get shaved; we had grown so used to seeing one another with long hair that afterward, we barely recognized our companions. We were starting to look human again, and some had even found the means to wash their underwear.

Meanwhile I went to the only Armenian drugstore in town, along with one of our pharmacist friends from Constantinople, to buy medicine for our sick. Then suddenly word came that I should rush back to our inn to deal with a problem that had come up.

When I returned, I was surprised to see that many from our group, carrying their large or small packages or bundles, were lined up in front of the door, waiting to depart . . . Meanwhile the police commissioner, along with about ten policemen and police soldiers, had gone to the upper story, and was driving those reluctant to go downstairs with his whip. After the official promises of an extra day's rest, such a quick and bitter disappointment was unbearable, and the initial discontent of our group turned to rage. Our joy had lasted barely a half hour, and our exaltation quickly changed to grief. No longer did we have time to think; in the months and years of our suffering, we couldn't be allowed one day of rest.

In this general confusion, policemen and police soldiers were dragging the resistant ones out of their rooms, and other policemen were pushing the poor deportees down the stairs. Some of us were being beaten with cudgels, while others were getting slapped in the face; it was pointless to counsel prudence. Yet it didn't seem likely that we would be killed at this moment, so I rushed over to the chief of police and, in a spontaneous and inexplicable act of rebellion, without any formality or civility, shouted in his face that I had personally received permission from the governor for one extra day of rest. I went on to tell him that we refused to leave and that it was preferable to die here than in some desolate place . . . I then told the deportees not go outside the main gate but to go to their rooms and stay there as if nailed to the floor . . . At the same time I invited the commissar to go with me to the *mutasarrif* to verify my statement.

Seeing that matters might get out of hand and perhaps feeling that he lacked the right to forcibly expel us, the police commissioner sought to settle things. He came over to me and told me to come with him to his headquarters so as to resolve the matter amicably.

It became clear that he was doing this to us because, in petitioning the *mutasarrif* directly, I had unwittingly overlooked him, and furthermore I had neglected to offer him a few gold pieces. Since, however, he had brought things to this point, and I had already obtained the permission directly from the governor, I elected not to try that approach now. As it was, we had no money to spare . . . we had been robbed and drained . . . and three-fourths of our companions were hungry and in need of medicine and treatment. Why should we throw away money, and where would we even get it from anyway? Especially since some fifty wretched deportees had been waiting days for a piece of dry bread, and many hadn't had a morsel for twenty-four hours.

Promising to see the governor later on, the commissar departed with the policemen and police soldiers he had brought and let us continue to go about the town, purchase what we needed, and engage in our urgent business. This storm had barely passed when our wretched companions surrounded me, asking that I find a piece of bread for them.

Oh, my own situation was dire. I was the shepherd of a dismembered flock, an exiled clergyman in a caravan of exiles. I too was deprived of all material and moral resources, yet everybody's eyes were on me . . . After all, had not the Armenian people for centuries known their clergyman to be a leader, as prelate or pastor? . . . This was my role. But I was also the leader of this decimated caravan of flotsam and jetsam headed for Der Zor . . . The lifeless, supplicating looks of those exhausted eighty-year-old Yozgat natives added to the torment of my soul. For one must have personally suffered to know the depth of grief and pain of such desperate souls, and one must have gone hungry in order to understand what hunger is like. I had suffered as much gut-wrenching hunger as my most starved companions; however, given my position, I had hidden my condition from the others. Often a piece of dry bread with a few dust-covered raisins, passed among us, had been my sole sustenance for an entire day.

I didn't know where to turn, but the hapless deportees had no one else to turn to. Whether by persuasion or threats, I had previously gotten money or bread from one or another, and by such means I had brought our wretched companions this far without leaving anyone at the mercy of the two-legged wolves or the four-legged ones.

Their doleful appearance alone was sufficient to soften stony hearts. To the credit of my wretched companions, I must say here that none of them had once said to me, "I am hungry." Rather, they communicated it through gestures, and I had learned this language very well . . . the language of the hungry—incomprehensible to those who are sated.

Hearing that the youngest [Matheos] of the three wealthy Nalbandian brothers, a local member of the Ottoman Parliament, was currently in Sis,

I aimed to find him, with the hope of obtaining a loan to buy bread. I sent word to Nalbandian that I wished to see him; he replied that he would come to see me at our inn.

But the day was almost over, and he had not come. I heard that he was in bed, supposedly ill, but in fact he was hoping that the authorities would soon force us to resume our journey so that he would escape the dangerous dilemmas we represented. He was unaware that we had obtained permission to remain and rest in Sis for an extra day.

The end of the first day was drawing near, and realizing that nobody was coming, and my hungry companions were starving and feeling tormented by the wait, I went to the Nalbandian residence. I was escorted to a small room on the second floor, where the youngest* brother was sitting up in bed in the company of two elderly relatives, ostensibly engaged in a heated discussion.

In this small room of this secluded residence, we spoke about various topics of the day. After coffee I stated the real purpose of my visit, describing in detail the exhausting journey to Sis of our caravan of 102 deportees. I told him that 60 or 70 of us were destitute and in extremely deplorable condition owing to our forced journey of the past thirty-five days. I related how I had accomplished the impossible in keeping these wretched deportees alive and bringing them as far as Sis—by begging in Turkish villages, accepting alms from our well-to-do, and personally giving loans. But I stressed that we had a long way to go before reaching Der Zor, and I asked him for a loan of twenty-five gold pounds in exchange for a receipt redeemable at the patriarchate. I assured him that when he delivered it to Constantinople, the patriarchate would gladly pay such a nominal sum for the cost of bread for Armenian deportees.

Nalbandian, however, responded hardheartedly that considering the numerous current difficulties in communications, it was not possible to redeem such a promissory note by sending it to the patriarchate in Constantinople. Obviously this man's heart lacked even an ounce of compassion toward those exiled survivors, in whose name and thanks to whose support his brother Matheos had taken his seat in the Ottoman Parliament. And thanks to his influential position, he, Matheos, had not only saved all his wealth and property but also further benefited materially from the deportation of Armenians, whose businesses were now left solely to the Nalbandians. In addition, as a member of the Ottoman Parliament, Matheos had been able to have his relatives exempted from deportation and from governmental seizure of their wealth.

*Since Matheos was the youngest, Grigoris Balakian is most likely referring to the oldest, Krikor.—trans.

I exerted every effort to persuade Nalbandian to lend us the nominal sum of twenty-five gold pounds, which would rescue more than half the members of our ill-starred caravan from starvation. I described the thousand and one tribulations and deprivations of our exile, and how we were emaciated and exhausted, many of us reduced to skeletons . . . but to no avail. He was totally indifferent and replied stonily that the condition of all Armenians was bad.

But not theirs, of course. [The Nalbandians] passed the time eating and drinking to excess and playing cards with high-level Turkish officials, all the while filling their wheat granaries by means of the forced-labor battalions of Armenian workers [*amele taburi*], whom they refused even to supply with a full measure of bread. Their reply to any protests was: "Thank God that here at least you are getting dry bread. If you do not do this work, you will end up in Der Zor." If bold Armenian soldiers had protested these fratricidal deprivations and constraints more vigorously, the Nalbandians would most likely have had the Turkish military officials drive them out.

Seeing his indifference, I made one final attempt. Without considering the likely insult to my own dignity, I requested that he deign to give only ten gold pounds to me personally as a loan. I hastened to add that, sending my receipt to Constantinople, he would receive immediate payment, even if I were to die in the desert.

I could see his displeasure at this new request. So in order to coax him, I declared that my brother in Melbourne and my relatives in Constantinople, being financially well off, would be glad to pay tenfold or more, without objection, in honor of my memory, along with accrued interest. He responded to me with such coldheartedness, he terrified me: "But I cannot make this kind of a loan to you, because you are being taken to Der Zor and nobody knows what end you will meet."

Further entreaties were superfluous; the individual facing me was morally bankrupt and unworthy of the honor of my request . . . For if he had a human heart, he would have not only granted me the modest loan of ten gold pounds but offered much more as a gift. It was impossible to talk anymore.

When I left the Nalbandian residence, it was nearing dusk, and the scorching spring sun was descending toward the west. I was so overcome, so morally crushed, and my distressed soul was so agitated, that I wanted desperately to find an out-of-the-way spot to cry by myself. Only tears could pacify my heart. When I was thinking about what answer I would give to my group when I got back, the sun simply appeared to my eyes as darkness.

On the way I stumbled over rocks and fell to the ground more than once because I had lost myself and did not know where I was going. All at once I forgot all the old miseries I had suffered at the hands of the enemy, so revolting was this disappointment caused by my fellow countryman—particularly since I had seen the comfort he enjoyed in his own home, sitting up in clean bedsheets, with savory foods on his table. When I compared all that with our present situation, I had to force myself as a servant of God to suppress the curses that wished to pass from my lips. For, after all, I was a giver of blessings.

To request only ten gold pounds for the cost of bread for sixty to seventy wretched compatriots on their death march and be refused . . . Yes, he refused, figuring that we were being taken to the deserts to be massacred, so his conduct would never be known.

When I had arrived at our caravan site, everybody, especially those from Yozgat, rushed to my side to hear whether I had succeeded. One can just imagine their bitterness and anguish to learn that I had returned empty-handed. Many uttered curses, and a few young intellectuals from Constantinople vowed: "Oh, if only we manage to survive, we will show the Nalbandians how much their cruelty will cost them . . . their wealth is had at the cost of the wretcheds' sweat . . . they considered a piece of bread too much for us . . . they will see . . . but, oh, if only we can survive."

Fortunately at this very moment an Armenian baker, having heard about the starving deportees, lost no time in offering me sixty loaves of bread to distribute to the neediest. This gesture relieved them somewhat, and each person received 250 drams [just under a pound] of bread. They were satisfied and blessed the donor's name.

Shortly thereafter, when an employee of the Nalbandian bakery came to sell bread, I personally told him that an Armenian merchant-baker had compassionately donated sixty loaves to the deportees and asked that he do likewise so that they would have some in reserve for the journey since, like famished beasts, they had devoured the bread they had just received.

Replying that without his boss's approval he could do nothing, the employee left the inn. Returning a little later, he handed over only forty loaves of bread. They had given twenty fewer loaves so they could make a profit on them . . . Some of the elderly natives of Yozgat cried out in justifiable rage . . . A few youths asked that I refuse these forty loaves and the great disrespect attached to them, but the supplicating look of the starving old folks obliged me to take the bread. We spent a peaceful night and the next day prepared for departure.

The local Armenians told us that about sixty of the eight hundred Armenian families of Sis were friends or relatives of the Nalbandians; they had been able to avoid deportation and were living in the town when we passed through. An elderly local priest* also had been able to remain in Sis,

*Father Avedis Achabahian.—trans.

as he was a cripple, but he was confined to his house and forbidden even to bury the dead. The monastery of Sis had been turned into a school for the sons of Turkish refugees, while the houses emptied of their Armenian inhabitants were assigned to the Muslim refugees from the interior provinces who were now overrunning Cilicia.

The bishops, who were the last to depart, had gathered all the sacred vessels, vestments, books, and manuscripts in the monastery for transport to Holy Jerusalem. As for those artifacts that could not be sent, as the final legacy of the dying Armenian people, they were buried in vaulted cellars. The catholicossal throne, an antique made of marble and decorated with carvings, was smashed to bits by Turkish schoolboys at the urging of their fanatical teachers. Even though this is known as the throne of Levon [King Levon I of Cilicia (1199–1219)], the catholicos of Cilicia has noted that it was no more than two hundred years old.[1]

As part of the exceptionally friendly treatment we had enjoyed in Sis, we were able to send letters and telegrams, informing our families of our whereabouts.

Our innkeeper was an Armenian from Hajin who, through a ruse, had managed to escape deportation and remain in Sis. He told us that there were fugitives from the military, [Armenian] families as well as Muslim, who were now in the employ of the German Berlin-to-Baghdad railway company, constructing railroad tunnels on the Amanos and Taurus line. Having found refuge on the railway line, he said, they could consider themselves saved, because the Turkish civil and military authorities could not arrest them: such action would violate the written agreement between the Turkish government and the German railway company. He suggested to us that when we reached the railway line, we all flee together and take refuge with the German railway company.

We were already convinced that our only chance of salvation was escape; if we had jobs for the railway, the Turkish government would have no authority over us. Since our caravan was composed entirely of men, it would be relatively easy for us, as employees, to escape at one of the stations.

Subsequently, thanks to the same Armenian innkeeper, we entered into secret negotiations with a clever Turk, an army deserter who worked for the line; he had come from Ayran to Sis for a few days' vacation. In exchange for generous compensation, this Turk undertook to go ahead of us to Ayran, the headquarters of the Amanos railway company, and prepare the ground for our escape. He planned to meet with interpreter P. of the German company and bring word to us in Keller, which we would be passing through prior to reaching Islahiye.

The Turk wanted something in writing sanctioning his action, but I was leery of giving him a letter, thinking that the request could be a trap: the government could use it as evidence against us and kill us. The Turk relented and departed from Sis, promising to wait for us at the designated place on our route.

The caravan set out from Sis toward Garzbazar, with hope of imminent freedom. The extra day's rest made all of us feel quite invigorated and like human beings again. We soon left the historic capital city of the Rubenid kings, with its lost ancient glory, and entered the Cilician plain.

Spread out beneath our feet were verdant grassy plots, and here and there we could see ears of wheat. The hot Cilician sun was warming the cold dampness that had followed the rainfall.

Our caravan advanced quickly along the road through the plain, which was flat and level as a sea, and made for easy walking. We had soon forgotten our adversities—the hunger, the thirst, and the beatings. The young members felt a new energy, and the idea that escape was at hand excited them to the point of their thinking that they were already saved. We were no longer terrified by death; previously an unknown and formidable enemy, it was now a familiar friend.

Like the star guiding the Magi coming from the East to worship the infant Jesus, "a comet" was leading us pilgrims of the desert too. This star was of the impending dawn of the Armenian people, now in agony; with a barely perceptible glitter, after five hundred long years of fruitless expectations, it had finally appeared on the distant horizon that had begun to redden and set fire to Ararat, the mountain sacred to Armenians.

Yes, all of us had the deep conviction that this widespread bloodbath, organized to annihilate the Armenian people, *was the last one* . . . that the deluge of innocent blood would not be in vain . . . Alas, only the fortunate few survivors would live to see that magnificent dawn.

In this excitement of ours, a few youths in the vanguard began to sing in spirited voices, audible to all, as if they were out on an excursion:

When the doors of hope open,
And winter leaves our land,
The exquisite land of mine, our Cilicia,
When sweet days shine,
When the swallow returns to its nest,
When the trees are covered with leaves,
I wish to see my Cilicia,
*Land where my sun shines.**

*From "Giligia" (Cilicia), words by Nahabed Rousinian.—trans.

From another direction, inspired by this nostalgic, poignant tune, a few other youths were singing in more martial ones:

Death is the same everywhere . . .
Man shall die once . . .
But fortunate is he . . .
Who sacrifices his life . . .
For the freedom of his nation.

Oh, how apt were these defiant words of the poet.* More than one million Armenians had been sacrificed on the altar of their people's freedom. And if a mountain were to be formed from the skulls of the Armenian martyrs, it would surely shade the snow-covered peak of sacred Ararat. Indeed, the vitality of the Armenian people was among the most marvelous in the annals of human history.

Periodically over the past twenty-five years, widespread massacres had been carried out in order to exterminate the race: the Erzerum massacre of 1890, the large-scale massacres of 1895–96, the Sassoun massacre of 1902, the Adana massacre of 1909, and the crown and laurels of all these, the massacres of 1915, organized for the final and total extermination of the Armenian people. These massacres were unparalleled in human experience. Each time, however, the Armenians had forgiven and kissed their executioners.

The Armenian people were noble, sublime in spirit, and forgiving; it sufficed for their merciless executioners to say a few conciliatory words, and their memory of every waste of blood soon faded. Their deep sores and wounds would quickly heal, and then they would forget every black day—until new massacres and new bloodbaths would again bring affliction and horror.

Thus it was that this handful of survivors of this oft-tortured people, subjected to martyrdom countless times, who ate their crust of dry bread with tears in their eyes, still walked, singing, despite knowing that they were probably going to their graves.

Oh, of course such a vital and heroic people, having gone through the baptism of blood and fire, suffering and tears, for thousands of years, could not utterly die. Yes, the future belonged to them, but the survivors would have to be lucky enough to see it.

The darkness had enveloped us, but we still hadn't come across a village where we could spend the night. It seemed that we had lost our way, and

*From the Armenian national anthem, "Mer Hairenik" (Our Fatherland), words by Mikayel Nalbandian, music by Parsegh Ganachian.—trans.

the policemen and police soldiers accompanying us also expressed concern. Being new to the job, they were unfamiliar with the roads. It was the third hour of the night, and we were groping our way in the dark, when suddenly—about fifty feet ahead of us—we heard the successive crackling of firearms. We panicked, thinking that the moment of our death had finally come. We scattered, and some fled without looking back, not knowing where they were going.

In the confusion none of us could tell who was firing or why. As the shots kept coming, our fear increased. Finally it became clear that two police soldiers had arrested four or five deserters and were threatening them with execution. We lost quite a bit of time before we assembled again and took a head count; we confirmed our official number at 109.* We continued on our way, walking cautiously, until fortunately we left the dreadful mountainous roads behind, and the road from here followed the plain.

We were able to spot a pale light shining far, far away in the night, but we could not make out whether it meant a village or a shepherd with his flock. Those experienced in nighttime travel know well that it is difficult to determine the distance of lights with any certainty. Thus, in the hope of resting soon, we quickened our pace, proceeding toward the light, but it seemed to recede from us. The nocturnal dew and frost had wet our clothes and chilled us. Then we reached a place where there was more than one shining light—a village. But to reach it, we had to cross a rather large body of stagnant water overlain with a fallen tree trunk. Some of us tumbled into the water, including quite a few of the older deportees, among them the elderly servant of God Father Housig Kachouni. Every time we traveled along a difficult road like this, he was the first to fall down; he was over seventy, but he would utter a curse only sometimes, when he was totally exhausted: *May God punish them* . . .

After waging quite a battle against wild mastiffs that attacked us from all sides, we entered a large stable, adjoined by a few sheepfolds. Our caravan settled into this stable and these sheepfolds, and without giving a thought to eating, we fell, utterly exhausted, onto piles of dried manure and slept.

The following day we got hold of some black barley bread resembling mud, then set out, and after a short midday respite, we reached Garzbazar quite early in the evening.

*When we left Sis, seven individuals from the local population joined our caravan.—G.B.

30

Garzbazar to Osmaniye

On the road from Sis we crossed a marvelous stone bridge in order to reach Garzbazar, which is a country town, the seat of the *kaymakam* on the banks of a rivulet that flows into the Jihun River. It had had a population of about one thousand households, two hundred of which were Armenian. But the local Armenians had been deported, and now none were left in the town. The local Turks, being immigrants from the town of the same name in the Caucasus, were fanatical Muslims and fierce enemies of the Armenians. Contrary to our expectations, they not only refused to accept us in Garzbazar, as custom required, but actually ordered us to leave immediately.

We pleaded, saying that we were very tired, and on top of everything we had no bread. We asked that they be kind enough to at least sell us some bread, which we were willing to pay for; then we would readily sleep outdoors near the bridge—or it would be enough if they permitted us to purchase our food from the town.

The police soldiers, however, considered this plea as defiance of the government, and about ten of them rushed upon us with whips and clubs and struck the head of anyone sitting in the meadow who got in their way. When the thick tree branches they used as clubs broke, they kicked our hapless people with the heels and spurs of their boots. Like sheep under the wolf's sudden attack, we rushed toward the road on which we were supposed to leave. But the violent Armenophobic passion of these human beasts had not yet subsided, and they ran after those lagging behind and beat them mercilessly; these were the most spent and elderly, who fell to the ground unconscious under the blows. Once in a while we could hear a sigh indicating that someone was alive. No one was looking back anymore; despite their bloodied heads, everyone was trying to get away from this hellish town as quickly as they could. The *kaymakam*, in turn, standing at some distance, was signaling the police soldiers with his hands to keep hitting the deportees.

Having run out of patience, I rushed over to pick up an emaciated seventy-year-old and request that they consider his beating concluded. This time the police soldier landed a severe blow on my shoulder as the *kaymakam* yelled from the distance, "Hit the infidel priest" [*Voor kiafir papaza*].

After chasing and beating us in this way for fifteen minutes, the police soldiers finally turned back. The young people in our caravan, provoked by the sight of the blood flowing from so many heads, were saying, "How long are we going to be patient? Is it possible that these abominable people are going to get away with these deeds? Oh, isn't anyone going to live to tell the survivors and future generations of all the suffering we have endured? Oh, Reverend Father, if only you at least could remain alive and write a book." And so I am carrying out your last sacred wish, ill-fated comrades in exile and suffering, now that you are resting in eternal sleep, without a grave and without even a black wooden cross.

As the day was coming to an end, we spent the night in a Turkish village that we happened on half an hour away and there bound our bloody wounds. But oh, who would bind the wounds of our hearts?

The Turkish peasants, seeing our condition and discovering what had happened, cursed the names of Talaat and Enver, saying, *How do you expect these irreligious, ungodly people who don't even have pity on their own nation to have pity on you?* . . . and adding: *The towns and villages were emptied of their inhabitants, and the few remaining males are being taken to the front to be done away with too . . . Yes, they finished you* [the Armenians] *off, but we too got finished off; let the Germans come and be masters of the country.*

The next day we started on the road again under the warm sun and trod upon the fertile plain of Anavarza, which is famous for its abundance. The plain begins outside of Sis and stretches up to the Jihun River; it is for the most part swampy and full of cane fields. If the tributaries were to be regulated with dams, however, it could become quite extensive, for on these virgin soils wheat and cotton could be grown with a 40 to 60 percent yield. Malaria is widespread owing to the swampy climate, but if the swamps and cane fields were drained, the nearby snowcapped Taurus mountains and the northerly wind would make the land very pleasant.

The entire plain stretched before us like the flat, smooth surface of the sea, but we could not see a single moving entity, neither human nor animal. It was spring, but no fieldwork was in progress; not even a flock of sheep or herd of goats could we see grazing on the green meadows. The Ittihad government had confiscated everything, and only scattered yearling foals, calves, lambs, and kid goats grazed around the villages.

When we reached the ruins of the historic fortress of Anavarza, the panorama that opened before us moved our souls. Built on an isolated mountain on the vast plain, it had played a major historic role in the days of the Rubenid Armenian kings. A natural fortress, it has strong high walls and huge comblike towers.

As the sons of an ancient nation rich in historic glories who were being taken to the desert to be destroyed, we were inevitably moved as we passed what remained of the craft of our forefathers. We looked intently toward the fortress, as if pleading for its help, as if calling on the spirits of our ancient kings and princes to rush to our aid.

Below the fortress there was a village surrounded by gardens and orchards, but we saw no sign of life. Well before sunset we reached the edge of the Jihun River, where there was another rather large village, also surrounded by gardens full of trees. In this village, as was by now our custom, we found a few large stables by the riverbank and settled down in them. Taking advantage of the opportunity, we hurried to the bank to wash ourselves and our undergarments, which had become leathery.

Fortunately the stables had not sheltered animals for quite some time, so they were dry; indeed, these stables were palaces for us, and we were content to be permitted to live in them. The Ittihad government had confiscated all useful and domestic animals from the towns and villages—horses, donkeys, cows, oxen, sheep, goats, etc. And as with the people, it had left only the crippled, blind, mangy, and sickly.

A short distance from the village where we had stopped to rest, a pleasant scene opened up before us. The Jihun River, which sprang up from the Albistan mountains, descended here with a rapid current to the Cilician plain and was the real source of Cilicia's fertility. This spring the melting snow had caused it to overflow its banks, and it irrigated all the nearby fields and meadows, its murky and muddy currents and eddies rolling through the fertile fields toward the Mediterranean. It had carried along large tree stumps and branches from the mountains—anything that tried to impede its powerful current and course.

Oh, if only this Jihun had a tongue! What stories it would tell of the Armenian massacres of 1909 in Adana, when the Jihun and its sister river, the Sihun, washed the smashed bodies of thousands of martyrs into the sea! Meanwhile, in the harbor of Payas, the officers of the large naval ships of the mighty European countries had calmly taken photographs of the bodies as if photographing a natural scene. The civilized Christian nations of Europe saw, heard of, and photographed this new carnage against the Cilician Armenians—and considered their duty done.

After spending a rather comfortable night, we took up a small collection so that we might once more fool the stomachs of our needy and most wretched comrades with single morsels. At sunrise we waited our turn to cross the wide inundated Jihun River. The little boat in which we were to reach its opposite bank was in reality a raft made from rough-hewn logs skillfully tied together. Six meters long and four wide, the deck was protected around the perimeter to prevent it from being swamped. Really, it was like a prehistoric ark, the type of craft that was probably still in use on all the rivers in the East.

So that this raft would not be driven by the powerful currents of the river, it moved to and fro by means of a thick metal hawser, whose two facing edges were attached to the raft by means of a thick pulley-shaped rope. Because it could barely accommodate fifteen people at a time, we could not all reach the opposite side of the river together, and the police soldiers had particularly great difficulty in getting their horses across.

As soon as the last group made it over, we hurried to cross the flat, rocky plain so we could reach Osmaniye before dusk. Being extremely tired and thirsty, we found a well, and although the police soldiers did not want us to drink the water, some bribes secured their permission. A wooden pail on an iron chain hung from a large beam above the well, and it took an hour for all of us, in turn, to satisfy our burning thirst, exacerbated by the scorching sun.

Finally, quite some time after sundown, we reached Osmaniye. The responsible government officials had already all gone home, however, and no one wanted to deal with us. A noncommissioned officer of the police soldiers informed us that we could spend the night on the stones in the courtyard of the government building. No one among us dared to complain or show dissatisfaction; on the contrary, remembering how in other towns we had been refused admission outright, we wanted to show our contentment.

Still, we could derive no other benefit from the exceptional honor of being admitted to the town. They did not allow us to buy bread or anything else, saying, "Tomorrow you will satisfy your hunger" . . . we had not eaten since before departing from the last village where we had spent the night, ten hours earlier, and then all we had eaten was a dry piece of dark bread.

The town of Osmaniye, located at the easternmost edge of the Cilician plain where the Amanos mountain chain starts, was the first railroad station we had reached since departing Constantinople. For one year we had been roaming through mountains and valleys deep in Asia Minor, far from any hopeful glimmer of civilization. We had become like wild creatures. So when we reached the German lines of the railroad leading to Baghdad, a new hope of salvation was born in us, and we congratulated one another on having come this far.

But our thoughts of salvation were unfortunately in vain; most of us—except only a rare lucky few, like me—would disappear without a trace in the vast, arid stretches of the Ras-ul-Ain, Nisibin, and Der Zor deserts.

31

Osmaniye to Hasanbeyli and Kanle-gechid

As I have noted, Osmaniye is the western gate to the Amanos mountain chain, where the Amanos tunnels start. The main city on the eastern side of Amanos is Islahiye, three hours by rail from Osmaniye. Osmaniye is only four hours by rail from Adana, and a half hour from the Mamure station, where the mountainous ascent of the Amanos tunnels actually begins. The city, a [provincial] government seat, is also five hours from the Cilician bay, namely the Gulf of Alexandretta.

The few hundred Armenian households once found in Osmaniye had all been deported, so no Armenians were left in the city. As we passed through, we saw that all their homes, stores, and orchards had been turned over to Turkish refugees. The older Turkish refugees had come to these parts after the Balkan War, in accordance with the government's secret intention to neutralize the [local] Armenian population and create an Islamic majority. The more recent Muslim refugees were from the Armenian provinces near the Russian border, which they had fled in great fear of reprisals by the Armenian volunteers. These refugees had left behind whatever was difficult to carry, as they ran for their lives.

They were wretched survivors, subject to epidemics and hunger, since the Turkish government, fixated on war operations, had been unable to deal with the Turkish, Kurdish, and other Muslim refugees and had abandoned them to their languishing fate. From day to day they were being decimated, as were the Armenians; the only difference was that the Armenians were being annihilated through the widespread massacres of the Ittihad government, while the Muslim refugee population was dying on its own.

With foreboding, we spent a sleepless night on the flagstone pavement in the courtyard of the government building, and only the next morning were we given permission to buy some bread. Near us, sitting on rags, we found four elderly Armenian women from Kayseri, sixty to seventy years old. They had been forced into exile during the storms of winter because they had refused to accept Islam and preferred to die instead. The Turkish women who were their neighbors [in Kayseri] couldn't tolerate these women, who clung so steadfastly to their Christian faith, and started a fight with them; they then went to the government and accused the Armenian women of having cursed the Prophet [Muhammad]. Muslims always held this accusation in ready reserve so that in the absence of any real transgression, they could use it to slander and sabotage their Christian, and particularly Armenian, enemies. It's true, after all, that in Turkey the saying "You cursed my faith" [*dinime seoydiun*] has become a mantra.

These Armenian grandmothers had been put on the road from Kayseri on foot and had walked to Osmaniye via the same route we had traveled for forty days. Because of heavy snowfall when they were going through the Gazbel pass, for two weeks they had been forced to stay in various villages where they were not allowed to budge, let alone walk freely. They had neither money nor bread nor shoes nor any other goods whatsoever, so the police soldiers entrusted to bring them to Der Zor took pity on them and collected bread for them from the Turkish peasants in the villages where they spent their nights. Two of the women were barefoot and wearing wooden clogs [*nalin*]. Unable to withstand the hardships of the journey, they had fallen ill, and the police soldiers had seized donkeys from the Turkish peasants to transport the women over certain stretches of the road.

So extreme was the Turkish government's Armenophobic policy that it assumed that these four elderly women, had they been left in Kayseri, would have started a rebellion. They had uttered such vehement curses at the Turkish government, in the presence of major and minor officials, that even the skeptics there feared that one day they would receive their just punishment for their malefactions.

When important officials entering and leaving the government building where we were passed them, the sobbing women would cry out loudly, insolently, and without restraint in Turkish: "Just as they separated the daughters from the mothers, the sons from their fathers, the husbands from the wives, and took away our properties and homes, may God also divide them . . . Just as they ruined our homes and property, let their homes and property be ruined also . . . Let them be ruined [*veran*], let the owls hoot."*

As the women shouted "*Eh, Allah, Allah*" [*sic*], sighing bitterly, the Turkish officials quickly walked by without saying a word or even looking in their faces, not daring to reprimand them. Upon seeing our pitiful condition, the Armenian grandmothers became particularly irate, and when they learned that we had come from far away, they said repeatedly: "The

*In Asia Minor owls were considered unlucky for millennia, and in some regions are still bad omens associated with death and evil spirits.—trans.

despicable ones consider a few men still alive to be too much. They want to destroy you too."

The commander of the local guardhouse—who despite my promise of a bribe, had prevented us from staying in a *khan* in the town—came and ordered us to be ready to leave. As we had arrived late at night, the Turkish officer had not been able to complete the formalities of transferring custody of us over to new authorities, so he did so just prior to our departure. While we stood in line in pairs, he called the roll from the official list. When he saw that no one was missing except for the one who had run away and been killed in Gazbel, he turned to the *chavush* of the police soldiers who had brought us here and, giving him the receipt of transfer, said, "These have been on the road for a month and a half. How is it that not one of them is missing [i.e., killed]?"

And then, turning to the noncommissioned petty officer of the police soldiers who was assigned to take us to Hasanbeyli, he said emphatically, "If any of them dares to escape, execute him immediately and put the responsibility on me." As we departed, they did not permit us even to buy bread from the bread peddlers circling us.

About an hour outside Osmaniye, at the edge of a small river, we bribed our guard soldiers to let us remain there for an hour and wash up before we got back on the road. After a few more hours on the Osmaniye-Hasanbeyli road we reached a place redolent of death, named, to our horror, Kanle-gechid, which means "Bloody Passage." Kanle-gechid lies in a deep valley in the Amanos mountains.

At the foot of the German railroad line, Kanle-gechid is where the climb toward the tunnels begins; it had been a construction center for both the German line and the major highway stretching to Islahiye. Because the Amanos tunnels were not yet opened, the only road to Aleppo was this Kanle-gechid highway. Battalions of laborer soldiers, mostly Armenians, worked all day repairing these roads, for hundreds of military vehicles traveled on this road toward Islahiye. From Islahiye, the railroad provided transportation to Aleppo in four hours. The Baghdad railway, stretching from Haydar Pasha to Aleppo, was interrupted in only two places, in Taurus and the Amanos mountains. During this time the Germans were intent on tunneling through these mountains as quickly as possible to facilitate military transports—of munitions, weapons, cannons, and so on—to the Palestinian and Mesopotamian fronts.

A large traffic hub due to its natural position, Kanle-gechid was at the same time a bloody passage point for the hundreds of thousands of Armenian exiles being driven to Der Zor. A guardhouse for police troops had been built on a small hill here to monitor the passage of people, carts, and all types of vehicles. The German railway company, in turn, had built a large oven so as to provide bread for the hundreds who were working on the railroad line or in the construction of military roads.

During the black days of the Armenian deportations, Kanle-gechid saw its most horrific history, at least the major details of which cannot be omitted here.

In the summer of 1915 one caravan after another passed through Kanle-gechid heading south—hundreds of thousands of Armenians from Adrianople, Rodosto, Bilejik, and Bursa and vicinity, as well as those living in Konya and along the railway line who were deported to Der Zor. In addition, about 200,000 Armenians from the towns of Cilicia had passed through here. When witnesses told us of the tragic and criminal episodes they had seen here, their words would have softened the most hardened of hearts.

Oh, no pen of any individual can possibly convey the suffering and misery of the exiled Armenians who passed through Kanle-gechid on their way to the southern deserts. If all the seas were ink and all the fields were paper, still it would be impossible to describe, in detail, the reality of the endless tortures of hundreds of thousands of them—men, women, elderly, sons, daughters-in-law, daughters, down to children and innocent suckling infants. Persecuted wanderers, surrounded by savage gangs of police soldiers, riding in thousands of wagons and carts and on beasts of burden, though most were on foot and many of those bare. Like dried leaves driven by the wind, they passed through this sole bloody passage of the Amanos and on to the arid deserts of Der Zor, to die without bread, without water, without a shroud, and without a grave.

Through this bloody gorge, according to estimates of high-ranking railroad officials, more than 450,000 Armenians had preceded us heading toward Syria, Mesopotamia, Ras-ul-Ain, Nisibin, or Der Zor. This figure did not include those exiled to the south from Erzerum, Bitlis, the shores of Lake Van, Erzinjan, Sivas, Harput, Diyarbekir, Malatya, and other provinces and interior regions.

Barely had the men from these regions been separated from the women and put on the road to exile when they were mercilessly slaughtered and their corpses thrown into the rivers or valleys as food for vultures and other wild animals. The young brides and virgins were yanked from the embrace of their crying mothers and taken to Turkish harems; even ten-year-old girls were subjected to all manner of savage, unbearable Turkish debauchery. The older women who managed to endure the terrible hardships of the road were taken to Der Zor, where they were brutally slaughtered during the summer of 1916 in the large-scale massacre committed by Zeki, the *mutasarrif* of Der Zor.

Here in Kanle-gechid we unexpectedly met two young Armenians from

Constantinople who were noncommissioned officers and graduates of the city's civil engineering school. As guard [*conducteur*] officers, they were overseeing the work of an Armenian labor battalion that was building the Kanle-gechid–Hasanbeyli–Islahiye mountain highway.

These two Armenian officers, having been on duty in Kanle-gechid since the spring of 1915, were the eyewitnesses to what had happened to their exiled race. In tears, they told me how in 1915, particularly in September and October, when the exodus had reached its peak, approximately eighty thousand Armenians of both sexes were encamped under tents made from bedsheets and rags on the plain near the Kanle-gechid valley, stretching all the way to the spacious swampy field by the Mamure railway station. Reportedly six hundred to seven hundred were dying daily from fever and various epidemics—when suddenly a lengthy nocturnal autumn rain came and finished the task left unfinished by the human beasts. The people were stuck in the standing pools of water for several days; severe cold ensued, and none of them had adequate shelter, clothing, or food. They froze to death by the thousands, falling like the autumn leaves, or they died from dysentery, diarrhea, bleeding, and the other plagues of overcrowding. The field was soon covered with mounds of unburied bodies. Under makeshift tents entire families were reduced to corpses by hunger and the cold, with no one to bury them. Nor could those Armenians who found their dead kinfolk find any spades or hoes to bury them with.

And behold, suddenly one morning—to bring this widespread and heartrending wretchedness to its ultimate perfection—the director of the exiled caravans [*sevkiyat mudur*] and hundreds of police soldiers bearing whips and clubs surrounded the poor people already at death's door and ordered them to get immediately on the road to Islahiye.

It isn't humanly possible to imagine the hue and cry, the begging and pleading, and the chaos that prevailed in and around those thousands of tents. Then the tents were taken down, and the portable goods and bundles representing the deportees' last bits of property were assembled; but they had neither carts, nor wagons, nor beasts of burden to carry them. The lamentation then began: many would not leave loved ones who were sick in their death throes lying on the ground, uncared for and abandoned; the dying, aghast, begged not to be abandoned in the open field as food for hungry wolves and corpse-eating hyenas that prowled at night. But they had no time to think; the military police and major and minor officials of the *sevkiyat* fell upon them. Without pity or human feeling they struck the hapless and confused left and right, hitting them everywhere: eyes burst open, skulls were crushed, faces were covered with blood, and new wounds were opened up. Nobody cared. Nobody took pity on them.

The survivors, seeing that they had no option but to leave, took down and folded thousands of tents in an instant and, throwing them over their shoulders, got on the road, leaving their ill and dying loved ones behind. The wretched Armenian mothers who were unable to take their underage children (two to six years old)—children who had fallen ill from starvation, extreme cold, and the hardship of the long road, half dead or in the throes of death—had to leave them on top of the already dead. Tearfully, the eyewitnesses told us how two large mounds of corpses of thousands of Armenian children rose up in front of Kanle-gechid, among them also numerous children who had not yet died and who extended their small hands, searching for their mothers. The eyes of these emaciated and neglected angels bore a look of pleading and protest, directed toward their mothers and toward God. And from their half-dead lips, some of them cried that sacred word "Mommy" [*Maariiiig*] for the last time.

Since their mothers could not possibly take the children along—in a few hours the little ones would be dead and would have to be left on the road anyway—it was perhaps better that all of them, the offspring of the same wretched and persecuted nation, lay down in heaps in one place; maybe God and men would finally have pity and see that this was suffering enough.

Instead of half-dead children, mothers carried on their bosoms the weakest and most exhausted of the children still alive—until they too had to be abandoned.

I wonder, is it possible for the human mind to imagine thousands of mothers clutching their near-dead or frozen children, leaving behind a mound of child corpses? . . . And walking away with their heads lowered and backs bowed, looking backward, their hearts rent and dried up, their tongues quivering with curses . . . "Let them get theirs [their just reward] from God"?

The angelic souls of thousands of Armenian children were rising to heaven, to tell God of their beloved mothers' endless sufferings and misfortunes. Those remaining in the caravans of Armenian exiles moved on and disappeared into the mountains of Amanos, heading toward Hasanbeyli and Keller. There was an all-encompassing deep silence as night came; then the howling and yelping of hungry wolves, jackals, and foxes, and occasionally the faint screams of Armenian children being eaten. The animals would eat the live ones first.

These same young Armenian officers told us of other equally horrific episodes from the autumn of 1915 in Kanle-gechid. From all directions caravans of thousands of Armenians heading toward Der Zor via Aleppo reached Kanle-gechid in succession. Then the high-ranking civil and military officials overseeing the exodus detained them so as to exploit the chaos among the tens of thousands in order to fill their own pockets. Thus, as the tents of the exiles increased by the hundreds and thousands, major and minor Turkish civil and military officials, police soldiers, and bandits came from all over to plunder the hapless people by night.

Turkish officials would pass through the dense rows of tents by day and mark the beautiful Armenian girls who caught their eye; then at night they would attack and kidnap those innocent virgins. Suddenly screeches would emanate from those tents, and the horrified girls would be dragged out by their hair. The mothers wouldn't let go of their children until the police soldiers hit them with their gun butts. In response to the screams, distraught Armenian youths, even knowing the danger, would rush from their tents, their sole concern to rescue an innocent sister and to try to protect the honor of their race, only to be struck by a bullet.

By night, the Turkish officials took the abducted virgins down into a valley to wantonly satisfy their bestial passions, often in groups, until the women were lifeless. The officials then dismembered the bodies, and threw them off the cliffs.

For this reason, to have a better chance of preventing an abduction, mothers with beautiful daughters would pitch their tents in the middle of the forest of tents.

In one of the wooden military barracks on the right side of the road from Kanle-gechid to Hasanbeyli, we sat with the two Armenian military officers, crying as we described what we had seen and heard. The more details we exchanged about these criminal events, the more agitated our souls became, and a blazing fire of revenge burned within us, but to no avail.

The two officers urged me to run away and save my soul; they promised to make all necessary arrangements and to personally escort me to safety. They tried to convince me that since I knew German, my salvation was assured, for the German civil engineers were only a half hour away and in need of German-speaking Armenians to work as translators. Once I got in with the Germans, they said, no one could touch me.

But they could not persuade me because I would save myself only if I could save my comrades, or flee with them, particularly since the Turk whom we had sent from Sis to Ayran was to meet us the very next day outside Keller. I would not think of myself alone and violate the benevolent ties that, even while being reminders of these black days, were more precious than all the memories of the good days.

They continued their attempts to persuade me that my more than one hundred comrades were for the most part finished and of no good to the nation, and that tomorrow's Armenians needed Armenian intellectuals and people who could reconstruct the homeland.

Seeing that I would not be moved from what had become an inner creed, they relented, and finally we agreed that I would write a letter in German to the head of the German civil engineers of the Amanos railway line, Morf, to inquire about employment on the railway. One of them would deliver the letter by horseback at night and bring an answer to Hasanbeyli without fail.

While I was busy writing this letter, suddenly the Turkish officer of the Kanle-gechid police soldiers came in and greeted us. You can imagine my dread: pen in hand, I had just at that moment finished the letter when I heard his voice. I hid the paper between my knees and, trembling with fear, turned to ascertain the reason for this sudden visit. The three of us were surprised that this officer had tracked us down, since we had taken precautionary measures before coming here. As it happened, he had come not to arrest us but rather to plead with us.

The head of the railway workers in Kanle-gechid was a Greek man who had seen the beautiful daughter of one of the exile families passing through town and fallen in love with her. He then made all material and moral sacrifices necessary to free both the girl and her entire family—father, mother, and two little brothers. Thanks to the intervention of this same officer of the Kanle-gechid police soldiers, the Greek had taken them to his home. Now, upon hearing that the newly arrived caravan included one "despot" and one priest, this same Greek man asked the Turkish officer if he would further use his influence to persuade me to perform the wedding ceremony for him and his beloved Armenian girl. So when the Turkish officer came and asked me politely, I accepted with great joy—and my fears abated.

That very night, together with Turkish police soldiers and the two Armenian officers, we went to the home of the Greek foreman, where I verified that the girl and her parents indeed earnestly wanted this marriage out of gratitude to their Greek son-in-law-to-be, who had saved them from exile. They also invited Father Housig Kachouni, and together we performed the marriage ceremony, more or less recalling the main prayers that we recited from memory as we had no copy of the missal. Then we were offered hospitality, and I had a chance to sit in a corner and finish my letter in German. The younger of the two Armenian officers then mounted his horse and with the letter got on the road to Ayran, only four hours away.

Because the poor, exiled people of my caravan could find no shelter, they were forced to spend the night outdoors on the rocks; the valley was so cold, they had to make fires close to one another. At sunrise, before we left Kanle-gechid, on the bridge we saw some German trucks that had come from Aleppo. In them were the first German officers we had encountered. My comrades asked that I approach the first military vehicle, and in German I said to the officer, a major: "We've come from far away and have been walking for more than a month and a half. We have suffered much, and we are no longer capable of enduring; we lack even dry bread to keep us going. Please intervene on our behalf and find us jobs on the German railroad line."

In a coarse tone the officer told me that he could do nothing, and pointing to the automobile behind him, he recommended that I ask for help and mercy from the person who was in it. When I went to the second automobile and opened the curtain, I found a Turkish pasha sitting inside . . . and I backed away, terrified . . . I had turned to the German officer for help, and he was sending me to our executioners.

When my comrades, who were standing behind me in their tattered clothing with their tired faces, saw the coldheartedness of the German officer, they were enraged and showered curses on him before quickly moving away. They believed the German no less cruel and merciless than the Turk and thought the two allies indeed deserved each other.

We asked another German, a noncommissioned officer, to allow us to buy bread from the German bakery, but he refused and even came and stood in front of the bakery with his whip to drive away our friends who, with money in hand, had gathered there. He bellowed that only those under the German administration could buy bread from that bakery—whose flour nevertheless was made from the wheat of our [Armenian] fields.

While we were in Kanle-gechid, many Armenians who had witnessed nearly half a million pass through uttered laments, shaking their heads in despair: "Reverend Father, look at the fate of the Armenians. This time the Turks have done something unthinkable. Surely we are finished . . . even if you look for an Armenian who has some medicine, you cannot find one. The ones who went to the desert will also perish from hunger. Oh, why did the heads of our nation not surmise and take preventive measures? . . . It is a pity, now it is too late. Who is left, and what can we do after this . . . ? Zeytoun also fell. Only Van, Shabin Karahisar, and Ourfa were able to salvage Armenian honor with their heroic resistance."*

Finally we departed from this hellish place, aptly named Bloody Passage. On the one hand, we were disconsolate to hear the eyewitnesses' stories; on the other hand, however, we were hopeful and excited by the idea that we might be saved through our imminent escape.

Through winding mountain roads our caravan slowly ascended to Hasanbeyli. We had entered the Amanos mountains, known in the region

*Also the Armenians of Musa Dagh resisted heroically in September 1915, which inspired Franz Werfel's 1934 novel, *The Forty Days of Musa Dagh*.—trans.

as Gyavoor daghi [Infidel mountains]. Because this was the only way from Adana to Aleppo, a wide highway had been constructed—by the Armenian soldiers of the labor battalion. For their ten hours of daily work, these workers received only a piece of dry black bread without even German soup [*Alman chorbaseh*]. In the event that they got sick, death awaited them; no care was available, neither doctors nor medicine, and their Turkish supervising officers constantly told them, "You should consider yourselves lucky to be alive as labor battalion soldiers and living for free. What more do you want?"

The idea of escape uplifted us all, especially the green youth. As exhausted as they were by the tribulations of a long, hard journey on foot, they nevertheless longed to stay alive and see joyful days. These young pilgrims of the desert, rising above all the difficulties they had endured so far, walked and sang:

Crane, where are you coming from? I'm hanging on your voice,
Crane, don't you have a bit of news from our country?
Don't hurry, you will soon catch up to your flock,
Crane, don't you have a bit of news from our country?

I have left my fields and orchards and come . . .
As much as I heave deep sighs, my soul gets plucked.
Crane, wait a while, your voice is my soul,
Crane, don't you have a bit of news from our country?

Our hearts desired and we got up and left . . .
We learned of the worries of this false temporary world
We are left yearning for the simple, decent folk . . .
Crane, don't you have a bit of news from our country? . . .

God, from you I ask for mercy and kindness,
The émigré's heart is wounded, his soul is like a consumptive's
His drinking water is bitter, his bread is inedible,
Crane, don't you have a bit of news from our country?

I don't care if I burn, I will die as an émigré . . .
Crane, don't you have a bit of news from our country?

I wonder whether the homesick Armenian poet, when he wrote these lines, had even imagined such black and bloody days, when the entire Armenian population would die as exiles in the deserts of Der Zor, without bread, without water, and without a grave.

And we, the remaining members of the caravan, were repeating from the depths of hearts filled with the fire of revenge and grief: "I don't care if I burn, I will die as an émigré . . . Crane, don't you have a bit of news from our country?"

As we walked we sang, and as we ascended the forest-covered mountains of Hasanbeyli, we cried. On the hill rising above Hasanbeyli, at last we saw the ruins of the Armenian church that had been destroyed by Adana's previous governor-general, Jemal Pasha (later minister of the marine and supreme commander of the Turkish army moving against Egypt). Its walls stood erect, witness to the screaming injustice of the Turks. One after another, two-story houses appeared, and the bazaar of Hasanbeyli, and finally we reached the town.

32

Hasanbeyli to Islahiye: The Sweet Smell of Bread

Hasanbeyli is a completely Armenian town deep in the forested Amanos mountains with a healthful climate and cold springs. As the seat of the *kaymakam*, it has been an important center, along with other Armenian and Turkish villages in the vicinity. The Armenians of this district in particular have been brave mountaineers, rebellious in the face of the despotic Turkish government. There they have been able to uphold their honor, refusing to be trampled on by the criminal hordes of bandits.

Before the war it had a population of more than eight hundred Armenian households, but when we were passing through in 1916, there were only forty left—tradespeople exceptionally lucky to be allowed to stay. As blacksmiths, textile weavers, furniture makers, carriage makers, carpenters, saddlers, harness makers, or furriers, they all worked in the army workshops. From what we could gather, there were at most 165 of them.

When our caravan reached Hasanbeyli, we entered a row of stores selling a variety of goods; lining both sides of the main road, they made up the town's marketplace. Since setting out from Kanle-gechid, we had been walking for almost seven hours and were terribly hungry, having not been permitted to buy bread at the time of our departure; on the road we had not come across any village or station where we could obtain bread for all of us. When we finally found ourselves in front of a bakery, we all rushed in. Immediately, however, the police soldiers fell upon us with whips, screaming, "It is forbidden!" [*Yasaktir*].

Some drops cause the cup to overflow; truly it became impossible to endure such cruelty. Our hunger tormented our stomachs and intestines with contortions. We saw the bread, but we could not buy it even though we could pay for it.

Brandishing their whips, they moved us away just as we were catching the aroma of the bread. Oh, it was so sweet—at that moment all the aromatic oils and perfumes of the world would not have smelled as sweet. But we were forbidden to go and buy it; forced to walk forward, our eyes were behind us from whence came the aroma of the bread. Even though our worn-out souls had endured torture and turmoil for over a year, our desperation for a piece of bread now exceeded all limits. Yes, we had spent many long days hungry, trying to swallow just a piece of unchewable and indigestible black dry bread. We had quieted and encouraged ourselves, saying that there wasn't any bread to be bought, and so we had no choice but to wait and hope. But now that sweet aroma of the bread was taunting our appetite, awakening the tired and spent love of life still lurking within, buried in our inner ashes. We kept seeing the bread we were forbidden to go near.

Many of us, old and young, reduced to skeletons, cried bitterly, saying, "Dying is a thousand times better than living like this. Oh, when are we going to die and be free of this suffering fit for a dog?"

When a soldier was whipping one of the elderly among us, an elderly Turk approached the soldier and said to him: "You who are not afraid of God, these people are already finished. Don't you even let them buy a piece of bread with their own money? Let them eat a piece of bread . . . These doings of ours are not going to be left to us [to enjoy], but those who remain alive will see and suffer [the consequences]." He was one Turk out of a hundred thousand to take pity on us.

After being forced to pass through the entire market, we reached the upper end of the town, where we encountered Armenian worker-soldiers from a labor battalion. Mostly from Constantinople, they were repairing roads that had been ruined by rain. A few of these workers recognized me. One came from the Balat neighborhood, where I had been a preacher—he had had occasion to see me frequently inasmuch as he was in the church choir. Now he fell on me, crying, and kissing my hands. Devastated, he said:

> Reverend Father, what are these days that have fallen upon us? That I should have seen you one day also like this, in rags, without shoes and without human appearance? . . . Oh, oh, oh, we are finished, see to it that you get away . . . Above all, don't go to Der Zor; if you do, then abandon any hope of being saved . . . Everyone who goes there is going to be massacred . . . For the love of God, run away and save yourself . . . Your only salvation is running away . . . The railway lines are a little beyond; once you get yourself there, then you will be saved. Don't be afraid.

As I had been forced to walk since Kayseri, my shoes were so worn that my toes were sticking out . . . and my chemise [*entari*] and overcoat were torn. I showed no trace of normal human appearance. Still, this worker, like his friends, was in no better condition.

Despite their military service, none of them wore military garb. Instead they were working in their civilian clothing, which was worn out, torn to shreds . . . And the tattered strips were hanging down, since the poor fellows didn't have a needle and thread to sew them. They worked ten to twelve hours per day in the cold, snow, rain and wind, and to eat, they were given only 250 drams [about a pound] of bread a day and nothing else. If they fell ill, they were good as dead, having no regular nutrition, no doctors or medication, and no real shelter.

The living quarters of the Armenian worker-soldiers were simply peaked military tents pitched on the meadows, several men in each. Many of them were torn, letting in the cold and rain. And yet these men were not dissatisfied, because they had been given the exceptional favor of being allowed to live. Their comrades, meanwhile—namely, the Armenian soldiers in the interior provinces, who were stationed in Kayseri, Boghazliyan, Yozgat, and Ankara—had met violent death, even at the hands of their Turkish fellow soldiers.

Negotiations were under way for an appropriate place in town to spend the night, and we were awaiting the result. Suddenly the corporal of the guard soldiers came and ordered our caravan to be on our way. Unable to withstand this much torture, we resisted, just as we had tried to do outside Hajin; we did not want to take another step. We were hungry and thirsty, night was approaching, and we were deprived of even a stable in which to rest our heads on manure. A cold northerly wind was blowing. How could we spend the night outdoors in the mountains and valleys?

The corporal told us that the reason for the order was a cholera epidemic in the city; the Turkish military and civil officials did not want us to become infected. But many of our group were in fact looking for an opportunity to die like that, so as to be spared further unbearable torment;

instead of dying and coming to life every day, once and for all they could be dead and delivered.

The officials said there was no appropriate place to house our hundred-person-plus caravan in town because all the abandoned Armenian homes and yards had been turned over to Turkish refugees; the military authority had appropriated the best residences for its own needs. We would have been glad to stay in any ruined building, as long as it provided shelter from the northern wind. But the officials told us in no uncertain terms that since Hasanbeyli was under military authority, we were not permitted to spend even one night at such an important base. They ordered us to move forward without further resistance. The police soldiers were ready with sticks to drive us away—when my comrades asked me to make one last attempt.

They beseeched me to go plead with the military commander to give us shelter for at least one night. I obviously had no authority left; subjecting my shattered dignity to another demeaning experience would be pointless. As the saying goes, however, he who falls into the sea will hug a snake; so it was for people who were caught up in a storm of blood. Wasn't it incumbent upon us to try every avenue and every person, even if these people were our perennial executioners? Perhaps in a fit of compassion they might pity us.

After making inquiries, I found the station commandant [*menzil komutani*], a thirty-year-old Ittihad Turkish officer named Husni, standing in front of the military command headquarters. Despite his youth, he had a rank above major because he was from Salonica [military base of the Ittihad leaders]. I greeted him with extreme politeness in the fawning Turkish style, then beseeched him, in the name of humanity, to be kind enough to let us have at least one night's lodging in the city. We had been walking on the roads for more than a month and a half, I explained, enduring horrific torment and misery, and we were exhausted and unable to move on. The continuous spring rains, I added, made it impossible even to step on the ground, let alone sleep outdoors, for all the water and mud; we were also hungry and wanted at least to purchase a bit of bread. Finally, in the name of their Prophet, I begged him to take pity on us [*merhamet*].

The Turkish officer looked me over from head to toe with a hard stare. Then he said in an irritated tone: "You Armenians are lower than dogs, and yet you have the gall to expect pity, you abominable enemies of the nation and the state? . . . Even if there is space in the city, I will not allow you to spend a night here. You'll sleep outdoors and then go to Der Zor, where you can establish an independent Armenian state . . . Go away and don't let me see you again."

Unable to tolerate such an insult to our entire race—such as I had never heard before—I put my fear aside and said: "Whatever you do to us, you are going to find the same done to you" [*Iden bulur, dunyase dir*]. Exasperated, the commander let me have a powerful slap on my right cheek, shouting, "You dog, get out of here! I'll kill you under my feet right now."

I hurried back to our caravan. On my way through the market, an Armenian tradesman rushed over to me and said, "Reverend Father, let it be over . . . I am going to give you one hundred loaves of bread. Take them and divide them among your exiled people; we saw what happened. Let them get theirs from God."

The Armenian tradesmen working nearby were so upset that the commander had slapped me that some of them wanted to attack him, but their older friends restrained them, warning them of the bloody consequences of such an act. Then to console me, they had hastened to buy some bread on credit, promising to pay for it afterward by taking up a collection among themselves; they gave it to me, to divide it up among my starving fellow deportees.

When I returned to our caravan, those who approached me hoping for good news saw how upset I was. "What has become of you, Reverend Father?" they asked. "What did they do to you? Why is your right cheek so red? What happened?" I was unable to control my emotions, and a few tears slid down my cheeks, burning me like granules of fire. Without my having to say anything, they understood what had happened—and consoled me by saying, "Let them get theirs from God . . . Write this too in one corner of your book." For now we each had the good fortune of eating a small 100-dram [6.25-ounce] loaf of bread, bought at the price of the slap I had received. These were the first morsels of bread we had put in our mouths in fourteen hours; though little, it was better than not eating at all.

Finally, having no recourse, we walked away from Hasanbeyli cursing and disconsolate. After walking for approximately fifty minutes, we reached a valley on the right side of the road. There our military guards decided we would spend the night. In this valley water flowed from all directions. It wasn't that there were no places to lie down; rather, wherever we set foot it was muddy. But it was night, and darkness was all around us, and so willingly or unwillingly we climbed the little hill next to the valley, which appeared to be comparatively dry, collected brushwood, and made fires. Gathering around the fires in groups, we got some relief from the cold northerly wind, which was common on these spring nights and particularly severe at such a high altitude.

None of us had any bedding or blankets, as it had been impossible for us to carry much on foot. A few had some light woolen covers [*batanyaner*], and some had heavy overcoats that served as both bedding and blanket.

At Kayseri, where we had all been forced to continue on foot, all those who had taken bedding or blankets from home, especially the natives of Chankiri, unable to carry heavy loads, were forced to sell their belongings for next to nothing. Others, needing money for bread, had sold their watches and chains as well as bedding, blankets, coats, and wool coverlets—finally, anything of any value. Never mind that the proceeds would buy them bread only once or twice.

But I had nothing to sell. My clergyman's cloak was my only wealth; it served as both bedding and coverlet . . .

During that night Dr. S. D. S., the military physician of Hasanbeyli, from the village of Geyve in the region of Izmit, paid us a surprise visit with the covert intention of helping me to escape. The doctor had come on horse; he was escorted by the young Armenian officer from Kanlegechid who had taken my letter to Ayran to the chief of the German engineers, Morf.

The daring undertaking of these two selfless Armenians, which brought honor on our race, touched me to the core—they were endangering their own lives to save me. In these horrendous times the slightest offense or even suspicion was sufficient grounds to punish an Armenian with death.

In order to satisfy the curiosity of my noble and self-sacrificing visitors, I took them aside and briefly related the tribulations of our journey, what we had seen and heard. Then both of them, unable to hold back any longer, began to weep. Suddenly, cutting me off, the doctor said:

> Reverend Father, later you can tell us at greater length about the tragic journey you have made; now we have come to help you to escape. I have brought the horse with me for that purpose. We are not going to let you continue your journey, because going further than this is going toward certain death. All the Turkish military officials are my acquaintances; I can protect you.

I interrupted the doctor here to tell him about the slap I had received from the commander a few hours before, and to relate the threats that officer had made.

"Don't be afraid," the doctor answered. "I'll take it upon myself to win the favor of them all. Just come with me; you ride the horse, and we will follow you on foot. Also, don't be afraid of the police soldiers guarding you. I know their chief and will bribe him to ignore your escape."

I explained that I could not abandon my comrades in suffering who had come with me, because the Turk whom we had sent from Sis to Ayran was coming to find me in the woods near Keller the following day. Furthermore, I told them, I had high hopes of helping them to escape too, and that after undergoing so many torments and tribulations, I would not do something that, should I survive, would burden my conscience for the rest of my life.

The young officer tried to dissuade me, saying that the people with me were already finished, that those I called my comrades in suffering were emaciated, worn out, and unable to escape even if given the opportunity. Their external appearance, he added, proved that the human spirit inside them had died, and no good could come from staying with them.

But they were unable to convince me, as long as I thought that there might be a bit of hopeful news tomorrow. If I fled, the poor people would not be able to benefit from a favorable opportunity. Also, none of them knew German, so they would have to continue their journey all the way to Der Zor, or to death. Thus I remained unwavering in my refusal.

The young officer warned me that the Germans wouldn't want to take on too much responsibility for helping Armenians escape; therefore, I should not put too much hope in the coming news.

Luckily, Dr. Samuel, who was acquainted with the corporal of our military police and had once saved him from a grave illness, secured from him permission for us to have this lengthy meeting undisturbed. Dr. Samuel had reason to hope that in the event of my escape, our corporal would close his eyes, even if his mouth was not shut in advance with money.

I, however, had resolved never again to trust any Turks, be they old or young, ignorant or educated, religious or irreligious, military or civilian, urban or rural, male or female. After all these near-death trials and experiences, I would have to be an incorrigible fool to still believe in the virtues of the Turks, or to attempt escape by trusting Hasanbeyli's Turkish military and civilian officials. I didn't want to take such a foolish step. If I had survived this far, it was only because of the grace of God and this conviction of mine. But any who decided to trust the Turks got caught and paid for their good nature and naïveté with their lives—sometimes on the very day when the danger seemed to have passed and they thought they had been saved.

Seeing that they were unable to convince me, the doctor and the officer bade me farewell; we kissed, and they left, saying, "You are going to regret losing such a rare opportunity." Prior to departing, Dr. Samuel also gave me a small gift of money, which I accepted with gratitude for our most deprived comrades from Yozgat.

My selfless guests disappeared into the night, brokenhearted. As the hoofbeats of the doctor's horse gradually faded and disappeared, my heart was filled with fire: I pondered whether I had made a mistake and had let slip my only chance of escape. We had completed four-fifths of our journey toward death, and we had little hope of an unexpected salvation on the morrow; under these circumstances, was it excessive for me to remain so committed to my comrades in suffering?

That same night produced one of our blackest memories; had it not been for the fires we made from brushwood, all of us would probably have fallen ill from spending the night in the open on the ground in the bitter north wind. Early in the morning we hurried away from these inhospitable mountains, cursing those miserable pitiless Turks.

The powerful rays of the hot Cilician sun revived our enervated limbs. Relishing the feeling, we gradually climbed to the forested summits of the Amanos mountain chain. We entered the black cedar forests, where the lush reawakening of vernal nature again reminded us of the bottomless depth of our wretched situation—my God, what a contrast, when nature around us had been resurrected, giving life and vitality to everything. The emerald-green grass underfoot and the warbling birds overhead were glorifying nature or the Creator, building nests and singing their love songs of spring. But while tree and flower, bush and fern, nightingale and blackbird, with sweet scents and songs received the good news of reawakening nature, we were being taken to an unknown and bottomless grave.

To die in spring is to die twice.

Passing through the forests, we began to descend the slope of Mount Keller, from which the plain of Islahiye was visible. Suddenly news was brought to me that the fugitive Turkish soldier, whom we had sent from Sis to Ayran, had arrived and wished to see me in secret. We had to slow down the caravan, so as to meet discreetly with our messenger, whom we had been awaiting anxiously since leaving Sis.

Though his arrival was unexpected, his news was not discouraging. The German railroad company people in Ayran had replied that they could not take the responsibility for our escape. If, however, we were to take that responsibility ourselves, and to seek refuge along the railway lines, they promised to give us all work and if necessary also to protect us. They were not, however, willing to take any steps whatsoever to free us forcibly from the police soldiers.

We received supplementary information as well to the effect that if 80 percent of the workers were Turks, then they were soldiers, and if they were Armenians, then they were fugitives from exile. Via our Turkish messenger we sent word to the Armenian foremen [*chavush*] of the Armenian laborers of Keller that a hundred-person caravan was waiting in the valley half an hour away and was asking for assistance and protection to escape.

In the meantime, bribing our police soldiers, we kept the caravan in place, on the pretext of having a rest; we all sat in the meadow and waited impatiently for the news on which our freedom truly depended. After an hour's delay, our Turkish messenger returned and told us that everything would be ready in one hour; we had only to carry out the instructions he brought us, point by point.

Having no option, we bargained with our police-soldier guards to let us stay put for one more hour. We needed this extra time to deliberate among ourselves about a collective escape; therefore we assembled the caravan's leading figures to review the chances of an escape under all circumstances, favorable and unfavorable.

Unfortunately, except for the exiles from Constantinople, the majority—particularly the natives of Chankiri—did not favor attempting escape; they considered it very risky and probably fatal. And when the critical hour to take action came, even those who had continually said that our only salvation lay in escape weakened, too afraid to act, even if we bought the complicity of our police-soldier guards with bribes.

Those who opposed the escape plan made this objection: even if they succeeded in the escape, the Turkish government, in revenge, would confiscate everything they had left behind in Chankiri and exile their wives and daughters too, subjecting them to all kinds of moral and material misfortune and persecution. As for themselves, they feared that during the escape, our police-soldier guards could shoot us dead. Very few believed that bribing them would protect us from being shot down by the guards. The hour was passing, and to buy more time, we doubled the bribes for our police-soldier guards, but unfortunately we were unable to reach a conclusion.

Without exception, all the youths of our caravan wanted to flee, being deeply convinced they would bitterly regret not taking this most auspicious opportunity. Their reason was that the German railway construction company, taking advantage of its written agreement with the Turkish government, was making the greatest overtures to escapees of all kinds and all nationalities: the agreement included the Turkish government's promise to let the company find its officials and laborers in whatever way and manner it pleased, even among military deserters. Only on this condition had the German company undertaken to expedite construction of the railway, which was necessary to ensure the transportation of soldiers and matériel.

In the end, however, we could not reach an agreement among ourselves. Those who had left riches behind did not want to risk losing their property or wealth; only those with no riches and nothing to risk wished to attempt escape at any cost.

Those who felt they had something to lose did not yet understand that, from the day that they had set out on the road to Der Zor, they no longer had either riches or family or children. Only when it was too late and they were standing at the ditch of their grave in the desert sands would they grasp this bitter fact. Meanwhile, unbeknownst to them, a new arrangement had been made with the Armenian foremen to facilitate our escape.

At the appointed time the caravan got on the road again, descending the slopes of Keller. The road took us right through the middle of the town, and then descended through winding cliffs toward the plain of Islahiye. Suddenly a multitude of Armenian laborers surrounded us; when we heard an explosion, they explained, we were all to flee in different directions. Then, using a red flag to signal danger, an Armenian guard-laborer sounded the horn—and suddenly, violently, with successive mighty blasts, chunks of the cliffs came plunging down, while from all directions came deafening shouts of "Escape! Escape!"

In this general chaos and confusion, everybody—laborer, exile, police soldier, animal—fled without looking back. The soaring boulders had fallen in an instant, the uproar and blasts were subsiding, and again peace prevailed—but there was no one to be seen. Then the police soldiers, recovering their composure, appeared on the road again. They bellowed orders to the exiles to assemble quickly and continue on our way or be shot.

The Armenian laborers roaming around us said, "Don't be afraid, don't turn back," but many members of our caravan nonetheless did gradually come out of their hiding places. The more valiant ones lingered before joining the caravan, but the police soldiers swore that they would not let the caravan move forward without accounting for everyone.

The matter dragged on a long time and became quite serious. Those who did not want to return finally had to yield to the pleas of those who insisted that not surrendering would subject the entire caravan to horrendous loss—so the remaining ten or so emerged, and we got back on the road to Islahiye.

The police soldiers, with unspeakable threats, had convinced these pitiful exiles that they would shoot down everyone . . . Indeed, all efforts and attempts to save the lot of them were in vain; our comrades in suffering were so emaciated and worn out that they had lost all strength and vigor. They had the psychology of a herd of dumb sheep, going to their death without complaint, convinced that the sacrifice of their lives was necessary for the ultimate salvation of the Armenian nation—never mind that this sacrifice would be made by the most merciless and torturous of deaths. "At least let future generations live free and not see these black days we have experienced," they would say as they walked toward the grave.

Some too, having lived among Muslims for many centuries, believed in fate and would often say that struggling or rebelling against what was decided was in vain. This doctrine of fate preached by Muhammad to urge the newly converted Muslims to war now instilled in a few of our unfortunate comrades a passivist resignation verging on the suicidal, killing in them all initiative and inclination to take decisive steps.

Among us a few good-natured—or perhaps more accurately, naïve—persons still believed that the Turkish government, having brought them to Der Zor, would give them land and work so they could make a living. They therefore thought it was foolish to endanger their chances of receiving these favors by escaping.

As the sun set, we reached Islahiye, all of us demoralized and despondent, since by then even those who had refused flight understood that they had lost their greatest opportunity.

Unfortunately, we were not allowed to enter the town here either; rather, we were led to an open meadow nearby, twenty minutes away, and were obliged to spend the night on ground soaked by continuous spring rains. The cold night air and mist, as well as the robbers, made it all even more unbearable.

33

Islahiye: A Field of Mounds for Graves

Islahiye is a low-level administrative country town (seat of the *kaymakam*), most of whose population is Muslim. It is located on a spacious plain on the eastern side of the Amanos mountain chain.

As I have noted earlier, in the spring of 1916 the Baghdad railway line extended from Constantinople directly to the Bozanti pass in the Taurus mountains. The line was interrupted here at Bozanti inasmuch as the tunnels through the Taurus hadn't yet been completed; it resumed at Injirli,* before reaching the Mamure station via Adana and Osmaniye. At Mamure, the last stop on the plain of Cilicia, the line was again interrupted, as the tunnels through the Taurus were still under construction. At Islahiye the line resumed, terminating in Aleppo.

In addition to this German railway line to Baghdad, there was the French line from Mersin to Tarsus; by connecting with the German line to Baghdad at Injirli station, it went straight to Adana. Thus when all the

*Injirli: a junction northwest of Tarsus now called Incirlikuyu.—trans.

Armenians living near the railway line were deported, the most fortunate reached Bozanti by train. Those who came on foot went from here via the Giuleg pass route to Injirli, and, paying double the usual fare, then continued by train to Osmaniye via Adana. From there they crossed the Amanos mountain chain on foot via Hasanbeyli until they reached Islahiye.

Islahiye was a special temporary encampment for deported Armenians. From here they were sent to Aleppo on foot unless, through a bribe, they had secured permission to go by train. Aleppo, in turn, was the ultimate site of encampment for the million-plus Armenians deported to the deserts; from there they were sent in caravans, by the luck of the draw or more typically by order of bribes, toward Homs, Hama, or Damascus, or toward Nisibin, Ras-ul-Ain, or Der Zor—the center of the desert and the largest cemetery of the exiled Armenians.

At the time of our arrival in Islahiye, we inferred, the town had a population of about 1,500 households, of which only about 250 had been Armenian. Inasmuch as most of the latter had by now been deported, only four or five Armenian families remained, as railroad employees or suppliers of wood for the locomotives. (The locomotives burned wood because, for the duration of the war, it was impossible to procure coal.) Armenian contractors furnished this firewood, which came mostly from the huge cedar forests of the Amanos and Taurus mountains. Some fifty to sixty Armenians worked along with these contractors as secretaries, laborers, or transporters.

Thus on the Baghdad railway line from Constantinople to Aleppo, three points—Bozanti, Kanle-gechid, and Islahiye—had been transitional gathering places for Armenian deportees who had traversed the roads. Caravans of hundreds or thousands had arrived from all sides, successively increasing the total to tens of thousands, and the number of Armenian deportees reaching the tens of thousands had soon doubled and tripled. The distinct intention was annihilation, for in a naturally disorganized country, under a disorganized government, and under such crowded conditions, to provide food every day for all would be impossible. Thus the Turkish government would be exonerated of having planned an extermination.

The natural consequence of the formation of these huge crowds was mass starvation and the spread of disease. Out of the thousands reaching Islahiye, only a few hundred were put on the road each day, with the excuse that there was no transportation or not enough police soldiers to guard them; as a result, the number of daily deaths from starvation and dysentery increased to incredible proportions. On some days not tens but hundreds of deaths occurred, in tens of thousands of tents, and healthy persons could not be found to gather up the dead and bury them; or if they could be found, there were not enough shovels and hoes to bury so many dead.

The first victims were children, of all ages and both sexes. In a single night the freezing-cold northern wind snatched thousands of them from their mothers. And so when our wretched caravan reached Islahiye, we saw before our eyes a horrific scene that is one of the blackest pages in the annihilation of the Armenians.

The land stretching before us from Islahiye seemed like a battlefield, for the plain was covered with innumerable large and small mounds of earth. These were the graves of Armenians who had been buried fifty or a hundred at a time, and though winter had passed, the mounds of earth had kept their convex shape—and alas, some were veritable hills . . . When we were seized by the thought that these were human hills, filled with Armenians . . . our despair and demoralization reached such a level that we contemplated suicide.

The corpses of tens of thousands of Armenians had been buried—not as the sacred obligation finally due to all mankind, civilized or savage, since prehistoric times. Rather, these corpses had been buried by Muslim laborers sent by the government simply to "cleanse the environment" of the pollution caused by tens of thousands of rotten or decomposed bodies.

The dying Armenians, without the tools or the vigor to bury those already dead, would depart in their caravans every day, leaving the corpses of their loved ones behind, without even the usual loud and protracted expressions of grief. The next day the same fate awaited the rest of the straggling survivors.

The following morning, after we spent a nerve-wracking and heartrending night outdoors in wet meadows, the police soldiers who had brought us this far officially handed our caravan over to the commanders of the Islahiye police soldiers; our names were read out, one by one, as was customary. Aside from our unlucky companion who was killed while fleeing in the snow-covered pass of Gazbel, all of us, despite the strenuous forty-eight-day journey, had managed, miraculously, to reach Islahiye—if not healthy, at least alive.

This quite exceptional circumstance—not unlike what had happened in Osmaniye—caught the attention of the Turkish officer overseeing the transfer operation. To the petty officer of the police soldiers who accompanied us, he expressed his surprise: "What a fortunate group this is! How is it that not one of them was lost? . . . You didn't properly grasp the orders given to you as petty officer." What he meant was, how is it possible for a caravan of a hundred Armenians to make it to Islahiye after walking for seven weeks and especially after traveling the bloodiest route—from Yozgat to Boghazliyan to Kayseri?

On the second morning after our arrival, I received special permission to go into town and purchase essentials for the caravan. I had further intentions, however; namely to learn about recent political events relevant to us and to find a means of escape.

While I was roaming around the Islahiye marketplace in my clerical habit, a Turkish major came over and grabbed me by the hand, saying that as a member of the Ittihad Central Committee and frequent visitor at the Armenian Patriarchate, he knew me personally. Indeed, he knew my surname and that I had studied in Germany. He began speaking to me in German. I couldn't place him, but his face looked familiar, and apparently he had had contact with leading Armenians, for he mentioned many familiar names. He could recall those numerous well-known Dashnak workers and even whether they were extremist or moderate. When he learned that I was being taken to Der Zor with a caravan of a hundred deportees, he expressed his desire to meet at length with all of us.

I objected, saying that we were staying not in a hotel but in an open field a quarter hour from the town, without even a chair to offer someone of his position. He replied that he was coming in an unofficial capacity to observe our situation for himself and to express sympathy. Thus, at the Turkish major's insistence, we made an appointment for that very afternoon. I rushed to make the purchases requested of me and to return to our gathering place before the designated hour.

At precisely the appointed hour, the major arrived on foot with another major, who was black-skinned, and while standing, we answered their questions one by one. These majors, along with eight thousand soldiers, were headed to the Baghdad front to fight the British. Both of them, about forty-five years old, had been educated in Europe (the one who had recognized me was a doctor); they were most polite and gave the impression of being great Armenophiles who regretted what had happened and empathized with our wretched state. I think, however, that they were actually amusing themselves by gaping at our caravan of emaciated and worn-out Armenian deportees and Constantinople intellectuals.

The physician-major, surrounded by our caravan, directed these words specifically to me:

> I very much regret that such a misfortune as this has struck the Armenian nation, which is dear to us. I have always been sympathetic toward the Armenians. When I studied medicine in Paris and Berlin, I got to know a number of Armenians who subsequently achieved important positions, and with whom I subsequently became good and close friends.

In particular, I established friendships with Minas Cheraz, Arshag Chobanian, Agnouni, Vartkes, and a number of revolutionary and Dashnak workers. When I came to Constantinople from Switzerland immediately after the Ottoman Constitution, as an active Ittihad member, I had a very close relationship with your official national circles, and I came to know you on these occasions.

I was with those who came to greet Patriarch [later Catholicos] Matheos Izmirlian, and I was on your steamship. At that time you, as a member of the administrative committee, paid me many honors, as I had come on behalf of the Ittihad Central Committee. But I regret that the Armenian nation has been practically exterminated on account of the unrealistic policy pursued by your political activists. Aram Pasha declared independence in Van, and now, for this betrayal against the fatherland by one of its crazy children, the entire nation has atoned with its blood. For hundreds of years you lived peacefully and prospered more than the Turks, thanks to the Ottoman government. But one day when you dreamed of forming an independent state and plotted against the Turkish government, you received your just punishment . . .

Barely had the war between the Russians and Turks started when an Armenian member of the Ottoman Parliament, Karekin Pastermajian, known as Armen Garo, formed a group of volunteers in the Caucasus and took up arms against the Turkish government. [He did so] without thinking that he would be subjecting his entire clan in Erzerum and his nation to a just course of revenge. But I regret that the innocent and the just were trampled underfoot along with the guilty. It couldn't be any other way, because the Ottoman government, while waging a great life-and-death struggle, didn't have time at all to separate the innocent from the guilty, and so the wet and the dry burned together.

Which government doesn't punish a rebellious people in its land with armed force? . . . Your revolutionary committees were responsible for the blood of these innocent ones. Despite the equality, freedom, fraternity, and justice proclaimed by the Ottoman Constitution, they continued their secret treacherous activity, which had begun during the reign of Sultan Abdul Hamid and caused the tragic deaths of thousands of innocent women and children.

Having walked four-fifths of our road to death, it didn't seem necessary to speak reservedly, and so I responded by saying:

> We have no news about the events in Van. This is the first time we are hearing the name of an Aram Pasha, and truly we were asking ourselves who this novice hero could be. However, it is my profound conviction that the real motive for the Ittihad government's policy to annihilate the Armenians is neither the alleged rebellion at Van nor the bombs found in Yerzenga [Erzinjan] and Kayseri, nor the weapons found in various towns populated by Armenians. On the contrary, the leaders of the Ittihad government had made a threat, both verbally and in writing, on which they made good by taking advantage of the world war: *When the European powers, after agreeing among themselves, attempt to destroy the Ottoman Empire for good, then we shall also destroy all the Christian minorities beneath our ruins.*

The two majors refused to accept what I had said, so I recalled in detail two events.

First, on the day after the [proclamation of the] Ottoman Constitution, Thursday, July 15 [1908], following the general requiem service for Armenian martyrs (which took place in the cathedral with the participation of more than ten thousand people and in the presence of Ittihad Turkish intellectuals and influential members), a few of the most influential Ittihadist leaders were invited to a reception at the patriarchate. Present there with me was Archbishop Yeghishe Tourian, who had been appointed patriarchal *locum tenens* following the fall, the day before, of the Patriarch Ormanian,[1] since deceased. One of the [Ittihadist leaders] made the following speech:

> We can never forget the large and small material, moral, and human sacrifices made by the Armenian nation to overthrow the despotic Hamidian regime. We confess with pleasure here that the Armenian revolutionaries, and particularly the Armenian Revolutionary Federation committee, became our teacher and pioneer in the Young Turk revolutionary movement, conducted by us against Sultan Hamid's tyranny. Yes, we are eternally grateful to the Armenians, who did whatever was humanly possible to cause the downfall of a detestable despotic regime, while being subjected to unheard-of persecutions and deprivations.
>
> However, now that, with the proclamation of the constitution, the Armenians too have achieved their sought-after freedom and rights like other nations, we hope that hereafter they will spiritually embrace the Ottoman state, which belongs to us all.
>
> But if the Armenian nation chooses to again resort to secret

> treachery, like that which occurred during Sultan Hamid's reign, by working against the new and free Ottoman regime, with the goal of separation, then I declare that we Ittihadists shall punish such a betrayal with a severity to make you wish for the blackest days of the sultan's tyranny.

The two majors with whom we were conversing found it improbable that any Ittihadist would have dared to make such candid statements in an official setting, but it was pointless to argue. I was present and heard all these words with my own ears, and I recorded them that very same day in my diary, from which I have inscribed them here, word for word.

The second event was a speech given in the Rumeli Hisar Ittihad club in March 1912, a year before the Balkan War. Here the Ittihad Central Committee member Abdul Reshid referred to the late great elderly statesman Gladstone, a sincere friend of the Armenian people, as "Donkey, son of a donkey" [*Esheg oghlu esheg*]. He then said, among other things: "If Europe attacks in order to wipe us out, then we will be forced to carry out such a plan of revenge against our subject Christian peoples, that the Europeans will be stupefied and unable to take even a single step against us."

To the two majors, I insisted that this was a long-term plan of the Ittihadists, which they carried out by taking advantage of the current world war. The European powers, engaged in ripping one another apart, were not in a position to prevent the execution of the horrific plan.

In reply, the black-skinned major asked me why, as a clergyman, I engaged in politics, intimating that perhaps the government was right in exiling such dangerous individuals as us from Constantinople. Who else had been exiled from Constantinople? he asked.

I responded that all the well-known intellectuals of Constantinople, including all the Armenian revolutionary leaders, had been exiled with me, and that we had no news from them whatsoever. When I asked the majors whether they had received any word, they quickly replied, "May God give you life, all of them are bound to have died." They expressed particular regret only at the deaths of Zohrab and Vartkes, saying that Vartkes had committed suicide, while Zohrab, who had a heart condition, had suffered a heart attack. We, however, knew that these two had been killed in a frightful martyrdom, just a few hours from Ourfa, at the hands of brigands sent by Dr. Reshid, the fanatical Armenian-hating governor-general of Diyarbekir.

When a few of the young Armenian intellectuals who had been with us since Constantinople complained bitterly about the suffering and misery of our caravan, the two majors responded indifferently: "Give thanks for your having been able to reach here alive, on account of your late deportation. What more do you want?"

Once again, I had to "grab hold of a snake," as the popular Oriental saying has it, and so I appealed to their sympathy. I requested their intercession with the local Turkish government officials to obtain permission to remain in Aleppo. But the black-skinned major quickly retorted, "Der Zor is a better place than Aleppo . . . since your official papers are for Der Zor, you must go there. You remaining Armenians can then establish an independent Armenian authority there one day."

Obviously these men had come not to comfort us but to increase our suffering and to deepen our bloody wounds. It was useless to continue the argument; both majors, with their derisive explanations, gave us to understand that we were worthy, as a nation, of this punishment. After the insincere Turkish formalities of leave-taking, they abandoned us to our fate.

Those of us with faint hopes that our misery might be relieved a bit by the visit of these two Turkish majors again became submerged in a sea of despair.

34

Bad News from Der Zor

By giving the customary bribe, I managed to get special permission to go into town again, unattended by a police soldier, in order to purchase things our companions had requested.

Wanting a bowl of soup, I went into a Greek restaurant that faced the railroad station. As it was long before noon, I had to wait quite a while, since nothing had been prepared yet. Sitting in a corner next to a window, I was observing the passersby, looking for Armenian survivors, when a little hand that was reduced to skin and bones suddenly passed through the half-open window. It was the hand of an eight-year-old boy whose skin had turned to black leather from the desert sun. He was not only bareheaded and barefoot but practically naked, for the rags hanging from the poor lad's shoulders didn't cover half his body.

He was obviously starving; his skin bore the yellow spots characteristic of those dying from hunger. His facial features had become so disfigured that he looked more like a monkey than a human being. In fact, this was not a human being but a human ghost, resurrected from the grave; a desiccated, moving shadow. Even those like us on the road to Der Zor, deserving no less sympathy, would have had to pity this hapless boy. As we were heading toward our graves, this living skeleton seemed to be returning from his . . . In a barely audible voice he begged in Turkish, "Give ten paras for the souls of your deceased ones" [*Effendi, olurerin jane ichun on para ver*]. Yes, he had returned from the grave and was begging for a crust of bread in the name of the dead . . .

I was so moved that, despite thinking that this poor little boy was an orphaned Muslim, I gave him five piasters so he would disappear from my sight . . . for my tormented soul couldn't take seeing him anymore; and then I thought I too would be like this tomorrow. But I had barely put the money into his hand when he raced over to his sister, who had been waiting just ten steps away, and shouted with all the breath he could summon, "Zarug, the priest [*Der baba*] gave me five piasters. Go over to him—he'll give you money too, for sure!"

I was pierced with grief, for the little boy I had taken for a Muslim turned out to be Armenian . . . and the shriveled-up shadow standing off in the distance, barely twelve years old, was his sister, Zarug . . . She could hardly stand, swaying like a stalk of wheat. Encouraged by her little brother Hagop, she slowly walked toward the window and, in turn, extended her leathery, bony hand, saying, "*Der babas*, give ten paras for the souls of your deceased ones . . . we haven't eaten anything for two days." Like her brother, the little girl was a living skeleton, a moving shadow, who might be able to drag her worn-out body around for another day or two.

For the sake of truth, I must mention that she was practically naked; the remnants of a dress hanging off her body didn't even cover her private parts, and the lascivious Turkish passersby made fun of her nakedness, uttering lewd curses . . . The innocent little girl was telling me all this as she was crying.

After looking around and making sure that there were no Muslims in the restaurant—as a matter of fact, there was no one else there because of the hour—I invited the two orphans to come to my window, and I asked them questions. Little Zaruhi related the following, in a schoolgirl's proper Armenian, of which this is a brief summary.

> *Der baba*, my brother and I are natives of Adapazar; my father was a merchant and one of the city's prominent men. I was attending the Hayuhyats [Armenian girls' school]; there were fourteen members in our family: my father, my mother, my sisters, my

> brothers, my maternal aunts and maternal uncles. All of them, in turn, died in exile, especially in Islahiye, and there are only the two of us left . . . how I wish [*keshge*] we hadn't survived . . .

Unable to continue, she began to cry, sobbing. Her little brother Hagop said, "Don't cry, Zarug," and encouraged her [to continue]. "Oh, *Der baba*, we too were rich; we had houses, stores, and gardens. Now we don't have anything, and my brother and I live by begging." At this point two Armenian soldiers with sunburned faces entered the restaurant, greeted me, and came over and sat down. They had come from Der Zor and were coachmen in the military administration. I continued asking questions, and Zarug continued her story.

> Oh, my *Der baba*, wherever we went, they threw us out. Through the windows we would enter the houses left empty by Armenians and sleep there at night, but now those houses are filled with Turkish refugees, so we go to the stables of the *khans* and bury ourselves in the refuse and sleep. But often they don't let us sleep in those places either, and so we go and bury ourselves in the dry garbage dumped in the gardens to sleep, with just our heads showing. When winter came, there were many Armenian orphans trying to live by begging; however, all of them died and we are the only ones remaining. Now I too am sick; I got it from the Turkish youths and now I have no energy and am done for . . . Oh, *Der baba*, can't you send us back to Adapazar? We have many properties; we can make a living there. Wherever we go, the Turks throw us out. If you can't send us back, take Hagop and me wherever you go so we can be free from this place; we would want to eat the scraps in the streets but now the dogs won't let us.

While this forlorn orphan was telling her story, one of the two Armenian soldiers, a native of Malatya, began to cry, like a boy having been bastinadoed: "If one of my children has survived," he exclaimed, "who knows where he is begging like these . . . My God, what a deplorable state we have reached! They've made us worse than the Gypsies."

So moved were we by these children that we hadn't noticed the many customers of various nationalities who had entered as lunchtime approached and were watching in amazement. After we gave what money we could to the two orphans, we sent them on their way, convinced that a few days later our paths would meet in eternity.

I was then left alone with the two Armenian soldiers, who expressed amazement at their luck in finding an Armenian clergyman still alive.

They asked me to tell them—briefly—of our journey. I had barely sketched out our way of the cross when they told me what they had seen on the roads to the Der Zor desert. The one from Malatya, a brave young man, fairly educated, told me the following:

> *Hayr sourp* [Reverend Father], what can I say? It's what is known to everybody. Don't think that there are any Armenians left, and if there are any hanging on, they won't last . . . It's true, the Turks are finished, but these detestable people have finished us off too, along with themselves.
>
> How can I tell you so you will understand? It is impossible for human language to describe what those who went to Der Zor experienced. Thousands of families put on the road from Aleppo, to be sent to Der Zor; of these, not even five percent reached Der Zor alive. Because bandits in the desert, called Yeneze, in groups on horseback and armed with spears, attacked these defenseless people; they killed, they abducted, they raped, they plundered, they selected those appealing to them and carried them off, subjecting those who resisted to horrific tortures, before picking up and leaving. Because it was forbidden and impossible to turn back, those who survived had no choice but to go forward and were subjected to new attacks and plundering. Not even five percent reached Der Zor.
>
> We saw caravans of women, completely naked because the Yeneze bandits who greeted the caravans had taken even their undergarments. We came across thousands of corpses as naked as the day they were born and with eyes gouged out; all their limbs had been cut off for sport and their bodies were swollen; their entrails were spilled out; during the daytime, the vultures would descend on these corpses and feast, while it was the wild animals' turn at night. Reverend Father, where is the God of the Armenians? . . . Where is the Jesus you preach about? . . . Could it be that he doesn't see this unheard-of wretchedness and suffering?
>
> If these stones, fields, and desert sands could speak, what stories they would tell . . . If only you had been here and seen the tribulations of the Armenian people! . . . Reverend Father, they killed people who were hungry and thirsty . . . They sold God's water for money only to those who could pay a lot . . . The poor people were willing to drink even fetid water, and even this water was sold for money. And wasn't it their intention to kill us anyway!
>
> Now I'll tell you, but you won't believe it, that while transporting goods across the deserts by military vehicle, many, many times

> I saw half-naked hungry women and children gathered around dead and stinking animals or camels, and eating the corpses . . . I saw mothers gone mad who had thrown their newly deceased little children into the fire then eating them half cooked or half raw . . . and those who ate rotten corpses got poisoned and died.

I asked him whether there weren't police soldiers with the caravans of deportees to defend them. He replied, "What are you saying? It was the police soldiers accompanying the deportees who sent word to the bandits and then joined in with them. The police soldiers robbed the helpless people and directed the bandits to the beautiful girls, as well as to those with gold or diamond jewelry and coins.

"Reverend Father, it's a shame for you to throw your life away at such a young age. Don't go beyond this point; look after yourself. It's a shame for you and the nation both. As it is, there are so few of us left."

I had no reason to doubt the Armenian soldier's account. He had told me all this just to warn me, so that as I continued, I wouldn't jump into the lap of death. Yes, it was naïve to think that the Turks had had their fill of Armenian blood.

Yes, it was necessary to flee. All those who had tried to convince me that those who had fled had managed to stay alive were right.

For sure, taking just one step forward was foolish; determination was required. What I had seen and heard that day convinced me that I had to take advantage of opportunity. I had decided to flee; now I had to follow through, because there was no time to waste.

Therefore I got to work planning my escape, occupying myself with the most tediously minute details, for I knew that a seemingly insignificant detail could abort the most serious plan. If I failed to escape, clearly I would end up dead.

35

Escape from Islahiye to Ayran

The plan had been made. Now I had to execute it.

Unfortunately, up to now every attempt at collective escape had failed because our men were so demoralized that they were incapable of making any definitive move, even one that could have saved them.

Now they were so emaciated and drained that they asked me to try to obtain permission from the government officials to stay a few days in Islahiye. When the police soldiers told us that we had to travel another seven days on foot to reach Aleppo, we all shuddered.

The train from Islahiye to Aleppo took just five hours, but it was forbidden to deportees, since the real aim of the Turkish government was to wear us down and then ax to death anyone who tried to escape. So petitioning government officials in Islahiye to travel by train was fruitless. But even getting a few days to recuperate in Islahiye would require fervent appeals. We had learned a bitter lesson in Sis—that instead of appealing to the governor, it was better to deal with the chief of police and the commander of the police soldiers, bribing them if necessary.

So I rushed into town again, alone, and went directly to the government building, where I had a private meeting with the deputy captain of the police soldiers. We quickly came to an agreement, with the aid of a few gold pounds, and special permission was granted us to remain two extra days.

The sentry officer of the police soldiers then informed his superior that there weren't enough police soldiers ready to accompany our caravan as required, and only when a group had returned would it be possible for us to depart. Time and again Turkish officials were willing to do this kind of surreptitious dealing if there was money to be had, even if it was against the law. When I returned to that caravan, everyone was most happy that we would have two days of rest.

In whatever way possible, everybody began to mend their torn clothes and shoes. A barber was brought in to rid us of our hair and the beards that choked our heads and faces, making us look truly uncivilized. Everybody wanted to get cleaned up and get hot food in preparation for the final road to the Armenian Golgotha—Der Zor. We were terrified at the thought of walking for more than a month through the deserts to Meskene and Ras-ul-Ain and then Der Zor.

During the two-day rest, I made an effort to see whether we could get on a train to Aleppo. The station chief at Islahiye, a Christian Arab, had told me that a German captain who lived at the station was in charge of special permissions. I hastened to find him.

The German officer was very friendly and listened sympathetically to the story of our horrific journey. He asked how I became fluent in the German language. When I told him that in the fall of 1914 I had been at the University of Berlin, he felt sympathy and promised to do what he could to help our caravan be transported to Aleppo by train. In my presence he sent a telegram to the German commander in chief of railway transportation in Aleppo, requesting special permission for a hundred-plus individuals of our caravan.

When, at his suggestion, I met with him again four hours later, he informed me with much joy that the order had come to allocate one railroad car to us. But a maximum of only sixty persons could accompany me; the remaining ones would have to go to Aleppo on foot. I returned to our caravan site with mixed feelings and relayed the news. It was most upsetting, for the Chankiri and Yozgat groups, who had been joined near Yozgat in such tragic circumstances, would now, for want of money, have to separate for good.

Thus it remained to divide the caravan into two—and oh, how difficult it was for me to be impartial. I had done much more service to the poor of the caravan, which comprised fifty-four natives of Yozgat. I had sheltered and fed them with care and affection throughout our journey, sometimes by begging, sometimes by using my own means to get bread for them. And now all my efforts might go for naught, because in separating them I would be submitting them to the evil winds of fate.

The day of separation finally arrived. The local Islahiye government received a telegram from Aleppo that said: "Whoever can pay the fare to Aleppo may go by train, whereas those who can't pay must immediately prepare to depart on foot." So the fifty-four deportees from Yozgat—the remaining survivors of the three thousand Armenian households of the town, ranging from sixteen to eighty-five years in age, one more emaciated than the next, and surrounded by some eight police soldiers—now came to take their leave of me and their remaining companions.

We were all assembled in one place when they approached, one by one, to kiss my right hand. All of them wept and muttered words of gratitude in barely audible voices. They were kissing my hand, and I, in turn, their sun-blackened foreheads. They were the remaining survivors of my martyred race, whom I was again, for the umpteenth time, putting on the road to death . . . not to see again. Only a few had enough money to buy a crust of dry bread; the remaining fifty had nothing at all.

In response to my urgent appeals and with the help of some of the natives of Chankiri, we raised 135 piasters in silver coins. I added to this sum the two gold pounds that I had been given by a friend the same day to aid my escape, and so I turned over a total of 250 piasters to their leader. This was all they would have until their death.

Having lived by bribes, we were, for the most part, without material means, and our anxiety about what might happen tomorrow or the day after that made the rest of us a bit cautious. Along with our gradually depleting physical energies, I must confess, our moral values had also diminished. The panic imminent death engendered had made us all more selfish and less sympathetic toward our wretched companions.

It's sad to admit this, but for truth's sake I must also note that some who had been selflessly heroic in earlier times of danger now fell into the egocentric ways of their weaker comrades.

It is impossible to forget this black day of separation. Oh, the Yozgat natives were so grateful, so noble, and so loyal to their nation and religion. Deprived of their loved ones and all else, and near the end of their lives, they still displayed a heroic spirit, disdainful of death. They would fall victim to the Der Zor massacres in Ras-ul-Ain in the summer of 1916; all of them now lie in eternal sleep in the sands of those deserts. The only Yozgat natives who managed to reach the southern deserts alive joined the other 160,000 Armenian deportees who were eventually martyred in Der Zor during that period.

After we saw our companions off, we proceeded to the third-class car allotted to us. Just at this moment a frightful downpour began to turn the plain of Islahiye into a lake. It was midday. An Armenian about fifty years old with a rather powerful physique approached, asking about the daily tribulations of our roads of exile. This man appeared just as I was racking my brain to figure out an escape route, having found all roads before me closed off. I couldn't entrust a stranger with my escape plan, as it could be ruined if he were loose-lipped. Hardly had this man left me, however, when I instinctively ran after him and grabbed him, then told him about my secret plan. After calmly listening to the details of my plan, he turned and said,

> I'm just the person you're looking for; God must have sent me to you. I said I was from Bardizag, but I'm really a native of Van. Since the Van resistance, I've been saying that I'm from Bardizag

> so I won't be harassed. My name is Hovhannes, I'm fifty-two, and for fourteen years I was involved in tobacco smuggling in the region of Izmit. I have "knocked off" many an inspector of the *reji.* Finally the government, having no recourse, made me a police soldier with special pay so I would chase down the tobacco smugglers, all of whom I already knew. I've often gone as far as Armash, and I think I've also seen you there.
>
> Reverend Father, at your young age it's a shame for you to sacrifice yourself for the sake of these deportees. They're done for; they will be useless after this. I'll help you flee and take you wherever you want—just tell me where you want to go.

I told him I wanted to go to Ayran, headquarters for the construction of the Amanos line of the German railroad. If I were to be arrested during the escape, however, I would be killed without fail, and so would he. I asked him what security measures he could take to protect us from being shot.

Without hesitation, he responded:

> I have a friend who is very brave, and both of us are armed. We shall go by untraveled mountain roads and through forests; if we unexpectedly come across a police soldier or any Muslim who, suspecting us, wishes to arrest us or threatens our lives, we'll kill him on the spot and keep going. They've killed so many Armenians—hundreds of thousands—are we perhaps committing a sin if we kill a few of them? Of course, you'll grant us forgiveness . . . You must wear a disguise and trust me. I have two children; I swear on their lives that I won't harm you as long as I live. The nation needs you; they've killed so many of our leaders. I feel that by saving you, I will have done a great favor for the survivors of our nation. May God protect and save his servant and us from the hands of these detestable ones. Pray tonight for the three of us. Tomorrow morning, before dawn, come to this pointed tent you see facing us. We'll be ready when you arrive, and we'll set out armed for Ayran.

Having lost all faith in people, we had trusted only in God and had survived until now. Without that trust it would have been humanly impossible to endure such suffering and grief for so long without becoming utterly demoralized.

Since all the arrangements [for the train to Aleppo] had fallen on me, I did what was necessary for the comfort of our sixty-plus companions. We were put in a dirty third-class car, and that night I took up a collection to cover the forty-piaster train fare for a few of the Constantinople natives who were unable to pay it.

I had divulged my secret plan to only one or two of my close friends. One of them, Setrak Shakhian, who had been kind enough to loan me 25 gold pounds, gave me 3 gold pounds at the last minute in the event a bribe became necessary to save my life. In turn, he prayed that I would remain alive by the grace of the Lord, and so he made his will to me verbally, revealing that he had 2,300 gold Ottoman and British pounds in a secret corner of his house. In the event that I survived, he asked that I get his money and allocate it in his memory for an important national need. In these days of death it was rather ironic to hear talk of gold.

For a moment he wished to accompany me on my escape, but then gave up the idea, saying, "I'm sixty-five years old, and I can't walk for long, so you may be endangered on my account. Your life is precious—mine is pretty much over. Save yourself and write the story of our suffering; let the future generations know what a steep price was paid for the salvation and freedom of their nation."

By the grace of God this kindhearted old man survived and lived by selling salt in Aleppo. During my escape from Islahiye, I had twenty-five gold pounds wired to him from Constantinople; it was the amount I had borrowed from him, and he had nothing else remaining to him. After the Armistice, upon my return to Chankiri, I heard that the local Ittihad club had had his house destroyed in an attempt to find his hidden savings. His wife, under threat, had disclosed the whereabouts of the money, and the Ittihadists had divided it among their leaders. Two other friends of mine made similar wills, explicitly entrusting their children to my care.

The night of April 2, 1916—almost one year since my arrest and exile from Constantinople—became one of the most momentous of my life. The train was to depart at 5:10 A.M., when it was still dark. A torrential spring rain had been falling for fifteen hours, with only minor interruption, turning the fields into little lakes; and the brooks and streams overflowed their banks, flooding fields and meadows.

The critical moment was here. I had to make a final effort to get back the freedom that had been stripped from me a year before. I was deeply convinced that my only salvation lay in escape. I had no time to become demoralized or pessimistic. I had to take the definitive step by summoning all my spiritual or moral powers. Only in that way would I ever see the birth of the Armenian nation that would follow centuries of painful labor.

The rosy-fingered dawn over the snow-covered peak of Mount Ararat shined rays of resurrection on the scattered children of Armenia who longed for their fatherland. The days of dying had passed; it was time to live, to see the marvelous revitalization of the Armenian people, with an excitement that recalled the souls of their ancestors.

Inspired by all these thoughts as I was still huddled up in a corner of our railway car, I was already considering myself saved. It was five o'clock, and the train would be leaving in ten minutes. A bayonet-wielding police soldier was posted at the door of the car, and I convinced him to let me leave for a few minutes to attend to an urgent matter. I took only a few dozen steps in the dark—then I removed my clerical overcoat and emerged in a disguise that made me unrecognizable. I took a few dozen more steps, then hesitated for a moment and wondered whether I was heading toward salvation or death.

But this was no time to hesitate. I had to shake free from this passivity and defeatism. From now on I had to be master of my fate. I knelt on the muddy ground and said from the depths of my heart: "Lord, guide me" [*Der ughya*], and mumbled a few short prayers, and then my fears and worries evaporated. I had taken heart. No longer was I looking back.

In ten minutes I was in front of the small pointed tent designated as our meeting place.

Barely had I called out "Hovhannes" when my two brave, selfless, armed compatriots came flying out, at risk to their lives, for the sake of saving me. While the downpour camouflaged our escape, our little band of three fugitives disappeared, along with the dawn, into the forests facing Islahiye. Because the rain had interrupted the traffic, the road was now clear before us. It would be eight hours before we reached Ayran.

Taking shelter from the rain under rocks in the forest, I hastened to change the style of my hair and beard with the scissors and small mirror that I had taken with me. As it was, I had become unrecognizable . . . and in two months my black hair had turned white. From here on, having put ourselves in the good Lord's hands, we avoided human contact and all moving creatures and proceeded toward an unknown destiny.

VOLUME TWO

The Life of a Fugitive

APRIL 1916–JANUARY 1919

PART I

In the Tunnels of Amanos

1

Escape on the Way to Ayran-Baghche (Vineyard)

The torrential rainfall lasted more than eighteen hours with scarcely an interruption. We walked nonstop, our goal to reach Ayran as soon as possible, the first stop on what we hoped would be the road to freedom. We were just three fugitives, but so confident were we that we felt as if an army were protecting us.

Woe to the one who became demoralized, for he would be lost and court danger. My transformation in the forest had made me a new man, bold and fearless; clothing can change one's disposition and spiritual power in ways I had not realized. A peace-loving and meek servant of the church had abruptly been transformed into a young adventurer ready to employ all of his physical, intellectual, and moral energies to save his life. But any misjudgment would result in death.

My two fellow travelers had displayed such devotion and self-sacrifice, voluntarily becoming fugitives just to save me; now they were facing the same mortal danger. But we banished every pessimistic thought and remained excited by the indestructible hope of salvation. We had been walking for five hours and were panting when we reached the base of Mount Intilli, from which emerged the tunnel that began at Ayran, the longest mountain railroad. We entered the construction zone of laborers and for the first time encountered passersby.

Our route to Ayran passed through Intilli on the eastern terrace of Mount Ayran, because it was the only way to get to the central office of the Ayran tunnels where Morf—the senior head of civil engineers and the construction supervisor of the Ayran-Baghche railroad tunnels—was stationed.

We avoided going through Keller, since our caravan had passed through there a few days before; I could well be recognized and betrayed. Thus, having no choice, we began to climb Mount Ayran. At the very first step we encountered a Turkish police soldier on horseback, carefully leading his horse by the reins down the mountain slope. We reacted calmly and with song, pretending to be part of the railway crew, greeting him and moving on. So tired were we from climbing the mountain that when we passed through Intilli and came upon a taverna owned by a Greek, we went in and sat down at a bare, dirty wooden table to have something to eat. We had finished half our meal when inquisitive looks from several Armenian and Greek customers alarmed us, so we left in haste.

We were starting up the mountain again, on the road alongside the newly built railway above the village, when we encountered a multitude of Armenian women and girls sitting here and there on piles of rocks. Hundreds of them, and children of all ages and sizes, were buried in rags, mud, dirt, and misery. Their sunburned, wrinkled, blackened faces spoke volumes; without exception they were emaciated. The mothers had set their little suckling infants down next to them on wet tattered haircloth sacks of cement. It was impossible not to be moved by their heartrending cries.

Under the torrential spring rain, these refugees were breaking stones with iron hammers, turning rocks into pebbles to prepare a base for the newly installed railway tracks. Both adults and children were hammering stones in exchange for half a kilogram of indigestible mixed-grain bread, so that they might carry on for—who knows?—a day, a week, a month? I found out that these mostly female laborers had fled their deportation caravans, which had been sent along the railroad and then into the mountains stretching from Kanle-gechid to Keller, and had sought refuge. They had come from Izmit, Bardizag, Adapazar, and the Armenian villages of the Izmit plain—Bilejik, Eskishehir, Konya, Eregli, and their surrounding areas.

These people were so demoralized and were accustomed to such contempt as to be amazed that anyone would still show interest in them . . . They did not know it was an Armenian pastor and fugitive now witnessing their tragic situation, who would carry their story to the hypocritical Christians of the civilized world.

What of their abodes? Oh, thousands of Armenian women and children who had once had happy homes, lands, vineyards, orchards, gardens, and wealth were now living under makeshift tents of bedsheets, whose tattered pieces fluttered in the northern winds. Inside these tents were dirty pieces of haircloth on which scrawny infants rolled about and cried for milk. Alas, there were neither mothers nor milk, for the mothers were far off breaking rocks and were not permitted to return to their tents until the workday was over.

Despite this miserable situation, these families were content because they were not on their way to Der Zor. For a while now rumors had been circulating that the Armenians who had fled and found refuge along the railway line were going to be deported to the southern deserts. These rumors caused great anxiety, and so the bread was indigestible and the water bitter. The Armenian poet had sung so prophetically of the life and bitter sufferings of the exiled, when he called out to the crane, harbinger of spring:

Groong, oosdi gookas, dzara em tsainit,
Groong, mer ashkharhen khabrig muh choonis?
Mee vazer, yeramit shoodov guh hasnis.
Groong mer ashkharhen khabrig muh choonis?

Togher eger em, miulkerus oo aikis,
Kani vor akh g'anem goo kaghvi hokis;
Groong bah muh getsir, tserniguh eh hokis;
Groong, mer ashkharhen khabrig muh choonis?

Surdernis gametsav yelank knatsank . . .
Ais sood asdunvoris darderun imatsank,
Aghoohatsger martgants garod mnatsank . . .
Groong, mer ashkharhen khabrig muh choonis?

Asdvadz, kezme g'uzem moorvet oo kerim,
Gharibin sirdun eh khots, jigerun eh verem,
Khumadz choorun eh leghi, oo hatsuh haram,
Groong, mer ashkharhen khabrig muh choonis?

Airilus chem hokar, gharib guh mernim . . .
*Groong, mer ashkharhen khabrig muh choonis?**

It was beyond the imagination of any Armenian that days would come, black days, when an entire nation would be killed, or in exile, homeless, without refuge, hungry, thirsty, and persecuted.

This was the first time since the summer of 1915 that we had come across groups of Armenian survivors—men, women, and children. We thanked God for this too, since the Turks had led us to believe that, besides those in our caravan, and those in Constantinople and Smyrna, there were no Armenians left in Turkey.

*See translation on page 229.

For a moment or two, on seeing this misery, we lost hope. And we asked ourselves: Why are we living and for whom are we living? . . . But then, suddenly, the flaming fire of life strengthened our weary steps. No! No! On the contrary, it was necessary to live at all costs . . . all that mattered was to stay alive and see the resurrection of the Armenian people.

With energetic strides we walked quickly up the mountain, then entered the dense forests of Ayran, in the Amanos mountains. We had been walking for six to seven hours, resting for only half an hour in Intilli, when we began to descend to the Ayran valley. From there, by making a small ascent, we would finally reach Ayran: the first stop in our life as fugitives.

For about two hours we hid out under the rubble of a ruined water mill in the valley while one of my traveling companions, Megerdich, a native of Bardizag, went to Ayran to find Armenian families who might hide us for a few days.

The first house he went to was that of the well-known Soghomonian family of Bardizag. No sooner had the elderly Mrs. Soghomonian heard that an Armenian clergyman from Constantinople—who had been deported across Asia Minor and reached the Ayran valley alive—was seeking refuge than she said to Megerdich: "You can't find a safer place than my house. Let him not fear. Let him come; I'll keep him. If we're going to get caught, we'll be arrested and die together . . . My God, to think that our clergymen and leaders would end up like this, wandering over mountains and deserts, subject to all kinds of danger and insults." And she wept.

My guardians had wanted to take me there when they first went, but I had refused to go without being invited, because I didn't want to compromise anybody or have them risk their lives. But given the cordial invitation, at dusk we entered the Soghomonians' house—a one-room wooden hut set off in a remote corner of Mount Ayran—in which Mrs. Soghomonian lived with her son and two daughters, all of whom were employed as laborers or seamstresses for the German railway company.

Throughout all the days of my life, I shall never forget the noble and fearless hospitality that the elderly Mrs. Soghomonian showed me, without even consulting her children; upon coming home in the evening, they found themselves facing an unknown guest.

As it was, I had long since ceased to have a human appearance. For two months I had been choking in dirt and lice. And like my comrades, I had become accustomed to this filth. We would often say to one another, "Oh, if we could just see a bathhouse for once and get cleaned up." Therefore I felt unspeakable joy when the kind and hospitable Mrs. Soghomonian—a deserving Armenian mother in the full sense of the word, owing to the likes of which the race had succeeded in surviving through its tragic history—heated water and bathed and cleaned me with maternal solicitude. She dressed me in her young son-in-law's clean underwear and put hot food she'd cooked in front of me to relish. Then she prepared a clean bed and laid me down to rest.

Resting in a clean, comfortable bed, I felt for the first time in long months that mine was a life fit for human beings. I pulled the blanket over my head—when an unstoppable sobbing burned my throat, and I began weeping bitterly. It was not tomorrow's worries that were causing me to break down: it was the memory of erstwhile happy days, when we had the good fortune of lying in a clean bed like this every night. For who knew, perhaps tomorrow I would again end up wandering over mountain or valley, and being hunted down.

The very next day Papazian, the interpreter who worked for the railroad company in Ayran, visited me at my hiding place and gave me every assurance that he would protect and employ me. All I had to do was put aside my monk's cowl and shave my beard so the police wouldn't recognize me. Because Papazian, a well-liked and respected interpreter, was very influential, I was given a temporary position in the Baghche station, about an hour from here. I had heard that a young priest who had also been a fugitive in Ayran had been caught and murdered, so I shaved quickly and became a new man.

During the four pleasant days I spent as a guest in the Soghomonians' home, I asked them to recount the events of their exile from Izmit to Islahiye, and they told me stories that brought honor to the Armenian clergy. For example, Archbishop Stepannos, the virtuous prelate of Izmit, had refused an exemption from deportation that the government had granted him. He responded to the governor: "Thank you for the benevolence of the government, but I cannot abandon my flock, which I have tended for forty-five years. I have spent good days with them, and I will spend bad days with them." And His Grace [Archbishop] Hovagimian, a majestic and giant figure, bent over by his more than seventy-five years, proceeded to the head of the deportation caravans, and like a modern-day Moses, he led his people toward Bozanti. From there he put his cart at the disposal of the sick members of his flock and went on foot as far as Aleppo.

The Soghomonians told me of the many sufferings and tortures the Armenian deportees had experienced, especially the priests, whom Archbishop Stepannos ordered to remove their habits and shave their beards so as to escape beatings and persecution by the police soldiers.

Four days later, at dawn on the morning of April 7, 1916, I left the Soghomonians with feelings of overwhelming gratitude for their warm and unforgettable hospitality. Traveling by train along the narrow-gauge track, I arrived unobtrusively at the Baghche station. After Islahiye, the

Baghche station would be the next critical juncture of my escape in the Amanos mountains. In these mountains, following the fall of the Pakradouni kingdom, the founders of the Rubenid kingdom had planted their first strongholds before becoming rulers of Cilicia's fertile mountain plains, from about A.D. 1100 to 1400.

A month later Mrs. Soghomonian died suddenly of typhoid fever. Although I wanted to, I couldn't pay my final respects to this selfless woman, who had become a second mother to me and endangered her life to save me. If I had left the Baghche station for even a quarter of an hour, it could have been disastrous for me.

2

The Remnants of the Armenians in the Amanos Mountains

Holzmann, a German company in Frankfurt, had undertaken the construction of the Constantinople-Baghdad railway with the goal of someday establishing a large German colony in Asia Minor. The railway, stretching continuously for almost three thousand kilometers, was to join the harbor of Constantinople (the shortest water-to-land route between Europe and Asia) directly with the Gulf of Basra.

In 1914, when the Great War erupted, only the Haydar Pasha–Bozanti section of this huge railway project had been completed; the train could reach only as far as Bozanti. There the line was suspended, for numerous tunnels had to be drilled through the huge Taurus mountain chain, the natural barrier between the marshy plains of Konya, Eregli, and Karaman and the beautiful and fertile Cilician plain.

Thanks to a French company, the railroad had been operating for years in the Adana plain, along the Mersin–Tarsus–Adana route, and the German company had already prepared the line from Adana to Osmaniye. Thus for the past ten years the railroad had crossed the fertile 42,000-square-kilometer Cilician plain, connecting its western end to its eastern end and its eastern end to the base of the Amanos mountains. In so doing it benefited all the villages and regions along the way, making a great contribution to the progress and civilization of this marvelous region.

Between Adana and Aleppo, the railroad line encounters a second major obstacle: the huge Amanos mountain chain, beginning near the Gulf of Alexandretta and rising north to join the Taurus mountain chain. After the declaration of the world war in August 1914, the German company, upon the urgent demand of the German government, began feverishly to construct many long tunnels through the Taurus and Amanos mountains. Without them it would have been impossible to send weapons and soldiers from Haydar Pasha station in Constantinople to the two major war fronts of Syria: Palestine and Mesopotamia.

The War Ministry, headed by Enver, made every effort and granted all kinds of special permission so that the German company, by building tunnels, could make direct railway transportation possible between the Taurus and Amanos mountains, allowing the many millions of Muslims in Egypt and India to participate in the war effort. But (without tunnels) the railway encountered a major obstacle when, outside of Bozanti, troops, munitions, travelers, and everything else had to be unloaded from the railroad cars and taken by carriage from the Gulek-Bozanti pass down to Adana. From there they had to be taken, again by rail, to Osmaniye or Mamure—a five-hour journey—and then by another carriage down to Islahiye via the mountainous road through Kanle-gechid and Hasanbeyli. From here, by rail again, it was a four-hour journey to Aleppo.

This disjointed way of travel caused great losses of time and money. Given the necessity of moving munitions and troops rapidly, the Ittihad government pressed the German company to complete the tunnels. It was General [Liman] von Sanders, the German chief of staff in Constantinople, who coerced the Turkish War Ministry to give the Holzmann company permission to employ whomever they chose—including army deserters and Armenians who had escaped deportation—and even to defend them against the government's pursuit.

Taking advantage of this unusual situation, thousands of Armenians, often with their families, bribed the police soldiers guarding them, escaped their caravans, and sought refuge around the construction sites of the Taurus and Amanos tunnels. There they were given work and compensation.

By this arrangement, the railway construction company had established "Arshagavans"[1] in these two centers of tunnel construction, and all kinds of people gathered there—criminals, army deserters, and fugitives, as well as intellectuals and people of all classes and nationalities: Armenian, Turkish, Kurdish, Circassian, and so on.

Because caravans of deportees, traveling sometimes by rail and sometimes on foot, were forced to pass through Kanle-gechid, it was very easy for individuals to escape at night and take refuge near the adjoining railway tracks. In this way more than ten thousand Armenians* had taken refuge around the Amanos tunnels, ranging from Injirli, near the Mamure station, all the way to the Yarbashi-Baghche-Ayran-Intilli-Keller area.

Ayran was the highest point of the tunnels in the Amanos mountains, so it became a center for the construction effort. A large factory for the production and repair of machines was established there with a powerful generator, and there were also facilities serving ancillary purposes: iron and copper fabrication; a foundry; a sawmill; cabinetmaking; and so on.

As Ayran now had thousands of laborers, and many upper- and lower-level employees, including European civil engineers, it also had numerous warehouses for flour, oil, salt, olives, legumes, and other staples. The construction company also made life more tolerable by providing basic items such as tents, blankets, clothing, and shoes.

Barely 5 percent of those working at the construction sites were Europeans, most of them civil engineers. Of the rest, most were Armenian locals, especially the artisans, blacksmiths, carpenters, woodcutters, cabinet- and furniture makers, tailors, cobblers, telegraph workers, and draftsmen. They had been selected from the deportee caravans by special foremen [*chavush*] who went around in search of artisans and brought them up to the line. Among the common laborers were thousands of Kurds and Turks, and because of the prudent precautions of the German engineers, they were not permitted to display enmity toward the Armenian laborers.

The laborers were divided into various grades: boys and girls between twelve and fifteen years of age received 5 piasters a day; women, 10 piasters; common laborers, 10 to 15 piasters; artisans, as much as 30 piasters in paper money. The railway workers could elect to receive their daily bread, provisions, and wood against wages, the cost deducted on the weekly payday. Although the bread given to the laborers was often virtually inedible, owing to exploitative and fraudulent vendors, nevertheless the Armenian workers were content at least to be able to save their lives for the time being.

With few exceptions, the German and especially the Austrian engineers and surveyors treated the Armenians in a kind and compassionate manner. They showed an especially Christian solicitude for Armenian women, girls, and orphans, and they had even opened an orphanage in Intilli. The orphanage was made possible by the initiative of the local Armenian doctor, who was of great service during the war to his suffering compatriots, and by the protection of Koppel, the principal engineer of Intilli.

*No one knew the exact number, for many Armenians were registered with Muslim, Greek, Assyrian, and other names; the number of Armenians in Amanos was estimated at fourteen thousand.—G.B.

Some Armenians complained that the German engineers weren't acting for humane reasons but were merely getting slave labor in exchange for a piece of bread. The truth is that if there were some unscrupulous German civil engineers and surveyors, the majority had noble feelings toward the Armenian people. The old man Winkler, in particular, who had been in charge of surveyors and civil engineers in the second construction division of Adana, treated the Armenians with great paternal concern; he was motivated not by sordid or venal interests but rather by human feeling; he upheld the banner of European civilization and Christianity.

Winkler's successor in Ayran was Morf, a former Austrian officer who also showed special compassion toward the Armenian survivors. His right-hand man was Papazian, the Armenian from Constantinople, who had used his considerable influence to help me obtain my job. He helped Armenians at all costs and was so careless in doing so that sometimes he almost paid for it with his life.

But in the name of truth I must also note that the senior and junior German officers passing through were not friendly toward the Armenians. With very rare exceptions, the German military men, no matter their rank or position, officer or soldier—but especially the officers—behaved inimically toward the Armenians. They were hostile, detached, and unreliable; they simply considered Armenians their enemy, partisans of the Allied powers.

The Armenians, having spoken against the Germans and in favor of the Allies, had perhaps instigated this feeling, even though Armenians within Turkey had not—as a nation at least—derived any benefit from their support. The Turks, spoiled by the protection of the German military and driven by criminal instinct, had fallen upon the wretched, leaderless, and defenseless Armenian people with the fundamental plan of uprooting and annihilating them—a plan they carried out in a fashion that was universally recognized as criminal. The Germans, for their part, wished simply to remain in the role of spectator, thinking that would exonerate them; they maintained that they had no right to interfere in the internal affairs of the Turkish state. In actuality, however, they had seized control of the government of Turkey and regarded it as a vassal state, subject to overthrow.

3

Signs of Imminent New Storms

The Baghche railroad station was the twelfth section in the Ayran construction project of the second division of Adana. The station was in a valley on the rail route, isolated from Baghche, a country town a half hour away by foot. The first division of the construction project was centered at Belemedik, and the third at Aleppo.

An Austrian German named Klaus was superintendent civil engineer-surveyor of the Baghche construction. An astute professional, he was an equally subtle politician and a noble man who rendered quite a bit of service to us Armenians. Through his clever arrangement, for the sake of appearances, I had assumed control of all professional surveying and safe accounts.

During the railroad construction (1916–18), this station served as a technical workplace, with six or seven Armenian employees besides me. One of these, Nishan Mavian, Klaus's assistant surveyor, performed great services to his compatriots, including me. There was a young Armenian surveyor-draftsman, a general secretary, and an Armenian foreman in charge of hundreds of laborers. A young Bulgarian oversaw all the foremen.

Two Turkish police soldiers under our command worked as guards of our station-workplace. It was only they who reminded us that we were living in the Turkish state; otherwise everything around us was European, even the hats everybody wore, for only the common laborers wore fezes.

I had given myself the name Krikor Garabedian in order to eliminate any trace of my being a fugitive, and I was registered accordingly in the official company ledger. I cultivated relationships with no one; I lived in seclusion, self-contained and isolated. This station was both our workplace and our mess; up at the top of the stairs, the first room was my bedroom, where Nishan Mavian had shown me exceptionally kind hospitality, making space for me in already tight quarters.

All of us Armenians were living in misery; in distressing isolation, we had become transformed, submerged in our anxieties over what might await us. I had long since forgotten what it was like to smile; every innocent look aroused my suspicion, with a terrifying effect, and the nightmare of imminent discovery and death again agitated my mind and soul. This was despite the fact that not a single Turkish governmental official, civilian or military, had occasion to visit our caravan, aside from an elderly Turkish major who was an engineer corps commander.

Our days were monotonous and gloomy and always full of worry, owing to rumors that the Armenians working on the Amanos construction would be exiled too. One day War Minister Enver Pasha, while passing through Amanos on his way to visit the fronts in Palestine and Mesopotamia, was surprised to see a large crowd of Armenians. He asked his adjutants, "Wasn't it said that there were no Armenians left in the provinces? Look at how many have survived and found work in the construction of this railroad!"

Free to study my surroundings on Sundays, I would often, on the pretext of strolling about, make unobtrusive visits to the homes of the Armenian men and women who worked at our center. At the Baghche sites there were more than two thousand laborers, some eight hundred of whom were Armenians—men, women, girls, and boys, all without exception fugitives from deportation marches and camps. Some who had found refuge along the lines of the railroad construction had even succeeded in bringing their families here. All, without fail, had lost a few loved ones, but they had not found time to cry, or mourn them, or for that matter, even to bury them.

All Armenians, having escaped the bloody massacres, felt a special connection to one another; seeing an Armenian was an instance of rare good fortune, and the show of concern and consideration was mutual. There were no longer any issues dividing us—neither politics nor class nor denomination. We were all Armenians; woe had struck us; and now we were the last survivors of a persecuted nation.

When I visited the peaked military tents that sheltered the Armenian laborers, I would be overcome with grief. Inside were a few dirty rags used as bedding or blankets or clothing. Nor was it uncommon to find suckling infants wrapped in horse cloth, hanging from ropes; their cries and screams couldn't but stir you. This was the cradle of exile. Alas, nothing was left of the past—it was a vain dream. And sometimes mothers tried to put their bawling infants to sleep with lullabyes:

Oror usem knatsir, mshig mshig knatsir,
Jampou hekiate mi mornar,
Vor chi mnas hayun odar . . .

I say a lullaby, you sleep, sleep soundly,
Don't forget the fairy tale of the road,
So you won't become estranged . . .

Hearing young mothers trying to comfort their infants, it was impossible not to weep. They would say things like "My child [*yavrum*], I don't have bread or milk to give you. What can I do? No matter what stone I beat my head upon, I come up with nothing. My God, what black days we have come upon!"

One day I came across a small tent with three persons in it lying on some rags. I asked one of them, a sixty-year-old man whose set of gold teeth had caught my attention, where he had been deported from and who he was. I was stupefied to hear that he was Holas, one of the wealthy Armenian Catholics from Ankara. I knew the name when I was the prelate of Kastemouni. I inquired further, wishing to know the details of his deportation.

His story was the same heart-wrenching one that I had seen and heard a thousand times. After his goats, houses, vineyards, stores, wagons, and horses—worth tens of thousands of gold pounds—were seized, he had been sent on foot on the road from Ankara, together with his fellow Armenian Catholics, and via Kayseri and Ulukishla arrived at Eregli-Bozanti-Adana-Kanle-gechid.

Having bribed the officials overseeing him, Holas had fled and found refuge along the route of the railroad construction. Holas's wife and daughters, for their part, were robbed by men working for Atif, the vice governor of Ankara, that monster of a man. They had then been exiled to Konya, where B. Avkerian—representative of Mr. Hugnen, director of the Anatolia railroad—rescued them. They managed to remain there. The Roman Catholic Avkerian was one of those self-sacrificing Armenians who did not only the possible but the impossible to rescue his wretched compatriots from the vicissitudes of exile.

I asked why the Armenian Catholics of Ankara—who didn't wish to consider themselves Armenian and remained aloof from all national movements—were exiled, and whether he now perhaps wished to be called Armenian. Holas answered in Turkish, "It was to remain exempt, to be free of these misfortunes, that we kept away from the [other] Armenians and Armenian activities. Now that we have been removed from our homes and lands, brought to these parts, and subjected to this misery, we accept our Armenian identity, like it or not."

I told him not to worry; the Armenian nation had seen many storms; this one too would certainly pass, and he would regain at least his properties, and good days would return. But he replied in Turkish (for most of the Armenian Catholics of Ankara don't know Armenian, and those who do don't want to speak it): "Your Grace, I have no desire but to see my family and children one more time before dying, since there's no joy left in living for me."

Days and weeks passed like this, and then we heard new rumors that a ringleader named Hagop, together with his sister and almost thirty other Armenians, was fighting against Turkish police soldiers and causing quite a bit of damage on the roads he traveled. He was truly a brave Armenian, having resorted to arms rather than suffer the death of an infidel by the ax blows of a Turk.

Time passed, and the Turks had not been able to catch some of the resisters. We often heard stories, with great joy, about a handful of fighters from Findijak and Zeytoun who had managed to evade the trap of deportation. Since 1915 they had taken up arms and sought refuge in their inaccessible mountains; from this base they would raid the surrounding Turkish villages for provisions, inflicting great losses on the regular and irregular Turkish police forces that tried to repulse them.

Now and then men from these two bands of Armenian fighters would come down in disguise to the Intilli and Baghche railway lines. After gathering precise information about domestic and foreign political events, they would return to their eagles' nests to inform their comrades. They had resorted to arms and the errant life of mountaineer adventurers not to prey on innocent people, not out of the avarice of brigands who engage in pillaging, but to save their own lives. The Turkish government, however, was looking for an excuse to wipe out the remaining Armenian survivors.

In June 1916 Jevad, governor-general of Adana, and Avni, commander of the police soldiers, received such orders from Constantinople. They proceeded to take measures to annihilate, according to plan, the more than ten thousand Armenians working in the Amanos construction projects.

Talaat, the interior minister and chief executioner of the Armenians, together with War Minister Enver, was putting pressure on Hugnen, director-general of the Baghdad railroad company in Constantinople, to release the hundreds of Armenian employees who constituted 75 percent of the company's personnel. Hugnen, however, knew full well the reason for this demand and refused to comply. If he were to release his Armenian employees, he contended, the railroad would cease to work, and the consequences for the war effort on the Palestine and Mesopotamian fronts would be disastrous. Talaat and his camarilla recommended replacing the Armenians with Muslim and Levantine employees, but Hugnen objected, saying that he could not at a moment's notice put inexperienced men in the place of ones he had trained for years, and that such rashness could subject the railroad company to huge losses and dangers.

Talaat wished to exile and eliminate even the Armenians who were working unofficially as porters in the railroad stations. But Hugnen refused this demand too, sending secret instructions to the stationmasters to register the Armenian porters in their official ledgers. If Hugnen was reluctant to surrender all Armenian employees, upper- and lower-level alike, his motivations were not purely humanitarian; nevertheless, no one can doubt the honorable role of this noble Swiss in upholding the banner of Christianity and civilization. The Armenian employees, for their part, were equal in worthiness to this stubborn defense and appreciation.

I wish to discharge a pleasant obligation close to my heart by pointing out that the Armenian railroad employees played a providential role in saving their compatriots in exile, irrespective of sex or age. Choked with thirst, dripping with sweat, and covered with dust, the deportees were passing nearby and in front of them, one caravan after another, on the way south to the deserts, to die without shroud, without coffin, and without grave. Risking their lives, under any sort of pretext, the railroad workers gave aid wherever they could, providing material and moral assistance to free innocent souls. Many of them married Armenian girls and thereby succeeded in saving whole families. I must confess that I never heard of an Armenian railroad employee treating his persecuted and exiled compatriots unkindly.

Seeing that it was impossible to annihilate the permanent Armenian employees by "peaceful means," Talaat and his camarilla undertook other plans to exterminate the thousands working in the railroad construction projects.

But as always, for appearances' sake, the Turkish government officials resorted to Machiavellian measures. First, they created comprehensive blacklists of Armenian workers, claiming that, for their protection, all Armenians working in railroad construction had to be registered in special government ledgers and obtain documents [*vesika*] proving and establishing their identity. In this way, the government said, they would once and for all be exempt from pursuit by the police, and from harassment by governmental and military authorities.

And so police commissars and policemen from Adana, assisted by senior and subordinate police officials of the district governments near the rail route through Haruniye and Baghche, went to the centers—Yarbashi, Baghche, Ayran, Intilli, and Keller—and undertook the governmental registration, or, more accurately, the preparation of blacklists.

All the Armenians working in the construction projects, whether specialists or laborers, were invited by the police officials, one by one, to the company's offices. And because the Turkish officials had the railroad company's registration ledgers in hand, no one could avoid this requirement.

The idea of gaining protection under the law was so enticing that all the Armenians rushed forward. Even those who had previously been registered under Greek, Assyrian, or Kurdish names corrected their false identities, registering under their real names in the new ledgers prepared by the government.

As the last person to be called, I presented myself to Yashar, the black-skinned commander of the police soldiers in Baghche. Captain Yashar, who was in charge of the registration operations there, trusted Klaus, chief conductor of the Baghche line, and so instead of taking the ledgers with him to the town of Baghche, quite a distance from the station, he put them in the company's safe.

A few of us high-level Armenian railway officials had occasion to examine the ledgers and found many mysterious things. Recorded in alphabetical order were the first and last names of every Armenian, with father's name, age, birthplace, and marital status; and then which caravan each one had fled from or where they had come from prior to working for the railroad. After all that information was denoted, several marks were written opposite the name of each person. Judging by which marks appeared next to names of the persons known to us, we were able to analyze them, more or less, and figure out the secret code.

We concluded that Captain Yashar had placed the sign *.oo.* in front of the names of those individuals whom he considered dangerous and suspicious. We found out later that a special questionnaire had been sent by telegram to the birthplaces of those persons. In any event, the individuals so marked would be taken to different places of exile and toward a different destiny.

After the examination we put the black ledger back in the safe, until the next night, when our special investigation would continue. When I appeared for registration, I had secretly reached an agreement with Klaus in advance. I gave incorrect answers to Yashar's questions, saying that my name was Krikor Garabedian, I was a native of Constantinople, my address was Tarla Bashi no. 451, Pera, I had an elderly mother, and I had been working for the past sixteen years for the German railroad company as a draftsman, or *ressam,* the Turkish word I was obliged to learn during these days. Klaus, standing near me, certified the accuracy of my statements with the utmost composure.

To complete the deception, I began to draw blueprints, which I based on printed copies. In so doing I used my knowledge of theoretical and applied mechanics, which I acquired during my first sojourn as a student in Germany in 1895.

Yashar, however, was always suspicious of me and a few other mysterious employees of the station's office-workshop. One day, quite exceptionally, he came over to where we were eating and sat right opposite me. His professed purpose was to gather information about the origin, history, religion, and language of the Armenian nation and about great national events of the past. In reality, however, his aim in enticing us to converse and quizzing us was to see which of us excelled in knowledge of Armenian life. That way he could assess to what degree we were Armenian intellectuals.

So about six or seven of us who were seated around the lunch table, feeling flattered, endeavored to display our knowledge. I didn't say anything. Yashar, at his wit's end, wished to break my stubborn silence; he turned to me and asked whether perchance I knew anything about all this. I responded simply, "I'm ignorant when it comes to old and new national issues, since nothing has value for me besides money; money makes the world go 'round. I don't like to think about anything but eating and drinking well; this is why I love money."

Only a few Armenians close to the office of the Baghche station knew who I was, and if a few artisans and laborers besides guessed my identity, it must be said to their credit that they exercised extraordinary discretion in not disclosing the secret to anyone—an act that would have had severe consequences.

Only once did someone by the familiar name of Nalbandian, a native of Smyrna who was a tablemate of ours, suddenly exclaim, "I know you from when you went to visit the German admiral in Mersin, on behalf of the catholicos of Cilicia . . ." I instinctively used body language to convey to him that he was going down the wrong path. Although he said no more, this great indiscretion was enough for my identity to become known to those compatriots of mine who had been my messmates for months without knowing who I was.

In order not to jeopardize my new assumed identity, I continued to live in extreme modesty, simply, and in isolation. But day by day, warnings of an imminent storm were increasing, and I soon faced a great new danger.

4

The Treatment of the Armenians by the German Soldiers

The Ayran tunnels had not been completely opened and cleared out for ordinary rail passage, but narrow-gauge trains were coming and going nonetheless from the Mamure station [in the western foothills of the Amanos mountains] to Islahiye. This auxiliary line was constructed especially to transport munitions that had arrived from Constantinople at Bozanti to Islahiye—from Bozanti via the Belemedik-Dorak tunnels in the Taurus mountains, then by regular railroad cars via Adana to Mamure.

This narrow-gauge line had substantial capacity to transport munitions, but it wasn't sufficient; large quantities had to be transported by horse-drawn carriages from Mamure via the mountain route through Kanlegechid and Hasanbeyli, to the fronts in Palestine and Mesopotamia. The German and Austrian soldiers on these fronts varied in number from ten thousand to twenty thousand. In exchange, a comparable number of Turkish forces had been transported to the Galician front to fight the Russian army. For this reason we often had contact with German officers.

Sadly, all the German officers whom we met during these bloody years of world war, with rare exceptions, were as Armenophobic as the Turks, some expressing themselves indiscreetly, others being more diplomatic.

The Kaiser's government, having embarked on a policy of penetration of the Orient, needed the agreement and assistance of the Turkish government, and so it could not be friendly toward the Armenians, who were seeking autonomy, if not independence, through the intercession of other European powers. The German policy in the Orient called for using Turkey to win over the pan-Islam movement, to build the Baghdad railroad, and to go as far as India, with the hope of wresting control of the crown jewel of the British Empire.[1]

Given this policy, the German leaders ascribed importance to the existence of a few million Armenians, who could pose a serious obstacle on the route to Baghdad, especially in Cilicia. For a while, during the Balkan

War, German officials, particularly Foreign Minister Gottlieb von Jagow and his assistant Arthur Zimmermann, showed a certain friendliness toward the Turkish Armenians. They saw them as a tool of the Russian government, and wished to manipulate and use them for their own purposes. At the initiative of the Armenologist Dr. Johannes Lepsius, they formed a German-Armenian Society in Berlin for this purpose. It must be borne in mind that the German Foreign Ministry wished to take advantage of Dr. Lepsius's good reputation among the Armenians by using him to find out about their secret plans: this was yet another trap.

In the winter of 1913, six months before the world war, an individual by the fictitious name of Kurd Aram, who was actually a German, was sent to Armenia on behalf of the German-Armenian Society, to discover the Armenians' plans. For appearances' sake, Kurd Aram had been financed by Armenians, and he arrived with a letter of introduction from the Patriarchate of Constantinople, addressed to the provincial leaders.

While I was in Berlin, I too was asked to furnish Aram with a letter of introduction to the patriarch and the provincial leaders, but suspecting the motives of a German agent traveling to Asia Minor under an assumed Armenian name, I flatly refused.

The German officers on their way to Palestine and the Mesopotamian front had no choice but to pass before the Baghche station. All of them used offensive language with regard to the Armenians. They considered us to be engaging in intrigue, ready to strike the Turkish army from the rear, and thus traitors to the fatherland . . . deserving of all manner of punishment.

Although most of the Armenians living in Turkey had been deported, scattered, and martyred in the spring of 1915, a few hundred thousand survivors were still perishing in the deserts to the south—wasting away to nothing. Nevertheless the German officers' Armenophobic fury continued, and not a word of compassion was heard from their lips. On the contrary, they justified the Ittihad government, saying, "You Armenians deserve your punishment. Any state would have punished rebellious subjects who took up arms to realize national hopes by the destruction of the country."

When we objected, asking if other states would dare to massacre women and children, along with men, and annihilate an entire race on account of a few guilty people, they replied: "Yes, it's true that the punishment was a bit severe, but you must realize that during such chaotic and frightful days of war as these, it was difficult to find the time and means to separate the guilty from the innocent." This was also the merciless answer of the chief executioners—Talaat, Enver, Behaeddin Shakir, Nazim—and their Ittihad camarilla.

The German officers pretended ignorance of the widespread slaughter of more than a million innocent Armenians, irrespective of sex and age, and referred only to deaths by starvation and the adversities of travel during the deportations. Thus they exonerated the Turkish government, saying that its inability to provide for hundreds of thousands of deportees in a disorganized land like Asia Minor was not surprising. Meanwhile Turkish government officials prevented the starving refugees from receiving bread distributed by the Austrians and Swiss, stating, "Orders have come from Constantinople not to give any assistance. We cannot allow either bread or medicine to be given. The supreme order is to annihilate this evil race. How dare you rescue them from death?" The German officers would often speak of us as Christian Jews and as bloodsucking usurers of the Turkish people.

What a falsification of the wretched realities prevailing in Asia Minor, and what a reversal of roles! Yes indeed, there was an oppressor. Either the Germans were consciously distorting the facts and roles, or the Turks had really convinced them that the Turks were victims and the Armenians were criminals. How appropriate it is to recall here this pair of Turkish sayings: "The clever thief has the master of the house hanged" and "The one who steals the minaret prepares its sheath in advance, of course."

Many German officers had no qualms about turning over to the Turkish authorities Armenian youths who had sought refuge with them; they knew full well that they were delivering them to their executioners. If an Armenian merely spoke negatively about a German—be he the emperor or von der Goltz Pasha, or the average German—or dared to criticize German indifference toward the Armenian massacres, he was immediately arrested and turned over to the nearest Turkish military or police authority. And if the Germans found a certain Armenian particularly irritating, they pinned the label of spy on him.

Mistaking me for an Austrian, a few German officers boasted of having turned over several Armenians to the Turkish police, adding with a laugh, "Only the Turks know how to talk to the Armenians."

There was a German woman called Sister Paula, who, in order to pass for an American and so be able to gain the trust of American benefactors, had changed her name to Miss Shepherd. In my presence and that of our head surveyor-engineer, Klaus, this woman would denounce the Armenians as vocal enemies of the Germans. She had informed on quite a few Armenian youths to the Turkish police in Marash, Baghche, and Hasanbeyli. Miss Shepherd particularly reviled Armenians belonging to the national church, but she was less hostile and often even friendly toward Armenian Protestants.

Having studied the German modus operandi, I was extremely careful not to reveal my identity. Only Klaus knew who I was during my time in the Amanos region, and if a few more Germans learned my identity two months later, they couldn't harm me, because by then I had made my second escape.

5

The Ghosts of Ten Thousand Armenian Women in the Deserts of Ras-ul-Ain

For twenty years the Austrian architect and engineer Litzmayer, who was from Dalmatia, had held a supervisory position in the construction of the Baghdad railway. In the autumn of 1915 he was in Mesopotamia and witnessed an episode in the Armenian deportations.

During the last days of October Litzmayer had been busy putting down narrow-gauge lines [*ducovil*] from Zormana to Ras-ul-Ain [site of an Armenian refugee camp] when he saw a large army slowly moving in his direction from the north. He thought it was a Turkish army heading for Mesopotamia, where at that time the British, having taken Basra, were trying to capture Baghdad, the capital and the major communications nexus between Asia Minor and the Orient. As the crowd came closer, however, he realized that it was not an army but a huge caravan of women, moving forward under the supervision of soldiers. They numbered, according to some estimates, as many as forty thousand.

These women were survivors of the Armenian deportations from Erzerum, Serena, Kemah, Sivas, Bitlis, Harput, Malatya, Diyarbekir, and their surrounding villages; among them there were no males, since they had been separated from their families in the first days of the deportations and had either been massacred or died in exile.

It is superfluous to say that during their long journey on foot, these women had been subjected to all kinds of travails. They had known hopelessness and physical hardship, starvation, filth, abduction by Kurdish and Circassian mobs, pillage, and so on. Eyewitnesses relate that many of the young women, guessing what an ordeal the deportation order would be, had elected to commit suicide by swallowing poison. Along the way others suffered mental and physical exhaustion and threw themselves into rivers, valleys, or swamps. Many thousands of others died of disease, lacking medicine and medical care, since no provisions had been made for the sanitary conditions of this unusual army. Some of them had been driven to such a state that they were mere skeletons enveloped in rags, with skin that had turned leathery, burned from the sun, cold, and wind. Many pregnant women, having become numb, had left their newborns on the side of the road as a protest against mankind and God.

When these wretched women met the Austrian engineer, who spoke Turkish, they surrounded him and begged him to give them each a piece of bread. Litzmayer made every effort. He sent a telegram to Baghdad and received a certain sum to help them. He found some bread to buy and wanted to divide it among them. But the policemen overseeing the women interfered with his act of charity in every way possible. Despite being a powerfully built man, Litzmayer had a tender heart, and he told me in detail about tragic episodes that remain a black mark on civilization. As he talked, tears rolled down his face, and he said that this was how the Ittihad government carried out the *jihad* against the European great powers—on defenseless men and women and innocent children.

"And," he went on, "while we were busy distributing bread and medicine, this pathetic caravan of women was being driven with cudgels and whipped, to move on with slow steps toward the Der Zor desert." Needless to say, the majority of these women met death in the desert sands, and the few who lived were later martyred in July 1916, victims of the horrendous massacre organized by the governor of Der Zor, Zeki, to which I shall devote a special chapter.

6

The Deportation and Murder of the Armenian Workers of Amanos

Several more weeks passed with travails and foreboding; sure enough, at the beginning of June 1916, ominous events signaled the approach of danger. For several days police soldiers in small companies were passing by on their way to Baghche. Their number gradually increased until it exceeded four hundred. When we asked about them, we were told that they had been sent out to capture marauding Armenian gangs in the Amanos and Findijak mountains.

Avni, the central commander of the police soldiers of the province of Adana, was famous for killing Armenians; he came and established himself in the city of Baghche, making it the center of his military operations. He proceeded to blockade the line along which the Ayran railroad was being built, from Mamure all the way to Islahiye. He then turned over the surveillance of Yenije, Yarbashi, Baghche, Ayran, Intilli, and Keller to companies of police soldiers.

Without doubt we had been encircled by a military chain: all the likely roads and passages for escape were occupied by stationary and roaming groups of guards, and mountain, valley, and forest alike were filled with police soldiers on the lookout.

A handful of fugitives from the caravans, who had found refuge in these hospitable mountains of Amanos, had become a thorn in the side of the Turkish government. And so, having come from all directions to reap the spoils, the commissioners and police, with their officers and heads of local government, decided to eliminate these remaining survivors.

In front of our workshop station in Baghche, a horrifying scene unfolded before our eyes. The commander of the Baghche police troops, the black captain Yashar, surrounded by a few dozen police soldiers, and with whip in hand, lined up in a row the Armenian laborers and their foremen [*chavush*], who had been brought from the nearby areas. Pale and trembling, docile in their demoralized state, they were being sent in groups, under police supervision, to Baghche, the new deportation center.

The laborers made not one escape attempt, not one effort to save themselves. Thousands of Armenians, gathered from Ayran, Intilli, Keller, and Yarbashi, passed by us, being led to Baghche in rows of caravans, surrounded by police soldiers with bayonets. We shuddered as we watched. Woe to the one who fell behind on the road; with the butts of their rifles, the police soldiers shoved the laggards forward—the lame, the sick, and the children.

On the distant horizons new caravans gradually came into view: from the shoulders of the mountains, the rolling sides of the valleys, and the precipitous heights of the hills. No one felt sorry; no one offered assistance—all hearts had become stone, all eyes filled with blood. In horror we watched barefoot little children, as young as five years old, unable to keep up with the caravans, be tortured by the police soldiers. Having lost their mothers, they would turn back in search of them, crying, only to be knocked to the ground with one blow, like a piece of straw, right in front of us.

At this point Litzmayer, no longer able to tolerate this scene, ran up to the Turkish policeman and drubbed him with his cane. Meanwhile, on the road descending from Mount Ayran toward Baghche, a young pregnant woman who had gotten married during the exile suddenly fell to her knees in front of the wooden barracks of the Italian foremen. She crumpled onto the ground, in the throes of a painful miscarriage. A few of the police soldiers guarding the caravans and bringing up the rear surrounded the poor woman and, laughing lewdly, forced her to get up and rejoin the group. Hearing her screams, a few European women ran out of the nearby barracks to defend the honor of their sex against these human beasts. They covered the ill-fated, blood-covered mother with white bedsheets and tablecloths, and when one of the police soldiers tried to stop them, a noble Italian woman pushed him to one side with a ringing slap in the face.

A German woman witnessed this scene and came to Baghche shortly thereafter. When she told the dreadful story, Klaus, covering his face with a handkerchief, burst into tears and cried uncontrollably.

The European civil engineers, be they German, Swiss, Austrian, or Italian, tried in vain to save at least the Armenian officials with whom they were friends. But the noncommissioned officers of the police soldiers would not hear them. The order had come from Constantinople, from the highest level; it was inexorable: every Armenian had to go into exile, whether laborer or official—all that mattered was that he was Armenian.

Some of the civil engineers, seeing the futility of their efforts, tried to delay the departure of their laborers by asking for time to pay the men their wages. However, the noncommissioned officers forbade them, saying, "Don't worry, the government will take care of their needs." Some of the engineers, like Klaus, were able to convince a few officers of the police soldiers at least to give their departing laborers food rations for the road, and in this way—with some baksheesh to the officers, of course—they were able to distribute plenty of bread to a few hundred laborers.

In a single day the commanders of the police soldiers succeeded in gathering all the Armenian laborers of Amanos into a caravan and bringing them to Baghche. They registered them, assembled them in large groups, and put them on the road to Marash.

After the Armenian laborers had been rounded up, it was the turn of the Armenian railway officials, both high- and low-ranking. Captain Yashar himself, blacklist in hand, sought out the officials one by one and on the spot turned them over to the police soldiers following him.

With palpitations, I waited. Were they going to arrest me too, I wondered? I was right there before their eyes, but they did not, and so I assumed that my name was not on the blacklist.

They did arrest Mr. Karabajian, who had a position in the construction branch of Baghche and who had worked for the railroad company for more than eight years. Klaus hastened to intervene, arguing that they had no right to arrest his longtime, faithful, and expert employee.

But no one listened to him. So he got on his horse and rode to Baghche to personally ask the central commander, Avni, who was directing these operations, to release Mr. Karabajian. Avni made it clear to Klaus that such meddling was futile—he could not possibly suspend orders given at the last hour.

Klaus, who had sent a telegram to Winkler in Adana informing him of these arrests, continued to report every new incident to the administrative center of the railway construction there, and he also requested a special favor for Hamamjian [an accountant for the company] and me. But Winkler replied that, while he [Klaus] should keep him informed of each situation, he should not ask special favors for individuals, since he [Winkler] was doing the impossible in Constantinople trying to save everyone.

Yashar came and personally arrested Hamamjian, who had been well known as a teacher and principal for many years in the Armenian schools of Constantinople, particularly Makerkoy, and who had come to Cilicia as superintendent of schools. When the Great War started in the summer of 1914, he had been forbidden to return to Constantinople, so he continued to work as superintendent in Marash, trying to help the Armenian population there. As the political situation gradually worsened, he, like many others, considered the railway construction the safest place to be, and he sought refuge in Baghche. Here he worked competently as a general accountant, appreciated and liked by his boss, Klaus, and everyone else.

As soon as the civil engineer Karabajian was arrested, Hamamjian guessed that, if it could happen to such a longtime expert, he could be next. He began to prepare. First he signaled to me to follow him to his abode on the bushy hill opposite our station. He opened his suitcase, took out photographs of his wife and two children, and in an agitated state, kissed them and cried bitterly. It was impossible for me not to be moved, and I burst into tears.

Summoning all my moral strength, I encouraged him to take heart and be brave. But my words were in vain, since he knew instinctively that his last day had come. Again and again he kissed the photos with trembling hands, and then he said to me, "Reverend Father, besides God and the two of us, there is no one here within earshot. I beg of you, listen to what I say. I am going to die; there is no salvation for me. I have only one son, aged three, and one daughter, aged fourteen; for the love of God, be a guardian to my children, whom I love very much. (Alas, inflexible fate has not allowed me to do my parental duty to the end and secure their future.) Make them your children, and don't let my orphans become destitute like their father . . . Here I have forty gold pieces that I've saved. Five are enough for me; I am going to my death—what more do I need than this? Let's see whether tomorrow at this time I'm still alive or not . . ."

Losing control, he beat himself on the knees and wailed, and my tears flowed as well. I exhorted him to compose himself and promised to hide him.

Amid the prevailing chaos, I escorted him to the water tower that served the locomotives. Climbing up a ladder, Hamamjian hid in one of the dark secret corners of the tower's roof, where a few young people had likewise taken refuge. I then managed to get exceptional permission to hide Hamamjian in Klaus's house, where no police official would dare search.

But poor Hamamjian lost heart and elected not to take advantage of this excellent opportunity; he came down from his hiding place suddenly and gave himself up to Captain Yashar, a supposed sympathizer and friend of his. Only upon my insistence would he take his forty gold pieces with him, with which he could bribe the police soldiers and save himself when the situation required it.

After all this anxiety and drama, the bitter moment of separation finally came. Hamamjian kissed the few of us remaining, and when he was about to exit the station with the police soldiers, a Jewish official who was antagonistic toward him came to wish him a sarcastic bon voyage: "Certainly we will see each other in Constantinople after the war." Hamamjian answered in French, "Be glad I am going to my death. They are cleaning up the Armenians—the field is left to the Jews." Thus, with his little bundle on his shoulder, he went peacefully, without looking back.

I cannot omit his characteristic last words when we were alone in the tent: "Reverend Father, it is a pity that those of us who are going won't see our Armenian nation's independence and freedom. I envy those of you who are staying, for you will be able to see the day of freedom that we've desired for so long."

All those who went to their death, on all occasions, repeated that deep conviction: that the blood of more than a million innocent Armenians, *at least this time*, would not be in vain, and that the survivors would have the good fortune to salute the flag of the free and independent Armenia.

Those who died believed without seeing; meanwhile those who remained saw—and did not believe it. Like many who were going to die, the late Hamamjian often asked me to chronicle this tragic story of the Armenian Golgotha.

And with this account, I think I have executed the will of those who are no more.

The caravans of deportees were sent away. Klaus made one last attempt to save the young wife of his beloved and faithful civil engineer Karabajian, together with her mother and sister. But it was not possible: the Turks were exiling him in order to acquire his beautiful wife, whom he had saved from exile by marrying, and at the same time saving her sister and mother. A great many had been exiled despite not appearing on the blacklist, just so the Turks could get their hands on the exiles' beautiful wives and sisters.

By his persistent efforts, Klaus did succeed in getting the fanatically anti-Armenian Major Avni to guarantee that the caravan of officials would be taken safely to Birejik, and to promise that an acknowledgment bearing the signatures of the exiles themselves would be brought back to Klaus.

Finally night fell, and everyone retreated to his hut or tent, exhausted. Of the eight hundred Armenian laborers and officials in the eleventh section of the Baghche railway construction, only a few Armenians remained: Klaus's helper, the civil engineer Nishan Mavian; one telegraph operator; two youths who were timekeepers; and me—a total of five.

Of course none of us could sleep. We could not forget the dreadful departure of our friends and the thousands of others, or avoid agonizing over tomorrow and the untold dangers it held. Half the night had passed without us closing our eyes when we heard Mauser fire from the nearby forests. All those youths who, rather than surrender, had dared to flee there were being pursued by Avni's roaming police soldiers, who had orders to execute them on sight.

In the morning we saw more than eighty corpses; they were being dragged, by ropes around their legs, to the forests in the Baghche valley. There they were buried in two large ditches far from the road and out of sight, to prevent the European engineers from photographing them.

The next day new caravans of deportees arrived from the distant ends of the railway construction, from Yenije and Intilli and Yarbashi and Keller. All were women, young girls, and small children, whom they had not been able to bring during the night, due to the protests of the European engineers.

Oh, the sight of these wretched people was so horrifying. When this dust-covered caravan passed before the station, Klaus's wife and Armenian maid went out to distribute bread to the small children (five- to eight-year-olds). The Turkish police soldiers took the bread from the hands of some of them and threw it away. A few little boys lagged behind hoping to get some of it; the police soldiers flattened them with their gun butts and then beat them some more, before the boys had a chance to catch up to their mothers' caravan.

The soldiers' savagery was so revolting that, ignoring the danger, a few of us Armenians jumped forth to protect the children. The wives of the European engineers were saying, "If these [soldiers] torture these innocent children in our presence, one can only imagine what they do on remote roads, where no one can see them."

Contrary to all expectations, the total number of Armenians deported from the region of the Amanos railway construction exceeded *eleven thousand five hundred*—11,500. The true identity of numerous Armenians who had registered under pseudonyms of various foreign nationalities had come to light; now they too were exiled and added to the caravans. All together only 135 of us were left along the entire line from Mamure to Keller. All were officials and specialists, whether engineers, telegraph operators, artisans, or master workmen in the tunnels.

For the sake of truth, we must remember the noble efforts of Winkler, the general manager of the second division of the Adana railway construction. This elderly humanitarian—together with the head engineers of his branches, such as Morf from Ayran, Koppel, from Intilli, Klaus from Baghche, and others—ardently tried to prevent the deportation of their employees, whose dedication, commitment, and discipline were specially valued.

Sending a torrent of long telegrams of protest, they had petitioned Hugnen, general director of the Baghdad Railway Company in Constantinople; the main headquarters of the Holzmann company in Frankfurt, Germany; the Foreign Ministry in Berlin; von Sanders Pasha, defender of the Dardanelles and high commander of the German military forces in Constantinople; the German central military staff in Constantinople; and anyone from whom they could hope to receive help. Each petition explained the disastrous consequences of the deportation of thousands of workers and experienced administrative officials.

But orders from the German staff in Constantinople forbade the German civil engineers to intervene, lest it complicate relations between the Germans and the Turks. The German staff did at least promise to obtain some kind of favorable arrangement from War Minister Enver. And indeed, on the fourth day of the exile, the joy of us few Armenians left in Baghche was great: the Armenian telegraph office clerk ran to us to bring the good news from Constantinople that all the Armenian deportees would be returning. I alone did not believe it, knowing that while the Turks had told Winkler and the governor-general that they were ordering the return of the deportees from Adana, they were also sending coded telegrams to Avni in Baghche or Marash to destroy "the harmful microbes."*

All the Germans were happy, proud of this success they had achieved—

*Dr. Mehmed Reshid, a high-ranking Ittihad party member and governor of Diyarbekir, referred to Armenians as "dangerous microbes" infecting the state, characterizing the extreme racism against Armenians.—trans.

which indeed did not last for long. The next day we heard that only the specialists would return. And then even that news was refuted. These messages were all a Turkish game, to buy enough time for the exiles to be taken as far away as possible, or just to be done away with.

On the second day Winkler even came from Adana in a special locomotive to inspect the construction of all the railroad lines, on which there was no activity. The elderly man was deeply moved, and in Ayran, on hearing of the demise of so many exiles, we later learned, he cried in Morf's presence.

Winkler sent another petition to Constantinople by telegram, again demanding the return of his many thousands of exiled workers. This time he threatened immediate cessation of matériel and munitions transport if his demands were not met in three days. True to his word, [after three days had passed] he ordered an immediate and indefinite halt of traffic on the little railroad line from Mamure to Islahiye.

Thereafter matériel and munitions that reached the Mamure railway station from Constantinople began to accumulate in the Yenije station's warehouses. Although the Turkish military administration tried to transport the supplies on carts via the mountainous Kanle-gechid–Hasanbeyli road, it was impossible by such primitive means to reach the fronts in Mesopotamia and Palestine, where two large Turkish armies totaling a few hundred thousand were fighting pitched battles. The army in Mesopotamia was led at that time by the infamous von der Goltz Pasha, while the supreme commander of the army in Palestine was the naval minister Jemal Pasha.

The German staff from Constantinople and von Sanders Pasha, under orders from Enver, sent urgent telegrams to Winkler, insisting that he resume the rail transportation. After thirteen days' interruption, Winkler had no choice but to order the movement of supplies on the narrow-gauge railroad via the tunnels to resume.

Here is undeniable evidence of the inhumane behavior of the German military. For I am deeply convinced that the most powerful German military leadership of those years, if it sincerely wanted to, could have returned those exiles. But for the sake of appearances, they sent a few formal petitions to Enver; then they telegraphed Winkler that, for the sake of avoiding military and political complications, he could not meddle in the internal affairs of the Turkish government.

One Armenian priest officiating at the burial of another

An Armenian woman strokes a dead child outside of Aleppo

Grigoris Balakian disguised as a German named Herr Bernstein working for the railway in the Taurus mountains, 1916

Adana, a city in southern Turkey, historic Cilician Armenia, where twenty thousand to thirty thousand Armenians were massacred in 1909 and thousands more were deported and massacred in 1915. Grigoris Balakian's final place of refuge before his return to Constantinople.

Hajin, a city populated almost entirely by Armenians in the mountainous region of historic Cilician Armenia. Balakian and his deported caravan arrived there in March 1916 to find the city largely destroyed.

Sis, the historic Armenian city, once the capital of the medieval Armenian kingdom of Cilicia and in 1915 still the seat of the Cilician Armenian church; when Balakian and his caravan passed through in March 1916, the city was nearly emptied of Armenians.

Armenian deportees in a concentration camp in the Syrian desert

Starving Armenian children

The remains of Armenians burned alive by Turkish soldiers in Sheykhalan, a village in the Moush region. The photograph was taken by Russian soldiers in 1915.

A starved Armenian woman and two small children

Constantinople (Istanbul), 1908

Grigoris Balakian disguised as a German soldier during his final escape by train from Adana to Constantinople in the late summer of 1918

The St. Garabed Monastery in Moush (historic Armenia/eastern Turkey today), which was built between the fourth and eighteenth centuries. The photograph was taken circa 1900.

Site of the same St. Garabed Monastery in Moush, village of Cankly, circa 2000. This is one example of the thousands of Armenian churches, monasteries, and schools that were destroyed during and after the Armenian Genocide. Raphael Lemkin, who coined the term "genocide," described cultural destruction as a component of genocide and intent to destroy an ethnic group.

Twenty-two thousand Armenian and Greek orphans being transported from interior Turkey to Syria and Greece by Near East relief workers

Grigoris Balakian as prelate and vicar of the Holy Trinity Armenian Church in Manchester, England, 1922, the year *Armenian Golgotha* was published in Armenian in Vienna

7

Bloodshed on the Way from Baghche to Marash: A German Nurse Goes Insane

For the past few days groups of caravans comprising tens of thousands of male and female Armenian workers on the Amanos construction projects had departed from Baghche toward Marash. We had received no word at all from them and were anxiously awaiting the good tidings of their arrival in Marash.

More than the others, I knew what it meant when the Turkish government said, "We will deport." In reality, *deport* was synonymous with *murder*.

We, the few remaining Armenians, were frightfully worried, but our anxiety was somewhat assuaged by the thought that the Turks would not be foolish enough to create new proof of their crimes by massacring the deportees right before the eyes of Europeans—even Germans.

As always, however, the Turks had calculated things very well . . . because on the great day of reckoning, if it ever came, a few tens of thousands of victims more or less wouldn't much figure in the overall balance sheet of their atrocities . . . Additionally, they were firmly convinced that they, along with the Germans, would emerge victorious in this titanic struggle of nations.

But if, contrary to all expectations, they lost, then previous experience led them to believe they could easily cede some territory in exchange for the silence of their most threatening enemy. . . . When the time for punishment came, the European powers would, no doubt, engage in the ancient Oriental art of bargaining . . .

After the general deportation of the Amanos Armenians, the German Sister Paula, known to us by her pseudonym, Miss Shepherd, accompanied by a German nurse, a Turkish servant, and two police soldiers, set out from Marash for Baghche to offer money and other assistance to the thousands of deportees.

Inasmuch as the Marash-Baghche road was mountainous, carriage travel was impossible, so they traversed the deserted mountainous paths on horseback. After riding for some six hours, they suddenly found themselves on a battlefield. The more they advanced, the more maddening and frightful the scene became. All around them they saw hundreds of bodies in pools of blood, and all of them, without exception, were naked. Most of the corpses had had their heads and limbs cut off, and entrails had spilled out of many of the torsos. They had been so ripped apart it was impossible to differentiate the men from the women.

It was obvious that the killers, after murdering these deportees, had played with their corpses for hours, stripping them naked and cutting them to pieces. That which centuries of human history had never witnessed in its blackest of pages was carried out here, in the name of the Koran, in the name of *jihad*.

Seeing this effusion of blood all over the ground, the German nurse accompanying Sister Paula became so agitated that she jumped from her horse and ran to hug the decapitated body of a six-month-old girl. She kissed the baby and wailed, saying she wanted to take her, that she was her daughter.

The German nurse had gone mad. She jumped from one corpse to the next, and wherever she found dismembered bodies of little children, she hugged and kissed them and would not let go. Sister Paula and her attendants hurried to bring her back to reality, but to no avail. And so it was necessary to pry her from the corpses by force. Her clothing covered with blood, she was tied to her horse, and they all returned to Marash, where the crazed German nurse was placed in the German hospital.

The next day, Sister Paula again set out for Baghche.

She, however, was unable to endure this horrific scene, and returned to Marash, sobbing and repeating: "But what do these monsters want from the innocent women, the young children, and the pregnant women?" All those listening to her were moved to tears—German, Austrian, Dalmatian, and Hungarian engineers and surveyors alike. This story was no exaggeration; it bore the stamp of authenticity, from its witness—this German woman.

In the front yard of Klaus's house Sister Paula told the European engineers and surveyors about these criminal episodes, and they all grew enraged, wanting to bear witness before the civilized world. Shortly thereafter confirmation arrived that the number of those martyred on the Baghche-Marash road had now exceeded 2,600.

Following the arrival of this news, a few engineers, including Klaus, went to the sites of these massacres, in secret and without attendants, to take photographs as proof of what had happened. We asked a few youths, who'd made a narrow escape from the carnage and had found refuge with us, to tell us what they had seen; and when we learned the main details, we took ill for days, unable either to eat or sleep.

This is what these few Armenian youths, who had miraculously survived, told us. When the long caravans reached the place where the road stretching from Baghche to Marash begins to climb uphill through forests toward the mountain, the commander of the center in Adana and the director of this general deportation, the Armenian-killing Avni, ordered his police soldiers to aim their bullets at the Armenians ascending the mountain.

What a frightful scene it was, with men, women, girls, and children, one by one, being shot to death! They tumbled to the ground, bathed in blood. What took place was nothing more than a hunt, with humans as the prey. In order to stir the morbid enthusiasm of his gendarmes, Avni promised to pay them ten piasters per head.

This human hunt continued; the carnage went on. The gendarmes, all between the ages of twenty-one and twenty-six, tried not to miss their mark, since besides the ten piasters a head, a promotion in rank was also promised them . . . Alas, at this point the life of an Armenian was worth even less than that of a chick or chicken.

About four hundred persons fell injured from these bullets, and every time, gendarmes ran to rob those in the throes of death. Then they stabbed them with their sabers and, with apparent relish, cut them into pieces . . . Some of the deportees made it to the mountaintop and entered the wide plain extending to Marash; there a mob of Turkish peasants living nearby, invited to participate in the plunder, attacked from all sides—killing, stripping, and plundering them. These youths told us that many of the Armenian boys snatched the gendarmes' guns from their hands and were able to kill some before falling under a fusillade.

Major Avni, the director of the Amanos deportation and the central commander of the Adana government, had studied in Germany. This sixty-year-old man had resigned from the regular army command and entered this new line of work. He ordered his soldiers to rob all the caravans but kept the lion's share for himself, gathering as spoils approximately fifteen thousand Turkish gold pieces and many valuable objects. And then Avni sent this booty from Marash to Adana by mail, in small sealed parcels addressed to his wife.

The Turkish official who was the forwarding agent of the post office in Marash had been transferred to Baghche. One day as he was drinking raki, in a paroxysm of sincerity brought on by inebriation, he spoke in confidence to an Armenian colleague who had converted to Islam, and who, in turn, related what he said to me.

A few months after these deadly events, Avni, having given immense satisfaction to Talaat, interior minister and the real organizer of the extermination of the Armenians, was given a promotion. He went to Smyrna. There on virgin soil he carried out the same bestial acts on defenseless Armenian women . . . since the Armenians of Smyrna, along with those of Constantinople, had miraculously been saved from the overall deportations.

In 1920, after the Armistice, the Greeks seized Smyrna. Avni fled to Bursa and committed suicide as the only means of saving himself from the vengeance of the Greeks.

8

The Suffering of British Prisoners of War at Kut-al-Amara

A few thousand of the Armenian workers from the Amanos region had survived the massacre and managed to reach the environs of Birejik, emaciated, worn out, and starving.

In the unforeseen calm after the storm, we who had miraculously escaped were living in days of terror, full of menacing uncertainties. We no longer had any desire to live, let alone eat or drink. We had long since forgotten how to sleep; barely would we close our eyes than all the latest tragic episodes would enter our imagination, like a moving picture. Every whisper of the wind haunted us; we felt constantly stalked by the police soldiers, who we believed were coming after us.

The forced removal of tens of thousands of Armenian laborers brought the construction of the Amanos tunnels and railroad lines to a complete halt. Scattered here and there, a few dozen Kurds and Turks were working against their will, but otherwise there was no one.

Every time the supervising Turkish military and police officials came across us Armenians, they looked at us with surprise, as if wishing to ask how it was that we were still alive. We thought it best to stay out of their sight as much as possible, but even this avoidance aroused the suspicions of our executioners that perhaps we had escaped from our workstations.

To prevent any attempt at escape, numerous police soldiers on horseback had been stationed under huge trees in the mountains, and on both the open and secret roads in the surrounding mountains and villages. Our nights were especially anxious; the nightmare of death weighed on our souls, exhausted from suffering. We knew from experience that the Turkish police officials and soldiers planned their crimes during the day but went hunting at night.

Just two or three weeks after the deportation of the Amanos Armenians, on a doleful spring night at around ten o'clock, we heard the footsteps of hundreds of men. We tried to imagine who it could be and couldn't help but think it was further caravans of remaining Armenian deportees being taken to that mass grave, Der Zor. But when the caravan arrived at the Baghche railway station, we were surprised to see British and Indian soldiers emerge, humpbacked, in tatters, covered in dust and reduced to skeletons.

During the very first days of the world war, we had attentively awaited our saviors, the victorious troops of our powerful friends, the Allies . . . but now we were witnessing with our own eyes their emaciated living ghosts. In the darkness it was impossible to tell whether they were a mob or remnants of a demobilized army.

They wore short pants that came down to their knees; their legs were covered with wounds and sores; they were dirty and desiccated . . . their cheekbones were protruding, their eyes withdrawn deep into their sockets. The Indians were practically naked, some with just a few rags on their heads, according to their custom; in the darkness, an illusion of moving ghosts.

"Are there any Armenians among you? . . . Give us a piece of bread . . . We haven't had anything to eat for days." We were dumbfounded that they spoke English . . . that they were British . . . distant friends sharing our fate, asking us for bread . . . What an irony, indeed!

We ran to find our chief, the engineer Klaus, and after he made a brief inspection, we offered them our entire bread ration for the next day. They were about two hundred in number, a vanguard of the British army, and had been taken prisoner in Kut-al-Amara. Despite their near-starving condition, they lined up according to their rank and, with exemplary military discipline, received their bread rations before falling onto the wet meadows utterly exhausted.

We stayed up that night, impatiently curious, because this was the first time we had had an opportunity to gather information about the outside world and especially about our great and mighty allies, Britain, France, and Russia. The next day we learned that these soldiers had been brought in to work in place of the thousands of Armenian laborers who had been exiled and killed. But these wretched fellows had suffered so much and were so emaciated that they were being given a week's rest and food to make it possible for them to work. Many had so wasted away that they couldn't digest the beef or some of the other food they had eaten until days and even weeks later.

Among these prisoners were specialists—engineers, architects, and physicians—from London and various other British cities, but the Turkish soldiers guarding them didn't distinguish between the common soldiers and the officers. Only the commander of the British army in Kut-al-Amara, General Charles Townshend, was taken directly by train to Constantinople, where he was given a private residence on Grand Island* and enjoyed comfortable circumstances. In cunning Turkish style, here they were putting on a show of treating the prisoners in a civilized manner. Meanwhile, in the remote deserts, far removed from observing eyes, they had subjected these same wretched prisoners to unspeakable tortures.

The German management of the railroad construction gave positions to the British officers who were specialists, based on their aptitude. Some, however, preferred kitchen duty because they had gone hungry for so long. As we gradually became familiar with these officers and enjoyed their friendship, they told us of the horrible suffering they had endured in the deserts. Thirteen thousand British and Indian soldiers, along with their general, had been awaiting reinforcements from the auxiliary British army in Kut-al-Amara, below Baghdad. They had been unexpectedly besieged by a large Turkish army and taken prisoner. They had walked for more than two months from Baghdad via Der Zor to Amanos. The high command of the Mesopotamian Turkish army had doubted that Arab officers and soldiers would wish to carry out the secret instructions of their superiors, so they entrusted only their own soldiers and Ittihad officers to transport these British captives from Mesopotamia to Cilicia. The Ittihad officers had selected the roads across the longest deserts, in order to subject the defenseless prisoners to "white massacre." They had committed all sorts of cruelties so that the prisoners would die along the way. For example, instead of being taken on the roads in the cool of the night, as was the local custom, they were made to walk in the scorching daytime sun for weeks and months. They were told that supplies hadn't arrived, or that they were on their way; or that there weren't any. They had been left hungry for days on end and made to drink foul water, which caused them to fall ill with dysentery and consumption. Having wasted away, they had collapsed along the roads, abandoned.

These loyal agents of the Turkish state, who had formerly sent propa-

*Most likely Büyükada Island of the Princes Islands.—trans.

ganda to the hundred million Muslims of India, now treated the Muslim Indian prisoners even more harshly for having dared to serve in Christian armies against the Muslim caliph and take up arms against the Turks.

Isn't it true that the Turks had always burned, broken, destroyed, violated, and massacred the Arabs, Albanians, Circassians, and Persians under their dominion, even though they were their Muslim brothers? For this reason all the Muslim races had wished to throw off the Turkish yoke, attempting revolt down through the centuries. British officers even told us that Turkish soldiers, on the order of their officers, had oftentimes struck straggling Muslim Indian prisoners with the butts of their rifles and smashed in their skulls when those prisoners, languishing and unable to move, could no longer walk with the caravan.

Thus the Turkish officers and soldiers had not only flouted the rules of engagement observed by civilized nations but had acted with such brutality that out of the thirteen thousand British and Indian soldiers and officers taken prisoner at Kut-al-Amara, only about sixteen hundred, as best I can remember, managed to reach our Amanos construction lines. And if they treated the men of the most powerful country on earth this way, you can imagine how they treated their subject Christian peoples.

When the British officers finished their heartrending stories of desert suffering, they told us, with great compassion, of the frightful scenes they had witnessed in Der Zor. In those vast deserts they had come upon piles of human bones, crushed skulls, and skeletons stretched out everywhere, and heaps of skeletons of murdered children.

If the Armenian historians who had chronicled the martyrdom of the forty infants massacred in Sivas by Tamerlane were living in the here and now, what lamentations would they have written at the sight of thousands of massacred children? In the end, through slaughter and starvation, 400,000 Armenian deportees were exterminated in the endless expanse of the burning desert sands.

The Turkish officers and soldiers had treated the British prisoners just as they had treated the many thousands of Armenian deportees—without fear of any subsequent accountability. For the Turks were deeply convinced that in the end, owing to the invincible German armies, they would defeat the Allies; they would occupy the Caucasus, Persia, India, Egypt, and all the Muslim lands of North Africa and establish a huge Muslim world empire . . . Imagine the likelihood that a Turkish race numbering barely four million—two-thirds of whose far-flung empire had already been lost, the remainder facing the threat of division—would be able to realize this dream. This says something about the extent of the chauvinism, pan-Islamism, and pan-Turkic dreams that the young leaders of Turkey had embraced.

It took about a month for the German management of the railroad construction project to bring the British prisoners back to health, organize new labor battalions, and resume the construction of the routes and tunnels that had ceased with the deportation of the thousands of Armenian laborers.

We few remaining Armenians in Baghche found noble and trustworthy friends among the British officers who were our colleagues. Without reservation, we told them about our current sea of troubles as well as our future hopes and expectations. These officers, in turn, gave us hope that when this world war ended with the victory of the Allied and Entente powers, our centuries-old suffering too would finally come to an end. With soldierly sincerity not to be expected from politicians and diplomats, the British officers consoled us with reports of what was being written in the London dailies, particularly the Armenophilic speeches of Prime Minister H. H. Asquith and Foreign Minister Edward Grey, which had reached them through secret channels.

As survivors of the Armenian people, thirsty for consolation and encouragement, we were eager to believe—and thus became convinced—that as our new friends were assuring us, the Entente powers were waging this crucial war for the triumph of right and justice and for the liberation of oppressed peoples—a claim that responsible [cabinet] ministers made a good many times.[1]

9

The Program of Forced Islamization: Escape from Baghche to Injirli

The deportation of more than ten thousand Armenian workers from the Amanos railroad construction projects left about two hundred of us on the line, as surveyor-engineers, draftsmen, and telegraph operators. Among us were also a few dozen Armenian master craftsmen: blacksmiths, carpenters, tinsmiths, and so on.

All around us the hustle and bustle had ceased; it was deserted except for a few Turkish peasants and Kurdish refugee laborers scattered here and there, working on the newly constructed lines. With 10,000 of the 15,000 workers gone, construction had naturally slowed, but now, as the British prisoners came on the job, there was a new excitement.

The attention of the Turkish employees was now centered on us, the remaining few Armenians, who had become thorns in their sides; every day they started new rumors about how the remaining Armenians would also be deported.

Even discounting these rumors, we were all bewildered and anxious. And then the director of the tobacco *reji*, born a Jew in Salonica, summoned us one at a time and suggested that we accept Islam as the only way of being saved.

Word gradually reached us that a few Armenian telegraph operators along the line had gone to the nearby town of Islahiye, the government seat, and accepted Islam at the suggestion of the very same *reji* director, himself a convert. Not only had they changed their names, they had also submitted to all the formalities required by their new religion.

Mavian, Klaus's assistant, did everything possible to resist forced Islamization. Finally my turn had come. One day the same *donme* Jew from Salonica came to our workshop at the Baghche station and winked at me to come outside with him. In confidence, he said, "Garabedian *Effendi*, when are you going to submit a written request to become a Muslim?" I hastened to reply that I was ready and that it remained for him to lead me, like other Armenians, through all the legal formalities.

The fanatical *donme* gladly made an appointment for me to go and see him at his office in Baghche two days later, on a Friday, to sign the application that he would prepare. The next day we would go to Islahiye together and see to all the other legal requirements.

The very same evening I hastened to find our chief, the engineer Klaus; I told him the details of the proposal that had been made to me and asked him to help me save myself. As a *vartabed* of the Armenian Church, I preferred to die rather than renounce my faith.

Klaus, moved, asked what I proposed he should do. I requested that he help me escape to Taurus or Belemedik. He, however, found my plan rash, because he considered such a long journey dangerous, especially with all the roads besieged by police soldiers. He had goodwill toward me, but because of his responsible position, he was leery of any action bound to arouse suspicion. He was willing to make overtures but not to assume responsibility for my escape, fearing that, in the event of my arrest, I would be lost, as he would not be able to rescue me from the Turkish police.

At my wit's end, I turned to another German, the mechanic Kegel, who knew I was a clergyman. As a good Catholic, he wished to do what he could to rescue me from the threat of Islamization. We had no time to waste—I needed to escape from the Baghche region before my appointment in two days.

The kindhearted Kegel, with typical German resolve, gave me his passport, from which we removed the photograph. He then gave me a letter of introduction to a close friend in Injirli, who lived about four hours by narrow-gauge railroad from Baghche, asking that he take me in until he [Kegel] arrived.

Injirli was the last station on the Amanos line, and the major station of Mamure was a half hour's walk from there. For this reason Injirli was the railroad supply depot; here were located large warehouses of railroad building materials as well as military stores that had come from Germany via Constantinople for the fronts in Syria, Palestine, and Mesopotamia.

Through Injirli ran a very deep valley, over which, in July 1916, a marvelous huge bridge was being built. On foundations that had been sunk more than ten meters in the ground, its numerous arched columns rose as high as thirty-five meters, depending on the depth of the valley at that point. My contact was Kegel's friend, the Swiss engineer of this bridge. Meanwhile the passing hours seemed like years, as Friday, the ill-starred day of my appointment, fast approached. Unexpectedly, the Austrian engineer Litzmayer, who oversaw the construction projects of the narrow-gauge railway, arrived in Baghche with his special little rail wagonette. Seeing no other choice, I revealed to him my unfortunate situation and my identity, then earnestly beseeched him to help me escape to Injirli, where he was going that same day for an official inspection.

A good Christian, he wanted to save this Armenian clergyman; he personally escorted me to his little private railway car, and with his whistle, he signaled to the engineer in the locomotive to depart immediately, ahead of schedule. I had no time to say goodbye to all those who had been such courageous aides in my escape. Soon our little derrick train was galloping from Baghche toward Injirli, without stopping anywhere for long.

The rough mountainous route of the four-hour journey seemed endless. But my companion Litzmayer kept saying he was prepared to defend me at all costs, rather than turn me over to any Turkish military or police official.

Finally we arrived at Injirli, and together we went to the company's private restaurant to eat. Here we met a Jew named Blanck, head of the local warehouses, whose Armenophobic reputation had reached Baghche. With devilish delight in catching one's prey, he asked me who I was. By this time I had decided to drop my pseudonym Garabedian and take the German-Jewish name Herr Braunstein. Blanck, who as an informant had caused the arrest of many an Armenian in hiding, did his best to unmask me by interrogating me in German. Doing my best to evade him, I said I was in a hurry and left the restaurant like any traveler leaving for Adana. I then disappeared behind some bushes and rushed to find the Swiss architect, to whom I was to present my letter of introduction. With friendly warmth he welcomed me to his home and saw to it that I was comfortable and secure until Kegel's arrival in Injirli.

In the evening two young German engineers, neighbors of the Swiss architect, came home from work, and I was introduced to them as the Austrian Jew Herr Braunstein. From the start these men treated me like a friend and we downed glasses of cold beer as we spent the evening in pleasant conversation about nonpolitical issues, then retired to the wooden cells in our barracks. Still the days passed in tedium and anxiety, because my noble friend Kegel, in whom I had placed all my hope, had yet to arrive.

Every night the creaking of carriages coming from Kanle-gechid along the riverbank in the valley, just a half hour away, filled me with terror. At this time the remnants of thousands of deportation caravans were being taken to the deserts via the Islahiye road. The German engineers, whose hospitality I was enjoying, confirmed this fact at dinner. Since they and the Swiss architect with whom I was living would leave early in the morning for work at the railway, it was only in the evening that we could get together and talk.

Eight to ten days had passed, and still I had no word of my friend Kegel. Then one evening the Armenian massacres and deportations incidentally became the topic of conversation between myself and the two German engineers. Showing an amazing lack of compassion, they accused the Armenian people of being rebels and deserving their horrible punishment . . . Only the Swiss architect defended the Armenians, condemning the acts of Turkish savagery with righteous indignation. The two engineers didn't know that I was Armenian because the kind and foresighted Swiss architect had kept my identity a secret from his colleagues, allowing them to express their convictions sincerely and unreservedly.

When I could no longer conceal my identity, I confessed that I was Armenian and told them the story of my exile. Taken by surprise, and stupefied, they listened to my account of the Golgotha of us Armenians.

As a result of my indiscretion, they were less friendly to me, and they continued to throw stones, directly or indirectly, at the martyred Armenian people. I felt such outrage that, after saying goodbye one day, I departed so as not to be seen again. With no shelter or place to hide, I had no choice but to seek cover in the nearby cedar forest a half hour away.

10

In the Forests of Injirli: Escape from Amanos to Taurus

Like a wild animal, I had taken refuge in the forest, deprived of the most elementary means of sustenance; I had done this impulsively, without weighing the consequences.

Only after the first day, when darkness fell, did I feel the full weight of my rash undertaking. Horrified, I found myself alone in the mysterious silence and darkness of the forest. I took cover in a natural underground hollow, passing the hours of night sleepless, in search of a means of escape. My only hope was my self-sacrificing defender Kegel, and there was nothing I could do but wait for his arrival.

After a few days in the forest I could no longer endure the hunger or, especially, the thirst. It was July, and the scorching Cilician sun was burning and destroying everything. The depths of the dense forest were cool, but still I was parched, aching for a drop of water. I wandered around looking for edible grasses; their bitter taste slightly cooled my burning lips and tongue.

The hunger was more bearable than the thirst, as I insatiably ate the sap that dripped from the cedar trees without thinking about the consequences. Just having something between my teeth to chew gave me solace and strength, and my will to endure redoubled. But still I was burning up with thirst. I picked off pieces of cracked bark from the cedar trees, sucking and licking their undersides for moisture, but to no avail; my thirst was irrepressible, to the point of jeopardizing my life. One night, at my wit's end, I tried to descend to the Kanle-gechid stream, an hour away. But hardly had I stepped out of the forest when suddenly I saw shadows—so I immediately returned to my hiding place, trembling with fear. My dread grew, however, when I saw the same shadow near my underground hollow; before me was a wolf, looking at me with surprise as if to say, *What are you doing here?* I rushed upon the beast, threatening it with an iron bar I had at hand, when it ran off. Jackals, always in packs, were circling me, but that didn't frighten me; only their nocturnal howling filled me with terror.

Unable to endure after four days, I decided to go to the military tents located on the summit of the valley, a half hour from the forest. I left at midnight to determine if their occupants were Armenian worker-soldiers or Turks.

When I overheard a conversation in Armenian in a nearby tent, my joy was indescribable. In one tent two of four comrades were sleeping while the other two exchanged tales of the heroic defense waged by the Armenians of Shabin Karahisar.[1] One of them seemed to have been an eyewitness, to judge by the way he spoke.

Without much thought I called out to them in Armenian. Intrigued by my unfamiliar voice, the two Armenian soldiers stepped forth fearlessly, and seeing me in the humble position of supplicant, they invited me into their tent. They awoke their two companions, and with anxious impatience, all listened to the story of my journey of suffering. Then they tried to find out my identity, but I couldn't risk revealing it, so I said that I was an exiled Armenian schoolteacher. One of the Armenian soldiers, however, refused to believe me and kept repeating, "*Effendi*, you are an important person. Tell the truth; who are you?" These concerned Armenians could think only about my importance, whereas I could think only about my hunger and insatiable thirst.

These were hapless Armenian labor battalion [*amele tabur*] soldiers; all the members of their families—mothers, wives, and children—had been deported and massacred, the government's payment for their services.

When I told them that I was hungry and thirsty, they were all moved and opened their knapsacks. One of them looked under the dirty rags of his bedding and could find nothing more than a piece of black bread, like dried mud; he handed it to me. I could not bite off a piece or even break it with my hand, so I asked for some water, and after carefully drinking it, I moistened the bread and tried to grind it with my teeth. Meanwhile the soldiers, deeply affected by my plight, asked the same question several times: "*Effendi*, what is to become of us? . . . There aren't any Armenians left . . . To whom shall Armenia be left?"

At last my own anxiety waned, for now I had protectors ready to provide me with assistance and share their daily bread ration, however insufficient.

The situation of these wretched Armenian soldiers, however, was tragic. Four of them lived in one small tattered military tent that could barely accommodate two lying down. They had no medicine, no doctors or pharmacists. They wore only a few pieces of tattered underwear, tattered clothing, and torn shoes; they did not even have soap. The indigestible, tasteless bread of bran, potatoes, and wheat, which was like mud, was all they had to eat.

Labor-battalion soldiers died regularly—dried up, emaciated, and jaundiced from malaria—and here maybe only a third were left. We shared the same fate, and yet as a fugitive, I was in need of these Armenian worker-soldiers, whose life was only a bit more bearable than mine.

Many of their comrades had died forlorn, unable to endure the deprivation and suffering. Those still alive told me how their Turkish reserve officers selected only swampy sites for their encampments, hoping that attrition by disease would reduce the numbers to be massacred.

Thanks to these Armenians, I finally had a tolerable existence. For about three weeks I spent my days hiding in the forests, and at night I stayed with them, sharing their dry bread.

One night they informed me that Kegel had come to Injirli to begin work on the high-rise warehouse towers for the railroad locomotives. Kegel, my savior, was horror-struck to see my sunken eyes and how much weight I had lost. He ordered a tent to be set up for him on the nearby hill, away from the encampment; it would be my hiding place, a safe refuge, far from human eyes and feet. At the top of the tent pole waved the German tricolor, giving notice that this site was inviolable. Although the superintendents were not in the habit of flying flags on their tents, Kegel raised this flag to ensure that nothing untoward happened in his absence.

Thanks to plentiful nourishment provided by this honorable man, I gradually regained my strength. An elderly Jewish worker who was loyal to Kegel and had won his trust provided all kinds of food and fruits from the railway company's private cafeteria adjoining the military warehouses. A month later I had fully recovered.

At night our main topic of conversation was planning the safest escape from Amanos to Taurus. Kegel told me that the head of the food warehouses under the local German railway administration, who happened to be a Jew, was a terrible Armenophobe who had betrayed many Armenians in hiding, turning them over to the Turkish police and military officials. Therefore I had to exercise the most extreme caution, particularly considering that this Armenophobe knew I was staying in Injirli, though he hadn't been able to track me down. Kegel also discovered that the two German engineers who had previously sheltered me in Injirli had known that I was Armenian even before I had revealed my identity.

I decided to flee these parts at all costs. Kegel aimed to do the impossible and facilitate my escape from Amanos to Taurus with the help of kind, self-sacrificing Armenian railroad officials. To forestall every possible danger, he had given me his own German passport.

On July 26, 1916, full of gratitude, I took leave of my selfless protector once and for all. At dusk I departed as a German named Kegel, expressing the wish that we might meet again in better days. Hardly had I left the tent, hadn't even reached the thickets, when I fell to my knees for a final time on the dried grass and prayed.

Indeed, the moment was frightful; I was about to cross a narrow bridge and find my fate, so I asked God for help. Strengthened by heavenly minded prayer, I rose to my feet, and fearless this time, I was at last free from the nightmare of death.

Christ rightly said, "If ye have faith as a grain of mustard seed, ye shall say unto this mountain: Remove hence to yonder place; and it shall remove; and nothing shall be impossible unto you." Yes, the defenseless, wandering clergyman who had dreaded taking a step was now propelled by an inexhaustible force.

Reciting from the psalm, "Lord, guide my course along the right path" [*Der ughya uzkanatsus im ee janabarhus ughigh*], I walked away from the Amanos and, without fear, toward the Taurus mountains.

"Your faith sustained you." *Havadk ko getsutsin uzkez.*

PART II

In the Tunnels of the Taurus Mountains

Black Sea
Bosphorus
Constantinople
Sea of Marmara
Gebze
Izmit
Adapazar
Arifye
Chankiri
Bilejik
Ankara
Eskishehir
T U R
Afyonkarahisar
N
Konya
Karaman
Gulf of Antalya
Taurus Mts.
Mediterranean Sea
CYPRUS
Constantinople-to-Baghdad Railway
(Section of the Berlin-to-Baghdad Railway)
German construction from Constantinople to Konya, completed 1896
German construction from Bozanti to Islahiye (as of 1917–early 1918)
French Mersin-Tarsus-Adana Railway, completed 1886
Additional construction toward Baghdad
Railway tunnel
0 MILES 150
0 KILOMETERS 150

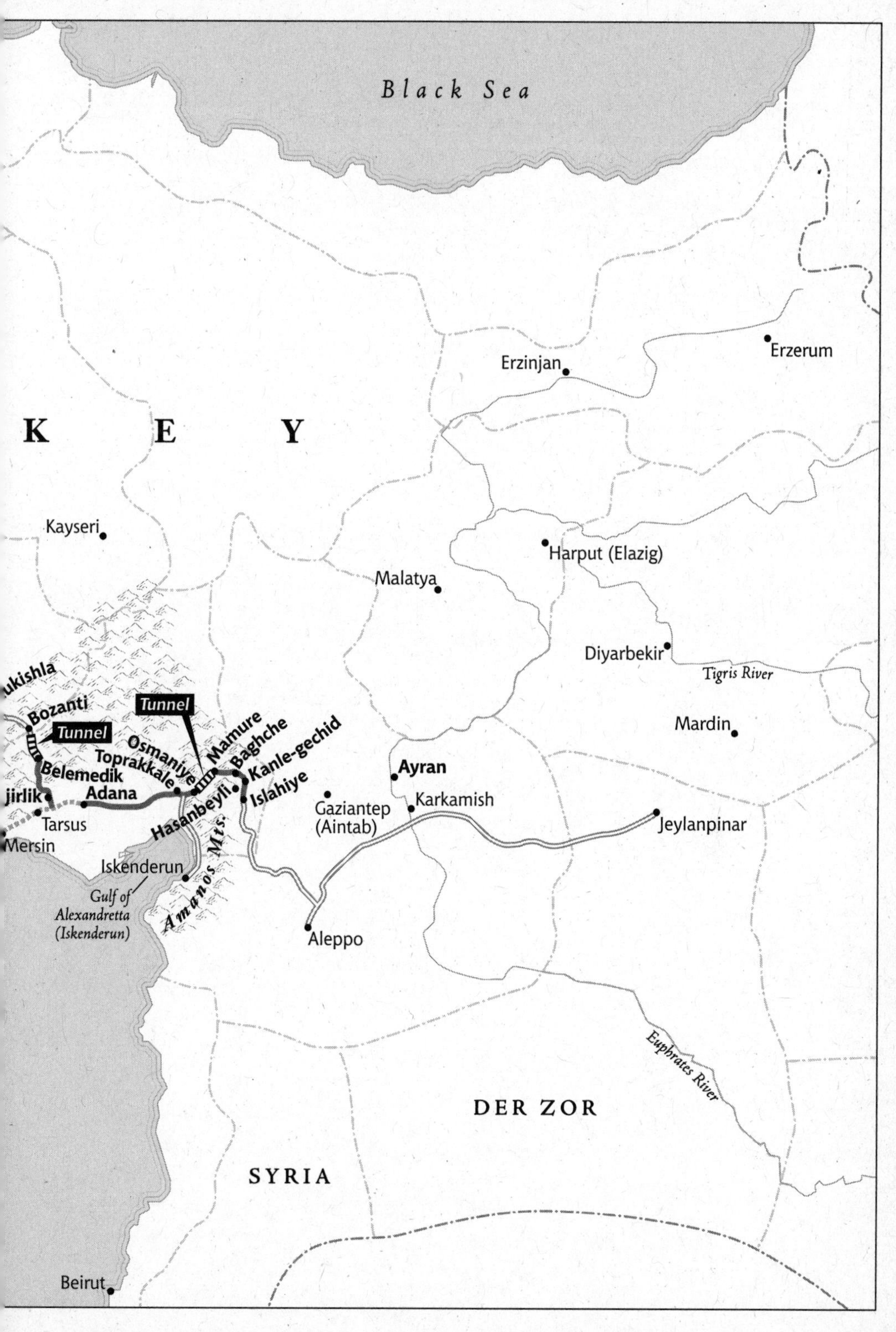
Black Sea
K E Y
Erzinjan
Erzerum
Kayseri
Harput (Elazig)
Malatya
Diyarbekir
Tigris River
Mardin
ukishla
Bozanti
Tunnel
Tunnel
Osmaniye
Mamure
Baghche
Kanle-gechid
Toprakkale
Belemedik
Adana
jirlik
Tarsus
Mersin
Hasanbeyli
Islahiye
Ayran
Gaziantep
(Aintab)
Karkamish
Jeylanpinar
Iskenderun
Gulf of
Alexandretta
(Iskenderun)
Amanos Mts.
Aleppo
Euphrates River
DER ZOR
SYRIA
Beirut

11

The Self-Sacrifice of the Armenian Workers of the Baghdad Railway

My savior Kegel, having spoken in advance with the Armenian officials of the Mamure station, had arranged the first requirement for my safety. Barely had he and I reached the station, an hour away from our hiding place, when he turned me over to an Armenian official, Mihran Melkonian. Together with another Armenian official, Melkonian took me to a first-class car hidden behind many other cars beyond the railway tracks. A little later a German major came to the same car; they introduced me to him, and he took a seat next to mine. In a friendly manner we conversed about varieties of fine wine.

The major's conversation was likely calculated. He never showed any interest in me; never asked who I was, where I was coming from, or where I was going. He wished to remain ignorant till the very end. But I had no doubt that I had been placed under his protection.

After about a quarter hour our isolated car was hooked onto the official train, and right before the eyes of the Turkish police and military officials, we set forth. They had missed what they were looking for.

Every time we came to a station, Turkish police and military officials of all ranks rushed onto our train, but for five hours, all the way to Adana, no one bothered us. Not one official dared to come to our car, with its sign SPECIAL WAGON FOR GERMAN OFFICERS, and there was no one in there but the two of us. Only the Armenian inspector, in accordance with his special assignment, frequently came by and looked me in the eye as if to say, *Do you need anything?* or, *Don't be afraid; I am here.*

Finally we reached the Adana station safely and without incident. The German major invited me to the station restaurant, and after eating, we went for an outing in town by carriage. On the way back to the station, we found out that the previous day Vahak, regional Dashnak leader of Cilicia, had been hanged in Adana's memorial fountain square, by order of Jemal Pasha, in whose close friendship Vahak had put much faith.

When we returned to the station, all the train cars, including ours, had changed, and new officials had replaced the old ones. While I was agonizing about that, another Armenian official came over and said, "Reverend Father, don't be concerned; I will take every precaution for your safety." When I asked him how he knew my identity, he answered, "Even though I was given this special assignment, I knew you from Scutari. I am from the Berberian school. You often came to our examinations." After that I felt safe, knowing that in case of danger a selfless compatriot was watching over me.

I was now traveling in such comfort that I forgot I was a fugitive. For the first time in sixteen months, seeing prosperous cities densely populated, I was in a good mood. The train moved, but no one demanded to see our passports or tickets. The usual haughty and contemptuous air of the German major and his companion made us unapproachable. Despite their obsession with hunting down Armenians, the military and police officials dared not ask me any questions.

As for the Turks, the German military personnel had so much mastery over them that no Turk, irrespective of rank, position, or class, dared to challenge them. Let one example suffice: When the Turkish major in charge of the Mamure station dared to show reluctance to put a whole car at the disposal of forty German soldiers, an ordinary German soldier killed him with a shot of his pistol. The matter—a German soldier's having killed the Turkish station commander—was not even brought before a court-martial. In fact, the case was quickly closed with the announcement that the major had been killed by a bullet fired by an unknown Turk.

The trip from Adana to Yenije, normally a one-and-a-half-hour journey, took us all of four and a half hours.[1] The kind German major continued to express his friendship, saying that he was the inspector-commander of the German military displacements of Gulek-Bogazi; he suggested that I go and live under his protection as a translator. But as my secret goal was to escape from Belemedik to Switzerland, I could not accept his good-faith offer. Thus, with reciprocal respect, we took leave of each other, and he repeated over and over that should I find myself in tight circumstances, I should not hesitate to take refuge with him. Despite my insistence, the Armenian official who had been helping me refused to accept any money, saying, "Instead of me giving it to you, you want to give it to me? I did my duty. I wish I could do more to save your life."

Indeed, although I benefited from the kindness of one or two German officers and a few German civilians, I remember with pride the selfless conduct of all the Armenian railway officials who, without expectation of gain, did all they could to save their unfortunate compatriots, sometimes even putting themselves in harm's way. During my fugitive exile and wanderings, I never met or heard of an Armenian railway official without compassion for the suffering of his race. And for this very reason, the many Turks viewed them with suspicion, accusing them of aiding the escape of the exiles, and sentenced them by court-martial to exile, imprisonment, and even hanging.

Barely had I set foot in the Yenije station when I hurried to see the Armenian stationmaster, a pleasant young man. Taking no chances, I introduced myself to the stationmaster as the German Herr Kegel and asked to rent a horse with a European saddle so I could go to Dorak.

The Armenian stationmaster, Diran Kooyoomjian, shrugged his shoulders indifferently and pointed to a dilapidated Turkish café. "I am a railway official," he said in German, "and I don't get involved in horse business; there are Turks sitting in the café facing us; go there, and they will find a horse for you." You didn't have to be a psychologist to sense that Germanophobia lay beneath his disdainful and unfriendly response, but a conversation with the Turks in the café could subject me to danger, so I went back and found the stationmaster in his office. Having no choice, I said in Armenian, "Dear friend, I am K. V. B. the clergyman, and I want to get to Dorak. But as a fugitive I am unable to move about freely and take care of my business. Thus I ask for your help. Please exercise the utmost discretion . . ."

And behold, this contemptuous stationmaster suddenly became a friendly and obliging person. With tear-filled eyes, he jumped to his feet and, taking my hand, led me to his personal apartment next to the station. He introduced me to his elderly mother, saying, "Mother, here is the only living Armenian *vartabed* left in the Armenian provinces. He owes his survival so far to his audacity and to his familiarity with the German language. He is our guest today; slaughter a chicken, and let us eat together."

In the parable of the Bible the prodigal son was lost and then found, was dead and then came back to life again. But at this moment it was a clergyman whose tracks had disappeared, who was dead and now had suddenly reemerged among his spiritual sons. After several extremely agonizing moments, I once more found myself in a safe place with trustworthy people, again recovering my inner peace and self-confidence.

In the intimate and unreserved conversations engendered by warm and sincere hospitality, the elderly Armenian woman, with pain in her heart, tears in her eyes, and curses on her lips, told me, one by one, many horrendous and tragic episodes of tens of thousands of Armenian deportees of both sexes who had come from Konya to Bozanti on foot and passed behind the Yenije station on the highway toward Adana. Without allowing the deportees to go into the city, the Turkish deportation officials and hundreds of savage police soldiers, cracking their whips, had driven them via Kanle-gechid toward the deserts of Syria and Mesopotamia.

This sobbing elderly woman told how in the summer of 1915 the Turkish police and soldiers did not allow even a drop of water drawn from the wells to touch the parched lips of these people; furthermore, they even snatched buckets of water from the hands of the deportees and emptied them out on the ground. The long-suffering Armenian mothers could do nothing but shout, fearless with bitterness: "You made us wretched, may God do the same to you . . ."

This hospitality, extended with a mother's solicitude, reminded me that I had a grieving mother anxiously awaiting my return. Oh, I wondered whether that blessed time would come, whether we would survive the bloody storm of the world war and return to our homes. Oh, to see that joyful day would be enough, and after that it would not matter if we died.

A fine horse and a trustworthy Turkish groom were now ready, and expressing my sincere gratitude, I got on the road toward Dorak, located on the west side of Adana. Under the scorching rays of the Cilician summer sun, I traveled on horseback nonstop for three hours while the young groom ran alongside me on foot. Firmly convinced that I was German, once in a while he uttered curses in Turkish against the German nation.

Toward noon we finally reached Dorak safe but spent. Following the suggestion of the hospitable Yenije stationmaster, I headed directly to the tent of a wealthy Armenian who was transportation contractor in charge of building materials for the Dorak railroad. This man was a native of Sassoun, a very patriotic individual who secretly helped every needy Armenian. Through the power of money and his unusual generosity, he had become friends with all the local government, police, and military leaders.

The Armenian stationmaster had heaped so much praise on this person that I had hardly dismounted when I went to his beautiful tent to ask for a horse or carriage to take me to Kushjlar. But when I got there, I found two other persons in the tent, one wearing a Turkish officer's uniform. Speaking a kind of Turkish peculiar to foreigners, I requested a means of transportation to Kushjlar. The official replied that it was not possible to accommodate my request since it was Sunday, and he asked me who I was, where I came from, and what work I did.

Seeing that the matter was dragging on and taking the form of an interrogation, I responded only, "I don't know Turkish" [*Ben yok bilir Turkje*]. But to my surprise, the officer, whom I had taken for a Turk, said to his friends in the proper Armenian of a schoolboy, "This man is not German; he looks like an Armenian. I wonder who he is." This was no time to lose my composure, so I pretended not to understand. Meanwhile the third person present, the Dorak railroad stationmaster, Yeghiazar Deyirmenjian, a noble and patriotic young man, turned and said to the others, "If he is not German but is Armenian and has managed to keep himself alive that way, bravo! He is a clever person. If only others too could have saved themselves through such ingenuity."

All three in the tent were clearly Armenian, but nevertheless, opting for prudence, I invited the young Armenian contractor outside. Taking him quite a distance behind the tent, out of sight, I revealed my identity and repeated that I needed to reach Kushjlar in a hurry.

He couldn't have been happier, and being familiar with my name from the newspapers, he led me back to the tent and said, "I present to you Most Reverend Father Grigoris Balakian—" Exclamations of joy flew out of the mouths of the two young officials, who ran up to embrace me.

In the evening we gathered around a table of tasty dishes and, with glasses of red wine in hand, stood up and drank toasts to an independent Armenia and the imminent resurrection of the undying Armenian race. The glasses were emptied, the toasts multiplied, and the enthusiasm grew, such that I forgot that I was a persecuted fugitive condemned to death.

We got so excited that we started to draw the borders of tomorrow's liberated Armenia on a map . . . and calculate the number of surviving Armenians. We concluded that there could be approximately 750,000 left: those in Constantinople and Smyrna, and those who escaped the deportations and were living along the railway line from Afyonkarahisar all the way to Aleppo, including the exiled Armenian refugees in Syria and Der Zor.

We didn't know then that in one week's time during these same days of July 1916, in accordance with orders from Talaat in Constantinople, 150,000 Armenian men, women, and children found on the banks of the Euphrates and in the remote desert areas of Der Zor had been murdered. This was done under the command of Governor Zeki, who had just arrived in Der Zor from Kayseri.

These two happy, illusory days of intimate, warm, and generous hospitality passed quickly. Physically and mentally rejuvenated, I departed for Kushjlar in the special carriage the Armenian contractor provided for me. There I was to deliver a secret letter of introduction from my savior Kegel in Baghche, addressed to the Swiss director of the electric company. In five hours I reached Kushjlar and immediately went to find the Swiss electrical engineer, who hosted me in his private residence with Christian hospitality, promising to take all precautions to ensure my safety.

12

Fragments of Armenians in the Taurus Mountains

As I have noted, hundreds of thousands of the escapees from the deportation caravans found refuge in the work of building tunnels in the Amanos mountains and had so far succeeded in lengthening their lives for practically a year. Toward the end of May 1916, the Turkish government leaders who had created and executed the plan to annihilate the Armenian race ordered them to be deported. In one week, more than eleven thousand Armenian laborers were thus deported for the second time. The majority, as noted in Chapter 7, were massacred on the desolate mountain roads and in the valleys of Baghche and Marash. But others, being families of soldiers and/or through bribes and other resourceful means, had succeeded in remaining in the cities along the railway line—Eskishehir, Afyonkarahisar, Soultaniye, and especially Konya and Eregli.

For the past year the Turkish government's police officials had constantly pursued these people and driven them southward toward Konya and its vicinity. Thanks to the kindness of the moderate local Muslim population, more than twenty thousand Armenians had gathered together in Konya, having come from Adrianople, Rodosto, and various regions of Thrace, as well as Bursa and its villages and the regions of Izmit, Adapazar, Bilejik, Eskishehir, and so on.

Konya was a historic and mighty center—first Seljuk and then Turkish—due to the peace-loving influence of the kind monastic Muslim Mevlevis.* The province's Muslim population had always maintained good neighborly relations with the Armenians, even during the Hamidian Massacres of 1895–96, in which they, like the Muslims of Kastemouni, took no part.

In noting the friendliness of the Kastemouni and Konya Muslims toward the Armenian people, however, one must also note that Kaste-

*Mevlevis: Sufi order of Islam, known in Konya as the Whirling Dervishes.—trans.

mouni and Konya were the only two provinces in Asia Minor in which the Armenian population was sparse. In 1910 the entire province of Kastemouni had but 2,000 Armenian households, while Konya had only 2,500.

The German management overseeing construction of the Taurus tunnels, starting from Bozanti, had established five main stations as construction centers: Belemedik, Tashdurmaz, Kushjlar, Yarbashi, and Dorak. In each, thanks to their industriousness and punctuality, Armenians had succeeded in gaining good positions as civil engineers, draftsmen, blacksmiths, carpenters, joiners, supervisors, clerks, bookkeepers, foremen, and cooks; a very few also worked as laborers. Altogether they were eight hundred.

Because of the wartime conscription of all available men, the German management had accepted the Armenians who applied and assigned them jobs according to their ability, grateful, given the circumstances, to have such dutiful employees specializing in all trades and fields, working under such unfavorable conditions. For clearly, even with good pay and under good material conditions, such people would not have come to this untamed Taurus wilderness of mountains and valleys in peacetime—prior to the deportations, having for the most part held enviable independent positions in their communities, often as owners of businesses. Now, however, removed from their birthplaces and deprived of their movable and immovable properties and possessions (which had been seized by the Turkish government), their sole concern was to save their lives, and they were satisfied with a piece of dry bread.

Fortunately, most of the construction officials were noble and humane Swiss who were sympathetic, kind, and friendly to the Armenians. With Christian compassion they shared their grief and protected them on every occasion. One time a Swiss official, seeing a Turkish laborer beating an Armenian laborer for no good reason, was so infuriated that he charged the Turk and landed him a powerful blow with a hammer, knocking him to the ground, while yelling in Turkish: "You committed all kinds of crimes in the unseen corners of the mountains and valleys. Now you have the audacity to continue your crimes against the hapless Armenians before our very eyes!" The unconscious Turk was in the hospital for quite a few weeks and barely managed to recover.

The head of construction for the Taurus tunnels, Mavrokordato, came from a wealthy, distinguished Greek family, but he was weak and timid, especially so because he was an Ottoman citizen. Thus while always careful not to defend the Armenians openly, secretly he had a special sympathy and even love for them. Mavrokordato supervised a Swiss engineer, an ex–military man named Leutenegger, who was bold and austere; and when it came to defending the Armenians, he made up for what was lacking in Mavrokordato.

Management of the construction work was centered in Belemedik, so Mavrokordato and Leutenegger lived and worked there, where the local Turkish military and police were afraid of the tough colonel-engineer. In the fall of 1915, during the black days of the Armenian deportation, when thousands of women and children from Eregli reached Bozanti hungry and thirsty, having been robbed in Konya by policemen and police soldiers, Leutenegger rushed there to provide material assistance for them. The Turkish officials overseeing the caravans refused to allow him to distribute bread to these starving people, and Leutenegger, filled with anger, pulled out his whip and unsparingly lashed all the police soldiers resisting him. "See, I am distributing the bread," he yelled. "Let me see which of you will dare to snatch it from the hands of these wretches!" The Turkish officials insisted that "there are strict orders from Constantinople not to help the Armenian caravans," but every time Leutenegger heard that caravans of Armenian deportees were arriving in Bozanti from Konya or Eregli, he would run there with bread and money.

After the deportation and massacre of the Armenians working on the Amanos tunnels, the Turkish government sought to fully implement its annihilation plan and took strict measures against the Armenians working on the Taurus tunnels as well. But the German construction office, arguing that it had barely eight hundred Armenians on these vital construction sites, had succeeded in preventing their deportation. To keep Talaat from meddling in the affairs of the railway construction office, War Minister Enver ordered all Ottoman subjects working on railway construction, without regard to ethnicity, to remain at their jobs as a form of military service. To indicate their military status, ribbons made from red cloth were sewn on the sleeves of all the officials and laborers. Nonetheless Talaat intervened and had all those who were suspect arrested in order to deport them.

13

In the Deep Valley of Tashdurmaz

A multitude of officials and laborers of all kinds were in Kushjlar because, after Belemedik, it was the second largest station of the Taurus tunnels. Electric and mechanical power plants stood at the summit of the valley, and as mentioned earlier, their director was the Swiss electrical engineer to whom I had brought a letter of introduction from Kegel, my kind protector in Baghche.

On the advice of my new protector in Kushjlar, I wore a blue workman's shirt as the most suitable disguise. Barely had I started to work in the electric power plant when, after a few days, I encountered familiar intellectuals from Constantinople, and so it became impossible to hide my identity any longer.

Among others, I met Sebouh Agouni and Yeghia Suzigian (both of whom have since died). As editors of Armenian papers in Constantinople, they had been my greatest critics and opponents in my public life. Now that we were all comrades in suffering, however, hounded by the same unrelenting fate, we greeted one another as old friends. Just the appearance of these two men stirred my compassion; they were thin and pale, their clothing and shoes torn.

My four days in Kushjlar had already convinced me that hiding my identity would be impossible here; every day I met new familiar faces and learned that word had spread that Balakian Vartabed was in Kushjlar. One night, without much thought, and at the recommendation of my kind Swiss host, I secretly departed on horseback, taking refuge an hour away at the secondary station between Kushjlar and Belemedik called Tashdurmaz. There I became the guest of another noble Swiss, who was the director of the electric power plant at that station.

But as there were Armenian officials and numerous Armenian artisans in Tashdurmaz as well, I saw that I probably couldn't keep my identity a secret here either. Therefore, after lengthy deliberations and on the advice of the Swiss electrical engineer, I descended the deep valley of Tashdurmaz to a water mill on the banks of the Chaket River. From here, the river water was channeled to the electric plants four hundred meters above, and to the huts of the workers who toiled in the various workshops.

Surrounded by the huge rocky and wooded Taurus mountains, buried in the deep inaccessible valleys of untamed nature—and above all, far removed from the company of any breathing creature, let alone human eyes—I started a life of deep solitude and silence. It did not frighten me because, for the time being, I was safe.

My only friend was a helper, an Armenian laborer, who was unaware of my secret. One of his responsibilities was to descend the winding trails of the mountain once a day and bring me cooked food and bread in closed containers from the special restaurant [*popote*] that catered to the Tashdurmaz officials. The trip would take him more than two hours. When I was alone, my job was to carefully monitor the movements of the giant mechanical water pump, since its sudden stoppage could cause the Tashdurmaz electric power plant to explode, which would result in huge losses to the company.

My Armenian helper knew me as a German machine operator, Herr Bernstein, and he obeyed my orders with utmost deference; it never crossed his mind that, like him, I was a wretched Armenian fugitive who had been thrown by some cruel twist of fate into this godforsaken wild valley.

In order to operate this giant hydraulic pump safely, I relied on what I could recall of the mechanical engineering I had learned during my first year at the Mittweida Technical University in Germany, in 1895. Only when the weather was bright and I could turn the responsibility over to my Armenian helper, an experienced machine operator, would I wander about the caves and forests in the deep recesses of the nearby valley. With admiration, I watched deer come hopping with their fawns to the edge of the Chaket River in the morning and evening to drink, and I envied these timid animals so peacefully roaming the woods, free from all pursuit.

After barely ten days, however, I began to feel physically weak. The air in the valley was extremely damp, and although it was August, the bright rays of Cilician sun did not find their way to me. Only for a few hours a day were the mountain peaks adorned by the sun; then once again storm clouds covered our narrow horizon. The name of this place was justified, as Tashdurmaz means "a rock can't stay." The mountains were so steep that rocks could not cling to their slopes; one way or another any loosened rock or boulder would tumble down to the valley, and so, large and small, they covered the banks of the river.

Despite my patience, little by little I became weaker. My spirit was willing, but my flesh was not. Ever since my deportation I had been losing physical and especially moral strength, because of the deprivations and fears caused by continual pursuit. I had not become totally demoralized, but the duration of the war and all the ordeals were making me irritable.

The hope of the Armenian rebirth and the imminent liberation of the fatherland comforted me like a shining star during the most agonizing moments, and I had had the strength to fly from mountain to mountain, valley to valley, to find a hiding place. But now, having found refuge in this valley cut off from civilization, it was becoming impossible for me to bear my suffering anymore. The main reason was sleeplessness. During the day the valley resounded with the deafening noise of dynamite shattering the cliffs, sending myriad pieces of rock tumbling down into the valley like hail. And at night the Chaket River, noisily eddying over the rocks, so disturbed the nocturnal silence that I could not close my eyes even for a few minutes.

After living in this valley for two weeks, I could not get out of bed and was no longer able to take any nourishment or drink; I couldn't even hold down a drop of water. At my wit's end, I wrote a letter to my Swiss electrical engineer friend in Kushjlar, asking for a remedy to my condition. At around this time a new situation further disturbed me: by some unknown means my Armenian helper, the machine operator, learned my secret. He came to kiss my hand with a provincial's piety and assured me that I should not worry, that he was ready to do all the work and to serve me. He tried to console me by telling me that he had engaged in many fights in the Yozgat region and killed Turks in revenge; furthermore, he said, it was because he was a wanted man that he had descended to this secret valley to hide out and cover his tracks. He swore that all the Armenian ironworkers of Tashdurmaz knew who I was and always asked about my health. So, I was known here too.

Thus one day about eight brave Armenian ironworkers came down into this deep valley with a stretcher to transport me up to the Belemedik hospital. I was unable to walk, but the ascent with a stretcher was impossible too. So the Armenian artisans, enduring much hardship, took turns carrying me up the mountain—which indeed was a new ascent of Calvary. After a few torturous hours, completely exhausted, we reached the Tashdurmaz railway line, where they had me lie down in a hut, leaving an Armenian youth to look after me. The next day at dawn they sent me in a carriage to Belemedik, to be admitted to the hospital.

14

Life in Belemedik

I was ill and enervated and, maintaining my disguise as a German, asked to be admitted, but the Armenian chief physician couldn't be bothered with me, saying coldly, "There is no space." Seeing that I could not persuade him, and being in no condition to wait outdoors for hours, I took advantage of a moment when we were alone to reveal my identity. The diffident Dr. Boyajian was suddenly kind; he took me by the arm to his private room and gave me a glass of cognac, saying:

> Don't worry, Reverend Father, I will get a bed readied for you now, and will do everything necessary to get you back on your feet as soon as possible. Besides this, the local chief, Leutenegger, is a close friend of mine; with his help, we will find a nice position for you, and you will be free of all stalking.

These encouraging words touched me so deeply that my eyes filled with tears. One month later, cured and recuperated, I was still in the hospital, but in hiding in a small storeroom for beds, waiting intently for a position.

In early September 1916 Teotig* [a journalist] had been sent from Constantinople to Bozanti. Although he had completed his one-year jail sentence, it had been considered dangerous for him to stay in the Turkish capital. Thus, Police Chief Bedri had condemned him to exile, with the intention of making him share the fate of the other martyred Armenian intellectuals. In Bozanti, Armenian youths had planned to help Teotig escape to Belemedik, provided they could find him a haven there. When they learned that no one would risk sheltering him, I suggested that they bring him to my hiding place. And so one night they brought a frightened and confused Teotig to my little cell in the hospital.

*See Biographical Glossary.

Adjacent to our room was the morgue, where every day the staff wheeled in corpses, and after wrapping them in shrouds, took them to the cemetery. But that didn't bother me, because being a neighbor to corpses was preferable to their eternal company. Furthermore, Teotig often demanded my protection when I myself needed the protection of others. But it was the first time I had had the opportunity to get news from Constantinople and hear about the political and community life of our people. From Teotig, I found out, among other things, that the Armenian Patriarchate, which had existed since the time of the conqueror of Constantinople, Fatih Sultan Mehmed II (1432–1481), had been closed and abolished; it had been transferred to Cilicia, and Catholicos Sahag II had been named patriarch of Jerusalem and Constantinople.

The patriarch of Constantinople, His Beatitude Zaven Der Yeghiayan,* had been exiled to his birthplace, Baghdad, and Archbishop Gabriel Jevahirjian had been named catholicossal and patriarchal vicar by the Turkish government. Publication of the religious newsletter *Dajar* continued under the editorship of the traitor Hrant Hovasapian, an imposter *vartabed* who, with Artin Megerdichian, *muhtar* of Beshiktash (who would be killed by an avenging bullet), had both put themselves at the service of the Turkish leaders. I learned that Armenians in the capital continued to live in fear of imminent deportation and that the *tekelif* (commission) organized by the government to collect war taxes consisted only of Muslims, who had undertaken the looting of Armenian stores.

In the name of the Turkish army they confiscated items of no military value such as perfumes, silk cloth, women's silk stockings, women's shoes, and boys' clothing. In the final analysis their goal was to strip the Armenian merchants bare. A red military vehicle would suddenly stop in front of a warehouse or a store belonging to Armenian merchants, and Turkish municipal and military officials would go inside and take whatever they wanted. Woe unto him who complained or protested; they would seize the merchant and take him also. Then the merchant would have to pay a further bribe in order to escape deportation or prison.

In those days, the triumvirate—Talaat-Enver-Jemal—controlled the fate of the Turkish empire. Internally they leaned on the Ittihad Central Committee and externally on the German armed forces and particularly on the commander in chief of the German troops in Turkey, von Sanders Pasha, who had become most powerful thanks to his successful defense of the Dardanelles.[1]

. . .

*See Biographical Glossary.

In our cramped hiding place Teotig and I consoled each other and exchanged information until finally, thanks to Dr. Boyajian, we both got jobs. Teotig got a position as a hospital attendant, and I became a bookkeeper of the provisions warehouses. And so our days passed peacefully and without incident, and I was satisfied finally to have a tolerable life. The German railway company customarily built wooden huts for its officials, and it assigned a furnished room in one of them to me, along with a servant to do the cleaning.

As the months passed, the circle of my acquaintances gradually expanded. Every Armenian fugitive who had escaped from the vicinity of Konya and Eregli came first to Belemedik and tried to find a job there; only if he could not would he leave for the more remote construction areas. Most Armenians taking refuge in Belemedik were students or youths exiled from Constantinople or Bursa, Izmit, Rodosto, or Thrace. Many, having attended Constantinople's Armenian secondary schools, had had the opportunity to get to know me from their examinations or school productions. As a result, despite all my efforts, the number of those who recognized me increased day by day, a circumstance that filled me with trepidation.

The increasing number of Armenian fugitives in Belemedik attracted attention, including that of the Turkish police commissar of the town. Like me, most of these Armenian refugees were registered in the company's official ledgers under false names—Greek, Assyrian, Levantine, and even Armenian; nevertheless the police found informers to reveal the identity of some of them. By a secret and urgent order from Talaat they went into action and prepared a blacklist of about twenty Armenian intellectuals.

The harsh and searching looks of the police officials led me to conjecture that a new danger was looming. Then one day I found out that Teotig and a few other Armenian youths had been arrested and sent into exile. With the strong help of the German engineers, we were able to win the release of this first group, and some youths succeeded in escaping on the road; nevertheless, if I was to avoid falling into another trap, I would have to think again about my own escape. Still, thanks to my position in Belemedik, I had succeeded in staying alive another six months.

The Germans in Belemedik celebrated New Year's 1917 with great pomp: there was plenty of food and drink, including beer and wine and even champagne—hundreds of glasses of champagne were emptied in toasts to the ultimate victory of Germany. We Armenians, however, passed the festive days within the confines of our huts, mourning and feeling like orphans. The hundreds of Russian, French, and Italian prisoners of war in Belemedik also spent the New Year in a melancholy frame of mind. But we Armenians felt not just melancholy but grief; the prisoners of war had the hope of seeing their loved ones again, but our beloved relatives had been martyred and had gone to eternity, leaving us inconsolable.

We who were left alive felt like pitiful wrecks, somehow still dragging our useless selves on; we envied those who had died . . . who, having paid their debt, were now resting forever. Meanwhile we remembered happy New Year celebrations of the past, with tables laden with fruit and *anushabour*;* surrounded by our loved ones, we had heartily wished one another Happy New Year and Merry Christmas. Would we ever see the old, happy days again?

The Germans—engineers as well as skilled and unskilled laborers—were shooting their firearms in celebration, not only because of the holiday but also to make a point to the Turkish crowd surrounding them. In the last months of 1916, after almost two and a half years of military alliance and close relations with the Turks, the Germans had become deeply convinced that the Turks were roguish, ill-intentioned, treacherous, and xenophobic, and that it would not be possible to develop a candid, long-term relationship with them. In a word, the Germans had lost trust in the Turks' intentions.

On the line at the Taurus tunnels I had met Turcophobic German engineers who had named their dogs Ahmed, Mehmed, Abdullah, Ismail, Ali, and so on. The Turkish laborers, unable to swallow these insults, would ask the Armenian translators to request of the Germans that they at least not call their dogs by the name of the great Prophet Muhammad. But the hatred between the Germans and the Turks had gradually reached such severity that the Germans had taken precautions against Turkish surprise attacks. Fearing vengeance over Turkish losses resulting from German routs, they had even set up special automatic-fire cannons. Fear of a sudden treacherous attack also caused the German soldiers to hide weapons in numerous storerooms intended for flour and potatoes.

Finally, hounded by the inexorable nightmare of getting arrested again, I saw no choice but to become a wanderer and disappear without a trace. I had made my decision. This time I did not know in which direction I would go to try to elude the specter of death that now was always following me.

*"Sweet soup": a traditional Armenian pudding served at the New Year, made of whole wheat kernels and dried fruits and flavored with cinnamon, nutmeg, and other spices.—trans.

15

The Deportation of Patriarch Zaven Der Yeghiayan from Constantinople to Baghdad

By August 1916 His Beatitude Zaven Der Yeghiayan had only nominal privileges, for the patriarchate no longer had any useful authority. His impotence had reached the point where, despite numerous urgent requests, Talaat refused even to receive him and once had even disrespectfully admonished him and sent him on his way.

The patriarchal agent Kamer Shirinian had acted as intermediary between the patriarchate and the Turkish government. In order to please the all-powerful Talaat, he had had the supreme responsibility of deceiving the patriarch, distorting every fact in favor of the Turkish government. Naturally, the secret services of this infamous agent of the patriarchate did not go unrewarded. Everyone observed with astonishment that at a time when responsible Armenians could not even go from one Constantinople suburb to another without arousing suspicion, Kamer Shirinian often traveled to and from Bulgaria.

The authority and management of the patriarchate had gradually passed into the hands of agent Shirinian, who had entered its service in 1904 at the age of twenty as an agent for Shahin Kasbarian. By now he had grown so powerful that he had managed to save his arrested friends from the clutches of Police Chief Bedri, and in exchange for generous financial compensation, he had secured permission for Armenian merchants to travel freely to Germany and Bulgaria.

In exchange for all his covert services—which amounted to the betrayal of the Armenian people—Kamer Shirinian received a special stipend from Talaat's secret credit chest. Having an enemy agent inside the patriarchate, Talaat easily attacked this administrative seat of the Armenian nation at its very base. While the Armenian people were being eliminated, inevitably the patriarchate was dissolved (on July 28, 1916); and then the Turkish government decided to deport Patriarch Zaven. The sheep had been destroyed, so there was no more need for a shepherd.

Patriarch Zaven—with the resignation of a passive spectator—witnessed the annihilation of the Armenian population that had been entrusted to his care. He lacked even the courage to voluntarily leave the patriarchal administration, which by now had become useless. By way of regret, he could only declare that he "could do no more than this." His explanation came to be like chewing gum in his mouth.

Since he could do "nothing more," his presence or absence no longer mattered; but by resigning, His Beatitude Zaven could at least have made a show of protest and provided himself with a good accounting before history.

Recall that in 1828, during the Greek rebellion, the Turkish government had hanged the Greek ecumenical patriarch, the martyr Grigorios, in front of the main door of the Greek cathedral in Fener. By contrast, His Beatitude Zaven used his position to protect only himself, and finally there was nothing else to save; his title became useless even to save him from exile and suffering. In August 1916, on the Monday following the Feast of the Holy Mother of God, officials from the Interior Ministry arrived at the patriarchate and, in Zaven's presence, sealed all the patriarchate's files. The patriarchate and the personal residence of the patriarch—located behind the cathedral—were now placed under police surveillance; luckily, just days before, special secret documents pertaining to the Balkan War and the Armenian Question of 1913–14 had been transported to an embassy.

Following the sealing of the patriarchate's files, on the day of Bayram,* two secret policemen escorted His Beatitude Zaven to the political section of the police administration, Kusmu Siyasi. After being held for one and a half hours, he was told, "Since you are originally from Baghdad, you must go back there, so get ready for the journey." The patriarch answered, "Since a patriarchal vicar will be designated, and since I myself have also sealed the archives of the patriarchate, let me wait. After transferring my position to the new vicar, I'll depart Constantinople." The Kusmu Siyasi director proceeded to telephone Talaat to request a command to this effect. But it was a holiday and he was unable to speak with him, so he released the patriarch to return to his residence under police surveillance.

Meanwhile, when the two secret police had arrested the patriarch and taken him to Kusmu Siyasi, a young Armenian lady from Erzerum had happened to be at his residence. She went to the American Embassy and met with Shmavonian, the first translator the embassy had had for years; she told him what had happened, hoping that American intervention could save the patriarch. Shmavonian, known for his genuine patriotism and

*Feast day; day of national rejoicing. In this case, August 30.—trans.

self-sacrifice for his unfortunate compatriots, hurried to bring this important news to the American ambassador, Henry Morgenthau.

Ambassador Morgenthau, whose unreserved sympathy for and defense of the Armenians had truly made him worthy of their eternal gratitude, rushed to the German embassy. Along with the German ambassador, he tried to convince Talaat to give the patriarch permission to remain in Constantinople. Talaat flatly refused, saying: "The authority and prestige of the Turkish government demand that Patriarch Zaven, in accordance with ministerial decision, depart for his birthplace, Baghdad, without fail." He did promise, however, to order the relevant provincial authorities to ensure the patriarch's safe journey.*

On Monday, August 2, 1916, approximately two weeks after his arrest, four secret policemen took the patriarch, together with his brother and his brother's daughter, from his residence to the Haydar Pasha station. From there he was taken toward Eskishehir by a military train guarded by the former Armenian Catholic priest Sislian, who was a spy using the alias Hidayet, and a Turkish policeman.

As soon as the train reached Eskishehir, the local Armenian [Apostolic] priest and an Armenian Catholic priest, who were still living there, miraculously, hurried to see him, having learned ahead of time of the patriarch's coming. But barely had they entered his first-class car when the *kaymakam* of Eskishehir arrived and forbade all communication with the patriarch.

When the train reached Eregli station, near Konya, a brave young Armenian station official hurried over to the patriarch and succeeded in conversing with him for a few minutes (as he himself told me). The patriarch told him that the German ambassador had assured him that he would reach Baghdad unharmed. This same young man, when Zohrab and Vartkes were being taken into exile, had offered to help them escape. They, however, had responded that they were *mebus*† and thus were in no danger, and had refused his assistance.

From Bozanti the patriarch, along with his brother and niece, took a two-horse spring-carriage to Tarsus. From there they continued by military train to Adana and, without going into town, went on to Osmaniye. Again by carriage, and with the same escorts, they reached Hasanbeyli and Islahiye. From there, via another military train, they arrived safely in Aleppo, where the local police chief reserved a special inn for the patriarch and his party.

*I have gleaned this episode of the patriarch's exile personally from his brother's daughter, who was his inseparable companion in exile, from Constantinople all the way to Baghdad and Mosul.—G.B. (Patriarch Zaven Der Yeghiayan's *My Patriarchal Memoirs* was published in English in 2002.—trans.)

†Member of Parliament; deputy.—trans.

On a visit to the governor-general of Aleppo province, the patriarch was treated with great respect. Meanwhile the spy Sislian and the Turkish policeman, having carried out their duty of guarding him all the way to Aleppo, returned to Constantinople, considering their job done.

The patriarch remained with his two relatives in Aleppo for eight days; then his party set out on the road to Der Zor in two carriages, escorted by six mounted police soldiers. On their way through the desert, between Meskene and Hamam, they passed hundreds of sepulchral mounds, under which were resting in eternal sleep tens of thousands of oft-tortured Armenian deportees who had died from starvation and thirst. By some horrific coincidence, the spiritual leader of the Armenians had come *involuntarily* to call on his martyred flock. In Meskene, the patriarch met surviving Armenian exiles, to whom he gave financial assistance from the sums remaining at his disposal.

Finally, after a six-day journey through the desert, the patriarch, with his two relatives, reached Der Zor and spent the night in a *khan.* But barely had he arrived when the government heard of his appearance and escorted him to the police station.

Coinciding with the patriarch's arrival was the general massacre of the remaining Armenian deportees from the interior provinces who had reached Der Zor. This massacre was carried out under the direction of Zeki, the *mutasarrif* of Der Zor, at whose hands more than 160,000 Armenians—men, women, children, and the elderly—were murdered, leaving only about 4,000 Armenian women and a few hundred children alive.

Even as *mutasarrif* Zeki was drowning the Armenian deportees in blood and throwing them into the Euphrates River, he was at the same time ceremoniously receiving the Armenian patriarch and inviting him to his official residence, where they took lunch together. The bloodthirsty Zeki lodged the patriarch as his personal guest for three days, then bade him farewell with great honor, setting him on the road from Der Zor to Baghdad.

For reasons easy to understand, the four police soldiers assigned to guard the patriarch took him to Baghdad via special routes so he would not come across the corpses of massacred and dismembered Armenians. And after an eleven-day journey, they finally reached Baghdad safe and sound.

Here is yet more proof that when the Turkish government wished, it could provide safe passage to caravans. Talaat's argument—"because the police soldiers have been taken to the front, the careless and inexperienced ones were not able to execute orders concerning the security of the caravans of exiled Armenians"—was totally baseless.

Patriarch Zaven was not only a native of Baghdad but also the son of a local deceased priest, Father Harutiun, so he, his brother, and his brother's daughter were able to remain in their ancestral home there for about five months. But then the British unexpectedly defeated the Turks at Kut-al-Amara, and the victorious army of Mesopotamia approached Baghdad. Eight days before the British occupation began, the patriarch and his brother and niece went by train to Samara and, after a five-day journey by carriage, reached Mosul. On this road, two hours from Samara, they met the German consuls assigned to Baghdad and the Austrian director of the Ottoman Bank, who were fleeing Baghdad for Mosul to avoid capture by the British.

Taking advantage of this unexpected encounter, the two German consuls met with the patriarch and informed him that the German ambassador in Constantinople had inquired by telegram whether he had reached Baghdad alive and well. Only then, five months later and on the occasion of an accidental meeting on the road at that, did the patriarch learn that the German ambassador had shown an interest in his well-being.

The Mosul police chief, Mehmed Khalid, was an Armenian who had converted to Islam during the 1895 massacres; thanks to him, for a time, the patriarch lived in Mosul without police surveillance and in comfortable circumstances. But a year later the governor-general of Mosul, Haydar, was replaced by Memduh, who had massacred the Armenians of Erzinjan. He would deal more harshly with the patriarch, even though he was an old acquaintance of his from Erzerum.

During the patriarch's stay in Mosul, the catholicos of Cilicia sent him five hundred Turkish liras in paper money as assistance. A large number of Armenian exiles lived there at this time, some two to three thousand, for the most part in frightful misery, oppression, and deprivation, since supplies were dwindling by the day. Fifteen to twenty daily were said to have died from hunger and suffering.[1]

16

Legions of Armenian Exiles in Konya and Bozanti

During the six months that I lived in Belemedik, reliable eyewitnesses among Armenians and Germans—and even Turkish soldiers—told me about the sufferings of the exiled and persecuted Armenian people.

In 1915, as I have mentioned, as the tunnels of Belemedik had not yet been opened, so the railway from Haydar Pasha Station reached only as far as Bozanti. Then, starting again in Dorak, it continued via Adana all the way to Mamure, where the Amanos mountains begin. Since the Amanos tunnels were not yet opened, here the line was interrupted again; all military transport had to go by carriages from Bozanti to Adana on the mountainous Gulek-Bogazi road, while from Osmaniye near Mamure, also via mountainous roads, carriages went to Kanle-gechid–Hasanbeyli-Islahiye.

The entire Armenian population of Adrianople, Rodosto, Malgara, and their vicinity; the large Armenian population of about 110,000 in Izmit, seat of the diocesan bishop; and the nearly 60,000 Armenians of Bilejik, Eskishehir, Kutahya, Afyonkarahisar, and their vicinity—about 170,000 in total—had been put on the road. On reaching Konya, the caravans of these exiles congregated, forming a large encampment on the plain near the town.

For the sake of appearances, the Turkish government tried to attribute this crowding of Armenian exiles to the lack of transportation, but actually, by creating an environment of overcrowding and filth, they hoped to start epidemics.

Trustworthy eyewitnesses reported the rise of a new tent city on the plain near Konya, tents made from sheets, whose number (according to knowledgeable Armenian and German sources), reached 28,000. This mass of human beings, deprived of any sanitary measures, would obviously be subject to all kinds of suffering and disease.

Since the city of Konya had a population of about 65,000, the bakeries could barely meet the local demand for bread; so when the caravans of Armenian deportees arrived, they suffered acute hunger. The exiled Armenians, even with money in hand, searched frantically for bread, but there was none; when they requested help, they received merciless blows from the whips of the guards. The Turkish government's secret goal was that these people would expire from hunger and epidemics instead of from massacres. Naturally the first victims were the small children, who fell like withered autumn leaves to the ground at the first dry wind, dying not by the hundreds but by the thousands.

Silent witnesses to this epidemic were the expansive plains of Konya, stretching all the way to Eregli and Bozanti, and those thousands of mounds that were the graves of Armenian martyrs. Outside Kanle-gechid (which I described in an earlier chapter) the bodies of thousands of innocent children formed similar hills.

One black day, as if this widespread misery were not enough, hundreds of high- and low-ranking deportation officials overseeing the caravans, assisted by numerous companies and battalions of police soldiers on horseback and on foot, with whips and cudgels—and making quite a din—suddenly fell upon this large encampment of Armenian deportees. "A strict order has come from Constantinople," they said. "Today all of you have to depart for Bozanti. There is no time; hurry . . ." Cracking their whips, they quickly forced the people onto the road. No brilliant imagination is needed to conceive the widespread terror of these helpless and suffering people when they heard that unexpected command.

The whips were cracking, the brutal blows were raining down. There was no time to think; it was necessary to move. But absolutely no means of transportation had been arranged, nor did any exist. Thus every family was forced to abandon all the belongings they could not carry. They hastily tried to gather bare essentials and anything that was of value and portable, such as jewelry, that might be exchanged for a piece of bread in the coming days.

The chaos was all-encompassing; crying, wailing, and pleading had no effect on the hardened hearts of the Turkish officials. It was as if they were not human beings. Men and women, youths and girls, cried and pleaded in vain for *at least one hour* so they could have time to gather their valuables. They would always receive the same impudent and cruel answer: *You are going to your death—what do you need your belongings for? If you don't leave them here, they will be taken from your hands anyway a few days from now in a different place. Why wear yourselves out for nothing?*

Some of the rich, by paying hefty bribes, succeeded in traveling to Bozanti by train, but the remaining multitude, crying, trudged along the road next to the railway line.

German eyewitnesses, officials traveling by train from Constantinople in those days, told me the following:

> When we were traveling in these same days on the train from Eregli to Bozanti, on the rough roads extending on both sides of the railway tracks we saw long lines of caravans of exiled Armenians, row after row, covered in dust, bent over and spent. Their number, although it was impossible to determine accurately, nevertheless must have been in the tens of thousands—men, women, youths, and girls. We found the pregnant women, and nursing babies in the arms of their mothers, even more deplorable and pitiful. They all had long been emaciated and ragged, and many fell onto the road or under a tree, or by a ditch or into a trench; wherever their strength finally failed, they fell, and were either in the throes of death or already dead.

When these wretched exiles saw a train approaching, they hastened to assemble from all directions, in dense rows on both sides of the tracks. And when the kindhearted passengers of various nations threw bread from the train windows, hundreds of starving women, girls, and children, stepping on one another, ran to get a piece.

Meanwhile hundreds of greedy Turkish officials, like hungry wolves, set upon their abandoned goods. High-level government officials came to the site of plunder with carriages, carts, and porters to cart away the valuables by the trunk load. More than the civilians, it was the military that engaged in that looting. They left the crumbs of these rich spoils to the poor Muslim people as their rightful share.

In exchange for a piece of bread, Armenian mothers, known for their maternal devotion, sold their beloved sons and beautiful daughters to the first comer, Christian or Muslim. Yes, for a piece of bread, Armenian mothers sold their dear children whom they had raised with tears and loving care, saying, "There is no salvation for us; we are going to our death. At least these poor children should be saved."

When the caravans arrived and clustered in Bozanti and its vicinity, the wretchedness and distress reached unspeakable proportions. These people, with no one to look after them, went hungry and thirsty for days under the pouring rain—without tents, since they had been forced to leave them on the Konya plain.

As I have noted, the German railroad company's headquarters for the construction of the Taurus tunnels was about an hour from Bozanti. Naturally the misery borne by the tens of thousands of this Christian nation could not go unnoticed, and all the company officials were deeply disturbed by it. The deputy director, the engineer Leutenegger, witnessed the travails of the deported Armenians. In the name of simple humanity, he rushed to have as much bread as possible baked in all the ovens of his company, then went to Bozanti to distribute it to the starving people, along with medical supplies.

But the deportation officials, reinforced by policemen and officers of the police soldiers, hastened to thwart Leutenegger's humane efforts. He later told me what they said to him: "The government is taking these people, as enemies of the state, to the deserts of Der Zor to be exterminated. It is not worth incurring expenses to save these people who are condemned to death."

This "sincere" but despicable answer was the same one Talaat and his comrades often gave to Ambassador Morgenthau and to the European officials who continually tried to intervene on behalf of the Armenian people. But the curtain had closed, and the time to fake and lie had already passed.

To confirm this, it is sufficient to consult Morgenthau's memoirs* as well as the book on the Armenian massacres written by James Bryce and published by the British government. There we learn that the kind and compassionate Leutenegger, who was a reserve colonel in the Swiss army, retorted in anger:

> If you are taking them to be killed, I, in turn, have orders from my company headquarters to help these people with bread and medicine; thus if you wish to impede me, I will forcefully distribute it; meanwhile you yourselves should think about the consequences to follow from this and the responsibility you will shoulder.

Following these indignant words from a former military man, the high-ranking deportation officials, fearing culpability, overlooked his humanitarian actions and hastened to move the caravans of deportees out of Bozanti.

Truly, as Armenian eyewitnesses told me, Swiss, German, and Austrian engineers often provided kind assistance in violation of the German government's policy of persecuting the Armenians. Their conduct was the antithesis of that of the Turks, who not only fulfilled the orders to the letter but surpassed them in cruelty.

*See Bibliography.

17

Meeting Armenian Intellectuals on the Road to Belemedik

During the last days of December 1916 two friends and I were taking a walk in the vicinity of Kara Punar, a half hour from Belemedik, when we came upon a caravan of Turks and Kurds, about four hundred in all.

All the humans and animals alike were emaciated and exhausted, and it was evident that they came from faraway lands. The forty or so animals—camels, horses, mules, and donkeys—all reduced to skin and bones, bore on their backs all the possessions of these wretched people—a black pot and ladle here, a dirty blanket there, and baskets of children, shriveled and scrawny.

Except for the children, this multitude of men and women, boys and girls, were walking; many were barefoot, their clothes in tatters. Even though they were Turks and Kurds, it was impossible not to feel pity for them. Are humanity, pity, and conscience limited by nation or fatherland?

Out of curiosity we approached the caravan, and pretending to be a German, I asked them in crude Turkish where they were coming from and where they were going. A well-built Kurd with a white beard, walking ahead of the caravan, answered haltingly, "We are coming from above" [*Yokardan gelioruz*]. I repeated my question in a compassionate tone, and another Kurd answered that they were coming from the Bitlis area.

Wanting to glean accurate information about the situation in the northern Turkish provinces on the Russian border, I gave these Muslim refugees quite a bit of tobacco and, according to the Eastern custom, became friendly with them. In the same tone I asked why they were traveling like this in the winter. An elderly Turkish peasant answered:

> For almost five months we have been traveling from the Bitlis region; the Russian Cossacks and Antranig Pasha's fedayeen seized all our lands. Fearing that we might become victims of reprisal, we gathered what we could take and hurried onto the road with the

> retreating Turkish army. Like this we have been walking for those many months; we are exhausted, but there's still more road to travel. When we got on the road, our caravan consisted of more than five thousand people, but as you can see, we have been reduced to barely four hundred. The children, unable to survive such a lengthy journey, died; many died from typhus and some from hunger. Whatever we did to the Armenians, Allah did to us and we got our punishment. Of course, the evildoer will get his punishment in this world. [*Helbet, eden bulur duyneaseh der*]. *Effendis,* when will the war end? If it does not end in a few months, no one will be left in Anatolia anymore.

These simple peasants rightfully acknowledged that whatever they did to the Armenians, they got their due punishment. Seen from a distance, they could have been a caravan of Armenian deportees, the only difference being that they had with them large and small pack animals, and there were no mounted or foot soldiers guarding them. Was it possibly the inexorable hand of eternal justice that was pursuing them?

During these days I received an unexpected visit from Yeghia Suzigian, the reporter-editor of the *Manzumeh* and later *Jamanak* newspapers, who often wrote lead articles under the name Nor-Kaghakaked [New Political Analyst]. He had been an unusually unbridled opponent of mine in public life. In March 1913, during the period of the Pangalti cemetery issue, when Patriarch Arsharuni, pretending to be ill, had left all responsibility to me, by decision of the Mixed Assembly of the Central National Administration* of Constantinople, I went to Bulgaria to negotiate by telegram on behalf of the patriarch with the catholicos in Holy Etchmiadzin. Yeghia Suzigian had written in the *Arshaluys* daily, which he published, that "Vartabed Balakian, having stolen fifty gold pieces from the patriarchate, has run away to Bulgaria; finally the time has come for the high ecclesiastical authority to defrock this adventurous and adventuresome vartabed."

When I returned from my successful trip to Bulgaria, the patriarchate and the Mixed Assembly reported it very favorably to all the Armenian papers, adding that not only had I refused the gratuity of *100* gold pounds offered to me, but that I had returned 26 gold pounds out of the 50 given to me for travel expenses. Yeghia Suzigian did not publish this information in his paper; rather, he accused the patriarch and the Central National Administration of defending me, and he slandered them as my puppets.

*The executive.—trans.

So here was Yeghia Suzigian again. He had been exiled from Constantinople after we were and for the past year had managed to survive by holding down a simple job at the railroad construction site a few hours from Belemedik. Then he became ill for several months in Khachkri. Emaciated, he came to Belemedik to enter the local German company hospital. But he had been refused admittance because no empty bed was available. Unable to stand on his feet, and physically spent, he had appealed for protection to a few longtime friends who were in Belemedik at the time.

His friends wished him well, but they were unable to help and recommended that he approach me. He told them that he did not have the nerve to go to me. Then two of his friends grabbed him by the arm and brought him to my room in the main building of the central branch of Belemedik's supply management.

Needless to say, persecution and suffering had united us on the road to perdition, such that our personal differences were forgotten. Forgiveness is a universal Christian virtue; under the present circumstances, it was a human obligation. Therefore I accepted him with open arms and gave him money to take care of his immediate needs. I also asked Dr. Boyajian to provide a bed in his hospital for our compatriot, who, after all, had been a man of the pen, even if he wrote only as he saw fit.

Yeghia Suzigian was immediately transported to the hospital, and I got permission to visit him every day, bringing him a few cigarettes and a piece of fruit or hard candy. While I was visiting, he often kept his head under the covers and sobbed inconsolably. A month and a half later, recovered, he entered my cell to say goodbye. With tears in his eyes, he murmured:

> When I unjustly criticized you in the papers I did not think that one day I would be at your mercy . . . Your fellow clergymen were the ones who convinced me to badger you, saying that it was a patriotic duty. How could I have imagined that you are a person with such a noble soul . . . ? I was often compensated financially for writing offensive articles against you in the papers . . . What inexorable fate, that the two of us should meet as exiles in these Taurus mountains! Now I have gotten to know your inner person . . . and may God grant that one day when we return to Constantinople . . . I will be the first campaigner to make you patriarch.

Having given himself over to alcoholism, a few months later Yeghia died in Khachkri in a most distressing state.

I had been stunned to hear straight from Yeghia's mouth that church officials, clergymen, in their ambition to ascend to the patriarchal throne, would blacken the name of one of their spiritual brothers whom they imagined might stand in their way. Nor did they hesitate to bribe journalists, even resorting to libel, while the same journalists would write panegyrics about one or another of them.

During these same months in Kushjlar I encountered Agouni, a reporter for various Armenian daily newspapers in Constantinople. He too was in an extremely wretched state, hungry and deserving of sympathy and assistance. He had often attacked me in the papers, and even then I had asked him the reason. He had replied, "Every vartabed once in a while gives me a present. Why don't you? Since you don't give, I will attack you." I told him that no one would believe what he wrote, and he answered, "If ninety of them don't believe, at least ten will, and that's enough to ruin your reputation."

Truly, from the day I entered the ecclesiastical profession, I never tried to bribe reporters, either to stop their attacks against me or to win their favor. I considered such demeaning behavior to be incompatible with my dignity and independence. Even the yellow journalists always used to say that if one wanted to advance rapidly in the ecclesiastical profession and become a bishop and then patriarch, one must pay.

Despite the nasty publicity that Agouni had generated against me, I saved him from death. When a fanatical young Dashnak teacher wanted to kill him, claiming that he was an informer, I convinced this agitated young man that if Agouni had been an informer in Constantinople, he wouldn't have been exiled and reduced to such wretchedness as we were.

By strange coincidence, the aforementioned teacher who wanted to kill Agouni had actually informed on me, revealing my identity to Syrian youths. Only by escaping was I able to be sure of saving myself. He had not forgotten that I had expelled him from the Sanassarian faculty in 1912 when I had gone to Erzerum to look into moving the Sanassarian Academy to Sivas.

In Belemedik I heard that Asdvadzadour Khachadourian, one of the worthy teachers from the Sanassarian Academy, a secret veteran of the Armenian liberation cause and one of my instructors, had been exiled from Constantinople and was now in Konya. Later Professor Khachadourian escaped Konya, finding refuge in the stations along the Belemedik line before reaching Nisibin and covering his tracks, just as Marzbed had.

But while Marzbed* had died accidentally after falling from his horse during the days of the Armistice, Asdvadzadour Khachadourian had the good fortune to live and to return to Constantinople. He joined in reconstituting the life of the surviving Armenians of Constantinople, whose

*Dashnak party worker.—trans.

devoted apostle and preacher he had been since 1885, until he was recruited to teach the Armenian language in the newly founded Sanassarian Academy in Erzerum, along with the poet Goriun Megerdichian, who had just graduated from the Gevorkian Seminary of Etchmiadzin when he died so young.

In Belemedik, I also had the opportunity to meet two youths, one of whom was Sebouh Sayabalian, the brother of Jack Sayabalian, martyred in Ankara; the other was Onnig Postajian of Rodosto. Both were exemplary patriots, doing as much as they could for their oppressed countrymen through their important positions in the German railway construction company. During my six months of exile in Belemedik, these two young men became my solace, often rendering me invaluable services. Later, in the autumn of 1918, a few weeks before the Armistice, when I was escaping from Adana disguised as a German soldier, Onnig Postajian would play a providential role, for which I remain eternally grateful.

18

Escape from Belemedik to Adana

Seeing that my serious worries of imminent arrest were in danger of becoming a reality, I hastened to make arrangements to escape. To elude the Turkish police, I used information I obtained by bribing the Turkish secretary of the military administration.

I went to see Kuterlen, director of our supply division in Belemedik, and an Armenophile. I told him in confidence that I was likely to be arrested, and I requested his protection in escaping. This noble native of Stuttgart—who had become a Turcophobe, owing to his necessarily close association with Turks—tried to dissuade me. He exhorted me instead to continue as a bookkeeper in the supply division under his protection. He would assist me in any way possible, he promised, even petitioning assistance from the local German military personnel close to him if necessary. Like me, he knew better than to believe the verbal or even written promise of a Turk. Nevertheless he insisted that he had many means at his disposal to rescue me from the Turkish military officials, even by force if necessary.

But I was hesitant to put my destiny in even his reliable hands. Finally I convinced this devout and noble man, who had protected me for six months as a guardian angel, to accept my escape plan. I pointed out to him my vulnerability. How, for example, I asked him, could he help me if Turkish policemen came for me one night and made me disappear in a deep valley or on a desolate road? He criticized my suspiciousness and fear but admitted that such a prospect was not impossible. To be entirely truthful, I never wanted to entrust myself to the German military either. The reason was, as I've written repeatedly, that 90 percent of the German soldiers were Armenophobes. At even the slightest discontent with Armenians serving under them, they would reportedly accuse them of spying and turn them over to the Turkish authorities. For this reason, in my three years as an exile, on the few occasions when I gained protection from German military personnel, I did not remain long in their employ, whether as a translator or in any other capacity.

Kuterlen asked that I give him a week to facilitate my escape—this time to Constantinople—with the help of his close friends among the German military personnel. I longed to go to Constantinople, even though I was deeply convinced that my presence would upset the comfort and safety of my family members. (I am happy to say that during my difficult years of exile and deportation, I never put anyone in danger for my sake or caused them to be suspected, and I am glad for a clear conscience in this regard.)

The compassionate Kuterlen selected the finest horse from the company stables, a fast steed that would be my principal means of escape. When it was finally time for me to bid him farewell, he asked that I come in the evening so we could have supper together.

I was in distress, but I could not refuse such a sincere invitation, no matter how little appetite I had for food or drink. After an intimate dinner, he gave me a personal gift of ten gold pounds. I have to confess that this sum represented my only wealth and would play a providential role in my escape.

These two selfless young Armenian men of Belemedik, Sayabalian and Onnig Postajian, stayed with me until midnight and then departed, expressing heartfelt good wishes. I was deeply moved, though my soul was like a stormy sea, as this escape plan would be the most dangerous of all to execute. Before, I had fled on empty roads into deserted mountainous locations, rarely seeing people, but this time I was going directly to Adana, the provincial center of Cilicia, which was full of Turks, and I would have to be vigilant.

It was the Armenian people's age-old hopes and dreams of future well-being and the dream of one day hailing the birth of a free Armenian nation that gave me the strength and wings to soar from mountain to mountain, from valley to valley, to conquer every obstacle. To calm my tortured soul during these turbulent times, I beseeched the inexhaustible unseen heavenly power, the eternal source of all powers. Prayer is the salvific balm for all souls in sorrow, grief, and despair.

In the loneliness of my room, with my arms outstretched, I came to my knees, asking for help for myself and for all the unfortunate and oppressed, for moral strength and vigor, from the inexhaustible treasury of eternal power. The wind of fear subsided, and with my soul recharged, my turmoil and agitation abated. The fear of unfamiliar and unexpected dangers that I had felt an hour before evaporated, as I received new strength and courage from the inexhaustible source. Didn't the Gospel say, "Thy faith hath saved thee" [Luke 7:50]? Woe unto those who knowingly or unknowingly are deprived of this limitless, comforting force inspired by faith.

Dawn was coming and it was essential for me to leave Belemedik quickly. On that winter day, January 4, 1917, the high mountains and black forests of the Taurus were covered with a thick layer of snow. A north wind swept through mountain and valley. Its whistling across the snow sounded like the howling of hungry wolves.

I emerged from my room disguised as a German engineer, wearing a European hat, leggings, a raincoat, a gun and whip, and leather gloves. I took the road from Belemedik to Kushjlar, where, by a cliff, the fast company horse was to be waiting. When I arrived, the horse was there; I mounted it without hesitation, and at a single crack of the whip, we were galloping forward, and I looked back no more.

The frisky, brave animal did all it could to run in the snow, but it hindered our progress all the same. The road wound through forests all the way to Kushjlar, the highest point between Belemedik and Dorak. I was indifferent to the cold and the blinding snow, surrounded on all sides by a vast panorama of untamed nature. Huge cliffs hundreds of meters high hemmed in the Chaket valley on both sides, and the black cedar forests amplified the mystery of their natural beauty.

I forged ahead, having yet to encounter anyone. Who would have been crazy enough to travel in such weather? About an hour from Kushjlar I passed a Turkish police officer, who, having burrowed under his fur coat, with his head hooded, scarcely took note of me; probably thinking that I was a German engineer, he continued on his way without a word.

Kushjlar stood on a plateau from which, on a clear day, one could see the Mediterranean. Indeed I wished that I had wings to fly to Cyprus. Actually, I was going to Adana to look for a way to get there.

As my horse galloped along, I reached Kushjlar and then Khachkri, once in a while having to pass in front of a police-soldier guardhouse. But the violent snowstorm had drawn everyone around crackling fires, so no one was paying any attention to travelers.

As I passed the German hospital in Khachkri, a few individuals cast curious glances my way, perhaps wondering what business a German engineer might have during such a blizzard.

Galloping for four hours without stop or even a ten-minute break, my horse brought me to Dorak. But by sinister coincidence, the railway was closed for the impending passage of a train, and so those on foot or on horseback were being stopped and interrogated in front of the police guardhouse. It was impossible to turn back, since I had been noticed—it would have created suspicion. So my only path to salvation was to proceed undaunted, cutting through the group of police, soldiers, and travelers, all of whom were Turkish peasants.

Just then the train passed, and the road in front of the guardhouse opened. Whipping my horse, I made a run for it, while from all sides came shouts of "You fellows, a German engineer is coming, make way so he can pass" [*Ulan, Alman muhendis gechior, yol verin, achelen*]. What an irony! The police were respectfully clearing the way for me, the fugitive Armenian clergyman whom they had been hunting for the past two years—because the Lord had blinded them.

A quarter of an hour later I reached the Dorak railway station and was received as the guest of the stationmaster, Deyirmenjian, whose hospitality and patriotism I had previously enjoyed while escaping from Amanos to Taurus six months earlier, as I have described.

A little later a policeman came into the station, supposedly having a job to do—in reality to investigate the passerby. Deyirmenjian introduced me as a German engineer with whom he was well acquainted. I, in turn, answered all the policeman's questions in the broken Turkish of the Germans: "I don't speak Turkish" [*Ben yok bilir Turkje*]. The policeman, convinced that he was indeed dealing with a German, left, enraged to have missed an opportunity to collect a bribe.

Deyirmenjian and I spent the entire night eating supper and engaging in joyful conversation, counting the survivors of the Armenian people, who we guessed numbered only some 600,000. We were nevertheless very hopeful about their future, being deeply convinced that the Entente powers would win the war—with their victory, the triumph of the Armenians would not be in doubt. Weren't the Entente powers waging this world war for the sake of liberating the small nations? Wasn't it a war for rights and justice against the despicable German military dictatorship and its expansionism?

After the Armistice, all such promises would soon be forgotten, as each victorious power aimed first to secure the lion's share of territory for itself. An oil field would prove much more valuable than the fate of a small and weak Christian people.[1]

After a comforting and rejuvenating night at the station in mountainous Dorak, I was strengthened by the mighty heavenly inspiration of my morning prayer. I got on the road to Adana at dawn, again on horseback this time, with a bodyguard following me. It was January 5, 1917.

After galloping madly for three and a half hours without incident or attracting scrutiny, we reached Adana by the Mersin highway. Wary lest two horsemen entering town might stir curiosity and even suspicion, I hastened to dismount in front of the Reji tobacco plant, then turned the horse over to my bodyguard and sent him back to Dorak. I boldly entered the Armenian quarter to look for the house of Dr. Karekin Vartabedian, of whose patriotism I had received ample testimony in Belemedik and Dorak.

PART III

In Adana

JANUARY 1917–SEPTEMBER 1918

19

The General Condition of the War at the Beginning of 1917

At the beginning of 1917 the world war had been raging in all its intensity and frenzy for two and a half years. Nearly 20 million or more soldiers were tearing one another apart, killing with indescribable fury.

By now the German people were facing a dozen different enemy countries and, with their unparalleled organization and power, trying to achieve victory at all costs. Invincible Britain, thanks to its ingenious minister of war, Lord Kitchener, transported an army of 7 million to the Western Front and elsewhere, gradually neutralizing the mighty German army. To date the Germans had succeeded not only in keeping the fighting far from their borders but also in giving incalculable military aid to their allies—the Austro-Hungarian Empire, Bulgaria, and Turkey—whose forces the Germans also had to defend.

France, with its valiant sons, stood against the oncoming German bayonets and cannons, defending its heart, the magnificent capital Paris, at great sacrifice.

In Russia the despotic regime of the tsar was no longer capable of resisting the stampede of the German armies, and that huge empire was gradually moving toward dissolution. And thanks to the intrigues and material assistance of the German government, Bolshevism was exploding in the capital, St. Petersburg.

Also thanks to the Germans, Turkey (whose forces during the Balkan War had disbanded and suffered a crushing defeat in the space of a month) had been able to send more than two million soldiers to seven fronts (the Caucasus, Persia, Mesopotamia, Palestine, the Dardanelles, Thrace, and Galicia), where they fought bravely. Eventually, however, Turkey was no longer able to continue this uneven struggle. As the Entente's forces kept increasing and becoming more organized from one day to the next, the forces of the Central Powers, deprived of overseas contacts and raw materials, were becoming exhausted. Nevertheless, the Ittihad regime in Turkey had no choice but to continue to fight, not because they believed they would achieve victory but, saddled as they were with criminal culpability, to save their own skins.

This was the situation at the beginning of 1917. I am omitting the details and the political implications, which are only indirectly related to this personal memoir. Let's just say that Germany, facing difficulties of rationing at home, enjoined the Turkish government to send grain and livestock to Central Europe. This further depleted the scanty food supply in Turkey, and the Turks began to complain that the Germans were taking the bread from their mouths. Relations between the two countries slowly cooled, growing into enmity.

These were the conditions as I was entering Adana.

20

A Mysterious Patient in Adana's German Hospital

On the road from Mersin, one of the first neighborhoods one encounters on the west side of Adana is the Christian neighborhood of Charchabook,* near the railroad station.

For about ten minutes I wandered through the muddy and winding streets of Charchabook with the aid of a ten-year-old Armenian boy, until I found the home of Dr. Vartabedian. Unfortunately, the doctor was not home; he was at the German company's hospital, where he was the principal—and sole—physician. Since he had the right to accept and treat whatever outside patients he wanted to, it was in effect his private hospital. He had also taken on the job of treating the staff of the railway construction company.

*At this time (January 1917), a large group of the remaining Armenians lived in Charchabook [meaning hastily built], so named because the houses there had been hastily built.—G.B.

At the doctor's house I got the address of a former classmate and old friend from Sanassarian, Sarkis Janjigian, and not wanting to wander through these streets too long, perhaps inviting attention, I hastened to find him.

Luckily, Janjigian's residence was only ten minutes away. I found it easily, and when I identified myself, I was received with impressive hospitality. So I took refuge there for a few days until I could find a convenient hiding place. Seeing that such a hiding place was impossible to find, and realizing that Janjigian's residence was not suitable either, I sent word to Dr. Vartabedian, asking whether he would be kind enough to come and help me. He did not know me personally and had only read my name in the newspapers, but he hurried over to put himself at my disposal. My worries, mental anguish, and troubled moods of the past several days dissipated when this noble and patriotic doctor said to me:

> Don't fret—I am ready to make every sacrifice to save your life. If high-ranking Turkish military personnel did not live next door to me, and in fact across the street, I would take you straight to my house. Such a step, however, would be very dangerous, and so I'm going to make a suggestion. I am the chief physician at the local German hospital, free to make all arrangements there. I will have a private room prepared for you on the top floor of the hospital—I even have a free room right now. You can come as a German patient and lie in bed pretending to be awaiting treatment, and I'll send you meals from my house. Since you know German, it will be very easy to admit you that way. If you find my plan suitable, I will make the arrangements as soon as I get to the hospital, and tomorrow I'll send my personal carriage to transport you there.

I would have been ready to go to a coal house if he had offered it. Being so hopeful about the future of the Armenians and so optimistic about the coming of happy days, I was perfectly ready to live in hiding for another few months. Yes, during the darkest hours, I had become a blind believer in the final victory of justice.

The next day I moved to the hospital. The room had six windows and plenty of light, and it was very clean. Though it was January, the warm Cilician sun drenched my quarters, and with German books at my disposal, I read constantly to pass the time. Every noon Dr. Vartabedian sent cooked food and sweets and even rare fruits in season. And in the evenings I was satisfied with plenty of milk and yogurt.

An Armenian from Bandirma by the name of Garabed was assigned to serve me; like me, he was a fugitive, working in the hospital as a servant. Garabed took me for a German patient and attended me dutifully. Every day he took my temperature and recorded it on the little board on which my name was written: *Engineer Mueller, 40 years old, diabetes.*

A doctor had once told me that if my temperature dropped suddenly from 40 to 37 Celsius I would die. After some weeks I began to put the thermometer under my tongue, and on a piece of paper I traced mountains and valleys, plotting points from 37 up to 40, then 41 degrees, and again gradually decreasing it. For a month I passed peaceful days this way without incident, and eventually, since I had food and books and gave praise to God, I grew accustomed to this imprisonment.

But the fact that I was confined to bed and never came out of my room, together with the abundant food brought to me daily from Dr. Vartabedian's house, aroused curiosity. So hospital staff would open my door, wanting to know who this mysterious German patient was.

Thinking that one day something untoward might happen, I called the doctor's attention to this circumstance. Right after he left my room, Dr. Vartabedian, an astute man, said to the staff, "You know, this German not only has diabetes, but having been in the war as an officer he has also gone a little mad . . . I'll not be responsible if you open his door, and he suddenly attacks and kills you. Better to be careful and not go into his room—not even pass by his door." The next time he came into my room, he told me what he had told everyone. I was amazed at his cleverness and said, "There has to be a humorous side to every misery." And we laughed quite a bit.

About two and a half months passed this way, without worrisome incident. Spring came. The trees and flowers bloomed prematurely, and I often saw the fragrant white blossoms of the orange trees in the hands of passersby in the street. But instead of making my soul happy, the chirping of the spring swallows and other birds at my windows filled it with even more sadness, because these happy creatures did not understand our misfortune.

Mrs. Vartabedian tired of providing these lavish services, dragging on for months, and one day Dr. Vartabedian got into an argument with her. She told her husband:

> Why do you need to send food to the German from home? Let them send it from the German restaurant. We have been sending it for months; isn't it enough? Now instead of being appreciated, we are being subjected to criticism. At least if he were British or French it would not have bothered me so much, but I'm not sending food for the German anymore. Find yourself another way.

Dr. Vartabedian couldn't say anything except,

> One day you also will be gratified and happy that I have honored and taken care of this German in this way; he is a very helpful person, an Armenophile . . . One day you will regret speaking like this. I'm going to write down what I just said on a piece of paper and give it to you; save it, and when that lucky day comes, show this piece of paper to me.

Dr. Vartabedian was one of our Protestant compatriots, while his wife belonged to the mother [Armenian Apostolic] church.

A week later Mrs. Vartabedian came to the hospital with her mother-in-law, determined to uncover the secret to this whole affair. Many German engineers had gone in and out of the hospital in the past, but the Vartabedians had never sent them food from their home.

When Mrs. Vartabedian visited me, without thinking, I thanked her in Armenian for the food she had sent me. Of course, having given myself away, I was forced to reveal my identity. In the following days the menu became even richer, as Mrs. Vartabedian seemed to want to surpass her husband's kindness and nobility.

One day a few weeks later, quite suddenly, the Turkish health inspector of Adana province came to the hospital on an official visit. He came to my room, wanting to interrogate me, and when I said that I did not know Turkish, he left, dissatisfied.

At the end of March I had to leave the hospital in a hurry to make room for a real German patient. Caught by surprise, Dr. Vartabedian had no choice but to take me home for a few nights, until other arrangements could be made. That same night a Turkish major from the Adana staff came to Dr. Vartabedian's house, and I was introduced as a German engineer. The major did not speak German, so it was impossible for him to get into our conversation.

Then a few days later, this time being introduced as Yorgi *Effendi,* I was transported to an orchard that belonged to a Greek. I remained there for a few months. I used to dig and sow and clear the grass under the hot sun, and it seemed to me that those were the most pleasant days of my exile, far from all prying eyes.

If I had not embraced the clerical profession, I would have wanted to work in orchards, so much did I enjoy the peaceful and clean atmosphere of nature, like those monks who, alongside their contemplative life, tilled the land, tending their orchards both spiritual and physical. Truly, the climate in Cilicia is wonderful—a veritable paradise, as the fertile soil, lush plant life, plentiful and varied fruits, and natural beauty of mountain and field, rivers and currents, join together to entice and excite the observer.

21

The Condition of the Remaining Armenians in Adana

By the beginning of 1917, the Ittihad government, in accordance with its radical plan to annihilate the Armenian race, had "cleansed" most of the Armenian people from the provinces of Asia Minor, and it was preparing to annihilate those who had survived.

Despite this radical measure of the Turkish government, in Adana,* some 7,000 to 8,000 Armenians remained. In part, they were the remnants of the more than 250,000 deportees from the Cilician regions near Adana, where a national law that exempted the families of soldiers from deportation had been at least partially respected. In addition to the families of soldiers, there were a few thousand Armenian artisans in Adana retained by the Turkish military authorities as tailors, shoemakers, blacksmiths, coach makers, carpenters, ironsmiths, weavers, saddle makers, tinsmiths, and workers in factories that produced military necessities.

It is worth remembering that within Turkish society the artisans were mainly Christians. The Turks and other Islamic peoples, generally speaking, were peasants, soldiers, clergymen, or government employees. Sometimes they were grocers, vegetable vendors, halvah sellers [*helvaji*], or chickpea sellers [*leblebiji*], but 90 percent of the Turkish people engaged in farming, under primitive and strenuous conditions.

Other Islamic states, such as Persia, Afghanistan, Belujistan, India, Malaysia, Egypt, Algeria, Morocco, and Tunisia, had ceased to be independent states and were vassals of European powers. In comparison the Ottoman Empire was able to occupy a dominant position in good part because it was not an entirely Islamic society but included millions of progressive Christian subjects, among whom the Armenians predominated. It is no exaggeration to say that the entire commercial life of Turkey's interior provinces was in the hands of the Armenians, and with the Greeks they shared in the foreign trade of the harbors.

*Adana refers here to both the province and its capital city.—trans.

When successive Turkish governments perpetrated their frequent acts of barbarism against Christians, Turkish government officials—as well as foreign Turcophile politicians, journalists, and even novelists—portrayed those acts as just retribution for Christian monopolies in the Turkish economy, particularly domestic and foreign commerce, retail trade, and shipping. The Christians were characterized as ferocious leeches that were sucking the blood of the poor Turkish people, getting rich at their expense.

The reality is that in the interior eastern provinces, where Armenians were a respectable minority, most Armenians made their living in agriculture and associated trades. In the main cities, inasmuch as all governmental positions—military and civil—were off-limits to them, they were forced to turn to private enterprise, commerce, and the arts.

In the provinces 95 percent of the pharmacies belonged to Armenians, and about the same percentage of the doctors were Armenian. Since university education was practically nonexistent in Constantinople for non-Muslims, Armenians, Greeks, and Jews would study in Europe and then return to Turkey to settle and fill this vacuum. Turks, for their part, preferred to become military doctors, pharmacists, or veterinarians.

The Christians and Jews kept up with nineteenth-century European scientific and technological advances, and having been educated in Europe, they were fluent in the languages used in European firms. Thus they were in a position to forge relationships with foreign commercial institutions. Furthermore, having little domestic industry, Turkey was forced to rely on imports to provide its people with necessities; Christians and Jews were importers of hardware, textiles, kerosene, petroleum oil, and coal. Without these imports the Turkish people would have been deprived of tools, clothing, light, and means of transportation on land and sea.

If performing these roles had fallen to the Christian and Jewish communities, was that a despicable crime to warrant revenge? Why weren't the Turks themselves undertaking those efforts?

They had left the steppes of Asia five hundred years before and settled in this region between Europe and Asia. Here radiant ancient civilizations had existed, their ruins visible in Greece, Thrace, Ephesus, Cilicia, and Syria, stretching to the land of Babylon, and greatly admired even today. Yet the Turkish people have remained militaristic, sectarian, and backward.

Perhaps the Turkish people themselves weren't fully responsible for this stagnation. But at no time, despite their victories and conquests, did their leaders ever have the wisdom to introduce a modern work ethic, education, and other sources of advancement. They were content to see their people engage as soldiers in fighting and pillaging, and to palliate their wretched condition, they finally pushed them to plunder and commit atrocities.

This truth underlies the execrable crime that claimed the lives of the Christian populations of Asia Minor. Unfortunately, the Great Powers of Europe, instead of putting this important region in an orderly state, pursued gains and privileges for themselves and in so doing became directly or indirectly responsible for this catastrophe. And in this unsettled state, sooner or later Turkey would join those who caused the world war and commit inexpiable crimes.

No, the civilized world cannot take pride in this outcome.

The buildings and monuments hailed as the work of Turkish civilization, the marvelous imperial palaces and mosques of the Turkish capital, are, almost without exception, the work of Armenian architects. May this digression suffice, with the promise of further details later.

In the Turkish army, not only were the artisans mostly Armenians, but so were the doctors, pharmacists, veterinarians, and dentists. Much to its dishonor the villainous Turkish government murdered more than a hundred Armenian physicians—victims of the jealousy, hatred, and perfidy of their Turkish colleagues. The Armenian Medical Association of Constantinople published a booklet that gives their names, as well as the sites and circumstances of their disappearance in full detail.

In Adana, aside from the remaining Armenians I mentioned earlier, there were also fugitives and survivors of the more than 400,000 from known and unknown caravans that had passed through on their way to Aleppo and Der Zor. Some of them had managed to flee the deportee caravans or survive by bribes: approximately 20,000 in Konya and 900 in Eregli. Finally, about 7,500 natives of Adana had avoided deportation.

It was comforting to see that almost all the Armenians of Adana had fashioned means of getting by, more or less. Women and girls were working in textile factories, making cloth for underwear for the Turkish soldiers and dyeing it yellowish or blue with onion skin or indigo. Others were occupied with their gardens and orchards, attending to their vegetables, grapes, and other fruits as well as grapevine branches, their source of wood for the winter.

Then highly exaggerated reports reached Adana that the Russian army had commiteed vengeful acts on the Caucasus front—and particularly the Armenian volunteers in the regions of Erzerum and Erzinjan—so the Turkish military, police, and municipal officials of all ranks redoubled their ill will toward the Armenians. Meanwhile, the Turkish people were ready to say to Armenians they encountered, whether they knew them or not: "We are going to massacre you too" [*Sizi de kesejeyiz bu gunlerde*].

In Adana the years 1916 to 1917 had passed in relative calm, but then the Muslim Turks began to show enmity toward the Armenians. They also criticized the Turkish government leaders, asking why they weren't deporting the Armenian survivors to finally rid Adana of them.

Even the handful of Armenians still alive in Adana had become a thorn in the side of the Turks there, who believed that they too deserved what the others had gotten. Having sold the possessions they had taken from the already deported Armenians and long since spent the money, they were now impatient for the remaining Armenians to be deported as well, creating new opportunities for plunder.

Hugnen, chief director of the Baghdad railway company, had been in its administration for thirty years, having risen from the bottom. He greatly appreciated the company's Armenian employees, because of whom the trains ran on time. Often he gave the Turkish leaders to understand that if they deported the Armenian employees, he would be forced to halt railway traffic.

The foreign journalists and novelists who have called the Armenians parasites forget that they had been held in high esteem by foreigners, not only in everyday life but in the greatest and most responsible of positions. In Russia, Loris-Melikov had held the rank of military dictator; in Egypt, Nubar Pasha had been prime minister. In Turkey, even under the rule of Sultan Abdul Hamid II, the latter entrusted the management of his personal treasury to Hagop Pasha, Portukalian Pasha, and Hovhannes Sakuz. I think it is fair to say that the Armenians, whom the Turks called ingrates [*namkeor*], have the right to use this term to describe the Turks, who didn't hesitate to annihilate this loyal, dynamic, and temperate people who made up a crucial part of the empire.

22

The Curse of Murdered Armenian Mothers

Toward the end of 1917 in Turkey, as in all the warring countries, poverty, epidemics, and misery wreaked horrendous havoc on the local population. The dominant Turks had long since exhausted the productive energy of their subject Christian peoples, especially the Armenians and Greeks, by whose just toil they lived.

The common Turkish folk had reached an extreme of indigence, but to whom could they protest? For ages, two classes have always existed in Turkey: the exploiters and the disadvantaged; the government officials and the common people. Among the common people Christians and Muslims alike are subjected to all kinds of extortion and cruelty.

Government officials enjoy great and rare opportunities to accumulate wealth, so their main ambition had been to maintain their positions. In order to meet wartime demands for food and supplies, the military authorities, under the martial law of requisition [*tekelife harbiye*], commandeered whatever they could from the homes of the Turkish peasants, down to the last animal in their stables. Thus the fields remained fallow; there were neither horses nor mules nor oxen with which to plow.

As for the Muslim city dwellers, especially the Turks, they had become so impoverished that they sold their valuables in the bazaar so they could buy bread. Veiled women had gotten hold of copper pots, braziers, mirrors, European kerosene lamps, tableware, toiletry containers, carpets, armchairs, and simple chairs that the Armenians abandoned during the deportations. Now they had to sell their booty in exchange for a few loaves of bread. An experienced eye could easily guess where these items had come from—and what an ironic twist it was that the Armenian women now working in cloth factories were the ones buying them!

As for the tens of thousands of Turkish and Kurdish people in Adana [province] who had sought refuge from the Russian borderlands and nearby provinces—Van, Bitlis, Erzerum, and Erzinjan—they were in an even more deplorable situation. They were the survivors of the hundreds of thousands of Muslims who had fled the Russian armies and the Armenian volunteer regiments. Decimated by starvation and epidemic, these Muslims would die in the severities of the coming winter.

It was the end of December 1917. Utilizing legal papers certifying me as an employee of a German company, I passed through the Turkish neighborhoods along the river and came upon thousands of Turkish and Kurdish refugees—women, girls, and children—on the flagstone pavements in front of the mosques. They were living ghosts, reduced by starvation to skeletons; for clothing they had only rags hanging from their shoulders, and the dirt that covered them rendered them unrecognizable. There was no visible difference at all between these refugees and Armenian exiles in the deserts of Der Zor.

While the Armenian people had been driven by the Turks to the deserts to perish, these Turkish and Kurdish refugees were subjected to their misery where they were. I often saw the sick—homeless, abandoned, and deprived of care—lying prostrate on the frozen flagstone courtyards of the mosques. No one paid any attention to these wretched people. Meanwhile government officials were saying, "We won't get an opportunity like this again," and went on plundering.

For the sake of appearances, the government gave these hapless ones a daily ration of one hundred drams of a mixture of bread, straw, and earth, which looked like mud, and a soup called *chorba*. Moral: The Turkish government had no more compassion for these poor people than they did for the Armenians. Instead of dying by fire or execution, they would perish from starvation and disease. This wretched, docile multitude had not understood the actual intent of its leaders.

23

The Natural Beauty of Cilicia: The Disguised Vine Grower

My hiding place in the Greek's vineyard behind the Adana railway station was not secure, inasmuch as high-ranking government officials would arrive at the station. And so I went to another vineyard more than a half hour from the city that Dr. Vartabedian had rented for me. I wasn't alone in this vineyard, for I brought with me my longtime friend Sarkis Janjigian and his wife and three children.

Janjigian, a draftsman in the central office of the railroad company in

Adana, would go into town every day and then return home with the latest news about the political and military situation. Again thanks to Dr. Vartabedian, I obtained the identity papers [*vesika*] of an Armenian soldier who had recently died in the German hospital. With these papers, I no longer had reason to be anxious. For the first time in my hard life in exile, my days went by peacefully and even pleasantly; in the mornings and evenings I worked in the vineyard with much enthusiasm, and I passed the rest of the day reading.

Although I was enjoying exceptionally good conditions now, I lacked the courage to write the story of the horrible suffering of the Armenians. But having a sharp memory, I stored in it all the principal events of my exile and all of the relevant details. I continually ruminated and mentally recorded everything; I analyzed all the events and occurrences; I examined them to determine their causes and reasons. During these days I decided, in the event of my survival, that I would write the horrific story, so that future Armenian generations would know the price of the freedom they enjoyed. And I decided that the title of this story would be *Armenian Golgotha.*

Spring was passing, and the hot Cilician summer would soon be upon us. The abundant grapes in our vineyard grew and swelled. In such a peaceful state, this marvelous and tranquil environment of Mother Nature, I would sometimes forget that I was a deported and fugitive clergyman. I could understand why the great Roman general Cincinnatus, after his wars of conquest, used to withdraw to his fields and cultivate vegetables. While planting cabbage, he would say, "Now I feel that I am living; now I see the sun's beauty." It is an irrefutable fact that under nature's wing, man is in his element, whereas the more he lives elsewhere, despite wealth and pleasures, the more he loses his health and happiness.

In 1909 I was living with Catholicos Matheos Izmirlian of blessed memory, as his immediate attendant, in the pontifical summer residence located in Byurakan, a small Armenian village three to four hours by coach from Holy Etchmiadzin. At that time I had felt this same marvelous enlivening influence of nature in the depths of my soul. Perched on the side of Mount Aragats, Byurakan was 4,000 meters above sea level and 800 meters above Etchmiadzin. His Holiness the Catholicos granted me permission to climb to the summit of Aragats with a small group that included Bishop Mesrop Movsesian, a member of the Synod of Bishops; Very Rev. Husik Zohrapian; and Father Komitas, the immortal messenger of Armenian peasant songs. During the forty-eight hours I spent on this huge high mountain, crowned with perpetual snow, 4,000 meters above human tumult and pollution, I felt so happy. Rising proudly and facing it was Mount Ararat.

Yes, the human races and nations of ancient times were not unreasonable in building temples to their pagan gods atop high mountains, believing that the gods received only prayers offered from such heights. For when one climbs a great mountain, it is impossible not to be affected by a sense of mystical elevation. The soul, jolted, sprouts wings and flies, soaring even higher into the boundless realms of the universe. This is perhaps the secret of the lovers of alpinism, who endanger their lives in order to enjoy this exquisite feeling.

Meanwhile our vineyard was giving me new life and vitality. On warm nights I would lie down on the roof of our cottage and sleep peacefully—and this relaxed my nerves and maintained my mental balance. So very many individuals had lost their minds in exile! My life in the vineyard was a providential blessing, an oasis of peace and tranquillity in a mortifying desert of grief, tears, and blood.

The more I looked at the marvelous elevation of the Taurus mountain chain, the forested sides of the huge mountains, and the wide Cilician plains, smooth as the surface of a sea, the more I would marvel—and the more I felt myself an expatriate, for these mountains, plains, and rivers had been the cradle of our erstwhile Cilician principality.[1]

With Catholicos Matheos Izmirlian of blessed memory, I had traveled on land and sea. By special royal railroad car we had crossed the vast plains of Great Russia, from Odessa to St. Petersburg, from Moscow to the Caucasus. I had toured the Ararat and Shirag plains of the Armenian homeland, the six large provinces of Asia Minor. I had traveled over almost all of Europe, but I had never come across such a marvelous land as this.

Where can you find a plain of 42,000 square kilometers that seems like a sea, as if the waters of the Mediterranean had only yesterday receded from the mountainsides? A land that since time immemorial has been formed from the alluvial flow from the Taurus and Amanos mountains, like the Nile River valley. Mother Nature spread a blanket of fertile soil over the land, a fecund land that bears fruit several times a year—and wheat, barley, corn, cotton, vegetables, and sesame. Its varied harvests can compete with the best anywhere else.

The fruits on the trees of Cilicia are the finest, the sweetest, and the juiciest. Consider the abundance, size, and taste of the oranges; if they are not better than the Jaffa variety, they are certainly as good. The oranges of Dort-Yol can vie with the finest anywhere in the world. In the spring, when the orange trees bloom and are covered like a bride with a veil of sparkling whiteness, they shine with ravishing beauty. Their aromatic fragrance pursues you for miles.

As much as the Cilician soil can boast of its orange groves and other fruit-laden trees, so too can it be proud of its olive trees, whose olives match in size and taste those of Bursa and Izmit, as well as those of the Greek islands of the Aegean.

The grapes grow in bunches as large as those of the promised land of Canaan. And the figs, like those we have in our orchard, are honey-flavored and sweet.

Yes, in what other land does the almond tree blossom near the apple tree, the apricot near the pear, the fig near the olive, the plum near the orange, and the walnut near the fig, and where else does the sugarcane grow near the pomegranate? All of them surpass in appearance, size, and taste those even in the countries famous for them.

As for the grapes, there are some twenty varieties of them, juicy and sweet. Every house with a vineyard has an abundance of grapes harvested for wine, raki, and *pekmez.**

What other land has a seacoast of about 300 kilometers and a serene port like Alexandretta that is large enough to accommodate a fleet of hundreds of commercial and naval vessels? And imagine—only about 100 kilometers from this marvelous seacoast, rising in the north, are huge mountains, with their perpetually snow-covered peaks at 3,000 to 4,000 meters. A few of them call to mind the two titans, Ararat (5,000) and Aragats (4,150), in the cradle of the Ararat plain.

These mountains, collectively called the Taurus, start between Mersin and Seleucia and extend northward as far as Armenia and the Partogh mountains; their main peak is the sacred Ararat. The Taurus mountains separate the Cilician plain from the plain of Konya, serving Cilicia as an impregnable natural rampart against any enemy coming from the north.

But this august mountain chain is not satisfied merely to defend Cilicia against enemies; it is also a reservoir of copious water for the fertile Cilician plains, where the Jihun, Sihun, and Galigatnos rivers originate. Their ever-flowing currents issue from the mountains' eternal lakes and springs. The rivers irrigate the fertile plains of Cilicia, turning this region into the Egypt of Asia Minor.

But while Egypt has only one Nile, whose source lies 3,000 kilometers away in Ethiopia, the Cilician plain has several. The German vice-admiral Pashich pointed this fact out to me with admiration when I went to pay a return visit to his battleship *Strasbourg*, on behalf of His Holiness Sahag II, catholicos of Cilicia.

On account of its scorching equatorial climate, Egypt can boast only of its cotton and wheat. But Cilicia, with its unique variety of climates, is a cornucopia of all kinds of fruits, grains, and vegetables.

The Taurus mountains are not only the perpetual reservoir for the Cili-

**Pekmez:* treacle; syrup made from grape juice.—trans.

cian plain but also a treasury of minerals and metals buried deep in the earth, which to date have remained unexploited. These same mountains are covered with leafy trees, rich virgin forests in which it is possible to travel for days without emerging; moreover, the forests are full of wild animals, an inexhaustible supply of game and fur.

This is Cilicia—which around 1045, after the destruction of Ani, became the second homeland of our forefathers. It was the cradle of the Rubenid kingdom, which was founded in 1220 and prevailed until 1385, when it succumbed to the continual attacks of the Mamluks from Egypt. If the history and sentiments of every Armenian had not been connected from time immemorial to prehistoric Urartu, the native homeland of Ararat, I would say that the only homeland worthy of the Armenian people would be Cilicia.

Sitting in my vineyard, looking out at the great summits rising majestically on the distant northern horizon, I was often immersed in such thoughts, my eyes and mind fixed deep in dreams. It mattered not that today I was an exile and fugitive clergyman; tomorrow would see the imminent resurrection of the Armenian people when we, as a junior member of the Allies, would receive our just due and reward for the blood we spilled in our common cause.

In autumn 1917 my friend Janjigian brought me a copy of the major German newspaper *Tageblatt*. Among other things, it reported that British prime minister Lord H. H. Asquith had said in a speech:

> The Turkish state shall not only be expelled from the territory of Europe but it will also not be able to maintain its independence on its Asiatic territories either. The Turkish government officials are personally responsible for the blood of the more than one million innocent Armenians massacred. This is the last massacre of Armenians, and this civilized and oldest Christian people shall, once and for all, be liberated from the despotic rule of the Turk, as our little ally.

My unspeakable grief was greatly consoled when I read this report, and those around me also felt great joy. During these years of our exile and torment, such encouragement from the Allies had been our only nourishment, the only refuge for our souls. Who could have foreseen that in 1922 the Turkish government officials held responsible for the Armenian atrocities, having been arrested and exiled to Malta, would then be set free by the very same persons who considered them to be criminals? Who could have imagined that the British prime minister Andrew Bonar Law would one day say to an Armenophile deputy, "We cannot alone act as the policemen of the world."

What Armenian would think that twenty-eight warships of the Allies—the same great powers that had declared "this massacre of the Armenians is the last"—would simply stand by as a great crime and fire engulfed Smyrna in September 1922; that they would merely watch the massacre and the abductions and the dumping into the sea of hundreds of thousands of Armenian and Greek refugees gathered on the quay of Smyrna; or that moving pictures of this carnage would be taken from their warships?

Whose mind would it have crossed that the Allies would fail to liberate us, and that the French would even return already-liberated lands, such as eastern Thrace and especially Cilicia, to the Turks? In December 1921, during a fifteen-day period, 120,000 Armenians would be forced to emigrate, subjected to the hardships of winter, just so the French could maintain economic control of Syria.[2]

Who could have imagined that the important government officials who had said the Turks would be expelled from Europe would then invite the defeated Turks to Europe, emboldening them to demand a return to the borders of 1913, prior to the post–Second Balkan War borders that diminished Ottoman territory?[3]

What pessimist, in his most pessimistic imagination, would have been tempted to think that the Turkish government, disarmed by the victorious Allies in the autumn of 1918 at the Mudros armistice, would be rearmed when the French left Cilicia—receiving tanks and airplanes worth 200 million francs from chivalrous France, pioneer of civilization, which the Turks would then use to drive the Greeks out of Smyrna and into the sea?

Who could ever have thought that the Christian minorities' undeniable need for protection, justice, and rights—included as an article of faith in all the treaties signed after the world war—would, with permissive complicity, end in the expulsion of the Christian remnants from Asia Minor? How did the Allies—defenders of Christian minorities—suddenly change their tune and say, "What can we do? If it's no longer possible to continue in neighborly relations with the Turks, go beyond the borders of the Turkish state."

And as they made this unsympathetic recommendation, these governments hastened to close their own borders so that naked, hungry, homeless refugees of various nationalities would not enter their countries and disturb them.

For the sake of accuracy, it must be allowed that, after the horrible Smyrna catastrophe, France alone opened her doors to Armenian refugees. Owing to this humane and chivalrous hospitality, more than

23,000 Armenian refugees settled in France and found work, food, and housing. As for Britain, home to a million Jews, she firmly shut her doors to Armenians—even those with relatives there. Parents, spouses, and children were prohibited from setting foot in that country.

In order to mask her moral bankruptcy, or at least to save appearances, she didn't even want to give 50,000 pounds sterling to each of the 200,000 Christian refugees who were forced to emigrate in October 1922 after the unexpected defeat of the Greeks, which resulted in 100,000 deaths. The Turkish government exiled the Christian male population as prisoners to the inner provinces. On this wretched situation, the League of Nations, under Dr. Nansen, spent but 100,000 francs for the 700,000 Christian refugees—amounting to 7 cents to each . . .

Of all the Christian minorities of the East, we Armenians are to blame for our fate. For although we are an alert nation, we believed in the Europeans' professed struggle for justice and rights, in their false words and deceptions. Our exemplary stupidity was a simplemindedness peculiar to peasants: we did not realize that on the scales of justice, the oil deposits of Mosul would weigh more than the lives of millions of Christians.

September came, the time for harvesting the grapes, which we crushed to make *pekmez* and vinegar. The work was so pleasant and invigorating. The months had passed without incident, and no one suspected who I was.

On one of those cool autumn nights I heard a song coming from the neighboring vineyard. A few young Armenian girls were singing Avetis Aharonian's "Nazei Orore" [Naze's Lullaby].

Sleep, my baby, look at the cradle,
Don't cry, I've cried a lot.
The blind cranes came and went
Across our black sky, lamenting in grief and sorrow,
Oh, they became blind in our mountains,
Don't cry, I've cried a lot.
The wind is sobbing in the black forests,
Baby is mourning an abandoned corpse,
There are many abandoned and unburied corpses,
Don't cry, I've cried a lot.

The caravan passed, loaded with tears,
It fell on its knees and remained in the black forests,
That is the suffering and cruelty of our world,
Don't cry, I've cried a lot.

I've strung beads, tied them to your cradle,
Against the evil eyes of our wicked enemy,
Sleep and grow, be quick about it, baby,
Don't cry, I've cried a lot.

My milk froze on your pale lips,
I know, it's bitter, you don't want it, baby,
Oh, my grief has squeezed poison in it . . .
Don't cry, I've cried a lot.

Suck the black poison along with my milk,
Let it become black vengeance in your soul,
Sprout, shoot up, I'll sacrifice to see you grow up,
Don't cry, I've cried a lot.

Although they were singing very softly, the harmonious strains of the tender lullaby reached me. The words *caravan . . . abandoned and unburied corpses . . . tears . . . black forests . . . enemy . . . vengeance . . .* echoed in my soul. My soul was agitated. One after another the bloody episodes of the thorny Armenian Golgotha moved across my mind. We were still living in a time of annihilation and terror.

I spent practically the whole night awake, as the unburied corpses near Keller, a few hours from Boghazliyan (which I described in Volume I), flashed before my eyes. Skeletons . . . skulls . . . oh, was there any chance of sleeping? If the Armenian bard had seen all that I had seen and heard all that I had heard, what would he have written . . . to describe for future Armenian generations in true colors these tragic episodes in this last great shipwreck of the Armenian people?

Might I not attempt, I wondered, to condense my impressions to verse form, in a poem? Providence had not endowed me with the talent of a poet. If I were to undertake such an effort, beyond my capacities, would it not be in vain? On the other hand, it seemed fitting to spill the sorrows amassed in my agitated soul onto white paper, instead of in tears.

After ruminating all night, at dawn I wrote the following lines:

Lullaby on the Way to Zor

(To the tune of "Knir im balik")

Oh, lullaby, lullaby, my baby, lullaby,
Expelled they're taking us toward Zor,
You don't have a cradle for me to rock you,
To give your little body a rest there.

My helpless orphan, we're left in fate's
Cruel hands, ridiculed by all,
I found a dirty rag as swaddling clothes for you,
Black grief gnaws at my heart, the fire of my life.

I want to live, willingly bear
All suffering, so you may be
A great pride to the ruined homeland,
Flaming revenge of innocent blood . . .

I always had a rock under my head, instead of a pillow,
Hungry, thirsty, I had not a hope;
Vengeance became the nourishment of my soul,
For this, I forgot all pain.

Oh, lullaby, lullaby my baby, lullaby,
Armenia will flower day by day;
May the victorious Armenian flag
Stand as perpetual remedy for our black sorrows.

Approximately a month later I heard another song, as stirring as the last, "Siretsi yarus daran,"* and based on its melody, I tried to express what I was feeling and thinking at that moment. I'm recording it here verbatim; in the original context I had drawn a symbol of death at the beginning of my poem.

The Death Procession Toward Zor

A series of processions,
Tens of thousands of Armenian deportees,
They're taking us toward Zor;
Worn out, emaciated every day,
We are dying with torment,
Abandoned by merciless fate.

We are walking toward Zor,
We are finally approaching
The grave day by day,
Where arid sunburnt deserts
Await us,
Where we shall die hungry.

*"I loved and they took away my sweetheart."—trans.

Our soldiers prisoners,
Our virgins abducted,
Our half-dead children
Piled up form hills.
As for our wretched Armenian mothers,
They walk barefoot for months.

But don't you cry, oh Armenians,
With our blessed blood
Will Armenia be born,
No longer being trampled
By the cruel feet of the evil Turk,
Always remaining the prisoner in their hands.

Smoking ruins,
Our populous, prosperous cities
Today abandoned by their owners;
When Armenia again sprouts
Blossoms day by day,
May DEATH IN ZOR *always be remembered . . .*

For, with our blood,
We bought reborn homeland,
Our sea of pains, tears,
Sufferings and griefs,
And rescued Armenia,
Let it be a monument to us.

With these hopes we closed
Our eyes forever,
We bore our pains without complaint,
We bore our cross without grumbling,
These became the salve
For our deep savage wounds.

Yes, every Armenian on the bloody roads of exile and in the sandy deserts, until his last breath, held the deep conviction that Armenia would be reborn at the cost of our blood, and that future Armenian generations would live free and independent from then on.

At the end of September 1917, all those who had gone to summerhouses in the vineyards descended to the city of Adana. But when our turn came,

I had no place to go. I couldn't remain here alone; again besieged with worry, I racked my brain, trying to think of a new place to go. I found another isolated vineyard an hour and a half from town where an elderly Armenian woman spent the summer with her young son, born an idiot. These two had no one else, and they made a half-decent living selling salted and spiced beef. So the same day that Janjigian left with his family for Adana, I went in Dr. Vartabedian's personal carriage to the vineyard of this elderly Armenian woman.

She was a paragon of the kind Armenian mother. She spoke to me with maternal solicitude, having no idea who I was and often asking questions about my identity in Turkish, for the inhabitants of Adana were Turkish-speaking. Having completed her work in her vineyard, she was preparing to return to her hut in Adana, having already laid in her modest winter stores as well as her stock of wood. I would gladly have accepted her invitation to hide out there, but the hut was in a district of Turkish homes. So my search for an appropriate hideout in an Armenian or Greek house in Adana ended in vain.

Once again my protector Dr. Vartabedian came to my aid. Visiting me at the vineyard where I was staying, he said:

> We searched long and hard but couldn't find a suitable place where you could live in secret. Therefore there is no alternative but for you to come and reside in our house. I'll furnish a special room and put it at your disposal; come live with us. Of course, this war will not go on forever; God is merciful. Later on we'll see what we can do . . .

I objected to this plan: since I was sentenced to death, I said, why should he put his family and children in danger, and why should his protection of so many relatives and other fugitives be risked on my account? Dr. Vartabedian wouldn't listen but simply reiterated, "Your life is valuable for us. Your life must be secured." I insisted on the contrary. But I was obliged to accept this decision whether I wanted to or not, so I moved to the home of my devoted friend. There was nothing else for me to do.

Hardly had I become settled in Dr. Vartabedian's house, however, when I realized that I had taken an imprudent step. Inasmuch as it was a doctor's house, many people came and went: Armenians, Greeks, Europeans—and especially Turks. My peaceful life in the vineyard was gone. So my days passed anxiously, and I wished to put an end to this perilous situation as soon as possible.

Dr. Vartabedian had no one but our acquaintance Winkler to ask for advice. I have earlier related in detail what exemplary self-sacrifice that kind and noble old man undertook in order to save his Armenian workers in Amanos from deportation. If he didn't succeed, it wasn't his fault but rather that of the German military authority, which looked upon his humane actions with contempt.

When Winkler heard Dr. Vartabedian's favorable account of me, he said laconically, "Bring him to my house tomorrow night. Let's have a meeting."

The next day we visited Winkler, whose house was a stone's throw from Dr. Vartabedian's.

24

The Clerk of the Office: Disappearance

Winkler received us with great respect, as if it were an official visit. He listened to my story with genuine compassion and was evidently moved. I waited with bated breath for his reply. Then he said to me:

> Don't worry; you needn't be afraid any longer. As long as I'm here, no one will dare to hound or torment you. As of tomorrow morning, I will make arrangements for you to carry out the job you had in Belemedik in the Adana office of our company. I will speak with the chief of the administrative branch and ask him to hire you. Even if there isn't a job opening, I'll have one created. We'll give you a suitable room in one of the special company houses, and I hope that when we give you our company voucher [*vesika*], no one will disturb you anymore, since you will be starting a normal life.

The very next day I was on the job. Everybody's eyes were on the new face that had suddenly appeared whom no one knew anything about. Everybody treated me with great respect, though they were nevertheless curious to learn who this newcomer was who enjoyed Winkler's special protection.

I had a suitable room, which Dr. Vartabedian had furnished with things he brought from his own home. Now and then I was able to take advantage of the freedom my job afforded me, roaming around town fearlessly to buy the things I sometimes needed.

The days and months passed peacefully, and I was thinking what good fortune it would be to hail the end of the world war like this, in ease and security. After the first month I received sixteen gold pounds as my monthly wage, a large sum, exceptional for the time.

But my Armenian friends, some of them old comrades from the Sanassarian Academy—of all places!—were jealous, and it was no use trying to keep my identity a secret. Also, quite quickly, I became the object of a kind of silent treatment, particularly from my Jewish colleagues. Worse, the director of our administrative branch, also first dragoman of the German consulate in Adana, was an Armenophobic German Jew. So it seemed that I had walked into a trap. As the number of people who knew who I was increased, the permanent military inspectors from the railroad's central office in Adana began to inquire about me too.

Incidentally I should mention that all the workers on the railroad construction projects were considered soldiers; we each wore a red ribbon on our sleeves indicating our employment on the railroad projects to protect us from persecution. To maintain nominal surveillance over us, a Turkish captain along with a few officials resided in a special section of our offices. They may have thought their prey had fallen into their hands, but they didn't want to get on Winkler's bad side by any untoward interference. Therefore, knowing that I was a runaway whom the police and military authorities had been seeking for two years, they went about beginning an inquiry, creating a legitimate pretext to point out my false identity and arrest me.

Unfortunately, at this moment, Winkler was on a two-month vacation in Germany, leaving me without his powerful aid. As soon as he departed for Constantinople, the glances had become wicked, and I encountered difficulties and hostility at every turn.

One day my young Jewish colleagues suggested that we go hunting on Sunday in the nearby mountains. I found this invitation to go hunting during wartime, from coworkers who had often treated me badly, quite strange. It was impossible not to suspect a trap, so I had to find a way to decline. I suspected that the director of our administrative branch was attempting to frame me as a spy for the Entente, so I had reason to believe that my every step was being watched. Indeed, one day when I was out of the house, the local policemen appeared, as if routinely, to question the naïve wife of an Armenian employee who also lived there.

Being well versed in Machiavellian ways, and determined not to be caught by surprise again, I took artful precautions. During this period the Ottoman telegraph agency was writing about Armenian volunteers every day, especially about their clashes with the Turkish army. Plans were under way to annihilate the remaining Armenians, and any who happened to be in the street were arrested and exiled, to be violently killed in the Amanos mountains.

One Sunday morning just after the European New Year of 1918, the Turkish captain of our office, together with the police commissioner and *muhtar* of the Charchabook ward, suddenly appeared at our house asking who lived there. My Armenian colleague's wife, as I had asked, told the officer that there were two Armenian families that worked in the office of the railroad construction company, and no one else. The commissioner asked again in an insistent tone whether anyone else was living there, and the woman said no. But the Turkish captain, now clearly irritated, asked: "Doesn't Krikorian live here?" The Armenian woman replied, indifferently, "Yes, there is such a man, but I don't know him . . ."

The government officials then pushed open the door of my room; they came in, questioned me, and departed. As soon as they left I stopped a little Armenian boy passing by and handed him my small bundle. Then, just in case, I hurried into town and took refuge for a few days at the home of an Armenian friend. To be extra cautious, I didn't even tell Dr. Vartabedian that I had fled, so for the moment I had disappeared. Even the Armenian boy didn't know where I had gone, for as I approached the house, I took the bundle from him, rewarded him, and sent him on his way.

25

The General Condition of the Armenians at the Beginning of 1918

The war that had begun in August 1914 had grown more complex as new states entered the fray: Italy on May 23, 1915; Siam on July 22, 1917; and Romania on August 27, 1916. China, Cuba, Guatemala, Honduras, El Salvador, Haiti, Brazil, and Panama were all standing up against Germany and its allies.

From the start the United States of America, unofficially and in the name of freedom of trade, had been assisting the Entente powers with money and arms. But it did not officially declare war until April 6, 1917, when German submarines sank the British steamship *Lusitania.*

It was now evident that Germany would not have the power to continue this struggle, especially since Austria-Hungary had begun to exhaust its military forces.

Just as powerful and rich America with its population of 120 million was entering the war, a revolution was taking place in Russia, toppling the cruel tsarist regime, which had expanded its power since Peter the Great's reign. By an ironic twist of fate, Tsar Nicholas II was exiled to Siberia, to which—simply out of his fear of losing power—he, like the other tsars, had exiled millions of people of various nationalities, and where he along with his family would subsequently be assassinated by the Bolsheviks, in Ekaterinodar* on July 18, 1918.

The revolution that overthrew the Russian regime handed the helm of state to Alexander Kerensky, whose term as premier was defined by the anarchy of transition. The ignorant Russian *muzhik* population, about 160 million people, drunk with new freedom, laid waste the cities, destroying palaces and appropriating private property. And so after seven months Kerensky's new revolutionary regime, unable to establish order, was gone.

During this period of anarchy Lenin, the great apostle of Bolshevik ideology, with the support of the Germans, traveled from Switzerland via Germany to Moscow and St. Petersburg. On November 6, 1917, he took control of the party, seized the capital St. Petersburg, and forced Kerensky to flee.

On December 15, during the second month of this great Bolshevik revolution, the Lenin-Trotsky regime signed a truce with Germany. The Russian army, in a state of dissolution, laid down its weapons, and the soldiers on the Caucasus front walked away from the Russo-Turkish war, retreating freely to Tiflis. In their wake they left hundreds of cannons, as well as much ammunition, foodstuffs, and booty.

The Armenian Military Council of Tiflis sent its great general Antranig to Erzerum, along with ten thousand volunteers, to take control of the Turkish front at Erzinjan, Erzerum, Bitlis, and Van. However, twenty times as many soldiers were needed to secure such an extensive front. When General Antranig reached Erzerum to take command, he hoped, with an invincible will that was unique to him, to do the impossible. The Russian-Armenian soldiers, however, like their fellow Russian soldiers in

*Balakian is mistaken here; actually the Romanovs were killed in Ekaterinburg, located in Central Russia.—trans.

the new Bolshevik army, laid down their weapons and hurried to return to their homes.

Nevertheless, General Antranig managed to retreat with minimal losses toward the old Russo-Turkish border at Sarikamish, taking with him caravans of about fifty thousand Armenian refugees. But the retreating Armenian refugees, who had been subjected to fire and the sword in their persecuted wanderings for the past three years, now met with further horrific sufferings.

In February 1918, with the Caucasus abandoned by the Russians, the Armenian, Georgian, and Tatar* leaders formed a temporary government called the Transcaucasian Federation [Seim], with ten ministers: four Georgian, three Armenian, and three Tatar. It was an artificial union; both the Georgians and the Tatars, having made a secret agreement with the Turks, were actually plotting against the Armenians. Because of this treachery, the Turkish armies, no longer thwarted, were able to advance toward Etchmiadzin and Yerevan.

Having scarcely established the brash Bolshevik-Soviet regime, Lenin and Trotsky engaged in negotiations, first for a truce, then for peace. On March 3, 1918, the Germans and the Russians concluded a peace treaty at Brest-Litovsk whereby, among other things, Russia was forced to evacuate not only the three Turkish provinces it had occupied (Erzerum, Bitlis, and Van) but also the three *sanjaks* of the southwestern Caucasus (Batoum, Kars, and Ardahan), leaving them to the advancing Turkish armies.

The disbanded Russian army's panicky retreat from the Turkish borders, and the Turkish armies' triumphant advance toward Sarikamish, Kars, and Ardahan, combined with the understandable excesses committed in reprisal by the retreating Armenian volunteer army, galvanized the Turks to continue the annihilation of the Armenians at a furious pace: they had the scattered remnants of the surviving Armenians in Syria and Cilicia massacred. And as part of the plan, they rounded up all the Armenians who had been employed as soldiers in military factories in Aleppo and Adana and sent them into exile.

In Adana, where I was hiding among hundreds of fugitives, the houses were searched daily, and Armenians were arrested and exiled to Aleppo. But many of those arrested were killed in the Amanos mountains, particularly in the forests and valleys near Keller.

Again, among the surviving Armenians the anguish of impending death prevailed. Would we ever hail the victory of freedom and justice, for the sake of which we had silently endured this suffering, torment, and persecution? We were thinking about this especially because, in the German

*Tatar: Azerbaijani.—trans.

newspapers, which we secretly obtained now and then, we were reading about such radical transformations as the dissolution of tsarist Russia, America's declaration of war, the Brest-Litovsk treaty, and so on. But when we read about the arrogant pronouncements and excesses of the Turks, who, drunk on their cheap victories in the Caucasus, were becoming ever more audacious and unruly, we were also demoralized.

We often heard that the Ittihad government had decided to deport all remaining Armenians in Constantinople and Smyrna to Der Zor. Oh, we became distraught, knowing that if these surviving remnants of the Turkish Armenian population were exiled too, then the Turks would have succeeded in wiping all of us out.

By chance I got hold of a few issues of a religious paper called *Dajar* [Temple], published in Constantinople, for which a group of traitors, both clergymen and laypersons, wrote. Led by the imposter *vartabed* Hrant Hovasapian and the infamous *muhtar* of Beshiktash, Artin Megerdichian, they justifed the martyrdom of their innocent countrymen and exonerated the Turks of killing them. With rage, we read their claims that the Armenian revolutionary organizations had incurred the massacres as just punishment for revolting against the righteous Turkish government, and that, faced with rebellious subjects, every state would speak the same language and punish them.

They condemned the innocent victims in order to justify the criminal murderer. Thus, in Constantinople, *Dajar* and [the Dashnak newspaper] *Hairenik* joined together in desecrating the sea of blood spilled by the Armenian people, by making arguments that would exonerate Talaat and his camarilla of committing this unprecedented crime.

With the cooperation of these traitors Talaat had a special illustrated book prepared, denouncing the Armenians and exonerating the Turks. Weapons that supposedly had been seized from Armenians were assembled and photographed by Armenian photographers for the book; but they were simply the rifles and swords of Turkish police soldiers and the pistols of Turkish policemen.

We consoled ourselves by thinking that this world war couldn't go on forever. The day of settling accounts would finally come, and the criminals, the traitors, and all those responsible for the sea of innocent Armenian blood would receive their just punishment. If only we could witness with our own eyes those redemptive days of punishment and eternal justice!

26

The Turkish Army Invades the Caucasus, and the Armenians at Sardarabad

As I noted in the previous chapter, when the Bolshevik Revolution took place in 1917, the Russian army was suddenly dissolved, and Russian troops in the Caucasus began a panicky retreat to Tiflis. The Brest-Litovsk treaty of March 3, 1918, between Russia and Germany, forced the Russian army to withdraw from the three provinces of Turkish Armenia that it had occupied—Van, Bitlis, and Erzerum.

Encouraged by this Russian retreat, the Turkish army went on the offensive, marching to Erzinjan and Papert as well as Erzerum, Bitlis, and Van. General Antranig tried in vain to keep the deserting Armenian volunteers on the firing lines, but the sudden withdrawal of the Bolshevik soldiers had affected them; amid general despair, they too were now hurrying home. The majority of these volunteers didn't want to fight, and once when General Antranig bared his sword and threatened to kill deserters, they even tried to attack him. Still, it was not possible to defend a battlefront of four to five thousand kilometers on the Russo-Turkish frontier with a volunteer army of ten thousand Armenians against an invading Turkish army five or six times as large.

Thus, after liberating the northern provinces of Turkey, formerly occupied by the Russians, the Turkish army crossed the 1914 Russo-Turkish frontier and occupied Sarikamish and the surrounding regions.

The Georgian leader Akakii I. Chkhenkeli—head of the Transcaucasian Democratic Federative Republic that had been formed on February 24, 1918—had made a secret agreement with Turkey. Without consulting with the Armenian leaders, he sent a telegram to the commander in chief of the Armenian army, General Nazarbekian. He instructed him to surrender the garrison town of Kars to Turkey without a fight and to withdraw with his troops to Alexandropol, in accordance with the Brest-Litovsk treaty.

General Nazarbekian—who had made Kars his base of operations by assembling all Armenian regular, volunteer, and irregular detachments there—thought that Chkhenkeli must have sent this order to retreat with the consent of the Armenian governmental body. He willingly or unwillingly withdrew to Alexandropol, taking with him hundreds of thousands of exhausted and emaciated Turkish Armenian refugees in their caravans.

The Turks, however, typically disrespected the treaty they had signed at Brest-Litovsk. Not content with their seizure of Kars, under Vehib Pasha, commander in chief of the third Turkish army, they kept advancing, with the objective of taking Etchmiadzin and Yerevan as well—the two historic religious and political centers of the Armenians.

It was Vehib Pasha's goal to destroy the new Transcaucasian Republic—to divide the three nations it comprised and strike them individually. This way the Turks could carry out their plan of pan-Turanic* expansion into the Caucasus, with the help of Caucasus Muslims, particularly the Tatars. First and foremost, however, Vehib Pasha planned to annihilate—or weaken as much as possible—the Armenians of the Caucasus.

Thus to the envoys of the Seim representing the Transcaucasian Republic, Vehib Pasha presented an ultimatum demanding the provinces of Akhaltsikhe, Akhalkalak, Alexandropol–Surmalu, Nor Nakhichevan, and Etchmiadzin.

In the spring of 1918, knowledgable Turks living in Adana were openly declaring, "Just as we annihilated the Armenians of Turkey at the root, we shall destroy the Armenians of the Caucasus and once and for all be rid of the headache the Armenians have caused us for centuries."

Despite the Brest-Litovsk treaty, after only a month (April 22, 1918–May 26, 1918) the demands of Vehib Pasha and the simultaneous advance of the Turkish army caused the Transcaucasian Republic to collapse. Now the Georgians and the Tatars went their separate ways, leaving to their own fate the Armenians hunted by the Turks. On the same day, the Georgians and Tatars declared their national independence—the former in Tiflis and the latter in Baku. Two days later, on May 28, in Tiflis, the Armenians announced the formation of the independent Republic of Armenia.

Ignoring these dramatic political developments, Vehib Pasha seized Kars. Then he proceeded toward Alexandropol and took this large provincial capital, populated entirely by Armenians. Finally he advanced toward the Ararat plain to strike the new Armenian cub in its den: a three-pronged formation of the Turkish army was proceeding simultaneously toward Lori, Karakilise, Etchmiadzin, and Yerevan.

When the Armenian people saw that the Turks were only three hours

*A popular nationalist belief and ideology that the Turks would conquer the Caucasus and Central Asia, reuniting the Turkic peoples there to create a new empire.—trans.

from Holy Etchmiadzin, they rose up as one—men, women, and youths, whoever could find a weapon, grab a stick, or perform some service. They did not wait for an order but rushed instinctively toward the battlefront, only three hours from Holy Etchmiadzin, on the outskirts of Sardarabad, at the foot of Mount Aragats on the Ararat plain. As if obeying the call of their race, they fought a second battle of Avarayr.*

There, under the leadership of Generals Movses Silikian, Daniel-Bek Perumian, and Dro, for four days and four nights, the Armenian people did battle with the Turkish army. Displaying heroic courage, they formed a human bulwark against the Turks' advance toward the ancient sanctuary of Holy Etchmiadzin. Strike followed strike, charge followed charge, until the Turkish army, unable to withstand this valiant popular resistance, was forced to retreat toward Alexandropol.

This epic victory of the second Avarayr inspired the Armenians of Lori and Pambak, following bloody assaults, to repulse the Turks from their mountainous regions. Simultaneously they mounted equal resistance to the third prong of the Turkish army outside of Karakilise.

There the elderly General Nazarbekian, commander in chief of the Armenian forces, defeated the Turkish army. The Turks left the Ararat province ashamed, infuriated, and confused by their failure to annihilate the Armenians—and at being forced to recognize the new Armenian Republic and its small territory of 16,000 square kilometers.

On the plain near Sardarabad, the Armenian people saved their race and their honor.[1]

His Holiness the Catholicos, along with the entire brotherhood of Holy Etchmiadzin, despite all the pressures on them to flee, remained in the Mother See during the four-day Battle of Sardarabad, refusing to abandon the fifteen-hundred-year-old sanctuary.

It is worth noting that the German army of the Caucasus had opposed the advance of the Turks toward Yerevan as a violation of the Brest-Litovsk treaty. The German staff headquarters in Tiflis sent a notice to Vehib Pasha demanding his compliance and threatening to prevent, by force if necessary, the advance of the Turkish army toward Yerevan and Etchmiadzin. In this way the Germans were attempting to atone for their unpardonable sin of being onlookers during the great crime of the extermination of the Turkish Armenians. Also, if the Germans considered the Turkish Armenians to be the enemy, they bore no special antagonism

*The Battle of Avarayr took place on a Persian plain by that name in 451. Here an army of Armenians along with other Christians who rejected forced conversion to Zoroastrianism valiantly fought a Persian army four times its size. The Persians were victorious militarily, and most of the Christians perished. But the Armenians preserved their Christian faith. Afterward the Persian king ceased proselytizing and caused churches to be built.—trans.

toward the Caucasus Armenians, the majority of whose intellectuals had studied at German universities.

While the Turks did not succeed in their radical plan of exterminating the Armenians of the Caucasus, they decimated the Armenians of Kars and Alexandropol in various ways. In 1919, after the Armistice, the Turks made yet another attempt to occupy the Armenian provinces of the Caucasus, this time led by Kazim Karabekir, commander in chief of the northern Turkish army, as we shall see in the next chapters.

The well-known Caucasus Armenian poet and chancellor of the Synod of Holy Etchmiadzin, Hovhannes Hovhannesian, became the voice of the indestructible hopes for the liberation of the Armenian people in the following poem, which he had written in Etchmiadzin in 1912.

We were going together on our way
You, tired, suddenly stopped, disheartened,
And said, "Look, the sky is dark,
It's preparing a fierce storm over our heads."

Let strata of clouds swell, become dense,
Thunderclaps crack, lightning flash on us,
Let us not despair and always proceed undisturbed,
I know, friend, the sun will get us there.

And we arrived, traversed a difficult road,
For a while the golden sun again rose,
But don't be deceived by this short-lived gleam,
Fate shall still place many adversities before us.

Evil rages, gets infuriated,
And we see the enemy face to face,
It is armed and formidable; we, powerless,
And our ranks are thinning day by day.

And it snatches the good ones from us,
And days of grief come as our share,
We are persecuted, we suffer at length,
But we live, this just seed shall not die . . .

Fertilized with the blood of the fallen,
The land will again give fruit, like childbirth,
The hour will come, the storm will cease,
And our sons will earn victory.

27

The Declaration of the Armenian Republic

The great day finally came when, after so much bloodshed, the Armenian people gave painful birth to national independence, thus breaking the rusty chains of 533 years of subjugation. Since 1385, when the Rubenid Cilician dynasty fell, all the succeeding generations had longed to see this day of Armenian liberation; but alas, they had passed on to eternity without seeing it.

Meanwhile the Georgians (who were protected by the Germans) and the Tatars (who were protected by the Turks) had proclaimed their national independence, on May 26, 1918, in Tiflis and Baku, respectively. Two days later, on May 28, 1918, in Tiflis, the leaders of the Armenian people proclaimed the Republic of Armenia.

The Armenian resistance against the regular Turkish army at Sardarabad and Karakilise had forced Vehib Pasha into retreat. But Armenia's success was bitter, for she was a poor country in wretched condition—depopulated, destroyed, and plundered by enemy armies. And the Armenian people of Kars and Alexandropol and its vicinity were so terrified that they sought refuge on the Ararat plain, joining more than 350,000 Turkish Armenians from Van, Bayazid, Erzerum, and Erzinjan who had fled with the Russian-Armenian army. Thus, practically half of the population of the new Armenian republic were refugees. Naturally, a homeless, defenseless, hungry, and wandering refugee population had no lack of epidemics; the people were being decimated by them. Adding to their wretchedness was starvation: the retreating Turkish army had carried off all kinds of farm animals—horses, cows, oxen, and sheep. The fields of the homeland had remained uncultivated, causing the hapless population to slowly waste away.

When the Transcaucasian Republic was dissolved, the Georgians seized almost half the movable and immovable property that the former Russian Empire had abandoned in the Caucasus. A third of it fell to the Tatar republic, while barely one-sixth was left to the Armenian Republic; for example, the new Republic of Armenia got only twenty locomotives, while Georgia and Azerbaijan together seized four hundred.

As for the reserve provisions and munitions stores of the Russian army, most were in Tiflis and so fell into the hands of the Georgians. Furthermore, the geographical position of the Armenian Republic was not favorable for economic development and growth, cut off as it was from the sea and surrounded by Turkey, Azerbaijan, and Georgia—three more or less hostile states. Meanwhile the Georgians were demanding Lori and Akhalkalak, while the Tatars were intent on gaining control of Zangezur and Karabagh [Artsakh (Armenian)]. And at the same time the Turkish and Tatar populations remaining within the boundaries of Armenia, particularly in Nakhichevan, were getting outside encouragement to revolt.

Adding to the complications, the leaders of the new Armenian Republic were inexperienced, shortsighted, and ambitious. Driven by fanatical partisanship, they attempted to control everything by putting incompetent loyalists in ministerial posts.

On June 4, 1918, six days after its proclamation, the Armenian Republic was finally recognized, under German pressure, by Vehib Pasha, supreme commander of the Ottoman army. An armistice* was signed, and Vehib Pasha invited the plenipotentiary envoys of the Armenian Republic to meet in Constantinople on June 11 for peace talks.

Thus on June 19, Avetis Aharonian, Alexandre Khatisian, and Mikayel Papadjanian arrived in Constantinople. And in accordance with Turkish custom, these three plenipotentiary envoys of the newly established Armenian government were put up in the largest Armenian hotel in the Turkish capital, located on the Pera side. They remained there until October 26, 1918, when the Armeno-Turkish peace treaty was signed, whereby Turkey withdrew its armies to within the borders established by the German-Russian-Turkish treaty of Brest-Litovsk.

But a few days later, with Turkey's defeat in the greater conflict, the general truce between Turkey and the Entente powers† created a new situation.

But for now, in Adana, we learned from the Turkish press of the arrival in Constantinople of the plenipotentiary envoys of the Armenian Republic and of the honors paid to them—and the proclamation of the Armenian Republic in the Caucasus. We were overjoyed that such a historic moment had come. We felt blessed that, after millions of Armenian martyrs had died with their eyes open, we had miraculously survived to see this day. The horror of the past four years was evaporating, and we were seeing the realization of our age-old hopes.

*Treaty of Peace and Friendship between the Republic of Armenia and the Ottoman Empire.—trans.

†Mudros armistice.—trans.

28

The Hospital-Slaughterhouse of Turkish Soldiers

Two weeks had passed since I disappeared into Adana [region], and worry began to haunt me. The house I was hiding in was surrounded by the houses of Turks; I was in danger of being seen. I had to flee this situation.

Thanks to a kind Armenian, a master cabinetmaker born in Constantinople but long since settled with his family in Mersin (he had, through bribery, succeeded in remaining in Adana during the deportations), we found a devout family from Kayseri that graciously lodged me for a week, until I could find a suitable hideout.

Despite the general decline in morals with the war, fellow Armenians and their families whom I was fortunate to encounter were always kind, self-sacrificing, compassionate, and friendly to me. Those who had once been thought indiscreet had become discreet; they would come to the aid of a compatriot in danger. I found solicitude and sincere respect in these two Armenian families, such that if I had visited them as the local prelate, they could not have accorded me more.

About three weeks after my disappearance, as the only means of pacifying my conscience, I sent word to my protector Dr. Vartabedian, asking him to pay me a visit. After a fraternal embrace, with tears in his eyes he chastised me:

> My friend, why did you suddenly disappear? What's there to be afraid of? You left us, our entire family, in a state of great anxiety. We thought perhaps that you had committed suicide in a fit of nervousness. I ordered a search for you by the riverbank and among the orchards by the station. After weeks had passed and we couldn't find any trace of you, we simply gave up all hope. I can only conclude that your having been a persecuted fugitive for so long has made you extremely distraught and distrustful. You are suspicious of everybody and everything. Did you begin to distrust

> me too . . . that you should have fled, disappeared without informing me? Did you think that I too would betray you?
>
> After you fled, men came from the railroad company and opened your room; they returned to me the goods I had sent you; the police learned of your disappearance; everybody thought that you had committed suicide; they felt very bad and attributed it to your abnormal mental state . . . There's nothing to be afraid of—come and resume your position . . . Winkler will be returning from Germany any day now. Too bad you left such an enviable position and fled, again subjecting yourself to such an unbearable situation. You've become more paranoid than Sultan Abdul Hamid. I'm not surprised; as a doctor, I'd say that your behavior is the logical result of all the suffering you've endured.

These remarks did not surprise me since the one who is sated cannot understand the condition of the hungry. How can one living free and fearless, who travels about town in his personal carriage, even identify, let alone understand, the seemingly insignificant signs of looming danger? As for suicide, during my three to four years of deportation and suffering, it never even crossed my mind. On the contrary, I was making every effort to live; I was gladly enduring every tribulation just so that one more misshapen column or stone of the destroyed temple of the Armenian people would remain standing . . . so that there would be one more living witness to the Armenian massacres.

Yes, naturally those who did not share that bitter experience were unaware of the mysterious events unfolding around them and were unable to discern the covert activity of the Turkish police. But when one had witnessed how the Turks took the whole nation—from cradled infants to octogenarians—to deserted mountains, valleys, and deserts in order to annihilate them, how could one not be afraid?

Every day my friends were bringing me information of new arrests. Yes, I had become extremely suspicious, not only because of my horrid and bloody experience but also because my only defense against unexpected and disastrous mishaps was my suspicious-mindedness. That is to say, I had come to trust nobody . . . I was detached from everybody . . . even from the most selfless of my friends . . . fearing that some noble friend could become the cause not only of my death but also, unwittingly, of his own.

After seeing the unprecedented events that had shaken and terrified the world, I would have had to be rather incorrigible or perverse to remain optimistic, naïve, and not suspicious-minded. Indeed, every day I was hearing about the tragic end of all those optimists who had wished to be good and sincere . . . but were deceived by the feigned smiles and fraudulent promises of the Turks. Now had arrived the deceptive news of an imperial pardon, whose sole purpose was to bring the Armenians still in hiding out into the open, where they could be arrested and killed.

Thinking *the danger had passed . . . the storm had died down*, hundreds were deceived by the false word being spread that it was all right to come out of hiding; thus they began to move about fearlessly in the towns. The first were purposefully not touched; they were to be decoys, so that others came forward, convinced that all danger had indeed passed. As soon as they did, the secret police identified them, prepared a blacklist, and arrested them all in one night—just as they had done to us on April 24, 1915. Telling them that they were to be exiled to Aleppo, the police took them into the cedar forests of Amanos between Hasanbeyli and Keller and there killed them with sticks and stones. A few whom the police soldiers left for dead washed their bloody wounds in nearby brooks and, walking along roads only at night, made their way back to Adana to tell their compatriots, me included, about what had happened to them. Therefore I had decided not to be seen, and once again I was to live the sleepless life of a fugitive, whom the cat's noise in the dark night fills a man with suspicion, rousing his imagination.

Thanks to my devoted friends, after a lengthy search I finally found Megerdich Arabian, a poor but trustworthy old Armenian whose house was located behind the store called Orosdi-Bach on the grounds of the Adana church. Even though his house faced the houses of Turks, it turned out to be a rather good hiding place. I would stay there for three months, then depart with the members of the household for their vineyard.

From my new hiding place behind the foreign store, I became the unwilling witness of some alarming and frightening things.

The Turkish military had converted this marvelous three-story Orosdi-Bach building into a hospital, which was now filled with thousands of sick Turkish soldiers. The soldiers were brought inside on stretchers that were lined up in long rows, then taken away a few days later, piled one upon the other, in hearses. Maybe 10 percent emerged alive from the hospital-slaughterhouse; with rare exceptions, the merciless sickle of death cut down almost everybody who entered. Resigning himself to fate, the Turkish soldier would say "Whatever fate has in store will be" [*Kader ne ise o olur*].

The Orosdi-Bach building was Armenian property and the site of the old dilapidated St. Giragos church. As soon as the Turkish military confiscated the building, they had removed the marble tombstones from the graves of Armenian clergymen and built a long row of latrines over their bones; the idea, of course, was to desecrate the graves.

The Turkish soldiers, most of them suffering from dysentery, entered the latrines by the dozens, and most of them died there. The dead became so numerous that the military administration prohibited the coming and going of hearses during the daytime; then every night until midnight, from a secret window in my hiding place, I watched the caravans of stretchers, ten, twenty at a time, that the horse-drawn hearses kept transporting. On some days there weren't enough closed hearses, and one-horse carts—usually used to transport manure—ferried the corpses to large pits that had been dug next to the Turkish cemeteries outside of the town.

The Armenian people had been taken to exile in caravans and brutally murdered; now I was watching caravans of dead Turkish soldiers.

Most of the doctors, druggists, and nurses in this hospital were Armenian, and they discharged their humanitarian obligation conscientiously, always careful not to give cause for complaint lest they be persecuted on the merest pretext. But what was such dedicated care worth, when neither medicine nor sufficient nourishment was available? A nurse at the hospital, related to my landlady, used to tell her of the goings-on there.

The Turkish military doctors, she said, separated as they were from their families in Constantinople, had turned the hospital into a den of immorality. They used to sit around with their friends and drink raki. When they got tipsy, the major would order his attendant to go and bring the Armenian nurses. And so the Turkish soldiers would drag in the Armenian nurses, who like snared birds would try to escape—but in vain. There was no limit to the shocking activities that these Turkish doctor-vampires conceived and carried out. As I listened to these stories, my Armenian dignity was racked with unspeakable anguish.

Many of the soldiers lying sick in this hospital reportedly confessed to their Armenian nurses: "It is punishment from God that I killed so many Armenian girls, and now needing help from one, I am asking you for water."

The particular nurse I knew told me that one day a badly injured soldier was brought from the front at Aleppo. The doctors were forced to amputate his legs. He was in tremendous pain, and the nurse compassionately tried to comfort him by wetting his burned lips with a sponge, putting ice on his head, and feeding him soup. Then the solider said with tears in his eyes:

> My sister, I don't deserve your help. Let me die like a dog. If you knew what acts of barbarity I have committed upon Armenian women, you would run away from me. Yes, everybody gets what

they've given. Now that my two legs have been cut off, I understand the meaning of this proverb.

A long catalog of Turkish soldiers made frightful pronouncements of contrition—not to the Armenian military doctors and pharmacists but rather to the Armenian nurses caring for them, and often on receiving no greater kindness than a glass of water.

As an experienced fugitive, I was able to stay here for almost three months, and my only consolation was the Psalms; King Solomon's prayers gave me inexhaustible strength.

> "Lord, how are they increased that trouble me! Many are they that rise up against me. Many there be which say of my soul, There is no help for him in God" (Psalm 3:1–2).
>
> "How long wilt thou forget me, O Lord? Forever? How long wilt thou hide thy face from me? How long shall I take counsel in my soul, having sorrow in my heart daily? How long shall mine enemy be exalted over me? Consider and hear me, O Lord my God: lighten mine eyes, lest I sleep the sleep of death; lest mine enemy say, I have prevailed against him; and those that trouble me rejoice when I am moved. But I have trusted in thy mercy; my heart shall rejoice in thy salvation. I will sing unto the Lord, because he hath dealt bountifully with me" (Psalm 13:1–6).
>
> "Let them be confounded and put to shame that seek after my soul: let them be turned back and brought to confusion that devise my hurt" (Psalm 35:4).
>
> "The fool hath said in his heart, There is no God. Corrupt are they, and have done abominable iniquity: there is none that doeth good" (Psalm 53:1).
>
> "Hear my prayer, O God; give ear to the words of my mouth. For strangers are risen up against me, and oppressors seek after my soul: they have not set God before them" (Psalm 54:2–3).
>
> "Deliver me from mine enemies, O my God: defend me from them that rise up against me. Deliver me from the workers of iniquity, and save me from bloody men. For, lo, they lie in wait for my soul: the mighty are gathered against me; not for my transgression, nor for my sin, O Lord . . . be not merciful to any wicked transgressors, Selah. They return at evening: they make a noise like a dog, and go around the city" (Psalm 59:1–6).
>
> "Reproach hath broken my heart; and I am full of heaviness:

> and I looked for some to take pity, but there was none; and for comforters, but I found none. They gave me gall for my meat; and in my thirst they gave me vinegar to drink" (Psalm 69:20–21).
>
> "O God, the heathen are come into thine inheritance; thy holy temple have they defiled; they have laid Jerusalem on heaps. The dead bodies of thy servants have they given to be meat unto the fowls of the heaven, the flesh of thy saints unto the beasts of the earth. Their blood have they shed like water round about Jerusalem; and there was none to bury them" (Psalm 79:1–3).
>
> "For they have devoured Jacob, and laid waste his dwelling place" (Psalm 79:7).

Oh! These last Psalms especially spoke so much to one's soul, in that blood was spilled like water and there was no one to bury the dead.

Indeed, the human soul is such an inexhaustible fountain of patience and moral power. Knowing how to exalt the faith latent in one's soul with pure conviction suffices to cause mountains to tumble to the sea—as Jesus explained. Moreover, all those who cling to material things and expect everything from them while having contempt for the spiritual life deserve much compassion and pity.

Strengthened through prayer and the inspired reading of the lyrical Psalms, I came to dismiss every danger, grief, and bitterness, taking solace in the fact that all these things are man's destiny in this world full of thorns.

Months passed, spring succeeded winter, and I accompanied this humble and kind family to their vineyard-orchard, thinking that there, an hour from town, I could safely pass the summer. Barely had I arrived at the vineyard, however, when the petty officer assigned to the police soldiers, passing by on horseback, noticed me. Suspecting that I was in hiding, he came to arrest me.

This time I had unexpectedly put the noose around my own neck. After he and I had set out for town, I immediately bargained with him and bought my freedom for fifty gold pounds Now we turned around and went back to the vineyard, sat down together at the dinner table, and became friends.

When I asked the petty officer why he let others go free in exchange for a few gold pounds while demanding such a large ransom from me, he replied, "It simply varies from one person to the next. You look like an educated man; the price is relative to each individual's social position." Thereafter he would often come and visit me, and I was no longer afraid, for if any police soldier were to arrest me, he would put this petty officer in charge of me, and I could securely return to the vineyard.

So the summer went by peacefully and safely, and through secret means

I received letters as well as money and clothing from Constantinople, so I was in need of nothing.

In Constantinople during these days policemen used to go to our house in Scutari Selamiye and ask, "Where perchance is your *vartabed*? There is favorable news about him." Knowing full well that the police wanted only to track me down for capture, my relatives would reply, "We received word of his death. We'd be thrilled to find out he is alive. If we hear anything, we'll let you know."

Because the governor-general of Adana was engaging in wheat speculation at this time, the price of bread rose as high as eighty piasters, depriving poor people of all nationalities of food. Often hundreds of women and girls would wait in front of bakeries for hours with their municipal vouchers, which gave them permission to receive bread. Those who didn't have such vouchers were condemned to go hungry.

I was one of the latter, but Dr. Vartabedian took care many times to send me bread from his home. For my part, I took care not to unreasonably monopolize his bread rations, which were limited. Sarkis Bakalian, a factory owner and a flour merchant, also came to my aid by sending me a sack of white flour. This gift, which cost eighty-five Turkish liras, was a comfort for me. So although some could not buy bread or flour even if they had money, I was relieved of that greatest of worries.

My landlady used to say to me, "There's proof of almighty God's power. Just with your Psalms, the white bread eaten by the governor-general came to your feet."

But the rationed bread resembled anything but bread; it was an indigestible mixture of corn, barley, millet, soil, ashes, straw, and so on. Many illnesses arose among the people because of it. During the war the bread business was one of the most profitable means of illicit gain, and government officials benefited from this black market, which it was supposedly their obligation to control.

After Dr. Vartabedian, my most fervent protector was the noble Sarkis Bakalian, a prudent, taciturn, and humble Kayseri native who secretly took care of many helpless Armenian families. When he heard that a defenseless Armenian woman and her children were hungry, he would immediately give her a measure of flour. Many neighboring Armenian families, whose unspeakable wretchedness I witnessed, appealed to his kindness, and he provided flour to them.

My life in the vineyard-orchard during the summer of 1918, as during the previous summer, revitalized my spiritual and physical powers. Sometimes I was tempted to be photographed, so I might have a personal memento. Even as the summer passed, however, the world war continued with an even more horrible momentum.

Fall came, and the village dwellers—Turks, Armenians, and Greeks—

having laid in winter provisions as best they could, hastened to make their descent into town. I had rendered certain services to the Armenian family that had provided me hospitality; with an ax I had cut down dried-up trees and chopped them into firewood. This pleasant work strengthened my muscles and sinews.

Once the vineyards and orchards were emptied of their occupants, it would not be prudent for me to remain. As we were about to leave, the Turks went about the abandoned vineyards and chopped down the huts, country houses, and cottages, the majority of which were made of wood. Then they loaded the wood onto their carts and carried it away for their winter supply.

Oh, what grief I felt when walking secretly through these abandoned Armenian vineyards and seeing these traces of vandalism everywhere.

We had a few beehives in the vineyard, and during the summer there I used to marvel at the wonderful organization of Mother Nature. Many days I would go and stand in front of these hives, hidden among the grapevines in the depths of the vineyard; for hours at a time, without getting bored, I watched the bees continuously coming and going. With their little feet they collected the sweet-scented pollen from the stamens of a thousand and one kinds of flowers—white, yellow, red, and blue—then brought it to the plank in front of the hive. Here their job was finished, for the bee bringing the nectar of the flower is the worker-porter bee, whereas the honey-making bee is different. The latter, with its front feet, takes the pollen from the feet of the worker bee, goes into the hive, and with the mortar of its saliva, makes honey in previously prepared cells.

Who had taught the bees such division of labor, such clever organization—architects and queen, workers and guard bees? The guard bees stand before the outer door to the hive to prevent foreign, pirate bees from entering the hive and partaking of the winter provisions prepared with such effort. Thus among bees there are also "Turks" that, without working themselves, freely enjoy the just fruits prepared by others . . .

How do these guard bees distinguish the foreign bees from among thousands of lawful entrants? A group of marauders approach the hive, intending to usurp it; the commotion begins immediately. Within and without the hive, the guard bees attack the foreign bees, the battle rages, and the workers return from flitting about in the fields. They must participate in the formidable struggle until the corpses of the attackers are strewn about the battlefield in front of the hive.

Sometimes the hive would be subjected to attack by mice, ants, hornets, wasps, or moles. Unable to hold their own against these more powerful foreign enemies, the poor bees, powerless like us Armenians, would abandon their hive—and also the honey—to the enemy and go off to make a new nest. Indeed, it is something to see armies of tens of thousands of bees flying high in the air led by their queen. When they tire, they descend on a tree to spend the night; all of them stick to their queen, one upon the other, forming a huge swarm.

Experienced beekeepers can hear the buzz of migrating bees from afar; for them, the sound is harmonious music, for the takeover of a hive by a regimen of bees means that a new colony of these industrious workers has been created. At summer's end, if the hive becomes too confining, the new generation selects its own queen and departs the paternal hive to make a new home.

If the observer does not bother the bees, the bees do not harm him. They are very good-natured; they can sit on your hands or your face without stinging. But if you are unaware of the ways of bees and kill one by accident, then the alarm is sounded, and the bees inside and outside the hive will attack and sting you badly.

Who taught the bees to make honey for winter? Who implanted the instinct for organization in these little insects, and who established their division of labor? Who taught them to distinguish the poisonous flowers from those good for making honey? Who taught the ant to work with exemplary discipline and carry its winter stock to its hole? Who taught architecture to the field mouse and the mole, so that they make nests with narrow passages and a back door for escape when the enemy attacks?

Who taught the cuckoo to lay its eggs in the nest of another bird, leaving the care of raising its chicks to the blackbird? Who taught the storks and swallows to pair off faithfully for many years, to migrate in the autumn when the climate is temperate, then return in the spring and find their nests?

Who taught the newborn lamb, barely having entered the world, to get on its feet for the first time, albeit wobbling, and to find its mother's teats and suck milk?

It is possible to multiply these marvelous examples—eloquent proofs of eternal wisdom. Whether Jehovah or God, providence or universal creation, the original atom or the creator atom, in the final analysis an eternal power governs the universe and the myriad celestial and terrestrial bodies, all with mathematical precision—planets, stars, and satellites. Who taught these bodies to revolve around their axes with perpetual punctuality in the infinite universe, then around their respective planets, then around the constellations and their suns? Fortunate is he who reasons with knowledge but concludes with divine faith!

. . .

As the political conditions for us Armenians worsened, I was forced to resort to new cautions. In the last week of September 1918, after my return to Adana from the vineyard, I found refuge in the hut of a poor washerwoman, a native of Kayseri, that was located in town near the Armenian school. The hut consisted of only one room; on top of it stood a cell with wood flooring, suitable for habitation. Hiding out in the basement, sitting on a pile of straw, I used to read the Psalms and Narek,* taking strength and resolve from these treasures. Furthermore, the guardian of my solace was simply prayer, the spiritual person's only bridge to the Creator. I was enduring my abject life with the patience of the blessed Job.

I conceived of a plan to escape to Cyprus, then seriously began to work out the details. I discussed it with a trustworthy Armenian family of military status who were staying in Mersin. But after considering that all previous attempts at escape had miscarried, I changed my mind and abandoned my plan.

29

The Victorious British Army Occupies Damascus: The Battle of Arara

Britain had brought a formidable Anglo-Indian army of half a million to the Dardanelles, yet it had failed to seize the Strait. The high commander of the German army, Liman von Sanders, had ingeniously thwarted their attempts to cross the Dardanelles.

The British had likewise failed in Mesopotamia. In the spring of 1916 their commander, General Sir Charles Townshend, and thirteen thousand Anglo-Indian soldiers had been taken prisoner at Kut-al-Amara. About a year later, they had occupied Baghdad, but only barely, and only because German general Baron von der Goltz, who managed the Mesopotamian battlefront, died of typhoid fever on the Baghdad front in April 1916.

On the Palestinian front, too, the British army had been unable to achieve great victories. At the beginning of the war the plan to occupy

*St. Grigor Narekatsi; see Biographical Glossary.—trans.

Egypt by crossing the Red Sea, which was under Turkish control, had "fallen into the water."* And thereafter the British army had made no significant progress, remaining stuck in the Sinai desert, outside Gaza.

In March 1917, the British army's Egyptian Expeditionary Force, commanded by General Sir Archibald Murray, advanced to Gaza with the objective of seizing Jerusalem, the holy city of the Jews and Christians. The Ottoman army, which was led by General Kress von Kressenstein, defeated Murray's force in late March, and again a month later, when the Egyptian Expeditionary Force took heavy casualties and withdrew.

At the same time the Anglo-Indian Army of the Tigris, under the command of General Sir Frederick Maude, advanced step by step and finally, on March 11, captured Baghdad. General Sir Edmund Allenby succeeded in taking Gaza on November 7 and seized Jerusalem precisely at noon on December 11, 1917, preventing the Turks from plundering the rich monasteries. Only at the last minute did the eldery catholicos of Cilicia, Sahag II, retreat with the Turkish army from the monastery in ravished Jerusalem.[1] Jemal Pasha, the high commander and one of Turkey's ruling triumvirate, scarcely had time to flee, along with his staff.

Thus Jerusalem passed undefiled into the hands of the British army. Among the notable institutions saved from destruction were the apostolic monastery of St. James, the great pride of us Armenians, and the Patriarchal See, with all its riches and antique treasures.

After seizing Jerusalem, the British army organized the existing railway lines, built new ones, and dug artesian wells. Its string of defeats was over: wherever British soldiers set foot, they established themselves so firmly that they were unmindful of possibly having to retreat.

Capturing Arara was the key to defeating the German-led Turkish army.

The Entente powers, particularly Britain and France, had negotiated with Boghos Nubar Pasha, president of the Armenian National Delegation, who had made many promises. At the beginning of 1918 these powers formed an army of four thousand Armenian volunteers. British and French officers trained them for months in Port Said and Cyprus, then transported them to the Palestinian front.

General Allenby had tried many times—as many as eight, according to well-informed sources—to seize the inaccessible heights of Arara, between Damascus and Jerusalem [near Nablus], where the Turco-German batteries were centered. This impregnable elevation, defended by hundreds of cannons, had succeeded in repelling all the successive advances of the British army.

But General Allenby trusted in the moral value of this small volunteer

*An Armenian expression for failure.—trans.

detachment. He was convinced that his Armenian volunteers, small in numbers but inflamed by the spirit of reprisal, would spark his large army of British, Indian, Egyptian, and Arab soldiers, 250,000 in all. With one further effort, he believed, he could push back the Turks.

Allenby situated about half of the Armenian volunteer army on the first line, keeping the last in reserve. In the morning the entire British artillery took aim at Arara. From the sky hundreds of British airplanes rained bombs on the Turco-German artillery, hidden on the heights. But the enemy artillery resisted with heroic force, repulsing the larger British one, just as it had always done in the past. This time, however, the Armenian volunteer detachment was ordered to attack these inaccessible and impregnable heights, with their mighty, modern batteries of Turco-German fire.

When the fearful moment arrived, a group of more than 2,500 valiant Armenians, inflamed with centuries of vengeful feeling, rushed forward. Every Armenian volunteer seemed to feel that the skeletons of more than a million martyred fathers, mothers, sisters, brothers, and children rose up and called on them to take vengeance for their innocently spilled blood.

These valiant Armenians, like those on the plain of Avarayr, moved forward like lion cubs. With hand tools they cut barbed-wire nets protecting Arara's heights and rushed toward the summit. The British and French officers urged caution on the Armenian soldiers but in vain.

The nightingale of Avarayr, in describing the Vartanantz war, had written: "Death is not meaningful death; meaningful death is immortality."*

The Armenians, consumed with love of nation and fatherland, justly hungry for vengeance, and excited by the prospect of meaningful death, attacked in order to achieve immortality. Later, in Cilicia in 1919, Armenian volunteers who had fought at Arara told me about that heroic battle with such passion, I shuddered and considered myself unfortunate for not having fought there.

The Turco-German artillery spewed fire and flames against the brave Armenians climbing up Arara mountain; finding natural protection on its rugged sides, however, they continued rushing toward the summit. Finally they reached the top, where German, Austrian, and Turkish artillerymen met the Armenians with bayonets.

The cannons that had been spewing hellish fire for months now fell silent because the men firing them had fallen. The Arara heights had been taken. British planes signaled the news of this great victory to General Allenby, and the entire British army rushed forward to complete this quite exceptional victory that the Armenian warriors had made possible. In his

*Quoted from Yeghishe, historian who chronicled the Vartanantz War.

daily address to his army, published in newspapers throughout the world, General Allenby extolled the bravery of the Armenian volunteer regiment.

After this victory Damascus fell too, and the victorious British army marched ahead toward Aleppo. Meanwhile the Turkish army of Palestine, in which there were sixteen thousand German soldiers, retreated in panic, practically disbanded.

Justice and right were finally triumphing, and we, the wretched survivors of the Armenian people, still groaning under the bloody Turkish yoke, were filled with hope of imminent salvation. After all, those approaching us with victorious steps were our great allies; the earth-shattering war they waged was a war for justice and right . . . and they were coming to smash the rusty chains of five hundred years of slavery and liberate the Armenian people.

30

The National Vow of the Turks to Exterminate the Surviving Armenians: The General Massacre in Der Zor

In September 1918 the world war was gradually coming to an end. The French general Marshal Louis Franchet d'Espérey defeated the Bulgarian army decisively. In Palestine Allenby's Anglo-Indian army, having beaten the Turkish armies at Megiddo on September 20, now seized the Haifa-Dera railway line. Then on September 21, as its advance continued unimpeded, the British army entered Nazareth and took more than 25,000 Turkish soldiers prisoner. A French naval squadron occupied Beirut, Syria's large port. Damascus, the great city of Syria and the ancient capital of the Muslim caliphs, was taken on September 30.

Day by day the Turkish army was disbanding: as many as 80,000 Turkish soldiers had become prisoners of the British; King Hussein of the Hejaz, who was assisting the British, took 8,000 Turkish prisoners on his own; 360 Turkish cannons were captured; and tens of thousands of wounded Turkish soldiers were being evacuated from the battlefront.

Without opposition, Allenby kept marching toward Aleppo, the largest interior center of Syria and the main station of the Constantinople-Baghdad railroad.

While Generals Allenby and Maude forced the Turkish armies in Palestine and Mesopotamia into retreat, Vehib Pasha's Turkish armies were enjoying cheap victories on the Caucasus front. Their sole objective was to isolate a small, crippled Armenia, so that under the imminent world peace settlement, she would be powerless to make any move, internal or external.

The official reports published daily by the Turkish national information bureau tried to conceal the sad truth, but we could easily conjecture that the Turkish armies were no longer able to resist the mighty pressure of the British and that the end of the war was approaching.

The hospitals of Adana were full of thousands of Turkish wounded, and thousands more were arriving daily. Since the military hospitals here had no more room, they were transported to Konya and other safe cities along the railway line.

At the start of the war the Turkish people, officials and civilians alike, had anticipated a decisive German-Turkish victory over the Entente powers. But now they were realizing that the war was lost. The more they contemplated a peace settlement, the more they feared punishment for the unspeakable crimes they had committed against more than a million and a half innocent Armenians and Greeks. But their fear, instead of making the Turks more prudent and lenient, drove them into a greater frenzy, like the dying bear that fights most fiercely at the end.

The Turks of Adana learned from the Turkish wounded, brought in daily, that the British army had occupied all of Palestine and Syria and would soon take Aleppo. They grew anxious that soon Adana would be occupied too. For ever since the occupation of Beirut, rumors had circulated that the Entente fleet would soon be discharging soldiers at Mersin to take Adana and all of Cilicia.

The Ittihad club in Adana held secret meetings to discuss what to do in case of an enemy invasion. They decided unanimously to deport the remaining Armenians—those who had been given special permission to remain as soldiers or families of soldiers, more than eight thousand in all—by caravans to the wooded mountains and valleys between Sis and Hajin and massacre them there.

Participating in these secret meetings were the governor-general of Adana, Enver's brother-in-law Jemil, and other high-ranking government officials. They made a vow to annihilate all the remaining Armenians so that when the Entente armies entered Adana, there would be no reprisals from survivors.

The Turks even talked to their close Armenian friends* about this secret vow, saying, "We will gladly keep you in our homes, but if the enemy enters the city and attacks us, you must defend us." In short, they expected protection from the surviving Armenians, all of whose loved ones they had murdered.

These bits of distressing news reached my ear by clandestine means, and I became extremely distraught. Our situation was now desperate, and ironic—we were to be murdered precisely when our salvation had arrived, when the Entente armies, the friends of us Armenians, were approaching and our final liberation was coming day by day, hour by hour.

But we had no time for despair; we needed to find a new road to salvation before it was too late and all the sufferings and tribulations we had endured came to naught. I had to completely disappear. I planned to create underground chambers in the house where I was hiding and fill them with a month's provisions.

The news I had heard was no rumor; at the beginning of September 1918 a few groups of Adana's Armenians had been arrested, taken to the mountains and forests of Amanos, and murdered. I abandoned my plan to create underground chambers and hastened to find a new hiding place. Thanks to devoted friends, I found a new place with an Armenian family near the Reji tobacco factories at the end of the Adana-Mersin road.

This family didn't know my identity and thought I was an Armenian teacher who had studied in Europe and been exiled. A few weeks later five elderly Armenian women, relatives of my landlord, came to visit and, curious and compassionate, wished to meet me. They asked my opinion about the escalating political and military events and about how we might avoid this final trap that the Turks had set for us. Following the local custom, the five women sat down in a circle and smoked a *nargile* [water pipe]—it was the first time I had ever seen women smoking such a pipe. And the Armenian women's optimism gave me great satisfaction.

A particularly intelligent one among them had been a teacher, and as we spoke about my situation, she related the following story, as if to console me:

> There is supposedly an exiled celibate priest presently in Adana who, having fled, is being intensely pursued by the Turkish police; he is reported to constantly change location, name, and status, in order to cover his tracks. He is supposedly very cunning; wherever he goes, he gives a new name to the members of the household. In

*Close Armenian friends of Adana's influential Turks would have been the wealthy landowners and international entrepreneurs who could be protected and who also had reason to hope for better prospects under the Kemalists.—trans.

> one place he says he is married; in another he says he is a bachelor. He tells one person that he has many children; to another, he asserts that he was married and his wife died. He tells one person that he is a merchant; he tells another that he's a moneychanger; he convinces yet another that he was the principal of a school in Constantinople . . . In this way, it becomes impossible to track him down. He has supposedly held many jobs and has brought upon himself the hatred and enmity of the Turkish government, particularly Talaat Pasha . . . One time he took refuge in Ayran Baghche, then Belemedik; one day he's German; the next day he's Greek. He spread rumors that he went to Aleppo and fled to Constantinople . . . Oh, charitable God, if only the priest were freed, at least all the miseries and misfortunes would not have been for naught. In the summers, he reportedly goes from one vineyard to another, and makes people think he is a vinedresser.

As this woman recounted my lengthy odyssey with such zeal, I turned pale, deeply disturbed that so many people knew about my life in exile, which I thought I had kept well hidden. Feeling tired, I excused myself and withdrew to my cell, and with my head in my hands, I fell into deep thought. Clearly my secret was public and the odyssey of "the fugitive celibate priest" had passed from mouth to mouth, drawing danger ever nearer. But this was no time for me to be demoralized; I had to find a new solution. As my concern was growing, one day the landlord came to my cell and gave me news of the British occupation of Aleppo. Suddenly he grabbed my hand and kissed it—and I realized that those women were entirely aware of whom they had come to see.

I have never been a believer in fate, always pitying those who hold to it blindly. Muhammad, the Prophet of the Muslims, invented the doctrine of fate to push the Arab populace to war, and he had his Jewish personal secretary write in the Koran:

> If it is decided that you shall die on so-and-so day, in so-and-so place, it's the same whether you go to the battlefront or stay home; death will find you. Therefore, it is better if you go to holy war for religion or *jihad* and become a martyr by dying.

A believer in the doctrine of fate kills, by his own hand, the most powerful inner willpower and drives himself to blind, passive compliance. But whoever believes that *where there is a will, there is a way* can work miracles and make possible the impossible.

During my four dreadful years of exile, what saved me was not an unreserved belief in fate, but rather pure faith in providence. Therefore I had to walk with powerful faith toward final salvation.

By a then inexplicable coincidence, an Armenian youth who had converted to Islam visited me. A native of Marash, he had been deported to Der Zor and was an eyewitness to the large-scale massacre of the Armenians there in the summer of 1915. He had later succeeded in becoming the secretary of the governor of Ras-ul-Ain, winning his confidence with his astuteness and knowledge of languages.

I learned that an Armenian military doctor who often came to visit me had sent this young man to tell me what he had seen. When I saw the doctor's business card, I felt less anxious about this unexpected visit. The doctor, a relative of his, was extremely confident of his discretion and patriotism. This is what this young Armenian man told me about how the remaining Armenian survivors were annihilated at Der Zor.

Der Zor is a city on the banks of the Euphrates River, a six-day journey by camel from Aleppo. The seat of the *mutasarrif*, it is part of the vast desert that extends across southeastern Turkey, Mesopotamia, and Syria. In early 1915 the Ittihad government had decided to exile the entire Turkish Armenian population to Der Zor and have them organize a new homeland there. By July 1915, however, barely 70,000 families—or let's say 350,000 Armenians—had reached Der Zor alive.

The governor at that time was Ali Suad Bey. Belonging to the older generation of Turkish government officials, he was reluctant to carry out the repeated orders for massacre that he had received from Constantinople. On the contrary, he attempted to alleviate the suffering of the Armenian deportees by forming a committee for refugees.

Thanks to Governor Ali Suad, in just a few months some 350,000 to 400,000 Armenians transformed their refugee camp in an arid desert (a half hour from the city of Der Zor) into a country town. Everyone dwelled in tents, and because there were many artisans among them, the neighboring tribes would come and offer considerable sums to learn from the Armenian craftsmen.

This newly established Armenian settlement gradually prospered to such an extent that Turkish officials came out of curiosity from the city to visit. Seeing a tent city with a marketplace, they were astonished, and said to the Armenians they knew: "Brother, what kind of people are you? You've barely arrived here, and you've made this desert bloom."

When Talaat learned of Ali Suad's refusal to massacre the Armenians, and of his humane treatment, he was enraged and immediately dismissed him. He replaced him with Salih Zeki, the Circassian who had been governor of Everek-Fenesse in the region of Kayseri.

In June 1916 the fanatical Zeki arrived at his new post at Der Zor and scattered the Armenian deportees by caravan to the surrounding villages. The desert tribes—nomadic, brigandlike, and half wild—began to chase down, torture, and rob the exiled Armenians, and kidnapping, rape, and murder of girls and women became ordinary occurrences.

Zeki sent hundreds of thousands of Armenians—men, women, girls, and children—to the cities and towns within the jurisdiction of Der Zor: Sisvar, Murat, Shedadiye, Hasishe. He formed bands of *chetes* from Chechens and other nomadic tribes of brigands and ordered them to spare nobody. An order had come from Constantinople, he declared, to "cleanse" the Armenians living in Der Zor once and for all.

These wild *chetes* attacked the unarmed and defenseless Armenians from the start of a feast day in August 1916. The pen is powerless to describe these massacres, which took the lives of more than 160,000 Armenians, irrespective of sex or age. The Murad and Khabur rivers were gorged with the dismembered corpses of tens of thousands. The waters of the Euphrates ran red with blood. Later some of the authors of these cruelties became possessed by the devil, suffered paralysis and blindness, and some confessed: "God punished us; we deserved it." But while a few felt contrite, most of these human monsters boasted of what they had done.

Armenian boys between the ages of three and ten were gathered together by the hundreds and starved for days. Then, to amuse themselves, the killers made them eat human and animal excrement. Finally they murdered them with axes. They filled wells with dozens of Armenian women at a time, or buried them alive in sand, and then danced around them rejoicing.

Governor Zeki personally supervised the massacres in Der Zor in August 1916. Police soldiers, *chetes*, and government officials who saved Armenians—hiding them in exchange for bribes—were subjected to severe punishment by Zeki. So severe was the governor's cruelty that no more than 5,000 Armenians survived this disaster.

Many Armenians were massacred even though they had paid off the executioners. One of these executioners, Agili Sultan Beg, took bribes from 250 rich Armenian families, then murdered them all with axes—and received a promotion from Zeki. Of the more than a million and a half Armenians deported from the Armenian interior provinces during the summer and fall of 1915, some 800,000 were massacred on the roads; 400,000, unable to endure the hardships of the journey, died of hunger and starvation before ever reaching Der Zor. Of the approximately 400,000 Armenians who did reach the deserts of Der Zor and Ras-ul-Ain from August 1915 to August 1916, 250,000 fell victim to starvation. In the late summer of 1916 most of the 150,000 to 160,000 who remained in Der Zor were massacred by the *chetes* organized by Zeki. About 5,000 did miraculously survive, but their ranks gradually dwindled as a result of disease and hunger, so that by the summer of 1918, only 400 to 500 of them were left.

Such massacres also took place in Ras-ul-Ain and its vicinity, and by the time they were over, the sands of Mesopotamia had become an open grave covered with the skulls and skeletons of martyred Armenians. Future Armenian generations must erect a monument[1] on these sands to this martyrdom.

31

Escape from the Land of Blood

I was coming to the conclusion that as long as I was in this land of blood, I was always in danger, and the specter of death would always be before me. But I wished to live.

I wished to live, not for life's frivolous pleasures—to which I had never attached value, even when I was twenty—but rather to gather up the scattered survivors of the shipwrecked Armenian people and build a community anew. I wasn't one of those who shook their heads pessimistically and said, "The Armenian nation is destroyed for good—there's nothing left for us survivors to do."

A poem by the well-known Caucasian Armenian poet Hovhannes Hovhannesian, which was published in his collection of poems of 1912, goes:

You say, brother, that we're waiting in vain,
That our hopes have already been dashed,
That you're hearing the sound of the final storm
And you're seeing the homeland in ruins.

It doesn't look to be in a good state at all
Yet I don't consider it ruins;
I'm not saying that our final hour has arrived,
And that we no longer have a place in this world.

As long as the fire in the hearth hasn't gone out,
The house is still standing, the owner is still alive,

There aren't any flames, but under the cold ashes
The sparks shall yet remain for a long time.

Time will come, we'll gladly give life
And we will kindle the hidden fire . . .
And you will see exquisite mansions,
Where now you see ashes.

All of us on the roads of the Armenian Golgotha and all of us miraculous survivors think as Hovhannes Hovhannesian does—

It doesn't look to be in a good state at all,
Yet I don't consider it ruins;
I'm not saying that our final hour has arrived,
And that we no longer have a place in this world.

The leaders of the British government rightly used to say that whoever has strong and tough nerves will triumph. Like nations, individuals must close their ears to all pessimism and rumors and steel themselves with an invincible will to achieve ultimate salvation.

A century ago the Armenian population of Turkey was barely one million. And in 1828, when the Russian armies under General Ivan Fyodorovich Paskevich seized Yerevan, Holy Etchmiadzin, and the Ararat plain, the Armenian population in the Caucasus was barely 450,000. Thus a hundred years ago the total number of Armenians scattered around the world did not exceed 1.5 million.

A hundred years ago there were only a few hundred Armenian households in Gyumri, which was then subject to Turkish rule. After Russia seized all the southern provinces of the Caucasus from the Persians and Turks, including Erzerum, General Paskevich was forced to vacate the latter in accordance with the treaty.* When the famous prelate Archbishop Garabed Pakradounian departed from Erzerum, he took with him more than 80,000 Armenians, and settled on the plain of Shirak in Gyumri, which was later called Alexandropol after the Russian tsar Alexander I.

The Armenian people of Erzerum chose Gyumri as their new homeland because, like the plain of Erzerum (1,800 meters above sea level), the plain of Shirak (about 1,350 meters above sea level) has a cool climate and is a historic granary.

There is therefore no reason to despair over the existence of the Armenian nation when, after such horrors and massacres, the number of

*Treaty of Adrianople, 1829.—trans.

Armenians living all over the world will probably again reach 3 million before long.

Consider that in less than a hundred years the number of Armenians in Russia quadradupled from 450,000 in 1828 to 1,870,000 by 1914. But in Turkey, over the course of a hundred years, the Armenian population of 1 million had managed only to double, more or less—because the government had tried to contain it by massacre. Therefore, despite the present tragic situation, I was viewing the future of the Armenians in this more positive way.

Moreover, in contrast to the horror of the last centuries, we now have to have an independent Armenia, where the people, known for their creativity and skill as builders, could assemble, grow, develop, and using their hands, make Hovhannesian's song a reality.

And you will see exquisite mansions,
Where now you see ashes.

This was my state of mind, and with the self-confidence and the masculine vitality befitting an Armenian man, I resolved to go from Adana to Switzerland.

When my friend Dr. Vartabedian learned of my plan to flee, he said, "Up to this point you have conceived so many plans, made preparations, and carried them out successfully. So I believe that this plan too will succeed because of your invincible will, your fearlessness, and your resolution."

When I asked him to lend me fifty gold pounds in paper money, he replied:

> This plan of yours won't work with fifty; I'll give you two hundred in paper money. Your life is valuable to us. Don't think about money. Just see to it that you succeed, and this time don't forget that these are the final cards you are playing.

In August 1920, during the trial following the assassination of Talaat, I traveled to Berlin, not only to save Soghomon Tehlirian [his accused assassin] but also to prove the fact of the Armenian massacres in a German court.* I was given about forty minutes to relate what I had seen and what

*Talaat Pasha, like many high-ranking Young Turks, fled to Germany after the Armistice. He was assassinated in daylight on a Berlin street by a young Armenian man who shouted, "This is to avenge the death of my family" when he pulled the trigger.—trans.

I knew, in the presence of a large courtroom full of people of all nationalities, and especially Turks, including the widow of Talaat, chief executioner of the Armenians.

A grieving Armenian woman, Mrs. Terzian, who had walked the bloody roads of the Armenian Golgotha, and an Armenian clergyman wrapped in his black cloak came forth in this Palace of Justice in Berlin as eyewitnesses to the annihilation of the Armenian race. When criminal Turks tried to obstruct the trial, they got caught in a downpour of spit, disparaging remarks, and curses—even from their allies and friends the Germans.

The German judges acquitted Soghomon Tehlirian, who represented just vengeance on behalf of the Armenians; there was general applause in the court, demonstrating that there are fair judges in Berlin.

Having made the decision to flee Adana for Switzerland, I wanted to make sure that I had planned for the small details as well as the larger ones, and fortunately, my noble and generous friend Dr. Vartabedian had promised me all sorts of material and moral assistance. During the period of my employment in management of the Adana railroad construction, I had had the chance to get to know Levon Kurkjian, an Armenian painter who had lived for many years in Paris, attaining fame and also winning the appreciation of prominent European artists.

For his professional work he came to Cilicia, and when the war broke out suddenly in 1914, he was forced to remain here and thus was saved from the fatal roads of exile. Noble and self-sacrificing, this fine artist became a very close friend, and an inseparable bond of love and compassion grew between us. He had been a willing companion in my pain and grief—even in my most miserable days he had visited my hiding places to comfort me.

One time in the spring of 1918, when the homes of Armenians were being searched and those in hiding were arrested, exiled, and killed, Kurkjian inquired about my perilous situation. He then requested moral support for me from Sarkis Bakalian. This other self-sacrificing and generous friend sent word to me through Kurkjian that I was not to fear if I were arrested; he was ready to give a bribe of two thousand gold pounds to secure my release.

As a factory owner and supplier of flour to the Ottoman army, Bakalian had great influence with the governor-general and genuine friends among the other Turkish high officials. I had no doubt that if I were arrested, he could help me. Kurkjian went to see Sarkis Bakalian, and he brought me a hundred Turkish pounds for my flight to Switzerland. Dr. Vartabedian also contributed a hundred gold pounds, and with two hundred gold pounds at my disposal, I already considered my plan a success. Then Bakalian invited the central stationmaster of the Adana railroad to my hiding place, and all the necessary arrangements were made for me to reach Kara Punar by rail.

By means of secret correspondence, I had negotiated with Onnig Postajian, vice-treasurer of the Belemedik railroad administration, receiving assurance that upon my arrival in Kara Punar he would assist me in all ways possible. Onnig was just twenty years of age and a most selfless and patriotic young man, the worthy son of a renowned family from Rodosto. His parents had managed to stay in Konya while he had come to Belemedik, like others, to find work, and owing to his good character and moral upbringing, everyone liked him; in a year's time, he had risen to the extremely important position of vice-treasurer.

As I mentioned in Chapter 18, Onnig Postajian and Sebouh Sayabalian were the very spirit of exiled Armenian youth, and they helped any countrymen who turned to them. Their assistance to me in this last flight was invaluable, and I must sadly note that Onnig Postajian is no longer among the living, having died of an unrelenting disease in the autumn of 1921.

Now everything was meticulously arranged. The closer I got to my day of departure, the more all the events preceding and following my original arrest crossed my terror-stricken mind like a motion picture. At six-thirty P.M. on the evening of Saturday, April 24, 1915, I had been eating supper with my mother, sister, brother-in-law, and nephews in our house in Scutari Selamiye. Suddenly there was a knock on the door, and one of my nephews came to tell me that the neighborhood Armenian *muhtar* was at the door and wished to see me. I sent my brother-in-law to inquire the reason, and he returned saying that the *muhtar* wished personally to convey important information to me. So I went to the door, and the *muhtar* said with the detachment befitting his position, "The neighborhood chief of police wishes to see you for a little while. Come, and you'll be able to return soon." Yes, let's say we were to go and come back . . . but how? . . . And by what route?

Instinct told me that I was leaving my family abode for the last time, and so I asked my brother-in-law to hide the items under my pillow and put my books somewhere safe. In particular, I asked him to guard my study *Kanonagir Hai Yegeghetsvo* [Canons of the Armenian Church] as a sacred legacy. Through a comparative study of parchment manuscripts, I had been collecting all the valid canons of the Armenian Church, which had come to us by decision of the apostles, holy fathers, universal councils of the Christian church, and Armenian ecclesiastical assemblies. I had been preparing this study with the encouragement of Adolf Deissman, one of my professors at the University of Berlin. A serious scientific study of its kind did not exist—that is, one that would distinctly classify a complete collection of the canons dealing with rituals, divorce, administration, punitive measures, worship, and so on, each in its own chapter. Each canon would contain an annotation indicating which article it was of which ecclesiastic council. I had distinguished the valid canons from the invalid ones and given historical and comparative data about all those set by the Apostolic Universal and Armenian ecclesiastical councils. My spiritual father, His Grace Yeghishe Tourian, had considered the completed book an innovation in its genre and had expressed the wish to write the preface.

In Chankiri I had written a study *Hai Endanik* [Armenian Family] about the external and internal reasons for the dissolution of the Armenian family and the increasingly frequent incidence of divorce. This book, which I completed at the time of my second exile from Chankiri in February 1916, I entrusted to the Armenian landlady of the house in which I was residing. Since these people were deported after my exile, however, this book was probably lost too.

A carriage sent by Dr. Vartabedian took me to the station. I was quite relaxed, like an ordinary traveler, and arrived there at five-thirty in the morning. By prior arrangement, my coachman went to inform the stationmaster, who hurried the train master—an Armenian—to meet me. This employee took me by an indirect route to a railroad car far from the station platform.

The farther one is from danger, the more one is afraid; when one is already in danger, there is nothing left to be afraid of. The same is true of death. When death waits in ambush far off, one is afraid, terrified . . . but when one comes face-to-face with it, one no longer fears.

The railroad car moved to the front of the station platform. At that moment the Armenian employee came running and said: "The Turkish policemen are searching every car. I beg you to climb into this trunk until the train departs. And if they find you, don't give my name. Say that you've come here on your own—otherwise I, too, will be a goner." I replied, "For almost four years now, nobody has been endangered on my account. Fear not—I won't give your name; I'll take responsiblity." Then I calmly got into this large wooden trunk, which could have accommodated two sitting down. A half hour later the men came with good news: the danger had passed, and I could come out of my trunk. I stretched out and took a deep breath. From the train window I saw the plains of Cilicia rushing by, with women harvesting cotton, the reapers of autumn.

Then we were in the tunnels, gradually climbing toward the Taurus gorges, and we made a half-hour rest stop outside of Dorak. Our train was on the first wide track, which went directly from Adana to Bozanti; the opening through the mountain for it had been newly completed. From Adana we arrived at Belemedik, and after a short stop, the train reached Kara Punar.

Only a half hour after the train's arrival, my car was transferred to the track in use, and an Armenian employee approached me and said, "Very Reverend Father, don't be afraid. Get off and follow me, but from a distance. Onnig Postajian and Bariur Hamamjian are waiting for you behind the station."

A few minutes later I entered Stationmaster Hamamjian's private room and embraced those two self-sacrificing young men who were waiting to help me continue my journey free and safe. Train schedules in wartime were not regular, but we had a one-hour break. The three of us concluded that it was safest for me to travel as a German, and so I secured a German soldier's uniform.

When I put it on, I was transformed. Through the intercession of Armenian employees, the German major supervising the railroad shipments had arranged the details of my escape. He recommended that I become the traveling companion of two other German soldiers departing for Germany. He wrote in our orders: "Three German soldiers are permitted to travel to Constantinople."

An open car was made available to us because we said we had a large broken-down hot-air stove that we were taking to Constantinople for repair. Now, we had only to wait on the platform for the train to come.

32

The Disguised German Soldier Toward Constantinople: The Longing of a Mother

The railroad train was proceeding across deserted plains. Nowhere on roads nearby or distant did we see any hustle and bustle—or any movement whatsoever. Our train, despite being an "express," was moving slowly because the shortage of coal made it necessary to fire the locomotives with wood from the cedar forests of the Taurus and Amanos.

The German soldiers with whom I was traveling were marveling at the fertile black soil of the far-flung Konya plain. As it was autumn, you could see the vineyards with their grape-laden vines, and the fruit trees loaded with fruit. The redness of the apples was causing the poor soldiers to salivate, for in the deserts of Mesopotamia they had seen no fruit.

We had become friends and were speaking about all topics pertaining to the war, especially the annihilation of the Armenian people. These Germans had socialist views and were extremely critical of the continuation of the war, convinced that Germany had lost and that to continue meant only more dead. Having fought beside Turkish soldiers in Palestine and Mesopotamia, they were also Turcophobic; there had been not only internal squabbles, but many times Turks and Germans had drawn their weapons on each other.

When I related what I had witnessed of the tragedy of the Armenian people, they expressed sincere compassion. Every time I alluded to the danger that might befall me, they assured me with righteous indignation that they would defend me with weapons if necessary. Our relations gradually became so cordial that they even promised to ensure my escape from Constantinople to Europe by obtaining for me the official papers of a German soldier.

We reached Konya without incident, as if on a pleasure trip. We were forced to stay there for almost eight hours because there was no locomotive available to change for ours. Taking advantage of the moment, I invited the two German soldiers to tour the city, do some shopping, and have a bite to eat. After we wandered for more than an hour, we were tired and so went to a large café, which I noted was full of unemployed Armenian exiles. Here I also encountered Constantinople Armenians of old acquaintance and a few teachers.

Two Armenian exiles, sitting quite close to us, were speaking softly about family matters. Suddenly one of them said bitterly to the other:

> Brother, I'd give anything to be in the shoes of these three German soldiers. The world is theirs; they can do anything they want. They've got all of Turkey in the palm of their hand, and they're crushing and squeezing it. They've got it made; they're happy; neither have they experienced exile, nor have they been out of work and hungry. They don't know what persecution is. Oh, if only we knew their language and could speak with them.

The other responded:

> They're Germans, aren't they? They deserve to die. After all, wasn't this detestable race responsible for our annihilation? It wasn't the Turks' idea to carry out deportation. It was the Germans who gave this idea to the Turks. If only they would receive a sound beating from the Allied powers, then my heart would cool off, and they, in turn, would come to their senses.

If they could only have known that one of the German military men sitting next to them was not a happy-go-lucky soldier but a fugitive Armenian celibate priest. When the German soldiers asked me what they were saying, I replied, "They're praising Germany."

After a stroll of a few hours in town, we returned to the station, and I gave each of my two comrades an amber smoking pipe as a memento. I approached the water pump to fill my brass canteen and saw two Armenian lads there. One said to his buddy: "Krikor, if you ask me, I'd say that the big guy among these Germans looks like an Armenian. Perhaps he's an Armenian deserter who's dressed like a German and fleeing to Constantinople. If only we could be like them and escape to Stambul." His buddy replied, "Hey, are you crazy or what? The Germans would never give a soldier's uniform to an Armenian. If it were up to them, they'd kill us before the Turks could. That guy doesn't resemble an Armenian at all. Just look at his eyes—they're blue." Besides, what Armenian could pull off such a stunt? During my entire journey from Adana to Constantinople, only this Armenian lad was able to see through my disguise.

In the evening, with a new locomotive finally ready, our train headed toward Kutahya and Eskishehir. At the Kutahya station, having a two-hour layover, we again went for a walk about town.

Konya had had barely 400 Armenian households before the war, but as the city had become a central refugee settlement, it was now densely populated, with almost 25,000 Armenians. Kutahya, on the other hand, was totally emptied of Armenians. Although many had been fortunate enough to avoid deportation at first, in the third year of the war most were driven toward Konya and Aleppo. Now half the stalls, shops, and stores were closed.

So it was in all the principal cities where we were forced to stop for an hour or two. We would disembark and roam around, and I would try to get a feel for the local situation. Forced to change trains in Eskishehir, we spent the night in a hotel.

The following morning we emerged into this historic city of volcanic white stone. Strolling about the city, I saw ten- to fourteen-year-old Armenian refugee boys going around selling bread, fruit, tobacco, vegetables, and so on. Then we departed Eskishehir, and the train passed Bilejik and Adapazar without stopping. We paused for an hour at Izmit, where a considerable number of Turkish travelers boarded for Constantinople.

We skirted the Gulf of Izmit and the shores of the Sea of Marmara, which were alternately rocky and verdant. The calm silvery Sea of Marmara, the clear blue sky, the intermittent splash of little waves, and a lovely autumnal sun had such a soothing and invigorating effect on me that for a while I forgot my exile state, my disguise, and everything.

But then all of a sudden memories of those horrible first days—of April 25–27, 1915—came back to me. Then we had traveled this same route toward Chankiri. Then too I had paid attention to the marvelous beauty of nature reawakening for spring, as Armenian intellectuals sat next to me, faced me, had been all around me, packed in rows; their heads had been down, and they were restless, sullen, and demoralized. The majority were now dead, and I was headed back to Constantinople, recalling them with deep sorrow.

My mother's face appeared before my eyes, and I wondered if I would be able to reach home safely and embrace her and say, "Mother, God heard your pious prayers, and behold—your lost child, resurrected from the dead, has returned to embrace you."

The train was now racing, but the closer we got to Haydar Pasha station, the more the clouds of danger tormented my mind and soul. Several times those going to and coming from Constantinople had said that there were Armenian spies, and that their leader, Artin Megerdichian, the detestable *muhtar* of Beshiktash, would be at the Haydar Pasha station. Like hunting dogs, they were searching for fugitives from the provinces. What if Megerdichian was there and recognized me?

I made final arrangements with the two Germans, who promised that the official German military papers that I needed would be ready four days after our arrival in Constantinople. Then we would depart together from the Sirkedji station, hopping onto the Constantinople-Berlin express.

I had told these German soldiers that I was going to Berlin, but my real intention was to remain in Bulgaria, specifically Philippe, from which—with the assistance of Armenian friends I knew well—I could depart for Switzerland.

Outside of Pendik I saw Turkish policemen drag a young Greek lad out of a wagon filled with wheat and beat him. He had managed to reach Pendik hiding in the wheat. Finally, six days after our departure, at four P.M. on Sunday, September 25, 1918, our train arrived at the Haydar Pasha station.

As at all the principal stations on our route, here too a German officer examined our papers before allowing us to pass. I could not have imagined that coming to Constantinople would be such an easy thing.

As my two German soldier companions and I passed in front of the station, we encountered two Armenian friends of old acquaintance returning with their families from their Sunday outing . . . I recognized them immediately, but it did not occur to them that the person passing them was the exiled clergyman whom they knew well and who they, like many, thought was dead. The large hat, unique to colonial soldiers, covered half of my face, making me unrecognizable.

The hours passed quickly. We three German soldiers, our hearts at ease, were freely roaming the quays of Kadikoy and Haydar Pasha. A multitude of people of all nationalities came and went, enjoying their Sunday in the clear autumnal weather, as though they were not living in wartime.

We had decided to take the last steamship from Haydar Pasha wharf and spend the night at a German military base in Pera. After finding a refuge in Constantinople, it was my aim to prepare my false papers for departure to Europe in a few days' time. But prior to leaving Constantinople, I wanted to see my poor mother, who had been anxiously waiting for the past four years for my return. But in order not to endanger my relatives, I had resolved not to remain in Constantinople or take refuge in our house.

We had gone as far as the entrance to the Haydar Pasha wharf and were about to board the steamship when I could go no farther. To the two German soldiers, I said, "Go, prepare my papers. I'll come and find you at noon on Thursday. I am going home to see my mother . . . If I don't come on Thursday, you'll know that I have been arrested." They took my address in case it became necessary to search for me, then boarded the steamship headed for Galata.

My longing for my mother made me take leave of my companions. She would have shed many tears since my exile and prayed much for my safety, I knew. How could I have walked by the door to her house without embracing her? I adored her—she had always been my pillar of strength in difficult moments. She was the head of the family, with her six children and fourteen grandchildren. I was proud to have such a mother, a model Armenian woman: patriotic, pious, loving of her children, extremely fond of learning, she had been the driving force for her children and grandchildren to receive college and university education.

She was the daughter of the much celebrated and wealthy Huesisian family of Shabin Karahisar and Tokat. In 1906 the well-known writer Melkon Gurdjian had described her in a special article sent from Kastemouni to the *Puzantion* newspaper. Her charity had become famous throughout Scutari; anyone afflicted or destitute would run to Diramayr.*

*Armenian word meaning "mother of a priest" here.—trans.

Everybody, especially wretched Armenian women, knew that Diramayr would not leave them in the lurch; she would have them sit by her side, and she would listen compassionately to their lengthy stories. She used to spend most of the money given her by my older brother to help the needy, even if it meant depriving herself. She would prepare dowries for poor girls, find suitable men and arrange their marriages, and then be made godmother to their newborn children.

Many times she would seek my intervention to protect individuals who had been wronged. And often I would have to fight and argue with my fellow Armenian officials in order to get them to redress an injustice. I did this gladly for my mother, for I was certain that she was on the side of justice. I not only loved her but idolized her, in the secular sense of the word. How could I have buried my longing throughout four years of suffering and gone to Europe without seeing her?

I sat in seclusion by the seashore and waited for darkness to fall. At about nine P.M. I set out for Scutari. It was already dark, and the gaslights were not lit, so there were no pedestrians in the streets.

The German soldier, with firm steps, proceeded past the marvelous building of the medical university of Haydar Pasha, then through the Turkish graves amid cypress trees, where, one could well say, deathly tranquillity and silence prevailed. Not only were the gaslights in the streets unlit, but I saw no light in any house; though it was barely nine-thirty, and there were only one or two faint lights in each street. Because of the war, kerosene had become so scarce and expensive that it was not possible to burn lanterns. Sometimes I caught sight of shadows moving behind the windows of houses, especially in the Christian neighborhoods.

At the military guardhouse on the Haydar Pasha and Scutari road, the guard soldier was making his rounds with an air of indifference. Then I came to the Armenian cemetery. Two roads forked in front of me. The short one would take me directly from Selamsiz to Ajibadem, passing the guardhouse of the same name; if I took it, however, suspicion could be raised, since our house was only a few feet from that guardhouse. Therefore I took the dusty Ijadiye road as far as the Jewish neighborhood, then went on to Selamsiz; from there I would be practically facing our house.

Amazingly, at ten P.M., there was a light on in the lower room, and the curtain was half open. Although my mother regularly went to bed at nine P.M. she was still sitting in front of the window. Was I dreaming? I couldn't believe my eyes. To think that I could come home and see my mother! I was moved to tears from my happiness. But considering her heart condition—my sudden appearance could be dangerous for her—I went first to my older sister's house, which was on the same street.

Climbing up the five marble steps to the front door, through the window I saw my brothers-in-law, my sisters, and my four or five nephews, and to my surprise I could hear them talking about me. I knocked softly on the windowpane, and one of my nephews, a soldier, came to the door. Thinking that I was a lost German soldier, he asked me in French what I wanted.

"Onnig!" . . . "Oh, my uncle . . ."

While we were overcome with emotion, crying and kissing each other, inside they were wondering why my nephew had not come back into the room. One by one they came out; then they were all gathered around me. They rained questions upon me, as they were impatient to hear my story. Meanwhile I was impatient to learn what had happened here since my arrest.

Our questions overlapped. Tears of joy had succeeded bitter tears of grief and anguish. But we were all infected with the dread of tomorrow. Everybody was stupefied by my audacity, surprised and amazed at my odyssey, however abbreviated my account of it. Then I told them that in four days, on Thursday, I would be departing by train for Europe.

All this seemed like a dream to them, and they too thought they were seeing an apparition. When they told me that immediately after my arrest the Turkish police had come and conducted a thorough search, taking all my books and manuscripts, including my *Kanonagir Hai Yegeghetsvo* [Canons of the Armenian Church], I was heartbroken.

With amazement they told me that just fifteen days earlier my mother had said to my sisters and nephews: "My son is making preparations to come to Constantinople." She always saw, with the eyes of her soul, what state I was in, and she often doubled her hours of prayer to enjoy my presence. Rising before dawn, she would go to the parlor to be alone and pray. "My son is again going through extremely difficult days; he's beset with dangers. If I can't do anything else, at least let me come to the aid of my poor child through prayer . . . May the dogs not kill my poor boy." God had heard her tearful prayers. How was it possible not to believe in this miracle?

At midnight I returned to our house. I couldn't sleep; I was thinking about my mother the whole night, and every footstep in the street gave me the illusion that policemen were coming to arrest me again, filling me with fear.

When morning came, my mother came out of her bedroom, and my sister, greeting her, gave her the good news: "Mother, a secret letter came last night from the Holy Father that my brother will be coming to Constantinople in a few days in order to go to Europe." And my mother, quite perturbed, replied, "My daughter, why are you deceiving me? My son is here. Why are you keeping it a secret from me?"

Finding it impossible to wait for the conclusion of my sister's preparatory ceremony, I emerged from my room and embraced my mother.

"Mother."

"Oh, my sweet child!"

33

Armistice: The Allied Fleet Victoriously Enters the Turkish Capital

In the spring of 1918 the tide of war was gradually turning against Germany, especially as the United States had entered on the side of the Entente powers. The United States brought an endless supply of manpower, money, and matériel to the Allied cause. Germany, on the other hand, was undergoing extreme hardship, especially with manpower and food supplies.

Thus, by the autumn of 1918 the war was approaching its end.

On the Western Front, the Allied victories at Saint-Mihiel, September 12–15; in the Meuse Argonne offensive, which began September 26; and at Ypres and Cambrai, September 28, were forcing the Germans to retreat. More than a quarter of a million prisoners, about ten thousand cannons, and many military stores fell into Allied hands.

On September 25, in a rapid advance, the commander in chief of the Entente armies, Marshal Ferdinand Foch, reached the banks of the Rhine. Meanwhile on the Western Front, day by day the Entente armies forced Germany and its allies into retreat. In the Balkan theater as well, General Franchet d'Espérey, the superior commander of the united French, Serbian, and Greek armies, attacked and seized Zovik, Stravena, Cherna, Perlepe, Manastir, Strumnica, Kochana, and Iskub, condemning the Bulgarian army to dissolution.

Because of the pressure the Entente armies exerted in the Balkans and their brilliant victories, ninety thousand soldiers from the Bulgarian army were taken prisoner, and two thousand cannons and extensive spoils were captured. Having no recourse, on September 26 Bulgaria sent General Georgi Todorov to Franchet d'Espérey to engage in negotiations, and the

Bulgarian armistice was signed in Salonica on September 29. With this truce, the line of communication between Turkey and Germany was finally cut.

Now separated from Germany and with all hopes of resupply lost, Turkey was condemned to follow Bulgaria's example. General Allenby, the senior commander of the Anglo-Indian army in the theaters of Palestine, Syria, and Mesopotamia, had crushed the Turkish offensive and, with about half a million soldiers, wiped out the remaining survivors of the eroding Turkish forces in Syria.

Now the ruling cabinet of Talaat-Enver-Jemal was forced to resign, and Sultan Mehmed VI turned over the premiership to the elderly Tevfik Pasha, who had held it many times before and whom the British considered trustworthy. The new premier sent the new minister of the marine, Reouf Pasha, together with the British general Townshend, who had fallen prisoner in Kut-al-Amara, to the British admiral Sir Arthur Calthorpe, to request a truce. About a month after the Bulgarian surrender, on October 30, 1918, an armistice with fourteen articles was drawn up in Mudros under the supervision of Admiral Calthorpe, supreme commander of the Entente fleet. According to this armistice, Turkey surrendered unconditionally, turning over to the Allies its capital city, the Dardanelles and Bosphorus straits, and all war matériel and weapons, as well as the administration of the railroads and the remnants of its fleet.

At the same time, the former ministers responsible for Turkey's destruction, Talaat, Enver, and Jemal, who were being held in detention, saw that the Entente fleet was soon to enter Constantinople and that the time of reckoning had come. They managed to escape by sea to Romania, and in disguise, they went from there to Berlin, where they lived to enjoy their immense booty.

After the world war Turkey lost all of Arabia, with 441,000 square kilometers and 1.8 million inhabitants; Mesopotamia (the provinces of Basra, Baghdad, Mosul, and the separate *sanjak* of Der Zor), with 448,000 square kilometers and 1,141,200 inhabitants; Palestine, with 18,000 square kilometers and 350,000 inhabitants; Syria and Lebanon, with 200,000 square kilometers and 2,750,000 inhabitants. In total Turkey lost 1,108,100 square kilometers and 6,041,200 subjects.

Thus Turkey was reduced to the territory of Asia Minor and the province of Adrianople [Edirne], not to mention the eastern provinces, whose fate had yet to be determined; all together it retained 702,300 square kilometers, and a population of approximately 10 million, according to the prewar statistics of 1914. But in 1918, after the Armistice, official Turkish announcements reported that scarcely half that population number existed—approximately 4.5 million were lost during the war, 2 million of whom were Armenians, Greeks, Syrians, and other Christians, and 2.5 million of whom were Muslims—soldiers, refugees, and victims of epidemic and starvation.

Four days before the signing of the October 30 armistice at Mudros, the Anglo-Indian armies seized Aleppo, and the Turks left tens of thousands of prisoners and many spoils to General Allenby. Four days after the signing, the Entente army, which contained well-trained Armenian volunteers under the command of French officers, occupied all of Cilicia, resulting in unprecedented euphoria among the Armenian survivors worn down from suffering.

Meanwhile the powerful Entente fleet swept the Dardanelles for mines, completing the job in ten days. All the dailies in the capital then reported that the united Entente fleet would enter Constantinople on November 13.

In Germany, as well, events were escalating rapidly, hastening its surrender and that of its allies. On September 29, 1918, the day of the truce with Bulgaria, the cabinet of imperial Germany tendered their resignations. On October 5 the new prime minister, Prince Max of Baden, proposed a general truce with America. Revolution was breaking out in Germany; the kings of Bavaria and Württemberg fled, and the former kingdoms of imperial Germany struggled to form a republic.

On November 6 Germany's plenipotentiary envoys, Matthias Erzberger, Captain Ernst von Salow, and General von Grünnel, presented themselves for negotiations with Marshal Foch. On November 8 the arrogant German Kaiser Wilhelm, the person truly responsible for this bloody war, abdicated the throne together with his son, the crown prince, and fled in terror to Holland. Germany proclaimed itself a republic, and the Armistice for this unprecedented war was signed on November 11, 1918, in the Compiègne forest in Picardy.

On November 13 the Entente fleet, consisting of forty-two large and small warships, passed through the Dardanelles Strait toward the Turkish capital.

As for me, having arrived in Constantinople on September 26, I was preparing to depart for Europe four days later; but the very same day the morning papers reported the unexpected Bulgarian truce. One didn't need to be a politician, diplomat, or strategist to see that this separate Bulgarian peace would bring a general armistice.

Therefore, postponing my departure, I began to write my memoirs. Hiding sometimes in our home and sometimes in my sister's home, I wanted to write the present history of the Armenian Golgotha while so many tragic and criminal episodes of the Armenian martyrology that I had experienced directly or heard directly from eyewitnesses were fresh in my memory.

While putting the outline of my memoirs in order, I anxiously followed daily events. No one knew of my return to Constantinople. But when the newspapers reported that the Entente fleet would be entering Constantinople on November 13, I put my pen aside to witness this momentous historical event. I felt I had the special privilege of sitting in the first rows of spectators welcoming the united Entente fleet. Like many, I believed that it represented the marvelous triumph of justice and right, and that henceforth we would be saved from the clutches of despotic governments.

Despite my elated feelings, I remained suspicious, exercised caution and prudence, and avoided indiscreet actions. Therefore I put on my black redingote, which I had brought from Berlin in 1914, and a top hat before I descended from Scutari to Kuzgunjuk. Knowing that if I were to go on to Beshiktash by steamboat I would run into many Armenian acquaintances, I preferred to cross the Bosphorus in a small boat.

The Turkish boatman, thinking that I was an Armenian doctor and hoping that I would commiserate with him, said:

> *Effendi*, what bad times we're living in! What black days we have fallen upon! Talaat and Enver have destroyed the fatherland, picked up and fled, and left us to our fate. Who would have believed that a foreign fleet would enter Constantinople so illustriously and that we Muslims would be simple spectators?

Spontaneously, and against my will, I tried to comfort him, saying, "These black dogs will pass too; don't worry."

As soon as I landed at the quay of Beshiktash I hurried up to Pera, and to Taksim by carriage via Gazhane, to watch from the hill on which the German embassy was located as the Entente fleet entered the Bosphorus. Indeed, the panorama was unique. Twenty-two British, twelve French, and ten Italian and Greek—all together forty-four—large and small warships of all kinds, with columns of smoke rising from their smokestacks, made a triumphant procession from the Marmara to the Bosphorus. The large British dreadnought leading this powerful fleet, HMS *Agamemnon*, with Admiral Sir Arthur Calthorpe on board, was coming to drop anchor in front of the imperial Dolmabahche Palace in Beshiktash.

There several ships separated; some anchored before Haydar Pasha and others in the open waters of Aya Stefano. Another group of torpedo boats stopped in front of Saray-Bournou [Palace Point], while a few cruisers went to anchor before the Ottoman forts in the Bosphorus strait, at the mouth of the Black Sea.

The populace of the capital, irrespective of ethnic identity, lined the seashore in rows, one above the other, and also the hills of Constantinople—particularly Ayaz Pasha, where I was—to watch the movement of the fleet, their mouths and eyes open wide.

A few British airplanes flew over the Bosphorus, adding even more dazzle to the historic event. The Greek people so rejoiced and swelled with pride at this scene that you would have thought it was they who had won the victory. They were fixed on the huge armored cruiser *Averof*, the crown jewel of the Hellenic fleet; along with two Hellenic torpedo boats, it had anchored between two British frigates in front of Kadikoy. When this Hellenic dreadnought sounded the national anthem, the thousands of Greeks gathered at the beach of Kadikoy shouted, "*Zito!*"* while the Turkish police beat and arrested the organizers of this demonstration.

After some hours I decided to go on foot from Taksim to Tunel to gather my impressions of the scene and the states of mind of the people. My God, what joy and exaltation! All of Pera, that European sector of Constantinople, resonated with the clamor of drunken Armenians and Greeks. All the prominent buildings and commercial houses, as well as the homes, were decorated with large and small British, French, Italian, Belgian, and Greek flags. Every time the large crowd saw an officer from the Entente army or fleet, they would shout giddily, "Hurrah for England, hurrah for France, hurrah for Greece!"

French, Greek, and Armenian girls threw flowers from their windows on the main boulevard of Pera as the joyful procession passed. The air resounded with "*Zito!*" Meanwhile the Muslims had withdrawn behind the grated windows of their houses, watching in silence.

When I was passing through Pera, right in front of the Greek embassy, I ran into two Armenians. One of them looked at me carefully. Then as I passed by, he said to his traveling companion, "Brother, I've seen this man somewhere, but I don't remember where. He resembles someone, but I don't remember whom." After a few steps, I turned around to get another look at them. Suddenly I saw that they too had turned around and were watching me in astonishment.

I went on, passing the confectionery stores adjoining Bon Marché. Surprisingly, the display windows were filled with all kinds of candies, pastries, and milk products, as they had been before the war, even though the Turkish capital was suffering from hunger. Naturally, the poor had no bread because of the corrupt Turkish officials. The rich, having made money easily during the war, ate, drank, and enjoyed life to the hilt, buying properties and spending recklessly.

The ridiculous styles and dress of the women with their made-up faces,

*Long live (Greek).—trans.

half-exposed breasts, and immodest manners occupied my special attention. In subsequent weeks, what I saw made me think that due to its reprehensible progress during the war, the Turkish capital had become a Babylon.

34

Did the Victors Come to Punish, or to Loot?

A few hours after the victorious demonstration outside Constantinople, the Entente fleet left a few warships in the waters around the capital and then dropped anchor in the Gulf of Izmit. The British, French, American, and Italian admirals got settled in their magnificent embassies in Pera, and the official representatives of the Turkish government rushed to pay their respects to them.

On behalf of the French community Bonet made an enthusiastic speech. In response the French admiral Ame, speaking at the French embassy, said in a patriotic tone:

> Dear compatriots, your prolonged nightmare is ending with the appearance of the victorious Allied fleet, which signifies final liberation. What pride to bear a Frenchman's name! Glory to marshals Joffre and Foch; glory to their assistants; glory also to Gen. Franchet d'Espérey for the victory of the eastern fortress, where the first upset took place. Glory and gratitude to the republican government. Glory and gratitude and respect to Georges Clemenceau, the organizer of this victory, our honorable and great liberator, against all internal and external enemies.

These were great historical days of excitement and frenzy that we were living. The greatest of admirals and commanders and the crowds of ordinary folk, all equally intoxicated with the victory celebration, were in a state of joy and exhilaration. Everyone was absorbed in the glory and honor of the victory, everyone expressing himself with more patriotic fervor than the one next to him.

The historic "Sick Man" of the East had indeed lost his head, but the

Turkish press, in keeping with popular sentiment, was sounding the trumpet of exoneration, exclaiming that the Turkish nation was not responsible for perpetrating the widespread carnage but that a few adventurers from Salonica had committed these crimes, and now that they had fled, the matter was closed.

All the Turkish papers expressed this view; all refused to acknowledge responsibility, writing: "We are innocent; we weren't the ones committing those crimes. It was those who've fled; those accursed ones destroyed our fatherland, reducing the country to ruin. And now they've fled, abandoning the poor innocent people to their fate." In order to give an accurate idea of the Turkish psychology during the days following the Armistice, here, word for word, is a front-page article by the Turkish writer Tevfik Khalid, from the influential Turkish daily *Zaman:*

DON'T BE DECEIVED, DON'T BELIEVE

> Yes, don't be deceived at all, don't believe, don't be convinced, this world is a deceitful world. First, they become shepherds, take charge; then they become wolves and swallow the flock. Along with peace, the society of politicians will again set up a tent and extract money. In this or that corner, the remaining political vocalists shall assemble; they will sing the song of freedom, they will chant the ballad of justice, they shall take up a collection, they shall do new magic tricks; snatching the rest that is in our hands, they will throw it into their hats. In short, it's the same comedy, the same ruse. Don't be deceived, don't believe, don't be convinced of the poet's song, the words of the deputy. My mouth is burned from them all. Again somebody will emerge and, shouting "Equality!" from Chamleja to Kanleja, will buy land, make the spring of Elmale his fountain, and will leave the people without water. Again someone will emerge and, shouting "Justice!" will burn fields the next day, will trounce upon farms, hang people. Again someone will come and, shouting "Freedom!" will shut our mouths and tie our hands. What "heroes of freedom" will emerge! Don't be deceived, don't believe, don't be convinced. It's too bad if you didn't take heed from the lessons of the past ten years! Neither believe in the new political parties, nor be lulled by sweet hopes; expect neither gain from Ali nor good from Veli. "Nothing's changed; it's always the same, the same worn-out heel, the same behavior." The forty-year Yani won't become Keani. For the sake of the nation, they say they are walking on foot, but they come and then they go by car from the Sublime Porte to the

> agency of public works. They say they're drinking water, but they drown in champagne. What haven't we seen over the past ten years! Supposedly they have gone up the mountain to enter the vineyard, they have put the owl to flight in order to take over its nest, they have overthrown tyranny in order to find open space. They say, "We shall have people wear furs," and steal the skins; they say, "We shall wear crowns," and they snatch the caps; they appear friendly, and they cause anguish. They say, "Come on, walk," they let you go in front of them, and then, one by one, they flee and throw you into the fire. The senators are like this. So are the representatives. God forbid, war breaks out, and like the magician's assistant, they say, "Very well, my *effendi*, that's right, my *effendi*, it's suitable, my *effendi*," peace looms ahead, and like the coffeehouse keeper, they say, "Welcome, *agha*," the Ittihad government comes, and like bathhouse servants, they sing, "You are mine, I am yours," the opposition fades, they sing the folksong "My Eyes Kept Staring at the Road." Today they sing the praises of the Germans; tomorrow they'll become friends of the British. Take these unprincipled functionaries, and put them in the drawer. Like expertly trained parrots, the press kept propounding these three phrases for the past four years: "Hurrah for the war! Bravo! Hindenburg, final victory!" Now it's like that too, again three phases, "Hurrah for peace! *Aferin* Wilson! Separate peace!" The dailies are already writing their editorials in such a way that you'd think they had come from the pen of Enver Pasha. Let's see hereafter whose carriage they will sit in and which folksong they will sing . . . Don't be deceived, don't believe, don't be convinced. Again that which is in our hands will be usurped and camels will be made of them. Those with full stomachs will go off to one side, and the hungry ones will get somewhat sated. You'll think someone is a policeman, and he'll turn out to be a bandit. Someone will look like an angel and turn out to be a devil. If you don't open your eyes, the eggs will again come out rotten. In short, don't think that every bearded man is your father, don't be deceived by the chiefs. My advice to you would be—open your eyes, hold your legs firm, don't be deceived, don't believe, don't be convinced again.

This editorial reveals how the Turkish leaders had perfected duplicity, deception, and perfidy. They have always had two faces; they have been merciless and cruel toward the weak, while fawning, cringing, obliging, friendly, and hospitable toward the strong. And this latter tendency was most evident when the victorious Entente powers entered Constantinople.

Turkish diplomacy and strategy were bankrupt, but Turkish duplicity, sycophancy, and deceit were inexhaustible capital, which they had exploited skillfully for centuries—not least during and after the Armistice. Now they became the victims, and the Armenians, having been smashed to smithereens, became the criminals. They became the accusers and put the Armenians in the dock. Therefore it is not at all surprising that prominent French writers such as Pierre Loti, Claude Farrère, and Mrs. Golis [Berthe Georges-Gaulis] have written so enthusiastically and with so much admiration about the Turks.[1]

The imperial palaces of the Turkish capital (Dolmabahche, Churaghan, Beylerbey), the various royal villas in Saray-Bournou, Kiaghudhane, and Beykoz, and the most famous mosques of Constantinople are the handiworks of an Armenian, the royal architect Balian Amiras. No one wishes to acknowledge it. For five centuries the porcelain tiles of Kutahya were used to decorate the *mihrabs* of the famous Turkish mosques or houses of prayer in the historic Islamic centers of Constantinople, Bursa, Kutahya, Kastemouni, Konya, Seoyud, and throughout Asia Minor. They are the works of the Armenian masters of Kutahya. In the large so-called "Turkish" rug industry, the designers, as well as the master wool-dyers, again are Armenian, though the rugs are called Turkish because they are exported from Turkey.

During their six-hundred-year rule, the Turks have left no trace or memory of civilization except massacre, plunder, forced Islamization, and abduction. The army of Janissaries was composed of rounded-up Christian boys. When they were murdered,* the luster of the Ottoman Empire began to dim.

And so after the world war, when the Turks saw that they lacked other means to recover after their severe loss, they resorted to deception and sycophancy in their dealings with the Entente powers. These fanatical apostles of *jihad* opened the well-fastened grated windows and doors of the harems. To the foreign officers they offered Turkish girls made up with rouge and redolent of perfume, thus winning an easy victory. Turk-haters became Turk-lovers, while judges became advocates.

Encouraged by how they were received, the Turkish women perfected their tactics with foreign officers, and the Turks presented their heroines to the latter as the houris of pashas, beys, or noble Turkish families. And so the victors entering the Turkish capital city soon forgot whether they had come to punish or reward.

While the Turks were waiting dumbfounded to receive their just pun-

*Janissaries, Christian boys taken in tax, Islamized, and reared in military barracks, were the Praetorian Guard of the Ottoman Empire. Unmarried, well paid, and self-indulgent, they became so powerful and uncontrollable that in 1826 Sultan Mahmud II ordered that the entire Janissary corps be slaughtered and the practice abolished.—trans.

ishment, they began to see that the foreign soldiers, supposedly there fighting for the freedom of small nations, gave precedence to pillaging. Thus the compliant vanquished gradually understood that, far from being disarmed, they would secretly begin to receive new weapons when the British army left Syria to the French.

The following article, written by a well-known American, William Ellis, under the title "The Nemesis," was published as a fair critique in an American daily in 1922 and was reprinted in all the Armenian dailies. Here is an excerpt:

> It is fair to say that only the British authorities undertook to punish the responsible Turks. After the Armistice, suddenly one night they arrested more than fifty prominent Turkish criminals, who were definitely responsible for the great crime of the extermination of the Armenians, and immediately transported them to the Malta fortress.

Among them were Tahsin, the governor-general of Erzerum; Muammer, the governor-general of Sivas; Sabat, that of Harput; Memduh, that of Erzinjan; Ali Ihsan, Fakhri, Jevad, Ali, and Mahmud Kiamil pashas, who were prominent in the workings of the Ittihad center; ranting editors of the Ittihadist newspapers; and so on.

But all of them, without trial, much less sentencing, were released from Malta in 1921 and returned to Constantinople or Ankara so that they could continue to pursue their plans against the remnants of the Armenians and Greeks who had miraculously survived. The curtain of the secret had fallen, making it no longer necessary to save appearances; and the demands of the days following the Armistice were satisfied; so the political climate gave rise to new imperatives that were contrary to the original realities.

Thus each victorious government bargained with the Turks for its own interests. All the same, envoys of those governments would never forget to repeat on official occasions, with an olive branch in hand, that they had come to the Orient to establish justice and rights for the Christian peoples.

35

The General Condition of Constantinople on the Eve of the Armistice

The flotsam and jetsam of the shipwrecked Armenian people, who had miraculously survived, were gradually returning in small caravans from the far corners of Asia Minor and from the deserts of Mesopotamia to their destroyed paternal hearths. The exceptions were those from the Armenian provinces of Erzerum, Van, Bitlis, Moush, and Erzinjan. There, everything having been fully destroyed, no Christians were left (aside from the few hundred Islamized Armenian women and girls, confined to Turkish harems), but there were also practically no Muslims left either.

In these extensive provinces along the Russian frontier, according to the testimony of reliable Turkish and Armenian military men arriving in Constantinople from these areas, a population of barely 450,000—Turks, Kurds, Circassians, *kizilbash*, and Yezidi—was left. The Armenian element had been annihilated, whereas the Muslim peoples either had been overrun by the Russian armies or, having migrated southward, had been decimated by illness, epidemic, and starvation.

A reliable and quite educated Kurd who had passed through these provinces on his way to Persia gave this eyewitness testimony:

> There is not a single Armenian in the city of Bitlis. The homes of the Armenians are destroyed. Not a single church remains standing. The St. Garmrorag monastery has been converted to a barracks. The Turks who emigrated from Bitlis have not yet returned to their homes.
>
> The city of Moush is a pile of ruins. There are barely fifteen Armenian homes, to which their inhabitants have returned. They are bakers and shoemakers. The Armenian neighborhood is completely burned down. The churches are destroyed. The Apostles monastery is in a half-ruined state. St. Garabed is half destroyed. The part that isn't destroyed is serving as a barracks.

There isn't a trace of Armenians in Sassoun. There are a few Islamized ones. St. Aghperag monastery is still standing, where there are two novices. The monastery is under the absolute authority of the Kurdish family named Shego. The famous despot Musa Beg tried several times to destroy the monastery but encountered opposition from the Shego family. There are some forty Armenian orphans and widows in the monastery; their situation is totally hopeless.

The Kurdish chieftain Musa Beg lives in the village of Vartenis. A few Armenian male servants wait on him. Also in his "service" are seven Armenian unmarried girls and women. Among those women are the daughters of the chieftain Kasbar, a native of Vartenis, and the well-known Armenian merchant of Bitlis, Mahdesi Cherchiz Krikorian. Even their names have been Kurdicized. Even the Armenian graves in this village have been destroyed. There are a considerable number of Islamized Armenian women and children in the possession of Kurds and Turks alike.

Not even a trace of Armenians is left in the towns of Diyarbekir, Sighert, and Hazo.

There are about a thousand Armenian women, elderly, and orphans in the city of Van. A few boats remaining from the Russians and Armenians are going and coming on Lake Van. Those working in the boats are Russian.

Khulat and Bulanough have been reduced to ruins. There aren't even Kurds now in the erstwhile hundred-plus villages. There are quite a few Armenians in Kurtantsots and Modgantsots, now living in a tragic state.

The number of Kurds in the above-mentioned areas is greater than that of the Turks. Thousands of Kurds and Turks are sentenced to death from starvation and nakedness. Thousands of villages are destroyed. The fields remain uncultivated. The vineyards of Moush and Hazo are destroyed. The Kurdish incursions are continuous. The dissatisfaction toward the government often ends with rebellion.

The deportees who returned to their birthplaces in Adrianople, Rodosto, Bursa, Izmit, Adapazar, Bilejik, Eskishehir, Afyonkarahisar, Kutahya, Konya, Kastemouni, Bolu, Inebolu, Samsun, and Trebizond were subjected to new grief as they saw their houses, gardens, vineyards, and shops destroyed, wrecked by Muslim refugees and plundered by government officials. Many faced further difficulties getting back their paternal properties, for the Turks were not easily inclined to give up the valuable, income-producing spoils they had seized. As for the unfortunate Armenian exiles who returned to their paternal homes and engaged in trying to rebuild their ruined nests, they too faced obstruction by Armenophobic officials and the hostility of the Turkish people.

They did not even receive spiritual comfort, for they had neither pastor nor church, the remaining churches having been converted to workshops, warehouses, and stables. Only the deportees returning to Constantinople succeeded in finding protection from local government and national authorities.

Despite these adversities, there was great excitement among the Armenian people.

The Armenians had begun rounding up the tens of thousands of Armenian orphans with great enthusiasm. Sometimes Turks would voluntarily turn over to Armenian organizations or orphan stations the female Armenian orphans who had been confined in their harems and had reached maturity. But in the majority of cases, it was necessary to resort to police intervention to gain possession of the orphan boys and girls. In the two or three months following the Armistice, the intercession of the Entente powers had made it possible to rescue as many as three thousand orphans of both sexes in Constantinople.

A few Turks—few and far between—wrote articles in the Turkish dailies harshly criticizing the crimes committed. But these articles served more to expose the excesses of the authorities—motivated by the desire for personal revenge, and to discredit the Ittihadists—than to defend the Armenians or pay a debt of justice and conscience.

However, *Zeman*, a nationalistic Turkish daily, in an issue of late November 1918, published a piece criticizing these exposés by Turkish writers:

> Isn't anyone defending the Turks?—Every government has the right to transport those seen as dangerous from areas considered the war zone to other parts of the country, and every government makes broad use of this right . . . Why are they tarnishing the reputation of the Turkish people in this moment of national crisis? Why this need to present the Turkish people as criminals?

Overall the Turkish press, in keeping with a general unspoken consensus, defended the idea that the Turkish people were innocent, not guilty of any crime, and that but a few Ittihad leaders—Talaat, Enver, Jemal,

Behaeddin Shakir, Dr. Nazim—had slaughtered the Armenians. The perpetrators had fled the country, and so what were we to do? What fault was this of the Turkish people? They had suffered as many losses as had the Armenians . . . cursed be those who did this!

The Ittihad party changed its name to Tejeddud and formed a committee to investigate the crimes committed against the Armenians; they opened the state records and conducted inquiries. As an example, and to satisfy public opinion, Mehmet Kemal—the bloodthirsty *kaymakam* of Boghazliyan who, during August–September 1915, as vice-governor of Yozgat, had had 42,000 Armenians massacred in this district, irrespective of sex and age—was hanged. A year later, though, he was canonized a martyr of the Ottoman fatherland; programs of mourning were organized, and a bounteous life pension was awarded to his family.

A few Armenian-hating governors-general and high-ranking government officials were thrown into jail for show. Dr. Reshid, the Ittihadist governor-general of Diyarbekir who had had hundreds of thousands from Armenian caravans massacred, committed suicide in prison when he heard that Kemal had been hanged. And with this atypical sentence, the Turkish courts believed they had fulfilled their obligation.

When the cabinet changed, the new interior minister announced that the government had never officially given an order for the massacres; rather, the irresponsible Ittihad [Central] Committee had done so—as if Talaat, Enver, and Jemal, the ruling triumvirate, had not simultaneously embodied the Turkish government and the committee.

Responding to the former justice minister Senator Ibrahim, an honorable Armenian senator, Manoog Azarian, said at an official session of the Senate (October 1918):

> I am a witness to the fact that the government officially ordered the annihilation of the Armenians. During the Armenian massacres Bedri Bey, head of the police administration, said in the Senate in the presence of Senator Zareh Dilber Effendi, "Do you think the government has time to separate the innocent from the guilty? We have decided to annihilate all the Armenians."

Under the presidency of Eomer Rushdi Pasha, a supreme court was formed to try the members of the wartime Turkish cabinet who had served while Sayid Halim Pasha was prime minister.[1] They were Khayri (Sheikh-ul-Islam), Talaat (interior), Khalil (foreign affairs), Enver (war), Jemal (marine), Javid (finance), Khayri (*evkaf*),* Ibrahim (justice), Shukri (educa-

*Estates in mortmain (trusts); religious foundations (or works).—trans.

tion), Mahmoud and Abbas Halim (public works), Ahmed Nesimi (commerce and agriculture), and Vosgan Mardigian (post, telegraph).

When Sayid Halim resigned, unable to bear the persecution of his clans, the Syrian Arabs, Talaat then became prime minister, and the cabinet members were Musa Kiazim (Sheikh-ul-Islam), Ahmed Nesimi (foreign affairs), Enver (war), Jemal (marine), Javid (finance), Musa Kiazim (*evkaf*), Khalil (justice), Shukri and Nazim (education), Ali Munih (public works), Mustafa Sherif (commerce, agriculture), and Halim (post, telegraph).

When the supreme court started its inquiry, Talaat, Enver, and Jemal had already fled Constantinople. It was then, as I mentioned earlier, that the British arrested fifty people in one night and transported them by warship from Constantinople to Malta, where they were imprisoned in the local fortress. Everybody, especially the Armenians, thought that the hour of justice had arrived. (But three years later those arrested were released and would be allowed to return to Constantinople and Ankara.)

While these unexpected and just arrests gave rise to a sense of anticipation of the hour of reckoning, the Entente military authorities took not a single step to disarm the Turkish government according to the terms of the armistice of Mudros. The Entente merely placed the Turkish arsenals in Constantinople under watch.

Meanwhile Italy, which was occupying Antalya, was arming the Turks to defend themselves against the French, considering it a simple commercial transaction.* And in Constantinople, French and Italian officers and soldiers were engaging in all kinds of disgraceful behavior with Turkish women and prostitutes. It was not uncommon to see military men wallowing in the streets, drunk.

In July, Georges Clemenceau, the eminent prime minister of France, made his historic and famous statement in the Senate: "Justice cannot be compromised, given the enormity of the crime." Never mind that when this statement was made the Turkish delegation to the Paris Peace Conference had arrived with trunks of the jewels plundered from the imperial palaces to engage in secret bargaining . . . and to enjoy privileges for which they had already acquired a taste.

As harsh as the Entente powers were toward Germany, they were forgiving, lax, and kindly toward the Turks, because they wanted to get the "Sick Man" back on his feet. Perhaps they hoped to rescue the billions in loans they had made to Turkey.

*The French had designs on Cilicia and were engaging Kemalist troops there.—trans.

Woodrow Wilson, the honorable president of a great nation, speaking right after the Armistice and with the authority of a victor and peacemaker, articulated the reality of Turkey's crimes brilliantly and defended the Armenian cause eloquently.[2] Indeed, in the history of civilized humanity of the past few centuries, no government figure has upheld so high the holy banner of peace, justice, and universal brotherhood, though Lord Curzon, David Lloyd George, Sir Edward Grey, Raymond Poincaré, Georges Clemenceau, and other heads of state made similar statements, both during the war and after the Armistice.

Unfortunately, a number of Armenian traitors had helped the Turks, informing on their compatriots in exchange for position and money. They had prepared the blacklists of Armenian intellectuals and located them for the Turks to exile; they were shameless and base and undeserving of mercy or compassion.

Bedri, police chief in Constantinople, confessed that more than 150 Armenian informers were registered with the police. The principal ones were Artin Megerdichian, the infamous *muhtar* of Beshiktash and former teacher and editor; Hmayag Aramiantz, one of the well-known old leaders of the Hunchak Party, a national representative and managing editor of the papers *Gohag* and *Tailailig*, published in Constantinople; the abominable Arshavir [Yasian], also a member of the Hunchak Party, who was responsible for the hanging of the twenty Hunchaks in 1915; Hrant, the imposter *vartabed* Hovasapian; Kamer Shirinian, the first chargé d'affaires of the patriarchate, who had been paid by Talaat ever since the Balkan War of 1912.

After the Armistice Kamer Shirinian saved his neck by resigning his position at the patriarchate and fleeing in shame. Hrant Hovasapian saved himself by throwing off the cowl and fleeing with his sweetheart to Zonguldak, where he did voluntary hard labor in the mines, dragging himself along in the unfamiliar darkness. He was nearly killed by an avenging bullet. Artin Megerdichian and Hmayag Aramiantz in Constantinople, and Arshavir in Adana, were killed by bullets fired in revenge by Armenians.

I must mention something else here, with bitterness. A delegation from the patriotic Armenian youth of Scutari went to the Armenian Patriarchate to demand the resignation of the traitor, its chargé d'affaires, Kamer Shirinian. Dr. Tavitian, the chairman of the National Administration, claimed to be unaware of Shirinian's authority and high position. When the Armenian youths zealously defended their people's honor, Tavitian simply tried to get rid of them, saying that he could not tolerate interference from irresponsible elements. Nevertheless, in the end he was forced to yield.

The National Administration [of the Armenian Apostolic Church] had so lost its moral compass that rather than punish or expel a disgraced employee, it tried to defend a traitor like Kamer Shirinian. Shirinian had been the cause of righteous uproar in the National Representative Assembly in 1912, when he was exposed as the seventeenth detestable informer who used to attend secret evening meetings of the security committee dealing with the Armenian Question, reporting to the minister of the interior on what he had heard. He also stole a few official letters and other documents, which he handed over to the minister Reshid Bey in Bab-i Ali. One can find extensive coverage of this in the November 23, 1918, issue (no. 7755) of *Puzantion*, and in the October 1918 issue (no. 2347) of *Jamanak*.

Following the Armistice, the political assembly gave further proof of its impotence by neglecting to expel this chargé d'affaires from the patriarchate. The religious assembly, similarly infected, did not dare to defrock the traitor Hrant *vartabed* Hovasapian, who had let loose every insult and curse against both Armenian political party members and the martyred Armenian people in his weekly newspaper *Dajar*.

Just as during the Hamidian tyranny, from 1895 to 1908, so too during the World War I period of 1914–18, the national patriarchate had become a veritable seat of corruption, where great and small, titled and untitled traitors alike would come and go, privy to national secrets and other information, all of which they systematically conveyed to our executioners. It was a den of all kinds of material and moral abuses and dirty deeds. Moreover, some of its employees, seeing the extremely propitious and exceptional opportunity for illicit gain, appropriated bequests [from estates of wealthy Armenians] and other funds, believing that no one would come forth in the midst of the prevailing chaos to demand an accounting of their disbursement.

Thus the considerable sum of 30,000 gold pounds from the Johanescu bequest to the patriarchate disappeared, and those who asked about it received only the briefest reply: "We sent it to the interior, to help the starving Armenian people in exile." And if anyone insisted on an accounting, that answer too was ready: "The National Representative Assembly gave the patriarch permission to act freely in accordance with the circumstances."

If such august sums had been at the patriarch's disposal to benefit the exiled Armenian people, why did the patriarchate send only a pitiful 150 gold pounds over the course of ten months, in response to the heartrending appeals of Constantinople's Armenian intellectuals deported to

Chankiri and Ayash? But the nation was buried, and so who was to care if these accounts were buried with it?

After the Armistice, fund-raising began among the Armenians of Constantinople on behalf of thousands of orphan boys and girls. Day after day orphanages were opened in all the main sections of the city, inspiring great solicitude as well as material and moral assistance. The Armenians' excitement and enthusiasm was so great and widespread that one might have been deluded into thinking that nothing had changed during the past four years of war. Members of the Armenian press, without exception, outdid one another in denouncing the Turks.

The Turks, meanwhile, were quietly organizing, laying the foundation of the Kemalist movement.

In 1918 the Turkish capital was still the very picture of ancient Byzantium in 1451, when the Turks had delivered the final blow to the rotten authority of Constantin XI of the Paleolog dynasty. Ever since then Constantinople had been a hotbed of palace intrigues and political and military crimes. Even in the past twenty-five years, while various Turkish administrations had tried to save the country from destruction, individual and mass crimes had become akin to natural phenomena.

Those who know history know that the principal causes of a country's downfall are internal dissension, violent partisan struggle, lack of religion, political crime, and economic unraveling; all these per se bring with them unbridled excesses. Naturally, the Turkish capital city was no exception to this process of dissolution.

Indeed, since the Ottoman Constitution was established in 1908, in the guise of freedom, nothing but disorder had prevailed. Under the Young Turks, women had begun to remove the veil and frequent clubs in European dress. The police tried in vain to enforce the Islamic laws designed to protect their closeted lives, raiding Turkish mansions near Sultan Bayazid Square, nests of debauchery where even palace women rendezvoused. Every day the Turkish newspapers would expose, especially for the police's attention, the scandalous behavior of Turkish women. Here is one Turkish newspaper's (*Ileri*) criticism and admission:

> According to the information received by us, there are many Turkish women roaming around Germany. They have lost their identity in the European environment, and having exhausted their ready cash and pledged their jewelry as security, they are leading a dissolute life. Among them are women belonging to the imperial family . . . whose names we do not wish to give, to spare the reputation of the imperial family . . .

In the capital city, French and Italian officers assigned to disarm the defeated Turkey were themselves disarmed by Oriental charms, becoming Turcophiles.

The Turkish women were not the only adherents of this new strategy. Greek and Armenian women followed their example, and something rare occurred: Armenian women began cohabiting with Turks and Persians, and their cohabitation with German officers drew biting criticism in the satirical paper *Gavrosh*.

After the war Armenian, Greek, and other Christian girls, as well as Turkish ones, took jobs in shops and official establishments, and thus began a major revolution in manners and mores.

The Ittihad government, as I said, had abolished the Armenian Patriarchate of Constantinople. The national constitution, established by imperial edict in 1864, ceased to exist, and in 1916 Archbishop Gabriel Jevahirjian, formerly patriarchal vicar, was summoned to fill the post of patriarchal *locum tenens*. After the armistice of Mudros, however, Archbishop Jevahirjian resigned so that the old order could be reestablished, and Bishop Mesrob Naroyian* was appointed patriarchal *locum tenens* until the return of the exiled patriarch, Zaven Der Yeghiayan, from Mosul. Everything was in need of reorganization.

I had always participated in the national life of Constantinople with fervor and disinterestedness. But I became disenchanted by this sad state and thought about leaving the vile chaos once and for all.

*See Biographical Glossary.

36

Irrevocable Departure from Turkey: From Constantinople to Paris

During the days following the Armistice I often went to the upper floor of our house and devoted my time to outlining the story of the Armenian martyrdom.

I faced a painful and weighty responsibility: writing this history meant reliving, on a daily basis, all those black days whose very reminiscence filled me with horror. While I felt physically healthy, I was spiritually ill. Yet I had a sacred obligation to write this bitter story for future generations.

Fortunately, I had inherited a sharp memory from my mother. Even at her advanced age, she easily remembered past events as well as the names of persons and places. She knew the genealogies of all the Armenian dynasties by heart.

But when I started to work, I realized that I had practically forgotten Armenian, my mother tongue; having lived in hiding in Adana and vicinity for two years, where the Armenian people are Turkish-speaking, I had spoken only Turkish. Only schoolchildren spoke their mother tongue, and only in school, not at home. Often I had difficulty remembering even common Armenian words and how to arrange them in order to appropriately express my thoughts and ideas. My attention would become diverted as I searched Armenian dictionaries for synonyms. Then I began to read the Armenian papers without difficulty, and gradually my mother tongue, which seemed to have been buried in mud, rose to the surface.

Six of my exiled companions* in Chankiri had returned from Smyrna to Constantinople. (As I mentioned in my first volume, they had departed Chankiri in September 1915 and had reached Smyrna via Ankara. From there they had been transported to Oushak, where they remained until the Armistice.) When I found out that this group had arrived in Constantinople, I sent a petition to French admiral Ame, asking for his protection so

*Balakian refrains from naming them, noting only that Dr. M.K., probably Dr. Mirza Ketenjian, was among them.

that I could come out into the open. I stressed to him that I did not trust the Turks at all. Ame told me that I could feel safe and secure moving about Constantinople but that I should not go to the interior provinces. Encouraged by the assurance of protection, I placed an announcement in the newspapers informing people that I had returned safe and sound to Constantinople, omitting to mention that I had actually arrived five weeks earlier disguised as a German soldier.

A week after this announcement, the Turkish police chief of the Selamorz ward of Scutari, the same one who had arrested me four years earlier, began a secret investigation of me. And so despite all the comforts I enjoyed at home, I wasn't able to sleep at night, because when I heard footsteps in the street, I thought policemen were coming to arrest me again. I had become suspicious of everything, and I had developed a persecution complex . . . a telling sign of mental illness.

Despite the fact that my mind was clear, I could not free myself of my nightmare. I went to my spiritual father, Archbishop Yeghishe Tourian, to ask for his advice. He embraced me with paternal affection, and when I declared my firm intention to leave Constantinople for Paris as soon as possible, he proposed that, as a living witness to the martyrdom of the Armenian people, I go to Paris as an auxiliary to the national delegation and participate in the Armenians' assembly. Indeed, Boghos Nubar Pasha had sent an invitation to the national patriarchate in Constantinople requesting that two members be appointed to that assembly.

The Armenian Patriarchate had not yet been reestablished, however, so national authority remained in the hands of Dr. Tavitian. He saw himself as a dictator, having held this authority for all four years of the Armenian massacres, during which he had been a mere spectator of the annihilation—and had not dared to resign his absolutely nominal post.

Archbishop Tourian, chairman of the Religious Assembly and consequently an active member of the National Administration, expected the national authority to appoint as delegates to the great national assembly in Paris Gabriel Noradoungian (the former foreign minister of Turkey) and Vosgan Mardigian (the former postal minister). Both of them were already in Switzerland. Hardly had Boghos Pasha's invitation to participate in the Paris assembly become known than the number of candidates for the national leadership in Constantinople increased. The Dashnak Party made a spirited entrance into the campaign and assigned a delegate. Weren't they the political party that had saved the Armenian republic by achieving independence? They, therefore, felt that the lion's share of perquisites should fall to them. They made extraordinary efforts to dominate the assembly membership, so that with a majority they would take the presidency of the delegation during the Paris Peace Conference.

Under these conditions, after lengthy behind-the-scenes struggles, the following members of the great national assembly in Paris were elected: former patriarch Archbishop Yeghishe Tourian; Abraham Der Hagopian, a professor at the American Robert College for many years; and Dr. Armenag Parseghian, an active member of the Dashnak Party.

Archbishop Tourian, seeing some advantage in my departure from Constantinople, put my name on the list presented to the British administration in Constantinople of the four individuals for whom he requested permission to depart as members of the national assembly. Prior to my going, the parish council of the Holy Cross Church of Scutari invited me to celebrate the liturgy in the neighborhood church and also to officiate at the opening of the nearby Armenian orphanage, whose administration had been undertaken by the Armenians of Scutari.

During my exile and suffering I had so wished to become worthy of this day—worthy of going up to the holy altar to celebrate divine liturgy. When the moment arrived and I lifted up the chalice, my soul was troubled to its very depths and was shaking my tortured being. I said: "Take, eat, this is my body which is given for you and for many for propitiation and for remission of sins." As I said it, tears ran down my face, burning my pale cheeks.

How could I not become emotional with the innocent blood of hundreds of thousands of Armenian martyrs reflected in the eyes of my soul? I had trouble seeing; my voice went hoarse, for it seemed that this time I had filled the chalice with the blood of chaste Armenian virgins and innocent children.

I had so wished to become worthy of this day, and a sigh flew out from the depths of my soul: "*Glory to you, God, that I became worthy of this day . . .*"

A fiery tongue was burning, scorching, and parching me.

I had always been a defender of justice, and I had faith in justice (perhaps my pious mother had given me this feeling in her milk), which had caused my miseries. But no matter, for hadn't Christ suffered? Hadn't he been tortured? Wasn't he betrayed because he preached justice in this world, while perhaps justice could be only celestial and eternal, not worldly? In this state of spiritual frenzy I had to stop my sermon several times because the sight of more than a thousand listeners, similarly moved and tormented, was so painful.

After the services we conducted the opening of the orphanage in a solemn manner.

Everything was in order now, and the day of my departure was approaching.

. . .

On January 4, 1919, together with Archbishop Yeghishe Tourian, Professor Der Hagopian, and Dr. Parseghian, I boarded the British admiral's ship at the quay at Galata. One of its tugboats took us to the British steamer that would transport us to Malta. There were a few dozen British families and war wounded on board.

Pulling up anchor at evenfall, the steamship slowly left Constantinople. Twilight had fallen as our ship entered the deep waters of the calm open sea. Withdrawn in the aft section, I looked back at the lights of the Turkish capital, at Scutari, where I was leaving behind a mother advanced in her years . . . a mother whose eyesight had weakened from praying and crying and waiting day and night for the return of her unlucky son.

Perhaps this time we were being separated for life.

Acknowledgments

I am most grateful to the Dolores Zohrab Liebmann Fund, which provided me with generous support during the time I worked on *Armenian Golgotha* and *The Burning Tigris*. I am grateful in particular to the late Suren Fesjian, cotrustee, and to Missak Haigentz of the Liebmann Fund for their support. The Liebmann Fund enabled me to have concentrated time to work, away from my teaching responsibilities. I applaud the Liebmann Fund for its consistent support of scholarly work on Armenian history and culture and the legacy that this support has created.

I am indebted to His Eminence Archbishop Khajag Barsamian, Primate of the Diocese of the Armenian Church of North America (Eastern), and to His Eminence Archbishop Oshagan Choloyan, Primate of the Eastern Prelacy of the Armenian Apostolic Church of North America, for the generous support they gave to the translation process of this book. Carol Aslanian and the Armenian General Benevolent Union were instrumental in bringing me together with the Liebmann Fund. Robert Setrakian was most generous in assisting my initial conversation with Archbishop Choloyan.

Out of her passion to see this book come into English, Anahid Yeremian at Stanford University began the first phase of translating *Armenian Golgotha* with me in 1999, and without her energy this project would not have begun when it did. And the scholarly opinions of Rouben Adalian, director of The Armenian National Institute; Aram Arkun; Taner Akçam; Vahakn Dadrian; and Robert Jay Lifton were most helpful at certain times. Thanks to Mary Jane Walsh, government documents librarian at Colgate University, and to Theresa Kevorkian, who provided stalwart assistance in the eleventh hour.

Without the generosity of Colgate University dean/provosts Jack Dovido and Lyle Roelofs, who assisted me with leave time, this book could not have been completed in the fashion it was; I am immensely grateful to them. As always, the extraordinary staff at the Colgate Document and Mail Services Department has made my work on this manuscript so much more efficient and easy, and Mike Holobosky's work in helping me prepare the images for the book is greatly appreciated. Thanks also to John Gallucci, John Naughton, and Alan Swensen for helpful translations from French and German; to Donna-Lee Frieze for texts on Raphael Lemkin; and gratitude to Tessa Hoffman, director of the Centre for Information and Documentation on Armenia (Berlin), and to Debby Paddock for their aid and expertise with photographs and images.

I express deep gratitude to Mr. and Mrs. Joyce and Joseph Stein and the Philibosian Family Foundation for their generous support of my work over the years and in particular the years of work on this book.

My agent, Eric Simonoff at Janklow & Nesbit, has been instrumental in guiding this book with wise counsel at every stage. My editor, George Andreou at Alfred A. Knopf, has done meticulous and brilliant editing, and Lily Evans, editorial assistant, has done extraordinary work at every stage of this complex process.

Without Doris V. Cross's editorial expertise, scholarly input, and extraordinary devotion to this book, *Armenian Golgotha* would not have achieved the whole shape and sharpness it has; my gratitude to her is immense.

Yaddo once again provided me with quiet and beauty in which to work. Finally, my family has been generous with aid and affirmation at needed times, and my brother and sister-in law Jim and Janet D. Balakian have graciously given me space and time in their house by the water to work in unimpeded ways. My wife Helen Kebabian's editorial expertise and support have been essential throughout.

Glossary

POLITICAL AND HISTORICAL TERMS

Adana Massacre The April 1909 massacres of 20,000 to 30,000 Armenians in Adana province in south central Turkey, by Ottoman counterrevolutionaries and Young Turk forces.

Armash Seminary Founded in 1889 in the province of Nicomedia (Izmit); Grigoris Balakian studied there beginning in 1896. The semimary was closed in 1915 and its collection of manuscripts was destroyed.

Armenian Mixed Assembly Armenian Political Assembly and Religious Assembly combined.

Armenian National Religious Assembly Body of ecclesiastics in the Ottoman Empire that oversaw Armenian religious affairs.

Armenian Patriarchate of Constantinople The office of the head of the Armenian church in Turkey, authorized by the Ottoman government to hold religious and some civil authority over Turkey's Armenians.

Armenian Political Assembly Twenty laymen who oversaw Armenian political affairs in the Ottoman Empire.

Cilicia The region of southern Turkey that lies between the Taurus mountains and the Mediterranean. It was ruled by Armenian kings from 1199 to 1375 and was known as Armenia Minor or Little Armenia.

Committee of Union and Progress (CUP) (*Ittihad ve Terakki*) A party originating in the Young Turk movement. Its nationalist wing staged a coup on January 26, 1913, and installed the Ittihad government.

Dashnak Member of the Armenian Revolutionary Federation (*Dashnaktsutiun*), a political party founded in 1890 in Turkey, dedicated to Armenian advancement and civil rights.

Holy Etchmiadzin The Holy See of the Armenian Apostolic Church.

Hunchak Member of an Armenian Socialist political party, founded in 1887 by Russian Armenians in Geneva.

Ittihad See Committee of Union and Progress (CUP).

Ittihad Central Committee Central authority of the Ittihad government, with jurisdiction over Turkey's local Ittihad committees.

Ittihad clubs Network of local Ittihad party groups throughout Turkey where party business (including the massacres of the Armenians) was overseen.

police soldier A type of military police; also known as "gendarme."

Ramgavar Member of the Democratic Liberal Party, Armenians in Turkey who favored Russian protection.

responsible secretary A tier of CUP bureaucrats who functioned as the eyes and ears of the Ittihad Central Committee and exercised strict control in the provinces.

Special Organization (*Teshkilati Mahsusa*) A bureau within the Ittihad Central Committee that was used for special projects; it planned, organized, and executed the annihilation of the Armenians.

Sublime Porte The office of the Ottoman Grand Vizier in Constantinople.

NON-ENGLISH TERMS

afushahane pardon

amele tabur labor battalion

chavush sergeant; petty officer

chete raiders, brigands; mobile killing unit made up of criminals released from prisons

dolap intrigue, deceit

donme a convert to Islam

giaour infidel; Turkish term for a non-Muslim

hoja wise one

kaymakam lieutenant; district governor; deputy mayor

khan coffeehouse-inn

kismetli lucky

kizilbashes Members of the Alevi strand of Shi'a Islam; these sectarians have always been friendly to Christians.

muhtar alderman, headman

murahhasa effendi Turkish title and form of address for an Armenian bishop

mutasarrif provincial governor; vice-governor-general

nakharar minister; satrap; proconsul

nikeah married according to Muslim tradition

oke, okka unit of weight. One oke equals 400 drams, or 2.83 pounds.

ortak partner, associate

paklayalum "cleanse"; euphemism for "kill"

para unit of currency

piaster unit of currency. Forty piasters equal one para.

posha Gypsies who speak Armenian; their origin is unclear.

reji Turkish tobacco monopoly

sanjak county, subprovince
sevkiyat caravan of deportees, traveling on horses or donkeys, in carts or carriages, or on foot
vali governor-general
vesika documents; identity papers; voucher
vilayet Ottoman province
yasaktir It is forbidden.

PLACE-NAME VARIANTS

ARMENIAN / TURKISH, GREEK, OR RUSSIAN

Alexandretta Iskenderun
Bitlis Baghesh
Bursa Brusa
Diyarbekir Dikranagerd
Erdine Adrianople
Erzerum Karin, Garin
Erzinjan Yerzenga
Gyumri Alexandropol, Leninakan
Hajin Hadjin, Siambeyli
Harput Kharpert
Izmit Nicomedia
Kayseri Caesarea
Moush Taron
Ourfa Edessa, Urfa, Shanliurfa
Sassoun Sasun
Sis Kozan
Sivas Sepastia
Yenige Enije, Yenice
Zeytoun Zeitun, Suleymanli

Biographical Glossary

Agnouni. ***See*** **Maloumian, Khachadour**

Aharonian, Avetis (b. 1866 Gharib, Igdir–d. 1948 Marseilles). Author, teacher, Dashnak leader, diplomat, journalist, and poet. President of the parliament of the Armenian Republic (1918–20). Delegate to the Paris Peace Conference in 1919. He represented Armenia at the signing of the Treaty of Sèvres in 1920 (with Boghos Nubar Pasha representing diasporan Armenians), which established the independent Republic of Armenia. He attended negotiations for the Treaty of Lausanne and unsuccessfully protested its nullification of the Sèvres Treaty's provision for an independent Armenia. He became an invalid in 1934 after being paralyzed by a stroke.

Andonian, Aram (1875–1952). Author and historian who wrote a detailed history of the Balkan Wars. Remembered most for having compiled *Memoirs of Naim Bey*, which contains official documents of the Committee of Union and Progress instructing its officials to eliminate the Armenians. Editions of this book were published in French, English, and Armenian.

Antranig (Ozanian), General (b. 1865 Shabin Karahisar–d. 1927 Fresno, California). Military leader of the Armenian struggle for independence. During the world war he commanded Armenian volunteer forces in the Russian Armenian provinces, seeking to secure Russian protection for an Armenian state. Following the Bolshevik Revolution and the independence of Armenia in 1918, he continued to protect refugee Armenians in Azerbaijan and in Karabagh, which his "Special Striking Division" was able to retain as Armenian territory. After the war he went to the United States, married in 1922, and settled in Fresno, California.

Aram Pasha. ***See*** **Manoogian, Aram**

Asaf, Mehmed (?–?). Served as lieutenant-governor of Chankiri from May 15 to July 28, 1915. A former pupil of Diran Kelegian, a professor at the civil service school (in Mülkiye), he had forewarned him and Balakian of their impending doom and urged them to try to secure a hasty return to Constatinople. He had been complicit in the 1909 Adana massacres of the Armenians and barely escaped the verdict of death by hanging. Although he was helpful to his Armenian colleagues and then resigned his post, he acknowledged that his decision was influenced by fear of being a bureaucratic scapegoat for the Ittihad government in case of a postwar trial.

Bedri, Osman (?–?). Constantinople police chief who, with the help of Armenian informants, compiled the blacklist of the city's most influential public figures. On April 24, 1915, he supervised their arrest and transportation to prison and, for most of them, to eventual murder. A few months later he ordered the arrest of thousands of Armenians from the provinces who had emigrated to Constantinople. They were held in cells at police headquarters for days, starved, tortured, and then exiled on foot via Bilejik toward Bozanti; they were subjected to brutal treatment and torture on their journey. Numbering some twenty thousand, 95 percent of them did not survive.

Boghos Nubar Pasha (b. 1851 Alexandria, Egypt–d. 1930 Paris). Son of the Egyptian prime minister and one of the founders of the Armenian General Benevolent Union. He used his considerable resources and influence to press the Armenian case with the European powers. With Avetis Aharonian he headed the Armenian delegation to the 1919 Paris Peace Conference and cosigned the Treaty of Sèvres in 1920.

Cheraz, Minas (b. 1852 Constantinople–d. 1929 Paris). Writer and editor; taught the history of literature and languages in Constantinople. In 1878 he was a member of the Armenian delegation to the Congress of Berlin, and in 1880 he met with British prime minister Gladstone to request his support for Armenian reforms. He published a literary and political paper called *L'Arménie* in Paris and London and authored literary, pedagogical, and historical works. In 1890 he founded and directed an Armenian chair at King's College, the University of London.

Chilingirian, Dr. Rupen (Sevag) (b. 1885 Silivri–d. 1915 Chankiri). Physician, writer, and public figure. He wrote poetry devoted to mankind, the fatherland, and love; his lengthy poem *The Last Armenians* seems to prophesy the martyrdom of the Armenian people. He wrote the *Red Book* in 1910, about the Adana massacres. After completing medical school in Switzerland, in 1914 he returned to Constantinople with his German wife and their children. He was a physician in the Makrikoy army when he was deported to Chankiri.

Chobanian, Arshag (1872–1952). Writer in Armenian and French and publisher of the magazine *Anahid;* devoted to Armenian literature and art. He acquainted many Frenchmen with Armenian literature, principally through a few volumes of Armenian poetry translated into French. He is the author of novels, biographies, and poems, which were translated into many languages. He received several awards for his work from the French and Romanian governments.

Daghavarian, Dr. Nazareth (b. 1862 Sivas–d. 1915 Ayash). Scientist and educator. Educated in Armenian schools in Turkey and in Paris, he became chief physician in the Armenian National Hospital in Constantinople. He was imprisoned during the Hamidian reign of terror. In 1905 he became a founder, with Boghos Nubar, of the Armenian General Benevolent Union. After the Young Turk revolution in 1908, he was elected a deputy from Sivas to the Ottoman Parliament. He authored several works in Armenian, Turkish, and French on historical, scientific, and religious topics, including an unpublished study of animal husbandry in ten volumes. In 1902 he was honored as Officier d'Académie by the French government, and in 1910 he received the Mérite Agricole. He was a founder, in 1908, of both the Ottoman Itilaf Party and the Armenian Constitutional Democrat (Ramgavar) Party.

Der Yeghiayan, Patriarch Zaven (b. 1868 Mosul–d. 1947 Baghdad). Presided over the Armenians of Turkey as Armenian Patriarch of Constantinople (1913–22). Educated in Baghdad and at Armash Theological Seminary, he became bishop and then prelate for Diyarbekir; in 1913 he became patriarch of Constantinople. Grigoris Balakian is highly critical of his leadership during the period of the Genocide, believing that with more foresight he could have saved more lives. The Ottoman government exiled him to Baghdad in 1916. In 1926 Zaven became director plenipotentiary of the Melkonian Institute in Cyprus. In 1927 he moved back to Baghdad. He is the author of *My Patriarchal Memoirs*.

Enver Ismail Pasha (1881–1922). Soldier; later the junior but most famous member of the Young Turk triumvirate, with Talaat and Jemal. Born in Istanbul, the son of a civil servant, he graduated in 1902 from Harbiye and was posted to the Third Army in Salonica. He joined the CUP in 1906. He rose to fame as one of the leaders of the 1908 Young Turk revolution; became a member of the Central Committee (1908); and was a military attaché in Berlin (1909), in Libya (1911), and in the Balkans (1913). In January 1913, with Jemal and Talaat, he led an attack on the Sublime Porte in which the minister of war was killed. A year later Enver was made war minister and was promoted to brigadier general. On December 25, 1914, he led the Ottoman Third Army of 95,000 in an attack on Russia. Two weeks later the 20,000 men who had not been killed or frozen to death retreated from Sarikamish. For this crushing defeat Enver and Talaat blamed the Armenians. They soon ordered the deportation from Turkey of all Armenians living near the Russian border. In 1918, after the Ottoman defeat, Enver escaped abroad with other CUP leaders. He was killed in Turkestan, fighting the Bolsheviks, in 1922.

Garo, Armen. ***See*** **Pastermajian, Karekin**

Hamid, Sultan Abdul II (1842–1918). Sultan from September 1876 to April 1909. After his older brother Mourad V was found to be incapable, Abdul Hamid took the throne. He faced a growing reform movement in his domain and the disapproval of the European powers for the Sublime Porte's brutal treatment of the Balkan Christians. Abdul Hamid first promulgated the Ottoman Constitution on December 23, 1876, and then on February 13, 1878, he dismissed the parliament. For the next thirty years he ruled autocratically. In 1894–96, in response to Armenian demonstrations, he ordered wide-scale massacres, resulting in the death of about 200,000 Armenians. These Hamidian

Massacres drew front-page headlines in the world's major newspapers; Abdul Hamid was dubbed the "Bloody Sultan." In July 1908 the Young Turks forced him to restore the constitution and allowed him to keep his title but not his power. When he tried to exploit their insurrection of April 1909 to regain his authority, he was deposed and removed to Salonica. In 1912 he was allowed to return to Constantinople, and he spent his last years there, in the Palace of Beylerbey.

Izmirlian, Matheos (b. 1848 Constantinople–d. 1911 Etchmiadzin). Dubbed the "Iron Patriarch," he was patriarch of Constantinople from 1894 to 1896 and from 1908 to 1909. Elected Catholicos of All Armenians in 1908, he served until 1910.

Jelal, Mehmed (?–?). Served as governor-general of Aleppo province in the July 1914–June 1915 period. Previously he was dean of the Ottoman Empire's famous civil service school, Mülkiye, and he served as governor-general of the provinces of Erzerum, Edirne, Izmit, and, after Aleppo, of Konya. The main reason for his transfer from Aleppo to Konya was his refusal to order and organize the massacre of the surviving deportees in his province; he responded to the orders to massacre the Armenians by saying: "Each human has the right to live." While serving only for a few months in Konya province in the summer of 1915, he continued his benevolent attitude toward the countless deportees passing through that main railroad station. After the Armistice he published a series of articles in the Turkish daily *Vakit* (December 10, 12, and 13, 1918) explaining the ordeal of the Armenians and his pain of commiseration.

Jemal Pasha (1872–1922). Soldier, later senior member of the triumvirate, with Enver and Talaat. After graduating from War College (1895), he was attached to the Third Army in Salonica. He joined the CUP in 1906. After the Young Turk revolution of 1908, he became a member of the Central Committee, then military governor of Uskudar (1909); he was promoted to the rank of colonel. He became *vali* of Adana (1909), Baghdad (1911); commander of Konya Reserves (1912); and military governor of Constantinople (1913). He served as minister of public works and then minister of the marine. In 1914 he was sent to Syria to command the Fourth Army. He was responsible for ordering the death of thousands of Armenians. On November 2, 1918, he resigned and escaped abroad. On July 25, 1922, he was assassinated in Tiflis by Petros Ter-Poghosian.

Jevdet Bey (?–?). Governor of Van, brother-in-law of Enver Pasha, governor of Hekiari, and organizer of massacres in Bashkale. His reign of terror against the Armenians of Van, including the massacre and arrest of community leaders, was a major factor in the self-defense of Van in April 1915.

Kalenderian, Very Rev. Ardavazt (b. 1876 Bursa–d. 1915 Diyarbekir). Celibate priest from 1901; vicar of Erzinjan (1902–07), then *locum tenens* of Tokat and prelate of Ourfa until 1915. With Vartkes Serengulian and Krikor Zohrab, he was put on the road from Ourfa, attacked by *chetes*, tortured, and killed.

Kelegian, Diran (b. 1862 Kayseri–d. 1915 Ayash). Editor, journalist, teacher, and scholar. During Izmirlian's term as patriarch, Kelegian was chief dragoman of the Armenian Patriarchate. After the Hamidian Massacres he went to Europe and became a correspondent for *Nineteenth Century* and *Contemporary Review*. He contributed to the *Daily Mail*, the *Daily Graphic*, and other papers. Later, in Egypt, he became the editor of *Journal du Carré*, then editor in chief of *Bourse Egyptienne*. At the same time he served as a correspondent of the Correspondents Bureau (Vienna) and the Press Association of Paris. Following the proclamation of the Ottoman Constitution (1908), he returned to Constantinople and was appointed editor in chief of the major daily *Sabah*. He was also the author of a French-Turkish dictionary.

Khajag, Karekin (b. 1867 Alexandropol–d. 1915 Ourfa). Teacher, writer, and Dashnak member. After graduating from the University of Geneva, he arrived in Baku, where he had joined the Dashnak Party. He began working for *Droshak*. In 1895 the editors sent him on a mission to the Balkans, where he pioneered the Dashnak organization. From 1906 onward he belonged to the editorial team of *Harach* in Tiflis, along with Avetis Aharonian and Yeghishe Tourian. He settled in Constantinople in 1912, working as director of the national school in the Samatia district and for *Azadamard*. He was killed on the road to Ourfa.

Komitas, Father (Soghomon Soghomonian) (b. 1869 Kutahya–d. 1935 Paris). Composer, musicologist, and celibate clergyman of the Armenian Church. He saved Armenian folk music from permanent loss by writing down more than three thousand songs. He contributed significantly to the modern Armenian Divine Liturgy and was the first non-European member of the International Music Society. One of the intellectuals arrested on April 24, 1915, he was deported to the Turkish interior. Although his life was spared, he never fully recovered, and he spent his last years in French mental hospitals.

Kuchag, Nahabed (d. 1592). Sixteenth-century Armenian troubadour and poet whose songs of love were known throughout the Caucasus and the Middle East.

Loris-Melikov, General Count Mikhail (b. 1825 Tiflis–d. 1888 Nice). Military commander in the Russo-Turkish War of 1877–78. A graduate of the Lazarian Institute and the Russian Military Academy (1843), he was Armenian by birth. In 1880 under Tsar Alexander II, who was supportive of the Armenians, he served as Russian minister of the interior. After Alexander III succeeded to the throne, his reactionary policies led Loris-Melikov to resign from his position. He died in exile.

Maloumian, Khachadour (Agnouni) (b. 1863 Meghri–d. 1915 Ourfa). Journalist, editor, and author. After studying at Nersesian College of Tiflis, he joined the editorial team of the review *Mshak* in 1883. He was on the editorial staff of *Droshak* after 1899 and wrote *Caucasian News* under the pen name E. Agnouni. He became a member of the Dashnak's western bureau in 1901 and was one of the organizers of the Paris congress that militated against repressive Ottoman policies (1907). He published several works including *The Wounds of the Caucasus* and *Toward Combat*. He lived in Constantinople after 1908. He was killed on the road to Ourfa, one of the first intellectuals to be victims of the genocide.

Manoogian, Aram (Aram Pasha) (b. 1879 Zeiva, Zangezur–d. 1919 Yerevan).

Dashnak organizer, teacher, and statesman. By 1903–4 he was a resistance leader. He helped organize many self-defense operations against the Turks and Kurds, traveling to regions where Armenians needed help. He was a leader in the defense of Van in 1915. He was the first minister of the interior and minister of supply of the Republic of Armenia. He also served as the magistrate of Yerevan. He is referred to as the "architect of Armenian independence." He died in the typhus epidemic of 1918–19.

Morgenthau, Henry (b. 1856 Mannheim, Germany—d. 1946 New York City). U.S. ambassador to Ottoman Turkey, 1913–16. He did everything in his power to get the United States and Germany to intervene to stop the massacres of the Armenians. He was forced out of his post because of his agitation on behalf of the Armenians and returned home to write *Ambassador Morgenthau's Story* (1918), one of the most critically acclaimed memoirs of World War I. It included the first extensive narrative in English about the Armenian Genocide. After the war Morgenthau did philanthropic work to help Greek, Armenian, Arab, and other refugees in the Middle East.

Narek (951–1002). Known as St. Grigor Narekatsi, also as St. Gregory of Narek. A tenth-century poet, monk, and theologian, he wrote a major religious poem, *Lamentations: Conversations with God from the Depths of My Heart.* He wrote at the beginning of a renaissance in medieval Armenian literature. His work was a source of inspiration to Grigoris Balakian.

Naroyian, Bishop Mesrob (b. 1875 Moush–d. ?). A graduate of the Armash Seminary, he was ordained a *vartabed* in 1901 and a bishop in 1913. Under the pen name Harmag, he wrote articles about religious and philosophical questions for the Constantinople Armenian press, but his heart was in the seminary, where he held administrative posts. On August 7, 1915, he was exiled from Armash by Ibrahim Khayri, director of the Central Prison of Constantinople. He ended up in Konya and eventually was moved to Constantinople, where he was imprisoned. He managed to gain his release and after the war served twice as vicar of the Armenian Patriarchate during Patriarch Zaven's absence.

Nazarbekian (Nazarbekov), Tovmas Hovhannesi (b. 1855–d. 1931 Tiflis). Russian Armenian military officer, major-general in the Russian army (1915). He graduated from Russian military academies and participated in the Russo-Turkish war of 1877–78 and the Russo-Japanese war of 1904–05. During World War I, he fought on the Caucasian front, first as brigade commander, then as commander of the Second Caucasian infantry regiment. In April 1915, the military units led by Nazarbekian defeated the Turkish corps under the command of Khalil Bey near Dilman. In 1916, he was appointed commander of the troops operating in the direction of Van-Kop; in 1917, of the separate Armenian army corps. Under Nazarbekian's command, in May 1918 the Armenian troops and volunteers halted the advance of Turkish forces in the battles of Karakilise, Bash Aparan, and Sardarabad. During the years of the Republic of Armenia (1918–20), Nazarbekian remained politically neutral and continued his military service, with the aim of creating a regular army. Following the Sovietization of Armenia, he was exiled in 1921; after his pardon, he settled in Tiflis.

Nazim, Dr. Mehmed (c. 1870–1926); also known as Selanikli Nazim. Doctor and Ottoman minister. He was one of the earliest members of the Committee of Union and Progress. By 1910 the CUP's liberal membership had been eclipsed, and extreme nationalists, Dr. Nazim chief among them, controlled the Central Committee. Nazim, Dr. Behaeddin Shakir, and Midhat Shukri, fueled by the pan-Turkic and racist ideas of Zia Gökalp, masterminded the plan to annihilate the Armenians. As members of the secret Special Organization of the Central Committee, they conceived of the *chetes*. Nazim came up with the idea of settling the half-million Turkish refugees of the Balkan Wars on Armenian lands and in Armenian houses. In August 1918 Dr. Nazim was appointed minister of education. In October he fled the country. He was hanged in 1926 for collusion in a plot to assassinate Mustapha Kemal Pasha.

Odabashian, Very Rev. Sahag (b. 1875 Sivas–d. 1915 Sooshehir). Teacher and clergyman. A graduate of Armash Theological Seminary, he was ordained a *vartabed* in 1901, at the same time as Grigoris Balakian. He taught in Constantinople, then in Sivas. Beginning in 1905, he served as vicar and prelate in Sivas, Amasia, Marsovan, Samsun, and Bursa (1912–14). On a patriarchal assignment to the interior (which had been offered to Balakian), Odabashian was brutally murdered, one of the first people to lose his life in the Genocide.

Ormanian, Patriarch Maghakia (b. 1841 Constantinople–d. 1918 Constantinople). Patriarch of Constantinople (1896–1908). Raised a Catholic, he later converted to the Apostolic faith. He did not support the patriotic fervor of the Armenians but did lend his support to individuals accused of crimes against Turks. He is known for his many works, including *Azkabadum* (a four-volume history of the Armenian nation and church), *Dictionary of the Armenian Church*, and *The Church of Armenia*.

Parseghian, Dr. Armenag (b. 1883 Tokat–d. 1949 Boston). Educated at the University of Leipzig, he became a professor of philosophy in Constantinople. He was one of the 250 Armenian intellectuals and cultural leaders arrested on April 24, 1915. He was sentenced to death but was granted a reprieve through the efforts of U.S. ambassador Henry Morgenthau. He left Constantinople in 1918 with Grigoris Balakian to attend the Paris Peace Conference. A Dashnak party worker, he served as secretary to Avetis Aharonian. He later emigrated to the United States (changing his name to Barseghian) and during the 1930s and 1940s he was an editor of *Hairenik*, an Armenian-American daily newspaper published in Boston.

Pastermajian, Karekin (Armen Garo) (b. 1873 Erzerum–d. 1923 Geneva). An activist and later a member of the Ottoman Parliament. In 1896, as a young man, he led the takeover of the Ottoman Bank in Constantinople. He was a leader in the 1905 Armeno-Azeri battles, then later, with Dro, in the volunteer campaigns. He was a member of the Ottoman Parliament from 1908 to 1912. He played a role in the establishment of the Armenian Republic in 1918. After the world war he was a member of the revised delegation to the 1919 Paris Peace Conference, and he organized the assassinations of some Turkish leaders.

Reshad, Sultan (1844–1918). Mehmed V. He was the brother of Sultan Abdul Hamid II, who was deposed on April 27, 1909. The Young Turk government installed him as Sultan Mehmed V.

Reshid, Dr. Mehmed (?–?). A member of the inner circle of the CUP. In 1915 he became governor of Diyarbekir and began a reign of terror that wiped out its Armenian population. A fanatical pan-Turkic nationalist, he referred to Armenians as "filthy microbes" anticipating the biological racism of the Nazis. As the Ottoman courts-martial were getting under way, Dr. Reshid was arrested but escaped from prison. Shortly thereafter, when police were closing in on him, he committed suicide.

Reshid Pasha (?–?). Served as governor-general in the provinces of Ankara, and in the 1914–July 1915 period, of Kastemouni. He steadfastly refused to order the deportation of his province's Armenian population, arguing that he had no reason or justification to do so. He, too, defied his superior, Interior Minister Talaat, declaring, "I cannot stain my hands with blood." This attitude earned him the derogatory label "the governor-general of the Armenians." Upon the insistent complaints of the local organizers of the Young Turk party, he eventually was relieved of his post.

Sayabalian, Jack (b. 1880 Konya–d. ?). Author, editor, and translator. After attending the Berberian School and then the American School of Smyrna, he entered the business world. In 1904 he returned to Konya and for five years served as an interpreter for the British consul there; during the consul's eighteen-month absence, he held the position of vice-consul. After returning to Constantinople in 1909, he was director of the *Shehbal* review. He wrote for various newspapers, reviews, and almanacs. He wrote a short novel, satirical pieces, and poems. He translated works of Sir Arthur Conan Doyle, Lamartine, Heine, Prudhomme, Sylvester, and others. His brother Sebouh helped Grigoris Balakian make his escape from Belemedik.

Serengulian, Vartkes (b. 1871 Erzerum–d. 1915 Diyarbekir). Dashnak leader. Imprisoned in 1896, upon his release he participated in the Ottoman Bank takeover. Then he was sent by the Dashnaks to Marseilles, Geneva, Bulgaria, the Caucasus, and Van to organize resistance to Turkish assaults. In 1903 he was betrayed and imprisoned again, then was sentenced to death, but with the 1908 restoration of the Ottoman Constitution, he was released and became a deputy in the Ottoman Parliament. In 1915 he was exiled and murdered, together with Krikor Zohrab, near Diyarbekir.

Sevag. *See* **Chilingirian, Dr. Rupen**

Shahrigian, Haroutiun (b. 1860 Shabin Karahisar–d. 1915 Ankara). Lawyer and prominent Dashnak. A graduate of the University of Constantinople, he practiced law in Trebizond from 1889 to 1895, where he narrowly missed being killed in the 1895 massacre. As a lawyer, he defended many Armenian political prisoners but was arrested himself in 1895 for being a Dashnak. In 1908 he went to Constantinople and became a member of the Armenian National Assembly. He wrote several works on Armenian reforms and the Ottoman Empire and contributed to several Dashnak papers.

Shakir, Dr. Behaeddin (1877–1922). Doctor and chief of the political section of the CUP's Special Organization, which planned and organized the extermination of the Armenians. Banished to Erzinjan for revolutionary activity in 1891, he escaped to Egypt and then to Paris. After the CUP came to power, he worked behind the scenes in the Special Organization. Following World War I he was sentenced to death in absentia by a Turkish court-martial but escaped to Berlin. He was assassinated by Aram Yerganian and Arshavir Shiragian in Berlin in 1922.

Shukri, Midhat (1874–1957). A member of the CUP's Special Organization. He worked as an accountant in a local education department in Salonica and in 1906 became a founder-member of the Osmanli Hurriyet Cemiyeti, precursor of the CUP. Forced to escape to Europe because of his revolutionary activity, he worked in the CUP's Geneva branch. After the CUP came to power, he was elected deputy for Serez (1908), Drama (1912), and Burdur (1916). With Dr. Nazim and Dr. Behaeddin Shakir, he planned and organized the *chetes.*

Siamanto. ***See*** **Yarjanian Adom**

Ali Suad (?–?). Ali Suad refused to carry out the slaughter of Armenian deportees in Der Zor as lieutenant-governor of the district, stating by telegram: "If the purpose, which you insist upon, is the massacre of these deportees, I can neither do it myself, nor can I have it done by others." His superior, the governor-general of the province of Aleppo, of which Der Zor was a major subunit, relayed that cipher to Interior Minister Talaat, with a request to dismiss Ali Suad. Talaat complied promptly. Ali Suad was replaced in May 1916 by Salih Zeki, who took on the task of mass killing tens of thousands of survivors of the deportations during the summer and fall of 1915.

Talaat Pasha, Mehmed (1874–1921). Minister of the interior in 1915 who planned and oversaw the Armenian Genocide. Of humble origins and a limited education, he taught Turkish at a Jewish school in Adrianople and worked in the post office. He was committed to solving the Armenian Question by obliterating Turkey's Armenian population and admitted it openly to U.S. ambassador Morgenthau, among others. He became grand vizier in 1917, resigning in 1918 upon the CUP's dissolution. He escaped to Europe and was sentenced to death in absentia in 1919 by an Ottoman court-martial. On March 15, 1921, he was assassinated on a Berlin street by Soghomon Tehlirian.

Tanielian, Bishop Nerses (b. 1868 Zeytoun–d. 1915 Yozgat). Clergyman. After graduating from the monastery school of Sis and the Sahagian School of Samatia, he assumed a teaching position in Adana. Until 1895 he was vicar of Alexandretta. Accused of being one of the organizers of the Zeytoun revolt, he was jailed in 1896 in Aleppo for seven months. He was pardoned but exiled from Alexandretta, so he went to Syria. After the Adana massacres, being one of the leaders of the self-defense of Hajin, he suffered greatly in prisons for three and a half months. Sent to Yozgat as prelate in 1914, he was one of about 8,500 males massacred in the *sanjak*, or so Grigoris Balakian was told by the Turkish captain, Shukri, who had been in charge of the slaughter.

Teotig (Teotos Lapjinjian) (b. 1873 Constantinople–d. 1928 Paris). Writer and philologist. Studied at the Scutari and Berberian schools, then attended Robert College in Constantinople. Contributed to various newspapers. Although he wrote travelogues, profiles, and other works, he is best known for his *Amenun Daretsuitse* (Everybody's Almanac), which he published annually, together with his wife, Arshagouhi, from 1907 to 1920 in Constantinople and from 1923 to 1928 in Paris. He was exiled to Der Zor in 1915 but managed to escape, and for some time he shared a hiding place with Grigoris Balakian in Bozanti. Under an assumed name he found work in the military construction of tunnels in the Taurus mountains and became treasurer of the Tashdurmaz railway construction. Upon his return to Constantinople, he wrote and published several works dealing with the Genocide: *Monument to April 24*, listing the names of 761 prominent Armenians killed during the Genocide; *The Oppression and Our Orphans;* and *Golgotha of the Armenian Clergy and Its Flock in the Catastrophic Year of 1915*.

Tehlirian, Soghomon (b. 1896 Kemakh–d. 1960 San Francisco). Armenian who assassinated Talaat Pasha in Berlin on March 15, 1921, and the traitorous Artin Megerdichian in Constantinople in December 1921. Tehlirian lost all of his relatives in the Genocide and had been left for dead. Immediately after he gunned down Talaat, he was arrested and tried in a German court. After a suspenseful trial (at which Grigoris Balakian testified), he was acquitted.

Tourian, Yeghishe (1860–1930). Archbishop; patriarch of Constantinople, 1909–10. Patriarch of the Holy See of Jerusalem, 1921–30. He wrote several books and translated classical Armenian works into modern Armenian. He contributed significantly to the Armenian Apostolic Church. He was the brother of the poet Bedros Tourian.

Varoujan, Daniel (b. 1884 Sivas–d. 1915 Ayash). One of the leading poets of his generation. A graduate of the University of Ghent in Belgium, he became headmaster of schools in Sivas and Tokat, then principal of the Armenian Catholic Lousavorchian School in Constantinople. His sensuous, rich lyric poems opened new horizons for Armenian poetry. He wrote about Armenian myth and legend as well as the pastoral world of Armenian agrarian life. His books include *The Heart of a Nation* (1909), *Pagan Songs* (1912), and *The Song of Bread* (1921). Grigoris Balakian was with Varoujan and Dr. Chilingirian just before they set out on the Chankiri-Kalayjek road, where appointed killers were waiting to rob and kill them.

Vramian, Arshak (b. 1871 Constantinople–d. 1915 Van). Dashnak leader who became secretary of the Constantinople Central Committee in 1895. During the

1896 Ottoman Bank takeover, he hid in the Russian Embassy and later escaped to Geneva, where he helped edit *Droshak*. He lived in the United States from 1899 to 1907. In 1913 he was elected deputy from Van in the Ottoman Parliament. Deceived into believing he would be safe, he was actually the target of a plot devised by Jevdet, the prefect of Van province, and was murdered on the eve of the 1915 Genocide.

Yarjanian, Adom; known as **Siamanto** (b. 1878 Egin–d. 1915 Ayash). A prominent poet and editor. Educated in Constantinople and at the Sorbonne in Paris, he wrote about the tragedy of his people, particularly the 1909 Adana Massacre (*Agony and Torch of Hope, Bloody News from My Friend*). He introduced a graphic realism into modern Armenian poetry as well as a bardic, national voice and an interest in Armenian myth and legend. He served as editor of the Dashnak *Hairenik* daily (in Boston) from 1909 to 1910, then returned to Constantinople. He was arrested on April 24, 1915, and deported to Ayash, where he was murdered.

Zartarian, Rupen (Aslan) (b. 1874 Severeg–d. 1915 Ourfa). Teacher, writer, and founder-editor of the Dashnak organ *Azadamard*. He studied in Harput and taught from 1892 on. He was jailed for revolutionary activities. In 1914 he became a member of the Dashnak Party's Armenian National Bureau. Martyred on the road to Ourfa, he was one of the first victims of the 1915 Genocide.

Zaven Der Yeghiayan, Patriarch. See Der Yeghiayan, Patriarch Zaven

Zohrab, Krikor (b. 1860 Constantinople–d. 1915 Diyarbekir). Short story writer, novelist, editor, attorney, and member of the Armenian National Assembly. After the 1908 Ottoman Constitution, he became deputy for Constantinople in the Ottoman Parliament. He was very active in national and political affairs. Thinking that his friendship with Talaat Pasha carried some weight, he forcefully protested the April 24, 1915, arrests and murders. Although he himself was arrested in June 1915, he thought he would be released, right up until the eve of his murder.

Appendix: Author's Preface

TO YOU, ARMENIAN PEOPLE

BY GRIGORIS BALAKIAN

A. I dedicate to you, dear people of Armenia, this bouquet of episodes from your martyrdom, which is your Armenian Golgotha. This bouquet is not made of the myriad sweet-smelling colored flowers of the green fields of Armenia, although it is holy and sacred. Rather, it is made of the pains suffered in seas of blood and tears, as well as the harrowing martyrdom of your countless ancestors who died of inconceivable tortures.

This bloody manuscript is your holy book: read it without tiring, never doubt my story of the great crime, and never think that what is written herein has been in any way exaggerated. On the contrary, I have written the bare minimum, because it is not humanly possible to describe the horrific and ineffable martyrdom of your over one million dead sons and daughters. If all the seas on the earth were to become ink, the fields paper, and the reeds pens, still it would be humanly impossible to describe your thorny and bloody ascent to the summit of the Armenian Golgotha.

Since the Armistice I have waited for others more capable than I to fulfill this onerous obligation. However, apart from the eyewitness accounts of some foreign missionaries and the brief travel accounts of a few Armenian deportees, nothing has been published that recounts the story of your annihilation and martyrdom—nothing with real human emotion (as much as the pen can convey) that would give future Armenian generations a brief idea, at least in general terms, of these horrific and unprecedented episodes, in which more than half of your population lost their lives.

Yes, I did not want to write it, because I myself felt weak both of heart and of pen, to write about the great annihilation that surpasses even the bloodiest pages of human history. If Yeghishe required an infusion of patriotic spirit to write down the golden episodes of the heroic war of Vartanantz in 451, and to perpetuate the glorious memory of the 1536 witnesses who fell on the plain of Avarayr, then one would need superhuman power in order to record the cruel deaths of your martyred sons and daughters from countless unheard-of tortures.

There was a time when the Armenian nation had one collective history. But today, oh . . . every martyred or surviving Armenian has his or her own special story of black days, and this is only one of those hundreds of thousands of stories.

Yes, I did not want to put it down on paper, because that would mean a second exile, and the very recollection of it all would make me shudder. Just to write a few episodes, I had to recall and visualize those thousand-plus black days of terror, those three years of blood, with all their mortifying episodes.

Although I have written, it was not to become a hero; only in the good old days could our heroes be counted on one hand or two. Today everyone—from the suckling Armenian baby in the cradle to the eighty-year-old grandmothers and grandfathers—has truly become a hero. Because they endured such unheard-of suffering and tortures and died such heroic deaths in the name of their nationality and religion, I am ashamed even to call my tribulations suffering.

But I wrote because I had a sacred bequest from your dying offspring who have achieved sainthood through martyrdom. All those who were with me on the thorny road to the Armenian Golgotha requested that I write about their suffering and exile—their ineffable mass annihilation. All those who became separated from us for good, never to return, made this sacred testament to me, as their last will. I, in turn, am executing that promise I made them at their graves, and so I make a gift of these few episodes from the Armenian Golgotha to you. I want all future Armenian generations to know that their sacred tricolor Armenian flag, which flies over Yerevan, and their freedom and independence have been bought so expensively—at the cost of more than one million innocent lives.

B. All the large and small victorious nations, burying the bones of an unknown soldier in the magnificent pantheons of their capital cities, solemnly celebrate their bloody victories as national holidays, with the thunderous blasts of cannons. Recently the British daily newspapers wrote that the great British nation has allocated four million pounds sterling to erect magnificent war memorials in honor of its brave and victorious sons who, as worthy soldiers of the endangered mother country, fell during the Dardanelles campaign that took so many, for the inextinguishable honor of Great Britain.

And so it is that when British fathers and mothers in mourning make pilgrimages to the graves of their dead children, who fell with honor on the battlefield and shall remain forever unforgettable, they will enjoy a hospitable reception with all modern facilities, for the British government built magnificent huge hotels and even special railway lines at the end of Cape Saros, expending huge sums that could feed a small nation for a year.

But how can we erect memorials for you, the countless martyrs of my poor and wretched race, for your eternal memory and glory, when the Armenians who have survived are starving and hungry, when the starving Armenian survivors, along with the hundreds of thousands of orphans you've left behind, are getting their fill of bread given by noble, humanitarian Christian American and British people, when there is there is nothing left behind us but smoking ruins?

We have no gold and silver to build marvelous pantheons for the myriad martyrs; nor can we organize glorious national parades to honor the memory of the unknown Armenian volunteer. Where there is mourning and wailing, how can there be victory celebrations?*

Oh, how and where can we make a pilgrimage to you, when none of you—who died willingly and violently for the sake of nation and religion—even left a grave behind as a memorial for us? Every mountain and valley of our fatherland is your grave, where you fell side by side under the blows of the ax or sword, irrespective of denomination, ideology, class, or party line; and thereby you left us the legacy of an unbreakable pan-national union. Thus I dedicate my *Armenian Golgotha* to the perpetual memory of your countless martyrs anointed with saintliness.

And so, as a humble monument, I place on the cover of my book a historic ornamental black grave-cross, in honor of your one million two hundred thousand unknown Armenian martyrs, the tens of thousands of your Armenian volunteers who perished heroically on all the battlefields of the war, and the thousands of your pious clergymen who took their sacred vows along with me and who became martyrs through deaths even more harrowing than those experienced by their flocks, irrespective of denomination.

Meanwhile, I shall donate the proceeds from the sale of both volumes of *Armenian Golgotha* to the hundreds of thousands of orphans that you have left behind, under the strict supervision of a special committee formed on this occasion. I am deeply convinced that future Armenian generations will erect full-scale replicas of this thousand-year-old ornamental *khachkar* (stone-cross) of the Spasalars of Sanahin monastery in every part of our free and independent homeland. And when Armenian travelers pass by, they will fall to their knees in front of these black gravestones symbolizing Armenian liberation, shed two tears, and say the Lord's Prayer for the repose of the souls of the countless martyrs.

c. One final word: stand up, my dear people, for Armenia; after crossing the seas of blood, now is not the time to be demoralized, with the days of reaping the fruits of your victory, purchased at so high a price, having come. To be demoralized now is tantamount to committing personal and national suicide, when the bones of your countless dead children are still scattered all over the fields and valleys of the fatherland, after the rivers of our fatherland vomited blood into the seas for a year

*Only the Armenians of Constantinople are an exception to this.

(1915–16), after your tens of thousands of selfless volunteers fell honorably and heroically from Ararat all the way to Arara, from the heights of Van and Erzerum all the way to the fertile southern plains of Cilicia, and from the Dardanelles and Balkan battlefronts to the deathly borders of Germany and France, surprising even the commanders of the most powerful armies.

Armenian people, rise to your feet. If you abandon your self-confidence to live as a nation for a day or even for an hour, you are already lost, and with your own hand, you will have made the sign of the cross over the glorious history of your three-thousand-year-old civilization, and your ancient name will be wiped away from the history of nations, and at that time, alas, your million-plus children will have died in vain . . .

You have fallen on a road of misfortune, drained of blood and exhausted, hungry and decimated; in vain do you wait for a good Samaritan to come, lift you up, and clean and bandage your bloody wounds. Don't wait in vain. Your centuries-old neighbor has still not gotten his fill of your just and innocent blood, and if he can, he is intent on massacring your remaining orphans.

The foreigner, oh, he will always be a foreigner; don't put your hopes in him anymore! Because he only has the ulterior motive of secretly wresting new concessions within the vast stretches of Asia Minor, by playing the cards of your bloody quest for national salvation, and already it is only with this reprehensible goal that he has held your cards for the past century.

Put your hope, first of all, in God, and then in yourselves; you must be thoroughly convinced that an ancient historic people like us, with such high moral and intellectual accomplishments, can be decimated, but will not die. People will think that our nation is finished and consign it to the dustbin of history, but it will again be marvelously resurrected.

Don't be afraid of your foreign enemies, but rather be more afraid of those of your offspring who, under the disguise of patriotism, previously took advantage of your oppression, yesterday took advantage of your short-lived freedom, and today are taking advantage of your martyrdom and your bones. If you had only ten sincere, self-sacrificing worthy sons among your leaders (whom you already have by the thousands among your humble populace), leaders who would have the nobility and courage to subordinate their jealousy, passion, ambition, and avarice for the benefit of their nation, yours would undoubtedly be a more fortunate lot today. Yes, it is extremely painful, but I must confess that, alas, I did not meet even ten unselfish, unpretentious, and magnanimous individuals among your leaders during this past quarter-century of my public life.

Although you had many writers, poets, novelists, playwrights, and especially journalists and editors, you never had a historian: one to make a critical analysis of your real inner life hidden behind the curtain, and to show impartially, honestly, and unreservedly the real causes of your continual misfortunes. There is no saving you as long as the actors are always the same, and as long as imprudent adventurousness and secret, invidious action always form the basis and direction of national policy. If you had achieved a fortunate situation under these conditions, then I would have been surprised.

As you had no historian, it was a thankless task to truthfully write this chapter of contemporary Armenian history with its veiled secret moments and, in so doing, to become everyone's enemy.

Meanwhile, since you had no history, your leaders, irrespective of class, rank, and political affiliation, acted without fear of being held accountable in the judgment of history. They never dreaded the horror of the curses of future generations. But if your present-day leaders scoff at and mock history, saying *après moi le déluge*, then the contemporary Armenian historian will also scoff at and mock them and nail them to history's pillar of infamy, sparing none of them.

Stand up and reflect, Armenian people—you have been deceived enough. At least after such loss of life and property never before recorded in human history, and after such enormous unheard-of sacrifices, don't acknowledge every single one who says, "Oh my fatherland, praise be to Armenia," and swears by your name, as your savior; don't applaud him and glorify him as a hero of the fatherland.

The fact is that I was aware of many great and small Armenian traitors during the bloody, tyrannical regime of Sultan Abdul Hamid (1895–1908), who later, in 1908, in the immediate wake of the proclamation of the so-called Ottoman Constitution, walked in front of the enthusiastic popular processions, as constitutional pioneers, carrying the red flag and intoxicated by unrestricted freedom!

As I said, you have been deceived enough; set aside the politics of zeal and emotion. Be reserved and discreet. Don't reveal all your plans and thoughts, whether individual or collective, to whomever you come across. Distinguish the one who deserves to know from the one who does not. Don't worship clay statues. Cling tightly to your age-old fatherland, religion, and marvelous language. Through multiple births, quickly fill the places of the hundreds of thousands of children that you lost. And don't doubt that twenty-five years later, between Asia Minor and the Caucasus, you will become a viable new Bulgaria, free and independent, your wounds healed, respected by your neighbors and all states large and small. From now on, hasten to manifest your individual and racial merits, which amaze the world, in the collective sphere too, as a nation-state.

Yes, the future is yours! It is sufficient that you walk forward, always with self-confidence; instead of getting demoralized and preparing for loss, do for yourself that which your enemy could not do. I am an admirer of your creative and constructive work and national characteristics; your history is a witness to this, so let your future also be a witness to this.

Forward! The future is yours, walk forward unafraid!

Vartabed Grigoris Balakian
Manchester, August 20, 1922

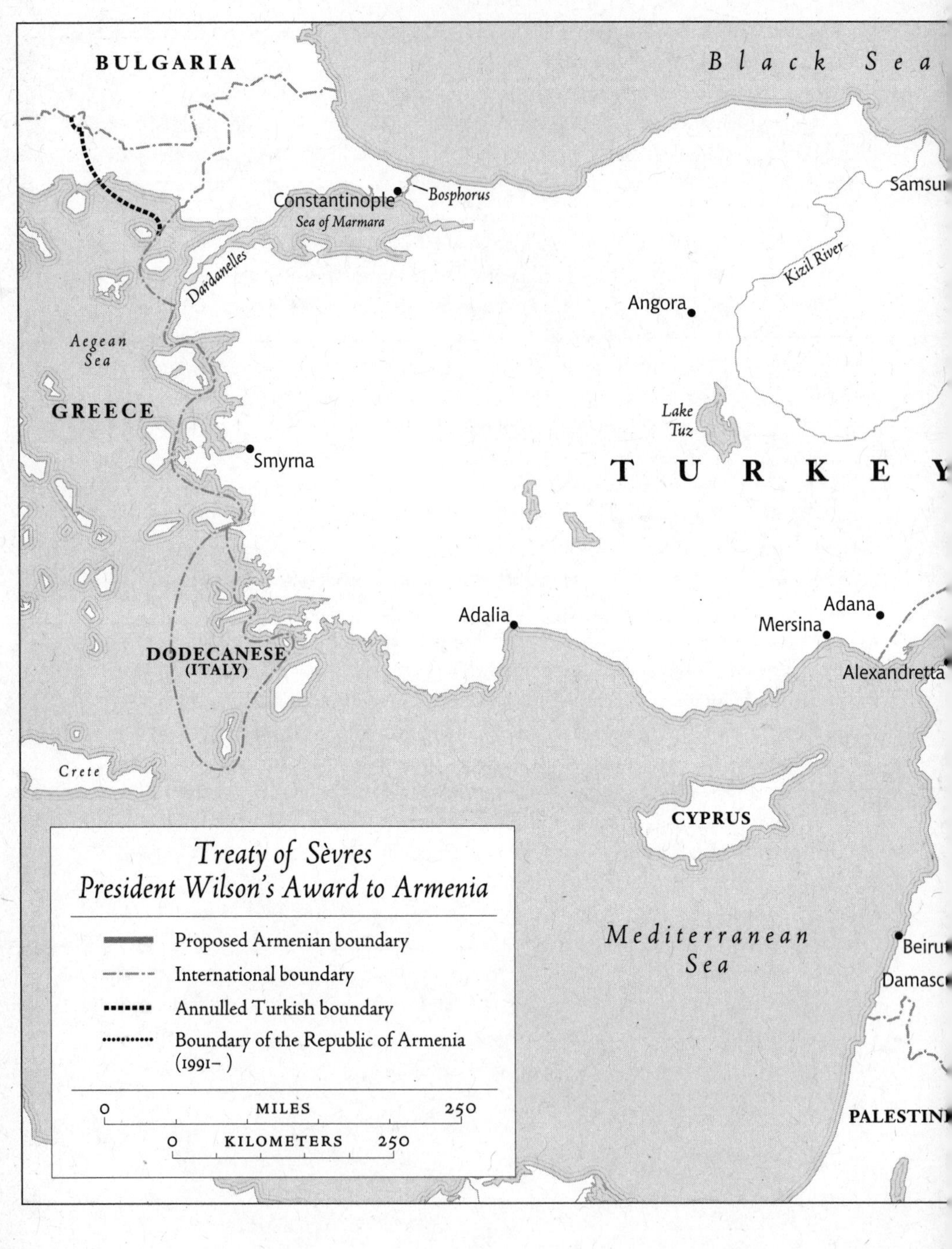

BULGARIA
Black Sea
Constantinople
Bosphorus
Sea of Marmara
Dardanelles
Samsun
Kizil River
Angora
Aegean Sea
GREECE
Lake Tuz
Smyrna
TURKEY
Adalia
Adana
Mersina
Alexandretta
DODECANESE (ITALY)
Crete
CYPRUS
Mediterranean Sea
Beirut
Damascus
PALESTINE
Treaty of Sèvres
President Wilson's Award to Armenia
Proposed Armenian boundary
International boundary
Annulled Turkish boundary
Boundary of the Republic of Armenia (1991–)
0 MILES 250
0 KILOMETERS 250

GEORGIA
Tiflis
Batum
Trebizond
Riza
Alexandropol
Kars
Lake Sevan
Erivan
Chorokh River
Kelkit River
Kura River
Erzerum
ARMENIA
Mt. Ararat
Arax River
Sivas
Moush
Lake Van
Murat River
Mezre
Harput
Bitlis
Tabriz
Malatya
Diyarbekir
Lake Urmia
Mardin
Ourfa
Aintab
PERSIA
Mosul
Aleppo
MESOPOTAMIA
SYRIA
N
Tigris River
Euphrates River

Notes

The following are the translators' notes, except where otherwise indicated.

INTRODUCTION

1. Ara Sarafian, "The Absorption of Armenian Women and Children into Muslim Households as a Structural Component of the Armenian Genocide," in *In God's Name: Genocide and Religion in the Twentieth Century*, ed. Omer Bartov and Phyllis Mack (New York and Oxford, Berghahn Books: 2001).

VOLUME 1

CHAPTER 1

1. Published in *Shant*, nos. 60–82 (Sept. 12/25–Oct. 4/17, 1914).

CHAPTER 2

1. "The Lion and the Mouse" is one of Aesop's *Fables*. A lion spares a mouse that has fallen under its paw; the lion is later ensnared in a net. The mouse reappears and, in gratitude, gnaws through the net to free the lion. The moral: The great and the little have need of each other.
2. As the Ottoman Empire was disintegrating during the nineteenth and early twentieth centuries, the European powers—primarily Austria, Britain, and Russia—debated future possession of the Balkan domains of the Ottoman sultan.

CHAPTER 4

1. Britain and France (with Russia's approval) secretly concluded the Sykes-Picot Agreement (May 16, 1916) on the partition of the Ottoman Empire. Both countries had assured Armenian leaders that their contributions to the Allied victory would be rewarded—and the tragic loss of Armenian lives compensated—by a grant of an independent Armenia under Allied protec-

tion. Yet France was awarded Cilicia, along with Syria and Lebanon, while Britain supported Azeri control of Karabagh (Artsakh).

2. In 1894 Armenian activists in the region of Sassoun organized resistance to punitive double taxation there. Other Armenians greeted the protest with enthusiasm. The result was the first organized massacre of Armenians by Ottoman troops. The massacre drew European and American attention to the human rights abuses that Armenians suffered under Ottoman rule.
3. In January 1919 the Ottoman sultan Mehmed VI assured Britain that those who were guilty of the Armenian massacres would be brought to justice. Trials were held, and prisoners were sentenced. But by the end of 1920 the political climate in Britain and Turkey had changed; the major perpetrators had fled the country, and a British–Ottoman prisoner exchange brought the Ottoman courts-martial to an end. For a concise summary of the courts-martial, see Peter Balakian's *The Burning Tigris.* For translations of related documentation in the Ottoman archives, see Taner Akçam's *A Shameful Act.*
4. On April 12, 1909, a military revolt against the ruling Committee of Union and Progress (CUP) failed. But afterward people throughout the Ottoman Empire were emboldened to stage protests. In the region of Cilicia (which had been an independent Armenian state until 1375) Armenian cultural pride and the hope of obtaining increased rights drew the attention of the province's officials and armed gangs. A rampage ensued. In Adana alone, the region's central city, the Armenian quarter was razed, its shops and homes were looted, and some two thousand were massacred. Several regiments that had been sent to restore order initiated another massacre, destroying thousands of houses and killing at least fifteen thousand Armenians. Eyewitness diplomats and journalists documented the carnage in detail. A special investigative commission of the Ottoman Parliament merely relieved the governor of his post and sentenced the military commandant to three months in jail.
5. In 1914, after the Balkan Wars, only 15 percent of Turkey's European territory remained in its hands. Armenians saw an opportunity to rally the European powers—Russia in particular—to press the ailing empire to institute some of the reforms they had been pursuing for decades. The result was the Armenian Reform Agreement of February 8, 1914, stipulating the appointment of European inspectors-general to administer reforms. The CUP (Young Turk) leadership, fearing that the reforms would touch off a repeat of the Balkan disaster, created a provincial network of party branches. A strain of nationalism that had been awakened with the emergence of the Young Turks took further hold, while an old pan-Turkic dream reemerged. Through the provincial party network the CUP instituted an organized plan of Turkification, laying the groundwork for the disenfranchisement of all non-Turks, including non-Turkish Muslims, and for the annihilation of Christians, most specifically, the Armenian people.
6. The Armenian Apostolic Church is one of the six Eastern Orthodox churches that are independent of the Roman Catholic, Eastern Orthodox,

and Protestant branches of the Christian faith. The Catholicos of All Armenians resides in Etchmiadzin, the Holy See, in Armenia, and the catholicos of Cilicia in Lebanon is leader of all churches belonging to the Holy See of Cilicia. There are also two Armenian Apostolic patriarchs, one in Istanbul and the other in Jerusalem.

7. Prince A. B. Lobanov-Rostovsky was given the post in 1895 and held it for only a year. He diminished the Russian state's traditional concern for the welfare of Christians under Ottoman rule.

CHAPTER 5

1. In Constantinople and all the other major cities of the Ottoman Empire, Christians—particularly Armenians, many of whom had been educated in Europe and had ties there—played a major role in the empire's financial dealings and its trade with the European powers. They held official positions in the Ottoman government. They thus comprised an elite who had minimal relations with provincial Armenians (the majority) and they were generally unaware of their travails.

CHAPTER 14

1. To document this fact, one need only scan the Armenian newspapers of Constantinople for the months of May, June, July, and August 1915.—G.B.

CHAPTER 15

1. In 1919, after the departure of General Antranig from Armenian Karabagh and Zangezur, this same Khalil subjected the Armenians of Shushi to a horrific massacre, adding yet one more chapter to this history.—G.B.

CHAPTER 21

1. In the wake of the Armistice, Kemal was sentenced to death and hanged in Constantinople. For this reason the Turks, considering him an innocent victim of the fatherland, sanctified him. In this way they stated their agreement with the horrific crimes committed by Kemal, which resulted in the loss of more than 42,000 innocent Armenian lives.—G.B.

CHAPTER 22

1. In October 1915 von Wangenheim, the Turcophile German ambassador in Constantinople, died suddenly. He was succeeded by Count Wolff Metternich, who issued a powerful protest against the widespread Armenian massacres. For this reason he was called back to Berlin.

CHAPTER 23

1. Now, in the wake of the Armistice, hasn't Turkey perhaps been put up for auction and might it not become the possession of the highest bidder?—G.B.

CHAPTER 24

1. Kastemouni was not one of the historic Armenian provinces.

CHAPTER 28

1. The Rubenid dynasty retained control of Cilicia and expanded its territory during the first three Crusades by forming alliances with the Europeans, particularly the Franks, who relied on Cilician matériel for their armies. Following the failure of the Third Crusade (1189–92) to recapture Jerusalem, Levon, the Rubenid ruler of Cilicia, received a crown, blessed by the pope, from the Holy Roman emperor. In 1199 he was crowned King Levon; the Byzantine emperor, who considered Levon a vassal of his empire, also sent him a crown. Levon established his capital at Sis and secured his reign over the Cilician plain and its ports. Cilicia flourished under Armenian rule until 1320. By then a faction of the Armenian Apostolic clergy and the Armenian nobility, through intermarriage, had become so Europeanized that they sought to recognize the supremacy of the pope. The Armenian Apostolic populace of Cilicia revolted, killing the Armenian heirs to the Cilician throne. So ended the bloodline of Armenian rule over the Kingdom of Cilicia. It passed to the Frankish Lusignan dynasty of Cyprus. In 1375, shortly after Levon V was crowned, invading Mamluks took him hostage, later releasing him for ransom. The last Armenian king, Levon died in France in 1393. His remains are entombed in Paris, in the Basilica of St. Denis.

CHAPTER 29

1. Sis was the Holy See from 1293 to 1375. The "throne of Levon" could refer to King Levon I (1199–1219) or to King Levon V (1374–75). In either case, a two-hundred-year-old throne could not have been the "throne of Levon."

CHAPTER 33

1. In 1896, Maghakia Ormanian was appointed Armenian Patriarch of Constantinople, as Armenians were being massacred throughout the Ottoman Empire at the instigation of Sultan Abdul Hamid II. An estimated 200,000 Armenians lost their lives during what became known as the Hamidian Massacres, which shocked the world and launched America's first international human rights movement. Patriarch Ormanian's ongoing cordial relations with the sultan on behalf of the Armenians angered those, particularly Dashnaks, who had long sought reforms that would grant Armenians and other minorities more rights and protections. On July 24, 1908, Ottoman-Turkish reformers (the Young Turks) staged a coup that disabled the government of the repressive Abdul Hamid. Reform-minded Armenians embraced the new regime. Six days later Ormanian was forced to resign.

VOLUME 2

CHAPTER 2

1. At the end of the 350s Arshagavan was founded by Arshag II as a bulwark in the struggle against centralist forces. Representatives of various social classes were given the right to reside there, including the landless and the unpropertied, the persecuted, and debtors. Located on the trade route between Tabriz and Erzerum, Arshagavan soon became a large populous city. But princes disgruntled with Arshag's policy combined forces and attacked the city, razing it and massacring most of its population. The city was never rebuilt.—G.B.

CHAPTER 4

1. If Armenians hated German policy, it was principally because ever since the Congress of Berlin, the Germans, being extremely pro-Turkish, had been preventing the realization of their demand for reforms.

CHAPTER 8

1. Balakian closes the chapter with a reference to an article in the London *Times*, September 2, 1920, that we could not locate.

CHAPTER 10

1. In June 1915 the Armenian men of Shabin Karahisar, west of historic Armenia, resisted an onslaught by Turkish troops and held them off for almost the entire month. Their resistance ended in their wholesale massacre.

CHAPTER 11

1. On account of the war and especially the shortage of coal, railway travel was extremely irregular. Thus the trees of the magnificent Amanos and Taurus forests were cut down for firewood. And as the wood chopping continued, the mountains of Cilicia became bare and barren. It was useless to become bitter about this, when millions of people were being massacred elsewhere throughout the country—Muslims in military service, and the Christians, particularly Armenians, on the roads of exile. Who was going to feel sorry for the loss of the forests?—G.B.

CHAPTER 14

1. It is worth mentioning here an episode from the life of von Sanders in Turkey. At the beginning of the world war, in September 1914, his two adult daughters went for a walk in the Baykoz woods with one of their father's Turkish bodyguards. Suddenly they were abducted by Turkish officers and violated. Von Sanders Pasha was satisfied with a payment of thirty thousand gold pieces in compensation, and the sentencing of a couple of ordinary soldiers . . . *raison d'état*.—G.B.

CHAPTER 15

1. After the Mudros Armistice, when the victorious British army entered Mosul, it treated the patriarch and the remaining Armenian survivors with great respect, materially helping the unfortunate Armenians who were in desperate need of bread.—G.B.

CHAPTER 18

1. After the Armistice the European powers and the United States vied for control over the Middle East's oil, particularly after the Wilson administration was succeeded by the isolationist Republican government of Warren Harding. The pledges that the Great Powers had made to support an independent Armenia were lost in the competitive frenzy to secure oil leases and develop other business interests in Turkey. For a full discussion of this history, see Christopher Simpson, *The Splendid Blonde Beast* (New York: Grove Press, 1993).

CHAPTER 23

1. During the eleventh century Ani, the capital of historical Armenia, fell to the Byzantines, and the ancient stronghold of Kars was overrun by the Seljuk Turks. Armenians then emigrated to Cilicia (in southern Turkey) in great numbers. Armenian nobles ruled the Kingdom of Cilicia (also "Lesser Armenia" or "Armenia Minor") from the end of the eleventh century until 1375.
2. Early in 1919, while the emerging Kemalist leadership of Turkey gathered force, the European powers competed for control over various portions of the disintegrating Ottoman Empire. France, even as it promised to help the Cilician Armenians keep Kemalist troops at bay, was secretly negotiating for economic ties with the new Turkish government. In late 1919 and early 1920 Kemalist forces who attacked French troops and Armenian resistance at Marash were on the verge of defeat; but the French were ordered to withdraw. The Kemalists overran Marash, then Ourfa, then Hajin—where Armenians held them off for seven months with no help from the French or any of the other powers. In mid-October 1920 the Armenians were forced to flee Hajin. The rest of Cilicia quickly fell to the Kemalists, and France received the mandate for Syria and Lebanon.
3. In 1912–13 a Balkan League (Bulgaria, Montenegro, Greece, and Serbia) was formed that retook Ottoman-held territory in Europe.

CHAPTER 26

1. The Battle of Sardarabad took place from May 24 to May 26, 1918. About twenty miles west of Yerevan a motley army of Armenians, outnumbered two to one, drove back the Turkish advance until the Turks retreated. They thereby prevented the Turks from reaching Etchmiadzin, in Armenia's heartland. The Turks asked for a truce, and though some argued against it, it

was accepted. Some scholars reason that had Armenians not resisted religious conversion in 451, or had they been unable to prevent the Turks from taking Holy Etchmiadzin in 1918, the Armenian nation (for which the Apostolic Church served as a government in exile for so much of Armenia's embattled history) might have ceased to exist.

CHAPTER 29

1. In the summer of 1916 the Turkish government abolished the Patriarchate of Constantinople, sending Patriarch Zaven into exile. It passed a new law combining the patriarchates of Constantinople and Jerusalem and making Jerusalem the catholicossal center.—G.B.

CHAPTER 30

1. Such a monument stands there today, a small chapel of white stone in Margadeh, in the Der Zor district, not far from the city of Der Zor. It was built in the 1990s after the Syrian government, while doing oil exploration, kept finding piles of bones in the steam shovels. They donated the land to the Armenian Prelacy of Aleppo for a memorial.

CHAPTER 34

1. Pierre Loti (Louis-Marie-Julien Viaud), 1850–1913; was a French naval officer and writer. Claude Farrère (1876–1957) was a popular French writer. Berthe Georges-Gaulis (1861–1942) was a journalist. All were Turcophiles who wrote about Turkey and supported its position after World War I.

CHAPTER 35

1. An ethnic Arab, Sayid Halim was the grandson of Muhammed Ali, the founder of modern Egypt. He had various disagreements with the leadership of the new CUP during these years.
2. The following excerpt from a speech G.B. attributed to Woodrow Wilson could not be located. We conjecture that it may have been something that appeared in an Armenian newspaper and was not well translated.

> Of all the countries in the war, Turkey is the most vulgar satellite ever seen in history, with a marvelous talent for evil and repugnance, with its atrocities copied from the Germans. It drags along its doubtful right to live in Europe, while remaining absolutely foreign to Western civilization. (Motions of general approval in the Congress.) Ever since the abominable leaders of Germany bound that wretched country under a military chain, it was from that day on that the incarnate Prussian militarism invaded Constantinople. Turkey became a veritable garbage heap of shameless and lying persons, murderers, brazen thieves and bestial oppressors. It became a worthy ally of the Kaiser

(applause). The Armenian massacres make it necessary that this ignorant and dirty horde be expelled from the European continent.

The widespread massacres would have happened to the Jewish people too, if the latter had not shown superb proof of adjusting to the time and circumstances with utmost cleverness in order to maintain political balance.

The Armenians must have that which history owes them. They have much more right to live than the Turks and they know how to govern themselves with much more talent. Sooner or later, the crimes of the Turks will find a court of justice and the goods stolen by them [spoils] shall be returned.

Bibliography

FURTHER READINGS

For readers who would like to learn more about the Armenian Genocide and the context of widespread upheaval and shifting alliances in which it took place, a range of works is listed herein (some of which the translators have drawn on for the Chronology, Glossaries, and Notes). From general histories and overviews to collections of archived documents of the time, these works are listed in sections for ease in locating those of interest.

Historical Overviews

Works on Armenian history and related works about Europe, the Near East, and the Ottoman Empire.

The Armenians

Bournoutian, George A. *A Concise History of the Armenian People*. Costa Mesa, Calif.: Mazda, 2005.

Chaliand, Gerard, and Jean-Pierre Rageau. *The Penguin Atlas of Diasporas*. New York: Viking Penguin, 1995.

Der Nersessian, Sirarpie. *The Armenians*. New York: Praeger, 1970.

Hewsen, Robert H. *Armenia: A Historical Atlas*. Chicago: University of Chicago Press, 2001.

Hovannisian, Richard, ed. *The Armenian People from Ancient to Modern Times*. Vol. 2. New York: St. Martin's Press, 1997.

Krikorian, Mesrob K. *Armenians in the Service of the Ottoman Empire, 1860–1908*. London: Routledge & Kegan Paul, 1978.

Lang, David Marshall. *Armenia: Cradle of Civilization*. 3d ed. London: George Allen & Unwin Hyman, 1980.

Lepsius, Johannes. *Armenia and Europe*. London: Hodder & Stoughton, 1897.

Mirak, Robert. *Torn Between Two Lands: Armenians in America, 1890 to World War I*. Cambridge, Mass.: Harvard University Press, 1983.

Nalbandian, Louise. *The Armenian Revolutionary Movement*. Berkeley: University of California Press, 1963.

Panossian, Razmik. *The Armenians: From Kings and Priests to Merchants and Commissars*. New York: Columbia University Press, 2006.

Redgate, A. E. *The Armenians*. Oxford: Blackwell, 1998.

Suny, Ronald G. *Looking Toward Ararat: Armenia in Modern History*. Bloomington: Indiana University Press, 1993.

Villa, Susie Hoogasian, and Mary Kilbourne Matossian. *Armenian Village Life Before 1914*. Detroit: Wayne State University Press, 1982.

Walker, Christopher. *Visions of Ararat*. London: I. B. Taurus, 1997.

The Ottoman Empire

Ahmad, Feroz. *The Young Turks: The Committee of Union and Progress in Turkish Politics, 1908–1914*. Oxford: Clarendon Press, 1969.

Davison, Roderick. "Turkish Attitudes Concerning Christian-Muslim Equality in the Nineteenth Century," *American Historical Review* 59 (1954): 846–47.

Dobkin, Marjorie Housepian. *Smyrna 1922: The Destruction of a City*. London: Faber & Faber, 1972.

Hanioglu, M. Sukru. *The Young Turks in Opposition*. Oxford: Oxford University Press, 1995.

———. *A Brief History of the Late Ottoman Empire*. Princeton, N.J.: Princeton University Press, 2008.

Harbord, James G. "Mustapha Kemal Pasha and His Party," *World's Work* 40 (June 1920).

Heyd, Uriel. *Foundations of Turkish Nationalism: The Life and Teachings of Ziya Gökalp*. London: Luzac, 1950.

Kansu, Aykut. *The Revolution of 1908 in Turkey: Social, Economic and Political Studies of the Middle East and Asia*. Leiden: E. J. Brill, 1997.

———. *Politics in Post-Revolutionary Turkey, 1908–1913*. Leiden: E. J. Brill, 2000.

Landau, Jacob. *Pan-Turkism: From Irredentism to Cooperation*. Bloomington: Indiana University Press, 1995.

Mardin, Serif. *The Genesis of Young Ottoman Thought*. Syracuse, N.Y.: Syracuse University Press, 2000.

Miller, William. *The Ottoman Empire and Its Successors, 1801–1927*, with an appendix, *1927–1936*. Cambridge, U.K.: Cambridge University Press, 1936.

Ramsaur, Ernest Edmondson. *The Young Turks: Prelude to the Revolution of 1908*. Princeton, N.J.: Princeton University Press, 1957.

Ramsay, William M. *Impressions of Turkey During Twelve Years' Wanderings*. New York: G. P. Putnam's Sons, 1897.

Sachar, Howard M. *The Emergence of the Middle East, 1914–24.* New York: Alfred A. Knopf, 1969.

Trumpener, Ulrich. *Germany and the Ottoman Empire, 1914–1918.* Princeton, N.J.: Princeton University Press, 1968.

Ye'or, Bat. *The Decline of Eastern Christianity Under Islam: From Jihad to Dhimmitude, Seventh–Twentieth Century.* Translated by Kochan and Littman. Madison, N.J.: Fairleigh Dickinson University Press, 1996.

Genocide in the Twentieth Century

Because the Armenian Genocide is the template for modern genocide, every book on comparative genocide studies in English has a segment on it. The following entries suggest the range of work done in this and other disciplines.

Bauer, Yehuda. *Rethinking the Holocaust.* New ed. New Haven, Conn.: Yale University Press, 2002.

Card, Claudia, and Armen T. Marsoobian, eds. *Genocide's Aftermath: Responsibility and Repair.* Oxford: Blackwell, 2007.

Chalk, Frank, and Kurt Johassohn, eds. *The History and Sociology of Genocide.* New Haven, Conn.: Yale University Press, 1990.

Dadrian, Vahakn. *Warrant for Genocide.* New Brunswick, N.J.: Transaction, 1999.

Fein, Helen. *Accounting for Genocide.* New York: Free Press, 1979.

Gaunt, David. *Massacres, Resistance, Protectors: Muslim-Christian Relations in Eastern Anatolia During World War I.* Piscataway, N.J.: Gorgias Press, 2007.

Gellately, Robert, and Ben Kiernan, eds. *The Specter of Genocide: Mass Murder in Historical Perspective.* Cambridge, U.K.: Cambridge University Press, 2003.

Gilbert, Martin. *A History of the Twentieth Century.* New York: William Morrow, 1997.

Graves, Sir Robert Windham. *Storm Centres of the Near East, 1879-1929.* London: Hutchinson & Co., 1933.

Jones, Adam. *Genocide: A Comprehensive Introduction.* London and New York: Routledge, 2006.

Kiernan, Ben. *Blood and Soil: A History of Genocide and Extermination from Sparta to Darfur.* New Haven, Conn.: Yale University Press, 2007.

Kuper, Leo. *Genocide: Its Political Use in the Twentieth Century.* New Haven, Conn.: Yale University Press, 1981.

Levene, Mark. *Genocide in the Age of the Nation State.* Vol. 1, *The Meaning of Genocide.* London: I. B. Tauris, 2005.

Lieberman, Benjamin. *Terrible Fate: Ethnic Cleansing in the Making of Modern Europe.* Chicago: Ivan R. Dee, 2006.

Mann, Michael. *The Dark Side of Democracy: Explaining Ethnic Cleansing.* Cambridge, U.K.: Cambridge University Press, 2005.

Melson, Robert. "Provocation or Nationalism." In *The History and Sociology of*

Genocide: Analysis and Case Studies, edited by Frank Chalk and Kurt Jonassohn. New Haven, Conn.: Yale University Press, 1994.

Midlarsky, I. Manus. *The Killing Trap: Genocide in the Twentieth Century.* Cambridge, U.K.: Cambridge University Press, 2005.

Power, Samantha. *A Problem from Hell: America and the Age of Genocide.* New York: Basic Books, 2002.

Rubenstein, Richard. *The Cunning of History: The Holocaust and the American Future.* New York, Harper & Row, 1975.

Simpson, Christopher. *The Splendid Blonde Beast: Money, Law, and Genocide in the Twentieth Century.* New York: Grove Press, 1993.

Staub, Ervin. *The Roots of Evil: The Origins of Genocide and Other Group Violence.* Cambridge, U.K.: Cambridge University Press, 1989.

Tatz, Colin Martin. *With Intent to Destroy: Reflections on Genocide.* New York: W. W. Norton & Co., 2003.

Valentino, Benjamin A. *Mass Killings and Genocide in the Twentieth Century.* Ithaca, N.Y.: Cornell University Press, 2004.

Weitz, Eric D. *A Century of Genocide: Utopias of Race and Nation.* Princeton, N.J.: Princeton University Press, 2003.

Woods, H. Charles. *The Danger Zone of Europe: Changes and Problems in the Near East.* Boston: Little, Brown, 1911.

The Armenian Genocide

This selection of comprehensive books provides background on what was taking place while Grigoris Balakian was on the run and in hiding. They are accounts of specific incidents, diplomatic reports, eyewitness reports of missionaries and others, collected news stories, and memoirs.

Scholarly Works

Akçam, Taner. *From Empire to Republic: Turkish Nationalism and the Armenian Genocide.* London: Zed Books, 2004.

———. *A Shameful Act: Turkish Responsibility and the Armenian Genocide.* New York: Henry Holt & Co., 2006.

———. "The Ottoman Documents and the Genocidal Policies of the Committee for Union and Progress (Ittihat ve Terakki) Toward the Armenians in 1915." *Genocide Studies and Prevention* 1, no. 2 (September 2006).

———. "Deportation and Massacres in the Cipher Telegrams of the Interior Ministry in the Prime Ministerial Archive (Basbakanlik Arsivi)." *Genocide Studies and Prevention* 1, no. 3 (December 2006).

Arkun, Aram. "Les relations arméno-turques et les massacres de Cilicie de 1909." In *L'actualité du génocide des Arméniens.* Paris: EDIPOL, 1999.

Astourian, Stephan H. "The Armenian Genocide: An Interpretation." *History Teacher* 23, no. 2 (February 1990): 111–60.

Auron, Yair. *The Banality of Indifference: Zionism and the Armenian Genocide*. New Brunswick, N.J.: Transaction Press, 2000.

Balakian, Peter. *The Burning Tigris: The Armenian Genocide and America's Response*. New York: HarperCollins, 2003.

Bardakjian, Kevork. *Hitler and the Armenian Genocide*. Cambridge, Mass.: Zoryan Institute, 1985.

Bloxham, Donald. *The Great Game of Genocide: Imperialism, Nationalism, and the Destruction of the Ottoman Armenians*. New York: Oxford University Press, 2005.

Bryce, J., Viscount. *The Treatment of the Armenians in the Ottoman Empire, 1915–16*. Compiled by A. Toynbee. London: British Governmental Document Miscellaneous, No. 31, 1916.

Dadrian, Vahakn. "The Naim-Andonian Documents on the World War I Destruction of Ottoman Armenians: The Anatomy of a Genocide." *International Journal of Middle East Studies* 18 (1986).

———. "The Role of Turkish Physicians in the World War I Genocide of Ottoman Armenians." *Holocaust and Genocide Studies* 1, no. 2 (1986).

———. "The Role of the Special Organisation in the Armenian Genocide During the First World War." In *Minorities in Wartime*, edited by Panikos Panayi. Oxford, U.K., and Providence, R.I.: Berghahn, 1993.

———. "The Secret Young Turk Ittihadist Conference and the Decision for the World War I Genocide of the Armenians." *Holocaust and Genocide Studies* 7, no. 2 (Fall 1993).

———. *The History of the Armenian Genocide*. Providence, R.I., and Oxford, U.K.: Berghahn Books, 1995.

———. *German Responsibility in the Armenian Genocide: A Review of the Historical Evidence of German Complicity*. Cambridge, Mass.: Blue Crane Books, 1996.

———. "The Historical and Legal Interconnections Between the Armenian Genocide and the Jewish Holocaust: From Impunity to Retributive Justice." *Yale Journal of International Law* 23, no. 2 (Summer 1998).

———. "The Armenian Question and the Wartime Fate of the Armenians as Documented by the Officials of the Ottoman Empire's World War I Allies: Germany and Austria-Hungary," *International Journal of Middle East Studies* 34 (2002): 59–85.

Des Pres, Terrence. "On Governing Narratives: The Turkish-Armenian Case," In *Writing into the World*. New York: Viking Press, 1991.

Gladstone, William E. "On the Armenian Question" (August 6, 1895). In Frederic Greene, ed., *Armenian Massacres or the Sword of Mohammed*. Philadelphia and Chicago: International, 1896.

———. "Bulgarian Horrors and the Question of the East." In Greene, *Massacres*.

Housepian, Marjorie. "The Unremembered Genocide." *Commentary* 42, no. 3 (September 1966).

Hovannisian, Richard, ed. *The Armenian Genocide in Perspective*. New Brunswick, N.J.: Transaction Press, 1986.

———. *The Armenian Genocide: History, Politics, Ethics*. New York: St. Martin's Press, 1992.

Kazarian, Haigaz K. "How Turkey Prepared the Ground for Massacre." *Armenian Review* 18, no. 4 (Winter 1965): 31–32.

Kloian, Richard D. *The Armenian Genocide: News Accounts from the American Press, 1915–22*. Berkeley, Calif.: Anto, 1987.

Kouymjian, Dickran. "Confiscation and Destruction: A Manifestation of the Genocidal Process." *Armenian Forum* 1, no. 3 (Autumn 1998): 1–12.

Kuper, Leo. "The Turkish Genocide of the Armenians, 1915–1917." In *The Armenian Genocide in Perspective*, edited by R. Hovannisian. New Brunswick, N.J.: Transaction Press, 1987.

Melson, Robert. *Revolution and Genocide: On the Origins of the Armenian Genocide and the Holocaust*. Chicago: University of Chicago Press, 1992.

Miller, Donald E., and Lorna Touryan Miller. *Survivors: An Oral History of the Armenian Genocide*. Berkeley: University of California Press, 1993.

Nassibian, Akaby. *Britain and the Armenian Question, 1915–1923*. London: Croom Helm, 1984.

Payaslian, Simon. "The Destruction of the Armenian Church During the Genocide." *Genocide Studies and Prevention* 1, no. 2 (September 2006).

Peterson, Merrill D. *"Starving Armenians": America and the Armenian Genocide 1915–1930 and After*. Charlottesville: University of Virginia Press, 2004.

Samuelli, Anna Maria, et al., eds. *Armin T. Wegner and the Armenians in Anatolia, 1915*. Milan: Guerini & Associates, 1996.

Smith, Roger W. "The Significance of the Armenian Genocide After Ninety Years," *Genocide Studies and Prevention* 1, no. 2 (September 2006).

Ternon, Yves. *The Armenians: History of a Genocide*. 2nd ed. New York: Caravan Books, 2004.

Toynbee, Arnold. *Armenian Atrocities; The Murder of a Nation*. London: Hodder & Stoughton, 1915.

Ungor, Ugur U. "When Persecution Bleeds into Mass Murder: The Processive Nature of Genocide." *Genocide Studies and Prevention* 1, no. 2 (September 2006).

Walker, Christopher. *Armenia: The Survival of a Nation*. New York: St. Martin's Press, 1980.

Winter, Jay, ed. *America and the Armenian Genocide of 1915*. Cambridge, Mass.: Cambridge University Press, 2004.

———. "Under the Cover of War: The Armenian Genocide in the Context of Total War." In *America and the Armenian Genocide of 1915*. Cambridge, U.K.: Cambridge University Press, 2004.

Eyewitness Accounts and Memoirs

Allitt, Patrick. "Disobedient Diplomats and Other Heroes," *Foreign Service Journal* (Oct. 1995).

Barton, James, ed. *Turkish Atrocities: Statements of American Missionaries on the Destruction of Christian Communities in Ottoman Turkey, 1915–1917*. Ann Arbor, Mich.: Gomidas Institute, 1998.

Bedoukian, Kerop. *The Story of an Armenian Boy*. New York: Farrar, Straus & Giroux, 1978.

Bjornlund, Matthias. " 'When the Cannons Talk, the Diplomats Must Be Silent': A Danish Diplomat in Constantinople during the Armenian Genocide." In *Genocide Studies and Prevention* 1, no. 2 (September 2006).

Davis, Leslie. *The Slaughterhouse Province: An American Diplomat's Report on the Armenian Genocide, 1915–1917*. Edited by Susan K. Blair. New Rochelle, N.Y.: Aristide D. Caratazas, 1989.

Der Yeghiayan, Zaven. *My Patriarchal Memoirs.* Translated and edited by Ared Misirlyan and Vatche Ghazarian. Barrington, R.I.: Mayreni, 2002.

Derderian, Mae M. *Vergeen: A Surivior of the Armenian Genocide (Based on a Memoir by Virginia Meghrouni)*. Los Angeles: Atmus Press, 1996.

Garo, Armen. *Bank Ottoman: Memoirs of Armen Garo*. Translated by H. Partizian, edited by S. Vratzian. Detroit: Topouzian Pub., 1990.

Knapp, Grace H. *The Tragedy of Bitlis*. New York and Chicago: F. H. Revell, 1919.

Morgenthau, Henry. *Ambassador Morgenthau's Story*. New York: Doubleday, 1918.

———. *Ambassador Morgenthau's Story*. Detroit: Wayne State University Press, 2003.

Riggs, Henry H. *Days of Tragedy in Armenia: Personal Experiences in Harpoot, 1915–1917*. Ann Arbor, Mich.: Gomidas Institute, 1997.

Shipley, Alice Muggerditchian. *We Walked, Then Ran*. Phoenix: A. M. Shipley, 1983.

Slide, Anthony, ed. *Ravished Armenia and the Story of Aurora Mardiganian.* London: Latham, 1997.

Surmelian, Leon Z. *I Ask You, Ladies and Gentlemen.* New York: E. P. Dutton, 1945.

Ussher, Clarence D. *An American Physician in Turkey*. Boston: Houghton Mifflin Co., 1917.

The Armenian Genocide in Government Records

UNITED STATES

Adalian, Rouben Paul, comp. and ed. *The Armenian Genocide in the U.S. Archives, 1915–1918.* Microfiche publication. Alexandria, Va.

Adalian, Rouben Paul, ed. *Guide to the Armenian Genocide in the U.S. Archives, 1915–1918*. Alexandria, Va.: Chadwyck-Healey, 1991–93. (37,000 pages of documents from the United States National Archives and the Library of Congress.)

United States Official Documents on the Armenian Genocide. Vol. 1: *The Lower Euphrates.* Collected by Ara Sarafian. Boston: Armenian Review Press, 1994.

United States Official Documents on the Armenian Genocide. Vol. 2: *The Peripheries.* Collected by Ara Sarafian. Boston: Armenian Review Press, 1994.

United States Official Documents on the Armenian Genocide. Vol. 3: *The Central Lands.* Collected by Ara Sarafian. Boston: Armenian Review Press, 1995.

TURKEY—OFFICIAL OTTOMAN RECORDS

Armenians in Ottoman Documents. Prime Ministerial Archives. The Turkish Prime Ministerial Archive, Istanbul. See General Directorate of the Prime Ministerial Archives, www.devletarsivleri.gov.tr./kitap/.

Documents from the Archive of the General Staff. Armenian Activities in the Archive documents, 1914–18, 7 vols., Ankara. Osmanli Belgelerinde Ermeniler 1915–20. Ankara: Basbakanlik Devlet Arsivleri Genel Mudurlugu, 1994.

Ottoman Parliamentary Gazette, Takvim–i Vekayi:/2303 (/27 September 1915)/; 3540 (/4 May 1919/); 3543, (/8 May 1919/); 3547 (/13 May 1919/); 3549 (/15 May 1915/); 3553 (/21 May 1919/); 3557 (/25 May 1919/): 3561 (/29 May 1919/); 3571(/13 June 1919/); 3575 (/15 June 1919/); 3577 (/17 June 1919/); 3586 (/28 June 1919/); 3589 (5 July 1919); 3593 (/9 July 1919/); 3594 (/10 July 1919/); 3595 (/12 July 1919/); 3596 (/13 July 1919/); 3604 (/22 July 1919/); 3616 (/6 August 1919/); 3617 (/7 August 1919/); 3618 (/9 August 1919/); 3771 (/9 February 1920/); 3772(/10 February 1920/); 3917 (/31 July 1920/); 3923 (/8 August 1920/); /Resmi Gazete, /say>: 2820, (/4 October 1934/); 2913 (/26 January 1935/)

AUSTRIA

Ohanjanian, Artem. Austria-Armenia 1912–1918, Austrian Documents on the Armenian Genocide, de Zayas, Alfred. Conference. "Human Rights—International Law—and the Armenian Genocide." Yerevan, April 20, 2005. www.armeniaforeignministry.com/conference/de_zayas_alfred.pdf.

FRANCE

Beylerian, Arthur. *Les Grandes Puissances: L'empire ottoman et les arméniens dans les archives françaises, 1914–1918.* 3 vols. Paris: Publications de la Sorbonne, 1983.

GERMANY

Gust, Wolfgang. *The Genocide of the Armenians 1915–16.* Documents from the Political Archives of the German Foreign Office. Hamburg: Klampen, 2005.

The Aftermath of the Genocide and the World War

After the November 1918 Armistice, the Ottoman government began a series of courts-martial for the perpetrators of the Armenian massacres. This section lists analyses of the Ottoman courts-martial; works that explore the crime of genocide and war crimes tribunals in the context of international law; and works on treaties, which left the Armenians bereft and at the mercy of a new Turkish army.

War Crimes Tribunals and Treaties

Bass, Gary Jonathan. *Stay the Hand of Vengeance: The Politics of War Crimes Tribunals*. Princeton, N.J.: Princeton University Press, 2000.

Dadrian, Vahakn, ed. "The Armenian Genocide in Official Turkish Records." *Journal of Political and Military Sociology* 22, no. 1 (Summer 1994); reprinted with corrections (Spring 1995).

de Zayas, Alfred. "Genocide as a Problem of National and International Law: The World War I Armenian Case and Its Contemporary Legal Ramifications." *Yale Journal of International Law* 14, no. 2 (1989).

———. "A Textual Analysis of the Key Indictment of the Turkish Military Tribunal Investigation the Armenian Genocide." *Armenian Review* 44, no. 173 (Spring 1991).

———. "The Documents of the World War I Armenian Massacres in the Proceedings of the Turkish Military Tribunal," *International Journal of Middle East Studies* 23 (1991).

———. "The Turkish Military Tribunal's Prosecution of the Authors of the Armenian Genocide: Four Major Court-Martial Series," *Holocaust and Genocide Studies* VII (Spring 1997).

———. Conference. "Human Rights—International Law—and the Armenian Genocide." Yerevan, April 20, 2005. www.armeniaforeignministry.com/conference/de_zayas_alfred.pdf

Falk, Richard. "The Armenian Genocide in Official Turkish Records." *Journal of Political and Military Sociology* 22, no. 1 (Summer 1994).

Gidney, James B. *A Mandate for Armenia*. Oberlin: Kent State University Press, 1967.

Hovannisian, Richard. *Armenia on the Road to Independence*. Berkeley: University of California Press, 1967.

Howard, Harry N. *The King-Crane Commission*. Beirut: Khayats, 1963.

Israel, Fred, ed. *Major Peace Treaties of Modern History, 1648–1957*. New York: Chelsea House Publishers, 1967.

Schabas, William A. *Genocide in International Law: The Crime of Crimes*. Cambridge, U.K.: Cambridge University Press, 2000.

———. "The 'Odious Scourge': Evolving Interpretations of the Crime of Genocide." *Genocide Studies and Prevention* 1, no. 2 (September 2006).

The Lausanne Treaty: Turkey and Armenia, 1926. New York: American Committee Opposed to the Lausanne Treaty, 1926.

Willis, James F. *Prologue to Nuremberg: The Politics and Diplomacy of Punishing War Criminals of the First World War.* Westport, Conn.: Greenwood Press, 1982.

Genocide Denial

Akçam, Taner. "The Genocide of the Armenians and the Silence of the Turks." In *Dialogue Across an International Divide: Essays Toward a Turkish-Armenian Dialogue*. Toronto: Zoryan Institute of Canada, 2001.

———. Review Essay, "Guenter Lewy's *The Armenian Massacres in Ottoman Turkey*," *Genocide Studies and Prevention* 3, no. 2 (Spring 2008): 111–45.

Auron, Yair. *The Banality of Denial: Israel and the Armenian Genocide*. New Brunswick, N.J.: Transaction Press, 2003.

Balakian, Peter. "Turkish Denial of the Armenian Genocide and U.S. Complicity." In *The Burning Tigris: The Armenian Genocide and America's Response.* New York: HarperCollins, 2003.

Dadrian, Vahakn. *The Key Elements in the Turkish Denial of the Armenian Genocide: A Case Study of Distortion and Falsification.* Toronto: Zoryan Institute, 1999.

Fein, Helen. "Denying Genocide from Armenia to Bosnia: A Lecture at the London School of Economics and Political Science, January 22, 2001." In *Papers in Comparative and International Politics* I.

Hovannisian, Richard, ed. *Remembrance and Denial: The Case of the Armenian Genocide*. Detroit: Wayne State University Press, 1998.

International Association of Genocide Scholars. "Open Letter Concerning Historians Who Deny the Armenian Genocide." October 1, 2006.

Lipstadt, Deborah. Correspondence to U. S. House International Relations Committee, Subcommittee on International Operations and Human Rights, Hon. Chris Smith, chair, concerning H. Res. 398, September 12, 2000. The United States Training on and Commemoration of the Armenian Genocide Resolution, 106th Cong., 2nd sess., September 14, 2000. Online at http://chrissmith.house.gov/uploadedfiles/Armenian%20Genocide%20Resolution%20Hearing%2009-2000.pdf, p. 136.

Smith, Roger, Eric Markusen, and Robert Jay Lifton. "Professional Ethics and the Denial of the Armenian Genocide," *Journal of Holocaust and Genocide Studies* 9, no. 1 (Spring 1995): 1–22.

Talaat, Mehmet. "The Posthumous Memoirs of Talaat Pasha." *Current History: A Monthly Magazine of The New York Times* vol. XV (October 1920–March 1922): 294–95.

Wiesel, Elie. Correspondence to U. S. House International Relations Committee, Subcommittee on International Operations and Human Rights, Hon. Chris Smith, chair, concerning H. Res. 398, September 12, 2000. The United States Training on and Commemoration of the Armenian Genocide Resolution, 106th Cong., 2nd sess., September 14, 2000. Online at http://chrissmith.house.gov/uploadedfiles/Armenian%20Genocide%20Resolution%20Hearing%2009-2000.pdf, p. 135.

Arts and Letters

Arax, Mark. *In My Father's Name* [memoir]. New York: Simon & Schuster, 1996.

Arlen, Michael J. *Passage to Ararat*. New York: Farrar, Straus & Giroux, 1975.

Balakian, Peter. *Sad Days of Light* [poems]. Pittsburgh: Carnegie-Mellon University Press, 1993.

———. "Arshile Gorky and the Armenian Genocide." *Art in America*, February 1996.

———. *Black Dog of Fate*. New York: Basic Books, 1997. New edition, 2009.

———. *June-tree: New and Selected Poems 1974–2000*. New York: HarperCollins, 2001.

Bedrossian, Margaret. *The Magical Pine Ring: Culture and Imagination in Armenian-American Writing*. Detroit: Wayne State University Press, 1990.

Charents, Eghishe. *Land of Fire: Selected Poems*. Translated by Diana Der Hovanessian and Marzbed Margossian. Ann Arbor, Mich.: Ardis, 1986.

Der Hovanessian, Diana. *Anthology of Armenian Poetry*. New York: Columbia University Press, 1978.

———. *Songs of Bread, Songs of Salt*. New York: Ashod Press, 1990.

———. *Selected Poems*. New York: Sheep Meadow Press, 1992.

Djankikian, Gregory. *So I Will Till the Ground*. Pittsburgh: Carnegie-Mellon University Press, 2007.

Edgarian, Carol. *Rise the Euphrates*. New York: Random House, 1994.

Forché, Carolyn, ed. "Poetry of the Armenian Genocide." In *Against Forgetting: 20th Century Poetry of Witness*. New York: W. W. Norton, 1992.

Frieze, Donna-Lee. "Cycles of Genocide: Stories of Denial, Atom Egoyan's Ararat." *Genocide Studies and Prevention*, 3, no. 2 (2008).

Hacikyan, Agop J., and Jean-Yves Soucy. *Summer Without Dawn*. Translated by Christina Vernoy and Joyce Baily. Toronto: McCelland & Stewart, 2000.

Hartunian, Abraham H. *Neither to Laugh nor to Weep: A Memoir of the Armenian Genocide*. Boston: Beacon Press, 1968.

Herrera, Hayden. *Arshile Gorky: His Life and Work*. New York: Farrar, Straus & Giroux, 2003.

Hilsenrath, Edgar. *The Story of the Last Thought*. Translated by Hugh Young. London: Scribner's, 1990.

Kalaidjian, Walter. *The Edge of Modernism: American Poetry and the Traumatic Past*. Baltimore: Johns Hopkins University Press, 2006.

Kalinoski, Richard. *Beast on the Moon* [play].

Kherdian, David. *The Story of an Armenian Girl*. New York: William Morrow, 1977.

Kricorian, Nancy. *Zabelle*. New York: Atlantic Monthly Press, 1998.

Kuyumjian, Rita Soulahian. *Archeology of Madness: Komitas, Portrait of an Armenian Icon*. Princeton, N.J.: Gomidas Institute, 2001.

Mandel, Maud. *In the Aftermath of Genocide: Armenians and Jews in Twentieth-Century France*. Durham: Duke University Press, 2003.

Marcom, Micheline Ahronian. *Three Apples Fell from Heaven*. New York: Riverhead Books, 2001.

Marsoobian, Armen. "Reconciliation After Genocide." In *Genocide's Aftermath: Responsibility and Repair*. London: Blackwell, 2007.

Matossian, Nouritza. *Black Angel: The Life of Arshile Gorky*. New York: Overlook Press, 2000.

Nichanian, Marc. *Writers of Disaster: Armenian Literature in the Twentieth Century*. Princeton and London: Gomidas Institute, 2002.

Peroomian, Rubina. *Literary Responses to Catastrophe: A Comparison of the Armenian and the Jewish Experience*. Atlanta: Scholars Press, 1993.

Saroyan, William. *The Daring Young Man on the Flying Trapeze and Other Stories*. 1935; reprinted New York: New Directions, 1997.

———. *The Saroyan Special* [collected short stories]. New York: Harcourt, Brace, 1948.

———. *An Armenian Trilogy* [three plays]. Fresno: California State University Press, 1986.

Siamanto. *Bloody News from My Friend* [poems]. Translated by Peter Balakian and Nevarte Yaghlian. Detroit: Wayne State University Press, 1996.

Tekeyan, Vahan. *Sacred Rage* [poems]. Translated by Diana Der Hovanessian and Marzbed Margossian. New York: Ashod Press, 1982.

Totovents, Vahan. *Scenes from an Armenian Childhood*. New York: Oxford University Press, 1962.

Werfel, Franz. *The Forty Days of Musa Dagh*. 1934; reprinted New York: Carroll & Graf, 1983.

Zarian, Gostan. *The Traveller and His Road*. Translated by Ara Baliozian. New York: Ashod Press, 1981.

Film and Video

The Armenian Genocide. PBS, Two Cats Productions. April 2006. 55 minutes.

The Armenians: A Story of Survival. Directed and produced by Andrew Goldberg. Two Cats Productions in association with National Education Telecommunications Association.

ABC World News Tonight with Peter Jennings. Five-minute segment on the Armenian Genocide. April 30, 1999.

Ararat. Directed by Atom Egoyan. Miramax. 115 minutes.

Foreign Correspondent. Australian Broadcasting Corporation. Australian documentary on the Armenian Genocide. April 22, 2008.

The Forgotten Genocide. Atlantis Productions. Directed by Michael J. Hagopian. With Mike Connors. 1987. 28 minutes.

The Great War and the Shaping of the Twentieth Century. A KCET/BBC coproduction in association with the Imperial War Museum (London). Produced and directed by Carl Byker, Lyn Goldfarb, et al. 1996. 8 videocassettes. (See cassette 3, *Total War*, for a discussion of the Armenian Genocide.)

The Hidden Holocaust. Pan-Optic. London, 1992. 45 minutes.

I Hate Dogs/Back to Ararat: A Forgotten Genocide. Directed by Pea Holmquist and Suzanne Kardalian. Pea Holmquist Productions. 2005.

Screamers. Documentary about rock band System of a Down. Directed by Carla Garapedian. BBC. 2007.

Voices from the Lake: A Film About the Secret Genocide. Directed by J. Michael Hagopian. Armenian Film Foundation, Thousand Oaks, Calif. 2000.

A Wall of Silence: The Unspoken Fate of the Armenians. Directed by Dorothee Forma. Humanist Broadcasting Foundation. The Netherlands. 1997. 54 minutes. Available through AIM Magazine, Glendale, Calif.

Index

Page numbers in *italics* refer to maps.
Page numbers beginning with 461 refer to endnotes.

Illustration Credits

FRONTISPIECE

Grigoris Balakian, 1913: courtesy of Peter Balakian

INSERTS

Grigoris Balakian, 1914: *Armenian Golgotha: Episodes from the Armenian Martyrology from Berlin to Zor, 1914–1920* (Vienna: Mekhitarist Press: 1922).

Sheik-ul-Islam announcing *jihad:* from *The History of the First World War* (Berlin: Union Deutsche Verlagsgesellschaft: n.d.). Informations-und Dokumentationszentrun Armenien, Berlin

Labor battalions: Informations-und Dokumentationszentrun Armenien, Berlin

Public executions: Wallstein Verlag, Göttenhiem, Germany

Armenians being marched out of Harput: Project SAVE archives, courtesy of an annonymous donor

Armenian deportees walking: © Armenian National Institute, Inc., courtesy of Sybil Stevens (daughter of Armin T. Wegner). Wegner Collection, Deutches Literaturarchiv, Marbach & United States Holocaust Memorial Museum

Armenians deported by Bagdad railway: Historical Institute of Deutsche Bank

Massacred Armenians: Informations-und Dokumentationszentrun Armenien, Berlin

CUP leaders: *Armenian Golgotha: Episodes from the Armenian Martyrology from Berlin to Zor, 1914–1920* (Vienna: Mekhitarist Press: 1922).

Ismail Enver Pasha: Collection of Mark A. Momjian

Mehmed Talaat Pasha: Informations-und Dokumentationszentrun Armenien, Berlin

Ottoman killers with victims' heads: Informations-und Dokumentationszentrun Armenien, Berlin

Bridge over Halys River: *Armenian Golgotha: Episodes from the Armenian Martyrology from Berlin to Zor, 1914–1920* (Vienna: Mekhitarist Press: 1922).

Daniel Varoujan: *Anthology of Armenian Poetry* (New York: Columbia University Press, 1978).

Krikor Zohrab: HYE-TERT Istanbul Ermenilerine Haberler

Siamanto: *Anthology of Armenian Poetry* (New York: Columbia University Press, 1978).

Komitas: Virtual Museum of Komitas Vardapet

Armenian priest burial: Informations-und Dokumentationszentrun Armenien, Berlin

Armenian woman and dead child: Library of Congress

Grigoris Balakian as Herr Bernstein: *Armenian Golgotha: Episodes from the Armenian Martyrology from Berlin to Zor, 1914–1920* (Vienna: Mekhitarist Press, 1922).

Adana: "Les Armeniens Dans Lempire Ottoman A La Ville Du Genocide," Kevorkian and Paboudjian

Hajin: Collection of Armen Aroyan

Sis: "Les Armeniens Dans Lempire Ottoman A La Ville Du Genocide," Kevorkian and Paboudjian

Armenian deportees in a concentration camp: © Armenian National Institute, Inc., courtesy of Sybil Stevens (daughter of Armin T. Wegner). Wegner Collection, Deutches Literaturarchiv, Marbach & United States Holocaust Memorial Museum

Remains of Armenians burned alive: courtesy of Armenian Genocide Museum Institute, Yerevan, Armenia

Starving Armenian children: Barton, James L., *Story of Near East Relief* (New York: Macmillan, 1930).

Starved Armeian woman and two children: © Armenian National Institute, Inc., courtesy of Sybil Stevens (daughter of Armin T. Wegner). Wegner Collection, Deutches Literaturarchiv, Marbach & United States Holocaust Memorial Museum

Grigoris Balakian as a German soldier: *Armenian Golgotha: Episodes from the Armenian Martyrology from Berlin to Zor, 1914–1920* (Vienna: Mekhitarist Press, 1922).

Constantinople: Sebah and Joallier Photographs Collection, Manuscripts Division, Department of Rare Books and Special Collections, Princeton University Library.

St. Garabed Monastery, circa 1900: *Armenian Architecture: A Cultural Genocide* (Montreal: Armenian National Committee, 2000).

Site of St. Garabed Monastery, circa 2000: *Armenian Architecture: A Cultural Genocide* (Montreal: Armenian National Committee, 2000). (Photo copyright © 2000, S. Karapetian)

Transport of Armenian and Greek orphans: Barton, James L., *Story of Near East Relief* (New York: Macmillan, 1930).

Grigoris Balakian as prelate and vicar: *Armenian Golgotha: Episodes from the Armenian Martyrology from Berlin to Zor, 1914–1920* (Vienna: Mekhitarist Press: 1922).

MAPS

Historic Armenia: Mapping Specialists, Madison, Wisconsin

Armenian Genocide: Mapping Specialists; from Robert H. Hewsen, *Armenia, A Historical Atlas,* (Chicago: University of Chicago Press, 2001).

Escape route: Mapping Specialists

Railway: Mapping Specialists

Treaty of Sèvres: Mapping Specialists

A NOTE ABOUT THE AUTHOR

Grigoris Balakian (1876–1934) was one of the leading Armenian intellectuals of his generation. In Ottoman Turkey he attended Armenian schools and seminary; and in Germany he studied, at different times, engineering and theology. He was one of the 250 cultural leaders (intellectuals, clergy, teachers, and political and community leaders) arrested by the Turkish government on the night of April 24, 1915, and deported to the interior. Unlike the vast majority of his conationals, he survived nearly four years in the killing fields. Ordained as a celibate priest *(vartabed)* in 1901, he later became a bishop and prelate of the Armenian Apostolic Church in southern France. He is the author of various books and monographs (some of them lost) on Armenian culture and history, including *The Ruins of Ani* (1910) and *Armenian Golgotha*, volume 1 (1922) and volume 2 (1959). He died in Marseilles in 1934.

A NOTE ABOUT THE TRANSLATORS

Peter Balakian is the author of *The Burning Tigris: The Armenian Genocide and America's Response*, winner of the 2005 Raphael Lemkin Prize, a *New York Times* best seller, and a *New York Times* Notable Book; *Black Dog of Fate*, winner of the PEN/Martha Albrand Prize for Memoir, also a *New York Times* Notable Book; and *June-tree: New and Selected Poems, 1974–2000*. He is the recipient of many awards, including a Guggenheim Fellowship and a fellowship from the National Endowment for the Arts. He is Donald M. and Constance H. Rebar Professor of the Humanities at Colgate University.

Aris G. Sevag is a writer, translator, and editor. Formerly managing editor of the *Armenian Reporter* weekly, he is currently editor of *Ararat* magazine. He has translated, from Armenian to English, and published more than a dozen literary and historical works, as well as hundreds of articles. Among his unpublished translations are accounts of several Armenian Genocide survivors, a study on the orphans from the Armenian Genocide, and histories of prominent Armenian families.

A NOTE ON THE TYPE

This book was set in Janson, a typeface long thought to have been made by the Dutchman Anton Janson, who was a practicing typefounder in Leipzig during the years 1668–1687. However, it has been conclusively demonstrated that these types are actually the work of Nicholas Kis (1650–1702), a Hungarian, who most probably learned his trade from the master Dutch typefounder Dirk Voskens. The type is an excellent example of the influential and sturdy Dutch types that prevailed in England up to the time William Caslon (1692–1766) developed his own incomparable designs from them.

Composed by Creative Graphics, Inc.,
Allentown, Pennsylvania
Printed and bound by Berryville Graphics,
Berryville, Virginia
Designed by Wesley Gott